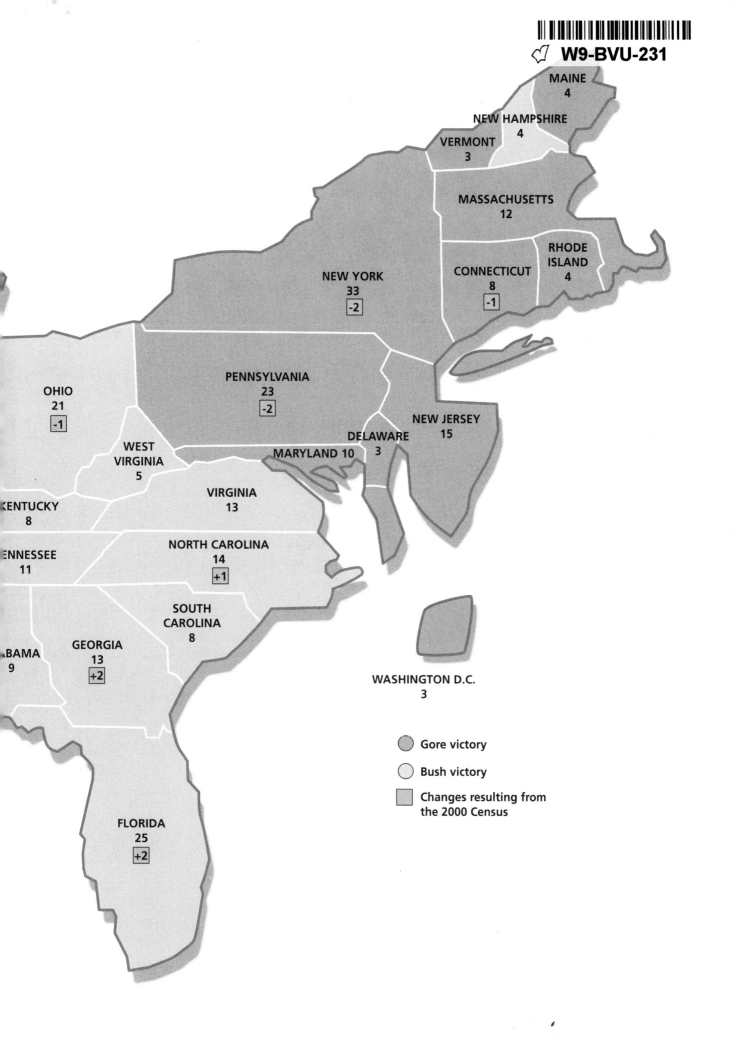

W9-BVU-231

MAINE
4

NEW HAMPSHIRE
4

VERMONT
3

MASSACHUSETTS
12

NEW YORK
33
-2

RHODE
ISLAND
4

CONNECTICUT
8
-1

OHIO
21
-1

PENNSYLVANIA
23
-2

WEST
VIRGINIA
5

NEW JERSEY
15

DELAWARE
3

MARYLAND 10

KENTUCKY
8

VIRGINIA
13

TENNESSEE
11

NORTH CAROLINA
14
+1

SOUTH
CAROLINA
8

BAMA
9

GEORGIA
13
+2

WASHINGTON D.C.
3

FLORIDA
25
+2

⬤ Gore victory

◯ Bush victory

◻ Changes resulting from
the 2000 Census

Yesterday:
dorm room
desk chair

Today:
political
hotseat

If you think politics is just a game,
think again.

Introducing PoliSim: Political Science Simulations in American Government—where YOU have the political power to control real politics.

Using the FREE ACCESS CODE found in this textbook, enter an exclusive *Companion Website*™ featuring **PoliSim**—12 interactive simulations in American Government that put YOU in the political hotseat, a.k.a. your dorm room desk chair. Sit down, log on, and experience the power of real politics with fully animated and interactive simulations of actual political situations in American Government, politically charged situations whose outcome depends on YOU:

★ **REAL DATA:** Powered by real data, **PoliSim** challenges you with multi-level simulations that require you to make simple and complex decisions, which are best made based on information drawn from real data:
  ★ *real* election results
  ★ *real* demographics, including sex, age, education level, race, and income
  ★ *real* maps, including political persuasion (Democratic or Republican) for specific areas
  ★ *real* score cards from real Senate members showing their votes on public interest issues
  ...and much more!

★ **REAL SITUATIONS:** Experience the concepts presented in your textbook using **PoliSim**, where you will be given the political power to:
  ★ Balance the nation's budget to gain popularity in the public eye.
  ★ Spend foreign aid dollars most effectively to reduce wars, terrorism, drug trade, and brutal dictatorship, and improve the U.S. standing from an international perspective.
  ★ Pass legislation by lobbying the Senate on a realistic budget and time frame—and use provided links to real senators' websites, where you will be exposed to their real views.
  ...and much more!

Notice that many chapter openers offer you an introduction to the specific **PoliSim** experience designed to help you bring the chapter content to life; and then:

Read the text. Log on using your access code included in this new book. Follow the *Companion Website*™ links to more information. Become an informed decisionmaker who considers the impact of political decisions before you make them.

And then log on to PoliSim and feel the power.

After all, isn't that what politics is all about?

GOVERNMENT BY THE PEOPLE

BASIC VERSION
2001-2002 EDITION

JAMES MACGREGOR BURNS
*University of Maryland, College Park
and Williams College*

J.W. PELTASON
University of California

THOMAS E. CRONIN
Whitman College

DAVID B. MAGLEBY
Brigham Young University

DAVID M. O'BRIEN
University of Virginia

Upper Saddle River
New Jersey 07458

Library of Congress Cataloging-in-Publication Data

Government by the people / James MacGregor Burns ... [et al]. — Basic version, 2001–2002 ed.
    p. cm.
  Includes bibliographical references and index.
  ISBN 0-13-031565-6
  1. United States—Politics and government. I. Burns, James MacGregor.

JK274.G66 2002b
320.473—dc21   2001034050

VP, Editorial Director: *Laura Pearson*
Senior Acquisitions Editor: *Heather Shelstad*
Development Editor and Project Manager: *Serena Hoffman*
Assistant Editor: *Brian Prybella*
Editorial Assistant: *Jessica Drew*
Director of Marketing: *Beth Gillett Mejia*
Copy Editor: *Ann Hofstra Grogg*
VP, Director of Production and Manufacturing: *Barbara Kittle*
Executive Managing Editor: *Ann Marie McCarthy*
Prepress and Manufacturing Manager: *Nick Sklitsis*
Prepress and Manufacturing Buyer: *Benjamin Smith*
Creative Design Director: *Leslie Osher*
Interior and Cover Designer: *Anne DeMarinis*
Director, Image Resource Center: *Melinda Reo*
Interior Image Specialist: *Beth Boyd*
Manager, Rights and Permissions: *Kay Dellosa*
Photo Researcher: *Linda Sykes, Abby Reip*
Manager of Production Services: *Guy Ruggiero*
Electronic Page Layout: *Joseph Lisa*
Illustrations: *Maria Piper*
Cover Art: *Corbis "American Destinations" collection
      and S. Wanke/Picture Quest*

This book was set in 10/12.5 Minion
by Prentice Hall Production Services and was
printed and bound by RR Donnelley & Sons.
The cover was printed by Phoenix Color Corp.

© 2002, 2000, 1998, 1995, 1993, 1990, 1989, 1987, 1985, 1984, 1981, 1978, 1975,
1972, 1969, 1966, 1963, 1960, 1957, 1954, 1952 by Pearson Education, Inc.
Upper Saddle River, New Jersey 07458

Printed in the United States of America
10 9 8 7 6 5 4 3 2 1

ISBN 0-13-031565-6

Pearson Education LTD., *London*
Pearson Education Australia PTY, Limited, *Sydney*
Pearson Education Singapore, Pte. Ltd
Pearson Education North Asia Ltd, *Hong Kong*
Pearson Education Canada, Ltd., *Toronto*
Pearson Educación de Mexico, S.A. de C.V.
Pearson Education — Japan, *Tokyo*
Pearson Education Malaysia, Pte. Ltd
Pearson Education, *Upper Saddle River, New Jersey*

BRIEF CONTENTS

CONTENTS

FEATURES

A MESSAGE FROM THE AUTHORS

The 2000 elections were a civics lesson for all Americans. Topics like the power of the Electoral College in close elections, the appropriate role of the Supreme Court, the function of the vice-president in an evenly divided Senate, and the discovery that neither major political party would dominate the national government suddenly became dinner-table conversation. More enduring lessons for the public were that every vote can make a difference, and that elections have policy consequences. In the aftermath of the 2000 elections, debates abounded about possible constitutional changes in our electoral process and proposals to modernize how Americans vote. These are indeed interesting times to study American government and politics.

Constitutional democracy—the kind we have in the United States—is exceedingly hard to achieve, equally hard to sustain, and often hard to understand without rigorous study. Our political history has been an evolution toward an enlarged role for citizens and voters. Citizens have more rights and political opportunities in 2000 and 2002 than they had in 1800 or 1900. The framers of our Constitution warned that we must be vigilant in safeguarding our rights, liberties, and political institutions. But to do this, we must first understand these institutions and the forces that have shaped them.

Many U.S. citizens take for granted civil liberties, civil rights, free and fair elections, the peaceful transfer of power, and economic freedom and prosperity. Yet many people live in places where these freedoms are nonexistent. This is a time of testing for new democracies as well as old ones. Contempt for government and politics is being expressed in the United States and abroad, yet politics and partisan competition are the lifeblood by which free societies can achieve the ideals of government by the people.

The world we live in remains highly volatile. Although our defense policy changed with the collapse of communism and the emergence of a less powerful Russia, the world has not suddenly become a safer place in which to live. Regional strife and terrorism continue to exist. The United States has entered a period of reassessment of its role in the world, in the United Nations, in regional defense organizations like NATO, and in its economic relations with other countries.

Although we constantly turn to government and to our elected officials with problems and requests, we are critical of their shortcomings. A recurrent theme of this book is the absolute need for politics and politicians, despite the widespread tendency to criticize nearly everything political. The reality is that our political system should not be taken for granted, even as we seek ways it can be improved.

We want you to come away from reading this book with a richer understanding of American politics, government, and the job of politicans, and we hope you will participate actively in making this constitutional democracy more vital and responsive to the urgent problems of the twenty-first century.

REVIEWERS

The writing of this book has profited from the informed, professional, and often sharp, critical suggestions of our colleagues around the country. This and previous editions have been considerably improved as a result of reviews by the following individuals, for which we thank them all.

David Gray Adler, Idaho State University
James E. Anderson, Texas A&M University
David Barnum, De Paul University
Robert Bartlett, Purdue University
Robert C. Benedict, University of Utah
Thad Beyle, University of North Carolina
Robert R. Bland, University of North Texas
Gary Bryner, Brigham Young University
J. Ranson Clark, Muskingum College
Jeanne Clarke, University of Arizona
Leif Carter, University of Georgia
Morgan Chawawa, De Kalb College
Richard Chesteen, University of Tennessee
Ray Christensen, Brigham Young University

Peggy J. Connally, North Central Texas College
Elmer Cornwell, Brown University
Gary Covington, University of Iowa
Douglas Crane, Georgia Perimeter College
Richard Davis, Brigham Young University
James D. Decker, Macon College
Robert DiClerico, West Virginia University
Lois Lovelace Duke, Georgia Southern University
Pat Dunham, Duquesne University
Robert Elias, University of San Francisco
Larry Elowitz, Georgia State College
Lee Epstein, Washington University

Steven Finkel, University of Virginia
Amy Fried, Colgate University
Earl H. Fry, Brigham Young University
Mark Gibney, Purdue University
L. Tucker Gibson, Trinity University
Eugene Goss, Long Beach City College
James A. Graves, Kentucky State University
Eugene R. Grosso, Long Beach City College
Gail Harrison, Georgia Southern University
Paul Herrnson, University of Maryland
Marjorie Hershey, Indiana University
Michael J. Horan, University of Wyoming
Ronald J. Hrebenar, University of Utah
Diane P. Jennings, De Kalb College

Loch K. Johnson, University of Georgia

Bill Kelly, Auburn University

Janet M. Kelly, Clemson University

J. Landrum Kelly, Georgia Southern University

Donald F. Kettl, University of Wisconsin

Dwight Kiel, Central Florida University

Ronald F. King, Tulane University

Michael E. Kraft, University of Wisconsin

Fred A. Kramer, University of Massachusetts

William Lammers, University of Southern California

Ned Lebow, Ohio State University

James P. Lester, Colorado State University

Paul Light, Brookings Institution

William Louthan, Ohio Weslyan University

Vincent N. Mancini, Delaware County Community College

Richard Matthews, Lehigh University

Robert McCalla, University of Wisconsin

Christopher B. Mobley, De Paul University

Theodore R. Mosch, University of Tennessee-Martin

Max Neiman, University of California

David Nice, Washington State University

Richard Pacelle, University of Missouri

Glen Parker, Florida State University

Kelly D. Patterson, Brigham Young University

William A. Pelz, Elgin Community College

B. Guy Peters, University of Pittsburgh

Richard Pious, Barnard College

George Pippin, Jones County College

John Portz, Northeastern University

Pamela Rodgers, University of Wisconsin

David Rosenbloom, American University

Alan Rosenthal, Rutgers University

Henry Shockely, Boston University

Steven Shull, University of New Orleans

Christine Marie Sierra, University of New Mexico

Christopher D. Skubby, Lakeland Community College

Robert W. Small, Massasoit Community College

Gregory W. Smith, Gettysburg College

Richard Smolka, American University

Neil Snortland, University of Arkansas at Little Rock

Michael W. Sonnleitner, Portland Community College

Jacqueline Vaughn Switzer, Northern Arizona University

Thaddeus J. Tocza, University of Colorado at Boulder

Roy Thoman, West Texas A&M University

John Tierney, Boston College

Richard Valelly, Massachusetts Institute of Technology

R. Lawson Veasey, University of Arkansas

Frank L. Wilson, Purdue University

Cheryl D. Young, Texas Technical University

Joseph F. Zimmerman, State University of New York at Albany

ACKNOWLEDGMENTS

Writing this book requires teamwork—first, among the authors, who read and rewrite each other's first drafts, then with our research assistants, who track down loose ends and give us the perspective of students, and with the editors and other professionals at Prentice Hall. Important to each revision are the detailed reviews by teachers and researchers, who provide concrete suggestions on how to improve the book. We are grateful to all who helped with this edition.

Research assistants for the current edition of *Government by the People* are: Kim Spears, Charles W. Ross, Mark Pickering, Chris Rees, Eric McArutur, and Chris Fillmore at Brigham Young University; Elizabeth Schiller at University of California, Irvine, and Neil G. Kornze at Whitman College. Donna Jones and JoAnn Collins at Whitman College provided secretarial assistance. We thank the Honorable David Sills, Presiding Justice of the California Court of Appeals, Fourth District, Division Three, for his most helpful comments.

Books for major college courses like this involve state of the art teaching tools and electronic ancillaries. Highly skilled professionals produced the various supplements and media: Larry Elowitz, Regina Swopes, G. David Garson, Brian Werner, Stuart Twite, and Bryon Wolfe.

Critical to the team that produces this book is Serena Hoffman, the production editor. She knows this book and cares about it. Her commitment to this edition, while at the same time tending to important family concerns, was extraordinary. We gratefully acknowledge her important contribution. We also thank Beth Gillett Mejia, who, as political science editor, brought her boundless energy and enthusiasm to this book and the entire political science list. Our thanks, too, to Brian Prybella and Jessica Drew, who assisted Beth and later the new political science editor, Heather Shelstad, in the numerous tasks involved in publishing a book of this scope. Others at Prentice Hall we wish to thank for their continued support are Phil Miller, Charlyce Jones Owen, and Nancy Roberts.

Many skilled professionals were important to the publication of this book. They include Joseph Lisa for page layouts, Linda Sykes for photo research, Guy Ruggiero for art coordination, Maria Piper for art creation, Anne DeMarinus for interior and cover design, and Leslie Osher for design supervision.

We also want to thank you, the professors and students who use our book and who send us letters with suggestions for improving *Government by the People*. We welcome your notes, phone calls, and e-mail. Please write us care of the Political Science Editor at Prentice Hall, 1 Lake Street, Upper Saddle River, New Jersey 07458, or contact us directly:

James MacGregor Burns   Academy of Leadership, University of Maryland, College Park, MD 20742

J.W. Peltason   School of Social Sciences, University of California, Irvine, CA 92717-5700   jwpeltas@uci.edu

Thomas E. Cronin   Office of the President, Whitman College, Walla Walla, WA 99362   cronin@whitman.edu

David B. Magleby   Department of Political Science, Brigham Young University, Provo, UT 84602   david_magleby@byu.edu

David M. O'Brien   Department of Government and Foreign Affairs, University of Virginia, Charlottesville, VA 22903   dmo2y@virginia.edu

A MESSAGE FROM THE PUBLISHER

*A*lways one step ahead. . . .

This edition marks a dynamic milestone for *Government by the People*. For 50 years *Goverment by the People*—in use in colleges and universities in every state in the nation—has been educating today's American citizens. In fact, *Government by the People* has set the standard that others strive to meet. *Government by the People* continues to innovate in response to changes in our democratic environment and changes in how the government course is taught. At Prentice Hall, we are extremely proud to continue to publish the book that always remains one step ahead of all others in its field by anticipating your needs as an educator and your students' needs as learners. This edition continues in that tradition.

Burns, Peltason, Cronin, Magleby, and O'Brien's *Government by the People, 2001–2002 Edition*, has been revised to provide you with the most current material. As we enter a political era with new leadership in office, no other book is better poised to take students from onlookers to participants in the fascinating world of American government. The gratifying success this text has enjoyed over the years results from a distinguished author team who treat each edition as a fresh challenge—and, in many ways, an entirely new book. As in the past, *Government by the People, 2001–2002 Edition*, remains one step ahead.

NEW TO THIS EDITION

- *New Co-Author:* With this edition we are honored to introduce a new member of our author team. David O'Brien of the University of Virginia joins the team to lend his knowledge to the areas of the courts, civil rights, and civil liberties. Professor O'Brien received his Ph.D. from the University of California–Santa Barbara. His research area is constitutional law, theory, and development, and he is renowned for his scholarship of the Supreme Court and judiciary processes. David O'Brien is the Leone Reeves and George W. Spicer Professor of the University of Virginia's Department of Government and Foreign Affairs. He has authored several works, including *Storm Center: The Supreme Court in American Politics*, 5th ed. (2000). Professor O'Brien is a Judicial Fellow at the Supreme Court of the United States, Russell Sage Foundation Visiting Fellow, and a Fulbright Lecturer at Oxford University.

- *Late-Breaking, Up-to-date Content:* This new edition has been thoroughly updated to reflect the happenings of the recent Election 2000. Virtually all chapters have undergone revisions to reflect events of the past two years—primarily the new leadership in Washington.

Highlights include data from the National Election Study and the latest information from the 2000 National Census. In addition, features within the text, such as A Closer Look, You Decide/Thinking It Through, We the People, and People Debate have been revised to address such important and timely issues as campaign finance reform and the Electoral College.

Finally, we continue our commitment to excellence, offering a balanced presentation with innovative treatment of political ideology and culture, political participation, voting turnout, voting behavior, and campaign financing.

These enhancements are present throughout *Government by the People, 2001–2002 Edition*. And there's more. . .

- *Improved Organization of Chapters:* In response to comments from reviewers and instructors, *Government by the People, 2001–2002 Edition*, now places the civil rights and civil liberty chapters *after* the explanation of the courts and judicial process. Although the chapters are self-contained and can be taught at any time during the course, this organization makes it easier to give students the background they need to understand these important topics.

- *New Chapter 13—Congressional-Presidential Relations:* This entirely new chapter examines how the president and Congress interact with each other. With the Senate almost equally divided and Republicans in the House with a very small majority, this timely topic will certainly dominate the news. Students will learn about similar periods in history and apply that knowledge to today's headlines.

- *Updated Chapter 5—The American Political Landscape:* This chapter examines social and economic diversity in American society today and some of the political consequences of living in a dynamic multicultural nation.

- *Greatly revised Chapter 11 (The Presidency), Chapter 12 (Congress), and Chapter 14 (Bureaucracy):* These chapters have been extensively revised to reflect current issues, including George W. Bush's proposed initiatives.

- *Improved Chapter 20—Making Social Policy:* This unique chapter is now updated to include current debates over welfare reform, health care, education, and crime control policies.

- *Substantially revised Chapters 19 through 21 (Policy Chapters):* These chapters have been thoroughly updated to reflect the current domestic and international policy initiatives and the priorities of the president and Congress.

NEW AND IMPROVED TECHNOLOGY

As in previous editions, *Government by the People* leads the industry in providing creative, innovative electronic solutions for your classroom. Whether in the form of tools that enable more effective communication or by providing dynamic presentation of content via the World Wide Web, Prentice Hall continues to anticipate your needs.

- **www.prenhall.com/burns**: This truly premium *Companion Website*™ is available to users of *Government by the People, 2001–2002 Edition.* This website is host to more than 15 dynamic resources to support the learning or teaching of your introductory government course.

  Among the many resources included are PoliSim, Politics Online, ContentSelect (Powered by EBSCO), Documents Online (provides full text of more than 150 source documents referenced in the text), as well as an abundance of online quizzing and assessment features. Chapter summaries, practice tests, links, glossary, video tips, interactive surveys, and interactive graphics are also available on this site.

  These resources are available free by using the access code found in new copies of *Government by the People, 2001–2002, Edition.* Access to the site may also be purchased separately.

- *PoliSim: Political Science Simulations for American Government:* Entirely new, these multistep, multimedia simulations are unique to *Government by the People, 2001–2002 Edition.* A simulation for most chapters is identified on the chapter openers. Not just scripted scenarios, these fully animated, interactive simulations invite your students into the context of what they are learning, requiring them to think critically and make decisions. Available on the *Companion Website*™.

- *ContentSelect: Powered by EBSCO: Government by the People* is proud to offer access to ContentSelect with the 2001–2002 Edition. From the convenience of their computers, students and instructors can now access thousands of current and archived articles from both scholarly and contemporary journals. Available on the *Companion Website*™.

- *Politics Online:* Entirely revised since the last edition, many of these end-of-chapter sections now contain interactive exercises in addition to thought-provoking situations and applicable links. Students will be prompted to participate in a brief interactive exercise, research relevant sites, or explore government in other nations, among other activities. Students can read the material in the Politics Online box, interactive in nature, and apply their knowledge by completing these activities and conducting research.

- *CourseCompass Edition:* For instructors who would like to implement the use of course management software to organize their course and communicate with students, Prentice Hall is pleased to offer *Government by the People CourseCompass Edition,* featuring a host of organizational tools, such as gradebook management, interactive syllabus, test preparation, and pre-loaded instructional content supporting the text. Instructors can save a great deal of time preparing for lectures and managing their course. Please see your Prentice Hall representative or visit **www.prenhall.com/burns** and select the link to CourseCompass.

- *Distance Learning Solutions:* For instructors interested in creating a distance learning course, Prentice Hall offers courses in both Blackboard and WebCT, in addition to our own CourseCompass Edition. Your local Prentice Hall representative can provide you with additional details, or you can visit **www.prenhall.com/burns** for a special demonstration and additional information.

ENDURING FEATURES OF THE TEXT

Among the many attributes of *Government by the People, 2001–2002 Edition,* are the features that have consistently supported the balanced presentation of topics within the text. Each of these features has been appropriately revised to reflect those issues that are most significant in our political environment today.

- THE PEOPLE DEBATE: These two-page spreads featured throughout the text have been completely revised to address contemporary topics such as Election 2000, Campaign Finance Reform, The Electoral College, and Social Security Reform. People Debates give students a chance to participate in a pro/con debate in the text, online, and through essays and links on the *Companion Website*™.

- YOU DECIDE/THINKING IT THROUGH: This participatory question-and-answer feature is designed to strengthen students' critical thinking skills as well as introduce controversal and challenging issues and ideas about American politics. A You Decide question is presented on the left page, and on the facing page, a Thinking It Through discussion examines possible answers.

- A CLOSER LOOK: These journalistic-style boxes combine text, photos, and art on relevant issues of high student appeal. Some of the topics include: Religion and Politics, Evaluating Bill Clinton's Presidency, The Politics of Capital Punishment, Campaign Finance Reform, and The "Don't Ask-Don't Tell" Controversy.

- WE THE PEOPLE: These unique boxes are designed to reflect the concerns and experiences of ethnic and minority groups in American politics. Some of the topics include: Oprah Winfrey: Achieving the American Dream, Distribution of Education in the United States, Portrait of the Electorate, and Women Governors.

SUPPLEMENTS FOR THE INSTRUCTOR

In addition to the abundance of material available in the Faculty Resources section of the *Companion Website™* (**www.prenhall.com/burns**) *Government by the People, 2001–2002 Edition*, offers instructors a wide range of instructional aids. These supplements have been completely revised, not only to incorporate material new to this edition, but also to ensure that standards of the highest quality are maintained.

- INSTRUCTOR'S RESOURCE MANUAL WITH LECTURE OUTLINER: In addition to a new section devoted to using our *Companion Website™*, this supplement provides the following resources for each chapter of the text: summary, review of major concepts, lecture suggestions and topic outlines, suggestions for classroom discussion, and a detailed content outline for lecture planning. An electronic version is also available in the Faculty Resources section of the *Companion Website™*.
ISBN: 0-13-0933724

- POWERPOINT GALLERY: For each chapter, the Power-Point Gallery provides electronic files for each figure and table in the text, along with pre-created PowerPoint slides ready for customization. With the use of this tool you may create a dynamic PowerPoint presentation or print your own customized 4-color transparencies. (Available in the Faculty Resources section of the *Companion Website™*.)

- PRESENTATION PACKAGE: A new resource designed to make your presentation preparation worry free, this supplement provides detailed instructions for using our PowerPoint Gallery to create your presentation. In addition, 8½ x 11 transparency masters for every figure and table in the text are provided, ready for duplication. Finally, a collection of the most widely used, 4-color transparencies is provided for your convenience.

- TEST ITEM FILE: Completely revised to ensure the highest level of quality and accuracy, this test item file contains over 2000 questions using multiple-choice, true/false, and essay format for covering factual, conceptual, and applied material from the text:
Basic, National, National/S/L versions: ISBN: 0-13-0326755
Brief version: ISBN: 0-13-0933686

- PRENTICE HALL TEST MANAGER: A computerized version of the test item file, this program allows full editing of the questions and the addition of instructor-generated items. Other special features include random generation, scrambling question order, and test preview before printing. Available for both the Microsoft Windows operating system and Macintosh computers:
MAC Basic, National, National/S/L versions:
ISBN: 0-13-0326712
MAC Brief version: ISBN: 0-13-0418129
WIN Basic, National, National/S/L versions:
ISBN: 0-13-0326607
WIN Brief version: ISBN: 0-13-0418110

- VIDEO: HOW A BILL BECOMES A LAW: This 25-minute video chronicles an environmental law in Massachusetts from its start as one citizen's concern to its passage in Washington, D.C. Students witness step-by-step the process of how a bill becomes a law. Complete with narrative and dynamic graphics:
ISBN: 0-13-0326763

- FILMS FOR THE HUMANITIES AND SCIENCES: With a qualifying order of textbooks from Prentice Hall, you may select from a high quality library of political science videos from Films for the Humanities and Sciences. Please contact your local representative for a complete listing.

- STRATEGIES FOR TEACHING AMERICAN GOVERNMENT: A GUIDE FOR THE NEW INSTRUCTOR: This unique guide offers a wealth of practical advice and information to help new instructors face the challenges of teaching courses in American Government. (Available in the Faculty Resources Section of the *Companion Website™*.)

SUPPLEMENTS FOR THE STUDENT

In addition to the wealth of content offered on the *Companion Website™* (**www.prenhall.com/burns**), *Government by the People, 2001–2002 Edition*, offers the following study material to maximize students' learning potential:

- STUDY GUIDE: In addition to a new section devoted to the *Companion Website™*, each chapter includes a detailed outline, study notes, a glossary, practice tests, Political Science Today study assignments, and data analysis worksheets that reinforce student learning. The guide was prepared by Larry Elowitz of Georgia College and State University:
Basic: ISBN: 0-13-0326674
National: ISBN: 0-13-0326682
National, State, and Local: ISBN: 0-13-0326690
Brief: ISBN: 0-13-09337A-3

- POLITICAL SCIENCE ON THE INTERNET: EVALUATING ONLINE RESOURCES: This timely supplement provides an introduction to the Internet and the numerous political sites on the World Wide Web. Not only does it describe e-mail, list servers, browsers, and how to document these sources, it also provides information on how to critically evaluate those sources. Furthermore, it includes addresses for the most current and useful politically-oriented websites. This 96-page supplementary book is FREE to students when shrink-wrapped with copies of *Government by the People*: ISBN: 0-13-0277584

- THE POLITICAL SCIENCE STUDENT WRITER'S MANUAL, 4TH ED.: Authored by Gregory Scott and Stephen Garrison, this comprehensive, practical writer's manual—created specifically for political science students—is designed to help students accomplish two goals: (1) improve their writing skills and strategies, and (2) learn about political science at the same time. Available to students for a discount when bundled with *Government by the People*: ISBN: 0-13-0404470

- THE WRITE STUFF: WRITING AS A PERFORMING AND POLITICAL SCIENCE ART, 2ND ED.: This brief booklet, written by Thomas E. Cronin, provides ideas and suggestions on writing style and methods in political science. Also available in the Student Resources section of the *Companion Website*™.

SUPPLEMENTARY BOOKS AND READINGS FOR AMERICAN GOVERNMENT

Each of the following books features specialized topical coverage allowing you to tailor your American Government course to suit the needs of your region or your particular teaching style. Featuring contemporary issues or timely readings, any of the following books are available for a discount when bundled with *Government by the People*. Please visit our Online Catalog at **www.prenhall.com/burns** for additional details.

American Politics: Core Arguments—Current Controversy, 2nd ed.
Peter Woolley, Fairleigh Dickenson University
Albert Papa, University of New Jersey
ISBN: 0-13-0879193 © 2002

Contemporary Readings in American Government
Mark Rozell, The Catholic University of America
John White, The Catholic University of America
ISBN: 0-13-0406457 © 2002

Issues in American Political Life: Money, Violence, and Biology, 4th ed.
Robert Thobaben, Wright State University
Donna Schlagheck, Wright State University

Charles Funderburk, Wright State University
ISBN: 0-13-0336726 © 2002

Choices: An American Government Reader—Custom Publishing
Gregory Scott, University of Central Oklahoma
Katherine Tate, University of California–Irvine
Ronald Weber, University of Wisconsin–Milwaukee
ISBN: 0-13-090399X © 2001

Civil Rights and Liberties: Provocative Questions and Evolving Answers
Harold Sullivan, The City University of New York
ISBN: 0-13-0845140 © 2001

Sense and Non-Sense: American Culture and Politics
J. Harry Wray, DePaul University
ISBN: 0-13-0833436 © 2001

21 Debated: Issues in American Politics
Gregory Scott, University of Central Oklahoma
Loren Gatch, University of Central Oklahoma
ISBN: 0-13-0219916 © 2000

Government and Politics in the Lone Star State: Theory and Practice, 4th ed.
L. Tucker Gibson, Trinity Univerity
Clay Robison, The Houston Chronicle
ISBN: 0-13-0340502 © 2002

Rethinking California: Politics and Policy in the Golden State
Matthew Cahn, California State University–Northridge
H. Eric Schockman, University of Southern California
David Shafie, Ohio University
ISBN: 0-13-4679121 © 2001

Real Politics in America series is another resource for contemporary instructional material. To bridge the gap between research and relevancy, we have launched a new series of supplemental books with the help of series editor Paul Herrnson of the University of Maryland. More descriptive than quantitative, more case study than data study, these books cut across all topics to bring students relevant details in current political science research. From exploring the growing phenomenon of direct democracy to who runs for the state legislature, these books show students that real political science is meaningful and exciting. Available for a discount when bundled with *Government by the People*. Please see your Prentice Hall representative or access **www.prenhall.com/burns** for a complete listing of titles in the series.

ABOUT THE AUTHORS

JAMES MACGREGOR BURNS

James MacGregor Burns is a Senior Scholar at the Academy of Leadership, University of Maryland, College Park, and Woodrow Wilson Professor Emeritus of Government at Williams College. He has written numerous books, including *The Power to Lead* (1984), *The Vineyard of Liberty* (1982), *Leadership* (1979), *Roosevelt: The Soldier of Freedom* (1970), *The Deadlock of Democracy: Four-Party Politics in America* (1963), and *Roosevelt: The Lion and the Fox* (1956). With his son, Stewart Burns, he wrote *A People's Charter: The Pursuit of Rights in America* (1991); with Georgia Sorenson, *Dead Center: Clinton, Gore, and the Perils of Moderation* (2000); and with Susan Dunn, *The Three Roosevelts* (2001). Burns is a past president of the American Political Science Association and winner of numerous prizes, including a Pulitzer Prize in History.

J.W. PELTASON

J.W. Peltason is a leading scholar on the judicial process and public law. He is Professor Emeritus of Political Science at the University of California, Irvine. As past president of the American Council on Education, Peltason has represented higher education before Congress and state legislatures. His writings include *Federal Courts in the Political Process* (1955), *Fifty-Eight Lonely Men: Southern Federal Judges and School Desegregation* (1961), and with Sue Davis, *Understanding the Constitution* (2000). Among his awards are the James Madison Medal from Princeton University, the Irvine Medal from the University of California, Irvine, and the American Political Science Association's Charles E. Merriam Award.

THOMAS E. CRONIN

Thomas E. Cronin is a leading student of the American presidency, leadership, and policy-making processes. He teaches at and serves as president of Whitman College. He was a White House Fellow and a White House aide and has served as president of the Western Political Science Association. His writings include *The State of the Presidency* (1980), *U.S. v. Crime in the Streets* (1981), *Direct Democracy: The Politics of Initiative, Referendum, and Recall* (1989), *Colorado Politics and Government* (1993), and *The Paradoxes of the American Presidency* (1998). Cronin is a past recipient of the American Political Science Association's Charles E. Merriam Award.

DAVID B. MAGLEBY

David B. Magleby is nationally recognized for his expertise on direct democracy, voting behavior, and campaign finance. He is Professor of Political Science at Brigham Young University and has taught at the University of California, Santa Cruz, and the University of Virginia. His writings include *Direct Legislation* (1984), *The Money Chase: Congressional Campaign Finance Reform* (1990), *Myth of the Independent Voter* (1992), and editor of *Outside Money: Soft Money and Issue Advocacy in the 1998 Congressional Elections* (2000). He was president of Pi Sigma Alpha, the national political science honor society, and has received numerous teaching awards. In 1996 he was a Fulbright Scholar at Nuffield College, Oxford University.

DAVID M. O'BRIEN

David M. O'Brien is the Leone Reaves and George W. Spicer Professor at the University of Virginia. He was a Judicial Fellow and Research Associate at the Supreme Court of the United States, a Fulbright Lecturer at Oxford University, held the Fulbright Chair for Senior Scholars at the University of Bologna, and a Fulbright Researcher in Japan, as well as a Visiting Fellow at the Russell Sage Foundation. Among his publications are *Storm Center: The Supreme Court in American Politics*, 5th ed., (2000); a two volume casebook, *Constitutional Law and Politics*, 4th ed., (2000); an annual *Supreme Court Watch;* and *To Dream of Dreams: Religious Freedom in Postwar Japan* (1996). He received the American Bar Association's Silver Gavel Award for contributing to the public's understanding of the law.

GOVERNMENT BY THE PEOPLE

BASIC VERSION
2001-2002 EDITION

1

CONSTITUTIONAL DEMOCRACY

THE CONSTITUTIONAL DEMOCRACY WE CALL THE
UNITED STATES OF AMERICA IS ABOUT TEN GENERATIONS
OLD, YET IT IS STILL AN EXPERIMENT, STILL A WORK IN
progress. We think of it as an enduring, solid government, but in a very real sense, our
constitutional political system is built on a fragile foundation. The U.S. Constitution
and its crucial Bill of Rights survive not because the parchment they were written on is
still with us, but because each generation of Americans respects, renews, and works at
understanding the principles and values found in these precious documents.

The political and legal struggles over whether George W. Bush or Al Gore was the
legitimate presidential victor in the 2000 election remind us once more about the
strengths and weaknesses of our political process. Many people believe that the voting
procedure in Florida and elsewhere was flawed, and the courts failed to provide nonpartisan remedies. Others believe the system worked, and that this extraordinarily
close presidential and congressional election created a unique opportunity to govern
from the political center.

Many observers view the Supreme Court's decision in the now landmark *Bush v
Gore* case as politically motivated, yet the public, weary after weeks of political haggling,
wanted an end to the counts and recounts and was willing to accept George Bush as the
Electoral College victor, even though Al Gore won the national popular vote.

Polls of the American people frequently ask whether Abraham Lincoln's famous
description—"government of the people, by the people, for the people"—is still true
today. Many say no. Moreover, people often say they do not trust their government to
do the right thing. A *Wall Street Journal*/NBC poll in late 2000 found that only 28 percent of the public had "a great deal of or even quite a bit of confidence in" the federal
government.[1] More than twice the percentage, in contrast, had confidence in the military and in small businesses.

We often hear people denouncing the government as if it were some alien empire.
The "government," some say, is out to get us, or is corrupt, or is engaging in a conspiracy,
whereas "the people" are thought to be all pure of heart. But government is not a thing.
The reality is that "government" is merely a shorthand term to refer to a lot of people in
our society—the people we elect and the people they appoint to promote the general
welfare, provide for domestic tranquility, and secure the blessings of liberty for us.

So, too, we often refer to "the people" as if it were some abstraction. But there is
no such "thing" as "the people" or "the public." The American people consist of over 285

CHAPTERMEDIA

POLITICS ONLINE
*The Internet and Your Study
  of Political Science*
www.prenhall.com/burns

POLISIM
The Map of Freedom
www.prenhall.com/burns

Let us define some of the basic terms we'll be using throughout this book. *Government* refers to the procedures and institutions (such as elections, courts, and legislatures) by which a people govern and rule themselves. *Politics* is the process by which people decide, at least in our system of government, who shall govern and what policies shall be adopted. Such processes invariably involve discussions, debates, and compromises over tactics and goals. *Politicians* are the people who fulfill the tasks of an operating government. Some politicians—legislators, mayors, and presidents—come to office through an election. Nonelected politicians may be political party officials or aides, advisers or consultants to elected officials. *Political science* is the study of the principles, procedures, and structures of government and the analysis of political ideas, institutions, behavior, and practices.

million highly diverse people of all kinds, colors, and sizes. And it is because these people do not all think alike, or have the same values or desires, that we engage in democratic politics to decide who should make our laws and hold government offices.

Americans love their country, revere their Constitution, and respect the free enterprise system, but they often don't like the politics and politicians that are central to a functioning government. A country and its heritage are easier to admire than are the people in office at any time who tax, regulate, penalize, and sometimes even conscript us. But can government also be a force for good? Is government merely "a necessary evil"? As this book will demonstrate, constitutional government and its elected officials often do use governmental power to improve our lives, protect our freedoms, and, in general, expand our liberties.

Consider, for example, the mundane regulations you are forced to follow in this country. You can be punished if you don't drive on the right side of the road, stop at red lights, or refrain from consuming alcohol when you drive. Moreover, both you and your vehicle must be licensed by a state agency. How can you be free, you might ask, when you are subject to so many regulations and have to give up so many rights? Author Garry Wills replies:

> Actually, these rules are immensely liberating. . . . Absent the rules of the road, we would all inflict suffering not only on those hit or hurt or killed, but on those who would have to live with the thought of having been the agent of another's death. It is an act of compassion and mercy to spare both the victim and the driver that kind of misery.[2]

Thus, greater governmental power is sometimes precisely what leads to greater rights, greater freedom. But this is not always the case. We know from our early history under the king of England and from our study of other nations that governmental power can be misused and misapplied. The challenge of a constitutional democracy is that its citizens must be constantly engaged in judging whether power is being used wisely, or whether power is being used to corrupt and to cause an undesirable loss of rights, freedoms, and liberty.

CONSTITUTIONAL DEMOCRACY IS NOT A SPECTATOR SPORT

The American Republic has endured and even prospered for more than two centuries. During that time we have held—even in the midst of a civil war, depressions, and world wars—54 presidential elections (including the recent 2000 election), and we have witnessed the peaceful transfer of power from one party to another on dozens of occasions.

Few democracies have survived this long. The United States has succeeded in large part because Americans have shared a common commitment to our Constitution, to one another, and to the belief that our differences are best reconciled by debate, compromise, and voting and that elected officials govern better than do military generals, or business entrepreneurs, or professors, or religious leaders.

But as recent events remind us, there are deep divisions in the United States. Many people are concerned about the persistence of racism, about religious bigotry, about the gap in economic opportunities between rich and poor, and about the gun violence that afflicts children and minorities.

The United States appears today to be more powerful and indestructible than any nation in history. With our thriving old and new industries, colleges and universities, vast governmental institutions, unrivaled military strength, and unprecedented breakthroughs in science, technology, and medicine, this country has an aura of invincibility. "But it is built" notes John W. Gardner, "on intangibles, every beam and

A government can regulate and restrict many of our ordinary actions, such as using cell phones. Some communities have outlawed the use of cell phones while driving because they have been found to distract drivers and cause accidents.

girder held together by mutual obligations and expectations, shared beliefs, laws and traditions, faith, caring, trust and responsibility. Weaken these beyond a certain point and the great edifice crumbles."[3]

More than any other form of government, the kind of democracy that has emerged under our Constitution requires active participation and a fine balance between faith and skepticism. Government by the people, however, does not require that *everyone* be involved in politics and policy making. Many citizens will always be too busy doing other things, and some people will always be apathetic toward politics and government. Government by the people does require a segment of the public that is attentive, interested, involved, informed, and willing, when necessary, to criticize and remove those in government.

Government by the people requires faith concerning our common human enterprise, a belief that if the people are informed and caring, they can be trusted with their own self-government and an optimism that when things begin to go wrong, the people can be relied upon to set them right. But a healthy skepticism is needed as well. Democracy requires us to question our leaders and never trust a group or institution that holds too much power. And even though constitutional advocates prize majority rule, they must remain skeptical about whether the majority is always right.

Thomas Jefferson

Constitutional democracy requires us to be constantly concerned about whether we are being tolerant and protective of the rights and opinions of others, and whether our democratic processes are, in fact, serving the principles of liberty, equality, and justice. Thus, the democratic faith depends on a peculiar blend of faith and skepticism when dealing with the will of the people.

Thomas Jefferson, one of our best-known champions of constitutional democracy, believed in the common sense of the people and in the flowering possibilities of the human spirit. Jefferson warned that every government degenerates when it is left only in the hands of the rulers. The people themselves, Jefferson wrote, are the only safe repositories of government. His was a robust commitment to popular control, to representative processes, and to accountable leadership. But he was no believer in the simple participatory democracy of ancient Greece or revolutionary France. The power of the people, too, must be restrained from time to time.

Our nation's founders set up a government that over the last two hundred years has become a government *by consent of the governed*. As Justice Robert H. Jackson wrote in a 1943 U.S. Supreme Court decision, "Authority here is to be controlled by public opinion, not public opinion by authority."[4]

Constitutional democracy is necessarily government by representative politicians. A central feature of democracy is that those who hold power do so only by winning an election. In our political system, the fragmentation of powers requires elected officials to mediate among factions, build coalitions, and work out compromises among and within the branches of our government to produce policy and action.

We expect a lot from our politicians. We expect them to operate within the rules of democracy, to be honest, humble, patriotic, compassionate, sensitive to the needs of others, well-informed, competent, fair-minded, self-confident, and inspirational. They must be candidates of all the people, not just those with money. They must not want power for itself, but lead because of their concern for the public good. And finally, they must be willing to do the job and get out when finished.

Why does such a gap persist between our image of the ideal politician and our views about actual politicians? The gap exists in part because we have unrealistic expectations. We want politicians to be perfect, to have all the answers, and to have all the correct (in our minds) values. We want politicians to solve our problems, yet we also want them to serve as scapegoats for the things we dislike about government: taxes, regulations, hard times, and limits on our freedom. It is impossible for anyone to live up to these ideals. Like all individuals, politicians live in a world in which perfection may be the goal, yet compromise, ambition, fund raising, and self-promotion are necessary.

Americans will never be satisfied with their political candidates and politicians. The ideal politician is probably a fictional entity, for the perfect official would be able to please everyone, make conflict disappear, and not ask us to make any sacrifices. Politicians become "ideal" only when they are dead.

But the love of liberty invites disagreements of ideology and values. Politicians and candidates, as well as the people they represent, have different ideas about what is best for the nation. That's why we have politics, candidates, opposition parties, heated political debates, and elections.

DEFINING DEMOCRACY

The word "democracy" is nowhere to be found in the Declaration of Independence or in the U.S. Constitution, nor was it a term used by the founders of the Republic. It is both a very old term and a new one. It was used at the time of the founding of this nation to refer to various undesirable things: mobs, lack of standards, and a system that encourages leaders to gain power by appealing to the emotions and prejudices of the rabble.

The distinguishing feature of democracy is that government derives its authority from its citizens. In fact, the word comes from two Greek words: *demos* (the people) and *kratos* (authority or power). Thus **democracy** means *government by the people*—not government by one person (a monarch, a dictator, a priest) or government by the few (an oligarchy or aristocracy).

Ancient Athens and a few other Greek cities had a **direct democracy** in which citizens came together to discuss and pass laws and select their rulers. These Greek city-states did not last. Most turned to mob rule and then resorted to dictators. Thus, when the word "democracy" came into English usage in the seventeenth century, it denoted this kind of direct democracy. It was a term of derision, a negative word, usually used to refer to mob rule.

James Madison, writing in *The Federalist*, No. 10, reflected the view of many of the framers of the U.S. Constitution when he wrote, "Such democracies [as the Greek and Roman] . . . have ever been found incompatible with personal security, or the rights of property; and have in general been as short in their lives, as they have been violent in their deaths" (*The Federalist*, No. 10, appears in the Appendix at the back of this book).

Today it is no longer possible, even if desirable, to assemble the citizens of any but the smallest towns to make their laws or to select their officials directly from among the citizenry. Rather, we have invented a system of representation. Democracy today means **representative democracy**, or, to use Plato's term, a *republic*, in which those who have governmental authority get and retain authority directly or indirectly as a result of winning free elections in which all adult citizens are allowed to participate. The framers preferred to use the term "republic" to avoid any confusion between direct democracy, which they disliked, and representative democracy, which they liked and thought secured all the advantages of a direct democracy while curing its weaknesses. Today, and in this book, *democracy* and *republic* are used interchangeably.

In defining democracy, several other terms need to be clarified. **Constitutional democracy** as used here refers to a government in which those who exercise substantial governmental powers do so as the result of winning free and relatively frequent elections. *It is a government in which there are recognized, enforced limits on the powers of all governmental officials.*

Constitutionalism is a label we apply to arrangements such as checks and balances, federalism, separation of powers, rule of law, due process, and the Bill of Rights that require our leaders to listen, think, bargain, and explain before they make laws. We then hold them politically and legally accountable for how they exercise their powers.

democracy
Government by the people, either directly or indirectly, with free and frequent elections.

direct democracy
Government in which citizens come together to discuss and pass laws and select rulers.

representative democracy
Government that derives its powers indirectly from the people, who elect those who will govern; also called a *republic*.

constitutional democracy
A government in which those who exercise governmental powers do so as a result of winning free and relatively frequent elections and are subject to recognized, enforced limits on the power of all government officials. It is the elections that make the government democratic; it is the recognized and enforced limits on power that make it constitutional.

constitutionalism
The set of arrangements such as checks and balances, federalism, separation of powers, rule of law, due process, and the Bill of Rights that requires our leaders to listen, think, bargain, and explain before they make laws. We then hold them politically and legally accountable for how they exercise their powers.

Like most political concepts, democracy encompasses many ideas and has many meanings. Democracy is a way of life, a form of government, a way of governing, a type of nation, a state of mind, and a variety of processes. We can divide these many meanings into three broad categories: democracy as a system of interacting values, a system of interrelated political processes, and a system of interdependent political structures.

Democracy as a System of Interacting Values

Today the democratic faith may be as near a universal faith as the world has. A belief in human dignity, freedom, liberty, individual rights, and other democratic values is widely shared in most corners of the world. The essence of democratic values is contained in the ideas of personal liberty, respect for the individual, equality of opportunity, and popular consent.

PERSONAL LIBERTY   Liberty has been the single most powerful value in American history. It was for "life, liberty, and the pursuit of happiness" that independence was declared; it was to "secure the Blessings of Liberty" that the Constitution was drawn up and adopted. Even our patriotic songs extol the "sweet land of liberty." The essence of liberty is *self-determination*, meaning that all individuals must have the opportunity to realize their own goals. Liberty is not simply the absence of external restraint on a person (freedom *from*); it is the individual's freedom and capacity to act positively to reach his or her goals (freedom *to*). Moreover, both history and reason suggest that individual liberty is the key to social progress. The greater the people's freedom, the greater the chance of discovering better ways of life.

RESPECT FOR THE INDIVIDUAL   Popular rule in a democracy flows from a belief that every individual has the potential for common sense, rationality, and fairness. Individuals have important rights; collectively, those rights are the source of all legitimate governmental authority and power. These concepts pervade all democratic thought. They are woven into the writings of Thomas Jefferson, especially in the Declaration of Independence: "All men . . . are endowed by their Creator with certain unalienable rights" (the Declaration of Independence appears in the Appendix). Constitutional democracies make the *person*—rich or poor, black or white, male or female—the central measure of value. The state, the union, and ideally even the corporation are measured in terms of their usefulness to individuals.

Not all political systems put the individual first. Some promote **statism**, considering the state supreme. In a modern democracy, the nation, or even the community, is less important than are the individuals who compose it.

EQUALITY OF OPPORTUNITY   The importance of the individual is enhanced by the democratic value of *equality*: "All men are created equal and from that equal creation they derive rights inherent and unalienable, among which are the preservation of liberty and the pursuit of happiness." So reads Jefferson's first draft of the Declaration of Independence, and the words indicate the primacy of the concept. Alexis de Tocqueville and other international visitors who have studied American democracy were all struck by the strength of egalitarian thought and practice in our political and social lives.

But what does equality mean? Equality for whom? For blacks as well as whites? For women as well as men? For Native Americans, descendants of the Pilgrims, and recent immigrants? And what kind of equality? Economic, political, legal, social, or some other kind of equality? Equality of opportunity? Does equality of opportunity simply mean that everyone should have the same place at the starting line? Or does it mean an effort should be made to equalize the factors that determine how well a person fares economically or socially?

"The Athenians are here, Sire, with an offer to back us with ships, money, arms, and men—and, of course, their usual lectures about democracy."

statism
The idea that the rights of the state (meaning nation) are supreme over the rights of the individual.

PEOPLE

BUSH V GORE: THE MAJORITY OPINION

The recount mechanisms implemented in response to the decisions of the Florida Supreme Court do not satisfy the minimum requirement for non-arbitrary treatment of voters.

In the 2000 election, for the first time in U.S. history, the Supreme Court played a decisive role in deciding who would win a presidential election when, in a 5 to 4 decision, it halted the manual recounting of ballots in Florida. After the automatic recount required under Florida law, George W. Bush's lead in the popular vote was 327 votes. The winner of Florida's 25 electoral votes would win the election. The issue before the court was whether manual recounts should proceed as ordered by the Florida Supreme Court in counties where the Gore campaign had asked for them, and what the standard of that manual recount should be. The Florida Supreme Court had not specified a standard.

Governor Bush appealed the Florida court's decision to the U.S. Supreme Court, and the majority of the justices ruled that the manual recounts violated the equal protection clause by applying different standards for counting the ballots in different counties; and that there was not time to remedy the problem before a congressional

deadline of December 12 for forwarding electoral votes to the Congress. The majority argued:

The right to vote is protected in more than the initial allocation of the franchise. Equal protection applies as well to the manner of its exercise. Having once granted the right to vote on equal terms, the State may not, by later arbitrary and disparate treatment, value one person's vote over that of another. . . The recount mechanisms implemented in response to the decisions of the Florida Supreme Court do not satisfy the minimum requirement for non-arbitrary treatment of voters. . . The formulations of uniform rules to determine intent based on these recurring circumstances is practicable, and, we conclude, necessary. . . The want of those rules here has led to unequal evaluation of ballots in various respects. . . it is obvious that the recount cannot be conducted in compliance with the requirements of equal protection and due process without substantial additional work. . . Because it is evident that any recount seeking to meet the December 12 deadline will be unconstitutional for the reasons we have discussed, we reverse the judgment of the Supreme Court of Florida ordering a recount to proceed. ★

DEBATE

BUSH V GORE: THE MINORITY DISSENT

One irony of the majority opinion is that the justices who joined it generally favored deference to state courts to set their own course. The dissent disputed the claim by the majority that U.S. Supreme Court had jurisdiction to decide this case and contended that while equal protection may have been an issue, there were alternative solutions to simply ending the recounts altogether. As Justice Stevens stated in his dissent:

The federal questions that ultimately emerged in this case are not substantial. . . The legislative power in Florida is subject to judicial review pursuant to Article V of the Florida Constitution, and nothing in Article II of the Federal Constitution frees that state legislature from the constraints in the state constitution that created it. . . It hardly needs stating that Congress, pursuant to [Section] 5 did not impose any affirmative duties upon the States that their governmental branches could "violate." Rather, [Section] 5 provides a safe harbor for States to select electors in contested elections "by judicial or other methods" established by law prior to the election day. Section 5, like Article II, assumes the involvement of the state judiciary in interpreting state election laws

and resolving election disputes under those laws. Neither [Section] 5 nor Article II grants federal judges any special authority to substitute their views for those of the state judiciary on matters of state law.

(Section 5 refers to the section of the Electoral Count Act of 1887 that provides a "safe harbor" for electoral votes receiving certification by December 12. Article II provides that "each state shall appoint, in such Manner as the Legislature thereof may direct" the electors for President and Vice President.)

Also speaking for the dissenting minority, Justice Breyer argued:

I agree that, in these very special circumstances, basic principles of fairness may well have counseled the adoption of a uniform standard to address the problem. . . Nonetheless, there is no justification for the majority's remedy, which is simply to reverse the lower court and halt the recount entirely. An appropriate remedy would be, instead, to remand this case with instructions, even at this late date, to permit the Florida Supreme Court to require recounting all undercounted votes in Florida... and to do so in accordance with a single uniform standard. ★

There is no justification for the majority's remedy, which is simply to reverse the lower court and halt the recount entirely.

For further information about this debate, go to **www.prenhall.com/burns** *and click on the Debate Icon in Chapter 1.*

POPULAR CONSENT   The animating principle of the American Revolution, the Declaration of Independence, and the resulting new nation was **popular consent**, the idea that a just government must derive its powers from the *consent of the people* it governs. A commitment to democracy thus entails a community's willingness to participate and make decisions in government. These principles sound unobjectionable intellectually, but in practice they mean that certain individuals or groups may not get their way. A commitment to popular consent must involve a willingness to lose when most people vote the other way.

DEMOCRATIC VALUES IN CONFLICT   The basic values of democracy do not always coexist happily. Individualism may conflict with the collective welfare or the public good. Self-determination may conflict with equal opportunity. For example, the right of a homeowner to add another floor to her home may conflict with the right of her neighbor to have an unobstructed view. Or the right of a person to smoke an after-dinner cigar in a restaurant may conflict with the right of others not to have to breathe tobacco smoke.

Much of our political combat revolves around how to strike a balance among democratic values—how to protect the Declaration of Independence's unalienable rights of life, liberty, and the pursuit of happiness while trying to "form," as the Constitution announces, "a more perfect Union, establish Justice, insure domestic Tranquility, provide for the common defence, promote the general Welfare, and secure the Blessings of Liberty to ourselves and our Posterity" (see the Preamble to the Constitution on page 43). Over the years the American political system has moved, despite occasional setbacks, toward greater freedom and more democracy.

A strong commitment to democracy was in many ways a twentieth-century idea. Although on dozens of occasions in the past century democracies collapsed and gave way to authoritarian regimes, even more democracies triumphed. Indeed, "the global range and influence of democratic ideas, institutions, and practices has made [the twentieth century] far and away the most flourishing period for democracy."[5]

Democracy as a System of Interrelated Political Processes

Far more people dream about democracy than ever experience it, and many new democracies fail. To be successful, democratic government requires a well-defined political process as well as a stable governmental structure. To become reality, democratic values must be incorporated into a political process, most importantly in the form of free and fair elections, majority rule, freedom of expression, and the right to assemble and protest.

FREE AND FAIR ELECTIONS   Democratic government is based on free and fair elections held at intervals frequent enough to make them relevant to policy choices. Elections are one of the most important devices for keeping officials and representatives accountable.

We previously described *representative democracy* as a government in which those who have the authority to make decisions with the force of law acquire and retain this authority either directly or indirectly as the result of winning free elections in which the great majority of adult citizens are allowed to participate. Crucial to modern-day definitions of democracy is the idea that opposition political parties can exist, can run candidates in elections, and can at least have a chance to replace those who are currently holding public office. Thus *political competition and choice* are crucial to the existence of democracy.

Although all citizens should have equal voting power, free and fair elections do not imply that everyone must or will have equal political influence. Some people, because of wealth, talent, or position, have more influence than others. How much extra influence key figures should be allowed to exercise in a democracy is frequently debated. But in an election, a president or a plumber, a corporate CEO or a ditch digger, each casts only one vote.

popular consent
The idea that a just government must derive its powers from the consent of the people it governs.

MAJORITY (PLURALITY) RULE **Majority rule**—governance according to the expressed preferences of the majority—is a basic rule of democracy. The **majority** candidate or party is the one that receives *more than half* the votes and so wins the election and takes charge of the government until the next election. In practice, however, majority rule is often **plurality** rule, in which the candidate or party with the *most* votes wins the election, even though it may not constitute a true majority of more than half the votes. About a third of our presidents have won with pluralities in the popular vote rather than majorities.[6] Once elected, officials do not have a right to curtail the attempts of political minorities to use all peaceful means to become the new majority. Even as the winners take power, the losers are at work to try to get it back at the next election.[7]

Should the side with the most votes prevail in all cases? Americans answer this question in a variety of ways. Some insist majority views should be enacted into laws and regulations. However, an effective representative democracy involves far more than simply ascertaining and applying the statistical will of most of the people. It is a more complicated and often untidy process in which the people and their agents debate, compromise, and arrive at a decision only after thoughtful deliberation.

The framers wanted to guard society against any one faction of the people acting unjustly toward any other faction of the people. The Constitution reflects their fear of tyranny by majorities, especially momentary majorities that spring from temporary passions. They insulated certain rights (such as freedom of speech) and institutions (such as the Supreme Court) from popular choice. Effective representation of the people, the framers insisted, should not be based solely on parochial interests or shifting breezes of opinion.

FREEDOM OF EXPRESSION Free and fair elections depend on access to information relevant to voting choices. Voters must have access to facts, competing ideas, and the views of candidates. Free and fair elections require a climate in which competing, non-government-owned newspapers, radio stations, and television stations can flourish. If the government controls what is said and how it is said, there is no democracy. Without free speech there are no free and fair elections.

THE RIGHT TO ASSEMBLE AND PROTEST Citizens must be free to organize for political purposes. Obviously, individuals can be more effective if they join with others in a party, a pressure group, a protest movement, or a demonstration. The right to oppose the government, to form opposition parties, and to have a chance of defeating incumbents is not only vital; it is a defining characteristic of a democracy.

Democracy as a System of Interdependent Political Structures

Democracy is, of course, more than values and processes. It also entails political structures that safeguard these values and processes. The Constitution and the Bill of Rights create an ingenious structure—one that both grants and checks government power. This constitutional structure is reinforced by a political system of parties, interest groups, media, and other institutions that mediate between the electorate and those who govern and thus help to maintain democratic stability.

The U.S. constitutional system has four distinctive elements: (1) *federalism*, the division of powers between the national and state governments; (2) *separation of powers* among the legislative, executive, and judicial branches; (3) *checks and balances* in which each branch is given the constitutional means, the political independence, and the motives to check the powers of the other branches; and (4) a judicially enforceable, written, explicit *Bill of Rights* that provides a guarantee of individual liberties and due process before the law.

majority rule
Governance according to the expressed preferences of the majority.

majority
The candidate or party that wins more than half the votes cast to win an election.

plurality
A candidate or party wins the most votes cast, not necessarily more than half.

Conditions Conducive to Constitutional Democracy

How do we explain the relatively small number of enduring, strong democracies? Although it is hard to specify the precise conditions that are essential for the establishment and maintenance of a democracy, here are a few things we have learned.

EDUCATIONAL CONDITIONS   The exercise of voting privileges takes some level of education on the part of the citizenry. But a word of caution: A high level of education does not cause or guarantee democratic government, as the example of Nazi Germany readily illustrates. And there are some democracies, such as India, where large numbers of people are illiterate. Still, voting makes little sense unless a considerable number of the voters can read and write and express their interests and opinions. The poorly educated and illiterate often get left out in a democracy.

ECONOMIC CONDITIONS   A relatively prosperous nation, with an equitable distribution of wealth, provides the best context for democracy. Starving people are more interested in food than in voting. Where economic power is concentrated, political power is likely to be concentrated. Well-to-do nations have a greater chance of sustaining democratic governments than do those with widespread poverty. The reality is that extremes of wealth and poverty undermine the possibilities for a healthy constitutional democracy. Thus the prospects for an enduring democracy are greater in Canada or France than in Rwanda or Russia.

Some measure of private ownership of property and a relatively favorable role for the market economy are also related to the creation and maintenance of democratic institutions. Democracies can range from heavily regulated economies with public ownership of many enterprises, such as Sweden, to those in which there is little government regulation of the marketplace. But there are no democracies with a highly centralized government-run economy and little private ownership of property, although there are many nations with a market economy and no democracy. There are no truly democratic communist states, nor have there ever been any.

SOCIAL CONDITIONS   Economic development generally makes democracy possible, yet proper social conditions are necessary to make it real.[8] In a society fragmented into warring groups that differ fiercely on fundamental issues, government by discussion and compromise is difficult, as we have seen in the Balkans. When ideologically separated groups consider the issues at stake to be vital, they may prefer to fight rather than accept the verdict of the ballot box.

In a society that consists of many overlapping associations and groupings, however, individuals are not as likely to identify completely with a single group and give their allegiance to it. For example, Joe Smith is a Baptist, an African American, a southerner, a Democrat, an electrician, and a member of the National Rifle Association, and he makes $50,000 a year. On some issues Joe thinks as a Baptist, on others as a southerner, and on still others as an African American. Sue Jones is a Catholic, a white Republican, an auto dealer, and a member of the National Organization for Women; she comes from a Polish background, and she makes $150,000 a year. Sometimes she acts as a Republican, sometimes as an American of Polish descent, and sometimes as a member of NOW. Jones and Smith differ on some issues yet agree on others. In general, the differences between them are not likely to be greater than their common interest in maintaining a democracy.[9]

Democracy is more likely to survive in a nation where the people have acquired democratic habits and are inclined to participate in social, cultural, and civic groups. Political scientist Robert Putnam calls this interest in participation **social capital**.[10] Democratic social capital is generated when there are a rich variety of associations and social institutions that bind people together. Participation in voluntary organizations such as women's groups, bowling leagues, and environmental and conservation groups help build and reinforce democratic habits of discussion, compromise,

social capital

Participation in voluntary associations that reinforce democratic and civic habits of discussion, compromise, and respect for differences.

IT'S NOT EASY TO BE FREE

New democracies often fail. It is one thing to espouse democratic values, another to put them into practice. Some people believe in democracy until they lose power in an election. Or the citizens grow weary of the political wrangling that comes with democracy and long for a strong charismatic leader with simple solutions for complex problems. The struggle to convert to a market economy in Russia has produced this kind of turmoil. Leaders like Napoleon or Adolf Hitler promise to make a

country work more smoothly, often by disbanding democratic institutions. Citizens may turn to such leaders when they face economic difficulties or are under threat from a foreign power. Sectional differences can also pull apart the fabric of democracy. Parts of a country that have a distinctive racial, religious, or ethnic composition often distrust the national majority and seek guarantees or special concessions—as have French-speaking residents in Quebec and ethnic Albanians in Kosovo.

Because democracies are so difficult to sustain, comparatively few have lasted long. More than half the world's constitutions have been written in the past four decades. On the entire continent of Asia, no democracy predates World War II, when a democratic constitution was imposed on Japan. In Africa, the oldest democracy is Botswana, which has had free elections and a multiparty system since 1966.

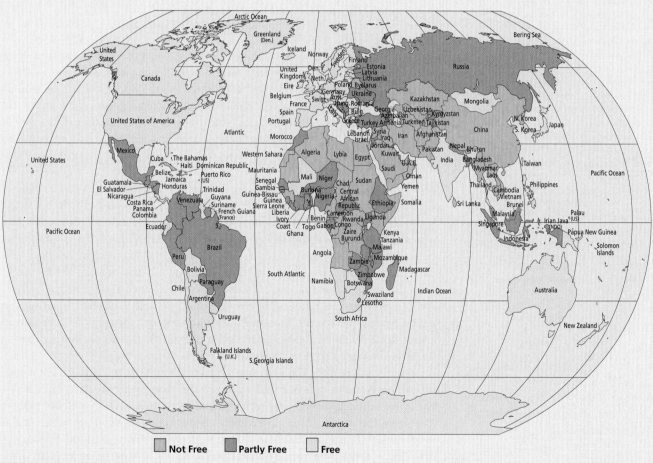

■ Not Free   ■ Partly Free   □ Free

The Map of Freedom 2000

SOURCE: *Freedom Review*, 1999–2000. © 2000 by Freedom House.

Political scientist Robert D. Putnam has pointed to a decline in American political involvement and a decline in confidence in our political institutions. He noted that in recent decades fewer people engage in politics—voting, attending a political rally, working for a political party, or taking part in the political process in other ways. There has also been a decline in church membership and attendance, membership in labor unions, involvement in the PTA, membership in civic and fraternal organizations, volunteering for the Boy Scouts, the Red Cross, and other organizations, and membership in Lions, Elks, Shriners, and Masons.

Putnam writes, "The most whimsical yet discomforting bit of evidence of social disengagement in contemporary America that I have discovered is this: More Americans are bowling today than ever before, but bowling in organization leagues has plummeted in the last decade or so." Noting that members of bowling leagues consume three times as much beer and pizza as do those who bowl alone, he theorizes that "The broader social significance . . . lies in the social interaction and even occasionally civic conversations over beer and pizza that solo bowlers forgo." Whether or not bowling beats balloting in the eyes of most Americans—more bowl than vote—"bowling teams illustrate yet another vanishing form of *social capital*."* Do you agree with him that Americans increasingly prefer social isolation over social involvement?

*Robert D. Putnam, "Bowling Alone: America's Declining Social Capital," *Journal of Democracy* 6, no. 1 (January 1995), p. 20.

ideology
One's basic beliefs about power, political values, and the role of government—beliefs that arise out of educational, economic, and social conditions and experiences.

theocracy
Government by religious leaders, who claim divine guidance.

Articles of Confederation
The first constitution of the American states, drafted in 1777, ratified in 1781, and replaced by the present Constitution in 1789.

and respect for differences. It can "provide the social resources and the civic training that citizens need to make democracy tick."[11]

Civic and social engagement has been changing in the Internet era. Today there are more advocacy and lobbying groups, and environmental groups are plainly on the rise. Beyond the traditional Boy Scouts, Girl Scouts, the YMCA, the YWCA, and the Red Cross, there are myriad local volunteer and service groups and a vast network of youth as well as adult soccer, basketball, hockey, and snowboarding leagues. Women and minorities have been recognized and are active in many new ways. As Michael Schudson notes, if measures of civic health include "measures of political inclusion and protection for individual rights," then "Americans are unquestionably better off in the past quarter century than at any prior moment in our history."[12]

IDEOLOGICAL CONDITIONS   **Ideology** refers to basic beliefs about power, government, and political practices—beliefs that arise out of the educational, economic, and social conditions individuals experience. Out of these conditions must also develop a general acceptance of the ideals of democracy and a willingness of a substantial part of the people to agree to proceed democratically. This acceptance is sometimes called the *democratic consensus*.

THE CONSTITUTIONAL ROOTS OF THE AMERICAN EXPERIMENT

Americans often take democracy for granted. Most of us probably consider it inevitable. We take pride in our ability to make it work, yet we have essentially inherited a functioning system. Its establishment was the work of others, nine or ten generations ago. The challenge for us is not just to keep it going but to improve it and make it adapt to the challenges of our times. To do so, however, we must first understand it, and this requires systematic consideration of our democratic and constitutional roots.

The Colonial Beginnings

There were many reasons one might have expected our democratic experiment to fail. The thirteen states (formerly colonies) were independent and could have gone their separate ways. Sectional differences based on social and economic conditions, especially southern states' dependence on slavery, were an obvious problem. Religious, ethnic, and racial diversity, which challenges so many governments around the world today, existed in substantial degree in the United States during its formative years.

Given these potential problems, how did democracy survive? How did this nation establish democratic principles for its government? How did it limit potential abuses? These questions are of importance not only to Americans but to all who value freedom and democracy everywhere.

The framers of the U.S. Constitution had experience to guide them. For almost two centuries, Europeans had been sailing to the New World in search of liberty—especially religious liberty—as well as land and work. While still aboard the *Mayflower*, the Pilgrims drew up a compact to protect their religious freedom and to make possible "just and equal laws." In the American colonies, editors found they could speak freely in their newspapers, dissenters could distribute leaflets, and agitators could protest in taverns or in the streets.

But the picture of freedom in the colonies was a mixed one. The Puritans in Massachusetts soon established a **theocracy**, a system of government in which religious leaders claimed divine guidance and in which not all religious sects were granted religious liberty. Dissenters were occasionally chased out of town, and some printers were beaten and had their shops closed. In short, the colonists were struggling with the balance of unity and diversity, stability and dissent, order and liberty. Puritans continued to worry "about what would maintain order in a society lacking an established church, an attachment to place, and the uncontested leadership of men of merit."[13] Nine of the thirteen colonies eventually set up a state church. Throughout the 1700s Puritans in Massachusetts barred certain men from voting on the basis of church membership. To the Anglican establishment in Virginia, campaigns for toleration were in themselves subversive. Women and slaves could not vote at all.

The Rise of Revolutionary Fervor

As resentment against British rule mounted during the 1770s and revolutionary fervor rose, Americans became determined to fight the British to win their rights and liberties. A year after the fighting broke out in Massachusetts, the Declaration of Independence proclaimed in ringing tones that all men are created equal, endowed by their Creator with certain unalienable rights; that among them are "life, liberty, and the pursuit of happiness"; that to secure those rights governments are instituted among men; and that whenever a government becomes destructive of those ends, it is the right of the people to alter or abolish it. (Read the full text of the Declaration of Independence in the Appendix.)

We have all heard these great ideals so often that we take them for granted. Revolutionary leaders did not. They were deadly serious about these rights and willing to fight and pledge their lives, fortunes, and sacred honor for them. Bills of rights in the new state constitutions guaranteed free speech, freedom of religion, and the natural rights to life, liberty, and property. All their constitutions spelled out the rights of persons accused of crime, such as knowing the nature of the accusation, being confronted by their accusers, and receiving a timely and public trial by jury.[14] Moreover, these guarantees were in *written* form, a sharp contrast to the unwritten British constitution.

Toward Unity and Order

As the war against the British widened, the need arose for a stronger central government that could pull the colonies together and conduct a revolutionary war. For a time the Continental Congress, which had led the way toward revolution, tried to direct hostilities against the British, but it took a man of George Washington's iron resolve to unify and direct the war effort. Sensing the need for more unity, Congress established a new national government under a written document called the **Articles of Confederation**. At first hardly worthy of the term "government," the Articles were not approved by all the state legislatures until 1781, after Washington's troops had been fighting for six years.

This new Confederation was a move toward a stronger central government, but a limited and inadequate one. Having fought a war against a strong central government in London, Americans were understandably reluctant to create another one, so the Articles established a fragile league of friendship rather than a national government. From 1777 to 1788, Americans made progress under this Confederation, but with the end of the war in 1783, the sense of urgency that had produced unity began to fade. Conflicts between creditors and debtors within the states grew intense. Foreign threats continued; territories ruled by England and Spain surrounded the new nation, which—internally divided and lacking a strong central government—made a tempting prize.

As pressures on the Confederation mounted, many leaders became convinced it would not be enough merely to revise the Articles of Confederation. To create a union strong enough to deal with internal diversity and factionalism as well as to resist external threats, a stronger central government was needed.

In September 1786, under the leadership of Alexander Hamilton, those who favored a truly national government took advantage of the **Annapolis Convention**—a meeting in Annapolis, Maryland, on problems of trade and navigation attended by delegates from five states—to issue a call for a convention that would have full authority to consider basic amendments to the Articles of Confederation. The delegates in Annapolis asked the legislatures of all the states to appoint

1. Congress had no direct authority over citizens but had to work through the states; it could not pass laws or levy taxes in order to carry out its responsibilities to defend the nation and promote its well-being.

2. Congress could not regulate trade between the states or with other nations. States taxed each others' goods and even negotiated their own trade agreements with other nations.

3. Congress could not forbid the states from issuing their own currencies, further complicating interstate trade and travel.

4. Congress had to handle all administrative duties because there was no executive branch.

5. The lack of a judicial system meant that the national government had to rely on state courts to enforce national laws and settle disputes between the states. In practice, state courts could overturn national laws.

Annapolis Convention
A convention held in September 1786 to consider problems of trade and navigation, attended by five states and important because it issued the call to Congress and the states for what became the Constitutional Convention.

Constitutional Convention
The convention in Philadelphia, May 25 to September 17, 1787, that framed the Constitution of the United States.

Shays' Rebellion
Rebellion by farmers in western Massachusetts in 1786–87, protesting mortgage foreclosures; led by Daniel Shays and important because it highlighted the need for a strong national government just as the call for a Constitutional Convention went out.

commissioners to meet in Philadelphia on the second Monday of May 1787, "to devise such further provisions as shall appear to them necessary to render the Constitution of the Federal Government adequate to the exigencies of the Union." The convention they called for became the **Constitutional Convention**.

For a short time all was quiet. Then, late in 1786, messengers rode into George Washington's plantation at Mount Vernon with the kind of news he and other leaders had dreaded. Farmers in western Massachusetts, crushed by debts and taxes, were rebelling against foreclosures, forcing judges out of their courtrooms, and freeing debtors from jails. Washington was appalled. "What, gracious God, is man?" he exclaimed. Ten years before, he had been leading Americans in a patriotic war against the British, and now Americans were fighting Americans!

Not all Americans reacted as Washington did to what became known as **Shays' Rebellion** after Daniel Shays, its leader. When Abigail Adams, the politically knowledgeable wife of John Adams, sent news of the rebellion to Thomas Jefferson, the Virginian replied, "I like a little rebellion now and then," noting also that the "tree of liberty must be refreshed from time to time with the blood of patriots and tyrants. It is its natural manure."[15]

Shays' Rebellion petered out after the farmers attacked an arsenal and were cut down by cannon fire. Yet this "little rebellion" sent a stab of fear into the established leadership. It also acted as a catalyst. The message now was plain: Action must be taken to strengthen the machinery of government. Seven states appointed commissioners to attend a convention in Philadelphia to strengthen the Articles of Confederation. Congress finally issued a cautiously worded call to all the state legislatures to appoint delegates for the "sole and express purpose of revising the Articles of Confederation." The suspicious congressional legislators specified that no recommendation would be effective unless approved by Congress and confirmed by all the state legislatures, as provided by the Articles.

THE CONSTITUTIONAL CONVENTION, 1787

The delegates who assembled in Philadelphia that May had to establish a national government powerful enough to prevent the young nation from dissolving but not so powerful it would crush individual liberty. What these men did continues to have a major impact on how we are governed. It also provides an outstanding lesson in political science for the world.

The Delegates

Seventy-four delegates were appointed by the various states, but only 55 arrived in Philadelphia. Of these, approximately 40 took a real part in the work of the convention. It was a distinguished gathering. Many of the most important men of the nation were there: successful merchants, planters, bankers, lawyers, and former and present governors and congressional representatives (39 of the delegates had served in Congress). Most had read the classics of political thought. Most had participated vigorously in the practical task of constructing local and state governments. Many had also worked hard to create and direct the national Confederation of the states. And 8 of the 56 signers of the Declaration of Independence were present at the Constitutional Convention.

The convention was as representative as most political gatherings at the time: the participants were all white male landowners. These well-read, well-fed, well-bred, and often well-wed delegates were mainly state or national leaders, for in the 1780s ordinary people were not likely to participate in politics. (Even today farm laborers, factory workers, and truck drivers are seldom found in Congress, although a haberdasher, a peanut farmer, and a movie actor have made their way to the White House.)

Although active in the movement to revise the Articles of Confederation, George Washington had been reluctant to attend the convention. He accepted only when persuaded that his prestige was needed for its success. He was selected unanimously to preside over the meetings. According to the records, he spoke only twice during the deliberations, yet his influence was felt in the informal gatherings as well as during the sessions. Everyone understood that Washington favored a more powerful central government led by a president. The general expectation that George Washington would likely be the first president played a crucial role in the creation of the presidency. "No one feared that he would misuse power. . . . His genuine hesitancy, his reluctance to assume the position only served to reinforce the almost universal desire that he do so."[16]

The proceedings of the convention were kept secret. To encourage everyone to speak freely, delegates were forbidden to discuss the debates with outsiders. It was feared that if a delegate publicly took a firm stand on an issue, it would be harder for him to change his mind after debate and discussion. The delegates also knew that if word of the inevitable disagreements got out, it would provide ammunition for the many enemies of the convention. There were critics of this secrecy rule, but without it, agreement might not have been possible.

Consensus

The Constitutional Convention is usually discussed in terms of its three famous compromises: the compromise between large and small states over representation in Congress, the compromise between North and South over the regulation and taxation of foreign commerce, and the compromise between North and South over the counting of slaves for the purpose of taxation and representation. There were many other important compromises; yet on many significant issues, most of the delegates were in agreement.

Although a few delegates might have privately favored a limited monarchy, all supported a republican form of government based on elected representatives

WE THE PEOPLE

The Framers: Hamilton and Madison

In the Constitution the framers offered perhaps the most brilliant example of collective intellectual genius—of combining both theory and practice—in the history of the Western world. How could a country 70 times smaller in population than it is today produce several dozen men of genius in Philadelphia, and probably another hundred or so equally talented political thinkers who did not attend? The lives of two prominent delegates, Alexander Hamilton and James Madison, help explain the origins of this collective genius.

Alexander Hamilton had been the engineer of the Annapolis Convention, and as early as 1778 he had been urging that the national government be made stronger. Hamilton had come to the United States from the West Indies and while still a college student had won national attention for his brilliant pamphlets in defense of the Revolutionary cause. During the war he served as General Washington's aide, and his experiences confirmed his distaste for a Congress so weak it could not even supply the Revolution's troops with enough food or arms.

James Madison was only 36 years old at the time of the convention, yet he was one of its most learned members. He had helped frame Virginia's first constitution and had served both in the Virginia Assembly and in the Continental Congress. Madison was also a leader of those who favored the establishment of a stronger national government.

Like most of the other framers, Hamilton and Madison were superbly educated. Both had extensive private tutoring—a one-to-one teacher-student ratio. Like scores of other thinkers of the day, both combined extensive practical experience with their schooling. Both were active in their political and religious groups; both took part in political contests and electoral struggles; both helped build political coalitions.

Both men were "moral philosophers" as well as political thinkers. They had strong views on the supreme value—liberty—as well as on current issues. Instead of simply sermonizing about liberty, they analyzed it; they debated what kind of liberty, how to protect it, how to expand it.

James Madison

Alexander Hamilton

of the people. This was the only form seriously considered and the only form acceptable to the nation. Equally important, all the delegates opposed arbitrary and unrestrained government.

The common philosophy accepted by most of the delegates was that of *balanced government*. They wanted to construct a national government in which no single interest would dominate. Because most of the delegates represented citizens who were alarmed by the tendencies of desperate farmers to interfere with the property rights of others, they were primarily concerned with balancing the government in the direction of protection for property and business.

Benjamin Franklin, the 81-year-old delegate from Pennsylvania, favored extending the right to vote to all white males, but most of the delegates believed that owners of land were the best guardians of liberty. James Madison feared that those without property, if given the right to vote, might combine to deprive property owners of their rights. Delegates agreed in principle on limited voting rights, but differed over the kind and amount of property one must own in order to vote. Because states were in the process of relaxing qualifications for the vote, the framers recognized they would jeopardize approval of the constitution if they made the qualifications to vote in federal elections more restricted than those of the states. As a result, each state was left to determine the qualifications for electing members of the House of Representatives, the only branch of the national government that was to be elected directly by the voters.

Within five days of its opening, the convention—with only the Connecticut delegates dissenting—voted that "a national government ought to be established consisting of a supreme legislative, executive, and judiciary." This decision to establish a supreme national government profoundly altered the nature of the union from a loose confederation of states to a truly national government.

Few dissented from proposals to give the new Congress all the powers of the old Congress plus all other powers necessary to ensure that the harmony of the United States would not be challenged by state legislation. The framers agreed that a strong executive, which had been lacking under the Articles of Confederation, was necessary to provide energy and direction. An independent judiciary was also accepted without much debate. Other issues, however, sparked considerable conflict.

Representing different constituencies and different ideologies, the Constitutional Convention devised a totally new form of government that provided for a central government strong enough to rule but still responsible to its citizens and to the member states.

Conflict and Compromise

There were serious differences among the various delegates, especially between those from the large and small states. One of the most contentious issues was how to distribute the land extending westward to the Mississippi, land that had been secured through the Revolution. Several large states asserted claims to these western lands, but small states generally objected. The large states also favored a strong national government (which they expected they could dominate), while delegates from small states were anxious to avoid being dominated.

This tension surfaced in the first discussions of representation in Congress. Franklin favored a single-house national legislature, but most states had had two-chamber legislatures since colonial times, and the delegates were used to the system. **Bicameralism**—the principle of the two-house legislature—reflected delegates' belief in the need for balanced government. The Senate, the smaller chamber, would represent the states, and to some extent the aristocracy, and offset the larger, more democratic House of Representatives.

THE VIRGINIA PLAN   The Virginia delegation took the initiative. They had met during the delay before the convention, and as soon as the convention was organized, they presented 15 resolutions. These resolutions, the **Virginia Plan**, called for a strong central government with a legislature composed of two chambers. The members of the more representative chamber were to be elected by the voters; those of the smaller and more aristocratic chamber were to be chosen by the larger chamber from nominees submitted by the state legislatures. Representation in both houses would be based on either wealth or numbers, which would give the wealthier and more populous states—Massachusetts, Pennsylvania, and Virginia—a majority in the national legislature.

The Congress thus created was to be given all the legislative power of its predecessor under the Articles of Confederation, as well as the right "to legislate in all cases in which the separate States are incompetent." Further, it was to have the authority to veto state legislation that conflicted with the proposed constitution. The Virginia Plan also called for a national executive with extensive jurisdiction who would be chosen by the legislature. A national Supreme Court, along with the executive, was to have a qualified veto over acts of Congress.

THE NEW JERSEY PLAN   The Virginia Plan dominated the discussion for the first few weeks. But by June 15 additional delegates from the small states arrived, and they began a counterattack. They rallied around William Paterson of New Jersey, who presented a series of resolutions known as the **New Jersey Plan**. Table 1–1 outlines the key features of both plans. Paterson did not question the need for a strengthened central government, yet he was concerned about how this strength might be used. The New Jersey Plan would give Congress the right to tax and regulate commerce and to coerce states, and it would retain the single-house unicameral legislature (as under the Articles of Confederation) in which each state, regardless of size, would have the same vote.

The New Jersey Plan contained the germ of what eventually came to be a key provision of our Constitution: the *supremacy clause*. The national Supreme Court was to hear appeals from state judges, and the supremacy clause would require all judges—state and national—to treat laws of the national government and the treaties of the United States as superior to the constitutions and laws of each of the states.

To adopt the Virginia Plan—which would create a powerful national government dominated by Massachusetts, Pennsylvania, and Virginia and eliminate the states as important units of government—would guarantee that many of the other states would reject the new constitution. Still, large states resisted, and for a time the

"Remember, gentlemen, we aren't here just to draft a constitution. We're here to draft the best damn constitution in the world."

bicameralism
The principle of a two-house legislature.

Virginia Plan
Proposal at the Constitutional Convention made by the Virginia delegation for a strong central government with a bicameral legislature, the lower house to be elected by the voters and the upper chosen by the lower.

New Jersey Plan
Proposal at the Constitutional Convention made by William Paterson of New Jersey for a central government with a single-house legislature in which each state would be represented equally.

TABLE 1-1 The Virginia and New Jersey Plans	
Virginia Plan	New Jersey Plan
Legitimacy derived from citizens, based on popular representation	Derived from states, based on equal votes for each state
Bicameral legislature	Unicameral legislature
Executive size undetermined, elected and removable by Congress	More than one person, removable by state majority
Judicial life-tenure, able to veto state legislation	No power over states
Legislature can override state laws	Government can compel obedience to national laws
Ratification by citizens	Ratification by states

convention was deadlocked. Small states believed all states should be represented equally in Congress, especially in the smaller "upper house" if there were to be two chambers. Large states insisted representation in both houses be based on population or wealth and that national legislators be elected by voters rather than by state legislatures. Finally, a Committee of Eleven was elected to devise a compromise. On July 5 it presented its proposals.

THE CONNECTICUT COMPROMISE   Because of the prominent role of the Connecticut delegation in constructing this plan, it has since been known as the **Connecticut Compromise**. It called for one house in which each state would have an equal vote and a second house in which representation would be based on population and in which all bills for raising or appropriating money would originate. This proposal was a setback for the large states, which agreed to it only when the smaller states made it clear this was their price for union. After equality of state representation in the Senate was accepted, most objections to a strong national government dissolved.

NORTH-SOUTH COMPROMISES   Other issues split the delegates North and South. Southerners were afraid a northern majority in Congress might discriminate against southern trade. They had some basis for this concern. John Jay, secretary of foreign affairs for the Confederation, had proposed a treaty with Great Britain that would have given advantages to northern merchants at the expense of southern exporters. To protect themselves, the southern delegates insisted a two-thirds majority be required in the Senate before presidents could ratify treaties.

Differences between the North and South were also evident on the issue of representation in the House of Representatives. The question was whether to count slaves for purposes of apportioning seats in the House. The South wanted to count slaves, thereby enlarging its number of representatives; the North resisted. After heated debate, the delegates agreed on the **three-fifths compromise**. Each slave would be counted as three-fifths of a free person for the purposes of apportionment in the House and of direct taxation; this fraction was chosen because it maintained a balance of power between the North and South. The issue of "balance" would recur in the early history of our nation as territorial governments were established and territories applied for statehood.

OTHER ISSUES   Delegates found other issues to argue about. Should the national government have lower courts, or would one federal Supreme Court be enough? This

Connecticut Compromise
Compromise agreement by states at the Constitutional Convention for a bicameral legislature with a lower house in which representation would be based on population, and upper house in which each state would have two senators.

three-fifths compromise
Compromise agreement between northern and southern states at the Constitutional Convention in which the slave population would be counted at three-fifths for determining direct taxation and representation in the House of Representatives.

issue was resolved by postponing the decision. The Constitution states that there shall be one Supreme Court and that Congress may establish lower courts.

How should the president be selected? For a long time the convention accepted the idea that the president should be chosen by Congress, but the delegates feared Congress would dominate the president, or vice versa. Election by the state legislatures was rejected because the delegates distrusted the state legislatures. Finally, the Electoral College system was devised. This was perhaps the most novel and contrived contribution of the delegates, and has long been one of the most criticized provisions in the Constitution.[17] (Consult Article II, Section 1, of the Constitution.)

After three months the delegates stopped debating. On September 17, 1787, they assembled for an impressive ceremony of signing the document they were recommending to the nation. All but three of those still present signed; others who opposed the general drift of the convention had already left. Their work well done, delegates adjourned to the nearby City Tavern to celebrate.

According to an old story, Benjamin Franklin was confronted by a woman as he left the last session of the convention.

"What kind of government have you given us, Dr. Franklin?" she asked. "A Republic or a Monarchy?"

"A Republic, Madam," he answered, "if you can keep it."

TO ADOPT OR NOT TO ADOPT?

The delegates had gone far. Indeed they had wholly disregarded Congress's instruction to do no more than revise the Articles. They had ignored Article XIII of the Articles of Confederation, which declared the Union to be perpetual and prohibited any alteration of the Articles unless agreed to by Congress and by *every one of the state legislatures*—a provision that had made it impossible to amend the Articles. The convention delegates, however, boldly declared that their newly proposed Constitution should go into effect when ratified by popularly elected conventions in nine states.

They turned to this method of ratification for practical considerations as well as for reasons of securing legitimacy for their newly proposed government. Not only were the delegates aware that there was little chance of winning approval of the new Constitution in all state legislatures; many also believed the Constitution should be ratified by an authority higher than a legislature. A constitution based on approval *by the people* would have higher legal and moral status. The Articles of Confederation had been a compact of state governments, but the Constitution was based on "We the People." Still, even this method of ratification would not be easy. The nation was not ready to adopt the Constitution without a thorough debate.

Federalists versus Antifederalists

Supporters of the new government, by cleverly appropriating the name **Federalists**, took some of the sting out of charges they were trying to destroy the states and establish an all-powerful central government. By calling their opponents **Antifederalists**, they pointed up the negative character of the arguments of those who opposed ratification.

The split was in part geographic. Seaboard and city regions tended to be Federalist strongholds; backcountry regions from Maine (then a part of Massachusetts)

Federalists
Supporters of ratification of the Constitution whose position promoting a strong central government was later voiced in the Federalist party.

Antifederalists
Opponents of ratification of the Constitution and of a strong central government generally.

1. *"All men are created equal"*: What kinds of equality are—and should be—protected by the Constitution, and by what means?

2. *"Government by the people"*: Does the evolving constitutional system, including political parties and interest groups, strengthen fair and effective representation of the people?

3. *Federalism*: Does the Constitution provide an efficient and realistic balance between national and state power?

4. *Checks and balances*: Does the constitutional separation of powers between the president and Congress lead too often to gridlock and stalemate?

5. *Minority rights*: Does the Constitution adequately protect the rights of women, African Americans, Native Americans, Hispanic Americans, other ethnic groups, and recent immigrants?

6. *Suspects' rights*: Can representative government uphold the rights of the criminally accused and yet protect its citizens?

7. *Individual liberties*: Are individual liberties adequately protected in the Constitution? Do big government and big business diminish the freedom of the individual?

8. *The judicial branch*: Is it too powerful? Are the federal courts exceeding their proper powers as interpreters of the Constitution?

9. *War and peace*: What are the responsibilities of the United States as the only superpower?

10. *Constitutional responsibilities*: Are Americans participating adequately in our democratic system? Do citizens have the social capital and understanding of our governmental processes to be heard and to make a difference?

The Federalist

Series of essays promoting ratification of the Constitution, written by Alexander Hamilton, John Jay, and James Madison in 1787 and 1788.

through Georgia, inhabited by farmers and other relatively poor people, were generally Antifederalist. But as in most political contests, no single factor completely accounted for the division between Federalists and Antifederalists. Thus in Virginia the leaders of both sides came from the same general social and economic class. New York City and Philadelphia strongly supported the Constitution, yet so did predominantly rural New Jersey.

The great debate was conducted through pamphlets, papers, letters to the editor, and speeches. The issues were important, but with few exceptions the argument about the merits of the Constitution was carried on in a quiet and calm manner. Out of the debate came a series of essays known as ***The Federalist***, written by Alexander Hamilton, James Madison, and John Jay to persuade the voters of New York to ratify the Constitution. *The Federalist* is still, said Charles Beard, "widely regarded as the most profound single treatise on the Constitution ever written and as among the few masterly works in political science produced in all the centuries of history."[18] (Three of the most important *Federalist* essays, Nos. 10, 51, and 78, are found in the Appendix of this book. We urge you to read them.) The great debate stands even today as an outstanding example of free people using public discussion to determine the nature of their fundamental laws.

The Antifederalists' most telling criticism of the proposed Constitution was its failure to include a bill of rights.[19] The Federalists believed a bill of rights was unnecessary because the proposed national government had *only* the specific powers delegated to it by the states and the people. Thus there was no need to specify that Congress could not, for example, abridge freedom of the press because the states and the people had not given it power to regulate the press. Moreover, the Federalists argued, to guarantee some rights might be dangerous, because it would then be thought that rights not listed could be denied. The Constitution already protected some important rights—trial by jury in federal criminal cases, for example. Hamilton and others also insisted that paper guarantees were weak supports on which to depend for protection against governmental tyranny.

The Antifederalists were unconvinced. If some rights were protected, what could be the objection to providing constitutional protection for others? Without a bill of rights, what was to prevent Congress from using one of its delegated powers to abridge free speech? If bills of rights were needed in state constitutions to limit state governments, why was a bill of rights not needed in the national constitution to limit the national government? This was a government farther from the people, they contended, with a greater tendency to subvert natural rights.

The Politics of Ratification

The absence of a bill of rights in the proposed constitution dominated the struggle over its adoption. In taverns and church gatherings and newspaper offices up and down the eastern seaboard, people were muttering, "No bill of rights—no constitution!" This feeling was so strong that some Antifederalists, who were far more concerned with states' rights than individual rights, joined forces with bill of rights advocates in an effort to defeat the proposed Constitution.

The Federalists were first to begin the debate over the Constitution that opened as soon as the delegates left Philadelphia in mid-September 1787. The Federalists' tactic was to secure ratification in as many states as possible before the opposition had time to organize. The Antifederalists were handicapped. Most newspapers were owned by supporters of ratification. Moreover, Antifederalist strength was concentrated in rural areas, which were underrepresented in some state legislatures and difficult to arouse to political action. The Antifederalists needed time to perfect their organization and collect their strength, while the Federalists, composed of a more closely knit group of leaders throughout the colonies, moved in a hurry.

In most of the small states, now satisfied by equal Senate representation, ratification was gained without difficulty. Delaware was the first state to ratify, and by early 1788, Pennsylvania, New Jersey, Georgia, and Connecticut had also ratified (see Table 1–2). Reports were coming in from Massachusetts, however, that opposition was broadening. The position of such key leaders as John Hancock and Samuel Adams was in doubt. The debate in the ratifying convention in Boston pitched some of the most polished Federalist speakers against an array of eloquent but plainspoken Antifederalists. The debate raged for most of January 1788 into February. At times it looked as though the Constitution would lose, as Antifederalists raised the cry of "Why no bill of rights?" and other objections. But in the end the Constitution was narrowly ratified in Massachusetts, by 187 to 168.

The struggle over ratification continued through the spring of 1788. By June 21, Maryland, South Carolina, and New Hampshire had ratified, putting the Constitution over the top in the number (nine) required for ratification. But two big hurdles remained: Virginia and New York. It would be impossible to begin the new government without the consent of these two major states. Virginia was crucial. As the most populous state, the home of Washington, Jefferson, and Madison, it was a link between North and South. The Virginia ratifying convention rivaled the Constitutional Convention in the caliber of its delegates. Madison, who had only recently switched to favoring the bill of rights after saying earlier it was unnecessary, captained the Federalist forces. The fiery Patrick Henry led the opposition. In an epic debate, Henry cried that liberty was the issue: "Liberty, the greatest of earthly possessions . . . that precious jewel!" But Madison quietly rebutted him and then played his trump card, a promise that a bill of rights embracing the freedoms of religion and speech and assembly would be added to the Constitution as the first order of business once the new government was established. At a critical moment, Washington himself tipped the balance with a letter urging ratification. News of the Virginia vote, 89 for the Constitution and 79 opposed, was rushed to New York.[20]

The great landowners along New York's Hudson River, unlike their southern planter friends, were opposed to the Constitution. They feared federal taxation of their holdings, and they did not want to abolish the profitable tax New York had been levying on trade and commerce with other states. When the convention assembled, the Federalists were greatly outnumbered, but they were aided by Alexander Hamilton's strategy and skill and by word of Virginia's ratification. New York approved by a margin of three votes. Although North Carolina and Rhode Island still remained outside the Union (the former ratified in November 1789, and the latter six months later), the new nation was created. In New York, a few members of the old Congress assembled to issue the call for elections under the new Constitution. Then they adjourned without setting a date for reconvening.

TABLE 1–2 Ratification of the U.S. Constitution	
State	Date
Delaware	December 7, 1787
Pennsylvania	December 12, 1787
New Jersey	December 18, 1787
Georgia	January 2, 1788
Connecticut	January 9, 1788
Massachusetts	February 6, 1788
Maryland	April 28, 1788
South Carolina	May 23, 1788
New Hampshire	June 21, 1788
Virginia	June 25, 1788
New York	July 26, 1788
North Carolina	November 21, 1789
Rhode Island	May 29, 1790

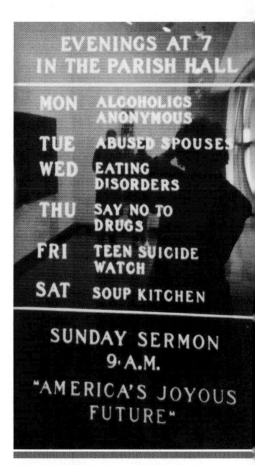

Despite the many serious problems facing our country, a spirit of optimism is still evident in our hopes for the future, as this church bulletin testifies.

POLITICS ONLINE

The Internet and Your Study of Political Science

Students of political science today have instant access to documents, journal articles, video, scholarly indexes, statistical data bases, and other resources that formerly took a trip to the library and hours of work to access. Your study of this subject, and any subject for that matter, is made much more accessible to you through the World Wide Web. Original documents, library catalogs, news reports, and research by public and private agencies are now at your fingertips and often free of charge.

One of the purposes of this Politics Online feature at the end of each chapter is to show you how you can use the Web to assist you in your study of political science and American government. Often in these boxes, we will also present an interesting example of how the Internet and related technology impact politics. Additionally, our publisher has invested heavily in web-based resources intended to reinforce key concepts and give you a chance to apply what you have learned through simulations and activities. In some chapters, we will invite you to explore your own ideology or assess how much you are investing in Social Security.

Many college students today are skilled in navigating the Web but can get lost in the enormous amount of information available. Politics Online will introduce you to relevant and interesting content you might not have known was there. Because websites are constantly changing, the place to start will always be the website for this book:
www.prenhall.com/burns

Politics Online will also demonstrate how the Internet impacts politics; how it is used by citizens, politicians, and government agencies; and some of the policy challenges it poses. Examples of this last category include e-mail privacy, sales taxes on Internet transactions, and pornography on the Internet.

Take, for example, the question of the extent to which the world's governments are democratic. In June 2000, 100 countries signed the Warsaw Declaration promoting democracy. To read this declaration and get a list of electoral democracies, go to:
www.fordemocracy.net.

We welcome your feedback on these boxes and hope they are helpful in opening up this remarkable resource, not only for this class but for other classes and in your future as an active citizen.

SUMMARY

1. Americans have long been skeptical of politicians and politics. Yet politics is a necessary activity for a democracy. Indeed politics and politicians are indispensable to making our system of separated institutions and checks and balances work.

2. "Democracy" is an often misused term, and it has many different meanings. We use it here to refer to a system of interacting values, interrelated political processes, and interdependent political structures. The vital principle of democracy is that a just government must derive its powers from the consent of the people and that this consent must be regularly renewed at free and fair elections.

3. Stable constitutional democracy is encouraged by various conditions, such as an educated citizenry, a healthy economy, and overlapping associations and groupings within a society in which major institutions interact to create a certain degree of consensus.

4. There has recently been some concern about a decline in *social capital*—the experiences people gain in working together in community groups. Lessons about compromise, accommodation, and participation are important building blocks for democracy. Some say we have a decline in civic engagement while others see a healthy level of voluntary and char-

itable engagement that is making our communities and nation better.

5. Constitutionalism is a general label we apply to arrangements such as checks and balances, federalism, separation of powers, rule of law, due process, and the Bill of Rights that force our leaders and representatives to listen, think, bargain, and explain before they act and make laws. A constitutional government enforces recognized and regularly applied limits on the powers of those who govern.

6. Democracy developed gradually. A revolution had to be fought before a system of representative democracy in the

United States could be tried and tested. It took several years before a national constitution could be written, and almost another year to be ratified. It took still another two years before a Bill of Rights could be adopted and ratified. It has taken more than two hundred years for democratic institutions to be refined and for systems of competition and choice to be hammered out. Democratic institutions such as free and fair elections and equal protection of the laws in the United States are still a work in progress, still in the process of being refined and improved.

KEY TERMS

democracy 4
direct democracy 4
representative democracy 4
constitutional democracy 4
constitutionalism 4
statism 5
popular consent 8

majority rule 9
majority 9
plurality 9
social capital 10
ideology 12
theocracy 12
Articles of Confederation 12

Annapolis Convention 14
Constitutional Convention 14
Shays' Rebellion 14
bicameralism 17
Virginia Plan 17
New Jersey Plan 17
Connecticut Compromise 18

three-fifths compromise 18
Federalists 19
Antifederalists 19
The Federalist 20

FURTHER READING

BERNARD BAILYN, ED., *The Debate on the Constitution: Federalist and Antifederalist Speeches, Articles, and Letters During the Struggle over Ratification*, 2 vols. (Library of America, 1993).

LANCE BANNING, *The Sacred Fire of Liberty: James Madison and the Founding of the Federal Republic* (Cornell University Press, 1995).

ROBERT A. DAHL, *On Democracy* (Yale University Press, 1998).

ALEXANDER HAMILTON, JAMES MADISON, AND JOHN JAY, *The Federalist Papers*, ed. Clinton Rossiter (New American Library, 1961). Also in several other editions.

SAMUEL P. HUNTINGTON, *The Third Wave: Democratization in the Late Twentieth Century* (University of Oklahoma Press, 1991).

EVERETT CARLL LADD, *The Ladd Report: Startling New Research Shows How an Explosion of Voluntary Groups, Activities and Charitable Donations Is Transforming Our Towns and Cities* (Free Press, 1999).

AREND LIJPHART, *Patterns of Democracy: Government Forms and Performance in Thirty-Six Countries* (Yale University Press, 1999).

DREW R. MCCOY, *The Last of the Fathers: James Madison and the Republican Legacy* (Columbia University Press, 1989).

RICHARD B. MORRIS, *Witnesses at the Creation: Hamilton, Madison, and Jay and the Constitution* (Holt, Rinehart and Winston, 1985).

PIPPA NORRIS, ED., *Critical Citizens: Global Support for Democratic Institutions* (Oxford University Press, 1999).

ROBERT D. PUTNAM, *Bowling Alone: The Collapse and Revival of American Community* (Simon & Schuster, 2000).

ROBERT D. PUTNAM, *Making Democracy Work: Civic Traditions in Modern Italy* (Princeton University Press, 1993).

JACK N. RAKOVE, *Original Meanings: Politics and Ideas in the Making of the Constitution* (Vintage Books, 1997).

MICHAEL SCHUDSON, *The Good Citizen: A History of American Civic Life* (Harvard University Press, 1998).

THEDA SKOCPOL AND MORRIS P. FIORINA, EDS., *Civic Engagement in American Democracy* (Brookings/Russell Sage, 1999).

ALEXIS DE TOCQUEVILLE, *Democracy in America*, 2 vols., 1835 (Vintage, 1955).

SIDNEY VERBA, KAY LEMAN SCHOLZMAN, AND HENRY E. BRADY, *Voice and Equality: Civic Volunteerism in American Politics* (Harvard University Press, 1995).

GARRY WILLS, *A Necessary Evil: A History of American Distrust of Government* (Simon & Schuster, 1999).

GORDON S. WOOD, *The Creation of the American Republic, 1776–1787* (University of North Carolina Press, 1969).

See also the *Journal of Democracy* (Johns Hopkins University Press).

2

THE LIVING CONSTITUTION

THE CONSTITUTION OF THE UNITED STATES, THE
WORLD'S OLDEST WRITTEN CONSTITUTION, IS ONE OF THE
SHORTEST. THE ORIGINAL, UNAMENDED CONSTITUTION, WHICH
went into effect in 1789, contains just 4,543 words, yet it established the framers' experiment in free-government-in-the-making that each generation reinterprets and renews.
The Constitution remains a document Americans revere. Optimists read it as expressing their hopes; pessimists put faith in its protections against tyranny and other abuses.

Why, after more than two hundred years, have we not written another constitution—let alone two, three, or more, as have other countries around the world? Part of
the answer is the widespread acceptance of the Constitution by optimists and pessimists
alike. But also part of the reason the Constitution endures is because of its brilliant
structure for limited government and because the framers built into the document the
capacity for adaptability and flexibility.

As the Constitution won the support of citizens of the early years of the Republic,
it took on the aura of **natural law**—law that defines right from wrong, law that is higher
than human law. "The [Founding] Fathers grew ever larger in stature as they receded
from view; the era in which they lived and fought became a Golden Age; in that age there
had been a fresh dawn for the world, and its men were giants against the sky."[1] This early
Constitution worship helped bring unity to the diverse new nation. Like the Crown in
Great Britain, the Constitution became a symbol of national loyalty, evoking both emotional and intellectual support from Americans, regardless of their differences. The
framers' work became part of the American creed and culture.[2] It stood for liberty,
equality before the law, limited government—indeed, for just about whatever anyone
wanted to read into it.

Even today, Americans generally revere the Constitution, yet many do not know
what is in it. A poll by the National Constitution Center found that nine out of ten
Americans are proud of the Constitution and feel it is important to them. However, a
third think the Constitution establishes English as the country's official language. One
in six believes the Constitution establishes America as a Christian nation. Only one out
of four could name a single First Amendment right. Although two out of three knew
that the Constitution creates three branches of the national government, only one in
three could name all three branches.[3]

The Constitution, however, is more than a symbol. It is a *supreme and binding law
that both grants and limits powers.* "In framing a government which is to be administered

CHAPTERMEDIA

POLITICS ONLINE
*What's Happening to the
Constitution?*
www.prenhall.com/burns

"And there are three branches of government, so that each branch has the other two to blame everything on."

by men over men," wrote James Madison in *The Federalist*, No. 51, "the great difficulty lies in this: you must first enable the government to control the governed; and in the next place oblige it to control itself." (See *The Federalist*, No. 51, in the Appendix of this book, or go on the Web to **http://www.mcs.net/knautzer/fed/fedpaper.html**.) The Constitution is both a positive instrument of government, which enables the governors to control the governed, and a restraint on government, which enables the ruled to check the rulers.

In what ways does the Constitution limit the power of the government? In what ways does it create governmental power? How has it managed to serve as a great symbol of national unity and at the same time a somewhat adaptable and changing instrument of government? The secret is an ingenious separation of powers and a system of checks and balances that check power with power.

CHECKING POWER WITH POWER

It may seem strange to begin by stressing the ways in which the Constitution *limits* governmental power, but you must keep in mind the dilemma the framers faced. They wanted a stronger and more effective national government than they had under the Articles of Confederation; at the same time, they were keenly aware that the people would not accept too much central control. Efficiency and order were important concerns, but they were not as important as liberty. The framers wanted to ensure domestic tranquillity and prevent future rebellions, but they also wanted to forestall the emergence of a homegrown King George III. Accordingly, they allotted certain powers to the national government and reserved the rest for the states, thus establishing a system of *federalism* (whose nature and problems we take up in Chapter 3). Even this was not enough. They believed they needed additional means to limit the national government.

The most important way they devised to make public officials observe the constitutional limits on their powers was through *free and fair elections*; voters would be able to throw out of office those who abuse power. Yet the framers were not willing to depend solely on political controls, because they did not fully trust the people's judgment. "Free government is founded on jealousy, and not in confidence," said Thomas Jefferson. "In questions of power, then, let no more be heard of confidence in man, but bind him down from mischief by the chains of the Constitution."[4]

Even more important, the framers feared that a majority might deprive minorities of their rights. "A dependence on the people is, no doubt, the primary control on the government," Madison admitted in *The Federalist*, No. 51, "but experience has taught mankind the necessity of auxiliary precautions." What were these "auxiliary precautions" against popular tyranny?

Separation of Powers

The first step was the **separation of powers**, that is, the distribution of constitutional authority among the three branches of the national government. In *The Federalist*, No. 47, Madison wrote, "No political truth is certainly of greater intrinsic value, or is stamped with the authority of more enlightened patrons of liberty, than that . . . the accumulation of all powers, legislative, executive, and judiciary, in the same hands . . . may justly be pronounced the very definition of tyranny."[5] Chief among the "enlightened patrons of liberty" to whose authority Madison was appealing were John Locke and Montesquieu, whose works were well known to most educated Americans.

The intrinsic value of the principle of dispersion of power does not by itself account for its inclusion in our Constitution. Such dispersion of power had been the general practice in the colonies for more than one hundred years. Only during the Revolutionary period did some of the states concentrate authority in the hands of the legislature, and that unhappy experience confirmed the framers' belief in the merits of separation of powers. Many attributed the evils of state government and the lack of

natural law
God's or nature's law that defines right from wrong and is higher than human law.

separation of powers
Constitutional division of powers among the legislative, executive, and judicial branches, with the legislative branch making law, the executive applying and enforcing the law, and the judiciary interpreting the law.

energy in the central government to the fact that there was no strong executive both to check legislative abuses and to give energy and direction to administration.

Still, separating power was not enough. There was always the danger—from the framers' point of view—that different officials with different powers might pool their authority and act together. Separation of powers by itself might not prevent governmental branches and officials from responding to the same pressures—from the demand of an overwhelming majority of the voters to suppress an offensive book, for example, or to impose confiscatory taxes on rich people. If separating power was not enough, what else could be done?

Checks and Balances: Ambition to Counteract Ambition

The framers' answer was a system of **checks and balances**. "The great security against a gradual concentration of the several powers in the same department," wrote Madison in *The Federalist*, No. 51, "consists in giving to those who administer each department the necessary constitutional means and personal motives to resist encroachments of the others: . . . Ambition must be made to counteract ambition." Each branch therefore has a role in the actions of the others (see Figure 2–1). Congress enacts laws, but the president can veto them. The Supreme Court can declare

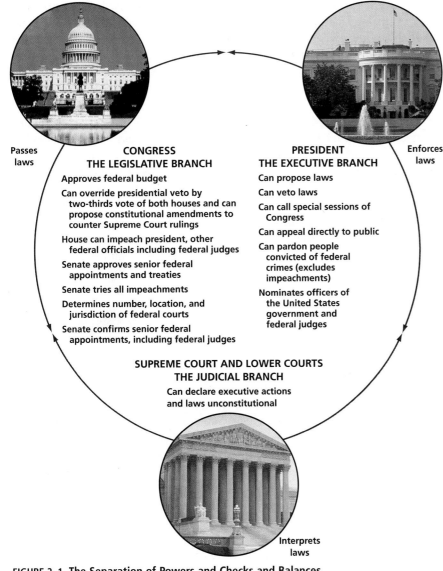

Passes laws

**CONGRESS
THE LEGISLATIVE BRANCH**

Approves federal budget

Can override presidential veto by two-thirds vote of both houses and can propose constitutional amendments to counter Supreme Court rulings

House can impeach president, other federal officials including federal judges

Senate approves senior federal appointments and treaties

Senate tries all impeachments

Determines number, location, and jurisdiction of federal courts

Senate confirms senior federal appointments, including federal judges

**PRESIDENT
THE EXECUTIVE BRANCH**

Can propose laws

Can veto laws

Can call special sessions of Congress

Can appeal directly to public

Can pardon people convicted of federal crimes (excludes impeachments)

Nominates officers of the United States government and federal judges

Enforces laws

**SUPREME COURT AND LOWER COURTS
THE JUDICIAL BRANCH**

Can declare executive actions and laws unconstitutional

Interprets laws

FIGURE 2–1 The Separation of Powers and Checks and Balances

checks and balances
Constitutional grant of powers that enables each of the three branches of government to check some acts of the others and therefore ensure that no branch can dominate.

vetoes The president has vetoed more than 2,500 acts of Congress. Congress has overridden presidential vetoes more than 100 times.

judicial review The Supreme Court has ruled 155 congressional acts or parts thereof unconstitutional. Its 1983 decision on legislative vetoes (*INS v Chadha*) affects another 200 provisions.

impeachment The House of Representatives has impeached 17 federal officials, 2 presidents, and 15 federal judges; of these, the Senate has convicted 7 judges but has not convicted a president.

confirmation The Senate has refused to confirm 9 cabinet nominations, and many other cabinet and subcabinet appointments were withdrawn because of likely Senate rejection.

For Internet resources on the Constitution, see our home page: www.prenhall.com/burns

laws passed by Congress and signed by the president unconstitutional, but the president appoints the justices and all the other federal judges with the Senate's approval. The president administers the laws, but Congress provides the money. Moreover, the Senate and the House of Representatives have an absolute veto over each other in the enactment of a law, because both houses must approve bills.

Not only does each branch have some authority over the others, but each is politically independent of the others. Voters in each local district choose members of the House; voters in each state choose senators; the president is elected by all voters. With the consent of the Senate, the president appoints federal judges, who remain in office until they retire.

The framers also ensured that a majority of the voters could win control over only part of the government at one time. Although in an off-year (nonpresidential) election a new majority might take control of the House of Representatives, the president would still have at least two years to go, and senators stay on for six years. Finally, independent federal courts, which have developed their own powerful checks, were also provided.

Modifications of Checks and Balances

Distrustful of both the elites and the masses, the framers deliberately *built inefficiency into our political system.* They designed the decision-making process so that the national government can act decisively only when there is a consensus among most of the interest groups and after all sides have had a chance to have their say. Even though the fragmentation of political power written into the Constitution remains, several developments have modified the way the system of checks and balances works.

THE RISE OF NATIONAL POLITICAL PARTIES   Political parties can serve as unifying factors—at times drawing together the president, senators, representatives, and sometimes even judges behind common programs. When parties do this they help bridge the separation of powers. Yet parties can be splintered and weakened by having to work through a system of fragmented governmental power, so they never become strong or cohesive. Moreover, when one party controls the Congress and the other the White House (**divided government**), as has generally been the case since the end of World War II, the parties may intensify checks and balances rather than moderate them, to the point that action on some important issues may be difficult.[6]

Divided government may lead to so much competition between the legislative and executive branches that we find "each institution protecting and promoting itself through a broad interpretation of its constitutional and political status, even usurping the other's power when the opportunity presents itself."[7] Thus we have had battles over presidential impoundment of funds appropriated by Congress, budget gridlock, and unseemly and angry confirmation hearings for the appointment of justices of the Supreme Court. Divided government also makes it difficult for the voters to hold anybody or any party accountable. "Presidents blame Congress . . . while members of Congress attack the president. . . . Citizens genuinely cannot tell who is to blame."[8]

Yet when all the shouting dies down, political scientist David R. Mayhew concludes, there have been just as many congressional investigations and just as much important legislation passed when one party controls Congress and another controls the presidency as when the same party controls both branches.[9] And Charles Jones, a noted scholar of Congress and the presidency, adds that not only is divided government not that important in determining how our government responds to crises, but divided government is precisely what the voters appear to have wanted through much of our history.[10]

Bill Clinton's first term as president confirmed Jones's thesis. There was more major legislation signed into law during his second two years (104th Congress,

divided government
Governance divided between the parties, especially when one holds the presidency and the other controls one or both houses of Congress.

1995–97) when Republicans controlled both houses, than during his first two years (103d Congress, 1993–95), when Democrats controlled Congress. During Clinton's second term (1996–2000), however, there was continual partisan conflict between the Republican-controlled Congress and the Democratic White House. Congressional committees spent most of their time investigating allegations of misconduct on the part of the president and members of his cabinet.

EXPANSION OF THE ELECTORATE AND CHANGES IN ELECTORAL METHODS The framers wanted the president to be chosen by the Electoral College—wise, independent citizens free from popular passions and hero worship—rather than by ordinary citizens. Almost from the beginning, however, that is not the way the Electoral College worked. Rather, voters actually select the president, because presidential electors chosen by the voters are pledged in advance to cast their electoral votes for their party's candidates for president and vice president.

The kind of "people" entitled to vote has expanded from white property-owning males to all citizens over 18 years of age. During the past century, American states have expanded the role of the electorate by adopting **direct primaries** in which the voters elect party nominees for the House and Senate and even for president; by permitting the voters in about half the states to propose and vote on laws (**initiatives**); by allowing voters to reconsider actions of the legislature (**referendums**) and even to remove elected state and local officials from office (**recall**). And with the passage of the Seventeenth Amendment, senators are no longer elected by state legislatures but are chosen directly by the people.

ESTABLISHMENT OF AGENCIES DELIBERATELY DESIGNED TO EXERCISE LEGISLATIVE, EXECUTIVE, AND JUDICIAL FUNCTIONS When the national government began to regulate the economy, it issued detailed rules on such complex matters as railroad safety, bank and stock-exchange practices, employment conditions, union negotiations, and automobile emissions. It was impossible to assign these regulatory responsibilities without providing the power to make and apply rules and to decide disputes. Beginning in 1887, Congress created *independent regulatory commissions* such as the Interstate Commerce Commission (which went out of business in 1995, although many of its functions were transferred to the Surface Transportation Board within the Department of Transportation) and the Federal Communications Commission. More recently it established *independent executive agencies* such as the Environmental Protection Agency.

CHANGES IN TECHNOLOGY The system of checks and balances operates differently today from the way it did in 1789. Back then there were no televised congressional committee hearings, no electronic communications, no *Larry King Live* or *Rush Limbaugh* talk shows, no *New York Times*, *Wall Street Journal*,

THE JAPANESE CONSTITUTION

The Japanese Constitution of 1947 created a parliamentary democracy and established the power of American-style judicial review. Although drafted in part by the United States and the Allied Occupation Forces after World War II, the Japanese Constitution was made easier to amend than ours. A proposed amendment needs only to be passed by a two-thirds majority of both houses of Japan's parliament and then be ratified by a majority vote of the people in a national referendum. Yet it has never been amended.

What explains the reluctance of the Japanese to amend their constitution? Part of the explanation may be that the Japanese Constitution goes well beyond our Bill of Rights to include a broad range of economic and social rights, so that progressive Japanese vigorously oppose changing it. Opposition also comes from older Japanese who remember World War II and revere their "Peace Constitution," while younger generations tend to be indifferent and more concerned with economic matters.

Another explanation is that the Japanese have learned to reinterpret controversial provisions of their constitution, as have Americans, in ways that make formal amendments unnecessary. For example, although Article 9 of the Japanese Constitution forbids the maintenance of "land, sea, and air forces," and includes a renunciation of war, the Japanese have interpreted Article 9 to permit them to maintain "self-defense forces," thus making it less urgent to change the constitution. Japan now ranks among the top five countries in terms of military spending and looks toward a larger role in international peacekeeping missions.

For more information on the Japanese Constitution, go on the Internet to www.home.ntt.com/jap/constitution/english-constitution.html

direct primary
Election in which voters choose party nominees.

initiative
Procedure whereby a certain number of voters may, by petition, propose a law or constitutional amendment and have it submitted to the voters.

referendum
Procedure for submitting to popular vote measures passed by the legislature or proposed amendments to a state constitution.

recall
Procedure for submitting to popular vote the removal of officials from office before the end of their term.

THE EUROPEAN UNION

The European Union was formed after World War II to promote economic integration. Through a series of treaties, the union has grown to include 15 countries in Western Europe. One of the most important institutions created by the union is the European Court of Justice (ECJ). The ECJ has the power to declare national laws invalid when they conflict with treaty obligations and has created a uniform system of law that takes precedence over national laws and constitutions.

The member states of the European Union have also signed the European Convention of Human Rights, which establishes a long list of civil liberties. They are subject to the jurisdiction of the European Court of Human Rights, which resolves allegations of human rights abuses and enforces the Convention on Human Rights. This court has interpreted its powers broadly and has asserted its right to invalidate national laws that contravene obligations that the nations accepted in signing the convention.

For the most part, the issues coming before the ECJ have been economic and commercial in nature, but it has struck down laws based on gender discrimination and advanced the right to equal pay for equal work. Critics of the ECJ complain that it has become too activist and compare it to the U.S. Supreme Court in the early nineteenth century under Chief Justice John Marshall, whose rulings striking down state trade barriers promoted the growth of our unified economy.

Even with these trends toward more active judicial review in the European Union, courts in the United States continue to exercise the power of judicial review more frequently and more broadly than do the newer constitutional and supranational courts.

For more information on the European Union go on the Internet to these addresses:
www.userpage.chemie.fu-berlin.de/adressen/eu.html
lib.berkeley.edu/gssi/eugde.html

The ECJ maintains a site at europa.eu.int/cj/en/ containing recent decisions and other information.

USA Today, CNN, or C-SPAN, no nightly news programs with national audiences, no presidential press conferences, and no live coverage of wars and of Americans being held hostage in foreign lands. Nuclear bombs, television, computers, cellular telephones, fax machines, the World Wide Web—these and other innovations create conditions today that are very different from those of two centuries ago. We also live in a time of instant polls that tell us what people are thinking about public issues.

In some ways these new technologies have added to the powers of presidents by permitting them to appeal directly to millions of people and giving them immediate access to public opinion. And these new technologies have also added leverage to organized interests by making it easy for them to target thousands of letters and calls at Congress, to organize letters to the editor, and to stage media events. New technologies have also given greater independence and influence to nongovernmental agencies such as the press. They have made it possible for rich people like Ross Perot and Steve Forbes and religious leaders like Pat Robertson, who have access to large resources, to bypass political parties and carry their message directly to the electorate.

THE EMERGENCE OF PRESIDENTIAL POWER   Today problems anywhere in the world—Israel, Kosovo, North Korea, and Iraq—often become crises for the United States. The need to deal with perpetual emergencies has concentrated power in the hands of the chief executive and the presidential staff. The president's role as the most significant player on the world stage and media coverage of summit conferences with foreign leaders enhance his status. Headline-producing events give the president a visibility no congressional leader can achieve. The office of the president has on occasion served to modify the system of checks and balances and provide some measure of national unity. Drawing on constitutional, political, and emergency powers, the president is sometimes able to overcome the restraints imposed by the Constitution on the exercise of governmental power—to the applause of some and the alarm of others.

JUDICIAL REVIEW AND THE "GUARDIANS OF THE CONSTITUTION"

Judges have become so important in our system of checks and balances that they deserve special attention. Judges did not claim the power of **judicial review**—the power of a court to refuse to enforce a law or a government regulation that in the opinion of the judges conflicts with the Constitution—until some years after the Constitution was in operation. From the beginning, however, judges were expected to restrain legislative majorities. "The independence of judges," wrote Alexander

judicial review
The power of a court to declare unconstitutional a law or a government regulation that in the opinion of the judges conflicts with the Constitution.

Hamilton in *The Federalist*, No. 78 (which appears in the Appendix), "may be an essential safeguard against the effects of occasional ill humors in the society."

Judicial review is a contribution of the United States to the art of government, a contribution that has been adopted at an increasing rate by other nations. In Japan, Germany, France, Italy, and Spain, constitutional courts are responsible for reviewing laws referred to them to ensure constitutional compliance, including compliance with the charter of rights that is now part of these constitutions.[11] The Canadian Constitution allows either a provincial legislature or the national parliament to override certain sections of the Charter of Rights for a renewable period of six years.[12] (See also the box on the growth of judicial review within the European Union.)

Origins of Judicial Review

The Constitution says nothing about who should have the final word in disputes that might arise over its meaning. Whether the delegates to the Constitutional Convention of 1787 intended to give the courts the power of judicial review is a question long debated. The framers clearly intended that the Supreme Court have the power to declare *state* legislation unconstitutional, but whether they intended to give it the same power over *congressional* legislation is not clear. Why then didn't the framers specifically provide for judicial review? Probably because they believed the power could be inferred from certain general provisions.

The Federalists—those who urged ratification of the Constitution and controlled the national government until 1801—generally supported a strong role for federal courts and favored judicial review. Their opponents, the Jeffersonian Republicans (called Democrats after 1832), were less enthusiastic. In the Kentucky and Virginia Resolutions (1798, 1799), Jefferson and Madison (who by this time had left the Federalist camp) came close to the position that state legislatures—and not the Supreme Court—had the ultimate power to interpret the Constitution. These resolutions seemed to question whether the Supreme Court even had final authority to review state legislation, something about which there had been little doubt.

When the Jeffersonians defeated the Federalists in the election of 1800, it was still undecided whether the Supreme Court would actually exercise the power of judicial review. Logical reasons to support such a doctrine were at hand, and some precedents could even be cited; nevertheless judicial review was not an established power. Then in 1803 came *Marbury v Madison*, one of the most famous Supreme Court decisions of all time.[13]

Marbury versus Madison

The election of 1800 marked the rise to power of the Jeffersonian Republicans. President John Adams and fellow Federalists did not take their defeat easily. Indeed, they were greatly alarmed at what they considered to be the "enthronement of the rabble." Yet there was nothing much they could do about it before leaving office—or was there? The Constitution gives the president, with the consent of the Senate, the power to appoint federal judges to hold office during "good Behaviour." With the judiciary in the hands of good Federalists, thought Adams and his associates, they could stave off the worst consequences of Jefferson's victory.

The outgoing Federalist Congress then created dozens of new federal judicial posts. By March 3, 1801, Adams had appointed and the Senate had confirmed loyal Federalists to all these new positions. Adams signed the commissions and turned them over to John Marshall, his secretary of state, to be sealed and delivered. Marshall had just received his own commission as chief justice of the United States, but he was continuing to serve as secretary of state until Adams's term as president expired. Working right up until nine o'clock on the evening of March 3, Marshall sealed, but was unable to deliver, all the commissions. The only ones left were for the justices of the peace for the

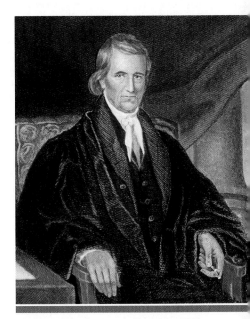

Chief Justice John Marshall (1755–1835), our most influential Supreme Court justice. Appointed in 1801, Marshall served until 1835. Earlier he had been a staunch defender of the U.S. Constitution at the Virginia ratifying convention, a member of Congress, and a secretary of state. He is one of those rare people who served in all three branches of government.

Supreme Court Justice Thurgood Marshall

I do not believe that the meaning of the Constitution was forever "fixed" at the Philadelphia Convention. Nor do I find the wisdom, foresight, and sense of justice exhibited by the framers particularly profound. To the contrary, the government they devised was defective from the start, requiring several amendments, a civil war, and momentous social transformation to attain the system of constitutional government, and its respect for the individual freedoms and human rights, that we hold as fundamental today. When contemporary Americans cite "The Constitution," they invoke a concept that is vastly different from what the framers barely began to construct two centuries ago.

For a sense of the evolving nature of the Constitution we need look no further than the first three words of the document's preamble: "We the People." When the Founding Fathers used this phrase in 1787, they did not have in mind the majority of America's citizens. "We the People" included, in the words of the framers, "the whole Number of free Persons." On a matter so basic as the right to vote, for example, Negro slaves were excluded, although they were counted for representational purposes—at three-fifths each. Women did not gain the right to vote for over a hundred and thirty years.

These omissions were intentional. The record of the framers' debates on the slave question is especially clear: the Southern states acceded to the demands of the New England states for giving Congress broad power to regulate commerce, in exchange for the right to continue the slave trade. . . .

And so we must be careful, when focusing on the events which took place in Philadelphia two centuries ago, that we not overlook the momentous events which followed, and thereby lose our proper sense of perspective. . . . If we seek, instead, a sensitive understanding of the Constitution's inherent defects, and its promising evolution through 200 years of history, the celebration of the "Miracle at Philadelphia" will, in my view, be a far more meaningful and humbling experience. We will see that the true miracle was not the birth of the Constitution, but its life, a life nurtured through two turbulent centuries of our own making, and a life embodying much good fortune that was not.

SOURCE: Remarks of Thurgood Marshall at the Annual Seminar of the San Francisco Patent and Trademark Law Association (Maui, Hawaii, May 16, 1987). It appears in David M. O'Brien, ed., *Judges on Judging* (Chatham House, 1997), pp. 195–200.

District of Columbia. The newly appointed chief justice left these commissions for his successor to deliver.

This "packing" of the judiciary angered Jefferson, now inaugurated as president. When he discovered that some of the commissions were still lying on a table in the Department of State, he instructed a clerk not to deliver them. Jefferson could see no reason why the District needed so many justices of the peace, especially Federalist justices.[14]

Among the commissions not delivered was one for William Marbury. After waiting in vain, Marbury decided to seek action from the courts. Searching through the statute books, he came across Section 13 of the Judiciary Act of 1789, which authorized the Supreme Court "to issue writs of *mandamus*." A **writ of mandamus** is a court order directing an official, such as the secretary of state, to perform a duty about which the official has no discretion, such as delivering a commission. So, thought Marbury, why not ask the Supreme Court to issue a writ of mandamus to force James Madison, the new secretary of state, to deliver the commission? Marbury and his companions went directly to the Supreme Court, and, citing Section 13, they made the request.

What could Marshall do? If the Court issued the writ, Madison and Jefferson would probably ignore it. The Court would be powerless, and its prestige, already low, might suffer a fatal blow. On the other hand, by refusing to issue the writ, the judges would appear to support the Jeffersonian Republicans' claim that the Court had no authority to interfere with the executive. Would Marshall issue the writ? Most people thought so; angry Republicans even threatened impeachment if he did so.

On February 24, 1803, the Supreme Court delivered its opinion. The first part was as expected. Marbury was entitled to his commission, said Marshall, and Madison should have delivered it to him. Moreover, the proper court could issue a writ of mandamus, even against so high an officer as the secretary of state.

Then came the surprise. Section 13 of the Judiciary Act seems to give the Supreme Court original jurisdiction in cases such as that in question. But Section 13, said Marshall, is contrary to Article III of the Constitution, which gives the Supreme Court original jurisdiction only when an ambassador or other foreign minister is affected or when a state is a party. Even though this is a case of original jurisdiction, Marbury is neither a state nor a foreign minister. If we follow Section 13, wrote Marshall, we have jurisdiction; if we follow the Constitution, we have no jurisdiction.

Marshall then posed the question in a more pointed way: Should the Supreme Court enforce an unconstitutional law? Of course not, he concluded. *The Constitution is the supreme and binding law,* and the courts cannot enforce any action of Congress that conflicts with it. Thus by limiting the court's power to what is granted in the Constitution, Marshall gained the much more important power to declare laws passed by Congress unconstitutional. It was a brilliant move.

Marbury v Madison might have been interpreted by subsequent generations in a very limited way. It could have been interpreted to mean that the Supreme Court had the right to determine the scope of its own powers under Article III, but Congress and the president had the authority to interpret their own powers under Articles I and II. But over the decades, building on Marshall's precedent, the Court has taken the commanding position as the authoritative interpreter of the Constitution.

Several important consequences follow from the acceptance of Marshall's argument that judges are the official interpreters of the Con-

THE BRITISH AND AMERICAN SYSTEMS: A STUDY IN CONTRASTS

Our political system is based on the Constitution; Britain has no such single document. Yet both systems are "constitutional" in the sense that the rulers are subject to well-defined restraints. Parliament is the guardian of the British constitution. In the United States it is the courts—ultimately the Supreme Court—that are the keepers of the constitutional conscience, not Congress or the president. The limitations in our written Constitution and the practices in the unwritten British constitution rest on underlying national values and attitudes to toward government.

In the British system, voters elect members of the House of Commons from districts, much as we elect members of our House of Representatives. Like us, the party with the most votes in a district wins the seat, so that even with three or more parties, a plurality of the popular vote usually results in a majority of the parliamentary seats. So long as the parliamentary majority stays together, it can enact into law the ruling party's program.

Leaders of the majority party in the House of Commons serve as executive ministers who collectively form the cabinet, with the prime minister at its head. The majority selects the prime minister. If the ruling party loses the support of the majority in the Commons on a major issue, it must resign or call for new elections. Formerly, the House of Lords could check the Commons, but it is now almost powerless.

The House of Commons, when it chooses to act, has almost complete constitutional power. There is no high court with the power to declare acts of Parliament unconstitutional, and the prime minister cannot veto them, although he or she may ask the Crown to dissolve Parliament and call new elections.

In British politics, parties are cohesive and disciplined; party members vote together and support their parliamentary leaders. In Britain the party that wins an election has a very good chance of seeing its policies enacted. By contrast, our system depends on the agreement of

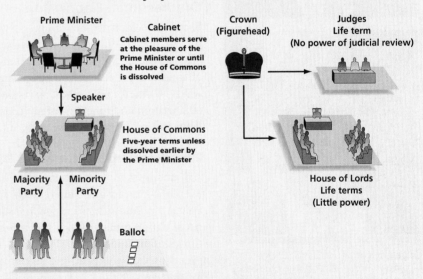

American System of Separation of Powers

House of Representatives Two-year term

Senate Six-year term

Judges Life-term

President Four-year term

Electors

Ballot

Ballot

Voter

British Parliamentary System of Concentration of Responsibility

Prime Minister

Cabinet
Cabinet members serve at the pleasure of the Prime Minister or until the House of Commons is dissolved

Crown (Figurehead)

Judges
Life term
(No power of judicial review)

Speaker

House of Commons
Five-year terms unless dissolved earlier by the Prime Minister

House of Lords
Life terms
(Little power)

Majority Party   Minority Party

Ballot

A Comparison of the British and American Systems

many elements of society. The party that wins a presidential or congressional election or even one that controls both these branches may still have a tough time carrying out its campaign promises.

In recent years the British system has been substantially modified. In addition to introducing elements of federalism by providing for regional parliaments in Scotland and Wales, the House of Lords has been stripped of its hereditary peers, peers who served as a result of hereditary titles. The House of Lords can still

delay implementation of acts of the House of Commons, but it now consists only of people appointed by the prime minister for their accomplishments in the arts, business, and public service.

In October 2000, England made the European Convention on Human Rights part of domestic law, giving ordinary citizens their first American-style bill of rights. Civil libertarians praised the move as the most important change to the British constitutional system in more than 300 years.

Impeachment of presidents: Charges against Andrew Johnson failed to receive the necessary two-thirds vote in the Senate; President Richard Nixon resigned when it became clear that the House of Representatives was prepared to pass articles of impeachment; the House passed two of the four articles of impeachment against Bill Clinton, but the Senate could not muster the two-thirds majority needed to convict.

writ of mandamus
Court order directing an official to perform an official duty.

impeachment
Formal accusation against a public official and the first step in removal from office.

stitution. The most important is that people can challenge laws enacted by Congress and approved by the president. Simply by bringing a lawsuit, those who lack the clout to get a bill through Congress can often secure a judicial hearing. And organized interest groups often find that goals unattainable by legislation can be achieved by litigation. Litigation thus supplements, and at times takes precedence over, legislation as a way to make public policy.[15]

THE CONSTITUTION AS AN INSTRUMENT OF GOVERNMENT

As careful as the Constitution's framers were to limit the powers they gave the national government, the main reason they had assembled in Philadelphia was to create a stronger national government. Having learned that a weak central government was a danger to liberty, they wished to establish a national government within the framework of a federal system with enough authority to meet the needs of all time. They made general grants of power, leaving it to succeeding generations to fill in the details and organize the structure of government in accordance with experience.

Hence our formal, written Constitution is only the skeleton of our system. It is filled out in numerous ways that must be considered part of our constitutional system in its larger sense. In fact, it is primarily through changes in the informal, unwritten Constitution that our system is kept up to date. These changes are found in certain basic statutes and historical practices of Congress, presidential practices, and decisions of the Supreme Court.

Congressional Elaboration

Because the framers gave Congress authority over many of the structural details of the national government, it is not necessary to amend the Constitution every time a change is needed. Rather, Congress can create legislation to meet the need. Examples of congressional elaboration appear in such legislation as the Judiciary Act of 1789, which laid the foundations of our national judicial system; in the laws establishing the organization and functions of all federal executive officials subordinate to the president; and in the rules of procedure, internal organization, and practices of Congress.

Impeachment and Removal Power

A dramatic example of congressional elaboration of our constitutional system is the use of the impeachment and removal power. An **impeachment** is a formal accusation against a public official and the first step in removal from office. Constitutional language defining the grounds for impeachment is sparse. Look at your copy of the Constitution, and note that Article II (the Executive Article) calls for removal of the president, vice-president, and all civil officers of the United States on impeachment for, and conviction of, "Treason, Bribery, or other High Crimes and Misdemeanors." It is up to Congress to give meaning to that language.

Article I (the Legislative Article) gives the House of Representatives the sole power to initiate impeachments and the Senate the sole power to try impeachments. In the event the president is being tried, the chief justice of the United States presides, as Chief Justice William H. Rehnquist did in the impeachment of President Bill Clinton. Article I also requires conviction on impeachment charges to have the agreement of two-thirds of the senators present. Judgments shall extend no further than removal from office and disqualification from holding any office under the United States, but a person convicted shall also be liable to indictment, trial, judgment, and punishment according to the law. Article I also exempts cases of impeachment from the president's pardoning power. Article III (the Judicial Article) exempts cases of impeachment from the jury trial requirement. That is all the relevant constitutional language about impeachment. We must look to history to answer most questions about the proper exercise of these powers.[16]

Fortunately, past experience has triggered few acute constitutional disputes about the interpretation of impeachment procedures, so there is little history to go on. The House of Representatives has investigated 67 individuals for possible impeachment and has impeached 17 (2 presidents and 15 federal judges). The Senate has convicted only seven, all federal judges.

Presidential Practices

Although the formal constitutional powers of the president have not changed, the office is dramatically more important and more central today than it was in 1789. Vigorous presidents—George Washington, Thomas Jefferson, Andrew Jackson, Abraham Lincoln, Theodore Roosevelt, Woodrow Wilson, Franklin Roosevelt, Harry Truman, Lyndon Johnson, Bill Clinton—have boldly exercised their political and constitutional powers, especially during times of national crisis. Their presidential practices have established important precedents, building the power and influence of the office.

A major practice involves **executive orders**, which carry the full force of law. They may make major policy changes, such as withholding federal contracts from businesses engaging in racial discrimination, or they may simply be formalities, such as the presidential proclamation of Earth Day.

Other practices include **executive privilege** (the right to confidentiality of executive communications, especially those that relate to national security), **impoundment** by a president of funds previously appropriated by Congress, the right to send our armed forces into hostilities, and, most important, the right to propose legislation and work actively to secure its passage by Congress. President Clinton requested a federal judge to extend executive privilege to two of his advisers to prevent testimony before the grand jury investigating his relationship with White House intern Monica Lewinsky, but the request was denied.

Foreign and economic crises as well as nuclear age realities have expanded the president's role: "When it comes to action risking nuclear war, technology has modified the Constitution: the President, perforce, becomes the only such man in the system capable of exercising judgment under the extraordinary limits now imposed by secrecy, complexity, and time."[17] The presidency has also become the pivotal office for regulating the economy and protecting the general welfare. Plainly, the president has become our chief legislator as well as our chief executive.

Custom and Usage

Custom and usage round out our governmental system. The development of structures outside the formal Constitution—such as national political parties and the extension of the suffrage within the states—has democratized our Constitution. Examples of custom and usage are televised press conferences and presidential and vice-presidential debates. Through such developments, the president has become responsive to the people and has a political base different from that of Congress. Consequently, the constitutional relationship between the branches today is considerably different from that envisioned by the framers.

Judicial Interpretation

As discussed earlier, judicial interpretation of the Constitution, especially by the Supreme Court, has played an important part in keeping the constitutional system up to date. As social and economic conditions have changed and new national demands have developed, the Supreme Court has changed its interpretation of the Constitution accordingly. Because the Constitution adapts to changing times, it does not require frequent formal amendment. The advantages of this flexibility may be appreciated by comparing the national Constitution with the rigid and often overly specific state constitutions. Many state constitutions are so detailed

executive order
An order issued by a president that has the force of law.

executive privilege
The right to confidentiality of executive communications, especially those that relate to national security.

impoundment
Presidential refusal to allow an agency to spend funds authorized and appropriated by Congress.

Leaving aside the first ten amendments (the Bill of Rights), the power of constitutional amendment has served a number of purposes:

To Add or Subtract National Government Power

The Eleventh took some jurisdiction away from the national courts.

The Thirteenth abolished slavery and authorized Congress to legislate against it.

The Sixteenth enabled Congress to levy an income tax.

The Eighteenth authorized Congress to prohibit the manufacture, sale, or transportation of liquor.

The Twenty-first repealed the Eighteenth and gave states the authority to regulate liquor sales.

The Twenty-seventh limited the power of Congress to set members' salaries.

To Expand the Electorate and Its Power

The Fifteenth extended the suffrage to all male African Americans.

The Seventeenth took the right to elect their United States senators away from state legislatures and gave it to the voters in each state.

The Nineteenth extended suffrage to women.

The Twenty-third gave voters of the District of Columbia the right to vote for president and vice-president.

The Twenty-fourth prohibited any state from taxing the right to vote (the poll tax).

The Twenty-sixth extended the suffrage to otherwise qualified persons 18 years of age or older.

To Reduce the Electorate's Power

The Twenty-second took away from the electorate the right to elect any person to the office of president for more than two full terms.

To Limit State Government Power

The Thirteenth abolished slavery.

The Fourteenth granted national citizenship and prohibited states from abridging privileges of national citizenship; from denying persons life, liberty, and property without due process; and from denying persons equal protection of the laws. This amendment has come to be interpreted as imposing restraints on state powers in every area of public life.

To Make Structural Changes in Government

The Twelfth corrected deficiencies in the operation of the Electoral College that were revealed by the development of a two-party national system.

The Twentieth altered the calendar for congressional sessions and shortened the time between the election of presidents and their assumption of office.

The Twenty-fifth provided procedures for filling vacancies in the vice-presidency and for determining whether presidents are unable to perform their duties.

that they tie the hands of the public officials and must be amended or replaced frequently.

CHANGING THE LETTER OF THE CONSTITUTION

The idea of a constantly changing system disturbs many people. How, they contend, can you have a constitutional government when the Constitution is constantly being twisted by interpretation and changed by informal methods? This view fails to distinguish between two aspects of the Constitution. As an expression of *basic and timeless personal liberties*, the Constitution does not, and should not, change. For example, a government cannot destroy free speech and still remain a constitutional government. In this sense the Constitution is unchanging. But when we consider the Constitution as an *instrument of government* and a positive grant of power, we realize that if it does not grow with the nation it serves, it will soon be ignored.

The framers could never have conceived of the problems facing the government of a large, powerful and wealthy nation of over 285 million people at the beginning of the twenty-first century. Although the general purposes of government remain the same—to establish liberty, promote justice, ensure domestic tranquillity, and provide for the common defense—the powers of government that were adequate to accomplish these purposes in 1787 are simply insufficient more than two hundred years later. Through its remarkable adaptability, our Constitution has survived democratic and industrial revolutions, the turmoil of civil war, the tensions of major depressions, and the dislocations of world wars.

The framers knew that future experiences would call for changes in the text of the Constitution and that some means for formal amendment was necessary. In Article V they gave responsibility for amending the Constitution to Congress and to the states. The president has no formal authority over constitutional amendments; presidential veto power does not extend to them, although presidential political influence is often crucial in getting amendments proposed and ratified. Nor may governors veto ratification of amendments by either state legislatures or state ratifying conventions.

Proposing Amendments

The first method for proposing amendments—and the only one used so far—is *by a two-thirds vote of both houses of Congress*. Dozens of resolutions proposing amendments are introduced in every session. Thousands have been introduced since 1789, but few make any headway. Throughout our history Congress has proposed only 31 amendments, of which 27 have been ratified—including the Twenty-seventh, which was originally part of the Bill of Rights but took more than two hundred years for ratification (see Figure 2–2).

In recent decades there has been a flurry of congressional attempts at constitutional amendments.[18] None has been formally proposed by both chambers; many are currently under consideration. One given serious consideration is the Balanced Budget Amendment. Such an amendment has several times secured the two-

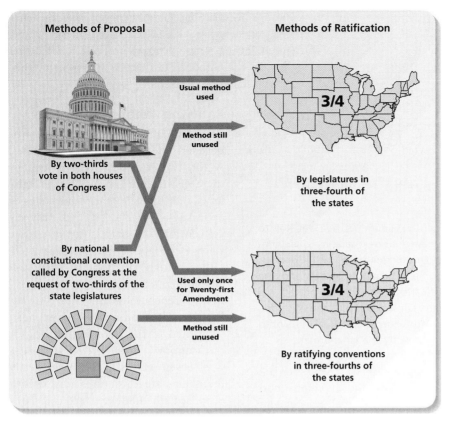

Methods of Proposal

By two-thirds vote in both houses of Congress

By national constitutional convention called by Congress at the request of two-thirds of the state legislatures

Methods of Ratification

Usual method used

Method still unused

Used only once for Twenty-first Amendment

Method still unused

3/4

By legislatures in three-fourth of the states

3/4

By ratifying conventions in three-fourths of the states

FIGURE 2–2 Four Methods of Amending the Constitution

thirds vote needed in the House, but failed to do so in the Senate. Republicans tend to favor it; most Democrats oppose it. The fact that, as a result of good economic times and some fiscal restraint, the budget actually started to generate a surplus for the first time in decades has reduced the pressure to pass a Balanced Budget Amendment. Nevertheless, in view of strong public support for it, this debate is likely to continue.

Why has proposing amendments to the Constitution become so popular? In part because interest groups unhappy with Supreme Court decisions seek to overturn them. In part because groups frustrated by their inability to get things done in Congress hope to bypass Congress. And in part because scholars or interest groups (not necessarily mutually exclusive categories) seek to change the procedures and processes of government to make the system more responsive.[19]

The second method for proposing amendments—*a convention called by Congress* at the request of the legislatures in two-thirds of the states—has never been used. This method presents some difficult questions.[20] First, can state legislatures apply for a convention to propose specific amendments on one topic, or must they request a convention with full powers to revise the entire Constitution? How long do state petitions remain alive? How should delegates be chosen? How should such a convention be run? Congress has considered bills to answer some of these questions but has not passed any, in part because most members do not wish to encourage a constitutional convention for fear that once in session it might propose amendments on any and all topics.

Under Article V of the Constitution, Congress could call for such a convention without the concurrence of the president. Under most proposals, each state would have as many delegates to the convention as it has representatives and senators in Congress. Finally—a crucial point—the convention would be limited to considering only the subject specified in the state legislative petitions and described in the congressional call for the convention. Scholars are divided, however, on whether Congress has the authority to limit what a constitutional convention might propose.[21]

WE THE PEOPLE

Gregory Watson and the Twenty-seventh Amendment

In March 1982, Gregory Watson, a student at the University of Texas writing a paper on the Equal Rights Amendment, came across an amendment proposed in 1789 as part of the Bill of Rights that would prohibit a pay raise for members of Congress until the intervention of an election for members of the House. He found that only 6 of the original 13 states had ratified it, and that during the intervening years only 3 more states had done so.

Watson decided to start a ratification movement. He got some publicity for his efforts and, with the help of Texas Republican State Representative Don Mielke, persuaded 6 more state legislatures to ratify this long-forgotten proposed amendment. (By the way, Watson got only a C on his paper, although he is credited with influencing 26 state legislatures to ratify the Twenty-seventh Amendment.)*

After members of Congress tried unsuccessfully in 1989 to avoid public anger by delegating their decision to increase their own salaries to an independent commission, anti-Congress sentiment began to grow, and the ratification movement picked up steam. On May 7, 1992, the Michigan legislature became the thirty-eighth state to ratify the amendment.

The first reaction of some congressional leaders was to question this action because the Supreme Court had made it clear that amendments must be ratified within a "reasonable time." However, when members of Congress realized that the issue could be used against them in the next election, they declared the Twenty-seventh Amendment to be "valid as part of the Constitution of the United States." The vote was 99 to 0 in the Senate, 414 to 3 in the House.

*Ruth Ann Strickland, "The Twenty-seventh Amendment and Constitutional Change by Stealth," *P.S.: Political Science and Politics* (December 1993), p. 720.

Ratifying Amendments

After an amendment has been proposed, it must be ratified by the states. Again, two methods are provided by the Constitution: approval by the legislatures in three-fourths of the states or approval by specially called ratifying conventions in three-fourths of the states (see Figure 2–3). Congress determines which method is used. All amendments except one—the Twenty-first (to repeal the Eighteenth, the Prohibition Amendment)—have been submitted to the state legislatures for ratification.

Seven state constitutions specify that their state legislatures must ratify a proposed amendment to the U.S. Constitution by majorities of three-fifths or two-thirds of each chamber. Although a state legislature may change its mind and ratify an amendment after it has voted against ratification, the weight of opinion is that once a state has ratified an amendment, it cannot "unratify" it.[22]

The Supreme Court has said that ratification must take place within a "reasonable time." When Congress proclaims an amendment to be part of

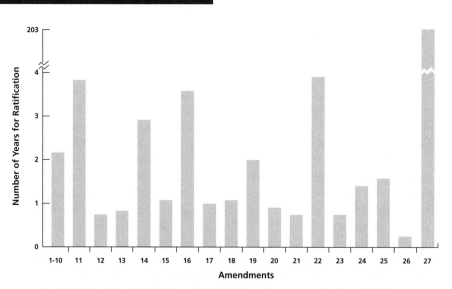

FIGURE 2-3 **The Time for Ratification of the 27 Amendments to the Constitution**

the Constitution, it must decide whether the amendment has been ratified within a reasonable time so that it is "sufficiently contemporaneous to reflect the will of the people."[23] However, Congress approved ratification of the Twenty-seventh Amendment, which had been before the nation for almost 203 years, so there seems to be no limit to what it will consider to be a "reasonable time." Because of the experience with the Twenty-seventh Amendment, Congress will probably continue the current practice of stipulating in the text of a proposed amendment that the necessary number of states must ratify it within seven years from the date of submission by Congress. In fact, ratification ordinarily takes place rather quickly.[24]

Ratification Politics

The failure of the Equal Rights Amendment to be ratified provides a vivid example of the pitfalls of ratification. First introduced in 1923 and frequently thereafter, the Equal Rights Amendment (ERA) did not get much support until the 1960s. An influential book by Betty Friedan, *The Feminine Mystique* (1963), challenged stereotypes about the role of women. The National Organization for Women (NOW), formed in 1966, made passage of ERA its central mission. By the 1970s the ERA had overwhelming support in both houses of Congress and in both national party platforms; not until 1980 did one party (the Republican) adopt a stance of neutrality. Every president from Harry Truman to Ronald Reagan, and many of their wives, endorsed the amendment. More than 450 organizations with a total membership of more than 50 million were on record in support of the ERA.[25]

Soon after passage of the amendment by Congress in 1972 and submission to the states, many legislatures ratified it quickly—sometimes without hearings—and by overwhelming majorities. By the end of 1972, 22 states had ratified the amendment, and it appeared that the ERA would soon become part of the Constitution.[26] Then the opposition organized under the articulate leadership of Phyllis Schlafly, a prominent spokesperson for conservative causes, and the ERA became controversial.

Opponents argued that "women would not only be subject to the military draft but also assigned to combat duty. Full-time housewives and mothers would be forced to join the labor force. Further, women would no longer enjoy existing advantages under state domestic relations codes and under labor law."[27] The ERA also became embroiled in the controversy over abortion. Many opponents contended that its ratification would jeopardize the power of states and Congress to regulate abortion and would compel public funding of abortions.[28]

After the ERA became controversial, state legislatures held lengthy hearings, and floor debates became heated. Legislators hid behind parliamentary procedures and avoided making a decision for as long as possible. Opposition to ratification arose chiefly in the same cluster of southern states that had opposed ratification of the Nineteenth Amendment, which gave women the vote. As the opposition grew more active, proponents redoubled their efforts.

In the autumn of 1978 it appeared that the ERA would fall three short of the necessary number of ratifying states before the expiration of the seven-year limit on March 22, 1979. After an extended debate, and after voting down provisions that would have authorized state legislatures to change their minds and rescind prior ratification, Congress, by a simple majority vote, extended the time limit until June 30, 1982. Nonetheless, by the final deadline the amendment was still three states short.

The framers intended that amending the Constitution should be difficult. The ERA ratification battle demonstrated how well they planned.

The Equal Rights Amendment

Proposed March 22, 1972.   Died June 30, 1982, three state legislatures short of the thirty-eight needed for ratification.

Section 1.   Equality of rights under the law shall not be denied or abridged by the United States or by any State on account of sex.

Section 2.   The Congress shall have power to enforce, by appropriate legislation, the provisions of this article.

Section 3.   This amendment shall take effect two years after the date of ratification.

People came from every state of the union to march in support of passage of the Equal Rights Amendment.

SUMMARY

1. Our Constitution both grants and limits powers. The framers established a government by the people. Yet the framers were suspicious of people, especially of those having political power, so they separated and distributed the powers of the newly created national government in a variety of ways.

2. The framers were also concerned to create a national government strong enough to solve national problems. Thus they gave the national government substantial grants of power, but these grants were made with such broad strokes that it has been possible for the constitutional system to remain flexible and adapt to changing conditions.

3. Judicial review is the power of the courts to strike down acts of Congress, the executive branch, and the states as unconstitutional. It is one of the unique features of the U.S. constitutional system.

4. The constitutional system has been modified over time, adapting to new conditions through congressional elaboration, presidential practices, custom and usage, and judicial interpretation.

5. Although adaptable, the Constitution itself needs to be altered from time to time, and the framers provided a procedure for its amendment. An amendment must be both proposed and ratified: proposed by either a two-thirds vote in each chamber of Congress or by a national convention called by Congress on petition of the legislatures in two-thirds of the states; ratified either by the legislatures in three-fourths of the states or by specially called ratifying conventions in three-fourths of the states.

6. The Constitution has been formally amended 27 times. The usual method has been proposal by a two-thirds vote in both houses of Congress and ratification by the legislatures in three-fourths of the states.

KEY TERMS

natural law 26
separation of powers 26
checks and balances 27
divided government 28

direct primary 29
initiative 29
referendum 29
recall 29

judicial review 30
writ of mandamus 34
impeachment 34
executive order 35

executive privilege 35
impoundment 35

FURTHER READING

BRUCE A. ACKERMAN, *We the People* (Harvard University Press, Belknap Press, 1993).

LANCE BANNING, *The Sacred Fire of Liberty: James Madison and the Founding of the Federal Republic* (Cornell University Press, 1995).

RICHARD B. BERNSTEIN, *Amending America: If We Love the Constitution So Much Why Do We Keep Trying to Change It?* (Time, 1993).

JAMES BRYCE, *The American Commonwealth* (Macmillan, 1889), vols. 1 and 2.

JAMES MACGREGOR BURNS, *The Vineyard of Liberty* (Knopf, 1982).

GERHARD CASPER, *Separation Powers: Essays on the Founding Period* (Harvard University Press, 1997).

ROBERT LOWRY CLINTON, *"Marbury v. Madison" and Judicial Review* (University Press of Kansas, 1989).

NEIL H. COGAN, *The Complete Bill of Rights: The Drafts, Debates, Sources, and Origins* (Oxford University Press, 1997).

LOUIS FISHER, *Constitutional Conflicts Between Congress and the President*, 4th ed. (University Press of Kansas, 1997).

MICHAEL KAMMEN, *A Machine That Would Go of Itself: The Constitution in American Culture* (Alfred A. Knopf, 1986).

BARBARA B. KNIGHT, *Separation of Powers in the American Political System* (George Mason University Press, 1989).

PHILIP B. KURLAND AND RALPH LERNER, *The Founders' Constitution*, 5 vols. (University of Chicago Press, 1987).

DAVID E. KYVIG, *Explicit and Authentic Acts: Amending the U.S. Constitution, 1776–1995* (University Press of Kansas, 1996).

LIBRARY OF CONGRESS, CONGRESSIONAL RESEARCH SERVICE, *The Constitution of the United States of America: Analysis and Interpretation*, Senate Document 100-9 (U.S. Government Printing Office, 1991). Updated on the Web at http://www.findlaw.com/case_code

J. W. PELTASON AND SUE DAVIS, *Understanding the Constitution*, 15th ed. (Harcourt College Division, 2000).

WILLIAM H. REHNQUIST, *Grand Inquests: The Historic Impeachments of Justice Samuel Chase and President Andrew Johnson* (Morrow, 1992).

JOHN R. VILE, *Encyclopedia of Constitutional Amendments, Proposed Amendments, and Amending Issues, 1789–1995* (ABC-CLIO, 1996).

On Reading the Constitution

More than two hundred years after its ratification, our Constitution remains the operating charter of our republic. It is neither self-explanatory nor a comprehensive description of our constitutional rules. Still, it remains the starting point. Many Americans who swear by the Constitution have never read it seriously, although copies can be found in the back of most American government and American history textbooks.

Justice Hugo Black, who served on the Supreme Court for 34 years, kept a copy of the Constitution with him at all times. He read it often. Reading the Constitution would be a good way for you to begin (and then reread again to end) your study of the government of the United States. Thus, we have included a copy of it at this point in the book. Please read it carefully.

The Constitution
of the
United States

The Preamble

We the People of the United States, in Order to form a more perfect Union, establish Justice, insure domestic Tranquility, provide for the common defense, promote the general Welfare, and secure the Blessings of Liberty to ourselves and our Posterity, do ordain and establish this Constitution for the United States of America.

Article I—The Legislative Article

Legislative Power

Section 1   All legislative Powers herein granted shall be vested in a Congress of the United States, which shall consist of a Senate and House of Representatives.

House of Representatives: Composition; Qualifications; Apportionment; Impeachment Power

Section 2   The House of Representatives shall be composed of Members chosen every second Year by the People of the several States, and the Electors in each State shall have the Qualifications requisite for Electors of the most numerous Branch of the State Legislature.

No Person shall be a Representative who shall not have attained to the Age of twenty five Years, and been seven Years a Citizen of the United States, and who shall not, when elected, be an Inhabitant of that State in which he shall be chosen.

Representatives and direct Taxes[1] shall be apportioned among the several States which may be included within this Union, according to their respective Numbers, *which shall be determined by adding to the whole Number of free Persons, including those bound to Service for a Term of Years, and excluding Indians not taxed, three fifths of all other Persons.*[2] The actual Enumeration shall be made within three Years after the first Meeting of the Congress of the United States, and within every subsequent Term of ten Years, in such Manner as they shall by Law direct. The Number of Representatives shall not exceed one for every thirty Thousand, but each State shall have at least one Representative; and until each enumeration shall be made, the State of New Hampshire shall be entitled to chuse three, Massachusetts eight, Rhode-Island and Providence Plantations one, Connecticut five, New-York six, New Jersey four, Pennsylvania eight, Delaware one, Maryland six, Virginia ten, North Carolina five, South Carolina five, and Georgia three.

When vacancies happen in the Representation from any State, the Executive Authority thereof shall issue Writs of Election to fill such Vacancies.

The House of Representatives shall chuse their Speaker and other Officers; and shall have the sole Power of Impeachment.

Senate Composition: Qualifications, Impeachment Trials

Section 3   The Senate of the United States shall be composed of two Senators from each State, *chosen by the Legislature thereof,*[3] for six Years; and each Senator shall have one Vote.

Immediately after they shall be assembled in Consequence of the first Election, they shall be divided as equally as may be into three Classes. The Seats of the Senators of the first Class shall be vacated at the Expiration of the second Year, of the second Class at the Expiration of the fourth Year, and of the third Class at the Expiration of the sixth Year, so that one third may be chosen every second Year; *and if Vacancies happen by Resignation, or otherwise, during the Recess of the Legislature of any State, the Executive thereof may make temporary Appointments until the next Meeting of the Legislature, which shall then fill such Vacancies.*[4]

No person shall be a Senator who shall not have attained to the Age of thirty Years, and been nine Years a Citizen of the United States, and who shall not, when elected, be an inhabitant of that State for which he shall be chosen.

The Vice President of the United States shall be President of the Senate, but shall have no Vote, unless they be equally divided.

The Senate shall chuse their other Officers, and also a President pro tempore, in the Absence of the Vice President, or when he shall exercise the Office of President of the United States.

The Senate shall have the sole Power to try all Impeachments. When sitting for that Purpose, they shall be on Oath or Affirmation. When the President of the United States is tried, the Chief Justice shall preside: And no Person shall be convicted without the Concurrence of two thirds of the Members present.

Judgment in Cases of Impeachment shall not extend further than to removal from Office, and disqualification to hold and enjoy any Office of honor, Trust or Profit under the United States; but the Party convicted shall nevertheless be liable and subject to Indictment, Trial, Judgment and Punishment, according to law.

Congressional Elections: Times, Places, Manner

Section 4   The Times, Places and Manner of holding Elections for Senators and Representatives, shall be prescribed in each State by the Legislature thereof; but the Congress may at any time by Law make or alter such Regulations, except as to the Places of chusing Senators.

The Congress shall assemble at least once in every Year, *and such Meeting shall be on the first Monday in December, unless they shall by Law appoint a different Day.*[5]

---

[1]Modified by the 16th Amendment
[2]Replaced by Section 2, 14th Amendment

[3]Repealed by the 17th Amendment
[4]Modified by the 17th Amendment
[5]Changed by the 20th Amendment

Powers and Duties of the Houses

Section 5   Each House shall be the Judge of the Elections, Returns and Qualifications of its own Members, and a Majority of each shall constitute a Quorum to do Business; but a smaller Number may adjourn from day to day, and may be authorized to compel the Attendance of absent Members, in such Manner, and under the Penalties as each House may provide.

Each House may determine the Rules of its Proceedings, punish its Members for disorderly Behaviour, and, with the Concurrence of two thirds, expel a Member.

Each House shall keep a Journal of its Proceedings, and from time to time publish the same, excepting such Parts as may in their Judgment require Secrecy; and the Yeas and Nays of the Members of either House on any question shall, at the Desire of one fifth of those Present, be entered on the Journal.

Neither House, during the Session of Congress, shall, without the Consent of the other, adjourn for more than three days, nor to any other place than that in which the two Houses shall be sitting.

Rights of Members

Section 6   The Senators and Representatives shall receive a Compensation for their Services, to be ascertained by Law, and paid out of the Treasury of the United States. They shall in all Cases, except Treason, Felony and Breach of the Peace, be privileged from Arrest during their Attendance at the Session of their respective Houses, and in going to and returning from the same; and for any Speech or Debate in either House, they shall not be questioned in any other Place.

No Senator or Representative, shall, during the time for which he was elected, be appointed to any civil Office under the Authority of the United States, which shall have been created, or the Emoluments whereof shall have been encreased during such time; and no Person holding any Office under the United States, shall be a Member of either House during his Continuance in Office.

Legislative Powers: Bills and Resolutions

Section 7   All Bills for raising Revenue shall originate in the House of Representatives; but the Senate may propose or concur with Amendments as on other Bills.

Every Bill which shall have passed the House of Representatives and the Senate, shall, before it becomes a Law, be presented to the President of the United States; if he approve he shall sign it, but if not he shall return it, with his Objections to that House in which it shall have originated, who shall enter the Objections at large on their Journal, and proceed to reconsider it. If after such Reconsideration two thirds of that House shall agree to pass the Bill, it shall be sent, together with the Objections, to the other House, by which it shall likewise be reconsidered, and if approved by two thirds of that House, it shall become a Law. But in all such Cases the Votes of both Houses shall be determined by yeas and Nays, and the Names of the Persons voting for and against the Bill shall be entered on the Journal of each House respectively. If any Bill shall not be returned by the President within ten Days (Sundays excepted) after it shall have been presented to him, the Same shall be a Law, in like Manner as if he had signed it, unless the Congress by their Adjournment prevent its Return, in which Case it shall not be a Law.

Every Order, Resolution, or Vote to which the Concurrence of the Senate and House of Representatives may be necessary (except on a question of Adjournment) shall be presented to the President of the United States; and before the Same shall take Effect, shall be approved by him, or being disapproved by him, shall be repassed by two thirds of the Senate and House of Representatives, according to the Rules and Limitations prescribed in the Case of a Bill.

Powers of Congress

Section 8   The Congress shall have Power To lay and collect Taxes, Duties, Imposts and Excises, to pay the Debts and provide for the common Defence and general Welfare of the United States; but all Duties, Imposts and Excises shall be uniform throughout the United States.

To borrow Money on the Credit of the United States;

To regulate Commerce with foreign Nations, and among the several States, and with the Indian Tribes;

To establish an uniform Rule of Naturalization, and uniform Laws on the subject of Bankruptcies throughout the United States;

To coin Money, regulate the Value thereof, and of foreign Coin, and fix the Standard of Weights and Measures;

To provide for the Punishment of counterfeiting the Securities and current Coin of the United States;

To establish Post Offices and post Roads;

To promote the Progress of Science and useful Arts, by securing for limited Times to Authors and Inventors the exclusive Right to their respective Writings and Discoveries;

To constitute Tribunals inferior to the supreme Court;

To define and punish Piracies and Felonies committed on the high Seas, and Offences against the Law of Nations;

To declare War, grant Letters of Marque and Reprisal, and make Rules concerning Captures on Land and Water;

To raise and support Armies, but no Appropriation of Money to that Use shall be for a longer Term than two Years;

To provide and maintain a Navy;

To make Rules for the Government and Regulation of the land and naval Forces;

To provide for calling for the Militia to execute the Laws of the Union, suppress Insurrections and repel Invasions;

To provide for organizing, arming, and disciplining, the Militia, and for governing such Part of them as may be employed in the Service of the United States, reserving to the States respectively, the Appointment of the Officers, and the Authority of training the Militia according to the discipline prescribed by Congress;

To exercise exclusive Legislation in all Cases whatsoever, over such District (not exceeding ten Miles square) as may, by Cession of particular States, and the Acceptance of Congress, become the Seat of the Government of the United States, and to exercise like Authority over all Places purchased by the Consent of the Legislature of the State in which the Same shall be, for the Erection of Forts, Magazines, Arsenals, dock-Yards, and other needful Buildings;—And

To make all Laws which shall be necessary and proper for carrying into Execution the foregoing Powers, and all other Powers vested by this Constitution in the Government of the United States, or in any Department or Officer thereof.   "Necessary + Proper" Clause

Powers Denied to Congress

give Congress power

Section 9   The Migration of Importation of such Persons as any of the States now existing shall think proper to admit, shall not be prohibited by the Congress prior to the Year one thousand eight hundred and eight, but a Tax or Duty may be imposed on such Importation, not exceeding ten dollars for each Person.

The privilege of the Writ of Habeas Corpus shall not be suspended, unless when in Cases of Rebellion or Invasion the public Safety may require it.

No Bill of Attainder or ex post facto Laws shall be passed.

No Capitation, or other direct, Tax shall be laid, unless in Proportion to the Census or Enumeration herein before directed to be taken.[6]

No Tax or Duty shall be laid on Articles exported from any State.

No Preference shall be given by any Regulation of Commerce or Revenue to the Ports of one State over those of another; nor shall Vessels bound to, or from, one State, be obliged to enter, clear, or pay Duties in another.

---

[6]Modified by the 16th Amendment

No Money shall be drawn from the Treasury, but in Consequence of Appropriations made by Law; and a regular Statement and Account of the Receipts and Expenditures of all public Money shall be published from time to time.

No Title of Nobility shall be granted by the United States; And no Person holding any Office of Profit or Trust under them, shall, without the Consent of Congress, accept of any present, Emolument, Office, or Title, of any kind whatever, from any King, Prince, or foreign State.

Powers Denied to the States

Section 10 No State shall enter into any Treaty, Alliance, or Confederation; grant Letters of Marque and Reprisal; coin Money; emit Bills of Credit; make any Thing but gold and silver Coin a Tender in Payment of Debts; pass any Bill of Attainder, ex post facto Law, or Law impairing the Obligation of Contracts, or grant any Title of Nobility.

No State shall, without the Consent of the Congress, lay any Imposts or Duties on Imports or Exports, except what may be absolutely necessary for executing its inspection Laws: and the net Produce of all Duties and Imposts, laid by any State on Imports or Exports, shall be for the Use of the Treasury of the United States; and all such Laws shall be subject to the Revision and Controul of the Congress.

No State shall, without the Consent of Congress, lay any Duty of Tonnage, keep Troops, or Ships of War in time of Peace, enter into any Agreement or Compact with another State, or with a foreign Power, or engage in War, unless actually invaded, or in such imminent Danger as will not admit of Delay.

ARTICLE II—THE EXECUTIVE ARTICLE

Nature and Scope of Presidential Power

Section 1 The executive Power shall be vested in a President of the United States of America. He shall hold his Office during the Term of four Years and, together with the Vice President, chosen for the same Term, be elected as follows:

Each State shall appoint, in such Manner as the Legislature thereof may direct, a Number of Electors, equal to the whole Number of Senators and Representatives to which the State may be entitled in the Congress: but no Senator or Representative, or Person holding an Office of Trust or Profit under the United States, shall be appointed an Elector.

The Electors shall meet in their respective States, and vote by Ballot for two Persons, of whom one at least shall not be an Inhabitant of the same State with themselves. And they shall make a List of all the Persons voted for, and of the Number of Votes for each; which List they shall sign and certify, and transmit sealed to the Seat of the Government of the United States, directed to the President of the Senate. The President of the Senate shall, in the Presence of the Senate and House of Representatives, open all the Certificates, and the Votes shall then be counted. The Person having the greatest Number of Votes shall be the President, if such Number be a Majority of the whole Number of Electors appointed; and if there be more than one who have such Majority and have an equal Number of Votes, then the House of Representatives shall immediately chuse by Ballot one of them for President; and if no person have a Majority, then from the five highest on the List the said House shall in like Manner chuse the President. But in chusing the President, the Votes shall be taken by States, the Representation from each State having one Vote; A quorum for this Purpose shall consist of a Member or Members from two thirds of the States, and a Majority of all the States shall be necessary to a Choice. In every Case, after the Choice of the President, the person having the greatest Number of Votes of the Electors shall be the Vice President. But if there should remain two or more who have equal Vote, the Senate shall chuse from them by Ballot the Vice President.[7]

The Congress may determine the Time of chusing the Electors, and the Day on which they shall give their Votes; which Day shall be the same throughout the United States.

No Person except a natural born Citizen, or a Citizen of the United States, at the time of the Adoption of this Constitution, shall be eligible to the Office of President; neither shall any Person be eligible to that Office who shall not have attained to the Age of thirty five Years, and been fourteen Years a Resident within the United States.

In Case of the Removal of the President from Office, or of his Death, Resignation, or Inability to discharge the Powers and Duties of the said Office, the same shall devolve on the Vice President, and the Congress may by Law provide for the Case of Removal, Death, Resignation, or Inability, both of the President and Vice President, declaring what Officer shall then act as President, and such Officer shall act accordingly, until the Disability be removed, or a President shall be elected.[8]

The President shall, at stated Times, receive for his Services, a Compensation, which shall neither be encreased nor diminished during the Period of which he shall have been elected, and he shall not receive within that Period any other Emolument from the United States, or any of them.

Before he enter on the Execution of his Office, he shall take the following Oath or Affirmation:—"I do solemnly swear (or affirm) that I will faithfully execute the Office of President of the United States, and will to the best of my Ability, preserve, protect and defend the Constitution of the United States."

Powers and Duties of the President

Section 2 The President shall be the Commander in Chief of the Army and Navy of the United States, and of the Militia of the several States, when called into the actual Service of the United States, he may require the Opinion, in writing, of the principal Officer in each of the executive Departments, upon any Subject relating to the Duties of their respective Offices, and he shall have the Power to grant Reprieves and Pardons for Offences against the United States, except in Cases of Impeachment.

He shall have Power, by and with the Advice and Consent of the Senate to make Treaties, provided two thirds of the Senators present concur; and he shall nominate, and by and with the Advice and Consent of the Senate, shall appoint Ambassadors, other public Ministers and Consuls, Judges of the supreme Court, and all other Officers of the United States, whose Appointments are not herein otherwise provided for, and which shall be established by Law: but the Congress may by Law vest the Appointment of such inferior Officers, as they think proper, in the President alone, in the Courts of Law, or in the Heads of Departments.

The President shall have Power to fill up all Vacancies that may happen during the Recess of the Senate, by granting Commissions which shall expire at the End of their next Session.

Section 3 He shall from time to time give to the Congress Information of the State of the Union, and recommend to their Consideration such Measures as he shall judge necessary and expedient; he may, on extraordinary Occasions, convene both Houses, or either of them, and in Case of Disagreement between them, with Respect to the Time of Adjournment, he may adjourn them to such Time as he shall think proper; he shall receive Ambassadors and other public Ministers; he shall take Care that the Laws be faithfully executed, and shall Commission all the Officers of the United States.

Section 4 The President, Vice President and all civil Officers of the United States, shall be removed from Office on Impeachment for, and Conviction of, Treason, Bribery, or other High Crimes and Misdemeanors.

ARTICLE III—THE JUDICIAL ARTICLE

Judicial Power, Courts, Judges

Section 1 The judicial Power of the United States, shall be vested in one supreme Court, and in such inferior Courts as the Congress may from time to time ordain and establish. The Judges, both the supreme and inferior Courts,

---

[7]Changed by the 12th and 20th Amendments

[8]Modified by the 25th Amendment

shall hold their Offices during good Behaviour, and shall, at stated Times, receive for their Services, a Compensation, which shall not be diminished during their Continuance in Office.

Jurisdiction

Section 2 The judicial Power shall extend to all Cases, in Law and Equity, arising under this Constitution, the Laws of the United States, and Treaties made, or which shall be made, under their Authority;—to all Cases affecting Ambassadors, other public Ministers and Consuls;—to all Cases of admiralty and maritime Jurisdiction;—to Controversies to which the United States shall be a Party;—to Controversies between two or more States; *between a State and Citizens of another State*;[9]—between Citizens of different States;—between Citizens of the same State claiming Lands under Grants of different States, and between a State, or the Citizens thereof, and foreign States, Citizens, or Subjects.

In all Cases affecting Ambassadors, other public Ministers and Consuls, and those in which a State shall be Party, the supreme Court shall have original Jurisdiction. In all the other Cases before mentioned, the supreme Court shall have appellate Jurisdiction, both as to Law and Fact, with such Exceptions, and under such Regulations as Congress shall make.

The Trial of all Crimes, except in Cases of Impeachment, shall be by Jury; and such Trial shall be held in the State where the said Crimes shall have been committed; but when not committed within any State, the Trial shall be at such Place or Places as the Congress may by Law have directed.

Treason

Section 3 Treason against the United States, shall consist only in levying War against them, or in adhering to their Enemies, giving them Aid and Comfort. No Persons shall be convicted of Treason unless on the Testimony of two Witnesses to the same overt Act, or on Confession in open Court.

The Congress shall have Power to declare the Punishment of Treason, but no Attainder of Treason shall work Corruption of Blood, or Forfeiture except during the Life of the Person attainted.

ARTICLE IV—INTERSTATE RELATIONS

Full Faith and Credit Clause

Section 1 Full Faith and Credit shall be given in each State to the public Acts, Records, and judicial Proceedings of every other State. And the Congress may by general Laws prescribe the Manner in which such Acts, Records and Proceedings shall be proved, and the Effect thereof.

Privileges and Immunities; Interstate Extradition

Section 2 The Citizens of each State shall be entitled to all Privileges and Immunities of Citizens in the several States.

A person charged in any State with Treason, Felony or other Crime, who shall flee from Justice, and be found in another State, shall on Demand of the executive Authority of the State from which he fled, be delivered up, to be removed to the State having jurisdiction of the Crime.

No person held to Service or Labour in one State, under the Laws thereof, escaping into another, shall, in Consequence of any Law or Regulation therein, be discharged from such Service or Labour, but shall be delivered up on Claim of the Party to whom such Service or Labour may be due.[10]

Admission of States

Section 3 New States may be admitted by the Congress into this Union; but no new State shall be formed or erected within the Jurisdiction of any other State; nor any State to be formed by the Junction of two or more States, or Parts of States, without the Consent of the Legislatures of the States concerned as well as of the Congress.

The Congress shall have Power to dispose of and make all needful Rules and Regulations respecting the Territory or other Property belonging to the United States; and nothing in this Constitution shall be so construed as to Prejudice any Claims of the United States, or of any particular State.

Republican Form of Government

Section 4 The United States shall guarantee to every State in this Union a Republican Form of Government, and shall protect each of them against Invasion; and on Application of the Legislature, or of the Executive (when the Legislature cannot be convened) against domestic Violence.

ARTICLE V—THE AMENDING POWER

The Congress, whenever two thirds of both Houses shall deem it necessary, shall propose Amendments to this Constitution, or, on the Application of the Legislatures of two thirds of several States, shall call a Convention for proposing Amendments, which, in either Case, shall be valid to all Intents and Purposes, as Part of this Constitution, when ratified by the Legislatures of three fourths of the several States, or by Conventions in three fourths thereof, as the one or the other Mode of Ratification may be proposed by the Congress; Provided that no Amendment which may be made prior to the Year One thousand eight hundred and eight shall in any Manner affect the first and fourth Clauses in the Ninth Section of the first Article; and that no State, without its Consent, shall be deprived of its equal Suffrage in the Senate.

ARTICLE VI—THE SUPREMACY ARTICLE

All Debts contracted and Engagements entered into, before the Adoption of this Constitution, shall be as valid against the United States under the Constitution, as under the Confederation.

This Constitution, and the Laws of the United States which shall be made in Pursuance thereof; and all Treaties made, or which shall be made, under the Authority of the United States, shall be the supreme Law of the Land; and the Judges in every State shall be bound thereby, any Thing in the Constitution or Laws of any State to the Contrary notwithstanding.

The Senators and Representatives before mentioned, and the Members of the several State Legislatures, and all executive and judicial Officers, both of the United States and of the several States, shall be bound by Oath or Affirmation, to support this Constitution; but no religious Test shall ever be required as a Qualification to any Office or public Trust under the United States.

ARTICLE VII—RATIFICATION

The Ratification of the Conventions of nine States, shall be sufficient for the Establishment of this Constitution between the States so ratifying the Same.

Done in Convention by the Unanimous Consent of the States present the Seventeenth Day of September in the Year of our Lord one thousand seven hundred and Eighty seven and of the Independence of the United States of America the Twelfth *In Witness whereof We have hereunto subscribed our Names.*

AMENDMENTS

The Bill of Rights

[The first ten amendments were ratified on December 15, 1791, and form what is known as the "Bill of Rights."]

AMENDMENT 1—RELIGION, SPEECH, ASSEMBLY, AND POLITICS

Congress shall make no law respecting an establishment of religion, or prohibiting the free exercise thereof; or abridging the freedom of speech, or of the press; or the right of the people peaceably to assemble, and to petition the government for a redress of grievances.

---

[9]Modified by the 11th Amendment
[10]Repealed by the 13th Amendment

Amendment 2—Militia and the Right to Bear Arms

A well regulated Militia, being necessary to the security of a free State, the right of the people to keep and bear Arms, shall not be infringed.

Amendment 3—Quartering of Soldiers

No Soldier shall, in time of peace be quartered in any house, without the consent of the Owner, nor in time of war, but in manner to be prescribed by law.

Amendment 4—Searches and Seizures

The right of the people to be secure in their persons, houses, papers, and effects, against unreasonable searches and seizures, shall not be violated, and no Warrants shall issue, but upon probable cause, supported by Oath or affirmation, and particularly describing the place to be searched, and the persons or things to be seized.

Amendment 5—Grand Juries, Self-Incrimination, Double Jeopardy, Due Process, and Eminent Domain

No person shall be held to answer for a capital, or otherwise infamous crime, unless on a presentment or indictment of a Grand jury, except in cases arising in the land or naval forces, or in the Militia, when in actual service in time of War or public danger; nor shall any person be subject for the same offence to be twice put in jeopardy of life or limb; nor shall be compelled in any criminal case to be a witness against himself, nor be deprived of life, liberty, or property, without due process of law; nor shall private property be taken for public use, without just compensation.

Amendment 6—Criminal Court Procedures

In all criminal prosecutions, the accused shall enjoy the right to a speedy and public trial, by an impartial jury of the State and district wherein the crime shall have been committed, which district shall have been previously ascertained by law, and to be informed of the nature and cause of the accusation; to be confronted with the witnesses against him; to have compulsory process for obtaining Witnesses in his favor, and to have the Assistance of Counsel for his defense.

Amendment 7—Trial by Jury in Common Law Cases

In Suits at common law, where the value in controversy shall exceed twenty dollars, the right of trial by jury shall be preserved, and no fact tried by a jury shall be otherwise re-examined in any Court of the United States, than according to the rules of the common law.

Amendment 8—Bail, Cruel and Unusual Punishment

Excessive bail shall not be required, nor excessive fines imposed, nor cruel and unusual punishments inflicted.

Amendment 9—Rights Retained by the People

The enumeration in the Constitution, of certain rights, shall not be construed to deny or disparage others retained by the people.

Amendment 10—Reserved Powers of the States

The powers not delegated to the United States by the Constitution, nor prohibited by it to the States, are reserved to the States respectively, or to the people.

Amendment 11—Suits Against the States
[Ratified February 7, 1795]

The Judicial power of the United States shall not be construed to extend to any suit in law or equity, commenced or prosecuted against one of the United States by Citizens of another State, or by Citizens or Subjects of any Foreign State.

Amendment 12—Election of the President
[Ratified June 15, 1804]

The Electors shall meet in their respective states, and vote by ballot for President and Vice-President, one of whom, at least, shall not be an inhabitant of the same state with themselves; they shall name in their ballots the person voted for as President, and in distinct ballots the person voted for as Vice-President, and they shall make distinct lists of all persons voted for as President, and of all persons voted for as Vice-President, and of the number of votes for each, which lists they shall sign and certify, and transmit sealed to the seat of the government of the United States, directed to the President of the Senate;—The President of the Senate shall, in presence of the Senate and House of Representatives, open all the certificates and the votes shall then be counted;—The person having the greatest number of votes for President, shall be the President, if such number be a majority of the whole number of Electors appointed; and if no person have such majority, then from the persons having the highest numbers not exceeding three on the list of those voted for as President, the House of Representatives shall choose immediately, by ballot, the President. But in choosing the President, the votes shall be taken by states, the representation from each state having one vote; a quorum for this purpose shall consist of a member or members from two-thirds of the states, and a majority of all states shall be necessary to a choice. And if the House of Representatives shall not choose a President whenever the right of choice shall devolve upon them, *before the fourth day of March next following*, then the Vice-President shall act as President, as in the case of the death or other constitutional disability of the President.[11] The person having the greatest number of votes as Vice-President, shall be the Vice-President, if such a number be a majority of the whole numbers of Electors appointed, and if no person have a majority, then from the two highest numbers on the list, the Senate shall choose the Vice-President; a quorum for the purpose shall consist of two-thirds of the whole number of Senators, and a majority of the whole number shall be necessary to a choice. But no person constitutionally ineligible to the office of President shall be eligible to that of Vice-President of the United States.

Amendment 13—Prohibition of Slavery
[Ratified December 6, 1865]

Section 1   Neither slavery nor involuntary servitude, except as a punishment for crime whereof the party shall have been duly convicted, shall exist within the United States, or any place subject to their jurisdiction.

Section 2   Congress shall have power to enforce this article by appropriate legislation.

Amendment 14—Citizenship, Due Process, and Equal Protection of the Laws
[Ratified July 9, 1868]

Section 1   All persons born or naturalized in the United States, and subject to the jurisdiction thereof, are citizens of the United States and of the State wherein they reside. No State shall make or enforce any law which shall abridge the privileges or immunities of citizens of the United States; nor shall

---

[11]Changed by the 20th Amendment

any State deprive any person of life, liberty, or property, without due process of law; nor deny to any person within its jurisdiction the equal protection of the laws.

Section 2 Representatives shall be apportioned among the several States according to their respective numbers, counting the whole number of persons in each State, excluding Indians not taxed. But when the right to vote at any election for the choice of electors for President and Vice President of the United States, Representatives in Congress, the Executive and Judicial officers of a State, or the members of the Legislature thereof, is denied to any of the male inhabitants of such State, being twenty-one[12] years of age, and citizens of the United States, or in any way abridged, except for participation in rebellion, or other crime, the basis of representation therein shall be reduced in the proportion which the number of such male citizens shall bear to the whole number of male citizens twenty-one years of age in such State.

Section 3 No person shall be a Senator or Representative in Congress, or elector of President and Vice President, or hold any office, civil or military, under the United States, or under any State, who, having previously taken an oath, as a member of Congress, or as an officer of the United States, or as a member of any State legislature, or as an executive or judicial officer of any State, to support the Constitution of the United States, shall have engaged in insurrection or rebellion against the same, or given aid or comfort to the enemies thereof. But Congress may by a vote of two-thirds of each House, remove such disability.

Section 4 The validity of the public debt of the United States, authorized by law, including debts incurred for payment of pensions and bounties for services in suppressing insurrection or rebellion, shall not be questioned. But neither the United States nor any State shall assume or pay any debt or obligation incurred in aid of insurrection or rebellion against the United States, or any claim for the loss or emancipation of any slave; but all such debts, obligations and claims shall be held illegal and void.

Section 5 The Congress shall have power to enforce, by appropriate legislation, the provisions of this article.

AMENDMENT 15—THE RIGHT TO VOTE
[Ratified February 3, 1870]

Section 1 The right of citizens of the United States to vote shall not be denied or abridged by the United States or by any State on account of race, color, or previous condition of servitude.

Section 2 The Congress shall have power to enforce this article by appropriate legislation.

AMENDMENT 16—INCOME TAXES
[Ratified February 3, 1913]

The Congress shall have power to lay and collect taxes on incomes, from whatever source derived, without apportionment among the several States, and without regard to any census or enumeration.

AMENDMENT 17—DIRECT ELECTION OF SENATORS
[Ratified April 8, 1913]

The Senate of the United States shall be composed of two Senators from each State, elected by the people thereof, for six years; and each Senator shall have one vote. The electors in each State shall have the qualifications requisite for electors of the most numerous branch of the State legislatures.

When vacancies happen in the representation of any State in the Senate, the executive authority of such State shall issue writs of election to fill such vacancies: *Provided*, That the Legislature of any State may empower the executive thereof to make temporary appointment until the people fill the vacancies by election as the legislature may direct.

This amendment shall not be so construed as to affect the election or term of any Senator chosen before it becomes valid as part of the Constitution.

AMENDMENT 18—PROHIBITION
[Ratified January 16, 1919. Repealed December 5, 1933 by Amendment 21]

Section 1 After one year from the ratification of this article the manufacture, sale, or transportation of intoxicating liquors within, the importation thereof into, or the exportation thereof from the United States and all territory subject to the jurisdiction thereof for beverage purposes is hereby prohibited.

Section 2 The Congress and the several states shall have concurrent power to enforce this article by appropriate legislation.

Section 3 This article shall be inoperative unless it shall have been ratified as an amendment to the Constitution by the legislatures of the several states, as provided in the Constitution, within seven years from the date of the submission hereof to the States by the Congress.[13]

AMENDMENT 19—FOR WOMEN'S SUFFRAGE
[Ratified August 18, 1920]

The right of the citizens of the United States to vote shall not be denied or abridged by the United States or by any State on account of sex.

Congress shall have power, by appropriate legislation, to enforce the provision of this article.

AMENDMENT 20—THE LAME DUCK AMENDMENT
[Ratified January 23, 1933]

Section 1 The terms of the President and Vice President shall end at noon on the 20th day of January, and the terms of the Senators and Representatives at noon on the 3rd day of January, of the years in which such terms would have ended if this article had not been ratified; and the terms of their successors shall then begin.

Section 2 The Congress shall assemble at least once in every year, and such meeting shall begin at noon on the 3rd day of January, unless they shall by law appoint a different day.

Section 3 If, at the time fixed for the beginning of the term of the President, the President elect shall have died, the Vice President elect shall become President. If a President shall not have been chosen before the time fixed for the beginning of his term, or if the President elect shall have failed to qualify, then the Vice President elect shall act as President until a President shall have qualified; and the Congress may by law provide for the case wherein neither a President elect nor a Vice President elect shall have qualified, declaring who shall then act as President, or the manner in which one who is to act shall be selected, and such person shall act accordingly until a President or Vice President shall have qualified.

Section 4 The Congress may by law provide for the case of the death of any of the persons from whom the House of Representatives may choose a President whenever the right of choice shall have developed upon them, and for the case of the death of any of the persons from whom the Senate may choose a Vice President whenever the right of choice shall have devolved upon them.

---

[12]Changed by the 26th Amendment

[13]Repealed by the 21st Amendment

Section 5   Sections 1 and 2 shall take effect on the 15th day of October following the ratification of this article.

Section 6   This article shall be inoperative unless it shall have been ratified as an amendment to the Constitution by the legislatures of three-fourths of the several States within seven years from the date of its submission.

AMENDMENT 21—REPEAL OF PROHIBITION
[Ratified December 5, 1933]

Section 1   The eighteenth article of amendment to the Constitution of the United States is hereby repealed.

Section 2   The transportation or importation into any State, Territory, or Possession of the United States for delivery or use therein of intoxicating liquors, in violation of the laws thereof, is hereby prohibited.

Section 3   This article shall be inoperative unless it shall have been ratified as an amendment to the Constitution by conventions in the several States, as provided in the Constitution, within seven years from the date of the submission hereof to the States by the Congress.

AMENDMENT 22—NUMBER OF PRESIDENTIAL TERMS
[Ratified February 27, 1951]

Section 1   No person shall be elected to the office of the President more than twice, and no person who has held the office of President, or acted as President, for more than two years of a term to which some other person was elected President shall be elected to the Office of the President more than once. But this Article shall not apply to any person holding the office of President when this article was proposed by the Congress, and shall not prevent any person who may be holding the office of President, or acting as President, during the term within which this Article becomes operative from holding the office of President or acting as President during the remainder of such term.

Section 2   This Article shall be inoperative unless it shall have been ratified as an amendment to the Constitution by the legislatures of three-fourths of the several states within seven years from the date of its submission to the States by the Congress.

AMENDMENT 23—PRESIDENTIAL ELECTORS
FOR THE DISTRICT OF COLUMBIA
[Ratified March 29, 1961]

Section 1   The District constituting the seat of Government of the United States shall appoint in such manner as the Congress may direct:

A number of electors of President and Vice President equal to the whole number of Senators and Representatives in Congress to which the District would be entitled if it were a State, but in no event more than the least populous State; they shall be in addition to those appointed by the States, but they shall be considered, for the purposes of the election of President and Vice President, to be electors appointed by a State; and they shall meet in the District and perform such duties as provided by the twelfth article of amendment.

Section 2   The Congress shall have power to enforce this article by appropriate legislation.

AMENDMENT 24—THE ANTI-POLL TAX AMENDMENT
[Ratified January 23, 1964]

Section 1   The right of citizens of the United States to vote in any primary or other election for President or Vice President, for electors for President or Vice President, or for Senator or Representative in Congress, shall not be denied or abridged by the United States or any State by reason of failure to pay any poll tax or other tax.

Section 2   The Congress shall have power to enforce this article by appropriate legislation.

AMENDMENT 25—PRESIDENTIAL DISABILITY,
VICE PRESIDENTIAL VACANCIES
[Ratified February 23, 1967]

Section 1   In case of the removal of the President from office or his death or resignation, the Vice President shall become President.

Section 2   Whenever there is a vacancy in the office of the Vice President, the President shall nominate a Vice President who shall take the office upon confirmation by a majority vote of both houses of Congress.

Section 3   Whenever the President transmits to the President pro tempore of the Senate and the Speaker of the House of Representatives his written declaration that he is unable to discharge the powers and duties of his office, and until he transmits to them a written declaration to the contrary, such powers and duties shall be discharged by the Vice President as Acting President.

Section 4   Whenever the Vice-President and a majority of either the principal officers of the executive departments, or of such other body as Congress may by law provide, transmit to the President pro tempore of the Senate and the Speaker of the House of Representatives their written declaration that the President is unable to discharge the powers and duties of his office, the Vice President shall immediately assume the powers and duties of the office as Acting President.

Thereafter, when the President transmits to the President pro tempore of the Senate and the Speaker of the House of Representatives his written declaration that no inability exists, he shall resume the powers and duties of his office unless the Vice President and a majority of either the principal officers of the executive departments, or of such other body as Congress may by law provide, transmit within four days to the President pro tempore of the Senate and the Speaker of the House of Representatives their written declaration that the President is unable to discharge the powers and duties of his office. Thereupon Congress shall decide the issue, assembling within forty-eight hours for that purpose if not in session. If the Congress, within twenty-one days after receipt of the latter written declaration, or, if Congress is not in session, within twenty-one days after Congress is required to assemble, determines by two-thirds vote of both houses that the President is unable to discharge the powers and duties of his office, the Vice President shall continue to discharge the same as Acting President; otherwise, the President shall resume the powers and duties of his office.

AMENDMENT 26—EIGHTEEN-YEAR-OLD VOTE
[Ratified July 1, 1971]

Section 1   The right of citizens of the United States, who are eighteen years of age, or older, to vote shall not be denied or abridged by the United States or by any State on account of age.

Section 2   The Congress shall have power to enforce this article by appropriate legislation.

AMENDMENT 27—CONGRESSIONAL SALARIES
[Ratified May 7, 1992]

No law, varying the compensation for the services of the Senators and Representatives, shall take effect, until an election of Representatives shall be intervened.

3

AMERICAN FEDERALISM

INNOR | DUR 2 | 4M A | MUR PUR | FEC UNE | NONE
S TAB | LISH | JUSTIZ | N SURE | DOME
ESTIK | TRAN | KWILI | T PRO | VIDE 4 | TH COM
UN DE | FENZ | PRO MOT | TH JEN R | L WEL
FARE N | C CURE | TH BLES | NGS OF | LIBBER | T 2 R
SELVS | N R POS | TERI T | DO R | DANE N
S-TAB | LISH | THIS | CON STI | 2 10 | 4 TH

S
INCE THE FOUNDING OF THE REPUBLIC, THE RELATIONSHIP OF THE NATIONAL GOVERNMENT TO THE STATES HAS BEEN DEBATED.[1] IN 1787 THE FEDERALISTS defended the creation of a strong national government, whereas the Antifederalists warned that a strong national government would overshadow the states. More recently, Republicans have led the charge against big government, urging the return of many functions to the states—a **devolution revolution.**[2] They had some success when President Bill Clinton agreed to turn over more responsibilities for welfare to the states and to put the brakes on the growth of the national government.

Federalism has recently emerged as a hot topic in other countries as well. Within the European Union, member states have given up some authority over economic regulation and have agreed to a common currency (the euro).[3] The Association of South East Asian Nations (ASEAN) is another example of countries joining together to compete effectively in the global economy. In contrast, the former Soviet Union—a highly centralized government that was federal in name only—broke apart into 15 independent nations. Now Russia (or more precisely, the Russian Federation) is redefining relationships with its 21 autonomous republics, conceding them more autonomy while trying to preserve its territorial integrity and economic power. The pressures of international economic competition are driving these developments.

Heightened interest in federalism also comes from demands for greater local self-governance for ethnic nationalities. The Canadian federal system strains under the demands of the French-speaking province of Quebec for special status and even independence. In the United Kingdom, devolution is occurring in Scotland and Wales, which have recently established their own parliaments. Belgium, Italy, and Spain are devolving powers from their central governments to regional governments. Central European nations have divided and subdivided over ethnic tensions, some of which have culminated in ethnic cleansing and war.

In contrast to these countries, the United States has had a relatively peaceful experience with the shifting balances of power under federalism. From the New Deal in the 1930s to today, there has been a drift of power and responsibility from the states to the national government. Although presidents from Richard Nixon to Bill Clinton slowed the growth of the national government, it was not until the late 1990s that the Republican-controlled Congress sought major reforms that heated the debate over federalism. As with welfare reform in 1996, Congress promoted decentralization in education with

CHAPTERMEDIA

POLITICS ONLINE
Should Internet Sales Be Taxed?
www.prenhall.com/burns

European Union negotiators meet with Chinese trade officials in Beijing to discuss conditions for China's entry into the World Trade Union.

the Educational Flexibility Partnership Demonstration Act of 1999, authorizing the secretary of education to grant states waivers from federal rules setting educational goals. Still, in spite of such moves toward decentralization, Congress continues to expand federal law by making federal crimes such offenses as car-jacking and church-burning, even though they are already state and local crimes.

After more than half a century, the Supreme Court is now placing some constraints on congressional powers in the name of federalism.[4] Like Congress, however, the Court's recent record on federalism is mixed. In spite of rulings in 1999 holding that Congress may not authorize individuals to sue states to enforce federal laws,[5] the Court ruled that state welfare programs may not restrict benefits to new residents to what they would have received in the states from which they moved[6] and that Congress may restrict states from selling drivers' personal information.[7]

devolution revolution

Movement beginning with the 1994 congressional elections to transfer functions and responsibilities from the national government to the states; for example, for providing welfare.

At the official opening of Scotland's parliament on July 1, 1999, Queen Elizabeth was presented with the Scottish crown. The 129-member assembly is Scotland's first parliament in nearly 300 years.

Debates over federalism resemble those over whether "the glass is half-empty or half-full."[8] People who think they can get more of what they want from the national government usually advocate national action. Those who view states as more responsive and accountable argue for decentralization. Although Republicans generally favor action at the state level and Democrats tend to support action by the national government, neither are consistent in their positions on the balance of power between the national government and the states. It depends on the issue at stake.

This chapter begins by defining federalism and discussing its advantages. We look next at the constitutional basis for our federal system. Then we see how court decisions and political developments have shaped, and continue to shape, federalism in the United States.

DEFINING FEDERALISM

Scholars argue and wars have been fought about what federalism means. Our own Civil War was one such war. One scholar counted 267 definitions.[9]

- *Dual federalism* views the Constitution as giving a limited list of powers—primarily foreign policy and national defense—to the national government, leaving the rest to sovereign states. Each level of government is dominant within its own sphere. The Supreme Court serves as the umpire between the national government and the states in disputes over which level of government has responsibility for a particular activity. During our first hundred years, dual federalism was the favored interpretation given by the Supreme Court.

- *Cooperative federalism* stresses federalism as a system of intergovernmental relations in delivering governmental goods and services to the people and calls for cooperation among various levels of government.

- *Marble cake federalism*, a term coined by political scientist Morton Grodzins, conceives of federalism as a marble cake in which all levels of government are involved in a variety of issues and programs, rather than a layer cake, or dual federalism, with fixed divisions between layers or levels of government.[10]

- *Competitive federalism*, a term created by political scientist Thomas R. Dye, views the national government, 50 states, and thousands of other units as competing with each other over ways to put together packages of services and taxes. Applying the analogy of the marketplace, Dye emphasizes that at the state and local levels we have some choice about which state and city we want "to use," just as we have choices about what kind of automobile we drive.[11]

- *Permissive federalism* implies that although federalism provides "a sharing of power and authority between the national and state government, the states' share rests upon the permission and permissiveness of the national government."[12]

- *New federalism*, favored by Richard Nixon, Ronald Reagan, and former president George Bush, emphasizes their position that many of the fiscal resources and responsibilities of the federal government should be returned to the states in the form of large block grants and revenue sharing.

Federalism, as we define it here, is a form of government in which a constitution distributes powers between a central government and subdivisional governments—usually called states, provinces, or republics—giving to both the national government and the regional governments substantial responsibilities and powers, including the power to collect taxes and to pass and enforce laws regulating the conduct of individuals.

The mere existence of both national and state governments does not make a system federal. What is important is that a *constitution divides governmental powers between the national government and the subdivisional governments*, giving clearly defined functions to each. Neither the central nor the subdivisional government

federalism
Constitutional arrangement whereby power is distributed between a central government and subdivisional governments, called states in the United States. The national and the subdivisional governments both exercise direct authority over individuals.

TABLE 3–1 **Number of Governments**	
U.S. government	1
States	50
Counties	3,043
Municipalities	19,279
Townships or towns	16,656
School districts	14,422
Special districts	31,555
Total	85,006

SOURCE: U.S. Bureau of the Census, *Statistical Abstract of the United States, 1998* (Government Printing Office, 1998).

receives its powers from the other; both derive them from a common source—the constitution. No ordinary act of legislation at either a national or a state level can change this constitutional distribution of powers. Both levels of government operate through their own agents and exercise power directly over individuals.

The number of federal nations is not large. Only 21 of the approximately 185 nation-states claim to be federal. But, they "cover more than half of the land surface of the globe, and include almost half of the world's population."[13] Federalism thus appears well suited for large countries with large populations.

Constitutionally, the federal system of the United States consists of only the national government and the 50 states. "Cities are not," the Supreme Court reminded us, "sovereign entities." But in a practical sense, we are a nation of about 85,000 governmental units—from the national government to the school board district (see Table 3–1). This does not make for a tidy, efficient, easy-to-understand system; yet, as we shall see, it has its virtues.

Alternatives to Federalism

Among the alternatives to federalism are **unitary systems** of government, in which a constitution vests all governmental power in the central government. The central government, if it so chooses, may delegate authority to constituent units, but what it delegates it may take away. England, France, Israel, and the Philippines have unitary governments. In the United States, state constitutions usually create this kind of relationship between the state and its local governments.

At the other extreme are **confederations**, in which sovereign nations by a constitutional compact create a central government but carefully limit the power of the central government and do not give it the power to regulate the conduct of individuals directly. The central government makes regulations for the constituent governments, but it exists and operates only at their direction. The 13 states under the Articles of Confederation operated in this manner, as did the southern Confederacy during the Civil War (see Figure 3–1). The European Union is another example.[14]

Why Federalism?

In 1787, federalism was an obvious choice. Confederation had been tried but proved unsuccessful. A unitary system was out of the question because most people were too deeply attached to their state governments to permit subordination to central rule. Federalism was, and still is, thought to be ideally suited to the needs of a heterogeneous people spread over a large continent, suspicious of concentrated power, and desiring unity but not uniformity. Federalism offered, and still offers, many advantages for such a people.

FEDERALISM CHECKS THE GROWTH OF TYRANNY   Although in the rest of the world federal forms have not been notably successful in preventing tyranny, and many unitary governments are democratic, Americans tend to associate freedom with federalism.[15] As James Madison pointed out in *The Federalist*, No. 10: If "factious leaders . . . kindle a flame within their particular states," national leaders can check the spread of the "conflagration through the other states" (*The Federalist*, No. 10, appears in the Appendix of this book). Moreover, when one political party loses control of the national government, it is still likely to hold office in a number of states. It can then regroup, develop new policies and new leaders, and continue to challenge the party in power at the national level.

Such diffusion of power creates its own problems. It makes it difficult for a national majority to carry out a program of action, and it permits those who control state governments to frustrate the policies enacted by Congress and administered by federal agencies. To the framers, these obstacles were an advantage. They

unitary system
A constitutional arrangement in which power is concentrated in a central government.

confederation
A constitutional arrangement in which sovereign nations or states, by compact, create a central government but carefully limit its power and do not give it direct authority over individuals.

Government Under the Articles of Confederation: 1781–1788

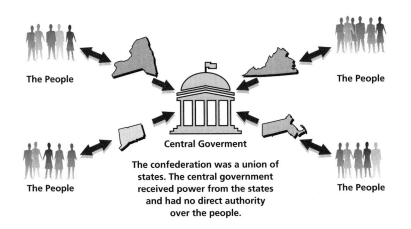

The People

The People

The People

The People

Central Goverment

The confederation was a union of states. The central government received power from the states and had no direct authority over the people.

Government Under U.S. Constitution (Federation): 1789–

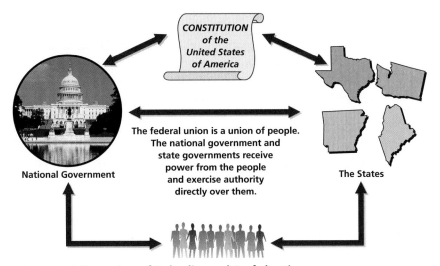

CONSTITUTION of the United States of America

National Government

The federal union is a union of people. The national government and state governments receive power from the people and exercise authority directly over them.

The States

FIGURE 3–1 A Comparison of Federalism and Confederation

feared that a single-interest group might capture the national government and attempt to suppress the interests of others. Of course the size of the nation and the many interests within it are the greatest obstacles to the formation of a single-interest majority—a point often overlooked today but emphasized by Madison in *The Federalist*, No. 10. If such a majority were to occur, having to work through a federal system would check its power.

FEDERALISM ALLOWS UNITY WITHOUT UNIFORMITY   National politicians and parties do not have to iron out every difference on every issue that divides us, whether it be abortion, same-sex marriages, gun control, capital punishment, welfare financing, or assisted suicide. Instead, these issues are debated in state legislatures, county courthouses, and city halls. But this advantage of federalism is becoming less significant as many local issues become national and as events in one state immediately affect policy debates at the national level.

FEDERALISM ENCOURAGES EXPERIMENTATION   Supreme Court Justice Louis Brandeis pointed out that state governments provide great "laboratories" for public policy experimentation, with states serving as proving grounds. If they adopt programs that fail, the negative effects are limited; if programs succeed, they can be

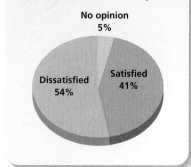

Are you satisfied or dissatisfied with the steps the federal government is taking to solve the major issues of concern to you?

No opinion
5%

Dissatisfied
54%

Satisfied
41%

FIGURE 3–2 The Public's Satisfaction with Government

SOURCE: Gallup Poll, August 24, 2000. For more information on trends in public opinion, go to: gallup.com/poll/releases.

express powers
Powers specifically granted to one of the branches of the national government by the Constitution.

implied powers
Powers inferred from express powers that allow Congress to carry out its functions.

necessary and proper clause
Clause of the Constitution setting forth the implied powers of Congress. It states that Congress, in addition to its express powers, has the power to make all laws necessary and proper for carrying out all powers vested by the Constitution in the national government.

inherent powers
Those powers of the national government in the field of foreign affairs that the Supreme Court has declared do not depend upon constitutional grants but rather grow out of the very existence of the national government.

adopted by other states and by the national government. Georgia, for example, was the first state to permit 18-year-olds to vote; Wisconsin has experimented with putting welfare recipients to work; California has pioneered air pollution control programs; Oregon and Hawaii are creating new systems for the delivery of health care; Nevada is the only state, so far, to legalize statewide gambling, but aspects of legalized casino gambling are now found in more than half the states. Not all innovations, even those considered successful, are widely adopted. Nebraska is the only state to have a unicameral legislature, although in recent years such a change has been discussed, not too seriously, in both Minnesota and California.

FEDERALISM KEEPS GOVERNMENT CLOSER TO THE PEOPLE   By providing numerous arenas for decision making, federalism involves many people and helps keep government closer to the people. Every day thousands of Americans are busy serving on city councils, school boards, neighborhood associations, and planning commissions. Since they are close to the issues and have firsthand knowledge of what needs to be done, they may be more responsive to problems than the experts in Washington.

We should be cautious, however, about generalizing that state and local governments are necessarily "closer to the people" than is the national government. True, more people are involved in local and state politics than in national affairs, and confidence in state governments has gone up while respect for national agencies has diminished. A majority of the public appears to be dissatisfied with the federal government's responses to major issues (see Figure 3–2). Yet national and international affairs are more often on people's minds than are state or local politics. Fewer voters participate in state and local elections than in congressional and presidential elections.

THE CONSTITUTIONAL STRUCTURE OF AMERICAN FEDERALISM

Dividing powers and responsibilities between the national and state governments has resulted in thousands of court decisions, hundreds of books, and endless speeches to explain—and even then the division lacks precise definition. Nonetheless, a basic understanding of how the Constitution divides these powers and responsibilities and of what obligations are imposed on each level of government is helpful (see Table 3–2).

The formal constitutional framework of our federal system may be stated relatively simply:

1. The national government has only those powers delegated to it by the Constitution (with the important exception of the inherent power over foreign affairs).

2. Within the scope of its operations, the national government is supreme.

3. The state governments have the powers not delegated to the central government, except those denied to them by the Constitution and their state constitutions.

4. Some powers are specifically denied to both the national and state governments; others are specifically denied only to the states; still others are denied to the national government, but not the states.

Powers of the National Government

The Constitution, chiefly in the first three articles, delegates legislative, executive, and judicial powers to the national government. In addition to these **express powers**, such as the power to appropriate funds, Congress has assumed constitutionally **implied powers**, such as the power to create banks, which are inferred from express powers. The constitutional basis for the implied powers of Congress is the **necessary**

and proper clause (Article I, Section 8, Clause 18). This clause gives Congress the right "to make all Laws which shall be necessary and proper for carrying into Execution the foregoing Powers, and all other Powers vested . . . in the Government of the United States."

In the field of foreign affairs the Constitution gives the national government **inherent powers**. The national government has the same authority to deal with other nations as if it were the central government in a unitary system. Such inherent powers do not depend on specific constitutional provisions. For example, the government of the United States may acquire territory by purchase or by discovery and occupation, though no specific clause in the Constitution allows such acquisition. Even if the Constitution were silent about foreign affairs—which it is not—the national government would still have the power to declare war, make treaties, and appoint and receive ambassadors.

Together, these express, implied, and inherent powers create a flexible system that allows the Supreme Court, Congress, the president, and the people to expand the central government's powers to meet the needs of a modern nation in a global economy. This expansion of central government functions rests on four constitutional pillars.

These four constitutional pillars—*the national supremacy article, the war power, the commerce clause, and most especially, the power to tax and spend for the general welfare*—have permitted a tremendous expansion of the functions of the national government, so much so that, despite the Supreme Court's recent declaration that some national laws exceed Congress's constitutional powers, the national government has, in effect, almost full power to enact any legislation that Congress deems necessary, so long as it does not conflict with those provisions of the Constitution designed to protect individual rights and the powers of the states.

An Expanding Nation

A great advantage of federalism—and part of the genius and flexibility of our constitutional system—has been the way in which we acquired territory and extended rights and guarantees by means of statehood, commonwealth, or territorial status, and thus grew from 13 to 50 states, plus territories.

Louisiana Purchase	1803
Florida	1819
Texas	1845
Oregon	1846
Mexican Cession	1848
Gadsden Purchase	1853
Alaska	1867
Hawaii	1898
Philippines	1898–1946
Puerto Rico	1899
Guam	1899
American Samoa	1900
Canal Zone	1904–2000
U.S. Virgin Islands	1917
Pacific Islands Trust Territory	1947

THE NATIONAL SUPREMACY ARTICLE   One of the most important pillars is found in Article VI of the Constitution: "This Constitution, and the Laws of the United States which shall be made in Pursuance thereof; and all Treaties made . . . under the Authority of the United States, shall be the supreme Law of the Land; and the Judges in every State shall be bound thereby; any Thing in the Constitution or Laws of any State to the Contrary notwithstanding." All officials, state as well as national, swear an oath to support the Constitution of the United States. States may not override national policies; this restriction also applies to local units of government since they are agents of the states. National laws and regulations of federal agencies *preempt* the field, so that conflicting state and local rules and regulations are unenforceable.

TABLE 3–2 The Federal Division of Powers

Types of Powers Delegated to the National Government	Some Powers Reserved for the States	Some Concurrent Powers Shared by the National and State Governments
▪ Express powers stated in Constitution	▪ To create a republican form of government	▪ To tax citizens and businesses
▪ Implied powers that may be inferred from express powers	▪ To charter local governments	▪ To borrow and spend money
▪ Inherent powers that allow the nation to present a united front to foreign powers	▪ To conduct elections	▪ To establish courts
	▪ To exercise all powers not delegated to the national government or denied to the states by the Constitution	▪ To pass and enforce laws
		▪ To protect civil rights

THE WAR POWER   The national government is responsible for protecting the nation from external aggression and, when necessary, for waging war. In today's world, military strength depends not only on troops in the field but also on the ability to mobilize the nation's industrial might as well as to apply scientific and technological knowledge to the tasks of defense. The national government has the power to do whatever is necessary and proper to wage war successfully. Thus the national government has the power to do almost anything not in direct conflict with constitutional guarantees.

THE POWER TO REGULATE COMMERCE   Congressional authority extends to all commerce that affects more than one state. Commerce includes the production, buying, selling, renting, and transporting of goods, services, and properties. The **commerce clause** (Article I, Section 8, Clause 3) packs a tremendous constitutional punch; it gives Congress the power "to regulate Commerce with foreign Nations, and among the several States, and with the Indian Tribes." In these few words the national government has been able to find constitutional justification for regulating a wide range of human activity, since very few aspects of our economy today affect commerce in only one state and are thus outside the scope of the national government's constitutional authority.[16]

The commerce clause can also be used to sustain legislation that goes beyond commercial matters. When the Supreme Court upheld the 1964 Civil Rights Act forbidding discrimination because of race, religion, or national origin in places of public accommodation, it said: "Congress's action in removing the disruptive effect which it found racial discrimination has on interstate travel is not invalidated because Congress was also legislating against what it considers to be moral wrongs."[17] Discrimination restricts the flow of interstate commerce; therefore, Congress could legislate against discrimination. Moreover, the law could be applied even to local places of public accommodation because local incidents of discrimination have a substantial and harmful impact on interstate commerce, though the Court has recently limited congressional powers to address such harms.[18]

THE POWER TO TAX AND SPEND   Congress lacks constitutional authority to pass laws solely on the ground that they will promote the general welfare, but it may raise taxes and spend money for this purpose. Congress, for example, lacks the power to regulate education or agriculture directly, yet it does have the power to appropriate money to support education or to pay farm subsidies. By attaching conditions to its grants of money, Congress may thus regulate what it cannot directly control by law.

When Congress puts up the money, it determines how the money will be spent. By withholding or threatening to withhold funds, the national government can influence or control state operations and regulate individual conduct. For example, Congress has stipulated that federal funds should be withdrawn from any program in which any person is denied benefits because of race, color, national origin, sex, or physical handicap. Congress has also used its power of the purse to force states to raise the drinking age to 21 by tying such a condition to federal dollars for highways.

Congress frequently requires states to do certain things—for example, provide services to indigent mothers and clean up the air and water. These requirements are called **federal mandates**. Often, Congress does not supply the funds required to carry out these mandates, and its failure to do so has become an important issue as states face growing expenditures with limited resources.

Powers of the States

The Constitution *reserves for the states all powers not granted to the national government*, subject only to the limitations of the Constitution. Powers not given exclusively to the national government by provisions of the Constitution or by judicial interpretation may be exercised concurrently by the states, as long as there is no conflict with

commerce clause
The clause (Article I) in the Constitution that gives Congress the power to regulate commerce among the states, with other nations, and with the Indian tribes. This clause provides the constitutional basis for most national regulations of our economy, as well as for much civil rights legislation.

federal mandate
A requirement imposed by the federal government as a condition of receipt of federal funds.

national law. Such **concurrent powers** with the national government include the power to levy taxes and regulate commerce internal to each state.

In general, a state may levy a tax on the same item as the national government does, but a state cannot, by a tax, "unduly burden" commerce among the states, interfere with a function of the national government, complicate the operation of a national law, or abridge the terms of a treaty of the United States. Where Congress has not preempted the field, states may regulate interstate businesses, provided these regulations do not cover matters requiring uniform national treatment or unduly burden interstate commerce.

Who decides what matters require "uniform national treatment" or what actions might place an "undue burden" on interstate commerce? Congress does, subject to final review by the Supreme Court. When Congress is silent or does not clearly state its intentions, the courts—ultimately the Supreme Court—decide if there is a conflict with the national Constitution or if there has been federal preemption by law or regulation.

CONSTITUTIONAL LIMITS AND OBLIGATIONS   To make federalism work, the Constitution imposes certain restraints on both the national and the state governments. States are prohibited from:

1. Making treaties with foreign governments
2. Authorizing private persons to prey on the shipping and commerce of other nations
3. Coining money, issuing bills of credit, or making anything but gold and silver coin legal tender in payment of debts
4. Taxing imports or exports
5. Taxing foreign ships
6. Keeping troops or ships in time of peace (except the state militia, now called the National Guard)
7. Engaging in war, unless invaded or in such imminent danger as will not admit of delay

The national government, in turn, is required by the Constitution to refrain from exercising its powers, especially its powers to tax and to regulate interstate commerce, in such a way as to interfere substantially with the states' abilities to perform their responsibilities. Today, the protection states have from intrusions by the national government comes primarily from the political process—because senators and representatives elected from the states participate in the decisions of Congress. However, the Court has held that Congress may not command states to enact laws to comply with, and state employees to enforce, unfunded federal mandates; for example, Congress may not require local law enforcement officials to make background checks prior to handgun sales.[19] It has also ruled that the Eleventh Amendment guarantee of states' sovereign immunity from lawsuits forbids state employees from suing states in federal and state courts in order to force state compliance with federal employment laws.[20] While Congress may not use those sticks, it may offer the carrot of federal funding if states comply with national policies, such as establishing a minimum drinking age or setting 55-mile-an-hour speed limits.

The Constitution also requires the national government to guarantee to each state a "Republican Form of Government." The framers used this term to distinguish a republic from a monarchy, on the one side, and from a pure, direct democracy, on the other. Congress, not the courts, enforces this guarantee and determines what is or is not a republican form of government. By permitting the congressional delegation of a state to be seated in Congress, Congress acknowledges that the state has the republican form of government guaranteed by the Constitution.

concurrent powers
Powers the Constitution gives to both the national and state governments, such as the power to levy taxes.

SAME-SEX MARRIAGES AND THE FULL FAITH AND CREDIT CLAUSE

The full faith and credit clause has become part of a national debate because one state now recognizes same-sex unions. In April 2000 Vermont enacted a law recognizing "civil unions," granting same-sex couples the same rights and protections of married couples. It was the first state to do so. As a result, same-sex couples were entitled to 300 state benefits, ranging from health care and inheritance rights to property transfers. However, in March 2001 the Vermont House of Representatives reversed course and passed a bill outlawing same-sex marriages.

Same-sex partnerships are legally recognized in several European countries, including Belgium, Denmark, France, Hungary, Luxembourg, Norway, and Sweden. However, such unions are banned in 32 states. Congress passed and President Bill Clinton signed the Defense of Marriage Act of 1996, which relieves states of any obligation to recognize same-sex marriages even if they are recognized in other states, and stipulates that the national government recognizes only heterosexual marriages for federal benefits such as Social Security.

The Defense of Marriage Act may well be challenged in the courts for going beyond the power of Congress to provide states with an exemption from their constitutional obligation under the full faith and credit clause. Those supporting the

Gay couples renew their vows to each other in this ceremony in San Francisco's Metropolitan Community church.

act point to the Constitution, which gives Congress the responsibility for prescribing the manner in which states are to comply with the clause.

The Supreme Court has not addressed the issue squarely, and precedents provide no clear answer. It is the view of one authority that in light of recent Court rulings showing the present Court's tilt toward states' rights and "the fact that

marriage has traditionally been an almost exclusive sphere of state authority, the Court would likely maintain the noncentralized and dual nature of American domestic relations that exist today, and allow the states to decide whether to recognize same-sex marriages."*

*John P. Feldmeier, "Federalism and Full Faith and Credit: Must States Recognize Out-of-State Same-Sex Marriages?" *Publius* 25, no. 4 (Fall 1995), p. 126. See also "Special Report, Shades of Gay," *Newsweek*, March 20, 2000.

In addition, the national government is obliged by the Constitution to protect states against *domestic insurrection*. Congress has delegated to the president the authority to dispatch troops to put down such insurrections when so requested by the proper state authorities. If there are contesting state authorities, the president decides which is the proper one. The president does not have to wait, however, for a request from state authorities to send federal troops into a state to enforce federal laws.

Interstate Relations

Three clauses in the Constitution, taken from the Articles of Confederation, require states to give full faith and credit to each other's public acts, records, and judicial proceedings; to extend to each other's citizens the privileges and immunities of their own citizens; and to return persons who are fleeing from justice.

FULL FAITH AND CREDIT   The **full faith and credit clause** (Article IV, Section 1), one of the more technical provisions of the Constitution, requires state courts to enforce the civil judgments of the courts of other states and accept their public records and acts as valid. It does not require states to enforce the criminal laws of other states; in most cases, for one state to enforce the criminal laws of another would raise constitutional issues. The clause applies especially to enforcement of judicial settlements and court awards.

INTERSTATE PRIVILEGES AND IMMUNITIES   Under Article IV, Section 2, states must extend to citizens of other states the privileges and immunities granted to their own citizens, including the protection of the laws, the right to engage in peaceful occupations, access to the courts, and freedom from discriminatory taxes. Because of this clause, states may not impose unreasonable residency requirements, that is, withhold rights to American citizens who have recently moved to the state and thereby have become citizens of that state. For example, a state may not set unreasonable time limits to withhold state-funded medical benefits from new citizens or to keep them from voting. How long a residency requirement may a state impose? A day seems about as long as the Court will tolerate to withhold welfare payments or medical care, 50 days or so for voting privileges, and one year for eligibility for in-state tuition for state-supported colleges and universities.

Financially independent adults who move into a state just before enrolling in a state-supported university or college may be required to prove that they have become citizens of that state and intend to remain after finishing their schooling by supplying such evidence of citizenship as tax payments, a driver's license, car registration, voter registration, and a continuous, year-round off-campus residence. Students who are financially dependent on their parents remain citizens of the state of their parents.

EXTRADITION   In Article IV, Section 2, the Constitution asserts that when individuals charged with crimes have fled from one state to another, the state to which they have fled is to deliver them to the proper officials upon the demand of the executive authority of the state from which they fled. This process is called **extradition**. "The obvious objective of the Extradition Clause," the courts have claimed, "is that no State should become a safe haven for the fugitives from a sister State's criminal justice system."[21] Congress has supplemented this constitutional provision by making the governor of the state to which fugitives have fled responsible for

FEDERALISM IN COMPARATIVE PERSPECTIVE

There is no single model for dividing authority between national and state governments or for power sharing in intergovernmental relations. The federal systems in Canada, Germany, and Switzerland are illustrative.

Canada combines a federal system with a parliamentary form of government that has authority to legislate on all matters pertaining to "peace, order, and good government." The system was established in 1867, in part to prevent conflicts similar to those between the states that led to the American Civil War. In each of the ten provinces, the lieutenant governor is appointed on the advice of the prime minister and must approve any provincial law before it goes into effect. The legislative powers of the provinces are thus checked and limited. However, the provinces retain residual powers, and unlike the U.S. Supreme Court, the Canadian judiciary has generally encouraged decentralization in recognition of its multicultural society. Thus, Canadian provinces exercise greater power and the national government is weaker than in the United States. In addition, the special status claimed by French-speaking Quebec has led to intergovernmental relations that alternate between periods of centralization and decentralization.

The Federal Republic of Germany, whose Basic Laws of 1949 became the constitution with the reunification of East and West Germany in 1990, is often referred to as an example of cooperative federalism. Its 16 states, or Länder, exercise a great deal of power, far more than states do in the United States. The central government has a president and a bicameral parliament composed of an upper house, the Federal Council, and a lower house, the National Assembly, as well as an independent judiciary. The central government has exclusive authority over foreign affairs, money, immigration, and telecommunications. But the Länder retain residual powers over all other matters and have concurrent powers over civil and criminal law, along with matters related to education, health, and the public welfare. Moreover, national legislation does not become law unless approved by a majority of the Federal Council, whose members are selected by legislatures in the Länder, not by popular elections.

Switzerland established a confederation on the basis of regional governments (cantons). The cantons reflect the ethnic and linguistic differences of their German-, French-, and Italian-speaking populations. All three languages are officially recognized by the central government. But of the 22 cantons, there are 18 that are unilingual, 3 that are bilingual, and 1 trilingual. They exercise most lawmaking powers and are represented in the National Council, a bicameral legislature, and the Council of States.

full faith and credit clause
Clause in the Constitution requiring each state to recognize the civil judgments rendered by the courts of the other states and to accept their public records and acts as valid documents.

extradition
Legal process whereby an alleged criminal offender is surrendered by the officials of one state to officials of the state in which the crime is alleged to have been committed.

Do we need a stronger or a weaker government in Washington?

Should responsibility for welfare, education, and health care be given back to the states? If the national government sets the standards, should it provide the funds but leave the details to the states? Do the facts, as you know them, support the need for federal standards? Or can state and local governments be trusted to handle most domestic problems in their own way?

interstate compact
An agreement among two or more states. The Constitution requires that most such agreements be approved by Congress.

national supremacy
Constitutional doctrine that whenever conflict occurs between the constitutionally authorized actions of the national government and those of a state or local government, the actions of the federal government take priority.

preemption
The right of a federal law or regulation to preclude enforcement of a state or local law or regulation.

centralists
Those who favor national action over action at the state and local levels.

decentralists
Those who favor state or local action rather than national action.

returning them. Despite their constitutional obligation, governors of asylum states have on occasion refused to honor a request for extradition.

INTERSTATE COMPACTS   The Constitution also requires states to settle disputes with one another without the use of force. States may carry their legal disputes to the Supreme Court, or they may negotiate **interstate compacts**. Interstate compacts often establish interstate agencies to handle problems affecting an entire region. Before most interstate compacts become effective, congressional approval is required. After a compact has been signed and approved by Congress, it becomes binding on all signatory states, and its terms are enforceable by the federal judiciary. A typical state may belong to 20 compacts dealing with such subjects as environmental protection, crime control, water rights, and higher education exchanges.[22]

THE ROLE OF THE FEDERAL COURTS: UMPIRES OF FEDERALISM

Although the political process ultimately decides how power will be divided between the national and the state governments, the federal courts—and especially the Supreme Court—have often been called on to umpire the ongoing debate about which level of government should do what, for whom, and to whom. This role for the courts was claimed in the celebrated case of *McCulloch v Maryland*.

McCulloch versus Maryland

In *McCulloch v Maryland* (1819), the Supreme Court had the first of many chances to define the division of power between the national and state governments.[23] The state of Maryland had levied a tax against the Baltimore branch of the Bank of the United States, a semipublic agency established by Congress. James William McCulloch, the cashier of the bank, refused to pay on the grounds that a state could not tax an instrument of the national government.

Maryland was represented before the Court by some of the country's most distinguished lawyers, including Luther Martin, who had been a delegate to the Constitutional Convention. Martin said the power to incorporate a bank was not expressly delegated to the national government in the Constitution. He maintained that the necessary and proper clause gives Congress only the power to choose those means and to pass those laws absolutely essential to the execution of its expressly granted powers. Because a bank is not absolutely necessary to the exercise of any of its delegated powers, Congress had no authority to establish it. As for Maryland's right to tax the bank, the power to tax is one of the powers reserved to the states; they may use it as they see fit.

The national government was represented as well by distinguished counsel, including Daniel Webster. Webster conceded the power to create a bank is not one of the express powers of the national government. However, the power to pass laws necessary and proper to carry out Congress's express powers is specifically delegated to Congress. Therefore, Congress may incorporate a bank as an appropriate, convenient, and useful means of exercising the granted powers of collecting taxes, borrowing money, and caring for the property of the United States. Although the power to tax is reserved to the states, Webster argued that states cannot interfere with the operations of the national government. The Constitution leaves no room for doubt; in cases of conflict between the national and state governments, the national government is supreme.

Speaking for a unanimous Court, Chief Justice John Marshall rejected every one of Maryland's contentions. He summarized his views on the powers of the national government in these now-famous words: "Let the end be legitimate, let it be within the scope of the Constitution, and all means which are appropriate, which are plainly adapted to that end, which are not prohibited, but consist with the letter and spirit of the constitution, are constitutional." Having thus established the doctrine of *implied national powers*, Marshall set forth the doctrine of **national supremacy**. No state, he said, can use its taxing powers to tax a national instrument. "The power to tax involves the power to destroy. . . . If the right of the States to tax the means employed by the general government be conceded, the declaration that the Constitution, and the laws made in pursuance thereof, shall be the supreme law of the land, is empty and unmeaning declamation."

The long-range significance of *McCulloch v Maryland* in providing support for the developing forces of nationalism and a unified economy cannot be overstated. The arguments of the states' righters, if they had been accepted, would have strapped the national government in a constitutional straitjacket and denied it powers needed to handle the problems of an expanding nation.

Federal Courts and the Role of the States

The authority of federal judges to review the activities of state and local governments has expanded dramatically in recent decades because of modern judicial interpretations of the Fourteenth Amendment, which forbids states to deprive any person of life, liberty, or property without *due process of the law*; nor can states deny to any person the *equal protection of the laws* and congressional legislation enacted to implement this amendment. Almost every action by state and local officials is now subject to challenge before a federal judge as a violation of the Constitution or of federal law.

Preemption occurs when a federal law or regulation takes precedence over enforcement of a state or local law or regulation. State and local laws are preempted not only when they conflict directly with federal laws and regulations, but also if they touch a field in which the "federal interest is so dominant that the federal system will be assumed to preclude enforcement of state laws on the same subject."[24] Examples of federal preemption include laws regulating hazardous substances, water quality, and clean air standards, and many civil rights acts, most especially the Civil Rights Act of 1964 and the Voting Rights Act of 1965.

Over the years federal judges, under the leadership of the Supreme Court, have generally favored the powers of the federal government over the states. In spite of the Supreme Court's recent bias in favor of state over national authority, few would deny the Supreme Court the power to review and set aside state actions. As Justice Oliver Wendell Holmes of the Supreme Court once remarked: "I do not think the United States would come to an end if we lost our power to declare an Act of Congress void. I do think the Union would be imperiled if we could not make that declaration as to the laws of the several States."[25]

The Great Debate—Centralists versus Decentralists

From the beginning of the Republic there has been an ongoing debate about the "proper" distribution of powers, functions, and responsibilities between the national government and the states. Did the national government have the authority to outlaw slavery in the territories? Did the states have the authority to operate racially segregated schools? Could Congress regulate labor relations? Does Congress have the power to regulate the sale and use of firearms? Does Congress have the right to tell states how to clean up air and water pollution? The debates in the past and those today are frequently phrased in constitutional language, with appeals to the great principles of federalism. But they are also arguments over who gets what, where, and how.

During the Great Depression of the 1930s, the nation debated whether Congress had the constitutional authority to enact legislation on agriculture, labor, education, housing, and welfare. Only 40 years ago some legislators and public officials—as well as some scholars—questioned the constitutional authority of Congress to legislate against racial discrimination. The debate continues between **centralists**, those who favor national action, and **decentralists**, those who favor action at the state and local levels.

Thinking It Through . . .

The great debate about which level of government can best perform functions continues to rage. The Republican party started its history as the party of the National Union, while the Democrats were then the champion of states' rights, but for the past several decades there has been a switch. After winning majority status in Congress in 1994, Republicans led the charge on Washington, demanding the return of functions back to the states. Democrats tend to be reluctant about removing all federal standards, especially with respect to regulation of the environment and of the workplace, and they tend to be in favor of providing minimum standards for programs, especially welfare and health care.

Centralists' Arguments

1. State and local officials tend to be less competent than national officials.

2. State and local officials tend to be concerned only with the interests of their own areas.

3. State and local governments are unable or unwilling to raise taxes needed to carry out vital government functions.

4. State and local governments are more apt to reflect local racial and ethnic biases as well as the biases of dominant local industries.

5. State and local governments are afraid to regulate industries for fear the industries will move elsewhere.

Decentralists' Arguments

1. Increased urbanization has made states more responsive to the needs of city people.

2. In recent years state and local governments have shown greater willingness to raise taxes than the national government.

3. State and local governments have become as sensitive to the needs of the poor and minorities as is the national government.

4. State and local governments have reformed and modernized and thus become more effective governments.

THE DECENTRALIST POSITION   Among those favoring the decentralist or states' rights interpretation were the Antifederalists, Thomas Jefferson, John C. Calhoun, the Supreme Court from the 1920s to 1937, and more recently, Ronald Reagan, George Bush, the Republican leaders of Congress, Chief Justice William H. Rehnquist, and Justices Antonin Scalia, Clarence Thomas, and Sandra Day O'Connor.

Most decentralists contend the Constitution is a treaty among sovereign states that created the central government and gave it very limited authority. As Justice Clarence Thomas, an ardent decentralist, wrote in a dissenting opinion supporting the argument that a state has the power to impose term limits on members of Congress, "The ultimate source of the Constitution's authority is the consent of the people of each individual State, not the consent of the undifferentiated people of the Nation as a whole."[26] Thus the national government is little more than an agent of the states, and every one of its powers should be narrowly defined. Any question about whether the states have given a particular function to the central government or have reserved it for themselves should be resolved in favor of the states.

Decentralists hold that the national government should not interfere with activities reserved for the states. The Tenth Amendment, they claim, makes this clear: "The powers not delegated to the United States by the Constitution, nor prohibited by it to the States, are reserved to the States respectively, or to the people." Decentralists insist state governments are closer to the people and reflect the people's wishes more accurately than does the national government. The national government, they add, is inherently heavy-handed and bureaucratic; to preserve our federal system and our liberties, central authority must be kept under control.

THE CENTRALIST POSITION   The centralist position has been supported by Chief Justice John Marshall, Abraham Lincoln, Theodore Roosevelt, Franklin Roosevelt, and throughout most of our history by the Supreme Court.

Centralists reject the whole idea of the Constitution as an interstate compact. Rather, they view the Constitution as a supreme law established by the people. The national government is an agent of the people, not of the states, because it was the people who drew up the Constitution and created the national government. They intended the central government's powers to be defined by the national political process and that it should be denied authority only when the Constitution clearly prohibits it from acting.

Centralists argue that the national government is a government of all the people, whereas each state speaks only for some of the people. Although the Tenth Amendment clearly reserves powers for the states, it does not deny the national government the authority to exercise, to the fullest extent, all of its powers. Moreover, the supremacy of the national government restricts the states, because governments representing part of the people cannot be allowed to interfere with a government representing all of them.

The Supreme Court and the Role of Congress

From 1937 until the 1990s the Supreme Court essentially removed federal courts from what had been their traditional role of protecting states from acts of Congress. The Supreme Court broadly interpreted the commerce clause to allow Congress to do whatever Congress thought necessary and proper to promote the common good, even if the federal laws and regulations infringed on the activities of state and local governments. In 1985 the Supreme Court went so far as to tell the states that they should look to the political process to protect their interests, not to the federal courts.[27]

In the last decade, however, the Supreme Court signaled that federal courts should no longer remain passive in resolving federalism issues.[28] In 1995 the Court declared that a state could not impose term limits on its members of Congress, but it did so only by a 5 to 4 vote. Justice John Paul Stevens, writing for the majority, built his argument on the concept of the federal union as espoused by the great Chief Justice John Marshall, as a compact among the people, with the national government serving as the people's agent. By contrast, Justice Clarence Thomas, writing for the dissenters, espoused a view of federalism not heard from a justice of the Supreme Court since prior to the New Deal. He interpreted the Tenth Amendment as requiring the national government to justify its actions in terms of an enumerated power and granting to the states all other powers not granted to the national government.[29]

The Court also declared that the clause in the Constitution empowering Congress to regulate commerce with the Indian tribes did not give Congress the power to authorize federal courts to hear suits against a state brought by Indian tribes.[30] The effect of this decision goes beyond Indian tribes. As a result, except to enforce rights stemming from the Fourteenth Amendment, which the Court explicitly acknowledged to be within Congress's power, Congress may no longer authorize individuals to bring legal actions against states in order to force their compliance with federal law in either federal or state courts.[31]

Building on those rulings, the Court continues to press ahead with its "constitutional counterrevolution"[32] in returning to an older vision of federalism not embraced since the constitutional crisis over the New Deal in the 1930s. Among other recent rulings,[33] the Court struck down the Violence Against Women Act, which had given women who are victims of violence the right to sue their attackers for damages.[34] Congress had found that violence against women annually costs the national economy $3 billion, but the Court held that Congress exceeded its powers in enacting the law and intruded on the powers of the states.

These Supreme Court decisions—most of which split the Court 5 to 4 along ideological lines, with the conservative justices favoring states' rights—may presage a major shift in the Court's interpretation of the constitutional nature of our federal system. Chief Justice Rehnquist, joined by Justices Scalia, Thomas, O'Connor, and frequently Justice Anthony M. Kennedy, veered the Court back to a decentralist position. President Clinton's two appointees, Justices Ruth Bader Ginsburg and Stephen Breyer, joined by Justices David Souter and John Paul Stevens, are resisting this movement back to a states' rights interpretation of our federal system. Consequently, federalism issues are likely to come up in future Supreme Court confirmation hearings, and the outcome of presidential elections—which determine who gets appointed to the Supreme Court—could well determine how these and other federalism issues will be decided.

REGULATORY FEDERALISM, FEDERAL GRANTS, AND FEDERAL MANDATES

Congress authorizes programs, establishes general rules for how the programs will operate, and decides whether and how much room should be left for state or local discretion. Most important, Congress appropriates the funds for these programs and, until recently, has had deeper pockets than even the richest states. One of Congress's most potent tools for influencing policy at the state and local levels has been federal grants.

Federal grants serve four purposes, the most important of which is the fourth:

1. To supply state and local governments with revenue.

2. To establish minimum national standards for such things as highways and clean air.

3. To equalize resources among the states by taking money from people with high incomes through federal taxes and spending it, through grants, in states where the poor live.

4. To attack national problems yet minimize the growth of federal agencies.

Types of Federal Grants

Three types of federal grants are currently being administered: categorical-formula grants, project grants, and block grants (or sometimes called flexible grants). From 1972 to 1987 there was also **revenue sharing**—federal grants to state and local governments to be used at their discretion and subject only to very general conditions. But when budget deficits soared in the second Reagan administration (1985–89) and there was no revenue to share, revenue sharing was terminated—to the states in 1986 and to local governments in 1987.

CATEGORICAL-FORMULA GRANTS   Congress appropriates funds for specific purposes, such as school lunches or the building of airports and highways. These funds are allocated by formula and are subject to detailed federal conditions, often on a matching basis; that is, the local government receiving the federal funds must put up some of its own dollars. Categorical grants, in addition, provide federal supervision to ensure that the federal dollars are spent as Congress wants. There are hundreds of grant programs, but two dozen, including Medicaid, account for more than half of total spending for categoricals.

PROJECT GRANTS   Congress appropriates a certain sum, which is allocated to state and local units and sometimes to nongovernmental agencies, based on applications from those who wish to participate. Examples are grants by the National Science Foundation to universities and research institutes to support the work of scientists or grants to states and localities to support training and employment programs.

BLOCK GRANTS   These are broad grants to states for prescribed activities—welfare, child care, education, social services, preventive health care, and health services—with only a few strings attached. States have great flexibility in deciding how to spend block grant dollars, but when the federal funds for any fiscal year are gone, there are no more matching federal dollars.

The Politics of Federal Grants

Republicans "have consistently favored fewer strings, less federal supervision, and the delegation of spending discretion to the state and local governments."[35] Democrats have generally been less supportive of broad discretionary block grants, favoring instead more detailed, federally supervised spending. The Republican-controlled Congress in the 1990s gave high priority to the creation of block grants, but it ran

revenue sharing
Program from 1972 to 1987 whereby federal funds were provided to state and local governments to be spent largely at the discretion of the receiving governments, subject to very general conditions.

into trouble by trying to lump together welfare, school lunch and breakfast programs, prenatal nutrition programs, and child protection programs in one block grant.

With President Clinton's enthusiastic support, however, the Republicans succeeded in making a major change in federal-state relations—a devolution of responsibility for welfare from the national government to the states. The Personal Responsibility and Work Opportunity Reconciliation Act of 1996 put an end to the 61-year-old program of Aid to Families with Dependent Children (AFDC), a federal guarantee of welfare checks for all eligible mothers and children. The 1996 act substituted for AFDC a welfare block grant to each state, with caps on the amount of federal dollars that the state will receive. It also put another big federal child care program into another block grant—Child Care and Development Block Grant (CCDBG).

Welfare block grants give states flexibility in how they provide for welfare, but no federal funds can be used to cover recipients who do not go to work within two years, and no one can receive federally supported benefits for more than five years. In order to slow down "the race to the bottom" in which states may try to make themselves "the least attractive state in which to be poor,"[36] Congress also stipulated that in order for states to receive their full share of federal dollars, they must continue to spend at least 75 percent of what they had been spending on welfare.

The battle over the appropriate level of government to control funding and to exercise principal responsibility for social programs tends to be cyclical. As one scholar of federalism explains, "Complaints about excessive federal control tend to be followed by proposals to shift more power to state and local governments. Then, when problems arise in state and local administration—and problems inevitably arise when any organization tries to administer anything—demands for closer federal supervision and tighter federal controls follow."[37]

Federal Mandates

Fewer federal dollars do not necessarily mean fewer federal controls. On the contrary, the federal government has imposed mandates on states and local governments, often without providing federal funds. State and local officials complained, and protests from state and local officials against unfunded federal mandates were effective. Congress, with President Clinton's support, passed the Unfunded Mandates Reform Act of 1995. The act requires the Congressional Budget Office (CBO) and federal agencies to issue reports about the impact of unfunded mandates. The act also imposed some mild constraints on Congress itself. A congressional committee that approves any legislation containing a federal mandate must draw attention to the mandate in its report and describe its cost to state and local governments. If the committee intends any mandate to be partially unfunded, it must explain why it is appropriate for the cost to be borne by state and local government.

Whether the Unfunded Mandates Reform Act significantly slows down federal mandates remains to be seen. So far it has had little effect. The Americans with Disabilities Act (1990), for example, called on state and local governments to build ramps and alter curbs—renovations that are costing millions. Environmental Protection Agency regulations require states to build automobile pollution-testing stations and take other actions to reduce pollution, but without corresponding federal dollars. Still, state officials praise the law for increasing congressional awareness of unfunded mandates. It has forced members of Congress to take into account how a bill would affect state and local governments, and to check with the Congressional Budget Office to avoid exposing a bill to procedural objections that could slow down or even block its passage.[38]

THE POLITICS OF FEDERALISM

The formal structures of our federal system have not changed much since 1787, but the political realities, especially during the last half-century, have greatly altered how federalism works. To understand these changes, we need to look at some of the trends that continue to fuel the debate about the meaning of federalism.

New Techniques of Federal Control

Direct Orders   In a few instances, federal regulation takes the form of direct orders that must be complied with under threat of criminal or civil sanction. An example is the Equal Employment Opportunity Act of 1972, barring job discrimination by state and local governments because of race, color, religion, sex, and national origin.

Cross-cutting Requirements   The first and most famous of these requirements (so called because a condition on one federal grant is extended to all activities supported by federal funds, regardless of their source) is Title VI of the 1964 Civil Rights Act, which holds that no person may be discriminated against in the use of federal funds because of race, color, or national origin. Other laws extend these protections to persons because of gender or handicapped status. More than 60 cross-cutting requirements concern the environment, historic preservation, contract wage rates, access to governmental information, the care of experimental animals, the treatment of human subjects in research projects, and so on.

Cross-over Sanctions   These sanctions permit the use of federal dollars in one program to influence state and local policy in another. One example is a 1984 act that threatened to reduce federal highway aid by up to 15 percent for any state that failed to adopt a minimum drinking age of 21 by 1987.

Total Preemption   This kind of control rests not on the national government's power to spend but on its powers under the supremacy and commerce clauses to preempt conflicting state and local activities. Building on this constitutional authority, federal law in certain areas just preempts state and local governments from the field. "There are fourteen types of total preemption laws, ranging from ones removing all regulatory powers from the states to ones authorizing states to cooperate in enforcing a statute."*

Partial Preemption   In these instances, federal law establishes basic policies but requires states to administer them. Some programs give states an option not to participate, but if a state chooses not to do so, the national government then steps in and runs the programs. Even worse from the state's point of view is *mandatory partial preemption*, in which the national government requires the state to act on peril of losing other funds but provides no funds to support the state action. The Clean Air Act of 1990 is an example of mandatory partial preemption; the federal government set national air quality standards and required states to devise plans and pay for their implementation and enforcement.** Medicaid is another example of the national government providing some funds but mandating states to provide services that cost more than the federal funds cover.

*Joseph F. Zimmerman, "Congressional Regulation of Subnational Governments," P.S.: Political Science and Politics 26 (June 1993), p. 179.

**Mel Dubnick and Alan Gitelson, "Nationalizing State Policies," in The Nationalization of State Government, ed. Jerome J. Hanus (D.C. Heath, 1981), pp. 56–57.

The Growth of Big Government

Over the past two centuries there has been a drift of power to the national government. "No one planned the growth, but everyone played a part in it."[39] How did this shift come about? For a variety of reasons. One is that many of our problems have become national in scope. Much that was local in 1789, in 1860, or in 1930 is now national—even global. State governments could supervise the relations between small merchants and their few employees, but only the national government can supervise relations between multinational corporations and their thousands of employees, many organized in national unions.

As industrialization proceeded, powerful interests made demands on the national government. Business groups called on the government for aid in the form of tariffs, a national banking system, subsidies to railroads and the merchant marine, and uniform rules relating to the environment. Farmers learned that the national government could give more aid than the states, and they too began to demand help. By the beginning of this century, urban groups in general and organized labor in particular pressed their claims. Big business, big agriculture, and big labor all added up to big government.

The growth of the national economy and the creation of national transportation and communications networks altered people's attitudes toward the national government. Before the Civil War, the national government was viewed as a distant, even foreign, government. Today, in part because of television and the Internet, most people identify as closely with Washington as with their state capitals. People are apt to know more about the president than about their governor, more about their national senators and representatives than about their state legislators, or even about the local officials who run their cities and schools.

The Great Depression of the 1930s stimulated extensive national action on welfare, unemployment, and farm surpluses. World War II brought federal regulation of wages, prices, and employment, as well as national efforts to allocate resources, train personnel, and support engineering and inventions. After the war the national government helped veterans obtain college degrees and inaugurated a vast system of support for university research. The United States became the most powerful leader of the free world, maintaining substantial military forces even in times of peace. The Great Society programs of the 1960s poured out grants-in-aid to states and localities. City dwellers who had migrated from the rural South to northern cities began to seek federal funds for—at the very least—housing, education, and mass transportation.

Although economic and social conditions created many of the pressures for expansion of the national government, so did political claims. Until federal budget deficits became a hot issue in the 1980s and early 1990s, members of Congress, presidents, federal judges, and federal administrators actively promoted federal initiatives. With the return of more balanced federal budgets, it will be interesting to see if Congress returns to active promotion of federal programs. True, when there is widespread conflict about what to do—how to reduce the federal deficit, adopt a national energy policy, reform Social Security, provide health care for the indigent—Congress waits for a national consensus. But when an organized constituency wants something and there is no counterpressure, Congress "responds often to everyone, and with great vigor."[40] Once established, federal programs generate groups with vested interests in promoting, defending, and expanding them. Associations are formed and alliances are made. "In a word, the growth of government has created a constituency of, by, and for government."[41]

The politics of federalism are changing, however, and Congress is being pressured to reduce the size and scope of national programs. At the same time, the cost of entitlement programs such as Social Security and Medicare are going up because there are more older people and they live longer. These programs have widespread public support, and to cut them is politically risky. "With all other options disappearing, it is politically tempting to finance tax cuts by turning over to the states many of the social programs . . . that have become the responsibility of the national government."[42]

The Devolution Revolution—A Revolution or Just Rhetoric?

The Republican sweep of the Congress in the 1994 elections carried with it a pledge to return many functions, most especially welfare, back to the states. President Clinton appeared to agree with the general tone of the Republicans. In his 1996 State of the Union Address, he proclaimed, "The era of big government is over." However, he tempered his comments by saying, "But we cannot go back to the time when our citizens were left to fend for themselves." Congress and the president came together for a major overhaul of welfare and, to a lesser degree, education. Congress also freed the states to set their own highway speed limits, changed the Safe Drinking Water Act to allow states to operate certain programs, and gave states a greater role over how federal rural development funds can be used.

Yet despite these shifts, recent Congresses, like their predecessors, have increased the authority of the national government in many areas. "Legislation cleared by the first Republican majority in four decades established national criteria for state-issued driver's licenses, ended state registration of mutual funds, created national food safety standards, nullified state laws that had restricted telecommunications competition, and extended federal criminal penalties to cover certain violent crimes."[43] Legislators made a host of offenses federal crimes, including car-jacking and stalking, and federalized the crime of rape committed while car-jacking. Appropriation bills pressured states to keep criminals behind bars by threatening to take grants away from states that failed to meet federal standards. As one reporter concluded, "The 'Devolution' promised by Congressional Republicans . . . has mostly fizzled. Instead of handing over authority to state and local governments, they're taking it away."[44]

THE FUTURE OF FEDERALISM

In 1933, during the Great Depression with state governments helpless, one writer stated, "I do not predict that the states will go, but affirm that they have gone."[45] Those prophets of doom were wrong. States are stronger than ever. During recent decades state governments have undergone a major transformation. Most have improved their governmental structures, taken on greater roles in funding education and welfare, launched programs to help distressed cities, and—despite new constitutional limitations—expanded their tax bases. Able men and women have been attracted to many governorships. "Today, states, in formal representational, policy making, and implementation terms at least, are more representative, more responsive, more activist, and more professional in their operations than they ever have been. They face their expanded roles better equipped to assume and fulfill them."[46]

Until the civil rights revolution of the 1960s, segregationists had feared that national officials would work for racial integration. Thus they praised local government, emphasized the dangers of centralization, and argued that the protection of civil rights was not a proper function of the national government. As one political scientist observed, "Federalism has a dark history to overcome. For nearly two hundred years, states' rights have been asserted to protect slavery, segregation, and discrimination."[47]

Today the politics of federalism, even with respect to civil rights, is more complicated than in the past. The national government is not necessarily more favorable to the claims of minorities than are state or city governments. When the Supreme

Court did not extend marital privacy rights to gays and lesbians, Vermont and some other state courts interpreted their state constitutions to provide more protection for these rights than does the U.S. Constitution. However, other states are passing legislation that would eliminate such protections.

As states more actively regulate the economy and as state attorneys general prosecute anticompetitive business practices, as they did in joining the suit against Microsoft in 2000, business interests have been arguing that conflicting state regulations are unduly burdening interstate commerce. They are asking for preemptive federal regulation, barring state taxes on e-commerce, for instance, in order to save them not only from stringent state regulations but from having to adjust to 50 different state laws. "One national dumb rule is better than 50 inconsistent rules of any kind," says a lawyer who represents trade groups in the food industries and medical devices.[48]

The national government is not likely to retreat to a pre-1930 posture or even a pre-1960 one. The underlying economic and social conditions that generated the demand for federal action have not been altered substantially. On the contrary, in addition to such traditional issues as helping people find jobs and preventing inflation and depressions—which still require national action—countless new issues have been added to the national agenda by the growth of a global economy based on e-commerce, an information explosion, and advancing technologies.

Most Americans have strong attachments to our federal system—in the abstract. They remain loyal to their states and show a growing and healthy skepticism about the national government. Some evidence suggests, however, that the anti-Washington sentiment "is 3,000 miles wide but only a few miles deep."[49] The fact is that Americans are pragmatists and are prepared to use whatever level of government—national, state, or local—necessary to meet their needs and new challenges.

POLITICS ONLINE

Should Internet Sales Be Taxed?

People can now buy virtually anything over the Internet; from groceries to automobiles to airline tickets, consumers find using their personal computer preferable to other forms of shopping. E-commerce is clearly a powerful new form of doing retail business. One problem e-commerce poses for government is that it makes collecting sales tax difficult. Conventional retail businesses collect sales taxes at the point of sale and forward those revenues to the government. Internet sales are generally not taxed, the exception being firms that operate a conventional retail business in the home state of the consumer. Hence, if a consumer purchased a book from *Amazon.com*, she would not pay sales tax, but if she purchased the same book via the Internet from the Barnes & Noble website, she would have to pay sales tax if her state had a Barnes & Noble store.

Conventional retail businesses have understandably cried "foul" to the non-taxable advantage enjoyed by many of their e-commerce competitors. Some state and local officials, like Utah Governor Mike Leavitt, have taken the lead in demanding tax fairness across the two types of retail business. On the other side of the issue are the Internet merchants, whose mantra is: "No Internet Taxes." Virginia Governor James Gilmore has been the leader of this group.

A national commission on this topic ended up so badly divided on what policy to recommend to Congress that it issued no formal recommendation, only majority and minority reports. We have archived the majority and minority report at:
www.prenhall.com/burns for this chapter.

For additional information on these issues go to:
www.ecomercetax.com.

SUMMARY

1. A federal system checks the growth of tyranny, allows unity without uniformity, encourages experimentation, and keeps government closer to the people.

2. Alternatives to federal systems are unitary systems in which all constitutional power is vested in the central government, and confederations, which are loose compacts among sovereign states.

3. The national government has the constitutional authority, stemming primarily from the national supremacy clause, from the war powers, and from its powers to regulate commerce among the states to tax and spend, to do what Congress thinks is necessary and proper to promote the general welfare and to provide for the common defense. These constitutional pillars have permitted tremendous expansion of the functions of the federal government.

4. States must give full faith and credit to each other's public acts, records, and judicial proceedings; extend to each other's citizens the privileges and immunities it gives its own; and return fugitives from justice.

5. The federal courts umpire the division of power between the national and state governments.

6. Today debates about federalism are less often about its constitutional structure than over whether action should come from the national or state and local levels. Recent Supreme Court decisions favor a decentralist position and may presage a major shift in the Court's interpretation of the constitutional nature of our federal system.

7. The major instruments of federal intervention in state programs have been various kinds of financial grants-in-aid, of which the most prominent are categorical-formula grants, project grants, and block grants. The national government also imposes federal mandates and controls some activities of state and local governments by other means.

8. Over the past 220 years there has been a drift of power to the national government, but recently Congress has been pressured to reduce the size and scope of national programs and to shift some existing programs back to the states. While responsibility for welfare has been turned over to the states, the authority of the national government has increased in many areas.

KEY TERMS

devolution revolution 52
federalism 53
unitary system 54
confederation 54
express powers 56

implied powers 56
necessary and proper clause 56
inherent powers 56
commerce clause 58
federal mandate 58

concurrent powers 59
full faith and credit clause 61
extradition 61
interstate compact 62
national supremacy 62

preemption 62
centralists 62
decentralists 62
revenue sharing 66

FURTHER READING

SAMUEL H. BEER, *To Make a Nation: The Rediscovery of American Federalism* (Harvard University Press, 1993).

MICHAEL BURGESS, *Federalism and the European Union: Building of Europe, 1950–2000* (Routledge, 2000).

CENTER FOR THE STUDY OF FEDERALISM, *The Federalism Report* (published quarterly by Temple University; this publication notes research, books and articles, and scholarly conferences).

CENTER FOR THE STUDY OF FEDERALISM, *Publius: The Journal of Federalism* (published quarterly by Temple University; one issue each year is an "Annual Review of the State of American Federalism").

TIMOTHY J. CONLAN, *From New Federalism to Devolution: Twenty-five Years of Intergovernmental Reforms* (Brookings Institution, 1998).

MARTHA DERTHICK, ed., *Dilemmas of Scale in America's Federal Democracy* (Cambridge University Press, 1999).

THOMAS R. DYE, *Politics in States and Communities*, 10th ed. (Prentice Hall, 2000).

DANIEL J. ELAZER AND JOHN KINCAID, *The Covenant Connection: From Federal Theology to Modern Federalism* (Lexington Books, 2000).

JOHN FEREJOHN AND BARRY WEINGAST, *The New Federalism: Can the States Be Trusted?* (Hoover Institute Press, 1998).

MICHAEL GREVE, *Real Federalism: Why It Matters, How It Could Happen* (American Enterprise Institute, 1999).

ELLIS KATZ AND G. ALAN TARR, eds., *Federalism and Rights* (Roman & Littlefield, 1996).

PAUL E. PETERSON, *The Price of Federalism* (Brookings Institution, 1995).

PAUL J. POSNER, *The Politics of Unfunded Mandates: Whither Federalism* (Georgetown University Press, 1998).

MARTIN REDISH, *The Constitution as Political Structure* (Oxford University Press, 1995).

WILLIAM H. RIKER, *The Development of American Federalism* (Academic Publishers, 1987).

ROBERT C. VIPOND, *Liberty and Community: Canadian Federalism and the Failure of the Constitution* (State University of New York Press, 1991).

DAVID B. WALKER, *The Rebirth of Federalism: Slouching Toward Washington* (Chatham House, 1995).

JOSEPH F. ZIMMERMAN, *Contemporary American Federalism: The Growth of National Power* (Praeger, 1992).

POLITICAL CULTURE AND IDEOLOGY

4

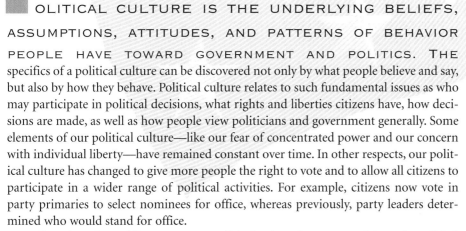

P

OLITICAL CULTURE IS THE UNDERLYING BELIEFS, ASSUMPTIONS, ATTITUDES, AND PATTERNS OF BEHAVIOR PEOPLE HAVE TOWARD GOVERNMENT AND POLITICS. THE specifics of a political culture can be discovered not only by what people believe and say, but also by how they behave. Political culture relates to such fundamental issues as who may participate in political decisions, what rights and liberties citizens have, how decisions are made, as well as how people view politicians and government generally. Some elements of our political culture—like our fear of concentrated power and our concern with individual liberty—have remained constant over time. In other respects, our political culture has changed to give more people the right to vote and to allow all citizens to participate in a wider range of political activities. For example, citizens now vote in party primaries to select nominees for office, whereas previously, party leaders determined who would stand for office.

Does it make a difference to our political culture how we participate in politics? The answer is yes. Contrast primary elections, in which individuals cast ballots on election day at voting places, with political caucuses, in which participants attend a meeting and listen to their neighbors making speeches about the candidates and issues of concern. The idea of people coming together, listening to each other, exchanging ideas, learning to appreciate each other's differences, and defending their opinions is thought to build community and relationships in ways that do not happen when citizens cast ballots. Even more impersonal are elections where voters cast ballots over the Internet.

Other places where citizens deliberate together include town council meetings, community groups, the PTA, labor unions, or business associations. Because of a decline of public participation in these institutions, some social scientists believe there has been a loss of the skills and learned behaviors people develop in such settings. Harvard professor Robert Putnam has defined **social capital** as "features of social organization such as networks, norms, and social trust that facilitate coordination and cooperation for mutual benefit."[1] But as we noted in Chapter 1, not all political scientists agree with Putnam's assessment of declining social capital.

The social capital debate has rekindled an interest in the nature and viability of the American political culture and an examination of how it is changing. Americans have conflicting ideas and beliefs about the proper role of government and where and how political power should be exercised. In this chapter, we look at the political culture that unites us as well as the ideologies that sometimes divide us.

CHAPTER MEDIA

POLITICS ONLINE
What's My Ideology?
www.prenhall.com/burns

POLISIM
What Do You Believe?
www.prenhall.com/burns

social capital

Participation in voluntary organizations that reinforce democratic and civic habits of discussion, compromise, and respect for differences.

political culture

The widely shared beliefs, values, and norms concerning the relationship of citizens to government and to one another.

natural rights

The rights of all people to dignity and worth; also called *human rights.*

THE AMERICAN POLITICAL CULTURE

Political scientists use the term **political culture** to refer to the widely shared beliefs, values, and norms concerning the relationship of citizens to government and to one another. American democratic values include liberty, equality, individualism, democracy, justice, the rule of law, nationalism, optimism, and idealism. There is no definitive list of American political values, however, for as we noted in Chapter 1, these widely shared democratic values overlap and sometimes conflict.

Shared Values

Before the American and French Revolutions, discussions about individual liberty, freedom, equality, private property, limited government, and popular consent were not widespread. Europe had been dominated by aristocracies, had experienced centuries of political and social inequality, and had been ruled by governments that were often arbitrary in their exercise of power. Liberal political philosophers rebelled against these traditions and proclaimed the principles of classical liberalism. They claimed individuals have certain **natural rights**—the rights of all people to dignity and worth—and that government, as a primary threat to those rights, must be limited and controlled. During this same period, the economic system was changing to a free market system. People began to think they could improve their lot in life and own property. Radical new ideas like these influenced the thinking of the founders of our nation.

LIBERTY   Americans have always been united by a commitment to liberty or freedom. No value in the American political culture is more revered. "We have always been a nation obsessed with liberty. Liberty over authority, freedom over responsibility, rights over duties—these are our historic preferences," wrote the late Clinton Rossiter, a noted political scientist. "Not the good man, but the free man has been the measure of all things in this sweet 'land of liberty'; not national glory but individual liberty has been the object of political authority and the test of its worth."[2]

EQUALITY   Jefferson's famous words in the Declaration of Independence express the primacy of our views of equality: "We hold these truths to be self-evident, that all men are created equal, that they are endowed by their Creator with certain unalienable rights, that among these are life, liberty, and the pursuit of happiness." Americans have always believed in social equality. In contrast to Europeans, our nation shunned aristocracy, and our Constitution explicitly bans titles of nobility.

Equality also refers to *political equality,* the idea that every individual has a right to equal protection under the law and equal voting power. Although political equality has always been a goal, it has not always been a reality. African Americans, Native Americans, and women have been denied political equality in the past.

Equality encompasses the idea of equality of opportunity, especially with regard to improving our economic status. Americans believe that social background should not limit our opportunity to achieve to the best of our ability, nor should race, gender, or religion. The nation's commitment to public education programs like Head Start for underprivileged preschool children, state support for public colleges and universities, and federal financial aid for higher education reflect this belief in equality.

INDIVIDUALISM   The United States is characterized by a persistent commitment to the individual. Under our system of government, individuals have both rights and responsibilities. Concern for preserving individual freedom of choice and what limits, if any, to place on individual choice generate intense political conflict. The debate over legalized abortion is often framed in these terms. Although Americans agree with individual rights and freedoms, they also understand that rights can conflict with other rights or with the government's need to maintain order.

POWER TO THE PEOPLE   Americans have faith in the common sense of the ordinary person. We prefer action to reflection. We are often anti-expert and sometimes anti-intellectual. The emphasis on practicality and common sense has become part of our image. Poets like Walt Whitman and Carl Sandburg and storytellers like Mark Twain, Will Rogers, Eudora Welty, and Garrison Keillor have helped shape this tradition. This reverence for the common person helps explain our ambivalence toward power, politics, and government authority. In the United States, government is often viewed as a necessary evil.

DEMOCRATIC CONSENSUS   The most important feature that binds us together is the **democratic consensus**, a fairly widespread agreement on fundamental principles of governance and the values that undergird them. We are a people from many different cultural and ethnic backgrounds, histories, and religions. Despite these differences, our political culture includes widely shared attitudes and beliefs about principles of government, procedures, documents, and institutions. Americans have strong opinions about who has power to do what, how people acquire power, and how they are removed from power. These are fundamental "rules of the game" in which widespread consensus is important.

We believe in **majority rule**—governance according to the expressed preferences of the majority at regular elections. Yet we also believe that people in the minority should be free to try to win majority support for their opinions. Despite the fact that large numbers of Americans lack strong party attachments, we favor a two-party system. Our institutions are based on the principle of representation and consent of the governed. We believe in **popular sovereignty**—that ultimate power resides in the people. Government, from this perspective, exists to serve the people rather than the other way around. The means by which the government learns the will of the people is through *elections*, perhaps the most important expression of popular consent. But there are instances when popular sovereignty and majority rule must be limited by other fundamental rights, as in the case of referenda limiting civil rights.[3] Examples include California's 1964 vote to permit people to discriminate in the sale of residential housing and 1996 vote to overturn affirmative action.

Many of the limits on government are specified in the Constitution and the Bill of Rights. The Constitution is revered as a national symbol, yet we often differ over the precise meaning of the framers' original intentions. We honor many of these rights more in the abstract than in the particular. More than half of us, for instance, think that books with dangerous ideas should be banned from public school libraries (see Table 4–1). Intolerance of dissenting or offensive views is amply demonstrated in many public opinion polls and is observed on college and university campuses. Still, Americans can ordinarily be characterized as affirming support for democratic and constitutional values.

JUSTICE AND THE RULE OF LAW   Inscribed over the entrance to the U.S. Supreme Court are the words "Equal Justice Under Law." The rule of law means that government is based on a body of law applied equally and by just procedures, as opposed to rule by an elite in which the whims of those in power decide policy or resolve disputes. Chief Justice John Marshall succinctly summarized this principle: "The government of the United States has been emphatically termed a government of laws, not of men."[4] Americans believe strongly in the principle of fairness: all individuals are entitled to the same legal rights and protections.

democratic consensus
Widespread agreement on fundamental principles of democratic governance and the values that undergird them.

majority rule
Governance according to the expressed preferences of the majority.

popular sovereignty
A belief that ultimate power resides in the people.

WHERE WE LEARN THE AMERICAN POLITICAL CULTURE

The Family

One of the important sources of political culture in the United States and in other nations as well is the family. Children are taught from an early age what it means to be an American. They are curious about why people vote, what the president does, and whether Grandpa fought in World War II. The questions may vary somewhat from family to family, but the themes of authority, freedom, equality, liberty, and partisanship are common. Families are the most important reference groups, and compared to families in other cultures, American families are much more egalitarian.

The Schools

Public schools are another source of the American political culture. Children and teachers often begin the school day by saluting the flag, reciting the Pledge of Allegiance, or singing the National Anthem. Teaching American political and economic values is part of the curriculum. Not only are values taught in American history classes, but they are put into practice in school elections and newspapers and in encouraging students to participate in small-scale economic ventures.

Colleges and universities also play a role in fostering the American political culture. Students who attend college are often more confident than other persons in dealing with bureaucracy and politics generally, more likely to participate in politics and vote, and more knowledgeable about government. Many states require students at state colleges and universities to take courses in American government or state government, in part to instill a sense of civic duty while imparting knowledge about state and national governments.

Religious and Civic Organizations

Religious freedom and diversity have played a part in the formation and maintenance of the American political culture. American churches, synagogues, and mosques have long fostered a common understanding of right and wrong. Freedom, including freedom of religion, individualism, pluralism, and civic duty, have all been fostered by churches. As churches do not all take the same positions on political issues, their impact is sometimes mitigated, but they have been important to such major social and political movements as abolition of slavery, expansion of civil rights, and opposition to war. Civic organizations like the Boy Scouts, 4-H, League of Women Voters, Rotary Club, and Chamber of Commerce encourage citizen participation and pride in community and nation.

The Mass Media

In modern times the mass media have taken over some functions previously performed by the family. By the time they are adults, children will probably have spent more time watching television than in conversation with their parents. They may have had more political instruction from MTV than from their parents or their schools.

Political Activities

Finally, Americans educate each other about political values in the workplace, at the PTA meeting, or in more expressly political activities.

TABLE 4–1 It Depends on What You Mean by Rights and Freedoms

	Agree	Disagree	Don't Know*
Freedom of speech should apply to groups such as communist and the Ku Klux Klan.	57%	39%	4%
There has been real improvement in the position of African Americans.	53	38	9
Books that contain dangerous ideas should be banned from public school libraries.	55	43	2
Affirmative action programs to help African American women get better jobs and education should be continued.	65	31	4
The police should be allowed to search the houses of known drug dealers without a court order.	45	53	2
School boards ought to have the right to fire teachers who are known homosexuals.	33	62	4

SOURCE: The Pew Research Center for the People and the Press, *Retro-Politics—The Political Typology*, November 14, 1999.

*Includes those who said "neither."

For government to adhere to the rule of law, its policies and laws should follow these five rules:

- *Generality*: Laws should be stated generally, not singling out any group or individual.
- *Prospectivity*: Laws should apply to the future, not punish something someone did in the past.
- *Publicity*: Laws cannot be kept secret and then enforced.
- *Authority*: Valid laws are made by those with legitimate power, and the people legitimate that power through some form of popular consent.
- *Due Process*: Laws must be enforced impartially with fair processes.

NATIONALISM, OPTIMISM, AND IDEALISM Americans are highly nationalistic, sharing a sense of values and identity. We are proud of our past and our role in the world today. We are optimistic, though more about people than about government. We believe in opportunity, choice, individualism, and most of all, in freedom to improve ourselves and to achieve success with as little interference as possible from others or from government. As Table 4–2 indicates, U.S. citizens are more satisfied with their democratic government than are citizens of other countries.

We know our system is not perfect. We often grumble that elected officials have lost touch with us, we are disgusted by scandals, and we are impatient with the slowness of the system to solve problems like health care, crime, drug abuse, and campaign finance. Yet we have an abiding faith in government by the people. Despite the dissatisfactions, a remarkable belief persists that this nation is better, stronger, and more virtuous than other nations. Like every country, the United States has interests and motives that are selfish as well as generous, cynical as well as idealistic. Still, our support of human needs and rights throughout the world is evidence of an enduring idealism.

TABLE 4–2 Satisfaction with the Way Democracy Works

	Satisfied	Dissatisfied
United States	64%	27%
Canada	62	24
Germany	55	27
Iceland	54	23
Thailand	54	27
Costa Rica	52	25
Chile	43	31
France	43	32
Dominican Republic	40	38
United Kingdom	40	43
Japan	35	32
India	32	43
Spain	31	30
Venezuela	28	59
Taiwan	25	18
Hungary	17	50
Mexico	17	67
China	na	na

SOURCE: "People Throughout the World Largely Satisfied with Personal Lives," *Gallup Poll Monthly*, June 1995, p. 6.

WE THE PEOPLE

Oprah Winfrey: Achieving the American Dream

Is the American Dream a reality? If you don't think so, ask Oprah Winfrey. Born in Kosciusko, Mississippi, in 1954 to parents who never married, Oprah had a less than ideal childhood. At age six, she moved from her grandmother's farm in Mississippi to live with her mother in Wisconsin. At age twelve a family member sexually molested her. Later she attempted to run away from home. To avoid being put in a detention center, she was sent to live with her father in Nashville.

Under her father's direction, Oprah began to straighten out her life. She enrolled in Tennessee State University but dropped out during her sophomore year to become the first African-American anchor for Nashville's WTVF-TV. She moved to Baltimore to anchor a TV news broadcast and was later fired. But she found her niche as host of a Baltimore morning talk show. Building on this success, she moved to Chicago and hosted *A.M. Chicago*, which was later syndicated as *The Oprah Winfrey Show*.

Today Oprah Winfrey is a household name, and for many, a household personality. She has amassed a net worth of over a half a billion dollars, owns her own production company, and has her own women's magazine. She has starred in several films and was nominated for an Academy Award for her role in *The Color Purple*. She has even been

Coming from humble beginnings, Oprah Winfrey—television host, movie actress, and one of the highest paid people in the country—epitomizes the American Dream.

active in the political arena. In 1994, Bill Clinton signed into law the "Oprah Bill," federal legislation to protect children from abuse.

SOURCES: Deborah Tannen, "The T.V. Host Oprah Winfrey" (http://www.time.com/time/time100/artists/profile/winfrey.html); "Oprah Winfrey: The Real Story," *Bibliobytes, 2000* (http://www.bb.com/looptestlive.cfm?BOOKID=1581&StartRow=1).

The American Dream

Many of our political values come together in the **American Dream**, a complex set of ideas holding that the United States is a land of opportunity, and that individual initiative and hard work can bring economic success. Whether realized or not, this American Dream speaks to our most deeply held hopes and goals. The essence of the American Dream can be found in our enthusiasm for **capitalism**, an economic system characterized by private property, competitive markets, economic incentives, and limited government involvement in the production and pricing of goods and services.

The concept of *private property* enjoys extraordinary popularity in our political culture. In many European democracies, the state owns and operates transportation systems, the media, and other businesses that are privately owned and operated in the United States, although there has been some privatization of communications systems like telephone companies and broadcast media. Americans cherish the dream of acquiring property. Moreover, most Americans believe that those who own property have the right to decide how to use it.

The right to private property is just one of the economic incentives that cement our support for capitalism and fuel the American Dream. This is the land of opportunity for the enterprising. Here the competitive, practical go-getter can make a fortune, build a dream home, and retire early. We assume that people who have more ability or work extremely hard will get ahead, earn more, and enjoy economic rewards. We also believe people should be able to pass most of what they have accumulated along to their children and relatives. Even the poorest Americans generally oppose high inheritance taxes or limits on how much someone can earn.

Americans believe the free market system gives almost everyone a fair chance, that capitalism is necessary, and that freedom depends on it. We reject communism and socialism—a rejection fortified in recent years as most communist nations shifted toward capitalism. In the United States, individuals and corporations have acquired wealth and, at the same time, exercised political clout. Their power has, in turn, bred some resentment.

The conflict in values between a *competitive economy*, in which individuals reap large rewards for their initiative and hard work, and an *egalitarian society*, in which everyone earns a decent living, carries over into politics. How the public resolves this tension changes over time and from issue to issue.

As important as the American Dream is to the national consciousness, Americans know it remains unfulfilled. An underclass persists in the form of impoverished families, ill-nourished and poorly educated children, and people living on the streets.[5] Many cities are actually two cities, where some live in luxury while others live in squalor. The gap between rich and poor has grown in recent years, and a sharp difference between white and black income persists tenaciously.[6] For more people than we want to admit, chances for success still depend on the family you were born in, the neighborhood you grew up in, or the college you attended.

Political and Economic Change

Political values are clearly affected by historical developments and by economic and technological growth. The Declaration of Independence and the Constitution identified such important political values as individual liberty, property rights, and limited government.[7] Early in our history we emphasized separation of powers, checks and balances, states' rights, and the Bill of Rights. It took an additional generation or two before we also began to take seriously the expansion of suffrage and competitive nominations and elections. Notions of political equality and effective participation emerged during the presidency of Andrew Jackson and matured in the course of the nineteenth century. By the end of the nineteenth century, populists and suffragists turned ideals into action and formed large-scale movements to achieve more democratic forms of participation and more responsive forms of governance.

THE INDUSTRIAL TRANSFORMATION   By 1900, the agrarian society the framers knew had been largely replaced by industrial capitalism and the growth of large corporations. With these changes, ideology was irreversibly transformed. Large privately owned corporations changed the economic order, including changes in the role of government and how people viewed each other. No one captures the implications of this shift better than political scientist Robert A. Dahl:

> One of the consequences of the new order has been a high degree of inequality in the distribution of wealth and income, and far greater inequality than had ever been thought likely or desirable under an agrarian order by Democratic Republicans like Jefferson and Madison, or had ever been thought consistent with democratic or republican government in the historic writings on the subject from Aristotle to Locke, Montesquieu, and Rousseau. Previous theorists and advocates had, like many of the framers of our own Constitution, insisted that a republic could exist only if the citizen body continued neither rich nor poor. Citizens, it was argued, must enjoy a rough equality of conditions.[8]

The success of the American industrial economy led to the accumulation of great wealth in the hands of a few—the robber barons or tycoons. Many had taken great risks or earned their fortunes through inventions and efficient production practices. But as disparities of income grew, so did disparities in political resources. Economic resources can be converted into political resources, like time to spend on politics and money to contribute to parties and candidates.[9]

At the turn of the century, the rise of the large corporation and the concentration of individual wealth in the United States created divisions and resentment. Muckraking journalists charged that the huge corporations had become **monopolies**, using their dominance of their industry to exploit workers and limit competition. Unsafe work conditions led to some regulation of the workplace by the states, but only the national government, it seemed, had the power to ensure fair treatment in the marketplace. This sentiment not only gave rise to the nation's first **antitrust legislation**—federal laws that try to prevent monopolies from dominating an industry and restraining trade—but also sowed the idea that government could—and

American Dream
The widespread belief that individual initiative and hard work can bring economic success, and that the United States is a land of opportunity.

capitalism
An economic system characterized by private property, competitive markets, economic incentives, and limited government involvement in the production and pricing of goods and services.

monopolies
Large corporations or firms that dominate their industries and are able to artificially fix prices and discourage competition.

antitrust legislation
Federal laws (starting with the Sherman Act of 1890) that try to prevent monopolies from dominating an industry and restraining trade.

should—as the Constitution asserts, "promote the general Welfare" by regulating working conditions, product safety, and labor-management disputes.

THE GREAT DEPRESSION AND THE NEW DEAL   Much of our thinking about the role of government in a capitalistic system was shaped by the Great Depression of the 1930s and the near collapse of the capitalistic system. Unrestrained capitalism and an unregulated market were faulted as causes of the Depression. The collapse of the stock market, massive unemployment, and a failed banking system brought the nation to the brink of disaster. There was no unemployment compensation, no guarantee on bank savings, no federal regulation of the securities exchanges, no Social Security. Americans turned to government to improve the lot of millions of jobless and homeless citizens. Beginning with Franklin D. Roosevelt's New Deal, the idea gradually gained widespread acceptance that government should use its powers and resources to ensure some measure of equal opportunity and social justice.

Roosevelt's State of the Union Address in 1944 outlined a "Second Bill of Rights" for all citizens in which he declared that this nation must make a firm commitment to "economic security and independence." Included in his Second Bill of Rights were:

- The right to a useful and remunerative job in the industries, shops, farms, or mines of the nation
- The right to earn enough to provide adequate food and clothing and recreation
- The right of every farmer to raise and sell his products at a return that would give him and his family a decent living
- The right of every businessman, large and small, to trade in an atmosphere of freedom from unfair competition and domination by monopolies at home or abroad
- The right of every family to a decent home
- The right to adequate medical care and the opportunity to achieve and enjoy good health
- The right to adequate protection from the economic fears of old age, sickness, accident, and unemployment
- The right to a good education.[10]

Roosevelt's policies and later efforts by John F. Kennedy and Lyndon Johnson in the 1960s to pass civil rights and voting rights legislation and launch a War on Poverty defined the ideological and political fights in the last half of the twentieth

Breadlines like this provided handouts of food to thousands of unemployed and destitute people during the Great Depression.

TABLE 4–3 Attitudes on Business and Welfare

	Agree	Disagree	Don't Know*
There is too much power concentrated in the hands of a few big companies.	74%	25%	1%
Business corporations make too much profit.	56	38	6
Regulation of business does more harm than good.	55	37	8
It is the responsibility of the government to take care of people who can't take care of themselves.	62	35	3
The government should help more needy people even if it means going deeper into debt.	49	47	4
The government should guarantee every citizen enough to eat and a place to sleep.	64	33	2

SOURCE: The Pew Research Center for the People and the Press, *Retro-Politics—The Political Typology*. November 14, 1999.

*Includes those who said "neither."

century. Modern-day liberalism and conservatism turn, in large measure, on how much one believes in Roosevelt's Second Bill of Rights and how much government assistance one thinks is owed to minorities, women, and others who have suffered discrimination or have been left behind by the industrial or technological revolutions of the twentieth century.

Today, free enterprise is no longer unbridled. Government regulations, antitrust laws, job safety regulations, environmental standards, and minimum wage rates all balance the freedom of enterprise against the rights of individuals. Most people today support a semiregulated or mixed free enterprise system that checks the worst tendencies of capitalism, but they reject excessive government intervention (see Table 4–3). Much of American politics centers on how to achieve this balance.

Currently, liberals and conservatives agree that some governmental intervention is necessary to assist those who fail in the competition for education and economic prosperity. In the 2000 elections, presidential candidates of both major parties debated the precise role and extent of government involvement in this area: Al Gore's campaign promised to provide health care to all Americans; George W. Bush's theme of "compassionate conservatism" would rely more on private charities to attend to human needs.

IDEOLOGY AND ATTITUDES ABOUT THE ROLE OF GOVERNMENT

Ideology refers to a person's ideas or beliefs about political values and the role of government. It includes the views people have about how government should work and how it actually works. Ideology links our basic values to the day-to-day operations or policies of government.

Two major schools of political ideology dominate American politics: *liberalism* and *conservatism*. Three lesser, but more defined, schools of thought, *socialism, environmentalism*, and *libertarianism*, also help define the spectrum of ideology in the United States. Table 4–4 provides a general distribution of political ideology in the United States.

Liberalism

In the seventeenth and eighteenth centuries, classical liberals fought to minimize the role of government. They stressed individual rights and perceived government as the primary threat to rights and liberties. Classical liberals favored *limited government* and sought ample protections from governmental harassment. Over time, the emphasis on individualism remained constant, but the perception of the need for government changed.

ideology
One's basic beliefs about political values and the role of government.

TABLE 4–4 Differences in Political Ideology

	Conservative	Moderate	Liberal
Sex			
Male	39%	45%	16%
Female	25	55	20
Race			
White	34	46	20
Black	10	78	12
Age			
18–34	19	58	24
35–45	37	44	18
46–55	35	44	21
56–64	36	55	10
65+	32	52	16
Religion			
Protestant	37	51	12
Catholic	25	55	20
Jewish	18	64	18
Education			
Less than high school	11	80	9
High school diploma	23	66	11
Some college	32	43	25
Bachelor's degree	44	34	21
Advanced degree	41	39	20
Party			
Democrat	15	54	31
Independent	26	58	16
Republican	71	24	6

SOURCE: Center for Political Studies, University of Michigan, *American National Election Study*, 2000.

Note: We have combined with the moderates persons who do not know their ideology or had not thought much about it. For party identification, we have combined Independent leaners with their respective parties. Rows may not add up to 100 percent due to rounding.

Today liberals view government as protecting individuals from being abused by a variety of forces, such as market vagaries, business decisions, and discriminatory practices.

CONTEMPORARY LIBERALS   In its current American usage, **liberalism** refers to a belief in the positive uses of government to bring about justice and equality of opportunity. Modern-day liberals wish to preserve the rights of the individual and the right to own private property, yet they are willing to have the government intervene in the economy to remedy the defects of capitalism. Liberals seek protection against inadequate or deficient health care, housing, and education. They generally believe in affirmative action programs, workers' health and safety protections, tax rates that rise with income, and unions' right to organize and strike.

On a more philosophical level, liberals generally believe in the possibility of progress. They believe that the future will be better, that obstacles can be overcome. This positive set of beliefs may explain their willingness to trust government programs. Liberals contend that modern technology and industrialization cry out for government programs to offset the loss of liberties suffered by the poor and the weak. Liberals such as Bill Bradley, Edward Kennedy, Hillary Rodham Clinton, and Jesse Jackson frequently stress the need for an involved and affirmative government.

liberalism
A belief in the positive uses of government to bring about justice and equality of opportunity.

Liberals charge that conservatives usually act in self-interest and follow the maxim, "Let the government take care of the rich, and the rich in turn will take care of the poor." Liberals, on the other hand, prefer that government take care of the weak, for the strong can always take care of themselves. "We have rejected the discredited theory that the fortunes of the nation should be in the hands of a privileged few," said President Harry Truman. "Instead, we believe that our economic system should rest on a democratic foundation and that wealth should be created for the benefit of all. . . . Every segment of our population and every individual has a right to expect from his government a fair deal."[11]

The liberal view holds all people equal. Equality of opportunity is essential, and to achieve that end, discriminatory practices must be eliminated. Some liberals favor the reduction of great inequalities of wealth that make equality of opportunity impossible. Most favor a certain minimum level of income. Rather than placing a cap on wealth, they want a floor placed beneath the poor. In short, liberals seek to lessen the impact of great inequalities of wealth and work to extend opportunities to all, regardless of their economic standing.

CRITICISMS OF LIBERALISM   Critics of liberalism say liberals place too much reliance on governmental solutions, higher taxes, and bureaucracy. These opponents argue that somewhere along the line liberals forgot that government, to serve our best interests, has to be limited. Power tends to corrupt, and too much dependence on government can corrupt the spirit, undermine self-reliance, and make people forget those cherished personal freedoms and property rights our Republic was founded to secure and protect. Too many governmental regulations and too much taxation tend to undermine the self-help ethic that "made America great." In short, critics of liberalism contend that the welfare and regulatory state pushed by liberals will ultimately destroy individual initiative, the entrepreneurial spirit, and the very engine of economic growth that might lead to true equality of economic opportunities.

In recent elections, Republicans have made liberalism a villain and positioned their own candidates more in the mainstream. George Bush, in 1988, consistently referred to Michael Dukakis as from the "liberal Democratic party." Bill Clinton was careful not to label his program as liberal, focusing on the need for economic growth, jobs, and a lower budget deficit. He insisted he was a "New Democrat." Al Gore positioned himself in the tradition of Clinton as a centrist, not a liberal, but George W. Bush charged that Gore was an advocate of big government.

The movement to the center by some Democrats and the conventional wisdom that liberal or progressive approaches are in decline is disputed by political commentator E. J. Dionne, Jr., whose book on how progressives can regain power is aptly titled *They Only Look Dead*. Dionne contends that the current political upheaval should be defined less as a revolt against *big* government than as a rebellion against *bad* government—government that has proven ineffectual in grappling with the political, economic, and moral crises that have shaken the country. Dionne challenges the claims that big government is bad or even over. Pointing to past progressive or liberal successes, Dionne contends Americans want a government that eases economic transitions, helps "preserve a broad middle class," and "expands the choices available to individuals."[12]

The popularity of liberalism and conservatism and the importance of particular issues change with world events. We were preoccupied with budget deficits until the budget surpluses of recent years. With the end of the cold war, we became more concerned about domestic policy than about foreign policy. But we live in a global economy in which our jobs and economic progress are linked to our neighbors and

Is Government a Necessary Evil or a Force for Good?

In his provocative book *A Necessary Evil: A History of American Distrust of Government*, historian Garry Wills explores the tension between widespread anti-government attitudes and the tendency of Americans to turn to government to solve problems. Hostility to government is deeply rooted and longstanding. In recent years it has been manifested in the tax revolt of the late 1970s and early 1980s, the movement to limit the number of terms legislators can serve in the 1980s and 1990s, and in the opposition to gun controls in the last two decades.

Wills identifies the following values as the core of anti-government hostility: the belief that government should be kept to a minimum; that local government is preferred to higher levels; that politicians should be amateur, spontaneous, voluntary, religious, and rotational.* Moreover, there is a tendency of the anti-government attitudes to cling together—take one and you are likely to end up with most or all of them.** Wills asserts that those who see government as a force for good believe that government is sometimes a positive good, and that good government is, among other things, expert, authoritative, efficient, secular, progressive, and regulatory.***

*Garry Wills, *A Necessary Evil: A History of American Distrust of Government* (Simon & Schuster, 1999, pp. 17–18).

**Ibid. p. 20.

***Ibid. p. 18.

Gary Bauer represented the strongly conservative position in the candidate debates for the Republican presidential nomination.

to other countries around the world. The net effect of these changes is that our national government, while focusing on domestic issues like health care and education, must also deal with international matters.

Conservatism

Private property rights and belief in free enterprise are cardinal attributes of contemporary **conservatism**. In contrast to liberals, conservatives want to keep government small, especially the national government, except in the area of national defense. However, because conservatives take a more pessimistic view of human nature than liberals do, they maintain that people need strong leadership institutions, firm laws, and strict moral codes to keep their appetites under control. Government, they think, needs to ensure order. Conservatives also believe that those who fail in life are in some way the architects of their own misfortune and must bear the main responsibility for solving their own problems. Conservatives prefer the status quo and desire change only in moderation.

TRADITIONAL CONSERVATIVES   Traditional conservatives are emphatically pro-business. They oppose higher taxes and resist all but the most necessary antitrust, trade, and environmental regulations on corporations. The functions of government should be to encourage family values, protect the nation from foreign enemies, preserve law and order, enforce private contracts, foster competitive markets, and encourage free and fair trade. Traditional conservatives favor dispersing power broadly throughout the political and social systems to avoid concentration of power at the national level. They favor having the market, rather than the government, provide services.

Until recent decades, conservatives opposed the New Deal programs of the 1930s, the War on Poverty in the 1960s, and most aggressive civil rights and affirmative action programs. Human needs, they say, can and should be cared for by families and charities. Conservatives put their faith in the private sector and consider social justice to be essentially an economic question. They dislike the tendency to turn to government, especially the national government, for solutions to societal problems. Government social activism, they say, has been expensive and counterproductive. They prefer private giving and individual voluntary efforts targeted at social and economic problems rather than government programs.

In the 2000 presidential campaign, George W. Bush attempted to build upon the successes of churches and other organizations in providing assistance to needy individuals, while at the same time trying to avoid the image of outright hostility to all government aid. Bush said early in his campaign, "Too often, my party has confused the need for a limited government with a disdain for government itself. . . . That love [of our country] is undermined by sprawling, arrogant, aimless government. It is restored by focused and effective and energetic government."[13]

SOCIAL CONSERVATIVES   Some conservatives focus less on economics and more on morality and lifestyle. Social conservatives favor strong governmental action to protect children from pornography and drugs. They want stringent limitations on abortions. This brand of conservatism—sometimes called the New Right, ultraconservatism, or even the Radical Right—emerged in the 1980s. The New Right shares traditional conservative's love of freedom and backs an aggressive effort to defend America's interests abroad. It favors the return of organized prayer in public schools and opposes policies like job quotas, busing, and tolerance of homosexuality. In sum, a defining characteristic of the New Right is a strong desire to impose various *social controls.*

A very active New Right or Religious Right group that supports social conservatism is the Christian Coalition, founded by Pat Robertson, a minister who sponsors a nightly cable television program. The Coalition has become a major political force. Although ostensibly working in a bipartisan fashion, it is more at

conservatism
A belief that limited government ensures order, competitive markets, and personal opportunity.

home in the Republican party. The Coalition lobbies for and funds candidates who are pro-family, anti-abortion, anti-gay. It favors a constitutional amendment that would guarantee the rights to prayer in public schools and religious symbols in public places. It works at all levels of government and especially targets candidates who have voted for abortion rights legislation.

Some conservatives are uncomfortable with the close association between the Republican party and the Christian Coalition. Former U.S. senator Warren Rudman, of New Hampshire, has observed, "Politically speaking, the Republican Party is making a terrible mistake if it appears to ally itself with the Christian right. There are some fine, sincere people in its ranks, but there are also enough anti-abortion zealots, would-be censors, homophobes, bigots, and latter-day Elmer Gantrys to discredit any party that is unwise enough to embrace such a group."[14] Rudman's statement was later used to justify phone calls by Reverend Pat Robertson to Christian Coalition members urging them to vote for George W. Bush in the 2000 South Carolina and Michigan primaries instead of for John McCain, whose campaign Rudman was managing.[15]

CRITICISMS OF CONSERVATISM   Not everyone agreed with Ronald Reagan's statement that "government is the problem." Indeed, critics of conservatism before and during the Reagan-Bush era saw hostility to government as counterproductive and inconsistent. Conservatives, they argued, have a selective opposition to government. They want more government when it serves their needs—regulating pornography and abortion, for example—but are opposed to it when it serves somebody else's.

Conservatives place great faith in the market economy—critics would say too much faith. This posture often puts conservatives at odds with labor unions and consumer activists and in close alliance with businesspeople, particularly large corporations. Hostility to regulation and a belief in competition leads them to push for deregulation. This approach has not always had the intended positive effects, as the collapse of many savings and loan companies in the 1980s and the energy crisis in California in the early 2000s revealed.[16] Conservatives counter that relying on market solutions and encouraging the free market are still the best course of action in most policy areas.

The policy of the Reagan years of lowering taxes was consistent with the conservative hostility to big government. Many conservatives embraced the idea that if

Bernard Sanders, a self-described Socialist, represents Vermont in the U.S. House of Representatives as an Independent.

we lower taxes on the rich, their increased economic activity will "trickle down" to the poor. This view was criticized by many Democrats, who pointed out that the growth in income and wealth in the 1980s was largely concentrated among the well-to-do.[17] They also pointed out that government spending, especially for defense, tripled the deficit during the 1980s when conservatives were in control.

Conservatives are also criticized for their failure to acknowledge and endorse policies that deal with racism and sexism in the United States. Their opposition to the civil rights laws in the 1960s and to affirmative action more recently are examples of this perspective. Not only have conservatives opposed new laws in these areas; they have hampered the activity of the executive branch when in power and have sought to limit the activity of the courts in these matters as well.

The selective application of government by liberals and social conservatives demonstrates the lack of consistency in both groups. Liberals favor vigorous governmental programs to help the poor but oppose governmental intrusion into citizens' private lives, while social conservatives preach less government except in promoting proper conduct.

Socialism

Socialism is an economic and governmental system based on public ownership of the means of production and exchange. Karl Marx once described socialism as a transitional stage of society between capitalism and communism. In a capitalist system, the means of production and most property are privately owned; in a communist system, property is controlled by the state in common for all the people. In the ultimate communist country, justice is achieved by having participants determine their own needs and take what is appropriate from the common product of society. Marx's dictum was, "From each according to his ability, to each according to his needs." Some aspects of socialism have been combined with democracy, as in Sweden. Communist countries like Cuba are ruled by one party, the Communist party.

In one of the most dramatic transformations in recent times, Russia, its sister republics, and its former European satellites abandoned communism and are attempting to establish free markets. These countries had previously rejected capitalism, opting for state ownership and centralized government planning of the economy. But by the end of the twentieth century, the disparities in economic well-being between capitalist and communist nations produced a tide of political and economic reform that left communism intact in only a few countries, such as Cuba and China.

American socialists—of whom there are only a few prominent examples—favor a greatly expanded role for the government. They would nationalize certain industries, institute a public jobs program so that all who want work would be put to work, place a much steeper tax burden on the wealthy, and drastically cut defense spending.[18] Most of the democracies of Western Europe are more influenced by socialist ideas than we are in the United States, but they remain, like the United States, largely market economies. Many countries appear to be turning to market solutions for problems once assumed to be the responsibility of government. Some of the most important debates of the next century are going to be about what is the proper role of government and what the market can do better.[19]

Debates about communist expansionism are increasingly dated and irrelevant in American politics. There is little fear today that the United States will become communist, and the communist threat around the world is greatly diminished. But people of varying ideologies do indeed worry about whether the United States is maintaining adequate military strength or losing ground in the global economy.

Environmentalism

Preoccupation with the environment and related matters is **environmentalism,** an ideology that has taken root in several democracies in recent decades. The so-called "Green movement" has elected members of parliament in Finland, Germany,

socialism

An economic and governmental system based on public ownership of the means of production and exchange.

environmentalism

An ideology that is dominated by concern for the environment but also promotes grass-roots democracy, social justice, equal opportunity, nonviolence, respect for diversity, and feminism.

Switzerland, Sweden, Luxembourg, Austria, and the Netherlands and is part of the liberal-left coalition governing Germany today. In the United States, the Green party emphasizes such values as grass-roots democracy, social justice, equal opportunity, nonviolence, respect for diversity, and feminism. In these areas environmentalism is little different from liberalism, but it is in their emphasis on ecology and the environment that "greens" are distinct.

The website of the U.S. Green party says, "We must practice agriculture which replenishes the soil; move to an energy-efficient economy; and live in ways that respect the integrity of natural systems."[20] Ralph Nader, the presidential standard-bearer for the Green party in 2000, enhanced the visibility of the party but still won less than 3 percent of the vote.

Libertarianism

Libertarianism is an ideology that cherishes individual liberty and insists on sharply limited government. It carries some overtones of anarchism, of the classical English liberalism of the past, and of a 1930s-style conservatism. The Libertarian party has gained a small following among people who believe that both liberals and conservatives lack consistency in their attitude toward the power of the national government.

Harry Browne, Libertarian candidate for president in 1996 and 2000, was on the ballot in all 50 states but received less than 1 percent of the total vote.

Libertarians preach opposition to just about all government programs. They favor massive cuts in government spending and an end to the Federal Bureau of Investigation, the Central Intelligence Agency, and most regulatory commissions. They oppose participation in the United Nations and favor a defense establishment that would defend the United States only if directly attacked. They oppose *all* government regulation, including, for example, mandatory seat-belt and helmet laws. Unlike conservatives, libertarians would repeal laws that regulate personal morality, including abortion, pornography, prostitution, and recreational drugs.

A Libertarian party candidate for president has been on the ballot in all 50 states in recent presidential elections, although never obtaining more than 1 percent of the vote. The Libertarian candidate for president in 2000, Harry Browne, ran on a platform that emphasized freedom from government. The 2000 Libertarian platform was committed to a smaller government, limited by the Constitution's specifications, and proposed immediate and complete removal of the federal government from education, energy, regulation, crime control, welfare, housing, transportation, health care, and agriculture; repeal of the income tax and all other direct taxes; decriminalization of drugs and pardons for prisoners convicted of nonviolent drug offenses; and withdrawal of overseas military forces. Libertarian positions are rarely timid; at the very least, they prompt intriguing political debates.[21]

A Word of Caution

Political labels have different meanings across national boundaries as well as over time. To be a liberal in certain European nations is to be on the right; to be a liberal in the United States is to be on the left. In recent elections, the term "liberal"—which back in Franklin Roosevelt's day had been popular—became "the L-word," a label most politicians sought to avoid.

But liberalism is more than a label. On big questions—such as the role of government in the economy, in promoting equality of opportunity, and in regulating the behavior of individuals or businesses—real differences separate conservative and liberal groups. This does not mean, however, that people who are conservative in one area are necessarily conservative in another, or that liberals always hold similar views.

It is important to appreciate that ideology both causes events and is affected by them. Just as the Great Depression resulted in a tidal wave of ideological change, so did our involvement in World War II, Korea, and Vietnam, each in its own way. World War II, with its positive example of how government can work to defend freedom, strengthened positive views about the role of the national government. The Vietnam War probably had the opposite effect, producing disillusionment with government.

libertarianism

An ideology that cherishes individual liberty and insists on a sharply limited government, promoting a free-market economy, a noninterventionist foreign policy, and an absence of regulation in the moral and social spheres.

> Conservatives are troubled by the inability of many individuals to accept the responsibility that living independently and morally in a free society entails.

CONSERVATIVE MANIFESTO

Pete DuPont

Former governor of Delaware and Republican presidential candidate Pete DuPont is a strong advocate for what he calls "contemporary conservatism." According to DuPont, conservatives are troubled by the inability of many individuals to accept the responsibility that living independently and morally in a free society entails.

Pointing to the Declaration of Independence, which states that "that all men are created equal, that they are endowed by their creator with certain unalienable rights," DuPont asserts that people receive their rights from God rather than from government. The problem is that today's government has unnecessarily restricted rights and freedoms by regulating the economy and replacing private initiative with publicly financed social programs. These actions have encouraged many individuals to abandon responsibility for their own welfare in favor of dependence upon government programs. DuPont asserts that, "Even in America, amidst the greatest success of political and economic freedom in the history of the world, generations of central social and economic planning have finally fostered a new culture—a culture of dependency, rampant crime, single parenthood, broken families, tribal-like group competition, and a turn away from personal responsibility."

Human beings, in the conservative view, are competitive and individualistic. Like many conservatives, DuPont applauds the open marketplace in which people can establish their own businesses and compete freely to build enterprises that contribute to the general welfare of society. Conservatives enjoy the exhilaration of risk and competition. They find personal dignity in facing adversity with courage and overcoming obstacles with determination. They find personal irresponsibility and immorality to be the two most negative features of human nature. Irresponsible people rely on government or private handouts or resort to crime to meet their needs; immoral people have extramarital affairs and desert their families in their pursuit of pleasure.

What, then, is the conservative vision of the good society? DuPont repeatedly emphasizes strength as he identifies explicit principles for creating a prosperous and just society. Conservatives would: (1) strengthen our national defense by increasing the military forces and improving technology; (2) strengthen law enforcement by building more prisons, reinvigorating drug enforcement programs, and reaffirming the public's right to own firearms; (3) strengthen our economy by reducing taxes, minimizing government regulation of business, abolishing affirmative action programs, and paring down social programs such as health and welfare subsidies; (4) strengthen families by making divorce and abortion more difficult and allowing families to select the schools their children will attend.)★

SOURCE: "Conservative Manifesto," *National Review* 46, March 21, 1994, pp. 32-38.

DEBATE

WHY I'M STILL LEFT

Mitchell Cohen

Mitchell Cohen, an editor of *Dissent* magazine, offers a different vision: one of American liberalism (or "social democracy," as he calls it). He explains that he uses the word "left" in order to identify with three "entwined" ideas: "liberty, equality, and solidarity." Conservatives, he says, have distorted what it means to be "liberal" or "left" and have tried to give these words negative connotations. Cohen maintains that at the heart of leftist values are democracy and social justice. This does not mean creating a utopia in which all people are forced to be equal. It does, however, include "siding with working people and the dispossessed, especially against private economic power." He hopes to convince people that "democracy ought to pervade socioeconomic in addition to political domains of life so that. . .the conditions for the freedom of one would be the conditions for the freedom of all."

Cohen insists that when conservatives claim that all people are equally free to pursue opportunity in our society, this is a myth. Citizens don't begin life at the same starting place. Our "free market" economy is in fact highly undemocratic because of the power of corporations and the advantages enjoyed by the upper social strata. People are not actually born with equal resources. We are born into a

world in which some possess considerable advantages and many others are at a disadvantage. Cohen writes (following philosopher John Rawls) that "Our parents are a matter of chance, not choice. Unless you can be said to have rated your progenitors, why should advantages or disabilities that attend accidents of birth be translated into social privileges?" He points to national income data that indicates that the top 20 percent of the population has nine times as much wealth as the bottom 20 percent. This imbalance, he believes, is inherently unjust.

Cohen also thinks that conservatives are too one-sided when they say that people are competitive, "rugged individualists" by nature. Cohen argues that we are "social individuals" who want freedom, but who also feel solidarity with other human beings. So while Cohen believes markets are an important part of economic life, he also contends that they need to be regulated on behalf of broader human values. Cohen advocates an "equality-friendly society" and "social citizenship." He wants to ensure equal access to education and health care and to restrain the power of large corporations. According to Cohen, a healthy political democracy requires economic democracy.) ★

SOURCE: Mitchell Cohen, "Why I'm Still Left," *Dissent* 44 (Spring 1997).

> We are "social individuals" who want freedom, but who also feel solidarity with other human beings.

For further information about this debate, go to **www.prenhall.com/burns** *and click on the Debate Icon in Chapter 4.*

The antigovernment sentiment in recent presidential elections is undoubtedly related to Vietnam, the Watergate scandal, and allegations of sexual misconduct by political leaders.

IDEOLOGY AND THE AMERICAN PEOPLE

Ideological controversy today centers on how we can improve schools, encourage a stronger work ethic, and stop the flow of drugs into the country; whether to permit openly gay people into the military or sanction same-sex marriages; and the best ways to instill moral values, build character, and encourage cohesive and lasting families.

Despite the twists and turns of American politics, the distribution of ideology in the nation has been remarkably consistent (see Figure 4–1). Conservatives outnumber liberals, but the proportion of conservatives did not increase substantially with the decisive Republican presidential victories of the 1980s or congressional victories of the 1990s.

Another important fact about ideology in the United States is that few people see themselves as extremists. In 2000 only 2 percent of the population saw themselves as extreme conservatives, and the same percent saw themselves as extreme liberals (see Figure 4–2). These percentages have changed very little over time. The tendency toward muted ideology is also demonstrated by the fact more people consider themselves *slightly* liberal or *slightly* conservative than liberal or conservative. Despite claims by ideological factions in both parties to move to the right or move to the left, there are simply more votes in the middle.[22]

Both major parties targeted moderate or centrist voters in the 2000 presidential election, as reflected in the stands of the candidates on key issues, including their efforts to minimize ideological battles at the conventions. Governor Tommy Thompson of Wisconsin, who chaired the Republican Platform Committee, stated that their more conservative partisans did not push their issues because "they want to win."[23] Democrats adopted a similar strategy. For example, they stressed the need to limit violence and sexuality in video games sold to children. This move to the center by both parties does not mean that there are not liberal and conservative wings in both parties, with the liberal wing more powerful in the Democratic party and the conservative wing more powerful in the Republican party. (We analyze party identification in greater detail in Chapter 7.)

For those who have a liberal or conservative preference, ideology provides a lens through which to view politics. It helps simplify the complexities of politics,

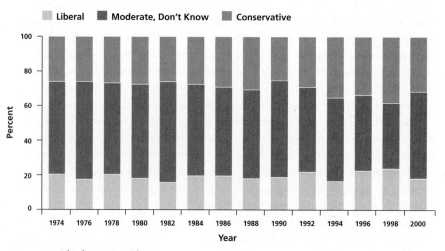

FIGURE 4–1 Ideology over Time

SOURCE: Center for Political Studies, University of Michigan, National Election Study Cumulative Data File, 1952–1992; *1994, 1996, 1998, and 2000 National Election Study*.

policies, personalities, and programs. An ideology may be an accurate or an inaccurate description of reality, yet it is still the way a person thinks about people, power, and society. However, most Americans do not organize their attitudes systematically. A voter may want increased spending for defense but vote for the party that is for reducing defense spending because he or she has always voted for that party or prefers its stand on the environment. Or a person may favor tax cuts and balancing the budget while at the same time be unwilling to see government programs cut back substantially.

Consistency among various attitudes and opinions is often relatively low. Much of the time people view political issues as isolated matters and do not apply an overall standard of performance in evaluating parties or candidates. Indeed, many citizens find it difficult to relate what happens in one policy situation to what happens in another. This problem becomes worse as government gets into more and more policy areas. Hence, many people, not surprisingly, have difficulty finding candidates who reflect their ideological preferences across a range of issues.

The absence of widespread and solidified liberal and conservative positions in the United States makes for politics and policy-making processes that are markedly different from those in many European and other nations. Policy making in this country is characterized more by coalitions of the moment than by fixed alignments that pit one set of ideologies against another. Our politics is marked more by moderation, pragmatism, and accommodation than by a prolonged battle among two, three, or more competing philosophies of government. Elsewhere, especially in countries where a strong Socialist or Christian Democratic party exists, things are different.

This does not, however, mean that policies or ideas are not elements in American politics. There has been, for instance, a shift to strongly partisan and ideological voting in the House of Representatives. Part of the explanation for the increasing importance of ideology in Congress is Republican gains in the South, with remaining southern Democrats becoming more liberal; in other parts of the country where moderate Republicans were once successful, liberal Democrats now hold many seats.

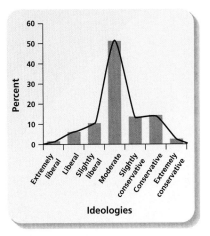

FIGURE 4–2 Ideology Curve

Source: Center for Political Studies, University of Michigan, *2000 National Election Study*.

IDEOLOGY AND TOLERANCE

Is there a connection between the ideologies of liberalism and conservatism and support for civil liberties and tolerance for racial minorities? Some political scientists assert that conservatives are generally less tolerant than liberals. This view is stoutly contested by conservatives, who have charged liberals with trying to impose a "politically correct" position on universities and the media. Liberals are usually more tolerant of dissent and the expression of unorthodox opinions. However, liberals, too, can be intolerant—of anti-abortion forces, for example, or the National Rifle Association, or the views of Pat Robertson.

Most liberals are strongly opposed to crime and lawbreaking, yet they are as concerned about the roots or causes of crime as they are about the punishment of criminals. Perhaps for this reason, liberals exhibit somewhat greater concern than conservatives for the rights of the accused and are more willing to expand the rights of due process. Conservatives usually take a harder line and, in recent years, have won widespread popular support for their greater concern for the victims of crime than for the rights of the accused.

Such differences are most evident in the responses of liberals and conservatives to questions of civil rights and civil liberties. In the area of free speech, conservatives are usually seen as less willing to permit speech that is out of the political or cultural mainstream. Perhaps conservatives are less tolerant because those who claim to be exercising the right of free speech often attack established values. Liberals favor limiting speech in areas like cigarette advertising or campaign spending.[24]

Conservatives believe that the United States has become too permissive. Many conservatives, especially in the New or Religious Right, are highly critical of homosexuals, drug users, prostitutes, unwed mothers, and pornographers. They worry about what they claim has been a decline in moral standards and, interestingly, call on government to help reverse these trends. Liberals, on the other hand, generally accept nonconformity in conduct and opinion as an inescapable by-product of freedom.[25] In this regard, liberals are like libertarians.

Ideologies have consequences. It is these sharp cleavages in political thinking that stir opposing interest groups into action. Groups such as the Christian Coalition, the American Civil Liberties Union, Amnesty International, Mothers Against Drunk Driving, Queer Nation, and countless others promote their views of what is politically desirable. It is also these differences in ideological perspectives that reinforce party loyalties and divide us at election time. Policy fights in Congress, between Congress and the White House, and during judicial confirmation hearings also have their roots in our uneasily coexisting ideological values.

Our hard-earned rights and liberties are never entirely safeguarded; they are fragile and are shaped by the political, economic, and social climate of the day. In later chapters we examine the interest groups and political parties that are battling to advance their values and compete in the American political culture. But before turning to those topics, we examine the social and economic diversity of the American political landscape in Chapter 5 and see why agreement on shared democratic values is all the more remarkable.

‣■■

POLITICS ONLINE

What's My Ideology?

Ideology is typically arrayed on a continuum from left to right, liberal to conservative. As we have noted in this chapter, there are several different dimensions on which people can classify themselves: economic policy, civil rights and liberties, foreign and defense policy, and lifestyle issues. Most people are moderate in their overall positions, and some do not even think in these terms.

At the www.prenticehall.com/burns site for this chapter, we have prepared a set of questions for you to answer that will give you a sense of your ideology for each of the four issue dimensions. Depending on which issue dimension you think most important, the exercise will also calculate an overall score for you. As you complete the self-assessment, do not hesitate to evaluate the extent to which the items capture the liberal/conservative concept.

Once you have used the questions to classify yourself, you may want to read more about different ideological perspectives. For example, libertarians may be a group you want to know more about; a useful website for to learn more about libertarians is:
www.lp.org.

There are a host of websites that advocate conservative positions; some you might find interesting include:
www.conservativedigest.net and ww.aei.org.

For a more liberal perspective, you can go to:
www.prospect.org or www.trunleft.com/ligeral.html.

■■■

SUMMARY

1. The United States, like every other nation or society, has a distinctive political culture. It consists of a widely held set of fundamental political values and accepted processes and institutions that help us manage conflict and resolve problems. In the United States, there is, at least in the abstract, respect for the Constitution, the Bill of Rights, a two-party system, and the right to elect officials on the basis of majority rule. Our belief in social equality has fostered acceptance of the

notion that government should guarantee equality of opportunity through programs like education and job training.

2. Americans share a widespread commitment to classical liberalism, which embraces the importance of individual liberty, equality, individualism, power to the people, private property, limited government, nationalism, optimism, idealism, the democratic consensus, and justice and the rule of law. They also believe that the American Dream should be something we can all pursue.

3. American political values have been affected by the industrial transformation, the development of large corporations and other large institutions, the Great Depression, and a global economy.

4. The sources of the American political culture include the family, schools, religious and civic organizations, the mass media, and political activities.

5. Two broad schools of thought are important in American politics today: liberalism, a belief in the positive uses of government to bring about justice and equality of opportunity; and conservatism, a belief that limited government ensures order, competitive markets, and personal opportunity. Socialism, environmentalism, and libertarianism also attract a following in America.

6. Most Americans are nonideological and are guided primarily by moderate pragmatism. Few Americans are extremists.

7. Ideological orientation has a bearing on how tolerant we are of the views and conduct of others. Liberals tend to be more permissive, whereas conservatives generally favor tradition, stability, and greater levels of "law and order." These differences have consequences for electoral contests and policy development in our political system.

KEY TERMS

social capital 74
political culture 74
natural rights 74
democratic consensus 75

majority rule 75
popular sovereignty 75
American Dream 79
capitalism 79

monopolies 79
antitrust legislation 79
ideology 81
liberalism 82

conservatism 84
socialism 86
environmentalism 86
libertarianism 87

FURTHER READING

WILLIAM F. BUCKLEY AND CHARLES R. KESLER, *Keeping the Tablets: Modern American Conservative Thought* (Harper & Row, 1988).

JAMES W. CEASER, *Reconstructing America: The Symbol of America in Modern Thought* (Yale University Press, 1997).

E. J. DIONNE, JR., *They Only Look Dead: Why Progressives Will Dominate the Next Political Era* (Simon & Schuster, 1996).

JOHN EHRMAN, *The Rise of Neoconservatism: Intellectuals and Foreign Affairs, 1945–1994* (Yale University Press, 1995).

JEAN BETHKE ELSHTAIN, *Democracy on Trial* (Basic Books, 1995).

DAVID FRUM, *What's Right: The New Conservative Majority and the Remaking of America* (Basic Books, 1996).

AMY GUTMANN AND DENNIS THOMPSON, *Democracy and Disagreement: Why Moral Conflict Cannot Be Avoided in Politics, and What Should Be Done About It* (Harvard University Press, 1996).

LOUIS HARTZ, *The Liberal Tradition in America* (Harcourt Brace, 1955).

LAWRENCE E. HARRISON AND SAMUEL P. HARRINGTON, EDS., *Culture Matters: How Values Shape Human Progress* (Basic Books, 2000).

IRVING KRISTOL, *Neoconservatism: The Autobiography of an Idea* (Free Press, 1995).

HERBERT MCCLOSKY AND JOHN ZALLER, *The American Ethos: Public Attitudes Toward Capitalism and Democracy* (Harvard University Press, 1984).

CHARLES MURRAY, *What It Means to Be a Libertarian: A Personal Interpretation* (Broadway Books, 1997).

JOHN J. SCHWARZMANTEL, *The Age of Ideology: Political Ideologies from the American Revolution to Post-Modern Times* (New York University Press, 1998).

ALEXIS DETOCQUEVILLE, *Democracy in America* (Knopf reprint, 1994).

GARRY WILLS, *A Necessary Evil: A History of American Distrust of Government* (Simon & Schuster, 1999).

J. HARRY WRAY, *Sense and Nonsense: American Culture and Politics* (Prentice Hall, 2001).

DANIEL YERGIN AND JOSEPH STAINSLAW, *The Commanding Heights: The Battle Between Government and the Marketplace That Is Remaking the Modern World* (Simon & Schuster, 1998).

5

THE AMERICAN POLITICAL LANDSCAPE

THE UNITED STATES IS A NATION OF IMMIGRANTS. WE CELEBRATE OUR IMMIGRANT PAST AND PROUDLY RECITE THE WORDS OF EMMA LAZARUS INSCRIBED AT THE BASE of the Statue of Liberty: "Give me your tired, your poor, your huddled masses yearning to breath free." And yet our borders are not open to all who wish to come here, and immigration is limited, with specific numbers of immigrants allowed to enter from each country each year. Hundreds of thousands avoid these limitations by crossing our borders illegally, seeking employment, refuge, and freedom.

The number of these illegal immigrants, as well as U.S. immigration policy generally, were the focus of television and newspaper ads in the 2000 Iowa caucuses, the South Carolina presidential primary, and some congressional contests. One group, the Federation for American Immigration Reform (FAIR), ran a television commercial about Storm Lake, Iowa, in the weeks leading up to the Iowa caucuses in January 2000. The commercial claimed that rising crime rates, increased costs for bilingual education, and increased public health care costs could be traced to the rise in immigrants who work in the town's meat-packing plants. FAIR was one of five anti-immigration groups that joined together in mounting an advertising campaign in 2000 on problems immigrants pose for our country. But the anti-immigration groups did not have much impact in the Iowa caucuses, in part because Iowa faces a net out-migration of population and needs the immigrants to fill jobs like the meat-packing jobs in Storm Lake. Elected officials in Iowa came out against the anti-immigration groups and strongly criticized the Storm Lake ad. Presidential candidates opposed the limits on immigration proposed. For instance, George W. Bush stated, "Family values don't stop at the Rio Grande. My administration will reform the INS, and make it worthy of a nation of immigrants."[1]

Disagreements about admission of aliens into this country and about their rights and privileges have been featured in political campaigns for the last two hundred years. In 1994 Californians passed a controversial ballot initiative, Proposition 187, restricting public services to illegal immigrants. Even though a federal judge found portions of the proposition unconstitutional, the furor about Proposition 187 demonstrated the intense feelings on both sides of the issue, especially in a border state like California.

Albert Einstein once said few people are capable of expressing opinions that differ much from the prejudices of their social upbringing.[2] This **ethnocentrism**— selective perception based on individual background, attitudes, and biases—is not uncommon, even among college students, who often assume that others share their

CHAPTERMEDIA

POLITICS ONLINE
Who Are My Neighbors?
www.prenhall.com/burns

POLISIM
The Great American Divide
www.prenhall.com/burns

How should people be counted?

The Census Bureau, which conducts the once-a-decade count of all persons in the United States, proposed using random sampling rather than attempting to count all households in the 2000 census. Republicans opposed sampling because they considered it unreliable. The proposed sample approach would contact 90 percent of the households in a census tract consisting of roughly 1,700 individuals. The bureau would then check the accuracy of the sample by surveying 750,000 households throughout the nation and adjusting the final total accordingly.

The sample approach responds to complaints about the flawed 1990 census, which cost $2.6 billion (a 400 percent increase over the cost of the 1980 census) and failed to account for 10 million people and double-counted 6 million others, according to a study by the National Academy of Sciences. Do you think that sampling is a fair and effective solution?

ethnocentrism

Selective perception based on individual background, attitudes, and biases that leads one to believe in the superiority of one's nation or ethnic group.

political socialization

The process by which we develop our political attitudes, values, and beliefs.

demographics

The study of the characteristics of populations.

political predisposition

A characteristic of individuals that is predictive of political behavior.

reinforcing cleavages

Divisions within society that reinforce one another, making groups more homogeneous or similar.

cross-cutting cleavages

Divisions within society that cut across demographic categories to produce groups more heterogeneous or different.

economic opportunities, social attitudes, sense of civic responsibility, and self-confidence. In this chapter we consider to what extent our social environment explains, or at least shapes, our opinions and prejudices. We also look at our diversity as Americans and the implications of geographic, social, and economic divisions for politics and government. Specifically, this chapter explores the effects of regional or state identity on political perspectives; the implications of differences in race, ethnicity, gender, family structure, religion, wealth and income, occupation, and social class for opinions and voting choices; and the relationship between age and education and political participation.

A LAND OF DIVERSITY

Most nations consist of groups of people who have lived together for hundreds of years and who speak the same language, hold the same concept of deity, and share a common history. Most Japanese citizens are Japanese in the fullest sense of the word, and it is generally the same in Germany, Sweden, Saudi Arabia, China, and France. The United States is different. We have attracted the poor and oppressed, the adventurous and the talented, from all over the world, and we have been more open to accepting these people than have other nations.

One reason so many people want to come to the United States is that it holds a promise of religious, political, and economic freedom. It is also a place of opportunity for the enterprising. Our economic system has provided widespread (but not universal) opportunity for individuals to improve their economic standing. The American Dream—that everyone can "make it"—is widely shared.

Some elements of our diversity have political significance. For example, sectional differences persist between the South and the rest of the country. Many Americans retain an identity with the native land of their ancestors, even after three or four generations. Holding onto such differences is often the result of socialization in families, churches, and other closely knit groups. **Political socialization** is the process by which parents and others teach children about political values, beliefs, and attitudes. This teaching occurs in the home, on the playground, in school, and in the neighborhood. In addition to fostering group identities, political socialization strongly influences how individuals see politics and which political party they prefer. Because where we live and who we are in terms of our age, education, religion, and occupation affect how we vote, many who study voting and make predictions about it do so in terms of these and other factors, referred to as **demographics**. A **political predisposition** is a characteristic of individuals that is predictive of political behavior. Although demographics can be important, there are large individual differences within socioeconomic and demographic categories.

When social and economic differences coincide, they reinforce each other and make the differences between groups more important. Social scientists call these differences **reinforcing cleavages**; where they occur, political conflict becomes more intense and there is greater polarization in society. In Italy, for example, the regional divide between North and South is reinforced by the tendency of the North to lean toward the Socialist or Communist parties and the South to be Christian Democratic and Catholic in orientation. Nations can also have **cross-cutting cleavages**, instances where differences do not reinforce each other. To illustrate, if all the rich individuals in a society are of one religion and the poor another, we would have reinforcing cleavages, and political conflict would be intensified. But if there are both rich and poor in all religions, and if people sometimes vote on the basis of their religion and sometimes on the basis of their wealth, then we would say the divisions are cross-cutting. American diversity has generally been more of the cross-cutting type than the reinforcing type, lessening political conflict because individuals have multiple allegiances.

In some societies, politics centers largely upon passions over economic and religious differences. Although socioeconomic differences are important to understanding American government and politics, they are not as central to the form and structure of politics as religion is in Bosnia or tribal identity in Rwanda. In Northern Ireland, the religious differences between Catholics and Protestants produced centuries of violent division that is yet to be resolved.

Despite the fact that America has been more hospitable to people from different religions, classes, or races than almost any other nation in the world, we often prefer to associate only with people "like us" and are suspicious of people "like them." From hostility toward different religions in the early colonies, to the anti-immigration movements of the late 1800s and early 1900s, to the various anti-immigration and anti–civil rights ballot initiatives of the 1990s, Americans have exhibited ethnocentrism, and for much of our history, minorities have been excluded from full participation in American political and economic life.

Geography and National Identity

The United States is a geographically large and historically isolated country. The French commentator Alexis de Tocqueville observed in 1835 that the country had no major political or economic powers on its borders "and consequently no great wars, financial crises, invasions, or conquests to fear."[3] Geographic isolation from the major powers of the world during our government's formative period helps explain American politics. The Atlantic Ocean served as a barrier to foreign meddling, giving us time to establish our political tradition and develop our economy. The western frontier provided room to grow and avoid some of the social and political tensions that Europe experienced. Two great oceans also reinforced our sense of isolation from Europe and foreign alliances. This reluctance to become involved in foreign wars and controversies still arises in debates over foreign policy.

In our entire history we have fought only one foreign enemy on our own soil—England in the War of 1812. (The war against Mexico of 1846–48 was fought almost entirely on Mexican land, some of which later became American land as a result of the war. The only other war fought on our soil was, of course, the Civil War.) In contrast, Poland has been invaded repeatedly and was partitioned by Austria, Prussia, and Russia in the eighteenth century and by Nazi Germany and the Soviet Union in the twentieth century. The difference is explained largely by location: Poland was surrounded by Europe's great powers. Had the United States been closer to Europe, it might have been overrun like

Part of our national identity is bound up with the physical isolation and hardship many families endured as pioneers.

Thinking It Through . . .

The battle over sampling was not so much about *how* to count as *whom* to count. The proposed sampling would have produced a more accurate count of inner-city Hispanics and African Americans—the most difficult to count. This approach would likely have resulted in a greater representation for Hispanics and African Americans in state legislatures and the U.S. House of Representatives. A more complete count of minorities could also mean that the Republican party could lose a few seats in the House to Democrats, which is why Republicans generally opposed the sampling approach while Democrats favored it. The constitutionality of sampling was also disputed, as the Constitution calls for an "actual enumeration" of the people. Democrats are quick to point out that under three presidents—Jimmy Carter, George Bush, and Bill Clinton—the Justice Department concluded that sampling is legal.

In 1998, in order to get a ruling on the constitutionality of sampling, then Speaker Newt Gingrich filed suit on behalf of the House of Representatives in the District Court of the Eastern District of Virginia and District Court of the District of Columbia. Both courts declared that sampling violated the Census Act 13 as amended in 1976. In January 1999 the Supreme Court upheld that decision and ordered an actual count.[*] The Census Bureau is supplementing its actual count with sampling in 2000, but the reapportionment of the House of Representatives will be based on the traditional mode of counting persons.

Source: Steven A. Holmes, "Political Interests Arouse Raging Debate on Census," *The New York Times*, April 12, 1998, p. 1; Holmes, "Gingrich Files Suit to Prevent Use of Sampling in 2000 Census," *The New York Times*, February 22, 1998, p. 21.

*Department of Commerce et al v United States House of Representatives et al, 119 S. Ct 765, January 1999.

Evidence of the persistent racial divide in this country was brought out by the dispute over the flag of the Confederacy (bottom flag) flying over the South Carolina capitol building. After bitter debate between descendents of slave-owning families and descendents of slaves, the flag was relocated near a small statue on the capitol grounds.

Poland, and our Constitution and institutions repeatedly changed or eliminated to suit the victorious invaders. Having powerful and aggressive neighbors makes it difficult for relatively weak nations to nurture democracy.

The United States is a large country. Its land mass exceeds that of all but three nations in the world. In contrast, India has a population more than three times larger than that of the United States on a land mass one-third the size. Geographic space gave the expanding population of the United States room to spread out. This possibility meant that some of the political conflicts arising from religion, social class, and national origin were diffused because groups could isolate themselves from one another. (See James Madison, *The Federalist*, No. 10, in the Appendix, for the "large republic" idea.) Moreover, the large and accessible land mass helped foster the perspective that the United States had a **manifest destiny** to be a continental nation reaching from the Atlantic to the Pacific oceans. This notion that the United States was "destined" to expand across the continent was used to justify taking land occupied by Native Americans and Mexicans, especially the land acquired following victory in the Mexican-American War.

The United States is also a land of abundant natural resources. We have rich farmland, which not only feeds our population but makes us the largest exporter of food in the world.[4] We are rich in such natural resources as coal, iron, uranium, and precious metals. All these resources enhance economic growth, provide jobs, and stabilize government. "The physical causes, unconnected with laws, which can lead to prosperity are more numerous in America than in any other country at any other time in history," observed Alexis de Tocqueville. "In the United States not legislation alone is democratic, for Nature herself seems to work for the people."

Geography also helps explain our diversity. Parts of the United States are wonderfully suited to agriculture, others to mining or ranching, and still others to shipping. These differences produce different regional economic concerns, which in turn influence politics. For instance, a person from the agricultural heartland may have a perception of foreign trade different from that of an automobile worker in Detroit. But if that automobile worker is African American, this fact may be more important to her politics than what she does or where she lives. To understand American politics, we must appreciate these differences and their relative importance.

Sectional Differences

Unlike many other countries, geography in the United States does *not* define an ethnic or religious division. All the Serbs in the United States do not live in one place, all French-speaking Catholics in another, and all German immigrants in another. Sectional differences in the United States are primarily geographic, not ethnic or religious.

The most distinct section of the United States remains the South, although the South's differences are diminishing. From the beginning of the Republic, the agricultural South differed from the North, where commerce and manufacturing were more significant. But the most important difference between the regions was the institution of slavery. Northern opposition to slavery, which grew increasingly intense by the middle of the nineteenth century, reinforced the sectional economic interests. The eleven Confederate states, by virtue of their decision to secede from the Union, reinforced a common political identity, and after the Civil War sectional differences were strengthened by the policy of Reconstruction and the problems of race relations.

Sectional differences have moderated in the last few decades. The South is becoming less distinct from the rest of the United States. A large in-migration has diminished the sense of regional identity, and the South has undergone tremendous economic change. The civil rights revolution gave African Americans the right to vote, opened up new educational opportunities, and helped to integrate the South into the national economy. African Americans still lag behind whites in voter registration, but the gap is now no wider in the South than elsewhere and is explained more by differences in education than by race.[5] In economic terms, the South, as a

manifest destiny
A notion held by nineteenth-century Americans that the United States was destined to rule the continent, from the Atlantic to the Pacific oceans.

region, still falls below the rest of the country in per capita income and education, but much less so than 50 years ago. The religious and moral conservatism of the South remains notable.

Until the 1970s, political observers spoke of the "solid South"—a region that voted for Democrats at all levels. The reason for the connection between the South and Democrats is simple: "The Civil War made the Democratic party the party of the South, and the Republican party, the party of the North."[6] The Democratic "solid South" was to remain a fixture of American politics for more than a century. Since 1968 that has changed dramatically, first at the presidential level and increasingly at the state and local levels. As two respected observers of the region comment, "The fall of the South as an assured stronghold of the Democratic party in presidential elections is one of the most significant developments in modern American politics."[7] The political alignment has shifted as African Americans have been enfranchised and become overwhelmingly Democrats, and many whites have become Republicans. In 1992 and 1996, even with two southerners (Bill Clinton and Al Gore) on the ticket, Democrats won only four of the eleven former Confederate states. In 2000, George W. Bush carried all 11 southern states, including Al Gore's home state of Tennessee.

What explains this dramatic reversal? Part of the explanation is that the Democrats' advocacy of aggressive action on civil rights in the 1960s alienated some southern whites. In addition, the debate within the Democratic party over Vietnam policy in the late 1960s and 1970s was "perceived by many southern voters as unpatriotic."[8] Republican presidential candidates have more recently emphasized family values, opposition to taxes, and law-and-order issues that appeal to conservative southern voters.

Republican success at the presidential level was slow to affect contests for Congress and state legislatures. Yet in recent years, Republicans had more than half of southern votes for the U.S. House of Representatives (see Table 5–1), and by 2000 they had seven of the eleven governorships in the former Confederate states. In the state legislatures of several southern states, remnants of the old "solid South" remain, but Republicans have made major inroads, and politics in the region is now much more competitive.

Another sectional division is the *sun belt*—the eleven former Confederate states plus New Mexico, Arizona, and the southern half of California. Sun belt states are growing much more rapidly than the rest of the country. Population shifts during the 1990s meant these states gained 12 seats in the House of Representatives after the 2000 census: Arizona, California, Colorado, Florida, Georgia, Nevada, North Carolina, and Texas.[9] Moreover, population growth in the South and West is occurring in different age groups. In the South, growth is largest among those over 65; in the West, it is younger persons who provide the growth. Sun belt states have also experienced greater economic growth as industries headed south and southwest, where land is cheaper and more abundant, and where labor is cheaper as well (see Figure 5–1).

State and Local Identity

Different states have different political traditions. Mention Wyoming, Mississippi, Oregon, New York, or Kansas, and it brings to mind a certain type of politics. The same is true for many other states. Like most stereotypes, these images are often misleading, yet they reflect the fact that there is a sense of identity to states as political units that goes beyond demographic characteristics and is supported by recent

TABLE 5–1 Voting Patterns in the Eleven Former Confederate States

Republican for President

1980	50%
1984	62
1988	59
1992	43
1996	46
2000	54

Republican Vote for U.S. Representatives

1980	40%
1982	39
1984	42
1986	41
1988	42
1990	43
1992	48
1994	58
1996	53*
1998	58
2000	53

Republican Share of State Legislators

	House	Senate
1980	18%	17%
1982	22	14
1984	23	17
1986	24	20
1988	27	24
1990	28	26
1992	31	31
1994	37	37
1996	44	44
1998	42	40
2000	44	42

SOURCE: U.S. Bureau of the Census, *Statistical Abstract of the United States*, 1993–2000. For 2000, www.cnn.com/elections/2000/results and *Congressional Quarterly Weekly Report*, November 11, 2000, pp. 2694–2703; and Todd Edwards, telephone interview, The Council of State Governments, Southern Office, 12/22/00.

*The 1996 Texas runoff elections are not included.

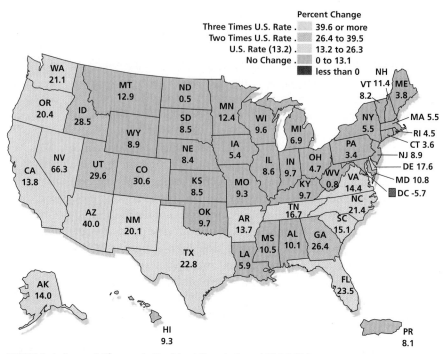

Percent Change

Three Times U.S. Rate .	39.6 or more
Two Times U.S. Rate .	26.4 to 39.5
U.S. Rate (13.2) .	13.2 to 26.3
No Change .	0 to 13.1
	less than 0

WA 21.1
MT 12.9
ND 0.5
MN 12.4
NH
VT 11.4
ME 3.8
OR 20.4
ID 28.5
SD 8.5
WI 9.6
MI 6.9
NY 5.5
MA 5.5
RI 4.5
CT 3.6
NJ 8.9
DE 17.6
MD 10.8
DC -5.7
WY 8.9
NE 8.4
IA 5.4
IL 8.6
IN 9.7
OH 4.7
PA 3.4
WV 0.8
VA 14.4
NV 66.3
UT 29.6
CO 30.6
KS 8.5
MO 9.3
KY 9.7
NC 21.4
CA 13.8
AZ 40.0
NM 20.1
OK 9.7
AR 13.7
TN 16.7
SC 15.1
MS 10.5
AL 10.1
GA 26.4
TX 22.8
LA 5.9
FL 23.5
AK 14.0
HI 9.3
PR 8.1

FIGURE 5–1 Percent Change in Resident Population, 1990-2000

SOURCE: U.S. Bureau of the Census home page: www.census.gov/population/cen2000/tab01.

empirical evidence. States have distinctive political cultures that affect public opinion and policy outcomes.[10] These state identities are reinforced by our electoral rules and other laws.

In American politics today, one state—California—stands out. More than one out of eight Americans is a Californian.[11] In terms of economic and political importance, California is in a league by itself; its 53 members of the House of Representatives exceed the total number of representatives from the smallest 20 states. Securing California's electoral votes is key for any presidential candidate.[12] In 2004, California will have 55 electoral voters.

WHERE WE LIVE

Most Americans, 80 percent of them, now live in central cities and their suburbs—what the Census Bureau calls *metropolitan areas*.[13] During the early twentieth century, the movement of population was from rural areas to central cities, but the movement since the 1950s has been from the central cities to their suburbs. Today the most urban state is California (93 percent of its population lives in cities or suburbs). Vermont is the least urban, with only 32 percent living in cities or suburbs.[14] Regionally, the West and Northeast are the most urban, the South and Midwest the most rural.

People move from cities to the suburbs for many reasons—better housing, new transportation systems that make it easier to get to work, the desire for cleaner air and safer streets. Another reason is *white flight*, the movement of whites away from the central cities so that children can avoid being bused for racial balance and attend generally better schools. White, middle-class migration to the suburbs means that American cities have become increasingly poor, increasingly African American, and increasingly Democratic. More than half of all African Americans now live in central cities, as opposed to only about one-quarter of whites, and the poverty level among blacks living in central cities is higher than whites living in the same cities.[15] The proportions are very nearly reversed for suburbs, where more than half of all white

Americans reside. Almost one-third of African Americans live in the suburbs, up from one-fifth in 1980.[16] In large cities such as Washington, D.C., Detroit, Baltimore, Atlanta, and New Orleans, the city population is now more than 50 percent African American (see Table 5–2). Hispanics constitute roughly two-thirds of the population of El Paso, Texas, Santa Ana, California, and Miami, Florida.[17]

As these population shifts occur, the tax base of cities declines because the richer people have moved to the suburbs. At the same time, service needs in the cities increase as the less-affluent remaining population must pay for education, police protection, and health care. Older suburban cities now face the same problems as the inner cities, as they too suffer from out-migration to newer cities and towns. High-tech and professional service companies frequently relocate to the suburbs to avoid traffic congestion and to be closer to the bedroom communities of their workers. Political boundaries, which define local governments and delineate responsibility for services, create understandable tensions among cities, suburbs, and rural areas. Tax revenues, legislative representation, zoning laws, and governmental priorities are hotly contested issues in most metropolitan areas.

WHO WE ARE

Sectional distinctions are less prominent today than they were a century or even a half century ago. Today Americans are more likely to define themselves by a number of characteristics, each of which may influence how they vote or think about various candidates, issues, or policies.

Race and Ethnicity

Racial and ethnic differences have always had political significance. **Race** can be defined as a grouping of human beings with common genetic characteristics. **Ethnicity** is a social division based on national origin, religion, and language, often within the same race, and includes a sense of attachment to that group. In the United States, race and ethnicity issues focus on African Americans, Asian Americans, and Hispanics.

There are more than 34 million African Americans in the United States, roughly 13 percent of the population. Asian Americans constitute just under 4 percent of the population, and Native Americans just under 1 percent. Most American Hispanics are classified as white by the Census Bureau, although Hispanics can be of any race. Hispanics are the fastest growing ethnic group; the Census Bureau estimates that there are 28 million American Hispanics, constituting over 10 percent of the population.[18] Because of differences in immigration and birth rates, whites in America will have declined to just under three-quarters of the population by the year 2050.

AFRICAN AMERICANS   Most people came to this country of their free choice in search of freedom and opportunity. African Americans came as slaves. Although they were freed as a result of the Civil War, racial divisions continue as one of the enduring issues of American politics. Until 1900, more than 90 percent of all African Americans lived in the South; by the end of the twentieth century, the figure was 54 percent.[19] Many African Americans left the South hoping to improve their lives by settling in the large cities of the Northeast, Midwest, and West. The reality for many was urban poverty. More recently, some African Americans have been returning to the South, especially to its urban areas.

In economic terms, most African Americans are worse off than most whites in the United States. African American median family income is close to $30,000, compared to more than $49,000 for whites.[20] More than one-quarter of African American incomes are below the poverty level, compared to 11 percent of whites.[21] Poverty

TABLE 5–2 Cities with Populations of 100,000 or More That Are at Least 50 Percent African American, 2000		
City	Population	Percent African American
Atlanta, GA	416,474	61.4%
Baltimore, MD	651,154	64.3
Birmingham, AL	242,820	73.5
Detroit, MI	951,270	81.6
Gary, IN	102,746	84
Jackson, MS	184,256	70.6
Memphis, TN	650,100	61.4
Newark, NJ	273,546	53.5
New Orleans, LA	484,674	67.3
Richmond, VA	197,790	57.2
Savannah, GA	131,510	57.1
Washington, D.C.	572,059	60.0

SOURCE: 2000 U.S. Census: www.census.gov/population/cen2000/phc-t6/tab05.pdf; release date April 2, 2001 Table 5.

race
A grouping of human beings with common characteristics presumed to be transmitted genetically.

ethnicity
A social division based on national origin, religion, language, and often race.

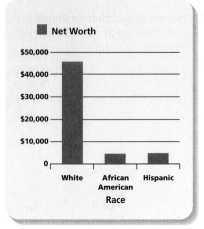

FIGURE 5–2 Wealth Distribution in the United States by Race, 1995.

SOURCE: U.S. Bureau of the Census, www.census.gov/hhes/www/wealth/wlth93f.html.

among Native Americans and Alaskan Natives has averaged 26 percent in recent years, a proportion quite similar to that found among African Americans and Hispanics.[22] However, many African Americans have recently become relatively prosperous; 21 percent of African American households have earnings of over $50,000, a proportion still only half that for whites.[23] Some African Americans, like Shaquille O'Neal and Oprah Winfrey, have risen to top earnings in their professions.

Another way to measure economic well-being is in terms of assets or wealth. *Wealth* encompasses the things of economic value (savings, stocks, property), as compared to *income*, which is how much money you make from your job or investments. As a group, African Americans' net wealth is only one-tenth that of whites, and Hispanics have only slightly more wealth than African Americans (see Figure 5–2).[24] As a result, most African Americans and Hispanics have fewer resources to fall back on in hard times, and they are less likely to have the savings to help a child pay for college.[25]

Middle-class African Americans, a growing category, are role models for the young of all races, yet their comparatively small number serves as a reminder that most African Americans remain behind whites in an economy that relies more and more on education and job skills. About 25 percent of whites graduate from college, whereas only about 15 percent of African Americans do.[26] Among 18-to-21-year-old high school graduates, 46 percent of whites go on to college, but only 33 percent of African Americans do.[27]

Finally, the African American population is much younger than the white population; the median age for whites in 1999 was 36.3, compared to 29.5 for African Americans.[28] The combination of a younger African American population, a lower level of education, and their concentration in economically hard-pressed urban areas has resulted in a much higher unemployment rate for young African Americans. Unemployment, in turn, can lead to social problems like crime, drug and alcohol abuse, and family dissolution.

African Americans had little political power until after World War II. Owing their freedom from slavery to the "party of Lincoln," most African Americans initially identified with the Republicans, but this loyalty started to change with Franklin Roosevelt, who insisted on equal treatment for African Americans in his New Deal programs.[29] After World War II, African Americans came to see the Democrats as the party of civil rights. The 1964 Republican platform position on civil rights espoused *states' rights*—then the creed of southern segregationists—in what appeared to be an effort to win the support of southern white voters. Virtually all African Americans voted for Lyndon Johnson in 1964, and in presidential elections between 1964 and 1996, their Democratic vote averaged 85 percent.[30]

Recently, African Americans have become much more important politically because of their increased voter participation and their concentrated population. African Americans constitute only .3 percent of the population in Montana and .6 percent of South Dakota, but 36 percent of Mississippi, 32 percent of Louisiana, and 30 percent of South Carolina.[31] Southern senators and representatives cannot afford to ignore the African American vote.[32] Evidence of growing African American political power is the dramatic increase in the number of African American state legislators, which rose from 168 in 1970 to 579 in 1998.[33] Mississippi has 45 African American state legislators, the most of any state. Alabama, Georgia, South Carolina, Maryland, and Louisiana all have over thirty.[34]

HISPANICS/LATINOS   Latinos are not a monolithic group, and while they share a common linguistic heritage, they often differ from one another, depending on which country they emigrated from. Cuban Americans, for instance, tend to be Republicans, while Mexican Americans and Puerto Ricans are disproportionately Democrats.[35] Latinos are politically important in a growing number of states. Nearly two-thirds of Cuban immigrants live in Florida, especially greater Miami; Puerto Rican immigrants are concentrated in or around New York City; and Mexican American immigrants in the southwest and California. Almost 11 million Hispanics live in California.[36]

Cuban Americans are more in the upper-middle income levels, while Puerto Rican Americans and Mexican Americans are generally in lower and lower-middle income categories.[37] A recent study found differences among Latinos of Mexican, Puerto Rican, and Cuban descent in partisanship, ideology, and rates of participation, but widespread support for a liberal domestic agenda, including increased spending on health care, crime and drug control, education, the environment, child services, and bilingual education.[38]

Given the overall growth of the Latino population, it is not surprising that both major parties are aggressively cultivating Latino candidates. Three Latinos, all from New Mexico, have won election to the U.S. Senate. Several Hispanics have been cabinet members: Manuel Lujan (Secretary of Interior), Laura F. Cavazos (Secretary of Education), Henry G. Cisneros (Secretary of HUD), Frederico Peña (Secretary of Transportation), and Bill Richardson (Secretary of Energy). In the George W. Bush administration, Mel Martinez is Secretary of Housing and Urban Development.

What's My Name?

The terms "Latino" and "Chicano" are preferred to "Hispanic" by some persons of Spanish-speaking descent to disassociate themselves from Spain, a colonial power against which their ancestors fought wars of independence. "Hispanic" is the term most widely used by government agencies and the media, while "Latino" appears more popular among leaders of the group. "Chicano" is often associated with the politically active Mexican American movement of the 1960s and 1970s. Most Mexican Americans, Puerto Rican Americans, and Cuban Americans prefer to be called American rather than Latino or Hispanic.

SOURCE: Richard Santillan and Carlos Munoz, Jr., "Latinos and the Democratic Party," in *The Democrats Must Lead*, ed. James MacGregor Burns, William Crotty, Lois Lovelace Duke, and Lawrence D. Longley (Westview Press, 1992), pp. 182–83; Rodolfo O. de la Garza, Louis DeSipio, F. Chris Garcia, John Garcia, and Angelo Falcon, *Latino Voices: Mexican, Puerto Rican, and Cuban Perspectives on American Politics* (Westview Press, 1992), p. 13.

ASIAN AMERICANS   Asian Americans are classified together by the Census Bureau for statistical purposes, but there are significant differences among them in culture, language, and political experience in the United States. Asian Americans include persons of Chinese, Japanese, Korean, Vietnamese, Filipino, and Thai origin, as well as persons from the Pacific Islands.

The United States is home to 10.6 million Asian Americans and Pacific Islanders, residing primarily in the western states, especially Hawaii, California, and Washington.[39] The numbers of Asian Americans grew during the 1970s and 1980s, largely as a result of Southeast Asian immigration. Immigrants from Asia have climbed to one of four of all foreign-born persons now living in the United States, and the Philippines was surpassed only by Mexico as the country of birth for foreign-born persons living in this country.[40]

Many Asian Americans have done well both economically and educationally. More than two out of every five Asian Americans have graduated from college, compared to one out of every four white Americans and one in seven African Americans.[41] Asian Americans are becoming more politically important and visible in politics. In 1996, Washington elected the first Chinese American governor of a state in the continental United States—Gary Locke. He was reelected in 2000.

THE TIES OF ETHNICITY   Except for Native Americans, all Americans are immigrants or are descended from immigrants. Early settlers were generally English-speaking Protestants; even today, people of English, Scottish, and Welsh background are the largest "ethnic" group in the United States. Irish immigrants, largely Catholics, started coming before the potato famine in the 1840s and came in larger numbers after it. Upon their arrival, they experienced economic exploitation and religious bigotry. The Irish American response was to retreat among themselves, forming a strong ethnic consciousness. Other ethnic groups that followed—Italians, Greeks, Chinese—each experienced a similar cycle: flight from their homeland and happy arrival here, then discrimination, exploitation, residential clustering, and the formation of a strong group identity.

The largest number of immigrants came between 1900 and 1924, when 17.3 million people relocated to the United States—by far the largest immigration to one country in any quarter-century in human history. From 1991 to 1997, there were more than 6.9 million immigrants,[42] primarily from the Caribbean and Mexico, and from Asian countries such as the Philippines, Vietnam, and China. The foreign-born proportion of the U.S. population has increased in recent years, rising from 14 million in

1980 to nearly 26 million in 1998, the largest number of foreign-born in U.S. history.[43] Recently the proportion of Asian and Mexican immigrants has pulled even with or surpassed the number of Europeans.

Having large numbers of immigrants can pose challenges to any political and social system. Immigrants are often a source of social conflict as they compete with more established groups for jobs, rights, political power, and influence.

WE THE PEOPLE

Percentage of the Population by Race and Origin

	1990	2000	2025	2050
White	83.9%	82.1%	78.3%	74.8%
African American	12.3	12.9	14.2	15.4
American Indian, Inuit, Aleut	0.8	0.9	1.0	1.1
Asian and Pacific Islander	3.0	4.1	6.6	8.7
Hispanic	9.0	11.4	17.6	24.5

SOURCE: U.S. Bureau of the Census, *Statistical Abstract of the United States, 1999* (Government Printing Office, 1999), p. 18.

Percentages do not equal 100 percent because Hispanics can be of any race. Figures for 2000, 2025, and 2050 are projections.

Gender

For most of U.S. history, politics and government were men's business. As will be discussed in greater detail in Chapter 17, women first gained the right to vote primarily in the western territories, beginning with Wyoming in 1869 and Utah in 1870, and then in Colorado and Idaho before the turn of the century.[44] The right was not extended nationally until 1920 with passage of the Nineteenth Amendment. The fears of some opponents of *women's suffrage* (the right to vote)—that women would form their own party and vote largely for women or fundamentally alter our political system—have not been realized. During Susan B. Anthony's suffrage campaign, Jonas H. Upton, editor of the *Democratic Salem Monitor* in Salem, Oregon, contended that women, if given the right to vote, would combine to vote for war because they were exempt from the draft.[45] Others said women would unite to vote for prohibition.[46]

For a half-century after gaining the right to vote, American women voted at a lower rate than women in other Western democracies.[47] But in the past 20 years, women have voted at nearly the same rate as men. Since women outnumber men, there are more female than male voters. Women have chosen to work within the existing political parties and do not overwhelmingly support female candidates, especially if they must cross parties to do so.

WOMEN IN POLITICS   The women's movement in American politics encompasses a comprehensive agenda, including voting and political rights as well as extending the basic liberties of the Bill of Rights and Fourteenth Amendment. In addition to rights and liberties, women seek equal opportunity, education, jobs, skills, and respect in what has been a male-dominated system.[48]

Since 1917, less than 6 percent of representatives in the U.S. House have been women, but the number of women in the House of Representatives and U.S. Senate reached new highs in the 1990s. Following the 2000 elections, there were 3 female governors, 13 women serving in the Senate, and 58 in the U.S. House of Representatives. The number of female officeholders is rising in part because women are increasingly running in contests with no incumbent running.[49]

Is there a **gender gap**? Do women vote differently from men? Women have typically divided their vote between the two major political parties. However, in recent elections women have been more likely than men to vote for Democratic presidential candidates (see Figure 5–3). In the 2000 presidential election, Al Gore's share of the vote among women was 12 percent higher than among men.[50]

Women are more likely to oppose violence in any form—death penalty, new weapons systems, or the possession of handguns. Women, as a group, are more compassionate than men and are more likely to favor government that provides

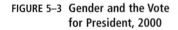

FIGURE 5–3 Gender and the Vote for President, 2000

gender gap
The difference between the political opinions or political behavior of men and of women.

health insurance and family services. Women generally are more concerned than men about women's rights—enforcement of child support, punishment for sexual abuse and rape, and equal treatment in the legal system. They also identify work and family issues such as daycare, prenatal and postnatal leave, and equal treatment in the workplace as important.[51] Other gender issues, some of them focal points in recent elections, include reproductive rights, restrictions on pornography, gun control, and sexual harassment.[52]

There are serious income inequalities between men and women. About 64 percent more women than men work at or below the minimum wage.[53] Because an increasing number of women today are the sole breadwinners for their families, the implications of this low income level are significant. Women earn on average less than men for the same work. Even among college graduates ages 25–34, women earn an average of 80 cents for every dollar earned by men of the same age and education. After controlling for characteristics such as job experience, education, occupation, and other measures of productivity, studies show that wage discrimination is somewhere between 89 to 98 cents on every dollar.[54] As age increases, the earnings gap widens. Increasing women's income is an important issue to the women's movement.

Sexual Orientation

Differences in sexual orientation have become important politically in recent years. The movement for expanded rights for gays and lesbians traces its roots to 1969, when New York City police raided the Stonewall Inn in Greenwich Village. Precise data on the number of homosexuals in the United States are in dispute. The gay and lesbian community talk in terms of 10 percent; other estimates come in much lower.[55] One source estimates that 2.8 percent of men and 1.4 percent of women identified themselves as homosexual or bisexual.[56] Regardless of its overall size, the homosexual community has become important politically in several cities, most notably San Francisco. Both parties have gay members of Congress.

In 2000 Vermont became the first state to enact legislation granting gay and lesbian couples "civil union" status, which in many respects is like marriage. Prior to this law taking effect, the Vermont Supreme Court had ruled that denying gay couples the same rights and benefits as heterosexual couples is unconstitutional. The legislation became an issue in the Vermont 2000 elections, and court challenges are also likely to arise.

The political agenda for gay and lesbian advocacy groups includes fighting discrimination, including the military's "Don't ask, Don't tell" policy. On some fronts the groups have been successful. In several cities and among some employers, gays and lesbians have been able to secure health care and other benefits for domestic partners. Antidiscrimination statutes protecting sexual orientation in housing and employment have been passed in several cities and states. Groups like the Human Rights Campaign are visible advocates of limiting restrictions based on sexual orientation. Hate crimes against gays and lesbians have led the Senate to include sexual orientation in federal hate crimes legislation.[57]

Conservative groups have, however, largely been successful in banning same-sex marriage in a series of statewide ballot initiatives. Among the groups who have been active in the protest movement have been conservative Christians, Catholics, and Mormons. The courts have also been drawn into the battle over sexual orientation. In a 5-to-4 decision, the Supreme Court upheld the right of the Boy Scouts of America to bar homosexuals from leadership positions, as well as general membership, in its organization.[58] As the Boy Scouts controversy illustrates, policies relating to sexual orientation are among the most contentious in our society.

The Boy Scouts do not permit homosexuals to be scout leaders. James Dale, an Eagle Scout who is gay, lost his lawsuit because the court said the Boy Scouts are a private association and can exclude gays.

FAMILY STRUCTURE

Over the past half-century the typical American family has been transformed from a "traditional family" (mother and father married with children in the home) to a variety of living arrangements and varying family structures. Today, Americans are much more likely to approve of premarital sex than in the early 1970s. And at some point in their lives, over half of Americans will *cohabit* (live with someone of the opposite sex to whom they are not married). Cohabitation raises public policy questions such as whether the live-in partner is eligible for employment benefits and welfare payments. Contraception is widely used and accepted, and yet one-third of all births are now illegitimate. These children will often be in need of social services and financial assistance.

People now marry later in life, with men marrying at average age 26 and women at 24.[59] Yet marrying later has not improved the chances of avoiding divorce. The average marriage today lasts only about 7.2 years. Before World War II, only 9 out of every 1,000 marriages ended in divorce; from 1950 to 1994 the divorce rate nearly doubled; today about one-half of all marriages are estimated to end in divorce.[60]

Divorce is one reason why many women go to work and why the number of households headed by women has risen. Attitudes about the role of women in marriage and the family have also changed. In 1972, one-third of Americans thought a woman's place is in the home (meaning she should not work outside the home), but in 1996, only one-sixth of all Americans felt this way.[61]

Religion

In many parts of the world, religious differences are a source of violent conflict. In Iraq and Turkey the Kurdish people have been subjected to expulsion and even to genocide. The war in Bosnia-Herzegovina was a religious and ethnic battle among Muslims, Serbs, and Catholics, as was the war between Serbs and Muslims in Kosovo. Countries like Afghanistan, Israel, Lebanon, India, and Sri Lanka have also experienced intense religious conflict. Jews have often been the target of religious discrimination and persecution (anti-Semitism), including the Holocaust, during which an estimated 6 million Jews were murdered.[62] The United States has not been immune, despite its principle of religious freedom. In 1838, Governor Lilburn W. Boggs of Missouri issued an extermination order against the Mormons.[63]

Our government is founded on the premise that religious liberty is more likely when there is not one predominant or official faith, which is why the framers of our Constitution did not sanction a national church. In fact, James Madison wrote in *The Federalist*, No. 51, "In a free government the security for civil rights must be the same as that for religious rights. It consists in the one case in the multiplicity of interests, and in the other in the multiplicity of sects" (see the Appendix).

The absence of an official American church does not mean that religion is unimportant in American politics; indeed, there were established state churches in this country until the 1830s. Some contend that "the root of American political and social values . . . is the distinctive Puritanism of the early New England settlers."[64] Politicians frequently refer to God in their speeches or demonstrate their piety in other ways. Democratic Vice-presidential candidate Joe Lieberman created some controversy in the 2000 campaign by his frequent references to deity and religion.

Many Americans take their religious beliefs seriously, more so than people of other industrial democracies.[65] Nearly two-thirds of Americans attend houses of worship several times a year, more than half attend a church or synagogue at least once a month, and more than one-third attend nearly every week.[66] Religion, like ethnicity, is a *shared identity*. People identify themselves as Baptist, Catholic, or Buddhist. Sometimes church attendance or nonattendance is more important than differences between religions in explaining attitudes. "Among both Catholics and Protestants, opposition to abortion increases with frequency of church attendance,

RELIGION AND POLITICS

At one time we thought a Catholic could not be elected president. With the election of 1960 that issue was resolved. John F. Kennedy directly confronted the question of whether a Catholic would put aside religious teachings if they conflicted with constitutional obligations. He said, "I am not the Catholic candidate for President. I am the Democratic party's candidate for President who happens also to be Catholic. I do not speak for my church on public matters, and the church does not speak for me." Nevertheless, today it is still the case that a candidate's religion may become an issue if religious convictions on sensitive issues such as abortion threaten to conflict with public obligations.

Religion can be an important catalyst for social change, as the Catholic church was in the overthrow of communism in Central Europe and the leadership of the black church was instrumental in the American civil rights movement. As writer Taylor Branch explains, the black church "served not only as a place of worship but also as a bulletin board to a people who owned no organs of communication, a credit union to those without banks, and even a kind of people's court."[*] African American ministers, like the Reverend Martin Luther King, Jr., became leaders of the civil rights movement; others, like the Reverend Jesse Jackson, have run for national office. Hence religion can be important not only as a source of personal values and attitudes but as a means of political activity and organization.

More recently there has been an increase in political activity among fundamentalist Christians. Led by ministers like Jerry Falwell and Pat Robertson, they have supported political organizations such as the Moral Majority and Christian Coalition. For the past two decades, they have sought to influence the national agenda, and Robertson taped telephone endorsements for George W. Bush in 2000. They also focus their attention at the local level—school boards, city councils, mayorships, and local GOP leadership.[**] Their agenda includes the return of school prayer, the outlawing of abortion, restrictions on homosexuals, and opposition to gun control.

In the 2000 presidential election, religion and deity were frequently raised by Joe Lieberman, Al Gore's running mate. Lieberman, the first Jewish candidate for vice president, was criticized by some for his frequent references to God and religion.[***] One of President Bush's first actions was to propose government use of churches to deliver social services, his "faith-based" initiative.

[*]Taylor Branch, *Parting the Waters: America in the King Years, 1954–63* (Simon & Schuster, 1988), p. 3.

[**]Kevin Lange, "An Energized Religious Right? Strategies for the Clinton Era," *Christian Century* 110 (February 17, 1993), pp. 177–79.

[***]Janine Zacharia, "The Role of God in U.S. Elections," *Jerusalem Post*, September 7, 2000, p. 6.

President John F. Kennedy

Pat Robertson

Joseph Lieberman

but the percentages expressing pro-choice and pro-life sentiments are almost identical for the Catholic and Protestant groups."[67]

One defining characteristic of religion in the United States is the tremendous variety of denominations. About half the people in the United States describe themselves as Protestant (see Figure 5–4). The largest Protestant denomination is Baptist, followed by Methodists, Lutherans, Presbyterians, and Episcopalians. Because

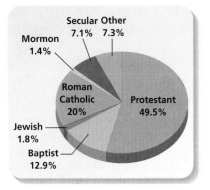

FIGURE 5–4 Religious Groups in America

SOURCE: "Largest Religious Groups in the United States of America" (www.adherents.com/relUSA.htm).

Protestants are divided among so many different churches, Catholics have the largest single membership in the United States, constituting more than one-quarter of the population. Jews constitute less than 2 percent of the population. Followers of Islam number more than 500,000.[68] Protestants came to the United States first; most Catholics and Jews immigrated after the 1840s. It was not until 1960, however, that Americans elected a Catholic president.

Religion is important in American politics in part because of the concentrations of people of particular religions in a few states. Catholics, as noted, make up about one-quarter of the U.S. population, yet they are more than 50 percent of the population of Rhode Island, Massachusetts, and Connecticut. Baptists represent 19 percent of the U.S. population, yet they are more than 50 percent of the population of Mississippi, Alabama, and Georgia. Mormons are only 2 percent of the U.S. population, yet they are more than 70 percent of the population of Utah. The South is the most Protestant—61 percent. The state of New York has the highest percentage of Jews, 7 percent; New York City is 14 percent Jewish.

In recent presidential elections, a majority of Protestants voted Republican, while majorities of Catholics and Jews voted Democratic.[69] The perception among many Catholics and Jews that the Democratic party is more open to them helps explain the strength of their Democratic identification. Democrats won the loyalty of many Catholics by their willingness to nominate Al Smith for the presidency in 1928 and John Kennedy in 1960. Jewish voter identification with the Democratic party was reinforced by Al Gore's selection of Joe Lieberman, an Orthodox Jew, to be his running mate in 2000. Southern Protestants have been Democrats for different reasons, having largely to do with the sectional issues discussed earlier. Religious groups vary in their rates of participation. Jews have the highest rate of reported voter turnout, 85 percent in 1996, while those who claim no religious affiliation have the lowest, 65 percent. Catholics voted at a slightly higher rate than Protestants.[70]

Religion can be related to other politically important characteristics. For instance, Jews are the most prosperous and best educated of any ethnic or religious group. More than 46 percent of Jewish adults graduated from college, compared to 22 percent of Protestants and 20 percent of Catholics.[71] In this example, as in others, religion is a cross-cutting cleavage in American politics; the differences do not reinforce one another. On the basis of income and education, Jews predictably should be Republicans, but 66 percent of American Jews are Democrats.[72] Similarly, southern Protestants should predictably be heavily Republican, but many are Democrats.

Wealth and Income

The United States is a wealthy nation. Compared to other nations, our purchasing power is higher than that of any other advanced democracy.[73] Indeed, to some knowledgeable observers, "the most striking thing about the United States has been its phenomenal wealth."[74] Most Americans lead comfortable lives. They eat and live well and have first-class medical care. But the unequal distribution of wealth and income still results in important political divisions and conflicts.

Wealth (total value of possessions) is more concentrated than income (annual earnings). The wealthiest families hold most of the property and other forms of wealth like stocks and savings. Traditionally, one of the problems with concentrated wealth has been that it fosters an aristocracy. Thomas Jefferson sought to break up the "aristocracy of wealth" by changing from laws based on *primogeniture* (the eldest son's exclusive right to inherit his father's estate) to laws that encouraged people to divide their estates equally among all their children, the result being smaller landholding. Jefferson sought to foster an "aristocracy of virtue and talent" through a public school system open to all for primary grades and for the best students through the university level.[75]

Education has been one of the most important means for Americans to achieve economic and social mobility. Those who have gone to college earn more than those

gross domestic product (GDP)
An estimate of the total output of all economic activity in the nation, including goods and services.

who have not, and those from wealthier families are more inclined to get an education. Most college students come from the top quarter of American families in income—those earning $50,000 a year or more. In fact, students from these families graduate from college at nearly twice the rate as those from the bottom 75 percent of the socioeconomic ladder.[76]

"The most common and durable source of factions has been the various and unequal distribution of property," wrote James Madison in *The Federalist*, No. 10 (reprinted in the Appendix). He continued, "Those who hold, and those who are without property, have ever formed distinct interests in society." Madison was right. Economic differences often lead to conflict, and Americans remain divided politically along economic lines. Aside from race, income may be the single most important factor in explaining views on issues, partisanship, and ideology. Most rich people are Republicans, and most poor people are Democrats, and this has been true since at least the Great Depression of the 1930s. In terms of income, the Northeast is the most prosperous region and the South the least prosperous.

Income has been rising in the United States. Even after adjusting for inflation, income doubled in the period between the 1950s and the 1970s. Since then, inflation-adjusted income has gone up and down, but the steady rise seen earlier has not occurred (see Figure 5–5).[77] Economists debate the causes for this change; some cite higher energy costs, low levels of personal savings, and the worldwide slowdown in productivity growth.[78]

Despite the general rise in income in the last quarter-century, roughly one in every ten Americans still comes from a family whose income is below the poverty line. In 1999 the official poverty level for a family of four was an income below $17,184.[79] Families headed by a female are three times more likely to fall below the poverty line than families headed by men, and nearly 35 percent of all households headed by females fall below the poverty line.[80] Close to 22 percent of the poor are children under 18 years of age, and many appear to be trapped in a cycle of poverty (see Figure 5–6). Both African Americans and Hispanics are nearly three times as likely to be poor than whites.[81]

The definition of poverty is itself political. It identifies persons who cannot meet a minimum standard in such basics as housing, food, and medical care. Regardless of how one defines poverty, however, the poor are a minority who lack political power. The poor vote less than wealthier groups and are less confident and organized in dealing with politics and government. During the last two decades there has been increasing inequality between rich and poor, a trend quite different from the 1960s, when the gap between rich and poor narrowed.[82] Although the gap did begin to decrease under the first Bush administration (1989–93), over the past decade inequality between rich and poor has again been on the rise.[83]

The distribution of income within a society can have important consequences for democratic stability. If there is a perception that only the few at the top of the economic ladder can hope to earn enough for an adequate standard of living, then domestic unrest and revolution may follow. Income is related to participation in politics. Poor people who need the most help from government are the least likely to participate. They are also the most likely to favor social welfare programs.

Occupation

Americans at the time of Jefferson and for several generations after worked primarily in agriculture, but by the end of World War I, the United States had become the world's leading industrial nation. This dramatic transformation also resulted in the expansion of American cities, as workers moved to find jobs. Labor conditions, including child labor practices, became important political issues. The invention and application of technology, combined with abundant natural and human resources, meant that the U.S. **gross domestic product (GDP)** rose, after adjusting for inflation, by more than 565 percent in real terms over the period from 1929 to 1998.[84]

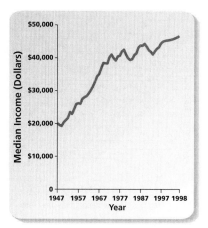

FIGURE 5–5 Median Family Income, 1947–1998

Source: U.S. Bureau of the Census home page: www.census.gov/hhes/income/histinc/f06.html; www.census.gov/hhes/poverty/ poverty98/ pv98est1.html.

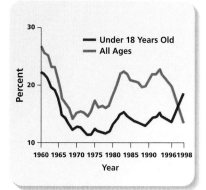

FIGURE 5–6 Percentage of Americans Living in Poverty, by Age, 1960–1998

Source: U.S. Bureau of the Census (www.census.gov/prod/3/97pubs/p60-198.pdf).

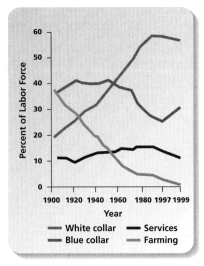

FIGURE 5–7 Occupational Groups, 1900–1999

Sources: U.S. Department of Labor, *Employment and Earnings*, vol. 43, no. 1 (Government Printing Office, 1996), p. 30; U.S. Department of Labor, *Employment and Earnings* 44, no. 1 (1997), p. 31; U. S. Department of Labor, *Employment and Earnings*, vol. 47, no. 1 (Government Printing Office, 2000), p.31.

The United States several years ago entered what Daniel Bell, a noted sociologist, labeled the "post-industrial phase of our development." "A post-industrial society, being primarily a technical society, awards less on the basis of inheritance or property . . . than on education and skill."[85] *Knowledge* is the organizing device of the postindustrial era. Postindustrial societies have greater affluence and a class structure less defined along traditional labor versus management lines.

The changing dynamics of the American labor force can be seen in Figure 5–7, which shows the percentage of the U.S. labor force in various occupations. There has been tremendous growth in the white-collar sector of our economy. This sector includes managers, accountants, and lawyers, as well as professionals and technicians in such rapid growth areas as computers, communications, finance, insurance, and research. This shift has been accompanied by a dramatic decline in the number of people engaged in agriculture and a more modest decline in the number of people in manufacturing (blue collar). Today only one in five working Americans produces goods, and only 2 percent work on farms.[86] Governments are among the biggest employers in this country. More than one-sixth of our gross domestic product is produced by federal, state, and local governments.[87]

Women and racial minorities have distinct occupational patterns. Women are much less likely than men to work in blue-collar jobs and more likely to work in clerical positions (30 percent) or in the service sector (15 percent).[88] As noted earlier, women generally earn less than men of the same age and education. Occupations in which women predominate, like teaching and clerical work, are generally lower paying than industrial or management jobs. And as women advance in their careers, especially in management, they encounter a barrier to advancement that has been labeled the "glass ceiling."

Social Class

Many observers have questioned why Americans do not divide themselves into social classes as Europeans do. American workers have not formed their own political party, nor does class seem to dominate our political life. Marxist categories of *proletariat* (those who sell their labor) and *bourgeoisie* (those who own or control the means of production) are far less important here than they are in Europe. Still, we do have social classes and what social scientists call **socioeconomic status (SES)**—a division of the population based on occupation, income, and education.

Most Americans, when asked what class they belong to, say "middle class." Very few see themselves as lower class or upper class. But what constitutes "middle class" is highly subjective. For instance, some individuals perform working-class tasks (such as plumbing), but their income is middle class or even upper middle class. A school teacher's income is below that of many working-class jobs, but in terms of status, the job ranks at least with middle-class fields. In many other industrial democracies, large proportions of the population think of themselves as working class instead of middle class.[89] In England, nearly three out of five persons see themselves as working class.[90] But to many Americans there is something undesirable about the label "working class."

One explanation for Americans' responses may be the elements of the American Dream that involve upward mobility. Or their responses may reflect the hostility many feel toward organized labor. In any case, compared to many countries, class divisions in the United States are less defined and less important to politics. As political scientist Seymour Martin Lipset has written, "The American social structure and values foster an emphasis on competitive individualism, an orientation that is not congruent with class consciousness, support for socialist or social democratic parties, or a strong union movement."[91]

Age

Americans are living longer, a phenomenon called the "graying of America" (Figure 5–8). Moreover, given the size of the population, fewer babies are being born. This demographic change is having important consequences; it has increased the

socioeconomic status (SES)
A division of population based on occupation, income, and education.

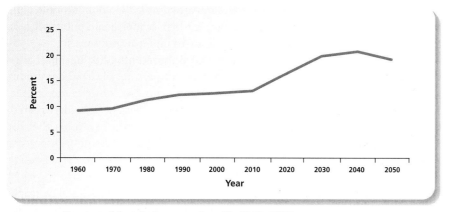

FIGURE 5–8 Percent of Population over Age 65, 1960–2050

Source: U.S. Bureau of the Census, "Aging in the United States, Past Present and Future," at www.census.gov/ipc/prod/97agewc.pdf.

demand for medical care, retirement benefits, and a host of other age-related services. Persons over the age of 65 constitute less than 13 percent of the population yet account for 31 percent of the total medical expenditures.[92]

Older Americans have political concerns, and they vote. Past legislative victories have changed the lives of older citizens. For instance, the poverty rate among this group dropped from 35 percent in 1959 to 10 percent in 1997, a change partly due to improved medical benefits passed during the 1960s.[93] As a group, older Americans fight to ensure that Social Security is protected; they value Medicare and favor prescription drug coverage. Despite their desire for services that benefit themselves, they also favor tax cuts.

In recent presidential elections, less than one-third of all 18-to-20 year-olds voted; in contrast, 70 percent of those 65 and older turned out to vote.[94] Their vote is especially important in western states and in Florida, the state with the largest proportion of people over 65. The "gray lobby" not only votes in large numbers but also has four other political assets not found in other age groups that make it politically powerful: disposable income, discretionary time, a clear focus on issues, and effective organization. When older Americans compete for their share of the budget pie, the young, minorities, and the poor often lose out. Al Gore, by championing Social Security, secured a majority of the vote of those over age 60.[95]

Age is important to politics in two additional ways: life cycle and generational. *Life-cycle effects* have shown that as people become middle-aged, they become more politically conservative, less mobile, and more likely to participate in politics. As they age further and rely more on the government for services, they tend to grow more liberal.[96]

There are also *generational effects* in politics that arise when a particular generation has had experiences that make it politically distinct. An example is the experience of those who lived through the Great Depression of the 1930s, which shaped their lifelong views of parties, issues, and political leaders. Some members of this generation saw Franklin Roosevelt as the leader who saved the country by pulling it out of the Depression; others felt he sold the country down the river by launching too many government programs. More recently, the baby boomers shared a common and distinctive political experience. These Americans came of age politically in the 1960s and 1970s during the civil rights movement and the Vietnam War.

Education

Education has long been linked to citizenship and civic virtue. Differences in education affect not only economic well-being but political participation and involvement. Thomas Jefferson wrote of education, "Enlighten the people generally, and tyranny and oppressions of body and mind will vanish like evil spirits at the dawn of day."[97]

"It's like this. If the rich have money, they invest. If the poor have money, they eat."

The vast majority of people in the United States are educated in public schools. Nine out of every ten students in kindergarten through high school attend public schools, and nearly four out of five students in college are in public institutions.[98]

Many people are surprised to learn that only recently did the number of college graduates in America surpass the number of persons who had not graduated from high school.[99] Just over half of all Americans have not gone to college, though many college students assume that the college experience is widely shared. The proportion of whites who are college graduates is nearly double that for African Americans and more than double that for Hispanics; roughly 24 percent of African Americans and nearly half of all Hispanics stopped their schooling before completing high school[100] (Table 5–3).

Education is one of the most important variables in predicting political participation, confidence in dealing with government, and awareness of issues. Education is also related to the acquisition of democratic values. Those who have failed to learn the prevailing norms of American society are far more likely to express opposition to democratic and capitalist ideals than those who are well educated and politically knowledgeable.[101]

UNITY IN A LAND OF DIVERSITY

As remarkable as American diversity is, the existence of a strong and widely shared sense of national unity and identity may be even more remarkable. Writing about the United States some years ago, a famous reporter, John Gunther, summarized his insights from extensive travels:

> Whoever invented the motto E Pluribus Unum [out of many one] has given the best three-word description of the United States ever written. The triumph of America is the triumph of a coalescing federal system. Complex as the nation is almost to the point of insufferability, it interlocks. Homogeneity and diversity— these are the stupendous rival magnets. . . . Think of the United States as an

TABLE 5–3 **Distribution of Education in the United States**					
	Population (1,000)	Not a high school graduate	High school graduate	Bachelor's degree	Advanced degree
Age					
25 to 34 years old	39,354	11.9%	31.9%	21.3%	6.2%
35 to 44 years old	44,462	12.0	34.0	18.3	8.0
45 to 54 years old	34,058	13.0	32.1	17.5	11.3
55 to 64 years old	22,255	20.5	37.3	13.0	9.2
65 to 74 years old	17,873	28.9	36.4	10.0	6.6
75 years old or over	14,209	38.0	33.2	8.1	4.4
Sex					
Male	82,376	17.2	32.3	17.1	9.4
Female	89,835	17.1	35.2	15.8	6.6
Race					
White	145,078	16.3	33.9	16.8	8.1
Black	19,376	24.0	36.0	10.3	4.4
Hispanic	16,044	44.5	26.8	7.8	3.2
Other	7,756	16.5	25.5	24.7	12.8

SOURCES: U.S. Bureau of the Census, *Current Population Reports*, P20–513 (Government Printing Office, 1999); U.S. Bureau of the Census, *Statistical Abstract of the United States, 1999* (Government Printing Office, 1999), p. 170.

immense blanket or patchwork quilt solid with different designs and highlights. But, no matter what colors burn and flash in what corners, the warp and woof, the basic texture and fabric is the same from corner to corner, from end to end.[102]

Social scientists sometimes speak of the *melting pot*, meaning that as minorities, especially ethnic groups, associate with other groups, they are assimilated into the rest of American society and come to share democratic values like majority rule, individualism, and the notion that America is the land of opportunity. The melting pot idea has been criticized as assuming that differences between groups are to be discouraged. In its place, critics propose the notion of the *salad bowl*, in which "though the salad is an entity, the lettuce can still be distinguished from the chicory, the tomatoes from the cabbage."[103]

As we have seen, important differences persist among groups, and in that sense the salad bowl analogy is accurate. Divisive issues like immigration, affirmative action, and programs for the poor have reinforced our differences. But in another way, our society has achieved a unity of commitment to democratic values and processes—a political culture that is, at least in part, a consequence of such elements of the melting pot theory as public schools, a common language, and hope for a better life for one's children. Ethnic divisions in the United States pose challenges to the institutions and processes of government, yet the public has generally accepted diversity in political appointments, government jobs and contracts, and other aspects of policy. This acceptance is in sharp contrast to the violent ethnic conflicts in other parts of the world. But we are still seeking the appropriate balance among recognition, preservation, and representation of ethnic groups and the needs for assimilation, common commitments, and a shared identity.

POLITICS ONLINE

Who Are My Neighbors?

We live in a diverse country. Some call it a melting pot; others call it a salad bowl or a patchwork quilt. Many different personal characteristics and associations distinguish people from one another: race, religion, ethnicity, gender, socioeconomic status, age, occupation, education, political ideology, and state or city of origin. As this chapter has demonstrated, these personal differences can often be important to politics. Although we may appreciate the importance of differences, we tend to know our own group's identities best, and we often project our own experience onto others (ethnocentrism). Once each decade, we get a chance to learn a lot more about social and economic differences through the census. The 2000 census gathered data on as many residents as it could find. You can access the census data at: www.census.gov.

A picture of the changing mosaic of the American people emerges out of the census data. *Indivisible: Stories of an American Community* is a project by Duke University and the Pew Charitable Trusts that gives you a glimpse of some of your neighbors. Photographers and interviewers recorded stories and snapshots of people who live in places ranging from Delray Beach, Florida, to Yaak Valley, Montana. To catch a glimpse of some of your neighbors, visit their website at: www.indivisible.org. Listen to their stories, learn who they are, how they live, how they are different from you, as well as what you have in common with them, and how they're trying to better our communities.

If you want to learn more about segments of the community more specifically, visit individual websites. For example, a good website for Latinos is: faclon.cc.ukans.edu/~droy/.

For Catholics or Mormons you can go to: www.catholic.net; or www.lds.org.

Use the search engine at www.prenhall.com/burns and you are likely to find links to groups that will help you learn more about them.

SUMMARY

1. The character of a political society and its social environment are important to understanding our politics and government.

2. As a nation of immigrants, Americans are more diverse than the citizens of most other nations. Diversity in race and ethnicity are reflected in different family structures and religions. The nation's citizens also differ in wealth and income, occupation, social class, age, and education. Divisions by gender and sexual orientation have recently become more important. This diversity is often significant in our politics, though most divisions cut across demographic categories, rather than reinforcing them.

3. Geography, room to grow, abundant natural resources, wealth, and relative isolation from "foreign entanglements" help to explain American politics and traditions, including the notions of manifest destiny, ethnocentrism, and isolationism.

4. Until recently, the South was a very distinct region in the United States, in large part because of its agricultural base and the issue of slavery and race relations. With in-migration and the impact of the civil rights movement, it is no longer solidly Democratic. Recently the most significant migration has been from cities to suburbs. Today large cities are increasingly poor, African American, and Democratic, surrounded by suburbs that are primarily middle class, white, and Republican.

5. Race has been among the most important of the differences in our political landscape. Although we fought a civil war over freedom for African Americans, racial equality was largely postponed until the latter half of the twentieth century. Race remains an important issue in our politics and government. Ethnicity, including the rising numbers of Hispanics, continues to be a factor in politics.

6. Gender is important in American politics. Women have gradually acquired political rights. They now play important roles in our government, and they differ from men in their attitudes on some issues. Sexual orientation policies are among the most contentious in our society.

7. Since World War II, attitudes toward sexuality, marriage, and family have changed in important ways. The use of birth control and contraception has risen, as has abortion and the number of illegitimate births. People cohabit at much higher rates, and those who marry are older. Divorce has also become much more commonplace. Changing family structures and attitudes affect our tax policies, child care, parental leave, and gender equality. They are also important political issues.

8. The U.S. has a large variety of religious denominations and these differences help explain public opinion and political behavior. Important differences also exist between those who are religious and those who are not.

9. While the United States is a land of wealth with a large middle class, not everyone has an adequate share in the American economic success. Poverty has grown over the past two decades, and it is most concentrated among African Americans, Native Americans, Hispanics, and single-parent households. Women as a group continue to earn less than men, even in the same occupations. Differences in income and wealth remain important.

10. America has shifted from an agricultural to an industrial to a postindustrial society, with consequences for occupations and politics. Governments are a major source of employment. Social class is less important in America than in other industrialized democracies.

11. Age and education are important to understanding American politics. Older citizens participate much more than young voters and are a potent political force. Education not only opens up economic opportunities in America but also explains many important aspects of political participation.

12. Despite our diversity, Americans share an important unity. We are united by our shared commitment to democratic values, economic opportunity, the work ethic, and the American Dream.

KEY TERMS

ethnocentrism 96
political socialization 96
demographics 96
political predisposition 96

reinforcing cleavages 96
cross-cutting cleavages 96
manifest destiny 98
race 101

ethnicity 101
gender gap 104
gross domestic product (GDP) 108

socioeconomic status (SES) 110

FURTHER READING

DOUGLAS L. ANDERSON, RICHARD BARNETT, AND DONALD BOGUE, *The Population of the United States*, 3d ed. (Free Press, 1996).

DAVID H. BENNETT, *The Party of Fear* (University of North Carolina Press, 1990).

EARL BLACK AND MERLE BLACK, *The Vital South: How Presidents Are Elected* (Harvard University Press, 1992).

URIE BRONTENBRENNER ET AL., *The State of Americans: The Disturbing Facts and Figures on Changing Values, Crime, the*

Economy, Poverty, Family, Education, the Aging Population, and What They Mean for Our Future (Free Press, 1996).

DAVID T. CANON, *Race, Redistricting, and Representation: The Unintended Conse-*

quences of Black Majority Districts (University of Chicago Press, 1999).

Rodolfo O. De La Garza, Louis Desipio, F. Chris Garcia, John Garcia, and Angelo Falcon, Latino Voices: Mexican, Puerto Rican, and Cuban Perspectives on American Politics (Westview Press, 1992).

Lois Lovelace Duke, ed., Women in Politics: Outsiders or Insiders? 2d ed. (Prentice Hall, 1995).

Sarah H. Evans, Born for Liberty: A History of Women in America (Free Press, 1989).

Geoffrey Fox, Hispanic Nation: Culture, Politics and the Constructing of Identity (Birch Lane Press, 1996).

Donald R. Kinder and Lynn M. Sanders, Divided by Color: Racial Politics and Democratic Ideals (University of Chicago Press, 1996).

Seymour Martin Lipset, Continental Divide: The Values and Institutions of the United States and Canada (Routledge, 1990).

Nancy E. McGlen and Karen O'Connor, Women, Politics, and American Society, 2d ed. (Prentice Hall, 1998).

Peter Nabokov, ed., Native American Testimony: A Chronicle of Indian-White Relations from Prophecy to the Present, 1492–1992 (Viking, 1991).

Kevin Phillips, The Politics of Rich and Poor: Wealth and the American Electorate in the Reagan Aftermath (Random House, 1990).

Steven J. Rose, Social Stratification in the United States: The American Profile Poster Revised and Expanded (New Press, 1992).

Arthur M. Schlesinger, Jr., The Disuniting of America (W. W. Norton, 1992).

Jeffrey M. Stonecash, Class and Party in American Politics (Westview Press, 2000).

Studs Terkel, Race: How Blacks and Whites Think and Feel About the American Obsession (W. W. Norton, 1992).

Alexis de Tocqueville, Democracy in America, ed. J. P. Mayer, trans. George Lawrence (Doubleday and Company, 1969).

Kenneth D. Wald, Religion and Politics in the United States, 3d ed. (CQ Press, 1996).

6

INTEREST GROUPS: THE POLITICS OF INFLUENCE

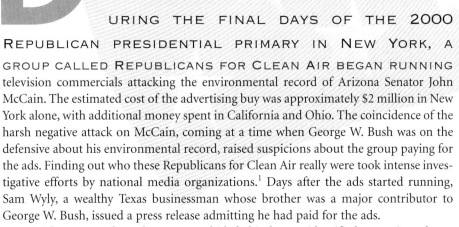

DURING THE FINAL DAYS OF THE 2000 REPUBLICAN PRESIDENTIAL PRIMARY IN NEW YORK, A GROUP CALLED REPUBLICANS FOR CLEAN AIR BEGAN RUNNING television commercials attacking the environmental record of Arizona Senator John McCain. The estimated cost of the advertising buy was approximately $2 million in New York alone, with additional money spent in California and Ohio. The coincidence of the harsh negative attack on McCain, coming at a time when George W. Bush was on the defensive about his environmental record, raised suspicions about the group paying for the ads. Finding out who these Republicans for Clean Air really were took intense investigative efforts by national media organizations.[1] Days after the ads started running, Sam Wyly, a wealthy Texas businessman whose brother was a major contributor to George W. Bush, issued a press release admitting he had paid for the ads.

Wyly was not the only person to hide behind an unidentified group in order to campaign for or against presidential candidates in 2000. A group named Keep It Flying, PAC sent out an estimated 200,000 letters to voters shortly before the South Carolina Republican primary incorrectly claiming McCain opposed flying the Confederate flag over the South Carolina state capitol. The letter quoted George W. Bush's wife, Laura, as having positive views on the Confederate flag and urging support for her husband. Who was Keep It Flying, PAC? After months of research, *The Wall Street Journal* reported that Richard Towell Hines, a native of South Carolina with close ties to George W. Bush and now a Washington, D.C. lobbyist whose major client is the Cambodian government, headed the group.[2]

Group-sponsored activity in recent elections has also included groups with names you will likely recognize: the Christian Coalition, American Federation of Labor–Congress of Industrial Organizations (AFL-CIO), National Education Association, National Abortion and Reproductive Rights Action League (NARAL), National Right To Life, and the Sierra Club. All these interest groups—dedicated to advancing specific interests through the political process—have run ads on television and radio and mounted telephone or mail campaign efforts in recent election cycles. When groups run ads that do not do not use words like "vote for" or "vote against," the U.S. Supreme Court defines these communications as **issue advocacy**. As such, they are not subject to the same disclosure requirements or contribution limitations as contributions to candidates. Groups can engage in issue advocacy in addition to the money they contribute to candidates and parties through their political action committees (PACs)

CHAPTER MEDIA

POLITICS ONLINE
In Whose Interest?
www.prenhall.com/burns

POLISIM
Lobbying America
www.prenhall.com/burns

and through contributions to political parties.[3] Much of this election activity is done late in the campaign and in ways designed to avoid media scrutiny.

How interest groups compete for influence, the role they play in elections, and how to limit their "mischiefs" are the subjects of this chapter. We begin by discussing the types of interest groups and the roles they play. Then we turn to one of their most important activities—lobbying. Finally, we examine the problems interest groups pose and ways to regulate them.

INTEREST GROUPS PAST AND PRESENT— THE "MISCHIEFS OF FACTION"

What we call interest groups today, founding father James Madison called **factions**. (Madison also thought of political parties as factions.) For Madison and the other framers of the Constitution, the daunting problem was how to establish a stable and orderly constitutional system that at the same time would respect the liberty of free citizens and prevent the tyranny of the majority or of a single dominant interest. As a good practical politician and a brilliant theorist, Madison offered both a diagnosis and a solution in *The Federalist*, No. 10 (reprinted in the Appendix). He began with a basic proposition: "The latent causes of faction are thus sown in the nature of man." Acknowledging that Americans live in a maze of group interests, Madison went on to argue that the "most common and durable source of factions has been the various and unequal distribution of property."

A Nation of Interests

As we noted in Chapter 5, some Americans identify with groups distinguished by race, gender, ethnic background, age, occupation, and sexual orientation. Others form groups based on issues like gun control or tax reduction. When such associations seek to influence government in some way, they are **interest groups**.

Interest groups are sometimes called "special interests." Politicians and the media often use this term in a pejorative way. What makes an interest group a "special" one? The answer is highly subjective. One person's special interest is another's national interest. Some interest groups claim to speak for the "public interest," yet so-called public interest groups like Common Cause or the Center for Responsive Politics support policies that not everyone agrees with. Politics is best seen as a clash among interests with differing concepts of what is in the public interest rather than a battle between the special interests on one side and "the people" on the other.

When political scientists call something an "interest group" or a "special interest," they are not calling it names. These are analytic terms to describe a group that speaks for some but not all of us. Much of our politics focuses on what is in the national interest. In a democracy there are many interests and many organized interest groups. The democratic process exists to decide among those national interests. Part of the politics of interest groups is to persuade the public that your group's interest is better, broader, more beneficial, and more general, and at the same time label groups that oppose yours as "special interests." For this reason we use the neutral term "interest groups."

Social Movements

Interest groups sometimes have their beginnings as movements. A **movement** consists of a large body of people who are interested in a common issue, idea, or concern that is of continuing significance and who are willing to take action on that issue. Examples include the abolitionist, temperance, civil rights, environmental, antitax, animal rights, and women's rights movements. Each movement represents groups who have felt "left out" of government. Such groups often arise at the grass-roots level and evolve into national groups. Movements tend to see their causes as morally right and the positions of the opposition as morally wrong.

issue advocacy
Unlimited and undisclosed spending by an individual or group on communications that do not use words like "vote for" or "vote against," although much of this activity is actually about electing or defeating candidates.

faction
A term used by James Madison and other founders of this country to refer to political parties as well as what we now call special interests or interest groups.

interest group
A collection of people who share some common interest or attitude and seek to influence government for specific ends. Interest groups usually work within the framework of government and employ tactics such as lobbying to achieve their goals.

movement
A large body of people interested in a common issue, idea, or concern that is of continuing significance and who are willing to take action on that issue. Movements seek to change attitudes or institutions, not only policies.

To a marked degree, our Constitution protects the liberties and independence of movements. The Bill of Rights guarantees movements—whether popular or unpopular—free assembly, free speech, and due process. Hence militants do not have to engage in terrorism or other extreme activities in the United States, as they do in some countries, and they need not fear persecution for demonstrating peacefully. In a democratic system that restricts the power of those in authority, movements have considerable room to operate *within* the constitutional system.

TYPES OF INTEREST GROUPS

Interest groups vary widely. Some are formal associations or organizations; others have no formal organization. Some are organized primarily to lobby for limited goals such as securing wage increases, conducting research, or broadly influencing public opinion by publishing reports and mass mailings.

Interest groups can be categorized into several broad types: (1) economic, including both business and labor, (2) ideological or single-issue, (3) public interest, (4) foreign policy, and (5) government itself. Obviously these categories are not mutually exclusive. The varied and overlapping nature of interest groups in the United States has been described as *interest group pluralism*, meaning that competition among open, responsive, and diverse groups helps preserve democratic values and limits the concentration of power in any single group.

Most Americans' interests are represented by a number of interest groups, some of which they are aware of and others of which they may not be and often with which they differ. For instance, older citizens may not be aware that the American Association of Retired Persons (AARP) claims to represent their interests. Others may not know that when they join the American Automobile Association (AAA), they not only purchase travel assistance and automobile towing when needed but also join a group that lobbies Congress and the Federal Highway Administration on behalf of motorists.

Economic Interest Groups

There are thousands of economic interests: agriculture, consumers, plumbers, northern businesses, southern businesses, labor unions, the airplane industry, landlords, truckers, bond holders, property owners, and so on and on.

BUSINESS   The most familiar business institution is probably the large corporation. Corporations range from small one-person enterprises to large multinational entities. Large corporations—General Motors, AT&T, Microsoft, Coca-Cola, McDonald's, Amazon, and other large companies—exercise considerable political influence, as do hundreds of smaller corporations. Corporate power and the implications of a changing domestic and global economy make business practices important political issues.

TRADE AND OTHER ASSOCIATIONS   Businesses with similar interests in government regulations and other issues join together as trade associations, which are as diverse as the products and services they provide. In addition, businesses of all types are organized into large, nationwide associations such as the Conference Board, the National Association for the Self-Employed, the Business Higher-Education Forum, and the Chamber of Commerce.

The broadest business trade association is the Chamber of Commerce of the United States. Organized in 1912, the Chamber is a federation of several thousand local Chambers of Commerce representing tens of thousands of business firms. Loosely allied with the Chamber on most issues is the National Association of Manufacturers, which, since its founding in the wake of the depression of 1893, has tended to speak for the more conservative elements of American business.

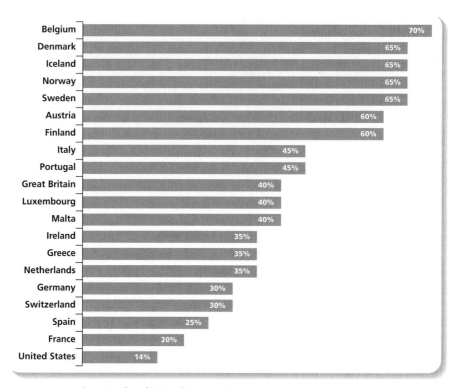

FIGURE 6–1 Union Membership in the United States Compared to Other Countries (Estimated Percentage of the Work Force)

SOURCE: *The World Almanac and Book of Facts, 2000*; based on data from Dr. Henri J. Wamenhoven, *Western Europe*, 5th ed. (Dushkin/McGraw-Hill, 1997), p. 46.

LABOR   Workers' associations have a range of interests, from professional standards to wages and working conditions. Labor unions are one of the most important groups representing workers. The American work force is the least unionized of almost any industrial democracy (Figure 6–1).

Probably the oldest unions in the United States were farm organizations. The largest farm group now is the American Farm Bureau Federation, which is especially strong in the corn belt. Originally organized around government agents who helped farmers in rural counties, the federation today is almost a semigovernmental agency, but it retains full freedom to fight for such goals as price supports and expanded credit. Other farm organizations are based on the interests of producers of specific commodities, such as the American Soybean Association.

Throughout the nineteenth century, workers organized political parties and local unions. Their most ambitious effort at national organization, the Knights of Labor, claimed 700,000 members. By the beginning of the twentieth century, the American Federation of Labor (AFL), a confederation of strong and independent-minded national unions mainly representing craft workers, was the dominant organization. During the ferment of the 1930s, unions more responsive to industrial workers broke away from the AFL and formed a rival national organization organized by industry, the Congress of Industrial Organizations (CIO). In 1955 the AFL and CIO reunited in the organization that exists today.

For some years the Committee on Political Education (COPE) of the AFL-CIO was one of the most respected—and most feared—political organizations in the country. In the Kennedy-Johnson years it won a reputation for political effectiveness. It encouraged and supervised grass-roots political activity, and at the national level it prepared and adopted a detailed platform that spelled out labor's position on issues. Labor contributed money to candidates, ran registration and get-out-the-vote campaigns, and otherwise supported its favorites. In recent elections COPE has had a fair, but not spectacular, record of wins for its endorsed House and Senate candidates.[4] Labor unions invested heavily in the fight against the North American Free Trade Agreement (NAFTA), claiming it would cost jobs. Labor's defeat in this battle was compounded by the 1994 election, which put Republicans in charge of Congress, and the 2000 election, which put the GOP in charge of Congress and the White House.

In recent elections the AFL-CIO has mounted vigorous campaigns to elect a Democratic majority in Congress and to keep the White House Democratic. Some foes of labor have proposed legislation and ballot initiatives called "paycheck protection," which would require annual authorization by union members for portions of their dues to be used for political purposes. Labor unions have successfully defeated these measures.

Unions have been effective in communicating with their members and organizing them for political purposes. In the 1998 elections and again in 2000, unions sent mailings to their members, organized get-out-the-vote drives, and paid for television advertising. The voter identification and mobilization done by the AFL-CIO for Al Gore in the Iowa caucuses and New Hampshire primary were important to his victories in those states. The strong labor backing of Gore continued through the general election and was also aimed at key congressional contests.

Union membership is optional in states whose laws permit the **open shop**, in which union membership cannot be required as a condition of employment. In states with the **closed shop**, union membership may be required as a condition of employment if most employees so vote. In both cases, the unions conduct negotiations with management, and the benefits the unions gain will be shared with all workers. In open shop states many workers choose not to affiliate with a union, as they can secure the same benefits without incurring the costs associated with union membership, a condition referred to as the **free rider**.

The AFL-CIO speaks for about 80 percent of unionized labor, but unions represent only about 13 percent of the nation's work force (see Figure 6–2).[5] The decline in the proportion of the work force belonging to unions is explained in part by the

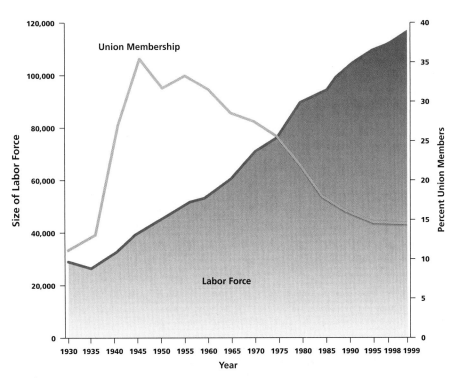

FIGURE 6–2 Labor Force and Union Membership, 1930–1999

SOURCE: *The World Almanac and Book of Facts, 2000*. Copyright © 1999 Primedia Reference, Inc. Reprinted with permission; all rights reserved. U.S. Bureau of Labor Statistics, www.stats.bls.gov/news.release/union2.toc.htm.

open shop
A company with a labor agreement whereby union membership cannot be required as a condition of employment.

closed shop
A company with a labor agreement whereby union membership is a condition of employment.

free rider
An individual who does not join an interest group representing his or her interests, yet receives the benefit of the influence the group achieves.

shift from an industrial to a service economy. Dwindling membership limits organized labor's political and lobbying muscle, and its prospects for increasing influence in the future are dim. Recently there has been growth in public sector unions, however, and even some doctors have unionized.

Traditionally identified with the Democratic party, unions have not enjoyed a close relationship with Republican administrations. Given labor's limited resources, one option for unions is to form temporary coalitions with consumer, public interest, liberal, and sometimes even with industry groups—especially on issues related to foreign imports. But labor pays a price for such collaboration. It must water down or give up some of its own goals. Few of labor's recent legislative initiatives have been successful, and with Reagan and Bush appointees in the majority, labor faces a much less sympathetic Supreme Court.

PROFESSIONAL ASSOCIATIONS   Professional people have organized some of the strongest unions in the nation. Some are well known, such as the American Medical Association and the American Bar Association. Others are divided into many subgroups. Teachers, for example, are organized into large groups such as the National Education Association, the American Federation of Teachers, the American Association of University Professors, and also into subgroups based on specialties, such as the Modern Language Association and the American Political Science Association.

Government, especially on the state level, regulates many professions. Lawyers, for example, are licensed by states, which, often as a result of pressure from lawyers themselves, have set up certain standards of admission to the state bar. Professional associations also use the courts to pursue their agenda. In the area of medical malpractice, for example, doctors lobby hard for limited liability laws, while the trial lawyers association resists such efforts. Teachers, hair stylists, and marriage therapists work for legislation or regulations of concern to them. It is not surprising, then, that among the largest donors to political campaigns through political action committees are those representing professional associations such as the American Medical Association and the American Realtors Association (see Table 6–1). Professional associations, in addition to lobbying legislative bodies, use the courts to pursue their agendas.

Ideological or Single-Issue Interest Groups

Ideological groups behave very much like economic interest groups, although they may not be driven by a desire to make money. Some of these groups are *single-issue groups*, often highly motivated and seeing politics primarily as a means to pursue

TABLE 6–1 PACs That Gave the Most to Federal Candidates (1996–2000)
(contributions in millions of dollars)

	2000	1998	1996
Realtors Political Action Committee	$3.42	$2.47	$2.10
Association of Trial Lawyers of America Political Action Committee	2.66	2.43	2.36
American Federation of State, County, and Municipal Employees	2.58	2.37	2.50
Dealers Election Action Committee of the National Automobile Dealers	2.50	2.10	2.35
Democrat Republican Independent Voter Education Committee	2.50	2.18	2.61
International Brotherhood of Electrical Workers Committee on Political Action	2.46	1.88	2.08
Machinists Non-Partisan Political League	2.18	1.64	2.00
United Auto Workers Voluntary Community Action Program	2.16	1.92	2.47
Service Emplyees International Union Politcal Acton Committee	2.15	1.30	.82
American Medical Association Political Action Committee	1.95	2.34	2.32

SOURCE: Federal Election Commission, "PAC Activity Increases in 1995–96 Election Cycle," press release, April 22, 1997, p. 19; FEC/Info: Political Action Committee and Party Committee home page: www.fecinfo/_pac.htm.

The Women's Christian Temperance Union, a movement dedicated to the prohibition of drinking liquor, succeeded in passing the Eighteenth Amendment, which outlawed the manufacture and sale of alcoholic beverages. It was later repealed by the Twenty-first Amendment.

their one issue. Such groups are often adamant about their position and unwilling to negotiate compromises. Right-to-life and pro-choice groups on abortion fit this description, as does the National Rifle Association.

Countless groups have organized around other specific issues, such as civil liberties, environmental protection, nuclear energy, and nuclear disarmament.[6] Such associations are not new. The Anti-Saloon League of the 1890s was single-mindedly devoted to barring the sale and manufacture of alcoholic beverages, and it did not care whether legislators were drunk or sober, as long as they voted dry. One of the best-known ideological groups today is the American Civil Liberties Union (ACLU), with roughly one-quarter million members committed to the protection of civil liberties.[7] Ideological religious groups are thriving in the otherwise pragmatic, pluralistic politics of today; examples include the Christian Coalition, which distributes Voter Guides the Sunday before the election.

Public Interest Groups

Out of the political ferment of the 1960s came groups that make a specific claim to promote "the public interest." For example, Common Cause, founded in 1970 by independent Republican John W. Gardner and later led by noted Watergate prosecutor Archibald Cox, campaigns for electoral reform and for making the political process more open. Its Washington staff raises money through direct mail campaigns, oversees state chapters, issues a flood of research reports and press releases on current issues, and lobbies on Capitol Hill and in major government departments.

Ralph Nader started a conglomerate of consumer organizations that investigates and reports on governmental and corporate action—or inaction—relating to consumer interests. Public Interest Research Groups (PIRGs) founded by Nader are among the largest interest groups in the country. PIRGs have become important players on Capitol Hill and in several state legislatures, promoting environmental issues, safe energy, consumer protection, and good government. Nader ran for president in 2000 as the nominee of the Green party. He received 3 percent of the popular vote.

A specific type of public interest group is the tax-exempt public charity. Examples include the American Heart Association, the Girl Scouts, and the American Cancer Society. These organizations must meet certain conditions, such as educational or philanthropic objectives, to qualify for this preferred status. Not only are public charities tax exempt, but donations to these organizations are tax deductible, and the

Environmental interest groups such as Greenpeace stage protests and even form political parties to protest the destruction of the beauty and safety of our natural resources.

organizations are not required to disclose information about their donors publicly. These organizations cannot participate in elections or support candidates, nor can they benefit an individual or small group. Despite these limitations, tax-exempt charitable organizations have been very active in voter registration efforts and in advertising campaigns designed to influence public opinion.

Foreign Policy Interest Groups

Domestic policy is not the only matter of concern to interest groups. More and more groups are organizing to promote or oppose certain foreign policies. Among the most prestigious foreign affairs groups is the Council on Foreign Relations in New York City. Other groups, devoted to narrower areas of American foreign policy, exert pressure on members of Congress and the president to enact specific policies. For example, interest group pressure influenced U.S. policy toward South Africa and played a role in South Africa's decision to abandon apartheid. Groups ranging from student organizations to national lobbies like the American Committee on Africa urged divestment, sanctions, or other policy measures that ultimately promoted change in South Africa from the outside.

The American-Israel Political Action Committee (AIPAC) has more than 50,000 members and has been very successful. Because AIPAC's primary focus is lobbying and not distributing campaign funds, it is not required to disclose where its money comes from or goes. Included in the long list of AIPAC lobbying successes are enactment of aid packages to Israel, passage of the 1985 United States-Israel Free Trade Agreement, and emergency assistance to Israel in the wake of the 1992 Gulf War. Its counterpart, the National Association of Arab Americans, lobbies for action in support of Arab causes and hosted events at both parties' 2000 national conventions. Efforts to secure a negotiated settlement between Palestine and Israel have meant that American interest groups on both sides of the dispute remain visible and important.

Government Interest Groups

Governments are themselves important interest groups. Many cities and most states retain Washington lobbyists, and cities also hire lobbyists to represent them at the state legislature. Governors are organized through the National Governors Associa-

A NEW MOVEMENT—OPPOSITION TO INTERNATIONAL TRADE AND GLOBALIZATION

Leaders such as Mahtma Gandhi and Martin Luther King have preached the use of "civil disobedience" to achieve governmental change. Civil disobedience is a peaceful, nonviolent demonstration against policy. Groups or movements trying to attract the attention of both the media and elected officials in support of their cause have often used civil disobedience tactics. As our own civil rights movement demonstrated, civil disobedience can be effective. A recent example of a movement that sought to use protest demonstrations to achieve its aims is the diverse set of interest groups that together assembled an estimated 10,000 protesters in Seattle, Washington, December 11–13, 1999, to oppose the labor, environmental, and trade practices fostered by the World Trade Organization (WTO). Though some groups, such as the AFL-CIO, applied for and were granted protest permits from the local government, other groups took a more confrontational approach.

What started out as a peaceful protest turned into riots. Peaceful groups like Public Citizen and the AFL-CIO were soon brushed aside by more violent protesters like the Ruckus Society and Direct Action Network. Vandals abandoned any pretense of peaceful protest by smashing store windows, and spray-painting the anarchist symbol of an "A" in a circle on buildings. The Seattle police, unable to control the situation and fearful they would be unable to protect delegates from 135 countries, used riot-control tactics like tear gas, rubber bullets, and pepper spray. They also arrested more than 400 protesters, many claiming to have committed no criminal act. Newspapers and television

Thousands of protesters from a great diversity of interest groups took over the streets of Seattle during the World Trade Organization meeting and caused much damage. The police battled back with tear gas and pepper spray.

around the world showed the confrontations, arrests, and destruction.

In the days and weeks that followed, the tactics of the protesters and the police were debated. By most accounts, the protests led to an abrupt ending to the meeting, and despite high hopes of important progress on international trade issues before the meeting, no new agreements were reached. More broadly, the protesters succeeded in forcing globalization and the negative consequences of increased international trade onto the political agenda. Before the protests in Seattle, it is doubtful many people had ever heard of the WTO or the concept of globalization.

Some of the same groups who protested in Seattle were also part of later demonstrations in Washington, D.C., aimed at the World Bank. This time the police were better prepared, and there were far fewer arrests and little damage to buildings. Whether those concerned about globalization and adverse consequences of international trade are able to turn protest into policy remains to be seen. But the use of protest demonstrations to force issues onto the agenda has once again been demonstrated.

SOURCES: Kim Murphy, "Anarchists Deployed New Tactics in Violent Seattle Demonstrations," *The Los Angeles Times*, December 16, 1999, p. A3; Marc Cooper, "Street Fight in Seattle," *The Nation*, December 20, 1999, pp. 3–4; Kenneth Klee, "The Siege of Seattle," *Newsweek*, December 13, 1999, p. 30.

tion, cities through the National League of Cities, and counties through the National Association of Counties.

Government employees form a large and well-organized group. The National Education Association (NEA), for example, claims more than 2.3 million members.[8] Public employees are also important to organized labor, and they are the fastest growing unions.

The American Association of Retired Persons (AARP) is a very large and effective interest group that influences legislation favoring the elderly.

Other Interest Groups

Americans are often emotionally and financially involved in a variety of groups: veterans groups such as American Legion or Veterans of Foreign Wars; nationality groups such as the multitude of German, Irish, Hispanic, and Korean organizations; or religious organizations such as the Knights of Columbus or B'nai B'rith. More than 150 nationwide organizations are based on national origin alone. In recent years there has been a virtual explosion in the number and variety of interests and associations. This is especially true for environmental groups (see Table 6–2).

CHARACTERISTICS AND POWER OF INTEREST GROUPS

Groups vary in their goals, methods, and power. Among the most important group characteristics are size, resources, cohesiveness, leadership, and techniques.

Size and Resources

Obviously size is important to political power; an organization representing five million voters has more influence than one speaking for five thousand. Perhaps even more important than size is the extent to which members are actively involved and fight for policy objectives. Often people join an organization for reasons that have little to do with its political objectives. They may want to secure group insurance, take advantage of travel benefits, participate in professional meetings, or get a job.

How do associations motivate potential members to join them? Organizations must provide incentives, material or otherwise, that are compelling enough to attract the potential free rider.[9] Unions are organized not just for lobbying but also to perform other important services for their members. They derive much of their strength from their negotiating position with corporations, which they use to obtain wage increases or improved safety standards. Similarly, the AARP, in addition to lobbying against Social Security cuts and speaking out on other issues of concern to older citizens, offers incentives such as a free subscription to its magazine, *Modern Maturity*, and member discounts at certain hotels. This combination of size and strength sets these groups apart from other large organizations in their effectiveness, as members derive numerous benefits from joining.

TABLE 6–2 Some Environmental Groups and How They Do Business

Group	Membership	Issues	Activities
Greenpeace USA	240,000	Oceans, global warming, genetically engineered foods	Media events; mass mailings; grass-roots activity; does not lobby government
Natural Resources Defense Council	400,000	Resources, energy, pollution	Lobbying; litigation; a watchdog; its scientists compete with experts from agencies and industry
Sierra Club	550,000	Wilderness, pollution, endangered species	Grass-roots action; media; hierarchy of 55 chapters and 400 local groups
Wilderness Society	200,000	Strictly public lands	Headquarters in Washington, D.C., with eight regional offices; mostly an analysis and advocacy group

SOURCE: www.sierraclub.org; www.greenpeace.org; www.wilderness.org; www.nrdc.org

While the size of an interest group is often important, so, too, is its *spread*—the extent to which membership is concentrated or dispersed. Automobile manufacturing is concentrated in Michigan and a few other states, and as a result the auto industry's influence does not have the same spread as that of the American Medical Association, which has an active chapter in virtually every congressional district. An association consisting of three million supporters concentrated in a few states will usually have less influence than another group consisting of three million supporters spread out in a large number of states.

Interest groups also differ in the extent to which they preempt a policy area or share it with other groups. Doctors and the AMA have effectively preempted the health care policy area because they play such an important role in the delivery of health care. But in the transportation policy area, railroads must compete with interstate trucking and even airfreight companies.

Groups also differ in their *resources*, which include money, volunteers, expertise, and reputation. Some groups can influence many centers of power—both houses of Congress, the White House, federal agencies, the courts, and state and local governments—while others cannot.

Cohesiveness

Usually a mass-membership organization is made up of three types of members: (1) a relatively small number of formal leaders who may hold full-time, paid positions or devote much time, effort, and money to the group's activities; (2) people intensely involved in the group who identify with the group's aims, attend meetings, faithfully pay dues, and do a lot of the legwork; (3) people who are members in name only, do not participate actively, and cannot be depended on to vote in elections or otherwise act as the leadership wants.[10] In a typical large organization, for every top leader there might be a few hundred hard-core activists and thousands of essentially inactive members.

Another factor in group cohesiveness is its *organizational structure*. Some associations have a strong formal organization; others are local organizations that have joined together in a loose state or national federation in which they retain a measure of separate power and independence. Separation of powers may be found as well: the national assembly of an organization establishes, or at least ratifies, policy; an executive committee meets more frequently; a president or director is elected to head and speak for the group; and permanent paid officials form the organization's bureaucracy.

Militia groups have sprung up in many parts of the country. They generally object to gun control laws and tend to be suspicious of government.

Power may be further divided between the organization's main headquarters and its Washington office. An organization of this sort tends to be far less cohesive than a centralized, disciplined group such as the army or some trade unions.

Leadership

Closely related to cohesion is the nature of the leadership. In a group that embraces many attitudes and interests, leaders may either weld the various elements together or sharpen their disunity. The leader of a national business association, for example, must tread cautiously between big business and small business, between exporters and importers, between chain stores and corner grocery stores, and between the producers and the sellers of competing products. The group leader is in the same position as a president or a member of Congress; he or she must know when to lead followers and when to follow them.

Techniques

Interest groups seeking to wield influence choose from a variety of political weapons and targets. They present their case to both houses of Congress, the White House staff, state and local governments, and federal agencies and departments. They also become involved in litigation. Other techniques include election activities, establishing political parties, and lobbying.

PUBLICITY AND MASS MEDIA APPEALS   Interest groups exploit the communications media—television, radio, newspapers, leaflets, signs, direct mail, and word of mouth—to influence voters during elections and to motivate constituents to contact their representatives between elections. Business enjoys a special advantage in this arena, and businesspeople have the money and staff to use propaganda machinery. As large-scale advertisers, they know how to deliver their message effectively or can find an advertising agency to do it for them. But organized labor is also effective in communicating with its membership through shop stewards, mail, and phone calls.

As people communicate more and more via e-mail, this technology will become an important means of political mobilization. John McCain effectively used e-mail in the 2000 primary campaign to turn out crowds in New Hampshire; after his big win in that state, he was able to raise campaign funds nationally. Candidates at all levels used e-mail for fund raising and to motivate supporters. E-mail will likely become part of political communication at the workplace, as management communicates information to its workers about the candidates and ballot issues.

MASS MAILING   One means of communication that has increased the reach and effectiveness of interest groups is computerized and targeted mass mailing.[11] Prior to computers, interest groups had to cull from telephone directories and other sources lists of people to contact, and managing these lists was time consuming. As a result, some groups sent out mailings indiscriminately. Today the computer permits easy data storage and efficient management of mailing lists. Mass mailing is now used by all kinds of interest groups. Today's technology can produce personalized letters targeted to specific groups, like the South Carolina "Keep It Flying" letter shown in Figure 6–3. Such targeted direct mail can also appeal to people who share a common concern, such as environmental groups.

INFLUENCE ON RULE MAKING   Organized groups have ready access to the executive and regulatory agencies that write the rules implementing laws passed by Congress. Government agencies publish proposed regulations in the *Federal Register* and invite responses from all interested persons before the rules are finalized. (The *Federal Register* is published every weekday. You can find it in your school, public library, or on the Internet at www.access.gpo.gov.) Well-staffed associations and corporations peruse the *Register*, ever alert for actions that will affect their interests.

Federal Register
This official document, published every weekday, lists new and proposed regulations of executive departments and regulatory agencies.

Keep It Flying

PAC

February 11, 2000

Dear Friend:

The NAACP has demanded that the Confederate Flag that flies over the South Carolina State House be taken down—calling it an "ugly symbol of racism" and even comparing it to the Nazi swastika.

The Confederate Flag flies over the State House to honor South Carolina's heritage. And the NAACP is just plain wrong to compare it to the swastika.

The liberal Democrats in the State Legislature have announced they will introduce a bill in the next few days to have the flag taken down. I hope you will help us keep it flying by doing three things today:

1. Display the enclosed "Keep the Flag! Dump Hodges!" sticker.

2. Call your State Senator or Representative and urge him or her to "Keep It Flying." The telephone number is 803-734-3000.

3. Send a contribution to Keep It Flying to help us rally grassroots supporters to "Keep It Flying."

Make no mistake: This fight isn't about whether the flag will fly over the State House or at another place of honor. The flag's opponents don't want it to fly at all. Anywhere.

Please act today. Remember: The liberal Democrats will introduce their legislation any day to take down the flag.

1. Call your State Representative or State Senator (803-734-3000). When the politicians hear from people across South Carolina, we will win.

2. Display the enclosed "Keep the Flag! Dump Hodges!" sticker.

3. Send a contribution to Keep It Flying. We need your contribution in the next few days to keep our TV and radio ads on the air. Please give $25, $50, $100—or if you can afford it, $250, $500, $1000.

Working together, we can win this fight. And keep the Confederate Flag flying to honor our heritage.

Yours truly,

John Brannen, Chairman
Keep It Flying PAC

P.S. Governor Hodges, the NAACP, Al Gore, and Bill Clinton all want to take down the Confederate Flag flying over the Senate House. Join us today to stop them.

FIGURE 6–3 A Sample of an Interest Group Mailing.

Source: Data Archive, "Getting Inside the Outside Campaign," David B. Magleby, ed. (Brigham Young University, Center for the Study of Elections and Democracy).

WE THE PEOPLE

Bernadette Budde, Senior Vice President, BIPAC

Thirty years ago, fresh out of Marquette University, Bernadette Budde started as a researcher for the Business and Industrial Political Action Committee (BIPAC). In college she had majored in journalism and wanted to be a newspaper reporter, but finding a reporter's low pay discouraging and not wanting to face "no news" days, she decided instead to go to Washington and find a job doing something related to government.

Her first assignment at BIPAC was typing numerous letters and checks perfectly, a task she did not enjoy. Her drive and ingenuity helped her move on to more analytic and strategic duties. Today she is one of the most respected PAC managers in the country. Her job is to decide which candidates BIPAC will support and with how much money. In the course of making these decisions, she interviews candidates and asks pointed questions about issues of importance to the business community.

In the 2000 election cycle, BIPAC contributed $226,000 to con-gressional candidates. While this is a relatively small sum compared to other donors, a contribution from BIPAC signals the business community at large that a candidate is a good investment. An early contribution from BIPAC can help secure contributions from larger business groups like the U.S. Chamber of Commerce and the Business Roundtable.

Budde's success is due in large measure to her ability to survey the political landscape and find new approaches. The traditional wisdom for PACs is to give money to incumbents and stay out of primaries, But Budde played a leading role in BIPAC's effort to mobilize pro-business voters in 2000, in much the same way that unions do. The effort was called "Project 2000" and provided businesses with a web-based "tool kit" that included voter registration forms and rules, candidates' voting records in a format ready for a customized voting guide, templates to create newsletters for employees, and get-out-the-vote materials. You can find these materials at www.politikit.com.

Lobbyists prepare written responses to the proposed rules, draft alternative rules, and appear at the hearings to make their case. These lobbyists seek to be on good terms with the staff of the agencies so that they can learn what rules are being considered long before they are released publicly and thus have input in the early stages. Administrative rules are defined over time through legal cases and agency modifications, so even if an interest group fails to get what it wants, it can fight the rules in court or press for a reinterpretation when the agency leadership changes hands.

Finally, an interest group can seek to modify rules it does not like by pressuring Congress to change the legal mandate for the agency or have the agency's budget reduced, making enforcement of existing rules difficult. In short, interest groups and lobbyists never really quit fighting for their point of view.

LITIGATION When groups find the political channels closed to them, they may turn to the courts.[12] The Legal Defense and Education Fund of the National Association for the Advancement of Colored People (NAACP), for example, initiated and won numerous court cases in its efforts to get rid of racial segregation and to protect the right to vote for African Americans. Urban interests and environmental groups, feeling underrepresented in state and national legislatures, turned to the courts to influence the political agenda.[13] Women's groups—such as the National Organization for Women and the American Civil Liberties Union's Women's Rights Project—also used the courts to pursue their objectives.[14] Conservative religious groups like the Washington Legal Foundation or groups identified with the Religious Right also actively used litigation as a strategy to pursue their objectives.[15]

In addition to initiating lawsuits, associations can gain a forum for their views in the courts by filing **amicus curiae briefs** (literally "friend of the court" briefs) in cases in which they are not direct parties. Despite the general impression that associations achieve great success in the courts, groups are no more likely than individuals to win their cases at the district court level.[16]

ELECTION ACTIVITIES Although nearly all large organizations say they are nonpolitical, almost all are politically involved in some way. What they usually mean when they say they are nonpolitical is that they are *nonpartisan*. A distinguishing feature of organized interest groups is that they often try to work through *both* parties.

Labor usually favors Democrats. The AFL-CIO has supported every Democratic candidate for president since the New Deal, although the Teamsters Union has often endorsed Republicans. In 2000 the Teamsters joined most other unions in backing Al

---

amicus curiae brief
Literally, "friend of the court" brief, this document is filed by an individual or organization to present arguments in addition to those presented by the immediate parties to the case.

Gore. Business groups generally endorse the incumbent but favor Republicans when no incumbent is running.

Some organizations are prevented from taking a firm position by the diversity of their members. A local retailers' group, for example, might be composed equally of Republicans and Democrats, and many of its members might refuse to openly support a candidate for fear of losing business.

Ideological groups target certain candidates, seeking to change the candidate's positions or, failing that, to influence voters to vote against that candidate. Americans for Democratic Action and the American Conservative Union publish ratings of members of Congress's voting record on liberal and conservative issues, as do the U.S. Chamber of Commerce and the AFL-CIO, among others.

How effective is electioneering by interest groups? In general, the mass-membership organizations' power to mobilize their full strength in elections has been exaggerated in the press. Too many cross-pressures are operating in the pluralistic politics of the United States for any one group to assume a commanding role. Some groups reach their maximum influence only by allying themselves closely with one of the two major parties. They may place their members on local, state, and national party committees and help send them to party conventions as delegates, but such alliances mean losing some independence.

FORMING A POLITICAL PARTY   Another interest group strategy is to form a political party. These parties are organized less with the intent to win elections than to *publicize a cause*. The Free Soil party was formed in the mid-1840s to work against the spread of slavery into the territories, and the Prohibition party was organized two decades later to ban the sale of liquor. Farmers have formed a variety of such parties. More often, however, interest groups prefer to work through existing parties. Today environmental groups and voters for whom the environment is a central issue must choose between supporting the Green party, which has yet to elect a person to federal office, and one of the two major parties. In a New Mexico congressional special election in 1997, the Green party candidate won 17 percent of the vote, helping elect a Republican to the seat. In the 1998 election, environmental groups campaigned aggressively for the Democrat, who obtained 53 percent of the vote, while all minor parties combined only got 4 percent.[17] In the 2000 presidential election, most environmental groups supported Al Gore over Green party nominee Ralph Nader.

COOPERATIVE LOBBYING   Often like-minded groups join together as cooperative groups. In 1987 the Leadership Conference on Civil Rights and People for the American Way brought together many groups in the battle to defeat the nomination of outspoken federal judge Robert Bork to the U.S. Supreme Court.[18] Different types of environmentalists work together, as do consumer and ideological groups on the right and on the left. Women continue to be represented by a large variety of groups that reflect diverse interests, but the larger the coalition, the greater the chance that members may divide over such issues as abortion.

Another example is the Food Group, a 30-year-old informal conference group in Washington that has represented more than 60 business and trade associations. In addition, it spawned an Information Committee on Federal Food Regulations to fight "truth-in-packaging" legislation. Although the Food Group has been fairly effective, it does run into the predictable problem of differences among its constituents over goals and priorities and has found it difficult to put strong and unified pressure on Congress and government agencies.

THE INFLUENCE OF LOBBYISTS

The terms "lobbying" and "lobbyist" were not generally used until around the middle of the nineteenth century in the United States. The root in these words refers to the lobby or hallway outside House and Senate chambers in the U.S.

Capitol. It was also used to refer to hotel lobbies in Washington where petitioners and agents of influence congregated. Thus a senator coming out of the Senate chamber might be accosted politely by several lobbyists seeking to influence his vote on some measure. Or a president might be dining at the Willard Hotel, a few blocks from the White House, and make reference to the number of "lobbyists" hanging around in the hotel lobby. The noun "lobby" has been turned into a verb in this political context. Thus "to lobby" is to seek to influence legislators and government officials, and we call this **lobbying** even if there is no lobby in sight.

Despite their negative public image, lobbyists perform useful functions for government. They provide information for the decision makers of all three branches of government, they help educate and mobilize public opinion, they help prepare legislation and testify before legislative hearings, and they contribute a large share of the costs of campaigns. Yet many people are concerned that lobbyists have too much influence on government and add to legislative gridlock by being able to stop action on pressing problems.

Who Are the Lobbyists?

The typical image is that of powerful, hard-nosed lobbyists who skillfully employ a combination of knowledge, persuasiveness, personal influence, charm, and money to influence legislators and bureaucrats. **Lobbyists** are the employees of associations who try to influence policy decisions and positions in the executive and especially in the legislative branches of our government. They are experienced in the ways of government, often having been public servants before going to work for an organized interest group, association, or corporation. They might start as staff in Congress, perhaps on a congressional committee. Later, when their party wins the White House, they gain an administration post, often in the same policy area as their congressional committee work. After a few years in the administration, they are ready to make the move to lobbying, either by going to work for one of the interests they dealt with while in the government or by obtaining a position with a lobbying firm.

Moving from a government job to one with an interest group is quite common, a practice called the **revolving door**. Despite the fact that it is illegal for former government employees to directly lobby the agency from which they came, their contacts made during government service are helpful to interest groups. Many former members of Congress make use of their congressional experience as full-time lobbyists.

The revolving-door tendency between government and interest groups produces networks of people who care about certain issues. These networks have been

Personal contact and access to decision makers continue to be key elements of lobbying today, as they were at the time of President Grant's administration.

called **iron triangles**—meaning mutually supporting relationships among interest groups, congressional committees and subcommittees, and the government agencies that share a common policy concern. Sometimes these relationships become so strong and mutually beneficial that the issue network becomes very powerful. Retired military officers, for example, can go to work for defense contractors after leaving the military, although they are banned for life from selling Department of Defense contracts. This restriction does not preclude them from providing advice to corporations on how best to compete for defense projects.

Legal and political skills, along with specialized knowledge, have become so crucial in executive and legislative policy making as to become a form of power in themselves. Elected representatives increasingly depend on their staffs for guidance, and these issue specialists know more about Section 504 or Title IX or the amendment of 1972—and who wrote that amendment and why—than most political and administrative leaders, who are usually generalists. It is in this gray area of policy making that many interest groups and lobbyists play a vital role, as people move freely from congressional or agency staff to association staff and perhaps back again. These groups of experts are sometimes called *issue networks*.

What Do Lobbyists Do?

Thousands of lobbyists are active in Washington, but few are as glamorous or as unscrupulous as the media suggest, nor are they necessarily influential. One limit on their power is the competition among interest groups. Rarely does any one group have a policy area all to itself. For example, transportation policy involves airplanes, trucks, cars, railroads, consumers, suppliers, state and local governments—the list goes on and on.

To members of Congress, the single most important thing lobbyists provide is money for their next reelection campaign. "Reelection underlies everything else," writes political scientist David Mayhew.[19] Money from interest groups has become instrumental in this driving need of incumbents. Interest groups also provide volunteers for campaign activity. In addition, their failure to support the opposition can enhance an incumbent's chances of being reelected.

Some people defend lobbyists as a kind of "third house" of Congress. Whereas the Senate and House are set up on a geographical basis, lobbyists represent people on the basis of interests and money. Small but important groups can sometimes get representation in the "third house" when they cannot get it in the other two. In a nation of vast and important interests, this kind of functional representation, if it is not abused, can be a useful supplement to geographical representation.

Beyond their central role in campaigns and elections, interest groups provide another essential commodity to legislators: information of two important types, political and substantive. The *political information* provided by lobbyists includes such matters as who supports or opposes legislation and how strongly they feel.[20] *Substantive information* such as the impact of proposed laws might not be available from any other source. Lobbyists often provide technical assistance on the drafting of bills and amendments, identify persons to testify at legislative hearings, and formulate questions to ask of administration officials at oversight hearings.

MONEY AND POLITICS

A **political action committee (PAC)** is the political arm of an interest group that is legally entitled to raise funds on a voluntary basis from members, stockholders, or employees in order to contribute funds to favored candidates or political parties. PACs link two vital techniques of influence—giving money and other political aid to politicians and persuading officeholders to act or vote "the right way" on issues. Thus PACs are the means by which interest groups seek to influence which legislators are elected and what they do once they take office.[21] PACs can be

lobbying
Activities aimed at influencing public officials, especially legislators, and the policies they enact.

lobbyist
A person who is employed by and acts for an organized interest group or corporation to try to influence policy decisions and positions in the executive and legislative branches.

revolving door
The employment cycle in which individuals work, in turn, for governmental agencies regulating interests and then for the interest groups or businesses with the same policy concern.

iron triangle
A mutually supporting relationship among interest groups, congressional committees and subcommittees, and government agencies that share a common policy concern.

political action committee (PAC)
The political arm of an interest group that is legally entitled to raise funds on a voluntary basis from members, stockholders, or employees in order to contribute funds to favored candidates or political parties.

You Decide...

Should PACs be abolished?

As a new member of Congress who almost lost to a candidate supported by PACs in the last election, you are urged by your local newspaper and some constituents to take a bold step and introduce legislation to abolish all PACs. If such legislation were introduced, how would you defend it?

categorized according to the type of interest they represent: corporations, trade and health organizations, labor unions, ideological organizations, and others.

The Growth of PACs

Ironically, considering that the explosion of PACs has occurred mainly in the business world, it was organized labor that invented this device. In the 1930s, John L. Lewis, president of the United Mine Workers, set up the Non-Partisan Political League as the political arm of the newly formed Congress of Industrial Organizations. When the CIO merged with the American Federation of Labor, the new labor group established the Committee on Political Education (COPE), whose activities we have already described. This unit came to be the model for most political action committees: "From the outset, national, state, and local units of COPE have not only raised and distributed funds, but have also served as the mechanism for organized and widespread union activity in the electoral process, for example, in voter registration, political education, and get-out-the-vote drives."[22] Some years later, manufacturers formed the Business-Industry Political Action Committee, but this committee played a limited role in the 1960s.

The 1970s brought a near revolution in the role and influence of PACs, ironically as the result of post-Watergate reforms. The number of PACs increased dramatically, from about 150 to nearly 4,000 today. Corporations and trade associations contributed most to this growth; today their PACs constitute the majority of all PACs. Labor PACs, on the other hand, increased only slightly in number, representing less than 10 percent of all PACs. But the increase in the number of PACs is less important than the intensity of recent PAC participation in elections and in lobbying.

How PACs Invest Their Money

PACs take part in the entire election process, but their main influence lies in their capacity to contribute money to candidates. Candidates today need a lot of money to wage their campaigns. It is no longer uncommon for House candidates to spend more than a million dollars, and for many senators or would-be senators to spend ten times that amount.[23] And as PACs contribute more, their influence grows. What

bundling
A tactic of political action committees whereby they collect contributions from like-minded individuals (each limited to $2,000) and present them to a candidate or political party as a "bundle," thus increasing their influence.

soft money
Unlimited contributions to a state or local political party for party-building purposes.

Labor PACs tend to favor Democratic candidates, as did these fire fighters.

counts is not only the amounts they give but to whom they give. PACs give to the most influential incumbents, to committee chairs, party leaders and whips, and to the Speaker. PACs give not only to the majority party but to key incumbents in the minority party as well, because they understand that today's minority could be tomorrow's majority.

PACs, like individuals, are limited by law in the amount of money they can contribute to any single candidate in an election cycle. The Federal Election Campaign Act of 1971 limits PACs to $5,000 per election or $10,000 per election cycle (primary and general elections). Individuals have a limit of $2,000 per candidate per election cycle. PACs have found some creative ways around this limit. They can host fund-raisers attended by other PACs to boost their reputation with the candidate, or they can collect money from several persons and give it to the candidate as a bundle. Through **bundling**, PACs and interested individuals can increase their clout with elected officials. PACs are not limited in how much they can give the political parties for "party building" purposes. Some of the largest PAC soft money contributors in the 2000 election cycle included several labor unions, AT&T, Philip Morris, and Microsoft.[24]

Campaign fund raisers such as this one often charge donors $1,000 a plate for the privilege of meeting the candidates and mingling with influential policy makers.

The Effectiveness of PACs

The strong tendency of PACs to give to incumbents has meant that challengers face real difficulties in getting their campaigns funded. Challengers have to rely more on individual contributors, and PACs can give five times as much to a candidate as can individuals. Moreover, PACs can help friendly incumbents with **soft money** contributions (unlimited contributions to political parties to be used for party building).

In highly competitive races, interest groups mount *issue advocacy* campaigns to help elect or defeat candidates. These campaigns are highly professional, often negative, and can be substantial in scope. Moreover, interest group electioneering includes all modes of communication with voters—phone calls, mail, personal contact, e-mail, radio commercials, and television. Groups—and even individuals—sometimes run their campaigns hiding behind phony names like Citizens for Good Sense, or the Foundation for Responsible Government, or Republicans for Clean Air or Keep It Flying. Mailings and ads by groups with names like these make it difficult for voters to evaluate the source of the communications. Voters assume that candidates are responsible for the tone and content of campaigns, but the growth in issue advocacy campaigns raises doubts about the validity of that assumption.

How much does PAC money influence election outcomes, legislation, and representation? One critic has written, "When politicians start to see a dollar sign behind every vote, every phone call, every solicitation, those other factors sometimes weighed during governance, like the public good and equal access to government, become less and less important."[25] In this area, as in others, money obviously talks. But it is easy to exaggerate that influence. While a candidate may receive a great amount of PAC money, only a fraction of that total comes from any single interest. In addition, it is debatable how much campaign contributions affect election outcomes and uncertain that winning candidates will be willing and able to "remember" their financial angels or that the money in the end produces a real payoff in legislation.

Much depends, however, on the context in which money is given and received. Many campaigns—especially state and local campaigns—are small-scale undertakings in which a big contribution makes a difference. Amid all the murk of campaigning, a candidate may feel grateful for so tangible and convertible a contribution as money. Studies demonstrate a significant relationship between the frequency of lobbying contacts and favorable treatment in the Ways and Means and House Agriculture Committees. Campaign contributions were found to predict lobbying patterns.[26]

Thinking It Through . . .

As an incumbent, your self-interest would dictate that you oppose a ban on PACs because you stand to benefit from them and your challengers do not. PAC contributions provide a major advantage to you and a huge obstacle to most challengers. This is why many incumbents who ran against PACs in their first race suddenly discover, once elected, that PACs are not all bad. Defenders of PACs label PAC contributions an important form of participation. They argue that such contributions are constitutionally protected. Or they point to a PAC from their district that has supported them and claim that PACs are merely groups of constituents.

If you want to stand by your original opposition to PACs and win others to your point of view, you will need to find a way to substitute "untainted" money like public financing of elections for what you see as "tainted" PAC money. You will have to overcome an intense lobbying effort by PACs to defend what they have been doing. Your best argument against them is that they give so heavily to incumbents (especially incumbents on committees that deal with their concerns) that they make competitive elections unlikely.

1. The struggle among factions is not a fair fight because highly organized and better-financed single-issue groups hold a decided advantage over more general groups.

2. The interest-group battle leads to great inequities, because lower-income people are grossly under-represented among interest groups, as compared to richer, more highly organized people, many of whom are represented by well-financed organizations and lobbyists.

3. Even though the organization of hundreds of single-issue groups has diffused power in government, as the Constitution's framers desired, it has led to incoherent policies, waste and inefficiency, endless delays, and the inability to plan ahead and anticipate crises.

4. The role of interest groups in elections has made incumbents more secure and enhanced the power of interest groups in relation to Congress and state and local governments.

CURING THE MISCHIEFS OF FACTION— TWO HUNDRED YEARS LATER

If James Madison were to return today, he would not be surprised by the existence of interest groups, nor would he be surprised by the variety of interest groups. He might be surprised, however, by the varied weapons of group influence, the deep involvement of interest groups in the electoral process, and the vast number of lobbyists in Washington and the state capitals. And doubtless Madison, were he alive today, would still be concerned about the power of faction, especially its tendency toward instability and injustice.

Concern about the evils of interest groups has been a recurrent theme throughout U.S. history. President Ronald Reagan in his Farewell Address warned of the power of "special interests,"[27] and President Dwight Eisenhower used his Farewell Address to warn against the military-industrial complex.

Single-interest groups organized for or against particular policies—abortion, handgun control, tobacco subsidies, animal rights—have aroused much concern in recent years. "It is said that citizen groups organizing in ever greater numbers to push single issues ruin the careers of otherwise fine politicians who disagree with them on one emotional issue, paralyze the traditional process of governmental compromise, and ignore the common good in their selfish insistence on getting their own way."[28] But which single issues reflect narrow interests? Women's rights—even a specific issue such as sexual harassment—are hardly "narrow," women's rights leaders contend, because they would help over half the population. Peace groups, too, claim that they represent the whole population, as do those who support prayer in schools. These issues may seem quite different from those related to subsidies to dairy farmers, for example.

What should be done about factions—if anything? For decades Americans have tried to find ways to keep interest groups in check. They have agreed with James Madison that the "remedy" of outlawing factions would be worse than the disease. It would be absurd to abolish liberty simply because it nourished faction. And the existence and activity of interest groups and lobbies are solidly protected by the Constitution. But by safeguarding the value of liberty, have Americans allowed interest groups to threaten equality, the second great value in our national heritage? The question remains: How can interest groups be regulated in a way that does not threaten their constitutional liberties?

Federal and State Regulation

Americans have generally responded to this question by seeking to regulate lobbying in general and political money in particular. Concern over the use of money—especially corporate funds—to influence politicians goes back well over a century, to the Crédit Mobilier scandals during the administration of Ulysses S. Grant. During the "progressive" first two decades of the twentieth century, Congress legislated against corporate contributions in federal elections and required disclosure of the use of the money.

In 1925, responding to the Teapot Dome scandal during Warren G. Harding's administration, Congress passed the Federal Corrupt Practices Act. It required disclosure reports, both before and after elections, of receipts and expenditures by Senate and House candidates and by political committees that sought to influence federal elections in more than one state. Note that these were *federal* laws applying to *federal* elections; regulation of state lobbying and elections was left to the states.

Federal legislation, including the 1925 Federal Corrupt Practices Act and the 1946 Federal Regulation of Lobbying Act, was not very effective. It was, in fact, largely unenforced. Many candidates filed incomplete reports or none at all. The reform mood of the 1960s brought basic changes. The upshot was the Federal Election Campaign Act (FECA) of 1971, which supplanted the earlier legislation.

FECA, which has been amended three times, establishes reporting or disclosure requirements for all candidates for the U.S. House of Representatives, the Senate, and the presidency, as well as their political parties and campaign committees. It also requires disclosure of the amounts spent to influence federal elections by others, including individuals and political action committees. The act established partial public financing for presidential candidates, financed by a voluntary check-off on federal income tax forms. *Spending by candidates* is not limited, but *contributions* to these candidates and to presidential candidates are limited. Two candidates for president in 2000, Steve Forbes and George W. Bush, turned down the federal matching funds and state-by-state limits in the primaries, a move likely to be copied by wealthy or well-funded candidates in the future.

There have been notable problems with the act, including an ineffective Federal Election Commission. The act has had its critics, and Congress has frequently debated reforming campaign financing. (We discuss these reform proposals in greater detail in Chapter 9.) There have also been significant attempts to regulate interest-group activity in elections at the state level. Some states, like Maine, Wisconsin, Minnesota, and Hawaii, provide for public financing of state offices and state legislative races; others, like Michigan, New Jersey, and Massachusetts, provide partial public financing of gubernatorial elections; a dozen more help underwrite parties with public funds.[29]

During President Bill Clinton's first term, Congress passed the first major overhaul of lobbying laws since 1946. Under the Lobbying Disclosure Act of 1995, the definition of lobbyist was significantly expanded to include part-time lobbyists, those who deal with congressional staff or executive branch agencies, and those who represent foreign-owned companies and foreign entities. This act was expected to increase the number of registered lobbyists anywhere from three to ten times its current level.[30] The act also included specific disclosure requirements and information requirements.

Just six months before leaving office, President Clinton signed into law legislation expanding disclosure requirements by interest groups running issue ads. Some groups had previously been able to avoid disclosure because they fell outside the disclosure requirements of either the Federal Election Commission or the Internal Revenue Service. An example previously discussed, Republicans for Clean Air, attacked Senator McCain's environmental record in the 2000 primaries. The new law will have only a minor impact, as interest groups desiring to engage in issue advocacy can continue to do so, hiding behind vague names like Foundation for Responsible Government, or Coalition to Make Our Voices Heard—two groups that have run ads in recent election cycles. These advertisements generally attack one candidate or praise another, and they are difficult to distinguish from candidate or party ads. But to limit them, as some reformers propose, means some wider limitation on freedom of speech.

Interest group issue advocacy ads as well as party ads paid for by soft money permit the interest group or party to circumvent the contribution limits and some of the disclosure requirements imposed on candidates. This strategic advantage has made issue advocacy and soft money increasingly important in competitive election contests. Interest groups are a major donor of soft money to the parties and also the primary donor to candidates. Under current rules, the same interest group may invest in elections through hard money (limited and disclosed) to candidates, soft money to the parties, and issue advocacy.

The Effects of Regulation

What have been the effects of past reforms on interest groups? Ironically, one has been to increase the number and importance of such groups. The strategy of the 1971 law was to authorize direct and open participation by both labor and corporate organizations in elections and lobbying in the hopes that a visible role for interest-group activity, backed by effective enforcement, would be constitutional under the First Amendment. The 1971 act allowed unions and corporations to communicate on political matters to members or stockholders, to conduct registration and get-out-the-vote drives, and to spend union and company funds to set up "separate segregated funds" (PACs) to use for political purposes.

Corporations, trade associations, and unions made PACs a central part of their government relations strategy. But what changed the rules of the game for corporate interests was passage in 1974 of limits on individual contributions, something not part of the 1971 act. An explosion of corporate PACs followed this 1974 amendment.[31] In 1978 there was little difference in the level of campaign activity of PACs representing corporations, labor unions, or trade associations.[32] But that has changed, with corporate PACs spending more than the others, and ideological PACs at roughly half the level of spending of trade and labor PACs. In the 1997–98 election cycle, corporate PACs spent $137.6 million, labor PACs spent $98.2 million, and trade PACs spent $114.4 million.[33]

The three major types of PACs all substantially expanded their contributions to candidates in 1999–2000. Labor PACs saw the greatest increase in spending, climbing to $126 million, or a 28 percent increase over 1997–98. Trade association PACs exceeded their past cycle contributions by $23 million, for a total of $114 million. Corporate PACs again led all PACs in contributions in 1999–2000, giving nearly $162 million, a 17 percent increase over 1997–98.

With each successive election cycle, PACs spend more money. Most of this money goes to incumbents, especially committee chairs and party leaders. The result, labor leaders contend, has been a greater imbalance than ever between the political action and power of a relatively small number of corporate executives and stockholders, on the one hand, and the labor unions on the other.

A centerpiece of past efforts to regulate interest-group activity was *disclosure* of how politicians fund their campaigns. Until the 1996 election cycle, with the important exception of soft money, we had a much better idea of how much money candidates raised and how they spent it. Without disclosure, much of what we have written here about PACs, for instance, would not be public knowledge. Disclosure permits the press and public to assess the implications of how candidates finance their campaigns. The growth of soft money and the advent of issue advocacy by interest groups now means that we know less and less about how campaigns are financed. Groups and individuals can avoid disclosure, and the public remains uninformed about who is trying to influence their vote.

Candidates and some appointed officials must also disclose their personal finances, permitting voters and the press to see what investments and resources candidates have that may affect their ability to be impartial. Such public disclosure of personal worth, the value of property owned, and outstanding debts no doubt discourages some persons from entering public life, but it also makes officeholders accountable for certain obligations and actions once they enter office.

Is Reform Possible?

Will Congress reform the PACs and campaign finance in general? Not only is reform itself complex and difficult, but it is doubtful that most members of Congress really want reform. Many members of Congress thrive on the present arrangements, and the leaders and members of both parties actually compete for

TABLE 6–3 The Big Givers, 1999–2000			
Donor	Republicans	Democrats	Total
Philip Morris Co. (tobacco)	$2,517,518	$ 481,518	$2,999,036
Joseph E. Seagram & Sons/MCA (liquor, music)	$ 685,145	$1,180,700	$1,865,845
RJR Nabisco (tobacco)	$1,188,175	$ 253,403	$1,441,578
Walt Disney Co. (entertainment)	$ 296,450	$ 997,050	$1,293,500
Atlantic Richfield Co.* (oil, gas)	$ 766,506	$ 486,372	$1,252,878
Communications Workers of America* (labor union)	$ 0	$1,128,425	$1,128,425

Source: Common Cause home page: www.commoncause.org/cgi-bin/ccause/soft_money.pl.

*Includes contributions from subsidiaries and/or executives.

PAC dollars (see Table 6–3). Although Republicans have generally received the larger amounts, Democrats in recent election cycles put pressure on the pharmaceutical and insurance industries to give more to Democratic candidates because Democrats might emerge from the election as the majority party, controlling all committee chairmanships and managing the floor of the House, Senate, or both.[35] One reason members of Congress become entrenched in their seats is that PACs fund them. Some of them are reluctant to give up such a cozy relationship. Thus the real question may not be whether Congress can reform the interest-group lobbies, but whether Congress can reform itself.

While PACs help secure incumbent victories with campaign contributions and their general tendency not to support challengers, interest groups also increasingly contribute soft money to the parties, who in turn spend this money to help elect or defeat candidates in competitive contests. This dual-track strategy is relatively new and, in the instance of some interest groups, substantial. For example, pharmaceutical industry PACs donated an estimated $5.2 million to federal candidates in 2000; they also gave another $15.2 million in soft money to the political parties.[36] The pharmaceutical industry exemplifies another recent development—the willingness of groups to spend money on issue advocacy. Beginning in 1999, the pharmaceutical industry contributed heavily to a group named "Citizens for Better Medicare," which reported it would spend $40 million in issue advertising in 2000.[37] Some of their ads ran in states with competitive Senate races, like Montana and Michigan.[38] This issue advocacy is unsettling to incumbents because it is unlimited and often not disclosed.

Interest groups and wealthy individuals have underwritten the dramatic surge in party soft money in recent elections. With control of the executive and legislative branches now so tenuous, both parties have turned up the pressure on interested groups and individuals to give large sums to win the battle for the White House or control of Congress, and groups and individuals responded vigorously. Probably the most conspicuous soft money fund raiser was Bill Clinton; George W. Bush waited only a few months into his new presidency before he started raising soft money for the Republicans.

The combination of issue advocacy and soft money spending invested in competitive races were factors in the Senate vote to pass campaign finance reform in 2001. The McCain-Feingold-Cochran legislation included a soft money ban as well as limits on issue advocacy and requirements for greater disclosure of groups supporting issue advocacy. Passage of the bill depended on whether the House would enact similar legislation, whether the House and Senate could agree on an identical bill, and whether President Bush would sign such a bill. The lengthy Senate debate and the ability of John McCain to mobilize media coverage of the issue enhanced its visibility and made passage more likely.

Strengthening the political parties might be another way to reduce the power of special interests. If campaign contributions were directed more to parties than to candidates, then candidates would be more accountable to the parties and less tied to any particular interest. Parties are also more likely to invest in challengers than are PACs. Finally, because parties must seek to broaden their appeal, they cannot risk becoming captive of a particular narrow interest. Yet politicians and the interest groups that finance their campaigns strongly favor the current system. This mutually beneficial system is likely to continue until public pressure for change increases.

POLITICS ONLINE

In Whose Interest?

One of the ways interest groups try to win friends and gain access to members of Congress is through campaign contributions, typically through their political action committee (PAC). There are over 4,000 political action committees registered with the Federal Elections Commission. You can access a list of most PACs by industry at:
www.opensecrets.org/pacs/index.asp.

Interest groups can attempt to influence the outcome of elections by spending money for or against a candidate through independent expenditures. The Supreme Court in *Buckley v Valeo* said that groups could not be limited in how much they spent to elect or defeat a candidate, so long as that expenditure was independent of the candidate or party campaigns. One group that engages in independent expenditures is the National Rifle Association (NRA). To learn how much they and other groups spend in this way, go to:
www.nra.org.

Since 1996, interest groups have found a new way to influence elections—issue advocacy—which permits them to spend unlimited and undisclosed amounts of money so long as they avoid using the words "Vote for—," as discussed earlier in this chapter. In 2000, money raised by interest group activity, combined with national political party activity, surpassed candidate activity. Many of these groups, in an effort to hide the identity of their donors and the goals of their group, take on innocuous names like Citizens for Good Common Sense, American Family Voices, and Americans for Hope, Growth, and Opportunity. Who are these groups? What do they advocate? Where do they get their money? In whose interest do they work?

During the 2000 election, The Annenberg Public Policy Center of the University of Pennsylvania tracked broadcast issue ads and the groups that paid for them. From this information, they compiled a database of groups and their activities. Visit the group index at: www.appcpenn.org/issueads/gindex.htm, and click on a specific group to find out who they are, who they represent, and what they did to influence the 2000 election. This site also contains links to many groups' home pages.

SUMMARY

1. Interest groups exist to make demands on government. The dominant interest groups in the United States are economic or occupational, but a variety of other groups—ideological, public interest, foreign policy, government itself, as well as ethnic, religious, and racial—have memberships that cut across the big economic groupings; thus their influence is both reduced and stabilized.

2. Movements of large numbers of people who are frustrated with government policies have always been with us in the United States. Blacks, women, and the economic underdogs have at various times organized themselves into movements.

3. Elements in interest-group power include size, resources, cohesiveness, leadership, and techniques, especially the ability to contribute to candidates and political parties as well as the ability to fund lobbyists. But the actual power of an interest group stems from the manner in which these elements relate to the political and governmental environment in which the interest group operates.

4. For many decades, interest groups have engaged in lobbying, but these efforts have become far more significant as groups become more deeply involved in the electoral process, especially through the expanded use of political action committees (PACs). Interest groups also take their messages directly to the public through mass mailings and advertising campaigns. Other interest group techniques include influencing rule making, litigation, election activities, and cooperative lobbying.

5. Concern for PACs centers on their ability to raise money and spend it on elections on behalf of endorsed candidates, typically incumbents. This concern has led to proposals to ban PACs or more strictly limit their activities. Yet their existence and rights are protected by the First Amendment.

6. Reforms of interest-group excess often include regulations that seek fairness, disclosure, and balance between interest groups. All reform efforts must operate so as not to take away basic constitutional rights of individuals. The key issue today in "controlling factions" is whether to allow groups to proliferate and so balance each other, to try to regulate groups, or to seek reforms outside the groups by fostering balanced power in political parties or elsewhere.

KEY TERMS

issue advocacy 118
faction 118
interest group 118
movement 118
open shop 121

closed shop 121
free rider 121
Federal Register 128
amicus curiae brief 130
lobbying 133

lobbyist 133
revolving door 133
iron triangle 133
political action committee
  (PAC) 133

bundling 134
soft money 134

FURTHER READING

JEFFREY M. BERRY, *The Interest Group Society*, 3d ed. (Longman, 1997).

JEFFERY H. BIRNBAUM, *The Lobbyists: How Influence Peddlers Get Their Way in Washington* (Times Books, 1992).

WILLIAM P. BROWNE, *Groups, Interests, and Public Policy* (Georgetown University Press, 1998).

ALLAN J. CIGLER AND BURDETT A. LOOMIS, EDS., *Interest Group Politics*, 5th ed. (Congressional Quarterly Press, 1998).

ALLEN D. HERTZKE, *Representing God in Washington: The Role of Religious Lobbies in the American Polity* (University of Tennessee Press, 1988).

RONALD J. HREBENAR, *Interest Group Politics in America* (M. E. Sharpe, 1997).

MANCUR OLSON, *The Logic of Collective Action* (Harvard University Press, 1965).

MARK P. PETRACCA, ED., *The Politics of Interests: Interest Groups Transformed* (Westview Press, 1992).

DAVID VOGEL, *Kindred Strangers: The Uneasy Relationship Between Politics and Business in America* (Princeton University Press, 1996).

JACK L. WALKER, JR., *Mobilizing Interest Groups in America: Patrons, Professions, and Social Movements* (University of Michigan Press, 1991).

CLYDE WILCOX, *Risky Business? PAC Decision Making in Congressional Elections* (M. E. Sharpe, 1994).

JOHN R. WRIGHT, *Interest Groups and Congress: Lobbying Contributions and Influence* (Allyn and Bacon, 1996).

7

POLITICAL PARTIES: ESSENTIAL TO DEMOCRACY

SOME YEARS AGO A COMMUNITY COLLEGE DISTRICT
IN LOS ANGELES HELD A NONPARTISAN ELECTION IN
WHICH ANY REGISTERED VOTER COULD RUN IF HE OR SHE PAID
the $50 filing fee and gathered 500 valid signatures on a petition. One hundred and
thirty-three candidates ran, and each voter could cast up to seven votes in the election.
Political parties were not allowed to nominate candidates, and party labels did not
appear on the ballot to help orient voters to the candidates.[1]

How did people vote in an election without parties? Candidates were listed alpha-
betically, and those whose names began with the letters A to F did better than those later
in the alphabet. Being well known helped. Endorsements by *The Los Angeles Times* also
influenced the outcome, as did campaigning by a conservative group. A Mexican-American surname also helped. In this election an important voting cue was absent: incumbency.
Because the board of trustees was newly created, none of the candidates were incumbents.

Rarely are American voters faced with such unorganized and plentiful choices,
because parties give structure to national and state elections. E. E. Schattschneider, a
noted political scientist, once said, "The political parties created democracy, and modern democracy is unthinkable save in terms of the parties."[2] This provocative statement
is true, but such a favorable evaluation of political parties runs counter to a long-
standing and deep-seated American fear and distrust of them. Experience has taught
us that free people create political parties to promote their own goals. Parties are a consequence of freedom, as we learned again with the fall of communism in Eastern
Europe. Even though our founders hoped to discourage them, political parties quickly
became an integral part of our political system.

Elections serve the vital task of deciding who can legitimately exercise political
power, and parties are an integral part of making national and state elections work. We
take for granted the peaceful transfer of power from one elected official to another, from
one party to another, yet in new democracies the transfer of power following an election is often problematic. Parties serve many functions, including an important one of
narrowing the choices for voters.[3] They are both a consequence of democracy and an
instrument of it. Parties need not be strong and cohesive like those in Britain and
Europe, but without some kind if party system, democracies are not likely to survive.

This chapter begins by examining the purposes parties serve that make them so
vital to the functioning of democracy. We then examine the evolution of American
political parties. Although American political parties have changed over time, they

CHAPTER MEDIA

POLITICS ONLINE
What's Your Party?
www.prenhall.com/burns

POLISIM
The Political Horizon
www.prenhall.com/burns

remain important in three different settings: as institutions, in government, and in the electorate. It is important to understand how parties facilitate democracy in all three settings. Finally, we turn to a discussion of the strength of parties today and the prospects for party reform and renewal.

WHAT PARTIES DO FOR DEMOCRACY

Party Functions

American political parties serve a variety of political and social functions, some obvious and some not so obvious. They perform some functions well and others not so well, and how they perform them differs from place to place and time to time.

ORGANIZE THE COMPETITION   One of the most important functions of parties is to organize the competition by choosing candidates to run under their label. Parties recruit and nominate candidates for office; they register and activate voters; they help candidates by training them, raising money for them, providing them with research and voter lists, and enlisting volunteers to work for them.[4] Recently campaign consultants rather than party officials have taken over some of these responsibilities; we explore this topic at some length in Chapter 8.

The ability of parties to influence the selection of candidates varies by the type of nominating system used in the state. A few states use a *caucus or convention system*, which permits party leaders to play a role in the selection of nominees. Other states utilize *primary elections*. As more and more states use primary elections, the ability of party leaders to influence who runs under their party label is reduced. Candidates with little party experience but with well-known names or ample personal funds can often win in a primary over a person with a known track record of prior party service or success in a less visible office.

A party's ability to organize the competition is also influenced by how states organize their ballots. In many states, candidates are listed in party columns—the **party column ballot**—which makes it easier for voters to vote a *straight ticket* for all the party candidates. Straight-ticket voting is also more likely in voting systems that permit flipping one switch or punching one chad to vote for all candidates from one party. Other states organize the ballot by office—the **office block ballot**—which makes straight-ticket voting harder. Even though many voters cast votes for candidates in more than one party, the party label of a candidate means something to most voters and is important in their voting decision.

Local and judicial elections in most states are **nonpartisan**, which means no party affiliation is indicated. Such systems make it more difficult for political parties to operate—precisely the reason why many jurisdictions have adopted this reform. Proponents of nonpartisan local and judicial elections contend that party affiliation is not important to being a good judge or school board member.

UNIFY THE ELECTORATE   Parties are often accused of creating conflict, but the fact is that they actually help unify the electorate and moderate conflict. There is a strong incentive in both parties to fight out their differences inside the party but then come together to take on the opposition. Moreover, in order to win elections, parties need to reach out to voters outside their party and gain their support. This action also helps unify the electorate, at least into the two large national political parties in our system.

Parties have great difficulty building coalitions when faced with controversial issues like abortion or gun control. Not surprisingly, candidates and parties generally try to avoid defining themselves or the election in single-issue terms. Rather, they hope that if voters disagree with them on one issue, they will still support them because they agree with them on other issues.

party column ballot
Ballot in which all candidates are listed under their party designations, making it easy for voters to cast votes for all the candidates of one party.

office block ballot
Ballot in which all candidates are listed under the office for which they are running.

nonpartisan
A local or judicial election in which party affiliation is not listed on ballots.

HELP ORGANIZE GOVERNMENT   Although American political parties are not as cohesive as those in England and most European democracies, parties are important when it comes to organizing our state and national governments. Congress is organized along party lines. The political party with the most votes in each chamber elects the officers of that chamber, selects the chair of each committee, and has a majority on all the committees. State legislatures, with the notable exception of Nebraska, are also organized along party lines.

Following the 2000 election, the U.S. Senate was evenly split between Republicans and Democrats, and the Republicans could have relied on Vice-President Cheney to cast a tie-breaking vote on which party would chair all committees. Instead, leaders of both parties negotiated a power-sharing arrangement in which Republicans chair all committees, but membership on committees is evenly split, with both parties having the same allocation of staff on all committees.[5]

The party that controls the White House, the governor's mansion, or city hall gets **patronage**, which means it can select party members as public officials or judges. Such appointments are limited only by civil service regulations that restrict patronage typically to the top posts, but these posts number about 4,000 in the federal government and are also numerous at the state and local levels. Patronage provides an incentive for people to become involved in politics and gives the party leaders loyal partisans in key positions to help them achieve their policy objectives.

TRANSLATE PREFERENCE INTO POLICY   One of the great strengths of our democracy is that even the party that wins an election usually has to moderate what it does in order to win reelection. For that reason, public policy does not change dramatically with each election. Nonetheless, the party that wins the election has a chance to enact its policies and implement its campaign promises.

American parties have had only limited success in setting the course of national policy, especially when compared with traditionally strong European parties. The European model of party government, which has been called a *responsible party system*, assumes that parties discipline their members through their control over nominations and campaigns. Officeholders in such party-centered systems are expected to act according to party wishes or they will not be allowed to run again under the party label. Moreover, candidates run on fairly specific party platforms and are expected to implement those policies if they win control in the election.

Because American parties do not control nominations, they are unable to discipline members who express views contrary to those of the party. The American system is *candidate centered*; politicians are nominated largely on the basis of their qualifications and personal appeal, not party loyalty. In fact, it is more correct to say that in most contests we have candidate politics rather than party politics. As a consequence, party leaders cannot guarantee passage of their program, even if they are in the majority. But in recent years parties have come to play an important role in competitive federal elections through their **soft money** expenditures. Soft money comes from unlimited contributions to the political parties from individuals, corporations, labor unions, and political action committees (PACs) for "party building" purposes, but it has come to be used for candidate promotion. Because such contributions are unlimited, parties put a premium on large donors.[6]

In our Congress, most, but not all, Democrats vote together, as do most, but not all, Republicans. And then there are times, rather unusual but not unprecedented, when a president of one party receives more congressional votes from the opposing party than from his own, as President Bill Clinton did in 2000 on legislation granting China permanent normal trade relations status with the United States.[7]

PROVIDE LOYAL OPPOSITION   Parties provide a loyal opposition. After a polite interval following an election—**the honeymoon**—the opposition party begins to criticize the party that controls the White House, especially when the opposition

patronage
The dispensing of government jobs to persons who belong to the winning political party.

soft money
Money contributed for party-building purposes that does not have to be disclosed under federal law.

honeymoon
A period at the beginning of a new president's term in which the president enjoys generally positive relations with the press and Congress, usually lasting about six months.

A precinct caucus in Des Moines, Iowa, discusses and votes on delegates to represent their choice for president.

party controls one or both houses of Congress.[8] The length of the honeymoon depends in part on how contentious the agenda of the new administration is and on the leadership skills of the new president. Early success in enacting policy can prolong the honeymoon; mistakes or controversies can shorten it.

The Nomination of Candidates

From the beginning, parties have been the mechanism by which candidates for public office are chosen. Massachusetts used the earliest method of nominating candidates—the **caucus**, a closed meeting of local leaders. The caucus played an important part in pre-Revolutionary politics. Elected officials organized themselves into groups or parties and together selected candidates to run for higher office, including the presidency. This method of nomination operated for several decades after the United States was established.

As early as the 1820s, however, charges of "secret deals" and "smoke-filled rooms" were made against this method. Moreover, it was not representative of people from areas where a party was in a minority or nonexistent, as only office-holders took part in the caucus. Efforts were made to make the caucus more representative of rank-and-file party members. The *mixed caucus* brought in delegates from districts in which the party had no elected legislators.

Then, during the 1830s and 1840s, a system of **party conventions** was instituted. Delegates, usually chosen directly by party members in towns and cities, selected the party standard-bearers, debated and adopted a platform, and built party spirit by celebrating noisily. But the convention method soon came under criticism that it was subject to control by the party bosses and their machines.

To involve more voters and reduce the power of the bosses to pick party nominees, states adopted the **direct primary**, in which people could vote for the party's nominees for office. Primaries spread rapidly after Wisconsin adopted them in 1905—in the North as a Progressive era reform and in the South as a way to bring democracy to a region that had seen no meaningful general elections since the end of Reconstruction due to one-party rule by the Democrats. By 1920 direct primaries were used for some offices in almost all states.

Today the direct primary is the typical method of picking party candidates. Primaries vary significantly from state to state. They differ in terms of: (1) who may run in a primary and how one qualifies for the ballot; (2) whether the party organization

caucus
A meeting of local party members to choose party officials and/or candidates for public office and to decide the platform.

party convention
A meeting of party delegates to pass on matters of policy and in some cases to select party candidates for public office.

direct primary
Election open to all members of the party in which voters choose the persons who will be the party's nominees in the general election.

can or does endorse candidates before the primary; (3) who may vote in a party's primary—that is, whether a voter must register with a party in order to vote; and (4) how many votes are needed for nomination—a plurality, a majority, or some other number determined by party rule or state law. The differences among primaries are not trivial; they have an important impact on the role played by party organization and on the strategy used by candidates.

In states with **open primaries**, any voter, regardless of party, can participate in whichever primary he or she may choose. This kind of primary permits **crossover voting**—Republicans and Independents helping to determine who the Democratic nominee will be, and vice versa. Other states use **closed primaries**, in which only persons already registered in a party may participate. Some states, like Washington and California, experimented with *blanket primaries* in which all voters could vote for any candidate, regardless of party. In 2000, blanket primaries were declared unconstitutional by the U.S. Supreme Court, in part because they permit people who have "expressly affiliated with a rival" party to have a vote in the selection of a nominee from a different party.[9]

Direct primaries were introduced to reduce the influence of party leaders, which they have done, but many critics believe that this change has had more undesirable than desirable consequences. Party leaders now have less influence over who gets to be the party's candidate, and candidates are less accountable to the party both during the election and after it. Along with modern communications and fund-raising techniques, direct primaries have diminished the influence of leaders of political parties.

The rise of direct primaries has not meant the death of caucuses or conventions. In some states local caucuses choose delegates to attend regional meetings, which in turn select delegates to state and national conventions, where they nominate party candidates for offices. The Iowa caucuses, in which roughly one hundred thousand Iowans in each major party participate, are highly publicized as the first important test of potential presidential nominees.[10]

In a few states, conventions still play a role in the nominating process. In Connecticut, for example, convention choices become the party nominees unless they are challenged. Candidates who attain at least 15 percent of the vote in the convention have an automatic right to challenge, but they do not always exercise this right.[11] In Utah, if a candidate gets 60 percent of the delegate vote at the convention, there is no primary. Should no candidate reach 60 percent, only the top two candidates are listed on the primary ballot. In other states, convention nominees are designated as such on the primary ballot; they may or may not receive help from the party organization. Conventions are also used to invigorate the party faithful by enabling them to meet with their leaders.

In most states candidates can get their names on the ballot as an Independent or minor party candidate by securing the required number of signatures on a nomination petition. This is hard to do, but it can be done, as Ross Perot demonstrated in 1992. He spent his own money to build an organization of volunteers who put his name on the ballot in all 50 states. Minor party gubernatorial candidates like the Minnesota Reform party's Jessie Ventura in 1998 or the Green party's presidential candidate Ralph Nader in 2000 secured their nominations through their existing parties. However, in 2000 Nader did not appear on the ballot in seven states.[12]

Party Systems

Although we have many minor parties, only the two major parties have much of a chance to win elections. Ours is a two-party system; most other democracies have a multiparty system. Multiparty systems are almost always found in countries that have a parliamentary government, in contrast to our presidential system. This is, however, not always true. For example, England has a parliamentary system but also a strong two-party system.

Parliamentary systems usually have a *head of the nation*, often called the president, but they also have a *head of the government*, often called the prime minister or

open primary
A primary in which any voter, regardless of party, may vote.

crossover voting
A member of one party voting for a candidate of another party.

closed primary
A primary in which only persons registered in the party holding the primary may vote.

ISRAEL'S COALITION GOVERNMENT

Israel has a multiparty system. Though Israelis vote for prime minister and parliament separately, the prime minister must still have the support of the majority of the members of parliament. If he doesn't, he is in danger of facing a parliamentary vote of no confidence. A vote of no confidence leads to new elections for prime minister and parliament. Because there are many parties, it is difficult—if not impossible—for any one party to gain a majority of the seats in the Knesset, the Israeli parliament. Usually one party can only get a plurality of the seats. A party with only a plurality of seats must form a coalition with other parties in order to rule. Certain concessions must be made to those parties to convince them to join. If the ruling party loses the support of its coalition partners, the prime minister and his party must form a new coalition or their government will be toppled by a parliamentary vote of no confidence.

In July 2000, three religious or rightist parties withdrew from Prime Minister Ehud Barak's coalition government in protest over the peace talks with the Palestinians. This left Barak without a parliamentary majority. Though he survived the subsequent vote of no confidence, he was forced into forming a new coalition government. This effort even led to talks of forming a unity party with

the Likud party. The Likud party leader, Ariel Sharon, was one of Barak's most outspoken critics. Sharon demanded that if his party were to join a unity government with Barak, it must have a veto over any future concessions in peace talks. These negotiations were ultimately unfruitful, and in a surprise move in November, Barak exercised his authority to call an early election for prime minister. On February 6, 2001, Ariel Sharon soundly defeated Ehud Barak. Now Sharon had to form a coalition government in a limited amount of time.

It is not clear what effect these developments will have on peace talks with the Palestinians. Sharon and the Likud party are much more reluctant to make concessions to the Palestinians than Barak and his government were, but to form a government, they must still make concessions to other parties. The peace policy they ultimately pursue may be a reflection of the concessions they must make to form a coalition government.

SOURCE: John Kifner, "Barak Seems in Position to Survive Vote in Parliament," *The New York Times*, July 31, 2000, p. A8; Joel Greenberg, "Barak and Sharon Open Talks on Forming a Coalition," *The New York Times*, October 24, 2000, p. A18; and Deborah Sontag, "Barak Declares Early Elections, in Surprise Move," *The New York Times*, November 29, 2000, p. A1.

chancellor, who is the leader of one of the larger parties in the legislature. In democracies with multiparty systems, such as Israel and Italy, because no one party has a majority of the votes, *coalition* governments are necessary. Minor parties can gain concessions—positions in a cabinet or support of policies they want implemented—in return for their participation in a coalition. Major parties need the minor parties and are therefore willing to bargain. Thus the multiparty system favors the existence of minor parties by giving them incentives to persevere.

In some multiparty parliamentary systems, parties run slates of candidates for legislative positions, and winners are determined by **proportional representation**, in which the parties receive a proportion of the legislators corresponding to their proportion of the vote. In our **winner-take-all** system, only the candidate with the most votes in a district or state takes office. Because a party does not gain anything by finishing second, minor parties in a two-party system can rarely overcome the assumption that a vote for them is a wasted vote.[13] Even if a third-party candidate can keep either major party candidate from receiving more than 50 percent (a *majority*) of the vote, the candidate with the most votes (a *plurality*) wins.

In multiparty systems, parties at the extremes are apt to have more influence than in our two-party system, and their legislatures more accurately reflect the full range of the views of the electorate. Political parties in multiparty systems can be more doctrinaire than ours because they do not have to appeal to masses of people. Even though parties that do not become part of the governing coalition may have little to say in setting government policy, they survive because they appeal to some voters. Under such a system, an incentive exists for third, fourth, or additional parties to run because they may win some seats. In contrast, our two-party system tends to create *centrist* parties that appeal to moderate elements and suppress the views of extremists in the electorate. Moreover, once elected, our parties do not form as cohesive a voting block as do ideological parties in multiparty systems.

Multiparty parliamentary systems make governments unstable, as coalitions form and collapse. In addition, swings in policy when party control changes can be quite dramatic. In contrast, two-party systems produce governments that tend to be stable and centrist, and as a result, policy changes occur incrementally.

Minor Parties: Persistence and Frustration

Although we have a primarily two-party system in the United States, we also have **minor parties**, sometimes called *third parties*. Those that arise around a candidate usually disappear when the charismatic personality does. Examples of such parties

proportional representation
An election system in which each party running receives the proportion of legislative seats corresponding to its proportion of the vote.

winner-take-all
An election system in which the candidate with the most votes wins.

minor party
A small political party that rises and falls with a charismatic candidate or, if composed of ideologies on the right or left, usually persists over time; also called a *third party*.

are Theodore Roosevelt's Bull Moose party and George Wallace's American Independent party. Wallace's party polled more than 13 million votes and won 46 electoral votes in 1968. Ross Perot won 19 million votes, for 19 percent of the total vote in 1992. He did only about half as well in 1996, despite the fact that he had organized a political party. Without Ross Perot to lead it, the Reform party was badly divided in 2000 and its presidential candidate, Pat Buchanan, failed to reach 1 percent of the national popular vote. More visible than the Reform party was the Green party, which mounted a major effort to reach 5 percent of the popular vote for presidential candidate Ralph Nader and thereby qualify the party for federal funding in the 2004 elections. The effort failed. The Green party mustered only 3 percent of the popular vote.

Minor parties that are organized around an *ideology* usually persist over a longer time than do those built around a particular leader. Communist, Prohibition, Libertar-

CANADA'S MULTIPARTY SYSTEM

In contrast to the two-party system found in the United States, Canada has a multiparty system. Following the general elections of 1997, the Liberal party, led by Jean Chrétien, formed Canada's government. In addition, seats were allocated in the House of Commons, Canada's preeminent legislative chamber, to the Progressive Conservative party, the New Democratic party, the Reform party, and the Bloc Québécois. Either the Liberals or the Progressive Conservatives have dominated the national political landscape since Canada became a sovereign nation in 1867, and both parties are basically centrist.

The New Democrats, which have formed several provincial governments in recent years, believe in social democracy and support a strong governmental role in the economy, an extensive social welfare system, and Canada's withdrawal from both the North Atlantic Treaty Organization (NATO) and the North American Free Trade Agreement (NAFTA). They are outspoken about too much American influence over Canada. The Reform party receives most of its support from voters in

Canada's western provinces and believes in a limited governmental role in the economic sector and cordial relations with the United States. The Bloc Québécois's primary mission is to promote Quebec's independence from Canada through democratic means. All of Canada's major parties are to the left of the Democratic and Republican parties in the United States, and Canadians in general are much more supportive than Americans of a major governmental role in the economic and social welfare sectors.

Because of the multiplicity of parties, Canadian voters have more options in linking their own policy preferences to specific party platforms. On the other hand, the multiparty system may occasionally result in a minority government, meaning that no party controls a majority of the seats in parliament. This can make governing a much more precarious process. In addition, Canada's multiparty system has accentuated regional biases and preferences within this vast northern nation, complicating efforts to promote national unity and a national vision of Canada's future.

ian, or Green parties are of the ideological type. Minor parties of both types come and go, and there are usually several minor parties running in any given election.[14] Some parties arise around a single issue, like the States' Rights party that split with the Democratic party in 1948 over President Harry Truman's civil rights policies.

Minor parties have had an indirect influence in our country by drawing attention to controversial issues and by organizing such groups as the antislavery and the civil rights movements. However, they have never won the presidency or more than a handful of congressional seats (see Table 7–1).[15] They have never shaped national policy from *inside* the government, and their influence on national policy and on the platforms of the two major parties has been limited.[16]

Minor parties have been criticized by major parties as "spoilers," diverting votes away from the major party candidate and costing that candidate the election. Green party candidate Ralph Nader was accused of doing this to Al Gore in 2000. Interest groups identified with environmental issues ran ads urging voters not to waste their vote on Nader, who could not win the election.

A BRIEF HISTORY OF AMERICAN POLITICAL PARTIES

Our First Parties

To the founders of the young Republic, parties meant bigger, better organized, and fiercer factions, and they did not want that. Benjamin Franklin worried about the "infinite mutual abuse of parties, tearing to pieces the best of characters." In his Farewell Address, George Washington warned against the "baneful effects of the Spirit of Party." And Thomas Jefferson said, "If I could not go to heaven but with a party, I would not go there at all."[17]

Ross Perot, organizer of the Reform party and its presidential candidate in 1992 and 1996.

Green party presidential candidate in 2000, Ralph Nader.

How, then, did parties get started? Largely out of practical necessity. The same early leaders who so frequently stated their opposition to political parties also recognized the need to organize officeholders who shared their views so that government could act. To get its measures passed by Congress, the Washington administration had to fashion a coalition among factions. This job fell to Treasury Secretary Alexander Hamilton, who built an informal Federalist party, while Washington stayed "above politics."

Secretary of State Jefferson and other officials, many of whom despised Hamilton and his aristocratic ways as much as they opposed the policies he favored, were uncertain about how to deal with these political differences. Their overriding concern was the success of the new government; personal loyalty to Washington was a close second. Thus Jefferson stayed in the cabinet, despite his opposition to administration policies, during most of Washington's first term. When he left the cabinet at the end of 1793, many who joined him in opposition to the administration's economic policies remained in Congress, forming a group of legislators opposed to Federalist fiscal policies and eventually to Federalist foreign policy, which appeared "soft on Britain." This party was later known as Republicans, then as Democratic-Republicans, then as Democrats.[18]

Realigning Elections

American political parties have evolved and changed over time, but some underlying characteristics have been constant. Historically, we have had a two-party system with minor parties. Our parties are moderate and accommodative, meaning that they are open to people with diverse outlooks. Political scientist V. O. Key and others argue that our party system has been shaped in large part by **realigning elections**, turning points that define the agenda of politics and the alignment of voters within parties during periods of historic change in the economy and society. Realigning elections are characterized by intense electoral involvement by the voters, disruptions of traditional voting patterns, changes in the relations of power within the community, and the formation of new and durable electoral groupings. They have occurred cyclically, not randomly. These elections tend to coincide with expansions of the suffrage or changes in the rate of voting.[19] We focus here on four realigning elections: 1824, 1860, 1896, and 1932.

TABLE 7–1 Minor Parties in the United States

Year	Party	Candidate	Percent of Vote	Electoral Vote
1832	Anti-Masonic	William Wirt	8%	7
1856	American (Know-Nothing)	Millard Fillmore	22	8
1860	Democratic (Secessionist)	J.C. Breckinridge	18	72
1860	Constitutional Union	John Bell	13	39
1892	People's (Populist)	James B. Weaver	9	22
1912	Bull Moose	Theodore Roosevelt	27	88
1912	Socialist	Eugene V. Debs	6	0
1924	Progressive	Robert M. La Follette	17	13
1948	States' Rights (Dixiecrat)	Strom Thurmond	2	39
1948	Progressive	Henry A. Wallace	2	0
1968	American Independent	George C. Wallace	14	46
1980	National Unity	John Anderson	7	0
1992	United We Stand, America	Ross Perot	19	0
1996	Reform	Ross Perot	9	0
2000	Reform	Pat Buchanan	0	0
2000	Green	Ralph Nader	3	0

1824: ANDREW JACKSON AND THE DEMOCRATS Party politics was invigorated following the election of 1824, in which the leader in the popular vote—the hero of the battle of New Orleans, Democrat Andrew Jackson—failed to achieve the necessary majority of the Electoral College and was defeated by John Quincy Adams in the runoff election in the House of Representatives. Jackson, brilliantly aided by Martin Van Buren, a veteran party builder in New York State, later knit together a winning combination of regions, interest groups, and political doctrines to win the presidency in 1828. The Whigs succeeded the Federalists as the opposition party. By the time Van Buren followed Jackson in the White House in 1837, the Democrats had become a large, nationwide movement with national and state leadership, a clear party doctrine, and grass-roots organization. The Whigs were almost as strong; in 1840 they put their own man, General William Henry Harrison ("Old Tippecanoe") into the White House. A two-party system had been born, and we have had that two-party system ever since—one of few such systems worldwide.

1860: THE CIVIL WAR AND THE RISE OF THE REPUBLICANS Out of the crisis over slavery evolved a new party: the second Republican party—ultimately the "Grand Old Party" (GOP).[20] Abraham Lincoln was elected in 1860 with the support not only of financiers, industrialists, and merchants, but also of large numbers of workers and farmers. For 50 years after 1860, the Republican coalition won every presidential race except for Grover Cleveland's victories in 1884 and 1892. The Democratic party survived with its durable white male base in the South.

1896: A PARTY IN TRANSITION The Republican party's response to industrialization and hard times for farmers transformed it in the late 1800s. A combination of western and southern farmers and western mining interests sought an alliance with workers in the East and Midwest to "recapture America from the foreign moneyed interests responsible for industrialization. The crisis of industrialization squarely placed an agrarian-fundamentalist view of life against an industrial-progress view."[21] This realignment of 1896 differs from the others, however, in that the party in power did not change hands. In that sense it was a *converting realignment* because it reinforced the Republican majority status that had been in place since 1860.[22]

The Progressive era, the first two decades of the twentieth century, was a period of political reform led by the Progressive wing of the Republican party. Much of the agenda of the Progressives focused on the corrupt political parties. Civil service reforms shifted some of the patronage out of the hands of party officials. The direct primary election took control of nominations from party leaders and gave it to the rank-and-file. And in a number of cities, nonpartisan governments were instituted, totally eliminating the role of a party. With the ratification of the Seventeenth Amendment to the Constitution in 1913, U.S. senators came to be popularly elected. Women obtained the right to vote when the Nineteenth Amendment was ratified in 1920. Thus within a short time, the electorate changed, the rules changed, and even the stakes of the game changed. Democrats were unable to build a durable winning coalition during this time and remained the minority party until the early 1930s, when the Hoover administration was overwhelmed by the Great Depression.

1932: FRANKLIN ROOSEVELT AND THE NEW DEAL ALIGNMENT The 1932 election was a turning point in American politics. In the 1930s the United States faced a devastating economic collapse. Between 1929 and 1932, the gross national product fell over 10 percent per year, and unemployment rose from 1.5 million to more than 15

Minor Parties

- **The Natural Law party** was started at the Mahirishi International University in Fairfield, Iowa, with the stated purpose to "bring the light of science into politics." The party's platform includes preventive health care and sustainable agriculture without pesticides; it favors using renewable energy to reduce pollution and create national energy self-sufficiency and advocates transcendental meditation as a solution to major health and crime problems, as well as a foreign policy tool. The Natural Law party also wants a 10 percent flat tax by 2002. The party had more than 700 candidates running for office in 1996.

- **The Libertarian party** places heavy emphasis on individual liberties, personal responsibility, and freedom from government. Its agenda calls for an end to the federal government's role in education and crime control. Libertarians believe the income tax is the "biggest intrusion into the lives of the American people," and they perceive Social Security as a "fraudulent scheme." They think the United States should wash its hands of foreign involvement—bring all U.S. troops home and only maintain sufficient military for our own defense. About 1,000 Libertarians ran for office in 1996.

- **The Green party** takes its name from other pro-environment parties throughout Europe. In the United States, the Greens not only embrace pro-environment positions but are committed to social justice, decentralization, respect for diversity, community-based economics, nonviolence, feminism, ecological wisdom, grass-roots democracy, and personal and global responsibility. Their 1996 and 2000 presidential candidate, Ralph Nader, called for public campaign financing, greater environmental protection, and affordable housing.

realigning election
An election during periods of historic change in the economy and society that proves to be a turning point, redefining the agenda of politics and the alignment of voters within parties.

- Parties began in this country as soon as people started taking sides in the debate over ratifying the U.S. Constitution, although it took a few years for them to organize into formal bodies.

- Political parties, and especially our two-party system, have persisted over the course of our history.

- Ours has almost always been a two-party system, differentiating us from most nations, which have a one-party or multiparty system.

- Since 1830 we have witnessed reasonably effective competition in our national party system.

- Our parties have historically been decentralized and fragmented. Parties are organized around states, congressional districts, counties, and cities, with state parties the most important units.

- Winning office and power has been more important to party leaders than specific issues or platforms; political parties in the United States are primarily organized to win and hold political power.

- Our parties can be characterized as moderate, centrist, and pragmatic, with only modest ideological cohesion and voting discipline, especially when compared to European political parties.

laissez-faire

Doctrine opposing governmental interference in economic affairs beyond what is necessary to protect life and property.

Keynesian economics

Economic principles based on the principles advocated by John Maynard Keynes: increasing government spending during business slumps and curbing spending during booms.

million, with millions more working only part-time. Herbert Hoover and the Republican majority in Congress had responded to the Depression by arguing that the problems with the economy were largely self-correcting and that their long-standing policy of *laissez-faire*, a hands-off approach to the economy, was appropriate.

Voters wanted more. Franklin D. Roosevelt and the Democrats were swept into office in 1932 by a tide of anti-Hoover and anti-Republican sentiment. Roosevelt rode this wave and labeled his response to the Depression the New Deal. He rejected *laissez-faire* economics and instead relied on **Keynesian economics**, which asserted that government could influence the direction of the economy through fiscal and monetary policy. After a century of sporadic government action, the New Dealers stepped in and fundamentally altered the relationship between government and society.

The central issue on which the Republicans and Democrats disagreed in this New Deal period was the role of government regarding the economy. Roosevelt Democrats argued that the government had to take action to pull the country out of the Depression, but Republicans objected to enlarging the scope of government activity and intruding it into the economy. This basic disagreement about whether the national government should play an active role in regulating and promoting our economy remains one of the most important divisions between the Democratic and Republican parties today, although, with time, the country and both parties accepted many of the New Deal programs.

For the two decades following the 1932 election, the Republican party was relegated to watching the majority Democrats—a new coalition of union households, immigrant workers, and people hurt by the Great Depression—implement their domestic policies. During World War II, both parties cooperated in embracing a bipartisan foreign policy.

We have gone a long time since the last critical or realigning election. You will note that each realignment lasted roughly 36 years, or a couple of generations. Some political scientists anticipated that we were ripe for such an election in 1968–1972, but it did not happen. Now, as memories of the New Deal fade and the agenda of American politics shifts, the alignments of the 1930s and 1940s hold less and less relevance. Yet, to a surprising degree, the parties are stable and closely competitive, as the 2000 elections demonstrated. Whether one party can seize the agenda of politics and fashion itself as the new majority party is one of the interesting political questions for the future.

Divided Government

Major shifts in the demographics of the parties have occurred in recent decades. The once "Solid South" that Democrats could count on to bolster their legislative majorities and help win the White House has now become the "Solid Republican South" in presidential and increasingly in congressional elections as well. Republican congressional leaders—House Majority Leader Dick Armey and Whip Tom DeLay, both of Texas, and Senate Minority Leader Trent Lott of Mississippi—came from states that once rarely elected Republicans. Further evidence of partisan change in the South is the fact that Vice-President Al Gore did not carry his home state of Tennessee in the 2000 presidential race and was also defeated in President Bill Clinton's home state of Arkansas. This shift in the South is explained by the movement of whites out of the Democratic party, largely as a result of the party's position on civil rights. The rise of the Republican South reinforced the shift to conservatism in the Grand Old Party. And as the South became more Republican, the Northeast became more Democratic and is increasingly the home of the Democratic party. This shift, combined with the diminished ranks of conservative southern

Democrats, made the Democratic party, especially the congressional Democrats, more unified and more liberal than in the days when many of its congressional members had "safe" southern seats.

Since 1953 we have had **divided government**, with one party controlling the Congress and the other the White House, twice as often as we have had one party in control of both legislative and executive branches. Until the 1994 election, Republican strength had been in presidential elections, where they often won with landslide margins. Part of the explanation was their ability to attract popular candidates like Dwight Eisenhower and Ronald Reagan, but Republicans also reaped the rewards of Democratic party divisiveness and generally weaker Democratic presidential candidates. Further evidence that voters are inclined to favor divided government came in the 1990s, when voters elected a Republican congressional majority in 1994 and then retained it in 1996 and 1998.

Republican victories in presidential elections between 1952 and 1992 were achieved with the support of some elements of Roosevelt's New Deal coalition. New Deal programs that benefited these voters had expanded the middle class and made possible the conservative "hold onto what we've got" thinking of voters in the 1980s, 1990s, and 2000. One way to interpret the closeness of the 2000 national elections is that the country is evenly divided, and while the election put Republicans in charge of both houses of Congress and the White House, their majorities are so slim that they effectively mean divided government.

The 2000 Elections–Into the New Century

Neither party could claim a mandate after the tightly contested 2000 elections, which resulted in a 50–50 partisan tie in the U.S. Senate, a slim Republican majority in the U.S. House, and a presidential contest whose outcome was unresolved for weeks as ballots were recounted in Florida. Although the outcome was essentially a tie, the breakdown of the vote was anything but random. The 2000 presidential results and exit polls demonstrated a divided nation. Al Gore carried the Northeast and Pacific states and a few urban states in the nation's midsection. George W. Bush carried the South and interior of the country, minus a few states like New Mexico. Demographically, the Democrats received large majorities of votes from African Americans, Hispanics, union households, Jews, and gays. Republicans did well among white males, religious conservatives, and higher income voters.[23] People's positions on most issues in the 2000 election were not as strongly held as on issues in the past, like Vietnam, civil rights, or the Great Society, but there were clear differences between Democratic and Republican voters on tax cuts, school vouchers, and privatization of Social Security.

AMERICAN PARTIES TODAY

Americans are largely indifferent about political parties. If anything, most people are critical or even fearful of the major parties. Parties are, in a word, distrusted. Some see parties as corrupt institutions, interested only in the spoils of politics. Critics charge that the parties evade the issues; they fail to deliver on their promises; they have no new ideas; they follow public opinion rather than lead it; or they are just one more special interest.

Still, Americans understand that parties are necessary. They want party labels kept on the ballot, at least for congressional and presidential elections as well as those for statewide offices. Most voters think of themselves as Democrats or Republicans, and typically vote for candidates from their party. They even contribute millions of dollars to the two major parties. Far more individual contributions go to the Republicans than to the Democrats.[24] Thus Americans appreciate, at least vaguely, that you cannot run a big democracy without parties.

Both the Democratic and Republican parties are moderate in their policies and leadership.[25] Successful party leaders must be diplomatic; to win presidential

Religion is sometimes linked to partisanship. In reality, devoutly religious people are found in both major parties.

divided government
Governance divided between the parties, especially when one controls the White House and the other controls Congress.

Jim Nicholson, Republican National Committee chair.

elections and congressional majorities, they must find a middle ground among more or less hostile groups. Members of the House of Representatives, in order to be elected and reelected, have to appeal to a majority of the voters from their own district. As more House districts have become "safe" for incumbents, the House of Representatives has become the home of partisan ideological clashes to a greater extent than the Senate or the White House.

Although each party usually takes its extremist supporters more or less for granted and seeks out the voters in the middle, both parties retain some ideological diversity. The Democratic umbrella encompasses the conservative Coalition for a Democratic Majority, the moderate Democratic Leadership Council (dominated by an array of southern governors and senators), and the liberal Americans for Democratic Action. The Democratic coalition embraces activists in the civil rights and other liberal-left movements. Republicans, while more homogeneous, have their contentious factions as well. On the more conservative side are the Religious Right, staunch supporters of the right to bear arms, and antitax activists.

Among Republicans the split has been between more liberal northeastern Republicans like Governors Christine Todd Whitman of New Jersey (now director of the Environmental Protection Agency) and Tom Ridge of Pennsylvania, and the dominant conservative wing. Democratic Senator Joseph Lieberman from Connecticut, known for his willingness to consider school vouchers and his concerns about affirmative action, had to reconcile with more liberal Democratic party activists after being selected by Al Gore to be his running mate in 2000.

Parties as Institutions

Political parties are organizations that seek political power by electing people to office so that their positions and philosophy become public policy. Like other institutions of American government—Congress, the presidency, and the courts—parties have rules, procedures, and organizational structure, and they make policy. What are the institutional characteristics of political parties?

NATIONAL PARTY LEADERSHIP   The supreme authority in both major parties is the **national party convention**, which meets every four years to nominate candidates for president and vice-president, to ratify the party platform, and to adopt rules. The delegates have only four days in which to accomplish their business, but many key decisions have been made ahead of time.

In charge of the national party is the *national committee*. In recent years both parties have strengthened the role of the national committee and enhanced the influence of individual committee members. The committees are now more representative of the party rank-and-file. But in neither party is the national committee the center of party leadership.

Each major party has a *national chair* as its top official. The national committee formally elects the chair, but in reality it is the choice of the presidential nominee. Even though he or she serves as a liaison between the party and the White House, the chair actually serves at the pleasure of the president and does the president's bidding. The chair of the party without an incumbent president has considerable independence, yet works closely with the party's congressional leadership. The national committee often elects a new head after electoral defeats. Although chairs are the heads of their national party apparatus, they remain largely unknown to the voters. The chair may play a major role in running the national campaign; after the election, the power of the national chair of the victorious party tends to dwindle.

National party organizations are often agents of an incumbent president in securing his renomination. When there is not an incumbent president seeking reelection, the national party committee is generally neutral until the nominee is selected. Although heated primary contests often preclude having a united party in the general election, national parties are helpless to prevent them.[26]

political party
An organization that seeks political power by electing people to office so that its positions and philosophy become public policy.

national party convention
The national meeting of delegates elected in primaries, caucuses, or state conventions who assemble once every four years to nominate candidates for president and vice-president, ratify the party platform, elect officers, and adopt rules.

In addition to the national party committees, there are also congressional and senatorial *campaign committees*. Senatorial campaign committees are composed of senators chosen for two-year terms by their fellow party members in the Senate; congressional campaign committees are chosen in the same manner by the House. Chairs of campaign committees are nominated by their party leadership and typically ratified by their party caucus. They have a lot of say about which candidates get campaign funds. In recent years congressional campaign committees have become much more active—recruiting candidates, training them, and assisting with campaign finance.[27]

The chair of the Republican House campaign committee is elected by the House Republican Conference after each congressional election (**www.nrcc.org/about/overview.htm**). A similar process is used to elect the chair of the National Republican Senatorial Committee. For more information on the process in the Democratic party, see **www.takebackthehouse.com/about/index.cfm** for information on the House and **www.dscc.org/2000revised/bobtorricelli.htm** for information on the Senate.

In the 1998 and 2000 elections, congressional campaign committees, following the lead of the national party committees in previous presidential elections, raised unprecedented amounts of soft money, contributions intended to support party activity in general, not a specific candidate. The soft money reform was enacted by Congress following the 1976 election, in which both parties complained that they did not have enough money for generic party activities like billboard advertising and get-out-the-vote drives. Amendments to the Federal Election Campaign Act and the interpretations of this legislation by the Federal Election Commission permitted unlimited contributions to the parties by individuals and PACs for these purposes. Over time both parties have found ways to spend soft money to promote the election or defeat of specific candidates, effectively circumventing the campaign finance reform rules. This is why banning soft money has become such a dedicated cause for Arizona Senator John McCain, a co-sponsor of the McCain-Feingold campaign finance reform legislation that finally passed the U. S. Senate in 2001.

Today soft money is spent in the most competitive races where it makes the biggest difference. The party committee leaders who make these allocations have grown in power as the amount of soft money raised has grown. Party committee leaders effectively used the close party balance, especially in the House of Representatives, to justify their soft money spending decisions.

What are the implications of this surge in soft money in presidential and congressional elections? First, because soft money contributions are unlimited, the priority given to raising soft money has elevated the importance of the large contributor. Although the reforms had lessened the power of wealthy individuals because they could give only $50,000 in total political contributions to candidates or parties in a two-year period, with the soft money loophole, such individuals can now give unlimited amounts. Parties rely heavily on these large donors.

A second implication is that those who allocate soft money are now very influential because they can contribute more money to a race than a candidate could have raised in months of fund raising. Decisions about which races will be targets for soft money spending are critical in an election outcome.

PARTIES AT THE GRASS ROOTS   The two major parties are decentralized, organized around elections in states, cities, or congressional districts. Like the government itself, they have national, state, and local organizations. Party organization at the state and local levels is structured much like the national level. Each state has a *state committee* headed by a *state chair*. State law determines the composition of the state committees and sets rules regulating them. Members of state committees are usually elected from local areas. Party auxiliaries such as the Young Democrats or the Federation of Republican Women are sometimes represented as well. In many states these committees are dominated by governors, senators, or coalitions of locally

Democratic Congressional Campaign Committee chair Nita Lowey of New York.

Republican Senatorial Campaign Committee chair Bill Frist of Tennessee.

A Closer Look

PARTY PLATFORMS

The typical party platform—the official statement of party policy—is often a vague and ponderous document that hardly anyone reads. Platforms are ambiguous by design, giving voters few obvious reasons to vote against the party. This generalization about party platforms does not mean that political parties do not stand for anything. Thus most business and professional people believe the Republican party best serves their interests, while working people tend to look to the Democrats to speak for them. The proportion of voters discerning important differences between the parties increased sharply in recent years, as the parties became more polarized.[*]

Many politicians contend that platforms rarely help elect anybody, but platform positions can hurt a presidential candidate. Because the platform-writing process is not always controlled by the nominee, it is possible for presidential candidates to disagree with their own party platform. But the platform-drafting process gives partisans, especially those motivated by particular issues, an opportunity to express their views, and it serves to identify the most important values and principles upon which the two parties are based. Once elected, politicians are rarely reminded of what their platform position was on a given issue. One major exception to this was former President George Bush's promise not to raise taxes if elected in 1988 with his memorable "Read my lips—no new taxes." He was forced to eat those words when taxes were raised.

Party platforms in 2000 were carefully controlled by the Gore and Bush campaigns. The Republican platform reflected Bush's compassionate conservative themes, but Bush was criticized for not softening the party position on abortion.[**] The Bush campaign decided not to risk a convention fight by removing the plank, preferring to present an image of a unified party, and pro-choice Republicans at the convention did not challenge the platform language. Vice-President Gore tried to reinforce centrist themes in his party's platform. For example, the Democratic platform included the death penalty as a means of fighting crime. In part because Al Gore and George W. Bush so thoroughly dominated the nomination process, neither party platform became the subject of attack from the opposing party.

Differences between 2000 Democratic and Republican platforms are highlighted below, and the platforms in their entirety are available at **www.democrats.org/hq/resources/platfom,/platform..html** and **www.rnc.org/2000/2000**.

[*]See Bruce E. Keith, David B. Magleby, Candice J. Nelson, Elizabeth Orr, Mark C. Westlye, and Raymond E. Wolfinger, *The Myth of the Independent Voter* (University of California Press, 1992), p. 148.

[**]Richard Benedetto, "Bush's Influence on Platform Results in 'More Upbeat' Tone," *USA Today*, July 31, 2000, p. A6.

Key Party Differences: Excerpts from Republican and Democratic Party Platforms, 2000

Democrats	Republicans
Abortion	
Support the right of every woman to choose, consistent with *Roe v. Wade*, and regardless of ability to pay. Individual—not government—can best take responsibility for making the most difficult and intensely personal decisions regarding reproduction.	Support a human life amendment to the Constitution and endorse legislation to make clear that the 14th Amendment's protections apply to unborn children. Oppose using public revenues for abortion and will not fund organizations which advocate it.

elected business and ethnic leaders. State chairs are normally elected by the state committees, although approximately one-quarter are chosen at state conventions. When the party controls the governorship, chairs are often agents of the governor, but some can remain independent.[28]

Some powerful state parties have developed in recent years. Despite much state-to-state variation, the trend is toward stronger state organizations, with Republicans typically much better funded.[29] In some states, third and fourth parties play a role in local elections. New York, for instance, has both a Liberal party and a Conservative party in addition to Democratic and Republican parties. The role minor parties play in statewide elections can be important, even though they rarely win office themselves.

Below the state committees are *county committees*, which vary widely in function and power. The key role of these committees is recruiting candidates for such offices as county commissioner, sheriff, and treasurer. The recruiting job often involves finding a candidate for the office, not deciding among competing contenders. For a party that rarely wins an election, the county committee has to struggle to find

Democrats	Republicans
Campaign Finance Reform	
Proposes tough new lobbying reform, publicly guaranteed TV time for debates and advocacy by candidates, a crackdown on special interest issue ads, and a public-private, nonpartisan Democracy Endowment which will raise money from Americans and finance Congressional elections—with no other contributions allowed to candidates who accept the funding.	Enact 'Paycheck Protection,' ensuring that no union member is forced to contribute to anybody's campaign. Preserve the right of every individual and all groups to express their opinions and advocate their issues.
Foreign Policy and Military Deployment	
"We cannot be the world's policemen, and we must be discriminating in our approach. But where the stakes are high, when nothing short of military engagement can secure our national interest, when we have the military forces available and have made our best efforts to join with allies, and cost is proportionate to the objective, we must be ready to act."	"The military is not a civilian police force or a political referee. . . A Republican president will identify and pursue vital American national interests, build and secure the peace. Republicans know what it takes to accomplish this: robust military forces, strong alliances, expanding trade, and resolute diplomacy."
Missile Defense	
Support the development of the technology for a limited national missile defense system. Any such system is compatible with the Anti-Ballistic Missile Treaty.	Favor deploying an effective missile defense . . . at the earliest possible date, and designed to protect all 50 states. America's deployed forces overseas, and our friends and allies . . . will seek a negotiated change in the Anti-Ballistic Missile (ABM) Treaty.
School Choice	
Favor public schools that compete with one another and are held accountable for results. Oppose private school vouchers.	Expand parental choice and encourage competition by providing parents with information on their child's school, increasing the number of charter schools, and expanding education savings accounts.
Gun Control	
Favor mandatory child safety locks, to protect our children, a photo license ID, a full background check, and a gun safety test to buy a new handgun.	Support background checks. Oppose federal licensing of law-abiding gun owners and national gun registration.
Status of Gays	
Support continued efforts . . . to end workplace discrimination against gay men and lesbians.	Support the traditional definition of 'marriage' as the legal union of one man and one woman.

SOURCE: *The New York Times*, August 14, 2000.

someone willing to run. When those seeking it value the job, however, primaries, not the party leaders, usually decide the winner.[30] Many county organizations maintain a significant level of activity, distributing campaign literature, organizing telephone campaigns, putting up posters and lawn signs, and canvassing door-to-door. Other county committees do not function at all, and many party leaders are just figureheads.

In recent elections the campaign efforts of state and county organizations have been aided by financial assistance from the party's national committee, which has distributed millions of dollars in soft money. In many instances broadcast ads paid for with soft money do not even mention the party.[31]

It is not clear that soft money helps build stronger parties at the state and local level. Some soft money spending may enhance such party activities as building a list of active partisans in the state or district, improving the computer technology of the party offices, or secondary benefits when party supporters are mobilized for a U.S. Senate or U.S. House race. But for most soft money spending, state parties simply become local bank accounts for candidate endorsements.

American government may be intensely partisan—some think much too partisan. In Congress the two parties have been locked in battle over legislation, investigations, and budget priorities. When legislators become intensely partisan, they become more concerned with advancing their own party's fortunes in the next election than with finding an acceptable compromise that would serve the public. And when there is divided government, with a governor or president from a party different from the legislative majority, that difference often leads to gridlock. Finally, partisanship in judicial or executive branch appointments means that qualified people may be excluded from consideration on the basis of party affiliation.

Would we be better off if we did not have political parties? Is intense partisanship destroying our political system?

One possible benefit of soft money would be strengthening parties at the grassroots level. At the base of the party pyramid—at the city, town, ward, and precinct level—strong local party organization is rare. Most local committees are poorly financed and inactive except during the few weeks before election day.[32] In a few places, local ward and precinct leaders still do favors for constituents, from getting more police patrols in a neighborhood, to organizing clambakes, or obtaining horse-racing passes in a state like Arkansas.

Parties in Government

Political parties are central to the operation of government in the United States. Party organizations play a more important role after the election in the operation of government than they play in the elections.

IN THE LEGISLATIVE BRANCH   Members of Congress take their partisanship seriously, at least while they are in Washington. Their power and influence are determined by whether their party is in control of the House or Senate; they also have a stake in which party controls the White House. The chairs of all standing committees in Congress come from the majority party, as do the presiding officials of both chambers. Members of both houses sit together with fellow partisans on the floor and in committee, leading to the expression often heard in floor debate, "the other side of the aisle."

In the wake of the tie in the U.S. Senate following the 2000 elections, with each party having 50 members, the Democrats suggested a power-sharing arrangement, including the possibility of co-chairs for some or all committees. The two parties agreed to equal membership and staff on all committees, but all chairs are Republicans.

Members of congressional staffs are also partisan. From the volunteer intern to the senior staffer, members of Congress expect their staff to be loyal first to them and then to their party. Should you decide to go to work for a representative or senator, you would be expected to identify yourself with that person's party, and you would have some difficulty working for the other party later. Employees of the House and Senate—from elevator operators to the Capitol Hill police and even including the chaplain—hold patronage jobs. With few exceptions, such jobs go to persons from the party that has a majority in the House or the Senate.

IN THE EXECUTIVE BRANCH   Presidents select almost all senior White House staff and cabinet members from their own party. However, it is not unusual for them to choose one or two advisers or cabinet members from the opposition party. Presidents, however, typically surround themselves with advisers who have campaigned with them and proven their party loyalty.

Partisanship is also important in presidential appointments to the highest levels of the federal bureaucracy. The party that wins the White House has more than 4,000 noncareer positions to fill.[33] Included in these positions are cabinet-level appointments and ambassadorships around the world. Party commitment, including making campaign contributions, is expected of those who seek these positions.

IN THE JUDICIAL BRANCH   The judicial branch of the national government, with its lifetime tenure and political independence, is designed to operate in an expressly nonpartisan manner. Judges, unlike Congress, do not sit together by political party. But the appointment process for judges has been partisan from the beginning. The landmark case establishing the principle of judicial review, *Marbury v Madison* (1803), concerned the efforts of one party to stack the judiciary with fellow partisans before leaving office.[34] Today party identification remains an important consideration in the naming of federal judges. While the party of a judicial nominee is not called for on any form, those responsible for

party registration

The act of declaring party affiliation; required by some states when one registers to vote.

screening and evaluating candidates certainly take party and ideology into account. Appointees must be acceptable to certain power centers in the party. For example, Republicans in the Ronald Reagan and George Bush administrations insisted on conservative judges; Bill Clinton, although nominating Democrats, gave more emphasis to gender and race than to ideology in selecting judges.

STATE AND LOCAL LEVELS   The importance of party in the operation of local government varies among states and localities. In some states, such as New York and Illinois, local parties play an even stronger role than they do at the national level. In others, such as Nebraska, parties play almost no role. In Nebraska, the state legislature is expressly nonpartisan, though factions perform like parties and still play a role. Parties are likewise unimportant in the government of most city councils. But in most states and many cities, parties are important to the operation of the legislature, governor, or mayor. Judicial selection in most states is also a partisan matter. Much was made by the Bush campaign of the fact that six of the seven Florida Supreme Court justices deciding the 2000 ballot-counting cases were Democrats. And the U.S. Supreme Court's decision on the Florida count was also said to be partisan.

Parties in the Electorate

Political parties would be of little significance if they did not have meaning to the electorate. Adherents of the two parties are drawn to them by a combination of factors: stand on issues; personal or party history; religious, racial, or social peer grouping; attractiveness of candidates. The emphases among these factors change over time, but they are remarkably consistent with those identified by political scientists more than 40 years ago.[35]

PARTY REGISTRATION   For citizens in most states, "party" has a particular legal meaning—**party registration**. At the time voters register to vote in these states, they are asked to state their party preference. They then become registered Democrats, Republicans, Libertarians, or whatever. Voters can subsequently change their party registration. The purpose of party registration is to limit the participants in primary elections to members of that party and to make it easier for parties to contact people who might vote for their party.

PARTY ACTIVISTS   This group tends to fall into three broad categories: party regulars, candidate activists, and issue activists. *Party regulars* place the party first. They value winning elections and understand that compromise and moderation may be necessary to reach that objective. They also realize that it is important to keep the party together as much as possible, because a fractured party only helps the opposition.

Candidate activists are followers of a particular candidate who see the party as the means to place their candidate in power. Candidate activists are often not concerned with the other operations of the party—with nominees for other offices or with raising money for the party. For example, people who supported Pat Buchanan in his unsuccessful run for the presidency as a Reform party candidate in 2000 would be classified as candidate activists. Buchanan, a former television commentator and unsuccessful Republican candidate for the Republican nomination in 1996, built a personal following. Reform party members who traced their roots in the party to Ross Perot were so disaffected from Buchanan that they split from him and nominated their own candidate for president. Buchanan fared poorly in the 2000 election, getting less than 1 percent of the vote and as a result losing millions of dollars in federal subsidies for the 2004 elections. The federal subsidy from Perot's 8 percent vote total in 1996 largely funded the Buchanan 2000 campaign.[36]

Issue activists wish to push the parties in a particular direction on a single issue or narrow range of issues: abortion, taxes, school prayer, the environment, or civil

Thinking It Through...

It is naive to believe that the removal of parties will negate conflict, self-interest, or ambition. A political system without parties would be a society without the means to deal with disagreements over policies, economics, or social values. Americans expect legislators to be partisan, to be contentious, and to make the most of partisan opportunities. Divided government may be inefficient, but that clearly has not bothered voters, who routinely elect legislators from one party and governors or presidents from another. Finally, people with judicial or administrative ambitions understand the role that parties play in appointments, giving them an incentive to get involved in a party. This is not all bad because, as we have seen, it is possible for idealistic individuals to redefine and reshape a party.

WE THE PEOPLE

Portrait of the Electorate

	Republican	Democrat	Independent
Sex			
Male	**41**	**49**	**10**
Female	35	54	11
Race			
White	42	47	11
Black	7	86	7
Hispanic	32	60	8
Age			
18–34	40	49	11
35–45	42	46	12
46–55	37	52	11
56–64	32	61	6
65+	31	58	10
Income			
Less than $10,000	34	54	12
$10,000–$19,999	29	62	9
$20,000–$29,999	35	53	12
$30,000–$39,999	32	54	14
$40,000–$59,999	37	53	10
$60,000+	48	42	10
Religion			
Protestant	41	51	8
Catholic	38	52	10
Jewish	18	82	0
Ideology			
Liberal	14	81	5
Moderate/Don't know	30	56	15
Conservative	67	28	5
Region			
Northeast	36	48	16
North-central	38	53	9
South	39	51	10
West	35	56	9
Total	**37**	**52**	**11**

SOURCE: *2000 American National Election Study*, Center for Political Studies, University of Michigan.

rights. To issue activists, the party platform is an important battleground because they seek party endorsement for their position. Issue activists are also often candidate activists if they can find a candidate willing to embrace their position.

Both issue activists and candidate activists insist on making their "statement" regardless of the electoral consequences. They prefer to lose the election rather than compromise. Party activists thus include a diverse group of people who come to the political party with different objectives. It is not surprising, then, that some of the most interesting politics you will observe are over candidate selection and issue positions within the political parties. Fights over strategy and party position are conducted in open meetings and under democratic procedures. Political parties foster democracy not only by competition *between* the parties but *within* the parties as well.

Party Identification

Most Americans are mere spectators of party activity. They lack the partisan commitment and interest needed for active party involvement. This is not to say that parties are irrelevant or unimportant to them. For them, partisanship is what political scientists call **party identification**—an informal and subjective affiliation with a political party that most people acquire in childhood, a standing preference for one party over another.[37] This type of voter may sometimes vote for a candidate from the other party, yet in the absence of a compelling reason to do otherwise, most will vote according to their party identification. Peers and early political experiences reinforce party identification, generally acquired from parents. It is part of the political socialization process described in Chapter 4.

Party identification is the single best predictor of how people will vote. Unlike candidates and issues, which come and go, party identification is a long-term element in voting choice. The strength of party identification is also important in predicting participation and political interest. Strong Republicans and Strong Democrats participate more actively in politics than any other groups and are generally more knowledgeable and informed. Pure Independents are just the opposite; they vote at the lowest rates and have the lowest levels of interest and awareness of any of the categories of party identification. This evidence runs counter to the notion that persons who are strong partisans are unthinking party adherents.[38]

Partisan Realignment and Dealignment

The current system of party identification is built upon a foundation of the New Deal and the critical election of 1932, events that took place nearly 70 years ago. How can events so removed from the present still be important in shaping our party system? When will there be another realignment—an election that dramatically changes the voters' partisan identification? Or has such a realignment already occurred, a question frequently debated in the literature of political science. Most scholars believe we have not experienced any major realignment since 1932.[39] Partisan identification for the past four decades has been stable, and while new voters have been added to the electorate—minorities and 18-to-21-year-olds—the basic character of the party system has not changed dramatically. Table 7–2 presents the party identification breakdown for the period from the 1950s to 2000.

Possible evidence of a voting realignment came in the early 1980s, when Republicans won several close Senate elections and gained a majority in that body. Democrats, however, won back the Senate in 1986, and until 1994 they appeared to have a permanent majority in the House. All that changed with the 1994 election, as Republicans were swept into office on a tidal wave of victories. Republicans made major inroads in the South and strengthened their share of the vote among white males.

The 1998 election gave the Democrats renewed hope that they could regain control of Congress, or at least the House of Representatives, in the 2000 elections. Overcoming their worst fears that the Clinton–Monica Lewinsky scandal would enlarge Republican majorities in the Senate and House, the Democrats effectively mobilized their core voters and actually picked up five seats in the House of Representatives. Allies of the Democratic party like organized labor were also encouraged by gains they saw in 1998. Republicans were disheartened by the congressional election outcome but pointed to their strength in several key governorships as cause for optimism.

The 2000 presidential and congressional elections were exceedingly close. The Republicans narrowly held onto their majority in the House in 2000, and the parties were evenly divided in the Senate after the election. While losing the White House to the Republicans through the Electoral College vote, Democrats see the 2002 election as their opportunity to regain the majority in both houses of Congress. The historic

party identification

An informal and subjective affiliation with a political party that most people acquire in childhood.

TABLE 7–2 Party Identification, 1950s to 2000

Decade	Strong Democrat	Weak Democrat	Independent-Leaning Democrat	Independent	Independent-Leaning Republican	Weak Republican	Strong Republican	Apolitical
1950s*	23%	23%	8%	7%	7%	15%	13%	4%
1960s	22	25	8	10	7	15	12	2
1970s	17	24	12	14	10	14	9	2
1980s	18	26	11	12	11	14	11	2
1990s	18	19	13	10	12	15	13	1
2000	19	15	14	11	13	12	13	2

SOURCE: American National Election Studies, Center for Political Studies, University of Michigan.

Note: Data may not sum to 100% due to averaged data.

*1950s percentages based on years 1952, 1956, 1958.

"*Very* Republican. I love it."

- Republicans usually wear hats. Democrats usually don't.
- Democrats buy banned books. Republicans form censorship committees and read them.
- Democrats eat the fish they catch. Republicans hang them on the wall.
- Republicans study the financial pages of the newspaper. Democrats put them on the bottom of the bird cage.
- On Saturday, Republicans head for the golf course, the yacht club, or the hunting lodge. Democrats get a haircut, wash the car, or go bowling.
- Republicans have guest rooms. Democrats have spare rooms filled with old baby furniture.
- Republicans hire exterminators. Democrats step on the bugs.
- Republicans sleep in twin beds—some even in separate rooms. That is why there are more Democrats.

SOURCE: The National Republican Congressional Committee Newsletter.

dealignment
Change in the composition of the electorate or its partisan preferences that points to a rejection of both major parties and a rise in the number of Independents.

pattern of the president's party losing seats in a midterm election works to their favor, and several of their key constituencies may be motivated to vote in large numbers in 2002 because of the perception of unfairness in the counting of Florida's presidential ballots and charges that election officials and procedures discriminated against minority voters.

In presidential voting, Republicans have done well, winning six of the last nine presidential elections, although they lost the popular vote in 2000. Bill Clinton's victories in 1992 and 1996 demonstrated, however, that Democrats could still assemble a winning coalition. But, as discussed previously, the 2000 presidential vote showed an evenly divided nation. Whether one party can expand its support to make it dominant remains an open question, especially in light of the strong feelings many people had about how the winner was determined in the Florida presidential contest.

Recent national elections can thus be characterized as a period in which voters have not demonstrated a consistent preference for one party over the other. In a time of such electoral volatility and low turnout, the winners and losers are determined by the basics of politics: who turns out their vote, who strikes a theme that motivates voters to participate, or who does a better job in communicating with the voters. Party identification remains important for those voters who come out to vote, and strength of partisanship remains positively correlated with turnout.

There are few signs of realignment, but there are signs of disengagement. Some think that, instead of a realignment, we are experiencing the rejection of partisanship in favor of becoming Independents, and there has indeed been an increase in the number of persons who characterize themselves as Independents. Journalist Hedrick Smith expresses a widespread view: "The most important phenomenon of American politics in the past quarter century has been the rise of independent voters who have at times outnumbered Republicans."[40]

The **dealignment** argument—that people have abandoned both parties to become Independents—would be more persuasive were it not that two-thirds of all Independents are really partisans in their voting behavior and attitudes. One-third of those who claim to be Independents lean toward the Democratic party and vote Democratic election after election. Another third of Independents lean toward Republicans and just as predictably vote Republican. The remaining third, who appear to be genuine Independents and who do not vote predictably for one party, turn out to be people with little interest in politics. Despite the reported growth in Independents, there were proportionately about the same number of Pure Independents now as there were in 1956.[41] There are, in short, at least three types of Independents, and most of them are predictably partisan. Table 7–3 summarizes voting behavior in contests for president in 1992, 1996, and 2000, and for U.S. House of Representatives since 1994.

Why has realignment moved so slowly? Why aren't all conservatives now happily ensconced in the Republican party and all liberals gladly lodged in the Democratic party? Americans do not casually cross party lines. If you grew up in a conservative New Hampshire family whose forebears voted Republican for a century, you are pretty much conditioned to stay with the GOP. Even if that party took a direction you disliked, you might continue to register as a Republican but quietly vote Democratic to avoid friction in the family. Or if you come from a "yellow dog" Democratic family in Texas (meaning your family would vote for a "yellow dog" before it would vote for a Republican), you might continue to vote for Democrats locally even though you disliked various Democratic candidates for president or senator. Evidence indicates that this pattern is common throughout the South.

TABLE 7–3 Voting Behavior of Partisans and Independents, 1992–2000

| | Percent Democratic Vote | | | | | | |
| | President | | | U.S. House | | | |
	1992	1996	2000	1994	1996	1998	2000
Strong Democrats	93%	96%	97%	88%	87%	77%	90%
Weak Democrats	68	82	89	73	70	57	73
Independent-leaning Democrats	70	76	72	68	69	63	73
Pure Independents	41	35	44	55	41	41	50
Independent-leaning Republicans	11	20	13	25	21	24	26
Weak Republicans	14	20	14	21	21	25	18
Strong Republicans	3	5	2	7	3	7	12

Source: *American National Election Study*, Center for Political Studies, University of Michigan.

Another reason for slow realignment is the local nature of the parties. For decades, conservative Democrats in the South have been voting for Republican candidates for president—not only George W. Bush and Ronald Reagan but also Richard Nixon and even Dwight Eisenhower—without changing their identification from the Democratic party to the Republican. Why? Partly because they still see themselves as Democrats, but also because the Democratic party remains stronger at the state and local level in many southern states. So if candidates and voters want to have an impact on local politics, in which the only meaningful elections may be in the Democratic primaries, they retain their Democratic affiliation.

ARE THE POLITICAL PARTIES DYING?

Critics of the American party system make three allegations against it: (1) parties do not take meaningful and contrasting positions on issues; (2) party membership is essentially meaningless; and (3) parties are so concerned with accommodating those on the middle of the ideological spectrum that they are incapable of serving as an avenue for social progress. Are these statements accurate, and if accurate, are they important?

Some fear parties are so meaningless they may be mortally ill, or at least in a severe decline. They point first to the long-run adverse impact on political parties of the Progressive reforms early in this century, reforms that robbed party organizations of their control of the nomination process by allowing masses of independent and "uninformed" voters to enter the primaries and nominate candidates who might not be acceptable to party leaders. They also point to the spread of nonpartisan elections in cities and towns and the staggering of national, state, and local elections that made it harder for parties to influence the election process.

Legislation limiting the viability and functions of parties was bad enough, say the party pessimists, but parties suffer from additional ills. The rise of television and electronic technology and the parallel increase in the number of campaign, media, and direct-mail consultants have made parties less relevant in educating, mobilizing, and organizing the electorate. Television, radio, the Internet, and telephones have strengthened the role of candidates and lessened the importance of parties. (See Chapter 10 for more on the media in this role.)

Advocates of strong parties concede that parts of this diagnosis may be correct: the demise of political machines at the local level, the decline in strong partisan affiliations, the weakness of grass-roots party membership. Yet they also see signs of party revival, or at least the persistence of party. The national party organizations—the national committees and the congressional and senatorial campaign committees—are significantly better funded than they were in earlier days; they even own permanent,

PEOPLE

Campaign contributions from a single source that run to the hundreds of thousands, or millions, of dollars are not healthy to a democracy.

SOFT MONEY IS BUYING OUR GOVERNMENT

Senator John McCain

For fifteen years Congress debated campaign finance reform, which passed the House only to die in the Senate. Early in 2001, Senate Majority Leader Trent Lott allotted two weeks for debate on the McCain Feingold campaign finance legislation. The number of debate amendments and its early scheduling were in part due to the persistance of Arizona Senator John McCain (R), a cosponsor of the bill and the nation's most visible campaign finance reform advocate.

The many sponsors of this legislation have but one purpose: to enact fair bipartisan campaign finance reform that seeks no special advantage for one party or another, but that helps change the public's widespread belief that politicians have no greater purpose than their own re-election, and to that end we will respond disproportionately to the needs of those interests that can best finance our ambition, even if those interests conflict with the public interest and with the governing philosophy we once sought office to advance.

Most Americans believe that we would let this nation pay any price, bear any burden, for the sake of securing our own ambitions, no matter how injurious the effect might be to the national interest.

Why can't we all agree to this very simple, very obvious truth that campaign contributions from a single source that run to the hundreds of thousands, or millions, of dollars are not healthy to a democracy?

Is that not self-evident? It is to the people. It is to the people.

Some will argue that there isn't too much money in politics. They will argue there's not enough; they will argue that soft money, the huge unregulated revenue stream into political party coffers, is necessary to ensure the strength of the two-party system.

I find this last point hard to understand, considering that in the 15 years or so that soft money has become the dominant force in our elections, the parties have grown appreciably weaker as independents become the fastest growing voter registration group in the country. . . .

Some will argue that the First Amendment of the Constitution renders unlawful any restriction on the right of anyone to raise unlimited amounts of money for political campaigns. Which drafter of the Constitution believed or anticipated that the First Amendment would be exercised in political campaigns by the relatively few at the expense of many.★

SOURCE: *The Congressional Record*, March 19, 2001.

DEBATE

SOFT MONEY IS FREEDOM OF SPEECH

Senator Mitch McConnell

The leading opponent of campaign finance reform, Senator Mitch McConnell, led the opposition in the 2001 debate. McConnell chaired the National Republican Senatorial Committee for the 1997–98 and 1999–2000 election cycles, a job in which he raised millions in soft money—money which is restricted under new reforms.

The real problem is not that there's too much money in politics; there's too little money in politics, particularly hard money, which is all limited and disclosed, directly given to parties and candidates to expressly advocate the election or defeat of a candidate. And yet nobody on the so-called reform side is trying to deal with the single biggest problem we have.

Now, the only way to really get at the core of this problem if senators believe that the influence of money in politics is so pernicious is to change the First Amendment. You have to go right to the core of the problem.

It's important to get the record straight about nonfederal money. The average soft money contribution to the Republican Senatorial Committee last cycle was $520. That's less than one-tenth of 1 percent of the money that the Republican Senatorial Committee raised.

If you look over at the Republican National Committee and the Republican Senatorial Committee, the largest contribution either of us got during the course of the year was $250,000. Admittedly that's a very large contribution. But any one of those $250,000 contributions would have represented less than one-half of 1 percent of the total money raised by either the senatorial committee or the Republican National Committee.

Each of those interests who care about what we're doing here, who believe that it may have an impact on their business or their interest, cannot be constitutionally restricted from speaking. Maybe some court somewhere would let us completely federalize the national parties, completely eliminate their ability to operate in state and local races in federal dollars. Maybe some court would let us do that. But no court in America, no federal court in America, is going to let us quiet the voices of all these interests who have a perfect right to go out and engage in issue advocacy up to and including the day of the election. There isn't a serious person who knows anything about the First Amendment who believes that we could do that. ★

SOURCE: *The Congressional Record,* March 19, 2001.

> **The real problem is not that there's too much money in politics; there's too little money in politics.**

For further information about this debate, go to **www.prenhall.com/burns** *and click on the Debate Icon in Chapter 7.*

modern headquarters buildings in Washington, D.C., located a few blocks from the U.S. Capitol. Moreover, the parties are more capable of providing assistance to candidates and to state and local party organizations because of their strong financial base from political contributions. They have defined their role as providing expertise to those who need it but cannot otherwise obtain it. Optimists hope these services will give the national parties some leverage over the positions that candidates and office-holders take on party issues.[42]

Since the first years of the Reagan administration, both the Republican and Democratic parties have demonstrated a remarkable cohesiveness in Congress on issues of importance. This trend can be measured by the *party unity score*, defined as the percentage of members of a party who vote together on roll call votes in Congress on which a majority of the members of one party vote against a majority of the members of the other party. Clinton had higher party unity scores from his party in 1993 than any party gave its president in the past 40 years; 85 percent of the Democrats voted together, while 84 percent of the Republicans voted together.[43] During the Republican-controlled 105th Congress (1997–98) as well as during the first half of the 106th Congress (1999), House and Senate Republicans voted together 86 percent of the time—a new all-time high. Democrats were only slightly less united.[44] Thus, while rank-and-file voters do not display strong partisan ties, party organizations and the party in government do show significant signs of strength.[45]

Reform Among the Democrats

After the 1968 election, the Democrats, responding to the disarray during their Chicago convention and disputes about the fairness of delegate selection procedures, agreed to a series of reforms. They put in place a process that led to greater use of direct primaries for the selection of delegates to the national convention and greater representation of younger voters, women, and minorities as elected delegates. Another reform was the abolition of the rule that a winner of a state's convention or primaries got all the state's delegates (the *unit rule*). This rule was replaced by a system of *proportionality* in which candidates won delegates in rough proportion to the votes they received in the primary election.

Chicago's mayor Richard Daley, father of the current mayor of Chicago, and many other party stalwarts argued that these reforms would make the party reflective of the views of college professors and intellectuals, and not working-class people, unionists, the elderly, and elected officials. Responding to this criticism, the party created "superdelegate" positions for elected officials and party leaders.

Reform Among the Republicans

Republicans have not been immune to criticism that their party conventions and party procedures were keeping out the rank-and-file. They did not make changes as drastic as those made by the Democrats, but they did give the national committee more control over presidential campaigns, and state parties were urged to encourage broader participation by all groups, including women, minorities, youth, and the poor.

The Republican party entered the 1980s with a party organization far superior to that of the Democrats. The GOP emphasized grass-roots organization and membership recruitment. Seminars were held to teach Republican candidates how to make speeches and hold press conferences, and weekend conferences were organized for training young professionals. Both parties now conduct training sessions for candidates on campaign planning, advertising, fund raising, using phone banks, recruiting volunteers, and campaign scheduling.[46]

Soft Money and Stronger Parties

Parties can spend unlimited and largely undisclosed amounts of soft money, but the candidate who benefits can deny any role in the message. Our election system lacks candidate accountability for the content and tone of the campaign. Accountability is also diminished by the large amounts of money spent by interest groups supporting one candidate or opposing another. Some of the largest soft money donors in the 2000 election cycle included the American Federation of State, County, Municipal Employees (AFSCME), which gave nearly $4.5 million in soft money to the Democrats, and AT&T, which gave over $2 million to the Republicans and over $1 million to the Democrats. Unions like AFSCME give most of their money to Democratic candidates and party committees. Unions were concerned in 2000 that if Republicans continued to hold both houses of Congress and won the White House, they would confront a national government controlled by Republicans for the first time in nearly 50 years. To avoid this, unions not only contributed to candidates but gave millions in soft money as well. Corporations like AT&T pursued a more bipartisan soft money strategy; this was a way of hedging their bet on who would win the election and ensuring friends in whichever party won. The volume of giving by labor and business entities shows how much soft money is now at play in national elections. If the system is not changed, we will certainly see more expensive campaigns and increasingly negative campaigning.

Despite their limitations, political parties have shown resilience. We have had Democrats and Republicans as the major parties in some form now for nearly 150 years. One reason for their resilience is they continue to serve a vital function in our constitutional democracy. Another reason is that our election rules clearly favor two parties. They do this through the winner-takes-all rule, which, unlike proportional representation, leaves the party with fewer votes no share of representation in that district or statewide race. This rule has served to moderate our major parties and makes it difficult to build minor parties into organizations that can win an election. State legislatures, generally under the control of a major party, have also strengthened the position of major parties over minor parties. As a result, we are likely to continue with the two parties we have for some time to come.

POLITICS ONLINE

What's Your Party?

Party identification is measured by political scientists by asking people the following question: Generally speaking, in politics do you consider yourself to be a Democrat, Republican, Independent, or what? As we have shown in this chapter, this measure of partisanship is a quite reliable predictor of voting behavior, and even Independents who lean towards a party are likely to vote for the party they lean towards. You might try out these questions on some friends or neighbors and see how often party leaners typically vote for the party towards which they lean. For the wording of the questions and the national data over time go to:www.prenhall.com/burns for Chapter 7.

Less academic but often fun ways to measure the degree to which you fit one party profile or another can be found on the Web. Often these quizzes will assess your party compatibility score. One example of such a site is: www.3pc.net/matchmaker/quiz.html. Among the categories covered are taxes, abortion policy, the role of the federal government, and government regulation in a variety of ways.

This kind of fun quiz does give you a sense of what some people see as differences between the national parties. One problem with quizzes like these is that they are not sensitive to differences between the party traditions in the states. Hence, Rhode Island Republicans are very different from Idaho Republicans, but these differences are lost in a national quiz like this. To see the differences, you might check out the websites of different state parties, looking for state party platforms or other position statements. The websites are: for the Republicans, www.rnc.org; for the Democrats: www.democrats.org; for the Green party: www.greenparties.org; and for the Libertarians: www.lp.org. Each party website has links to state parties.

SUMMARY

1. Political parties are essential to democracy—simplifying voting choices, organizing the competition, unifying the electorate, helping to organize government by bridging the separation of powers and fostering cooperation among branches of government, translating public preferences into policy, and providing loyal opposition.

2. Political parties help structure voting choice by nominating candidates to run for office. Before the advent of direct primaries, in which voters determine the party nominees, the parties had more control of who ran under their label. States determine the nomination rules. While most states employ the direct primary, some use a caucus or mixed caucus system where more committed partisans have a larger role in the decision of who gets nominated.

3. American parties are moderate. Bringing factions and interests together, they are broad enough to win the presidency and other elections. Third parties have been notably less successful. One reason for this is our single-member district, winner-take-all election rules. In systems with proportional representation or multimember districts, there is a greater tendency for more parties and the need to assemble governing coalitions across parties.

4. American parties have experienced critical elections and realignments. Most political scientists agree the last realignment occurred in 1932. In recent years, there has been divided government and an increase in the number of persons who call themselves Independents. This trend is sometimes called dealignment, but most Independents are closet partisans who vote for the party toward which they lean.

5. For the last 50 years, it has been routine to have divided government, with one party in control of the presidency and the other in control of one or both houses of Congress. Because of the partisan shift in the South toward Republicans, Republicans won control of the White House, often with Democrats controlling one or both houses of Congress. Successful presidents have found ways to cope with divided government and enact important parts of their agenda.

6. Parties are governed by their national and state committees, and the focal point of party organization is the national and state party chairs. When the party controls the executive branch of government, the executive (governor or president) usually has a determining say in selecting the party chair. With the rise of soft money in recent elections, parties now have more resources to spend on politics.

7. Party platforms are vague and generalized by design, giving the other party and voters little to oppose.

8. Parties are vital in the operation of government. They are organized around elected offices at the state and local levels. Congress is also organized around parties, and judicial and many executive branch appointments are based in large part on partisanship.

9. Parties are also active in the electorate, seeking to organize elections, simplify voting choices, and strengthen party identification.

10. Frequent efforts have been made to reform our parties. The Progressive movement saw parties, as then organized, as an impediment to democracy and pushed direct primaries as a means to reform them. Following the 1968 election, the Democratic party took the lead in pushing primaries and stressing greater diversity in those elected as delegates. Republicans have also encouraged broader participation, and they have improved party structure and finances.

11. Compared to some European parties, ours remain organizationally weak. There has been some party renewal in recent years as party competition has grown in the South and the parties themselves have initiated reforms.

KEY TERMS

FURTHER READING

JOHN H. ALDRICH, *Why Parties? The Origin and Transformation of Party Politics in America* (University of Chicago Press, 1995).

PAUL ALLEN BECK, *Party Politics in America*, 8th ed. (Longman, 1997).

JOHN F. BIBBY, *Politics, Parties, and Elections in America*, 3d ed. (Nelson-Hall, 1996).

DAVID BOAZ, *Libertarianism: A Primer* (Free Press, 1998).

MARY C. BRENNAN, *Turning Right in the Sixties: The Conservative Capture of the GOP* (University of North Carolina Press, 1995).

STEPHEN C. CRAIG, ED., *Broken Contract: Changing Relationships Between Ameri-*

cans and Their Government (Westview Press, 1996).

LEON EPSTEIN, *Political Parties in the American Mold* (University of Wisconsin Press, 1986).

JEFF FAUX, *The Party's Not Over: A New Vision for Democrats* (Basic Books, 1996).

J. DAVID GILLESPIE, *Politics at the Periphery: Third Parties in Two-Party America* (University of South Carolina Press, 1993).

JOHN C. GREEN AND DANIEL M. SHEA, EDS., *The State of the Parties: The Changing Role of Contemporary American Parties,* 2d ed. (Rowman and Littlefield, 1996).

PAUL S. HERRNSON, *Party Campaigning in the 1980s: Have the National Parties Made a Comeback as Key Players in Congressional Elections?* (Harvard University Press, 1988).

PAUL S. HERRNSON AND JOHN C. GREEN, EDS., *Multiparty Politics in America* (Rowman and Littlefield, 1997).

WILLIAM J. KEEFE, *Parties, Politics, and Public Policy in America,* 8th ed. (Congressional Quarterly Press, 1998).

BRUCE E. KEITH, DAVID B. MAGLEBY, CANDICE J. NELSON, ELIZABETH ORR, MARK C. WESTLYE, AND RAYMOND E. WOLFINGER, *The Myth of the Independent Voter* (University of California Press, 1992).

G. CALVIN MACKENZIE, *The Irony of Reform: Roots of American Political Disenchantment* (Westview Press, 1996).

L. SANDY MAISEL, ED., *The Parties Respond: Changes in American Parties and Campaigns,* 3d ed. (Westview, 1998).

WILLIAM G. MAYER, *The Divided Democrats: Ideological Unity, Party Reform, and Presidential Elections* (Westview, 1996).

SIDNEY M. MILKIS, *The President and the Parties: The Transformation of the American Party System Since the New Deal* (Oxford University Press, 1993).

WARREN E. MILLER AND J. MERRILL SHANKS, *The New American Voter* (Harvard University Press, 1996).

KELLY D. PATTERSON, *Political Parties and the Maintenance of Liberal Democracy* (Columbia University Press, 1996).

STEVEN J. ROSENSTONE, ROY L. BEHR, AND EDWARD H. LAZARUS, *Third Parties in America: Citizen Response to Major Party Failure,* 2d ed. (Princeton University Press, 1996).

JAMES SUNDQUIST, *Dynamics of the Party System: Alignment and Realignment of Political Parties in the United States,* rev. ed. (Brookings, 1983).

MARTIN P. WATTENBERG, *The Decline of American Political Parties, 1952–1992* (Harvard University Press, 1994).

JOHN K. WHITE AND DANIEL M. SHEA, *New Party Politics: From Jefferson and Hamilton to the Information Age* (Bedford/St. Martin's, 2000).

PUBLIC OPINION, PARTICIPATION, AND VOTING

8

UNDECIDED OR "SWING VOTERS" GOT A LOT OF
ATTENTION IN 2000 IN STATES OR DISTRICTS WITH COMPETITIVE
CONTESTS FOR PRESIDENT, U.S. SENATE, OR U.S. HOUSE.
Because so much was at stake in the 2000 elections—no incumbent running for president, and Republicans holding only a narrow majority in both houses of Congress—the candidates, parties, and interest groups made voter registration and turnout high priorities. Voters who had already made up their minds were bombarded with postcards reminding them to vote and phone calls reminding them it was election day and that their vote was needed. For example, the National Abortion and Reproductive Rights Action League (NARAL) made phone calls to pro-choice women under 40 years of age with a recorded message from Sarah Jessica Parker of HBO's *Sex and the City*, reminding them of the importance of electing pro-choice candidates.[1]

Candidate preferences and issue positions of possible voters are discovered by interviewing them on the telephone or in person, a process called a *canvas*. If these voters are undecided, they receive numerous pieces of mail and telephone calls aimed at persuading them to support one candidate over another. Mailings emphasize the stand of the candidate on such issues as Social Security, education, and prescription drug benefits. Interest groups and political parties send out similar persuasion pieces to undecided voters, often reinforcing the same themes as do the candidates. For example, in the U.S. House race in Washington's Second Congressional District, parties and interest groups sent out a total of 78 different mailings. In California's Twenty-seventh Congressional District—the most expensive U.S. House race in the country—parties and interest groups sent 71 different mailers on top of 45 different pieces of mail from the candidates' own campaigns.[2] No single household received all this mail; most of it was sent to voters who were for some reason thought to be persuadable. Consultants used all kinds of creative strategies like sending oversized mail and even a pop-up mailer like a children's book.

Some voters received conflicting messages. For instance, Michigan voters who were union members as well as gun owners received many communications from the National Rifle Association urging them to vote Republican, at the same time that their union was pushing a vote for the Democrats. In such cases, how do voters respond? Is a contact by telephone more persuasive than a piece of mail? Is the recorded voice of Sarah Jessica Parker more likely to get a person to vote than a live voice from someone calling from a telemarketing firm?

CHAPTER OUTLINE

■ Public Opinion

■ Participation:
  Translating Opinions
  into Action

■ Voting Choices

CHAPTER MEDIA

POLITICS ONLINE
Who Votes? Why Not You?
www.prenhall.com/burns

POLISIM
The Spin Effect
www.prenhall.com/burns

How you ask a polling question makes a lot of difference in the responses people give, as demonstrated by the way three different polls asked about special interests and campaign finance. The first question was written by Ross Perot's organization, not by a survey researcher. It was published in *TV Guide* and asked individuals to send in their answers. Perot's survey was criticized widely by survey organizations for its skewed sample and biased questions. The second and third questions were part of national surveys conducted by professional polling firms using random samples.

1. Should laws be passed to eliminate all possibilities of special interests giving huge sums of money to candidates?

Yes	99%

2. Should laws be passed to prohibit interest groups from contributing to campaigns? Or do groups have a right to contribute to the candidate they support?

Prohibit contribution	40%
Groups have right	55%

3. Please tell me whether you favor or oppose this proposal: New laws should eliminate all possibility of special interests giving large sums of money to candidates.

Favor	70%
Oppose	28%

SOURCE: Daniel Goleman, "Pollsters Enlist Psychologists in Quest for Unbiased Results," *The New York Times*, September 7, 1993, pp. C1, C11.

In addition to polls conducted by Gallop, Pew, and other such organizations, newspapers and TV networks conduct polls on election preferences and numerous other subjects.

What we learned from the 2000 election is that a few hundred votes can determine an election outcome. Candidates cannot take any votes for granted, so in close contests, voter mobilization is critical. In this chapter we look at the nature of public opinion, how to measure it, the factors that affect the formation of opinions, the nature and level of political participation in the United States, and why people vote as they do.

PUBLIC OPINION

All governments in all nations must be concerned with public opinion. In nondemocratic nations unrest and protest can topple them. And in a constitutional democracy, citizens can express opinions in a variety of ways, including demonstrations, letters to newspaper editors, and voting in free and regularly scheduled elections. Elected officials refer often to public opinion as the basis for their policy-making decisions. In short, democracy and public opinion go hand in hand.

What Is Public Opinion?

Everybody talks about "public opinion." Everybody claims to speak for "the public." But social scientists use the term more precisely: we define **public opinion** as the distribution of individual preferences for, or evaluations of, a given issue, candidate, or institution within a specific population. *Distribution* means the proportion of the population that holds a particular opinion, as compared to people with opposing opinions or those with no opinion at all. For instance, final pre-election polls in 2000 by the Gallup Organization found that among potential voters, 48 percent reported they would vote for George W. Bush, 46 percent for Al Gore, and 4 percent for Ralph Nader.[3] The actual vote was Bush 48 percent, Gore 48 percent, and Nader 3 percent.[4]

TAKING THE PULSE OF THE PEOPLE   *Proper sampling* is based on randomly selecting people to survey. *Random sampling* means that every individual has an equal chance of being selected. The sample of randomly selected respondents should be appropriate for the questions being asked. For instance, a survey of 18-to-24-year-olds should not be done solely among college students, since roughly three-quarters of this age group do not attend college. Even with proper sampling, surveys have a *margin of error*, meaning the sample accurately reflects the population within a certain percentage—usually plus or minus 3 percent for a sample of at least 1,500 individuals.

The art of asking questions is also important to scientific polling. The wording of questions can influence the answers. Question order can also alter the responses. Good questions have been pretested to be sure that the way the question is asked does not bias how it is answered. They should be delivered by trained and professional interviewers, who read the questions exactly as written and without any intonation in their voices. Questions can be worded in different ways to measure factual knowledge, opinions, the intensity of opinion, or views on hypothetical situations. Sometimes *open-ended questions* are asked that permit respondents to answer in their own words rather than in set categories.

Thorough analysis and reporting of the results as well as random sampling and clearly worded questions are required of scientific polls. Scientific polls inform the public of the sample size, the margin of expected statistical error for a standard question, and when and where the poll was conducted. It is also important to realize that public opinion can change and that most polls are really snapshots of opinion at a point in time rather than moving pictures of opinions over time.

Individual preference means that when we measure public opinion, we are asking *individuals*—not groups, elected officials, or journalists—about their opinions. The *universe* or *population* is the relevant group of people for the question. When a substantial percentage of a sample agree on an issue—for example, that we should honor the American flag—there is a *consensus*. But on most issues, opinions are divided. When a large portion of opposing sides feels intensely about an issue, voters are said to be *polarized*. Vietnam in the 1960s and currently abortion are polarizing issues (see Table 8–1).

TABLE 8–1 How Opinions Differ on Abortion

| | Percent saying abortion should be | | | |
	Legal under any circumstances	Legal under certain circumstances	Illegal under all circumstances	Don't know
Total Adults	28%	51%	19%	2%
Age				
18–29	25	58	17	—
30–49	27	55	17	1
50–64	22	63	14	1
65+	13	64	21	2
Sex				
Men	21	62	16	1
Women	24	56	18	2
Education				
High school graduate or less	18	61	19	2
Some college	22	61	15	2
College graduate	35	47	18	—
Postgraduate	33	55	11	1
Race				
White	22	60	17	1
Nonwhite	25	55	18	2
Black	21	55	23	1
Religion				
Protestant	21	61	17	1
Catholic	23	57	19	1
Political Philosophy				
Liberal	35	55	9	1
Moderate	27	59	13	1
Conservative	11	63	26	—
Party Identification				
Republican	18	62	19	1
Democrat	27	57	15	1
Independent	25	55	19	1
Income				
Less than $20,000	17	57	25	1
$20,000–$29,999	21	59	19	1
$30,000–$49,999	24	59	15	2
More than $50,000	29	60	10	1

SOURCE: Data for total adults and for sex are from a national survey by the Gallup Organization, May 2000 and January 1998; other data are from the Gallup Organization, January 1992.

Note: Figures may not add up to 100 percent due to rounding.

public opinion
The distribution of individual preferences for, or evaluations of, a given issue, candidate, or institution within a specific population.

"It should be 'yes' or 'no' or 'undecided'—we don't accept a 'don't give a damn' answer!"

Cartoon Features Syndicate.

INTENSITY   The factor called *intensity* produces the brightest and deepest hues in the fabric of public opinion. The fervor of people's beliefs varies greatly. For example, some individuals mildly favor gun control legislation and others mildly oppose it; some people are emphatically for or against it, and some have no interest in the matter at all; still others may not even have heard of it. Intensity is typically measured by asking people how strongly they feel about an issue or about a politician. Such a question is often called a *scale*.

LATENCY   *Latency* refers to political opinions that exist merely as a potential; they may not have crystallized, yet they are still important, for they can be aroused by leaders and converted into political action. Latent opinions set rough boundaries for leaders who know that if they take certain actions, they will trigger either opposition or support from millions of people. If leaders have some understanding of latent opinions—people's unexpressed wants, needs, and hopes—they will know how to mobilize them and draw them to the polls on election day. Many who lived in communist Poland, East Germany, Czechoslovakia, or Yugoslavia must have had latent opinions favorable to democracy—opinions supporting majority rule, freedom, and meaningful elections. The speed with which these countries embraced democratic reforms was possible when leaders encouraged widespread expression of such ideas.

SALIENCE   By *salience* we mean the extent to which people believe issues are relevant to them. Most people are more concerned about personal issues like paying their bills and keeping their jobs than about national issues, but if national issues somehow threaten their security or safety, salience of national issues rises sharply.

The saliency of issues may change over time. During the Great Depression of the 1930s, Americans were concerned mainly about jobs, wages, and economic security. By the 1940s, foreign affairs came to the fore. In the 1960s, problems of race and poverty aroused intense feeling. In the 1970s, Vietnam and then Watergate riveted people's attention. By the early 2000s, concern about drugs, crime, health care, education, and the state of the environment had become salient issues.

How Do We Get Our Political Opinions and Values?

No one is born with political views. We learn them from many teachers. The process by which we develop our political attitudes, values, and beliefs is called **political socialization**. This process starts in childhood, and the family and the schools are probably the two most important political teachers. Children learn the content of our culture in childhood and adolescence but reshape it as they mature.[5] Socialization lays the foundation for political beliefs, values, ideology, and partisanship.

A common element of political socialization in all cultures is *nationalism*, a consciousness of the nation-state and of belonging to that entity. Robert Coles describes it this way:

> As soon as we are born, in most places on this earth, we acquire a nationality, a membership in a community. . . . A royal doll, a flag to wave in a parade, coins with their engraved messages—these are sources of instruction and connect a young person to a country. The attachment can be strong, indeed even among children yet to attend school, wherever the flag is saluted, the national anthem sung. The attachment is as parental as the words imply—homeland, motherland, fatherland. . . . Nationalism works its way into just about every corner of the mind's life.[6]

The sources of our views are immensely varied in the pluralistic political culture of the United States. Political attitudes may stem from religious, racial, gender, ethnic, or economic beliefs and values. But we can make at least one generalization safely: We form our attitudes in *groups*, and not only in groups such as schools and social organizations, but especially in close-knit groups like the family. When we

political socialization

The process by which we develop our political attitudes, values, and beliefs.

identify closely with the attitudes and interests of a particular group, we tend to see politics through the "eyes" of that group.[7]

Group affiliation does not necessarily mean that individual members do not think for themselves. Each member brings his or her own emotions, feelings, memories, and resistance to groups. The extent to which people are captive to groups is indeed a running argument among scholars from different disciplines. Sociologists tend to emphasize the pervasive influence of groups over their members. Psychologists focus more on the developmental stages within individuals that prompt them to be joiners or loners. Political scientists have traditionally tended to agree more with the sociological approach.[8] Political psychologists seek to combine both approaches.

Children in the United States tend at an early age to adopt common values that provide continuity with the past and legitimize the American political system. Young children know what country they live in, and their loyalty to the nation develops early. Although the details of our political system may still elude them, most young Americans acquire a respect for the Constitution and for the concept of participatory democracy, as well as an initially positive view of the most visible figure in our democracy—the president.

FAMILY   American children typically show political interest by the age of ten, and by the early teens their interest may be fairly high. Consider your own political learning process. You probably formed your picture of the world by listening to a parent at dinner or by absorbing the tales your older brothers and sisters brought home from school. Perhaps you heard about politics from grandparents, aunts, and uncles. You, in turn, influenced your family, if only by bringing some of your own hopes and problems home from school. What we first learn in the family is not so much specific political opinions as basic *attitudes* that shape our opinions—attitudes toward our neighbors, political parties, other classes or types of people, particular leaders (especially presidents), and society in general.

Studies of high school students indicate a high correlation between the political party of the parents and the partisan choice of their children. This relatively high degree of correspondence continues throughout life. Such a finding raises some interesting questions: Does the direct influence of parents create the correspondence? Or does living in the same social environment—neighborhood, church, socioeconomic group—equally influence parents and children? The answer is *both*, and one influence often strengthens the other. For example, a daughter of Democratic parents growing up in a small southern town with strong Democratic leanings will be affected by friends, by other adults, and perhaps by youngsters in a church group, all of whom may reinforce the attitudes of her parents.[9] What happens when a young person's parents and friends disagree? Young people tend to go along with parents rather than friends on party affiliation, with friends rather than parents on issues like the death penalty or gun control, and somewhere in between in their actual votes in presidential elections.[10]

SCHOOLS   Schools also mold young citizens' political attitudes. American schools see part of their purpose as preparing students to be citizens and active participants in governing their communities and nation. At an early age, schoolchildren begin to pick up specific political values and acquire basic attitudes toward our system of government. Education, like the family, prepares Americans to live in society.

From kindergarten through college, students generally develop political values that will enhance their citizenship and legitimize the American political system. In their study of American history, they are introduced to our nation's heroes and heroines, the important events in our history, and the ideals of our society. Other aspects of the their experience, such as the daily Pledge of Allegiance, usually reinforce respect of country. Children also gain practical experience in the workings of

The Chicago Herald Tribune was so sure of its polling data in the 1948 election, they predicted a win for Republican Thomas Dewey before the results were final. A victorious Harry Truman displays the mistaken headline.

democracy through elections for class or school officers and student government. In some high schools and colleges, the state legislature or college trustees have made courses in U.S. history or American government a graduation requirement.

Do school influences give young people greater faith in political institutions? Yes and no. A classic study examined civics texts and students' attitudes in three Boston communities—one upper-middle class, one lower-middle class, and one working class. The textbooks in all three communities stressed the right of citizens to try to influence government, but only the texts used in the upper-middle-class community stressed politics as conflict and as a process for resolving differing group demands. Edgar Litt, a political scientist, concluded that the lower-middle-class students were learning that government was a process carried out by institutions on their behalf, while the upper-middle-class students were learning that the political process was something they could influence.[11]

The debate about whether there is peer pressure on college campuses to conform to certain acceptable ideas—*political correctness (PC)*—highlights the role higher education can play in shaping attitudes and values. How does college influence political opinions? One study suggests that college students are more likely to be knowledgeable about politics, more in favor of free speech, and more likely to talk and read about politics.[12] Is this the influence of the professors, the curriculum, the students, or the party leadership in the White House? It is difficult to generalize. Parents sometimes fear professors have too much influence on their college-age children; however, most professors doubt they have significant influence over the political views of their students.

MASS MEDIA   Like everybody else, young people are exposed to a wide range of media—school newspapers, national newspapers, the Internet, movies, television—all of which influence what they think. They, like adults, pick and choose the media with which they agree, so their exposure is *selective*. The mass media also serve as agents of socialization by providing a link between individuals and the values and behavior of others. When people watch, listen, and read, they discover which values and role models are considered important. News broadcasts present information about our society; events that get intensive media coverage often focus our attention on certain issues. For example, the hours of TV coverage of the presidential vote count in Florida in 2000 directed widespread attention to voting systems and the Electoral College.

OTHER INFLUENCES   Religious, ethnic, and racial attitudes also shape opinions, both within and outside the family. Generalizations about how people vote are useful, but we have to be careful about stereotyping people. True, Jewish families tend to be more liberal on both economic and noneconomic issues than either Catholics or Protestants, but there are lots of conservative Jewish families and lots of liberal Catholic and Protestant ones. It is dangerous to assume that because we know a person's religious affiliation or ethnic background we can know his or her political opinions.

Stability and Change in Public Opinion

Adults are not simply the sum of all their early experiences, but most of us do not change our opinions very often. Even if the world around us changes rapidly, we are slow to shift our loyalties or to change our minds about things that matter to us. In general, people who remain in the same place, in the same occupation, and in the same income group throughout their lives tend to have stable opinions. But people carry their attitudes with them, and families who move from cities to suburbs often retain their big-city attitudes long after they have moved. Political analysts are becoming more interested in the ways in which adults modify their views. A major factor may be a harsh experience—a war, economic depression, or loss of a job—that shocks people out of their existing attitudes.

Some of our political opinions change very little because they are part of our core values. Thus our views on abortion, the death penalty, and doctor-assisted suicide remain relatively stable over time. On issues that are less central to our values, such as our view of how a president is performing his job, opinions can show substantial change over time. On many issues, public opinion can change once the public learns more about the issue or perceives there is another side to the question. It is on these issues that politicians can help shape attitudes.

Public Opinion and Public Policy

For much of human history it has been difficult to measure public opinion. "What I want," Abraham Lincoln once said, "is to get done what the people desire to be done, and the question for me is how to find that out exactly." Politicians in our day do not face the uncertainty about public opinion faced by Lincoln. Modern polling tells them what public opinion is on all major policy issues. In addition to polls the politicians commission, they can turn to public or media polls. More than 80 percent of newspapers and half of all television stations conduct or commission their own polls.[13]

Here are some examples of how public opinion can shape policy and in turn how policies shape opinion. During the Vietnam War, antiwar demonstrations on college campuses spread to cities all over the country. "Public opinion had a substantial impact on the rate of troop withdrawals."[14] In the Persian Gulf War, opposition to the use of U.S. forces was greatly reduced after a few days of success in the air and ground war. When American forces were dispatched to Somalia in Operation Restore Hope in January 1993, 79 percent approved of the use of troops to ensure the delivery of humanitarian aid, food, and medical provisions. But when U.S. soldiers were killed and dragged through the streets of Mogadishu, support fell to only 17 percent in October of the same year.[15]

Typically, elected officials seek to follow public opinion. Winning reelection is a strong motive for members of Congress.[16] "Legislators show greater attention to public opinion as election day looms," and the closeness of the fit between constituent opinion and roll call voting reflects that connection.[17] Candidates use polls to determine where to campaign, how to campaign, and even whether to campaign. In the years and months preceding a national convention, politicians watch the polls to determine who among the hopefuls has political appeal.

Surely polls are no substitute for elections. Faced with a ballot, voters must translate their opinions into concrete decisions. They must decide what is important and what is not. Democracy is more than the expression of views, more than a simple mirror of opinion. It also involves choosing among leaders, taking sides on certain issues, and selecting the governmental actions that may follow. Democracy is the thoughtful participation of people in the political process. It means using heads as well as counting them. Elections, with all their failings, still establish the link between the many voices of "We the People" and the selection of their leaders.

Awareness and Interest

For most people, politics is of secondary importance to earning a living, raising a family, and having a good time; some Americans are more concerned about which team wins the Super Bowl than they are about who wins the school board elections,

These college students feel responsible to vote and line up on campus to fill out absentee ballots.

who gets to be mayor, or even who gets to be president of the United States. Most people find politics complicated and difficult to understand. And they should, for democracy *is* complicated and difficult to understand. But it helps to understand the mechanics and structures of our government: how the government operates, how the Electoral College works, how many chambers there are in Congress, the length of terms for the president and for members of the Senate and House of Representatives, for example.

Details about how the government works are typically best known by younger adults, who remember learning them in school. The general adult public, however, fares poorly when quizzed about their elected officials. Just over a quarter of Americans are able to recall the name of their member of Congress, and only 60 percent can name even one of their U.S. senators.[18] With so many voters not knowing who represents them in Congress, it is not surprising that "on even hotly debated congressional issues, few people know where their Congress member stands."[19]

Although the public's knowledge of institutional and candidate issues is poor, its knowledge of important public policy issues is worse. In 1982, after years of debate over ratification of the Equal Rights Amendment, nearly one-third of the adults in the United States indicated they had never heard of it. In late August 1993, several weeks before the vote in Congress on the North American Free Trade Agreement (NAFTA), six out of ten Americans reported they were not following the NAFTA story at all.[20]

Fortunately, not all Americans are uninformed or uninterested. About 25 percent of the public are interested in politics most of the time. They are the **attentive public**, people who know and understand how the government works. They vote in most elections, read a daily newspaper, and "talk politics" with their families and friends. They tend to be better educated and more committed to democratic values than are other Americans.

At the opposite end of the spectrum are *nonvoters*, people who are rarely interested in politics or public affairs and who rarely vote. About 35 percent of Americans have indicated that they have little interest in politics or are only occasionally interested.[21] A subset of this group might be called *political know-nothings*. These individuals not only avoid political activity but also have little interest in government and limited knowledge about it.

attentive public
Those who follow public affairs carefully.

Between the attentive public and the nonvoters are the *part-time citizens*, roughly 40 percent of the American public. These individuals participate selectively in elections, voting in presidential elections but usually not in others. Politics and government do not greatly interest them; they pay only minimal attention to the news, and they rarely discuss candidates or elections with others.

Democracy can survive even when a large number of citizens are passive and uninformed, as long as a substantial number of people serve as opinion leaders and are interested and informed about public affairs. Obviously, these activists will have much greater influence than their less active fellow citizens.

PARTICIPATION: TRANSLATING OPINIONS INTO ACTION

Americans influence their government's actions in several different ways, many of which are protected by the Constitution. They vote in elections, join interest groups, go to political party meetings, ring doorbells, call friends urging them to vote for issues or candidates, sign petitions, write letters to the editors of newspapers, and make calls to radio talk shows.

Protest is also a form of political participation. Our political system is remarkably tolerant of protest that is not destructive or violent; boycotts, picketing, sit-ins, and marches are all legally protected. Rosa Parks and Martin Luther King, Jr., used the peaceful breaking of the law to protest what they saw as unfair laws. The number of Americans who participate in protests is small, but the impact of their actions in shaping public opinion can be substantial.

A distinguishing characteristic of a democracy is that citizens can influence government decisions by participating in politics. In totalitarian societies, participation is very limited, forcing people who want to influence government to resort to violence or revolution. When the citizens of Belgrade turned out night after night to protest the nullification of their election, they forced Slobodan Milosevic to permit the victorious candidate, Vojislav Kostunica, to take power. But protests and demonstrations are not always peaceful or successful. The protest of Chinese students in Tiananmen Square failed to stop the onslaught of tanks and the repression that followed. Americans sometimes forget that our democracy was born of revolution, but that maintaining a constitutional democracy is also difficult and demands public participation.

Even in an established democracy, people may feel so strongly about an issue that they would rather fight than accept the verdict of an election. The classic example is the American Civil War. Following the election of 1860, in which an antislavery candidate who did not receive a single electoral vote from a slave state won the presidency, the South took up arms. The ensuing war marked the breakdown of democracy. Examples in our own time include antiabortion groups that use violence to press their political agenda and militia groups that arm themselves for battle against government restrictions.

Large numbers of Americans routinely participate in such rituals of democracy as singing the National Anthem or reciting the Pledge of Allegiance. They communicate their views about government and politics to their representatives in Washington and the state capitol. They serve as jurors in courtrooms and enlist in the military. They express concern about the involvement of American military forces in foreign hostilities. They complain about taxes and government regulations. And each year millions of Americans visit Washington, D.C., and other historic sights.

Street demonstrations in Belgrade, Yugoslavia, finally forced Slobodan Milosovic to concede defeat and permit the victorious candidate, Vojislav Kostunica, to take power. He was later taken into custody.

TABLE 8–2	Political Participation and Awareness in the United States	
Vote in presidential elections		49%
Vote in congressional elections		34
Know name of U.S. representative		28
Sign a petition		48
Write U.S. representative or state representative		30
Vote in local elections		10–30
Try to persuade vote of others		19
Display campaign button, sticker, or sign		7
Attend dinner, meeting, or rally for candidate		5
Contribute to candidate		4
Contribute to party		4

SOURCES: U.S. Bureau of the Census, *Statistical Abstract of the United States, 1998* (Government Printing Office, 1998), p. 297; 1998 American National Election Study, Center for Political Studies, University of Michigan.

For most people, politics is a private activity. Some books on manners still consider it impolite to discuss politics at dinner parties. To say that politics is private does not mean people do not have opinions or will not discuss them when asked by others, including pollsters. But often politics is avoided in discussions with neighbors, work associates, even friends and family, as too divisive or upsetting. Typically, less than one person in four attempts to influence how another person votes in an election. An even smaller number actually work for a candidate or party. Only one in 20 people make a contribution to a candidate, and only one in six designate three dollars of their taxes to the fund that pays for presidential general elections (see Table 8–2).[22]

Few individuals attempt to influence others by writing letters to elected officials or to editors of newspapers for publication. Even smaller numbers participate in protest groups or activities. Despite the small number of persons who engage in these activities, it would be a mistake to assume that small numbers of individuals cannot make a difference to politics and government. An individual or small group can generate media interest in an issue and expand the impact. Peaceful protests for civil rights, about environmental issues, and both for and against abortion have generated public attention and even changed opinions.

Voting

Americans' most typical political activity is voting. The United States is a constitutional democracy with more than 200 years of free and frequent elections and a tradition of the peaceful transfer of power between competing groups and parties.

Originally the Constitution left it to the individual states to determine the crucial question of who could vote, and the qualifications for voting differed considerably from state to state. All states except New Jersey barred women from voting, many did not permit African Americans to vote, and until the 1830s, property ownership was often a requirement. By the time of the Civil War, the franchise had been extended to all white male citizens in every state. Since that time, eligibility standards for voting have been expanded by legislation and constitutional amendments:

1870 Fifteenth Amendment forbade states from denying the right to vote because of "race, color, or previous condition of servitude."

1920 Nineteenth Amendment gave women the right to vote.

1924 Congress granted Native Americans citizenship and voting rights.

1961 Twenty-third Amendment permitted District of Columbia residents to vote in federal elections.

1964 Twenty-fourth Amendment prohibited the use of poll taxes in federal elections.

1965 Voting Rights Act removed restrictions that kept blacks from voting.

1971 Twenty-sixth Amendment extended the vote to citizens age 18 and older.

The civil rights movement in the 1960s, which made voting rights a central issue, secured adoption of the Twenty-fourth Amendment and passage of the 1965 Voting Rights Act. The Voting Rights Act banned literacy tests, eased registration requirements, and provided for the replacement of local election officials with federal registrars in areas where the denial of the right to vote had been most blatant. Its passage resulted in a dramatic expansion of African American registration and voting. Once African Americans were permitted to register to vote, "the focus of voting discrimination shifted . . . to preventing them from winning elections."[23] In southern legislative districts where African Americans are in the majority, however, there has been a "dramatic increase in the proportion of African American legislators elected"[24] (see Figure 8–1).

Registration

One peculiarly American legal requirement—**voter registration**—discourages voting. Most other democracies have automatic voter registration. Average turnout in the United States is more than 30 percentage points lower than in countries like Australia, Austria, Belgium, Denmark, Germany, and Italy; only Switzerland has lower average turnout.[25] This was not always the case. In fact, in the 1800s, turnout in the United States was much like that of Europe today. Turnout began to drop significantly around the turn of the century, in part as a result of election reform (see Figure 8–2).

American elections in the 1800s were different from those of today. Ballots were prepared by the parties, often using different colors of paper that allowed party officials to monitor how people had voted. In some areas charges of multiple voting generated a reform movement that substituted the **Australian ballot**, a secret ballot printed by the state, and initiated voter registration to reduce multiple voting and limit voting to those who had previously established their eligibility.

Registration laws vary by state, but in every state except North Dakota registration is required in order to vote. Three states permit election-day voter registration. The most important provision regarding voter registration may be the closing date. A few years ago it was not uncommon for closing dates to be six months before the election; now, by federal law, no state can stop registration more than 30 days before a federal election.[26] Voter registration places a responsibility on voters to take an extra step—usually filling out a form at the county courthouse, when renewing a driver's license, or with a roving registrar—some days or weeks before the election. Other important provisions include places and hours of registration.[27]

Motor-Voter

The burdens of voter registration were eased a bit when, on May 20, 1993, President Bill Clinton signed the National Voter Registration Act—called the "Motor-Voter" bill because it allows people to register to vote while applying for or

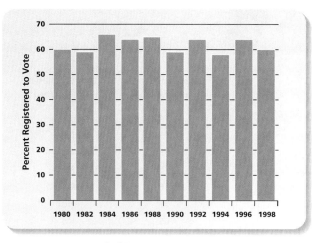

FIGURE 8–1 Percent of African American Registered Voters, 1980–1998

SOURCE: U.S. Bureau of the Census, *Statistical Abstract of the United States, 1999* (Government Printing Office, 1999), p. 300.

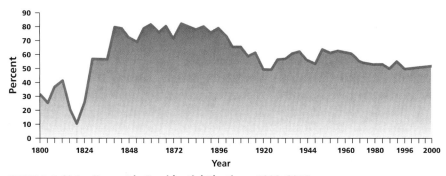

FIGURE 8–2 Voter Turnout in Presidential Elections, 1800–2000

SOURCE: Howard W. Stanley and Richard G. Niemi, *Vital Statistics on American Politics, 1999–2000* (Congressional Quarterly Press, 2000). See also www.infoplease.com/ipa/A0781453.html.

voter registration
System designed to reduce voter fraud by limiting voting to those who have established eligibility by submitting the proper form.

Australian ballot
A secret ballot printed by the state.

REGISTRATION AND VOTING IN THE WORLD'S DEMOCRACIES

	Turnout as percent of eligible vote	Compulsion penalties*	Automatic registration**
Australia	94%	Yes	No
Austria	91	No	Yes
Belgium	93	Yes	Yes
Canada	76	No	Yes
Denmark	86	No	Yes
Finland	78	No	Yes
France	66	No	No
Germany	84	No	Yes
Greece	85	Yes	Yes
Ireland	69	No	Yes
Israel	80	No	Yes
Italy	91	Yes	Yes
Japan	71	No	Yes
Netherlands	86	No	Yes
New Zealand	87	No	No
Norway	84	No	Yes
Spain	71	No	Yes
Sweden	86	No	Yes
Switzerland	46	No	Yes
United Kingdom	75	No	Yes
United States	53	No	No

SOURCES: Thomas T. Mackie and Richard Rose, *The International Almanac of Electoral History*, 3d ed. (Congressional Quarterly Press, 1991); G. Bingham Powell, Jr., "American Voter Turnout in Comparative Perspective," *American Political Science Review* 80 (March 1986), p. 38. Iceland, Luxembourg, Malta, and Portugal were not included in the Powell study and were therefore omitted from this table.

*Compulsion penalties are fines or other possible state actions against nonvoters.

**Automatic registration utilizes other forms of citizen identification like a driver's license.

renewing a driver's license. Offices that provide welfare and disabled assistance can also facilitate voter registration. States have the option to include public schools, libraries, and city and county clerks' offices as registration sites. The law also requires states to allow registration by mail using a standardized form. Motor-Voter requires a questionnaire be mailed to registered voters every four years to purge for death and change of residence, but forbids purging for any other reasons, such as nonvoting.

The law has been successful, at least in terms of numbers of new voters registered.[28] Early data on the impact of Motor-Voter suggest that neither Democrats nor Republicans are the primary beneficiaries because most who have registered claim to be Independent.[29] Yet even with the increase in registration, Motor-Voter does not appear to have increased turnout.[30]

Turnout

Americans hold more elections for more offices than do citizens of any other democracy. In part because there are so many elections, American voters tend to pick and choose which elections to vote in. Americans elect officeholders in *general elections*, determine party nominees in *primary elections*, and replace senators who have died or left office in *special elections*.

Elections held in years when the president is on the ballot are called *presidential elections*, elections held midway between presidential elections are called *midterm elections*, and elections held in odd-numbered calendar years are called *off-year elections*. Midterm elections (like the one in 2002) elect about one-third of the U.S. Senate, all members of the House of Representatives, and most governors and other statewide officeholders as well as large numbers of state legislators. Many local elections to elect city councils and mayors are held in the spring of odd-numbered years.

Turnout—the proportion of the voting-age public that votes—is highest in presidential general elections (see Figure 8–3). Turnout is higher in general elections than in primary elections and higher in primary elections than in special elections. Turnout is higher in presidential general elections than in midterm general elections, and higher in presidential primary elections than in midterm primary elections.[31] Turnout is higher in elections in which candidates for federal office are on the ballot (U.S. senator, member of the House of Representatives, president) than in state elections in years when there are no federal contests. Some states elect their governor and other state officials in odd-numbered years to separate state from national politics. The result is generally lower turnout. Finally, local or municipal

turnout

The proportion of the voting-age public that votes.

elections have lower turnout than state elections, and municipal primaries have even lower rates of participation.

Turnout peaked in 1960 at more than 65 percent of persons over 21 years of age, but it has since declined to 36 percent in 1998, and 51 percent in 2000.[32] Turnout should have gone up since 1960 because the Voting Rights Act of 1965 added large numbers of African Americans to the pool of registered voters. Women, another historically underrepresented group, have also increased their voting levels.[33] Finally, our electorate has grown richer and more educated since the 1960s, and since wealth and education are related to voting, we should have seen an increase instead of a decrease in voting. However, 85 million of eligible Americans failed to vote in recent presidential elections; the nonvoting figures are even higher for congressional, state, county, and local elections.[34]

Who Votes?

The extent of voting varies widely among different groups. The level of education especially helps predict whether people will vote; as education increases, so does the propensity to vote. "Education increases one's capacity for understanding complex and intangible subjects such as politics," according to one study, "as well as encouraging the ethic of civil responsibility. Moreover, schools provide experience dealing with a variety of bureaucratic problems, such as coping with requirements, filling out forms, and meeting deadlines."[35] Race and ethnic background are linked with different levels of voting, in large part because they correlate with education. Blacks in general turn out at lower rates than whites. However, women, another historically underrepresented group, increased their voting levels to the point where since 1984 more women than men vote.[36]

Income and age are also important factors. Those with higher family incomes are more likely to vote than those with lower incomes. Income, of course, corresponds to occupation, and those with higher-status careers are more likely to vote than those with lower-status jobs. Poor people are less likely to feel politically involved and confident, and their social norms tend to deemphasize politics.[37] Older people, unless they are very old and infirm, are more likely to vote than younger people. Women's recent higher turnout is generally attributed to increasing levels of education and employment.

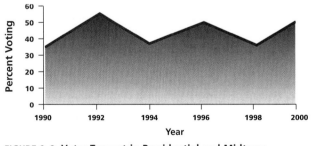

FIGURE 8–3 Voter Turnout in Presidential and Midterm Elections, 1990–2000

Sources: U.S. Bureau of the Census, *Statistical Abstract of the United States, 1998* (Government Printing Office, 1998), p. 97; Louis V. Gerstner, "Next Time, Let Us Boldly Vote As No Democracy Has Before," *USA Today*, November 16, 1998, p. A15. For 2000 data, www.infoplease.com/ipa/A0781453.html.

League of Women Voters

This poster, published by the League of Women Voters, urged women to use the vote the Nineteenth Amendment had given them.

How Serious Is Nonvoting?

Although Americans can hardly avoid reading or hearing about political campaigns, roughly 85 million Americans fail to vote in presidential elections. Who are they? Why don't they vote? Is the fact that so many Americans choose not to vote a cause for alarm? If so, what can we do about it?

The simplest explanation for low turnout is that people are lazy, but there is more to it than that. Of course, some people are apathetic, but the vast majority of Americans are not. Paradoxically, we compare favorably with other nations in political interest and awareness, but for a variety of institutional and political reasons, we fail to convert these qualities into votes (see Table 8–3).

The difficulty of voting in the United States, the cost in time and effort, is higher than in other democracies. In our system, individuals are required to register to vote, and they must make sense of a range of political alternatives that do not necessarily meet their interests.

Another factor in the decline of voter turnout since the 1960s is the Twenty-sixth Amendment, which lowered the voting age to 18. It increased the number of eligible voters, but that group is the least likely to vote. With ratification of the amendment in 1971, turnout fell from 62 percent in 1968 to 57 percent in 1972.[38] The effect of adding this low turnout group to the electorate has been to lower the overall turnout rate.

Some political scientists argue that nonvoting is not a critical problem. "Nonvoting is not a social disease," contends Austin Ranney, a noted scholar of politics. He points out that legal and extralegal denial of the vote to African Americans, women, Hispanics, persons over 18, and other groups has now been outlawed, so nonvoting is voluntary. He quotes the late Senator Sam Ervin of North Carolina: "I don't believe in making it easy for apathetic, lazy people to vote."[39]

Those who argue that nonvoting is a critical problem cite the "class bias" of those who do vote. The social makeup and attitudes of nonvoters are significantly different from those of voters and hence greatly distort the representative system. "The very poor . . . have about two-thirds the representation among voters than their numbers would suggest." Thus the people who need help the most from the government lack their fair share of electoral power to obtain it. And, it is argued, this situation is growing worse.[40]

Low voting, according to those who see a class bias in voting, reflects "the underdevelopment of political attitudes resulting from the historic exclusion of low-income groups from active electoral participation." In short, part of the problem of nonvoting among low-income, less-educated people is their failure to be conscious of their interests. Dynamic leadership or strong party organization, or both, would not only attract the poor to the polls but also make clear their "class grievances and aspirations."[41]

Others reject this class-bias argument. They admit nonvoters are demographically different, yet they cite polls showing that nonvoters' attitudes are not much different from voters' attitudes. One study, comparing the party identification of voters with that of all Americans, found the proportion of Democrats was nearly identical (51.4 percent of all citizens and 51.3 percent of voters), while Republicans as voters were slightly overrepresented (36 percent of citizens and 39.7 percent of voters). All other political differences are considered to be much smaller than this 3.7 percent gap. Further, voters are not "disproportionately hostile" to social welfare policies.[42]

TABLE 8–3 Why People Don't Vote

Not registered to vote	35%
Didn't have time to go	6
No campaign or organization contacted them	6
Was not convenient	24
Not interested in the candidates	22
Election just didn't seem important	10
Too young at the time	1
Other	2
Not sure	8

SOURCE: Roper Center at University of Connecticut, February 1997, Public Opinion Online, Question ID (Ushare.97govn, rf03b).

Note: Results add up to more than 100 percent due to multiple responses.

What effect might increased voter turnout have in national elections? It might make a difference, since there are partisan differences between different demographic groups, and candidates would have to adjust to the demands of an expanded electorate. A noted political scientist, while acknowledging that no political system could achieve 100 percent participation, pointed out that the entire balance of power in the political system could be overturned if the large nonvoter population decided to vote.[43] However, others argue that the difference may not be as pronounced. Nonvoters are not more in favor of government ownership or control of industry, and they are not more egalitarian. Nonvoters are, however, more inclined to favor additional spending on welfare programs.[44]

Another way to think of low voter turnout is to see it as a sign of approval with things as they are, whereas high voter turnout would signify disapproval and widespread desire for change. Even on the subject of how to interpret low turnout there is disagreement.

VOTING CHOICES

Why do people vote as they do? Political scientists have identified three main elements of the voting choice: party identification, candidate appeal, and issues. These elements often overlap.

Voter Turnout by Demographic Factors

	1992	1994	1996	1998
Sex				
Men	60.2%	44.4%	52.8%	41.4%
Women	62.3	44.9	55.5	42.4
Race				
White	63.6	46.9	56.0	46.5
Black	54.0	37.0	50.6	40
Hispanic	28.9	19.1	26.7	20
Education				
Some high school	41.2	27.0	33.8	24.6
High school graduate	57.5	40.5	49.1	37.1
Some college	68.7	49.1	60.5	46.2
College graduate	81.0	63.1	73.0	57

SOURCE: U.S. Bureau of the Census, *Statistical Abstract of the United States, 2000* (Government Printing Office, 2000), p. 290.

Voting on the Basis of Party

Party identification is the subjective sense of identification or affiliation that a person has with a political party, (see Chapter 7). Party identification often predicts a person's stand on issues. It is part of our national mythology that Americans vote for the person and not the party, but, as you will see, the person we vote for is most often from the party we prefer.

Partisanship is typically acquired in childhood or adolescence as a result of the socialization process in the family, then reinforced by peer groups in adolescence. In the absence of reasons to vote otherwise, people depend on party identification to simplify their voting choices. Party identification is not the same as party registration; it is not party membership in the sense of being a dues-paying, card-carrying member, as in some European parties. Rather, it is a psychological sense of attachment to one party or another.

There has been a dramatic increase in the number of Independents since the mid-1970s. Nominally there are more Independents in the electorate today than Republicans. But two-thirds of all Independents are, in fact, partisans in their voting behavior. Independent-leaning Democrats are predictably Democratic in their voting behavior, and Independent-leaning Republicans vote heavily Republican. Independent-leaners are thus very different from each other and

party identification
An informal and subjective affiliation with a political party that most people acquire in childhood.

A Closer Look

PROBLEMS COUNTING BALLOTS AND ADMINISTERING ELECTIONS

The chaos in the counting of ballots in Florida in the 2000 election surprised many Americans, who assumed that vote counting is simple and precise. They were wrong. The problems were not isolated to Florida's clogged voting machines, defective punch cards, and inconsistent standards for dealing with problems. Ballots were misplaced in New Mexico, voting machines broke down in several states, people's names were incorrectly purged from voting lists, and long lines of people waiting to vote led to court challenges in many states. In the weeks and months following the election, at least half the states launched efforts to study the problems and propose solutions; in addition, national commissions, advisory groups, and experts undertook extensive analyses of our voting procedures.

Most people agree that many communities need new voting equipment, and that the antiquated and flawed punch card technology used by "roughly 30 percent of the nation's voters" must be abandoned.* Whether jurisdictions adopt the less expensive optically scannable ballots or more expensive high-tech computer systems will depend in part on how much money Congress is willing to provide. Estimates vary, but the cost could be as high as $6.5 billion, depending on which new voting system is adopted.

The National Association of Secretaries of State—the state officials charged with election administration—issued recommendations that included: better pay

Angry voters in Palm Beach County protested that the "butterfly ballot" caused them to vote incorrectly and demanded an opportunity to vote over again, but were not allowed to do so.

for poll workers; aggressive voter education on matters like how to ask for a second ballot if the first is spoiled; equal access to balloting for minorities, poor, and elderly voters; maintaining up-to-date voter lists; ensuring the integrity of absentee ballots; and providing federal money to local communities to upgrade their voting systems.**

The debate over electoral reform growing out of the 2000 election is not limited to machines and ballots but includes standards for recounts, ways to ensure the process is open to all citizens, and concerns about the news media projecting winners before the polls close.

*Robert Tanner, "Ballot Reforms Are Slow in Coming, Despite Hundreds of Ideas, Studies," *Deseret News*, March 4, 2001, p. A3.

**Katharine Q. Seelye, "Panel Suggests Election Changes That Let States Keep Control," *The New York Times*, February 5, 2001, p. A16.

from the Pure Independents. Pure Independents have the lowest rate of turnout but generally do side with the eventual winner in presidential elections. These data on Independents only reinforce the importance of partisanship as an explanation of voting choice, because when we consider Independent-leaning Democrats and Independent-leaning Republicans as Democrats and Republicans respectively, there were only 11 percent Pure Independents or others without a party in 2000, and the average for the period 1952–2000 was only 11 percent.[45]

Although party identification has fluctuated somewhat in the past 40 years, it remains more stable than attitudes about issues or political ideology. Fluctuations in party identification appear to come in response to economic conditions and political performance, especially of the president. The more information voters have about their choices, the more likely they are to defect from their party and vote for a candidate from the other party.

Voting on the Basis of Candidates

While long-term party identification is important, it is clearly not the only factor in voting choices; otherwise the Democrats would have won every presidential election since the last realignment in 1932. In fact, since 1952, Republicans have been more successful in winning the White House than Democrats. The answer to this puzzle is largely found in a second major explanation of voting choice—candidate appeal.

Permission of Harley Schwadron.

The elections of the 1980s marked a critical threshold in the emergence of the candidate-centered era in American electoral politics. This change in focus from parties to candidates is an important historical trend that has been gradually taking place over the last several decades.[46]

Candidate appeal often involves an assessment of a candidate's character. Is the candidate honest? Is the candidate consistent? Is the candidate dedicated to "family values"? Does the candidate have religious or spiritual commitments? The press in recent elections has sometimes played the role of "character cop," asking questions about private lives and lifestyles. The press asks these questions because voters are interested in a political leader's background—perhaps even more interested in personal character than in a political position on hard-to-understand health care or regulatory policy issues.

Ronald Reagan's effort to generate positive candidate appeal was successful. Carter had hoped that Reagan would behave more like Barry Goldwater, who in his acceptance speech in 1964 had said, "Extremism in the defense of liberty is no vice. . . . Moderation in the pursuit of justice is no virtue."[47] Lyndon Johnson, Goldwater's opponent, benefitted from public perception that Goldwater and those who nominated him were out of the mainstream of American politics.

Like Barry Goldwater in 1964, George McGovern, who ran as the Democrat in 1972, was a candidate with negative appeal. Many of his supporters, by their dress and manner, appeared out of the mainstream of American politics. McGovern raised doubts about his judgment and leadership by how he handled his choice of a vice-president. McGovern named Missouri Senator Tom Eagleton as his running mate, only to discover that Eagleton had once been hospitalized for emotional exhaustion and depression and received electric shock therapy. McGovern initially stood behind Eagleton, but as press coverage and criticism of McGovern's lack of investigation into Eagleton's past grew, McGovern dropped Eagleton and named a new running mate, Sargent Shriver. In the end, "only about one-third of the public thought McGovern could be trusted as president."[48]

Candidate appeal or the lack of it—in terms of leadership, experience, good judgment, integrity, competence, strength, and energy—is often more important than party or issues. Dwight Eisenhower had great candidate appeal. He was a five-star general, a legendary hero of the Allied effort in World War II. His unmilitary manner, his moderation, his personal charm, and his lack of a strong party position made him appealing across the ideological spectrum. Ronald Reagan generated positive candidate appeal, in part by asserting characteristics the public found lacking in Jimmy Carter—leadership and strength. Neither George W. Bush nor Al Gore were able to convey a vision that lead to decisive victory in 2000. Bush was seen as more "likeable" and Gore as more "competent." But both candidates had liabilities. Bush

You Decide . . .

Should we allow voting by mail and on the Internet?

During the past two centuries of constitutional government, this nation has gradually adopted a more expansive view of popular participation. Not only has the right to vote been extended to more people, but what decisions will be made in the voting booth have been expanded as well, to include primary elections to nominate party candidates and ballot referenda in which state constitutional amendments and state laws are adopted.

It seems logical that the next step in our democratic progress is permitting voters to cast ballots through the mail or through the Internet. Not only would such a reform make voting easier, but it would permit us to have more elections. For example, when a city council wants voters to decide whether to build a new football stadium, or when there is need for a special election to fill the term of a member of Congress who has died or resigned, election officials could mail out the ballots, and then in two or three weeks count up those that have been returned. The state of Oregon has already conducted several general elections by mail, and other states are considering adopting the Oregon system.

What do you think? Should we move toward a system in which we replace the ballot box with the mailbox or the computer? What arguments would you make for and against such an idea?

---

fought the image of not being up to the job and Gore tried to make himself more likeable.

Increasingly, campaigns today focus on the negative elements of candidates' history and personality. Opponents and the media are quick to point out the limitations or problems of any given candidate. The political parties and interest groups did most of the attacking in 2000. Bush was attacked for his stand on abortion, his lack of support for hate crime legislation, his environmental record, and his competence.[49] Gore was attacked for the 1996 fund-raising scandals, his misstatement about inventing the Internet, and his position on gun control.[50] Voters indicated that the candidate quality that mattered most was "honest/trustworthy," which one in four voters mentioned. For these voters, Bush was preferred by 80 percent over Gore, Nader, and Buchanan. All other candidate attributes—"understands issues," "cares about people," "has experience," "strong leader," and "good judgment" were mentioned by 12 to 15 percent of voters as the quality that mattered most. For voters who saw understanding issues as most important, Gore got 75 percent of the vote. Gore also was the preferred candidate for voters who valued "cares about people" and "has experience," where he got 63 and 82 percent, respectively of the vote. Bush got nearly two-thirds of the vote of respondents who said strong leadership mattered most; among the 2 percent who said "likeable" was the candidate quality that mattered most, Bush got 82 percent of the vote.[51]

Voting on the Basis of Issues

Most political scientists agree that issues, while important, are not as central to the decision process as party identification and candidate appeal.[52] Part of the reason is that candidates often intentionally obscure their positions on issues—an understandable strategy.[53] Richard Nixon said he had a plan to end the Vietnam War in 1968, clearly the most important issue in that year, but he would not reveal the specifics of that plan. By not detailing his plan, he stood to gain votes from those who wanted a more aggressive war effort as well as those who wanted a cease-fire.

For issue voting to become of major significance, the issue must be important to a substantial number of voters, opposing candidates must take opposing stands on the issues, and voters must know these positions and vote accordingly. Rarely do candidates focus on only one issue. Voters often will agree with one candidate on one issue and with the opposing candidate on another. In such an instance, issues will likely not be the determining factor. But lack of interest by voters in issues does not mean candidates can take any issue position they wish.[54]

More likely than *prospective issue voting* (voting based on what a candidate pledges to do in the future about an issue if elected) is *retrospective issue voting* (holding incumbents, usually the president's party, responsible for past performance on issues such as the economy or foreign policy).[55] In times of peace and prosperity, voters will reward the incumbent; if the nation falls short on either, voters will elect the opposition.

But good economic times do not always lead to the retention of an administration, as Al Gore learned in 2000. Part of Gore's problem in 2000 was that only half of the public saw their family's financial situation as having gotten better. Of these voters, Gore received 61 percent of the vote.[56] But his inability to effectively claim credit for the good economic times hurt him, especially when Republicans contended that it was the American people, not the government, that produced the strong economy.

The state of the economy is often the central issue in midterm elections as well as presidential ones. Several studies have found a positive relationship between the state of the economy and "out" party gains and "in" party losses in congressional seats.[57] Political scientists have been able to locate the sources of this effect in individual voter's decision making. Voters tend to vote against the party in power if they perceive a decline or standstill in their personal financial situations.[58] Voters see responsibility for the economy resting with the president and Congress more than with governors or local officials.[59]

Despite generally good economic news and success in lowering the federal budget deficit, Democrats suffered a substantial defeat in 1994. Why? Part of the explanation lies in Bill Clinton's low approval ratings. The public continued to have doubts about his leadership. Clinton, who had won election in 1992 on the theme of change, found that he and Democrats in Congress were targets of the same voter frustrations they had directed at the Republicans. Republicans in Congress had used the filibuster and other tactics to defeat much of the Clinton agenda and then succeeded in arguing that Congress was in need of wholesale change. Newt Gingrich captured the "change" theme in 1994 by presenting the Contract with America, which included a commitment to a Balanced Budget Amendment, term limits for members of Congress, and other reforms. This strategy kept Democrats off balance and enabled Republicans to take advantage of voter anger.

Democrats focused the 1998 midterm election on four issues: Social Security, education, health care, and the environment. In contrast, the Republicans wanted to emphasize the accomplishments of the 105th Congress and the reasons to return that Congress to power. The Republican party also decided to raise the impeachment issue late in the campaign. Exit polls demonstrated that this strategy did not resonate well with voters, who wanted to move beyond the impeachment debate. The Democrats' emphasis on concrete issues, when combined with strong candidates in the relative few competitive races, helped them surprise even themselves by picking up a net gain of five House seats. This reinforced the sense that both parties would have a lot to gain or lose in the 2000 elections.

Republicans in 2000 worked hard to deny Democrats the kind of issue advantage they enjoyed in 1998. They had their own plans to privatize Social Security, foster better public schools, and provide prescription drugs for seniors. Democrats complained that Republicans were stealing their issues, something Republicans accused Bill Clinton of doing in 1996 with welfare reform. While Democrats retained an advantage on most issues in 2000, it was not enough for them to win in the Electoral College or secure a majority in either congressional chamber.

The bitterness and partisanship of the protracted ballot counting controversy in Florida following the 2000 vote, which was brought to an end by the Supreme Court, provides the Democrats with an issue for the future. The claim that the election was unfairly decided and that not all the votes were officially counted is one that Democrats may find still rankles many voters. Moreover, the fact that the greatest number of *undervotes* (what happens when a punch card ballot is not read by a card reader) occurred in counties with large minority group populations may help them mobilize those constituencies in future elections.

The 2000 presidential election was exceedingly close. Voters and political gurus learned anew the importance of just a few votes. Bush strategists may regret they had not mobilized Republicans, even in safe states, so their candidate could have won the popular vote. And had Gore carried his home state of Tennessee, or Clinton's home state of Arkansas, he would be president. Both parties, no doubt, will cite the 2000 election as a reason never to take votes for granted and to do all possible to get out their supporters.

Thinking It Through . . .

One of the problems with making elections more frequent is that voters will get fed up. Americans already vote more frequently and for more offices than citizens of any other democracy do. Asking them to make voting choices even more frequently could result in lower turnout and less rational consideration. Many voters may be unaware an election is going on. Yet the advantage of the vote-by-mail system employed by Oregon and some cities and counties is that it increases turnout, at least initially. What political scientists dispute is whether such increases in participation will continue when the novelty wears off.

Some critics of voting by mail or electronic democracy worry about fraud. Even when voters are required to sign their mailed-in ballots, the possibility for forgery still exists. Also voting by mail or computer has the possibility of allowing people to pressure or harass voters. Another concern is late returns, as occurred in 2000.

Another criticism is that mail and electronic voting could be skewed toward participation by better-educated and higher-income voters, who routinely pay their bills by mail, make purchases on their computer, and own a personal computer with Internet access. Advocates of these new voting procedures contend that voters who do not own computers can drop off their ballots in some public building, and that eventually computers will be available widely enough that access will not be a problem.

However, if voting can be made easier and more convenient, why not do it? If the integrity of the vote can be protected and the new ways of voting become widely accessible, then such changes are probably inevitable.

Sources: David B. Magleby, "Participation in Mail Ballot Elections," *Western Political Quarterly* 40 (March 1987), pp. 79–91; Michael W. Traugott, "An Evaluation of Voting by Mail in Oregon," paper prepared for workshop co-sponsored by the University of Michigan and the League of Women Voters, Washington, D.C., August 27, 1997.

POLITICS ONLINE

Who Votes? Why Not You?

You have a wide variety of elections and political process you can engage in if you are registered to vote. You can sign a petition to place a proposed law on the ballot if you live in a state that allows initiatives. You can vote in as many as four or more federal, state, or local elections per year in many localities. To get a sense of the different levels of participation in America, go to the website for this book and Chapter 8 at:

www.prenhall.com/burns.

The age cohort that is least likely to vote is 18–24-year-olds. There are several reasons for this, including the higher mobility of this age group. When you move often, it becomes a hassle to register to vote, especially if you have to do so in person. Many states have moved to simplify and streamline voter registration, and some even permit you to register online. To register to vote, you can go to the Federal Elections Commission website at: www.fec.gov.votregis/vr.htm, where you will find a National Mail Voter Registration form that can be downloaded and returned. Most states accept this form. The site also has links to learn about how to register in your state. State registration requirements are found at:

www.fec.gov/pages/voteinst.htm.

Elections have consequences. As the 2000 election demonstrated, elections can be decided by a few votes. Close elections were not limited to the presidential race. Some House and Senate races went into recounts, and the same is likely to happen in 2002 and 2004. Make use of the resource of the Web to learn how to register to vote, and then exercise your franchise.

SUMMARY

1. Public opinion is a complex combination of views and attitudes individuals acquire through various influences from childhood on. Public opinion takes on qualities of intensity, latency, consensus, or polarization—each of which is affected by people's feelings about the salience of issues.

2. The American public has a generally low level of interest in politics, and most people do not follow politics and government closely. The public's knowledge of political issues is poor.

3. Those Americans who are interested in public affairs can participate by voting, joining interest groups and political parties, working on campaigns, writing letters to newspaper editors or elected officials, attempting to influence how another person will vote, or even protesting.

4. Better educated, older, and party- and group-involved people tend to vote more; the young tend to vote the least. Voter turnout tends to be higher in national than in state and local elections, and higher in presidential than in midterm elections.

5. Party identification remains an important element in the voting choice of most Americans. It represents a long-term attachment and is a "lens" through which voters view candidates and issues as they make their voting choices. Candidate appeal, including character and record, is another key factor in voter choice. Voters decide their vote less frequently on the basis of issues.

KEY TERMS

public opinion 173
political socialization 174

attentive public 178
voter registration 181

Australian ballot 181
turnout 182

party identification 185

FURTHER READING

JOSEPH A. AISTRUP, *The Southern Strategy Revisited: Republican Top-Down Advancement in the South* (University of Kentucky Press, 1996).

HERBERT ASHER, *Polling and the Public: What Every Citizen Should Know*, 3d ed. (Congressional Quarterly Press, 1995).

EARL BLACK AND MERLE BLACK, *The Vital South: How Presidents Are Elected* (Harvard University Press, 1992).

M. MARGARET CONWAY, *Political Participation in the United States*, 4th ed. (Congressional Quarterly Press, 2000).

ROBERT S. ERIKSON AND KENT L. TEDIN, *American Public Opinion: Its Origins, Content and Impact*, 5th ed. (Allyn and Bacon, 1995).

WILLIAM H. FLANIGAN AND NANCY H. ZINGALE, *Political Behavior of the American Electorate*, 10th ed. (Congressional Quarterly Press, 1998).

JOHN G. GEER, *From Tea Leaves to Opinion Polls: A Theory of Democratic Leadership* (Columbia University Press, 1996).

ROBERT HUCKFELDT AND JOHN SPRAGUE, *Citizens, Politics, and Social Communication: Information and Influence in an Election Campaign* (Cambridge University Press, 1995).

LAWRENCE R. JACOBS AND ROBERT Y. SHAPIRO, *Politicians Don't Pander: Political Manipulation and the Loss of Democratic Responsiveness* (University of Chicago Press, 2000).

BRYAN D. JONES, *Reconceiving Decision-Making in Democratic Politics: Attention, Choice and Public Policy* (University of Chicago Press, 1994).

BRUCE E. KEITH, DAVID B. MAGLEBY, CANDICE J. NELSON, ELIZABETH ORR, MARK C. WESTLYE, AND RAYMOND E. WOLFINGER, *The Myth of the Independent Voter* (University of California Press, 1992).

V. O. KEY, JR., *Public Opinion and American Democracy* (Alfred A. Knopf, 1961).

ANTHONY KING, *Running Scared: Why America's Politicians Campaign Too Much and Govern Too Little* (Free Press, 1997).

PHILIP A. KLINKNER, ED., *Midterm: The Elections of 1994 in Context* (Westview Press, 1996).

WARREN E. MILLER AND J. MERRILL SHANKS, *The New American Voter* (Harvard University Press, 1996).

MICHAEL NELSON, ED., *The Elections of 1996* (Congressional Quarterly Press, 1997).

RICHARD G. NIEMI AND HERBERT F. WEISBERG, *Classics in Voting Behavior* (Congressional Quarterly Press, 1993).

RICHARD G. NIEMI AND HERBERT F. WEISBERG, *Controversies in Voting Behavior*, 3d ed. (Congressional Quarterly Press, 1993).

BENJAMIN I. PAGE AND ROBERT Y. SHAPIRO, *The Rational Public: Fifty Years of Trends in Americans' Policy Preferences* (University of Chicago Press, 1992).

FRANK R. PARKER, *Black Votes Count: Political Empowerment in Mississippi After 1965* (University of North Carolina Press, 1990).

GERALD M. POMPER, ED., *The Election of 1996: Reports and Interpretations* (Chatham House, 1997).

SAMUEL L. POPKIN, *The Reasoning Voter: Communication and Persuasion in Presidential Campaigns* (University of Chicago Press, 1991).

JACOB SHAMIR AND MICHAL SHAMIR, *The Anatomy of Public Opinion* (University of Michigan Press, 2000).

SUSAN J. TOLCHIN, *The Angry American: How Voter Rage Is Changing the Nation* (Westview Press, 1996).

JOHN ZALLER, *The Nature and Origins of Public Opinion* (Cambridge University Press, 1992).

See also *Public Opinion Quarterly, American Journal of Political Science,* and *American Political Science Review.*

CAMPAIGNS AND ELECTIONS: DEMOCRACY IN ACTION

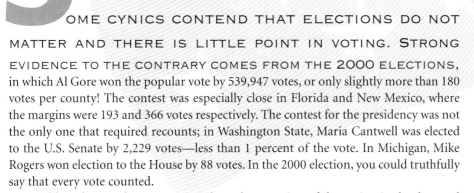

SOME CYNICS CONTEND THAT ELECTIONS DO NOT MATTER AND THERE IS LITTLE POINT IN VOTING. STRONG EVIDENCE TO THE CONTRARY COMES FROM THE 2000 ELECTIONS, in which Al Gore won the popular vote by 539,947 votes, or only slightly more than 180 votes per county! The contest was especially close in Florida and New Mexico, where the margins were 193 and 366 votes respectively. The contest for the presidency was not the only one that required recounts; in Washington State, Maria Cantwell was elected to the U.S. Senate by 2,229 votes—less than 1 percent of the vote. In Michigan, Mike Rogers won election to the House by 88 votes. In the 2000 election, you could truthfully say that every vote counted.

Although several contests were close, the attention of the nation in the days and weeks after the election was focused on Florida, where the counting and recounting of ballots, the legitimacy of some absentee ballots, and problems with punchcard ballots all ended up in court. At issue in Florida was whether partially punched ballots were valid. Experts debated in the media and testified in court about "dangling chads" (when part of the card is not fully detached) and "pregnant" or "dimpled chads," which show a depression from the stylus used by the voter but are not detached. This confusion meant the officials doing the recount would hold up the punch cards to see if they could see light through the ballot at the spot of the "dimple."

How could it be that in the United States, with computers in every high school, voting technology is so antiquated? The answer in part is that American elections, even presidential elections, are largely governed by *state* law and administered by *local* election officials—typically county clerks. Consequently, the mode of voting can vary from county to county. As a result of the nation's attention being focused on the Florida elections, governments at all levels have started to look for ways to improve voting and election procedures.

In the United States, citizens vote more often and for more offices than citizens of any other democracy. We hold thousands of elections for everything from community college directors to county sheriffs. About half a million persons hold elected state and local offices.[1] In 2000 we elected a president, a vice-president, 33 U.S. senators, all 435 members of the U.S. House of Representatives, 11 governors, plus dozens of treasurers, secretaries of state, and, in most states, judges.

In addition to electing people, voters in 27 states vote on laws or constitutional amendments proposed by initiative petitions or on popular referendums put on the

CHAPTER MEDIA

POLITICS ONLINE
Who Donates to Which Campaigns in Your Neighborhood?
www.prenhall.com/burns

POLISIM
Election in Action
www.prenhall.com/burns

ballot by petition. In all states except Delaware, voters must approve all changes in the state constitution.

In this chapter we explore our election rules. We note four important problems: the lack of competition for some offices, the complexities of nominating presidential candidates, the distortions of the Electoral College, and the influence of money in our elections. We also discuss proposed reforms in each of these areas.

ELECTIONS: THE RULES OF THE GAME

The rules of the game—the electoral game—make a difference. Although the Constitution sets certain conditions and requirements, most electoral rules remain matters of state law.

Regularly Scheduled Elections

In our system, elections are held at fixed intervals that cannot be changed by the party in power. It does not make any difference if the nation is at war, as we were during the Civil War, or in the midst of a crisis, as in the Great Depression; when the calendar calls for an election, the election is held. Elections for members of Congress occur the first Tuesday after the first Monday in November of even-numbered years. Although there are some exceptions (special elections or peculiar state provisions), participants know *in advance* just when the next election will be. In many parliamentary democracies, such as Great Britain and Canada, the party in power calls elections at a time of its choosing.

Fixed, Staggered, and Sometimes Limited Terms

Our electoral system is based on *fixed terms*, meaning that the length of a term in office is specified, not indefinite. The Constitution has set the term of office for the U.S. House of Representatives at two years, the Senate at six years, and the presidency at four years.

Our system also has *staggered terms* for some offices; not all offices are up for election at the same time. All House members are up for election every two years, but only one-third of the senators are up for election at the same time. Since presidential elections occur two or four years into a senator's six-year term, senators can run for the presidency without fear of losing their seat. But if their Senate term expires the same year as the presidential election, the laws of many states require them to give up their Senate seat to run for president or vice-president or any other position. An example of a state that permits a candidate to stand for election to two offices is Connecticut, where Joe Lieberman was reelected to the U.S. Senate in 2000 while being narrowly defeated in his race for vice-president. Had he been victorious in both campaigns, he would have resigned his Senate seat.

Term Limits

The Twenty-second Amendment to the Constitution, adopted in 1951, limits presidents to two terms. Knowing that a president cannot run again changes the way members of Congress, the voters, and the press regard the president. A politician who cannot, or has announced he or she will not, run again is called a "lame duck." Efforts to limit the terms of other politicians have become a major issue in several American states. The most frequent targets have been state legislators. One consequence of term limits is more lame ducks.

Term limits are popular. Voters in 22 states have enacted them for their state legislature, and even more states limit the term of governors.[2] Three-fourths of all voters favor term limits (9 out of 10 strong Republicans and 7 out of 10 strong Democrats).[3] Still, despite their popularity, proposals for term limits have repeatedly lost when they have come to a vote in recent sessions of Congress.

The Supreme Court, by a vote of 5 to 4, declared that a state does not have the constitutional power to impose limits on the number of terms for which its members of the U.S. Congress are eligible, either by amending its own constitution or by state law.[4] Congress has refused to propose a constitutional amendment to impose a limit on congressional terms.

Winner-Takes-All

An important feature of our electoral system is the **winner-takes-all** rule.[5] In most American electoral settings, the candidate with the most votes wins. The winner does not need to have a *majority* (more than half the votes cast); in a multicandidate race, the winner may have only a *plurality* (the largest number of votes). In 2000, three senators and seven House members were elected by pluralities.

Most American electoral districts are **single-member districts**, meaning that in any district for any given election—senator, governor, U.S. House, state legislative seat—the voters choose *one* representative or official.[6] When a single-member-district system is combined with the winner-takes-all rule, minor parties find it hard to win. For example, even if a third party gets 25 percent of the vote in several districts, it still gets no seats.

The single-member-district and winner-takes-all system is different from a **proportional representation** system, in which political parties secure legislative seats and power in proportion to the number of votes they receive in the election. Let's assume a hypothetical state has three representatives up for election. In each of the three contests, the Republican defeats the Democrat, but in one district by only a narrow margin. If you add up the statewide vote, the Republicans get 67 percent and the Democrats 33 percent. Under our single-member-district and winner-takes-all system, the Republicans get all three seats. But under a system of proportional representation, in which the three seats represent the whole state, the Democrats would receive one seat because they got roughly one-third of the vote in the entire state. Proportional representation thus rewards minor parties and permits them to participate in government. Countries that practice some form of proportional representation include Germany, Israel, and Japan.

The Electoral College

We elect our president and vice-president not by a national vote, but by an indirect device known as the **Electoral College**. The framers of the U.S. Constitution devised this system because they did not trust the choice of president to a direct vote of the people. Under this system each state has as many electors as it has representatives and senators. Thus California will have 55 electoral votes and Vermont 3 for the election of 2004.

Each state legislature is free to determine how its electors are selected. Each party nominates a slate of electors, usually longtime party workers. They are expected to cast their electoral votes for the party's candidates for president and vice-president. In our entire history, no "faithless elector"—an elector who does not vote for his state's popular vote winner—has ever cast the deciding vote. There were no faithless electors in 2000, but one elector from the District of Columbia abstained.

The Twelfth Amendment requires electors to vote separately for president and vice-president. To demonstrate how this works, if you voted for the Republican candidate in 2000, you actually voted for the Republican slate of electors pledged to support George W. Bush for president and Dick Cheney for vice-president.

Candidates who win a plurality of the popular vote in a state secure all that state's electoral votes, except in Nebraska and Maine, which allocate electoral votes to the winner in each congressional district plus two electoral votes for the winner of the state as a whole. Winning electors go to their state capital on the first Monday after the second Wednesday in December to cast their ballots. These ballots are then sent to Congress, and early in January, Congress formally counts the ballots and

winner-takes-all
An election system in which the candidate with the most votes wins.

single-member district
An electoral district in which voters choose one representative or official.

proportional representation
An election system in which each party receives the proportion of legislative seats corresponding to its proportion of the vote.

Electoral College
The electoral system used in electing the president and vice-president, in which voters vote for electors pledged to cast their ballots for a particular party's candidates.

The Electoral Commission of 1877 met in secret session to decide the controversial presidential election between Rutherford B. Hayes and Samuel Tilden. After many contested votes the presidency was eventually awarded to Hayes.

declares to the world what everybody already knows—who won the election for president and vice-president.

It takes a majority of the electoral votes to win. If no candidate gets a majority of the electoral votes for president, the House chooses among the top three candidates, with each state delegation having one vote. If no candidate gets a majority of the electoral votes for vice-president, the Senate chooses among the top two candidates, with each senator casting one vote.

When there are only two major candidates for the presidency, the chances of an election being thrown into the House are remote. But twice in our history the House has had to act: in 1800, before the Twelfth Amendment was written, the House had to choose in a tie vote between Thomas Jefferson and Aaron Burr; in 1824 the House picked John Quincy Adams over Andrew Jackson and William Crawford. Henry Clay, who was forced out of the race when he came in fourth in the Electoral College, threw his support behind Adams. When Adams was elected, he made Clay his secretary of state. The 1824 vote in the House was especially contentious. Jackson, winner of the popular vote, was passed over when the vote went to the House. This outcome infuriated Jackson, who won the Electoral College vote by a wide margin four years later.

As we were reminded in 2000, our Electoral College system makes it possible for a presidential candidate to receive the most popular votes, as Al Gore did, and not get enough electoral votes to be elected president. Al Gore won the popular vote by over 500,000 votes but lost the Electoral College 271 to 266.[7] This also happened in 1824, when Andrew Jackson won 12 percent more of the vote than John Quincy Adams; in 1876, when Samuel Tilden received more popular votes than Rutherford B. Hayes; and in 1888, when Benjamin Harrison won in the Electoral College although Grover Cleveland received more popular votes. It almost happened in 1960 and 1976, when the shift of a few votes in a few key states could have resulted in the election of a president without a popular majority. In a year with a serious minor party candidate, the result could be the election of a president without a plurality of the vote, as happened in 2000, when the Green party took enough votes away from Al Gore to have made the difference in Florida and New Hampshire.

In two of the four elections in which winners of the popular vote did not become president, the Electoral College did not decide the winner. The 1824 election was decided by the U.S. House of Representatives. In 1876 the electoral vote in three southern states and Oregon was disputed, resulting in an Electoral Commission deciding how those votes should be counted. In 1888 and 2000 the Electoral College awarded the presidency to the candidate with fewer popular votes.[8]

Concern about the Electoral College is renewed every time there is a serious third-party candidate for the presidency. Even a candidate like Green party candidate Ralph Nader, who got less than 5 percent of the popular vote in 2000, prompted pre-election discussions about his impact on the Electoral College vote. People began to ask: Which Congress casts the vote, the one serving during the election or the newly elected one? The answer is the new one, the one elected in November and taking office the first week in January. Since each state has one vote in the House, what happens if a state's delegation is tied in its vote, 2 to 2 or 3 to 3? Then its vote does not count. Would it be possible to have a president of one party and a vice-president of another? Yes, if the election were thrown into the House and Senate, and each chamber were controlled by a different party.

The Electoral College sharply influences presidential politics. To win a presidential election, a candidate must appeal successfully to the big states of California, Texas, Ohio, and Illinois.[9] California's electoral vote of 54 in 2000 exceeded the combined electoral votes of the 14 least populous states plus the District of Columbia. The map inside the front cover of this book provides a visual comparison of state size based on electoral votes.

Presidential candidates do not ordinarily waste time campaigning in a state unless they have at least a fighting chance of carrying that state; nor do they waste time in a state in which their party is a sure winner. Richard Nixon in 1960 was the last candidate to campaign in all 50 states, but he lost valuable time traveling to and from Alaska, while John Kennedy focused on the more populous states in which he had a chance to win. The contest usually narrows down to the medium-sized and big states, where the balance between the parties tends to be fairly even.

RUNNING FOR CONGRESS

How candidates run for Congress depends on the nature of their district or state, on whether candidates are incumbents or challengers, on the strength of their personal organization, on how well-known they are, and on how much money they have to spend on their campaign. We can, however, note several similarities in House and Senate elections.

First, most congressional elections are not close. In districts where most people belong to one party or where incumbents are popular and enjoy fundraising and other campaign advantages, there is often little competition.[10] Those who believe competition is essential to constitutional democracy are concerned that so many officeholders have **safe seats**. When officeholders do not have to fight to retain their seat, elections are not performing their proper role.[11]

Competition is more likely when funding is adequate for both candidates, which is not often the case in U.S. House elections. Elections for governor and for the U.S. Senate are more seriously contested and adequately financed than those for the U.S. House of Representatives.

Presidential popularity affects both House and Senate elections during presidential election years as well as midterm elections. The impact of presidential popularity in a presidential election is the **coattail effect**, the boost candidates from the president's party get from a popular presidential candidate running in the same election. But winning presidential candidates do not always provide such a boost. The Republicans suffered a net loss of six House seats in 1988, even though George Bush won the presidency, and the Democrats suffered a net loss of ten house seats in 1992 when Bill Clinton won the presidential election. Democrats fared better in 1996, picking up a net gain of nine house seats. There were no discernible coattails in the 2000 elections. Overall, "measurable coattail effects continue to appear," according to congressional elections scholar Gary Jacobson, but they are "erratic and usually modest" in their impact.[12]

safe seat
An elected office that is predictably won by one party or the other.

coattail effect
The boost candidates of the president's party receive in an election because of the president's popularity.

In midterm elections, presidential popularity and economic conditions have long been associated with the number of House seats a president's party loses.[13] These same factors are associated with how well the president's party does in Senate races, but the association is not as strong.[14] Figure 9–1 shows the number of seats in the House of Representatives and U.S. Senate gained or lost by the party controlling the White House in midterm elections since 1938. Republicans did better in 1994 than in any midterm election since 1946, picking up 53 seats. The Republican tide was not limited to the House but included a net gain of nine Senate seats.[15] In each of these elections until 1998, the party controlling the White House lost seats in the House. The range of losses, however, is quite wide, from a low of 4 seats for the Democrats in 1962 to a high of 71 seats for the Democrats in 1938. The robust economy and President Bill Clinton's high job approval ratings contributed to the success of the Democrats in the 1998 elections.

When presidential landslides occur, as they did with Lyndon Johnson in 1964, the victorious party is especially vulnerable and likely to lose seats in the next midterm election, as the Democrats did in 1966. Given the historic pattern of the president's party losing seats and the close party balance resulting from the 2000 elections, Democrats believe they are well positioned in 2002 to recapture control of both houses of Congress.

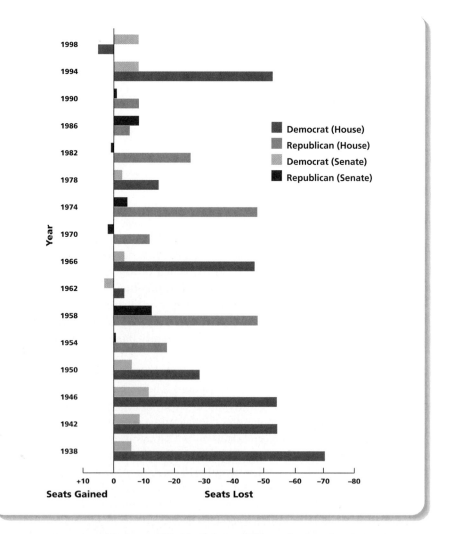

FIGURE 9–1 **Seats Lost by the President's Party in Midterm Elections for the House of Representatives and the Senate (1938–1998)**

The House of Representatives

Every two years, as many as 1,000 candidates—including approximately 400 incumbents—campaign for Congress. After deciding to take the plunge, candidates must first plan a primary race, unless they face no opponents for their party nomination. Incumbents are rarely challenged for renomination from within their own party, and when they are, the challenges are seldom serious. In the 1990s, for example, on average only two House incumbents were denied renomination each election cycle. Challengers from other parties running against entrenched incumbents rarely encounter opposition in their own party.[16]

MOUNTING A PRIMARY CAMPAIGN   The first step for would-be challengers is to raise hundreds of thousands of dollars to mount a serious campaign. This requires asking friends and acquaintances as well as interest groups for money. Parties can sometimes help, but they shy away from giving money in primary contests. The party organization usually stays neutral until the nomination is decided.

The second step is to build a *personal organization*. A candidate can build an organization while holding another office, such as a seat in the state legislature, or by serving in civic causes, helping other candidates, and being conspicuous without being controversial.

The next steps are to hire campaign managers and technicians, buy television and other advertising, conduct polls, and pay for a variety of activities. All these things depend on raising funds, which most candidates find difficult before they have secured the nomination.

A candidate's main hurdle is gaining visibility. Candidates work hard to be mentioned by the media. In large cities with many simultaneous campaigns, congressional candidates are frequently lost in media "noise," and in rural areas the press often plays down political news. Candidates rely on personal contacts, on hand shaking and door-to-door campaigning, and on identifying likely supporters and courting their favor—the same techniques used in campaigns for lesser offices. The turnout in primaries tends to be low, except in campaigns in which large sums of money are expended on advertising.

New York U.S. Senate Republican candidate Rick Lazio shakes hands with Democratic candidate Hillary Rodham Clinton in their first televised debate. Here Lazio is challenging Clinton not to use soft money in their race.

"My former opponent is supporting me in the general election. Please disregard all the things I said about him in the primary."

Dunagin's People. Tribune Media Services.

CAMPAIGNING FOR THE GENERAL ELECTION   As we have mentioned, most incumbent members of Congress win reelection.[17] Since 1970, over 95 percent of incumbent House members seeking reelection have won, and in 2000, 98 percent of incumbent House members running for reelection were successful[18] (see Figure 9–2). Incumbents outspent their challengers roughly 3 to 1; in the Senate the difference was closer to 1.75 to 1.[19] Most challengers spend little money, run campaigns that are not significantly more visible than primary campaigns, contact few voters, and lose badly.

Serious challengers in House races are hard to find. Many are scared away by the prospect of having to raise close to a million dollars in campaign funds; others realize the district has been drawn with fewer persons from their party than the incumbent's; and some do not want to face the media scrutiny that comes with a serious race for Congress. Nonetheless, in each election a few challengers mount serious challenges because of the incumbent's perceived vulnerability, the challengers' own wealth, party, or political action committee efforts, or a combination of factors.

Why is keeping a House seat so much easier than gaining it? Incumbents have a host of advantages that help them gain reelection. These "perks" include free mailings to constituents (the *franking* privilege), the free use of broadcast studios to record radio and television tapes to be sent to local media outlets, and perhaps most important of all, a large staff to perform countless favors for constituents and send a stream of press reports and mail back to the district.[20] Representatives also try to win committee posts, even on minor committees, that relate to the needs of their districts and build connections with constituents.[21]

If incumbents win so often, how do we get any significant turnover in the House of Representatives? Turnover comes when incumbents die, decide to retire, or seek some other office. *Redistricting*, which happens once each decade, often promotes some turnover, as it will in 2002, when incumbents are forced to run in new districts. More than one-third of the U.S. House retired between 1992 and 1996. This amount of turnover was unusual and included some members who were disillusioned by partisan bickering.

These retirements and redistricting create *open seats*, which can result in more competitive elections. Potential candidates, as well as political action committees and political party committees, all watch open seat races closely. But as noted, most races have incumbents and most incumbents win, lending credibility to the charge that we have a "permanent Congress."

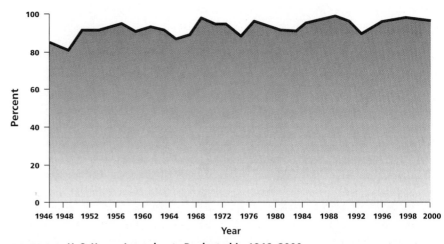

FIGURE 9–2 U. S. House Incumbents Reelected in 1946–2000

SOURCES: Federal Election Commission, press release, April 14, 1997, pp. 32–51; "House Membership in the 106th Congress," *Congressional Quarterly Weekly Report*, November 7, 1998, p. 3010; *Congressional Quarterly Weekly Report*, November 11, 2000, p. 2652.

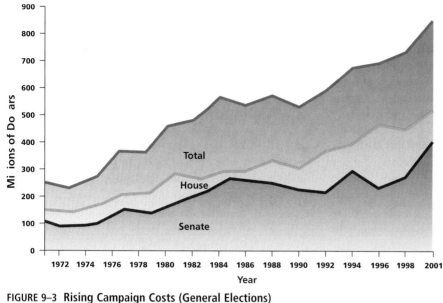

FIGURE 9–3 Rising Campaign Costs (General Elections)

Source: Federal Election Commission: ftp.fcc.gov/fec.

The Senate

Running for the Senate is big-time politics. The six-year term and the national exposure make a Senate seat a glittering prize, so competition is usually intense. Senate campaigns generally feature state-of-the-art campaign technology; a race normally costs millions of dollars[22] (see Figure 9–3). The essential tactics are to raise lots of money, get good people involved, make as many personal contacts as possible (especially in the states with smaller populations), avoid giving the opposition any positive publicity, and have a simple campaign theme. Incumbency is an advantage for senators, although not as much as for representatives.[23] Incumbent senators are widely known, but so are their opponents, who often raise and spend significant amounts of money.[24]

When one party controls the Senate by only a few seats, as has been the case in recent years, more good candidates run, and the number of competitive elections increases. The cost of Senate campaigns can vary greatly. California has 69 times the number of potential voters as Wyoming;not surprisingly, running for a seat from Wyoming is much cheaper than a seat from California. As a result, interest groups and parties direct more money to competitive races in small states when the stakes for control of the Senate are high.[25]

RUNNING FOR PRESIDENT

Presidential elections are major media events, with candidates seeking as much positive television coverage as possible and trying at the same time to avoid negative coverage. The formal campaign has three stages: winning the nomination, campaigning at the convention, and mobilizing support in the general election.

Stage 1: The Nomination

Presidential hopefuls must make a series of critical tactical decisions. The first is when to start campaigning. For the presidential election of 2000, some candidates, like Steve Forbes and Lamar Alexander, began almost as soon as the 1996 presidential election was over. Early decisions are increasingly necessary for candidates to raise the money and assemble an organization. Campaigning begins well before any actual declaration of candidacy, as candidates try to line up supporters to win caucuses or primaries in key states and to raise money for their nomination effort.

One of the hardest jobs for candidates and their strategists is calculating how to deal with the complex maze of presidential primaries and caucuses that constitutes the delegate selection system. The system for electing delegates to the national party convention varies from state to state and often from one party to the other in the same state. Although the process is influenced somewhat by federal regulation of campaign financing and national party rules, within broad limits states can set up the systems they prefer.

PRESIDENTIAL PRIMARIES   State presidential primaries, unknown before 1900, have become the main method of choosing delegates to the national convention. Today more than three-fourths of the states use presidential primaries. In 2000, 84 percent of the Democratic delegates and 89 percent of the Republican delegates were chosen in the primaries.[26] The rest of the delegates were chosen by party caucuses or conventions.

Voters in states like Iowa and New Hampshire, which are the first states to pick delegates, bask in media attention for weeks and even months before they cast the first ballots in the presidential sweepstakes. Because these early contests have had the effect of limiting the choices of voters in states that come later in the process, there has been a tendency for states to move their primaries up. This process is called "front loading." California, which traditionally held its primary in June, moved it to March in 2000 so that its voters would play a more important role in selecting the nominee. Other states did the same thing. On March 7, 16 states had primaries, forcing candidates to pick and choose where they would campaign aggressively. In effect, the 2000 primary season was compressed into several weeks of intense activity in the spring of 2000.

Presidential primaries have two main features: a *beauty contest*, or popularity vote in which voters indicate which candidate they prefer but do not actually elect delegates to the convention, and *actual voting* for delegates pledged to a candidate. Candidates may win the beauty contest and find their opponents doing better in actual delegates elected because they failed to put a full slate of delegates on the ballot or because local notables were listed on the ballot as delegates pledged to another candidate. Different combinations of these two features have produced the following systems:

1. *Proportional representation:* Delegates to the national convention are allocated on the basis of the votes candidates win in the beauty contest. This system has been used in most of the states, including several of the largest ones. The Democrats now mandate a proportional representation rule for all their primaries.[27] In some states Republicans use this same system, but Republicans are much more varied in their delegate selection processes.[28]

2. *Winner-takes-all:* In some states there is a winner-takes-all rule that whoever gets the most votes wins all that state's delegates, as George W. Bush did in the California Republican primary in 2000. To win all the delegates of a state like California is an enormous bonus to a candidate. Republicans still use the winner-takes-all system at the state level, and in 1996 about half of all states used this rule at either the state or congressional district levels.

3. *Delegate selection:* In several states, large and small, voters choose delegates who may or may not have pledged how they will vote in the national party convention. The names of the presidential hopefuls do not appear separately on the ballot, and there is no declared presidential preference. Under this arrangement, delegates are free to exercise their independent judgment at the convention. Only Republicans use this system; in 2000 it was used most prominently in New York and Illinois.

4. *Delegate selection and separate presidential poll:* In several states voters decide twice: once to indicate their choice for president, and again to choose delegates pledged, or at least favorable, to a presidential candidate.[29]

CAUCUSES AND CONVENTIONS   A **caucus** is a meeting of party members and supporters of various candidates. About a dozen states use a caucus and/or convention system for choosing delegates.[30] Each state's parties and legislature regulate them. The caucus or convention is the oldest method of choosing delegates and differs from the primary system because it centers on the party organization.

Delegates who will attend the national party conventions are chosen by delegates to state or district conventions, who themselves are chosen earlier in county, precinct, or town caucuses. The process starts at local meetings open to all party members, who discuss and take positions on candidates and issues and elect delegates to represent their views at the next level. This process is repeated until national nominating convention delegates are chosen by conventions of delegates throughout a district or state.

The best-known example of a caucus is in Iowa, because Iowa has held the earliest caucuses in the most recent presidential nominating contests. Every January or February in a presidential election year, Iowans have the opportunity to attend Republican and Democratic precinct meetings. Large numbers of voters attend these small town meetings and have a chance to meet and exchange views on issues and candidates, rather than merely pulling a lever in a voting booth or placing an *X* on a ballot.

Presidential hopefuls face a dilemma: to get the Republican nomination you have to appeal to the more intensely conservative Republican partisans, those who vote in primaries and support campaigns. Democratic hopefuls have to appeal to the liberal wing of their party as well as minorities, union members, and environmental activists. But to win the general election, candidates have to win support from moderates and pragmatic voters, many of whom do not vote in the primaries. If candidates get out too far from the moderates in their nomination campaign, they risk being labeled extreme in the general election.

STRATEGIES   Strategies for gaining delegates to the national convention have changed over the years. Some candidates think it wise to skip some of the earlier contests and enter first in states where their strength lies. John McCain pursued such a strategy in 2000, ignoring Iowa and concentrating on New Hampshire. Most candidates choose to run hard in Iowa and New Hampshire, hoping that early showings in these states, which receive a great deal of media attention, will move them into the spotlight for later efforts.

During this early phase, especially important is the ability of candidates to manage the media's expectations of their performance. Lyndon Johnson actually won the New Hampshire primary in 1968, but because Eugene McCarthy did better than the press had predicted, McCarthy was interpreted as the "winner."

Winning in the primaries thus becomes a game of expectations, and candidates may intentionally downplay their expectations so that "doing better than expected" might generate momentum for their campaign. John McCain's surprise victory in New Hampshire in 2000 generated a lot of free publicity and garnered campaign contributions via the Internet.[31] As the race moved to more friendly turf for George W. Bush in South Carolina, Bush won. Al Gore's early victories in Iowa and New Hampshire knocked Bill Bradley out of the race and effectively gave Gore the Democratic nomination.

Stage 2: The Convention

The delegates elected in primaries, caucuses, or state conventions assemble at their **national party convention** in the summer before the election to pick the party's presidential and vice-presidential candidates. In the past, delegates arrived at national nominating conventions with differing degrees of commitment to presidential candidates; some delegates were pledged to no candidate at all, others to a specific candidate for one or two ballots, and others firmly to one candidate only. Recent conventions have merely ratified decisions already made in the primaries and

caucus
A meeting of local party members to choose party officials and/or candidates for public office and to decide the platform.

national party convention
The national meeting of delegates elected in primaries, caucuses, or state conventions who assemble once every four years to nominate candidates for president and vice-president, ratify the party platform, elect officers, and adopt rules.

Every four years since 1856 both major parties have held conventions to nominate candidates for president and vice-president. Conventions bring together delegates from the state parties to represent the wishes of their voters. Successful conventions build party unity, mobilize support for the party nominees, and capture the interest and attention of the nation. Conventions also decide on rules and regulations governing the party, settling controversies surrounding delegate selection (credentials) and party platforms.

The 1968 Democratic National Convention will long be remembered for the more than ten thousand protesters who came to Chicago to oppose the war in Vietnam. Security concerns were high because earlier in 1968 Martin Luther King, Jr., and Robert Kennedy had been assassinated. Televised images of Chicago police using tear gas and night sticks to disperse the crowd not only hurt the Democrats in 1968 but meant neither party held a convention in Chicago for the next 28 years.

The intense battle in the streets of Chicago carried over onto the convention floor as delegates debated the Vietnam plank of the party platform into the early hours of the morning. Civil rights issues nearly tore the Democratic party apart as some southern states still had all-white delegations to the convention. African American delegates sought recognition, and the convention voted to seat some of them over the protest of the white delegates. The party remained badly divided after the Chicago convention and later changed its rules to encourage greater diversity in delegations and more extensive use of direct primaries.

Who attends conventions? Delegates come from all walks of life, yet many are former party leaders or public officials. Republican delegates are more likely to be male than their Democrat counterparts. Aside from the candidates and delegates, the most important people at the conventions are journalists and TV reporters. Thousands from all over the world view these festivities. The parties have an interest in getting a positive "spin" out of the convention, so they work hard to manage the news coverage. Reporters, on the other hand, have an interest in stirring up controversy.

Because the choice of the party nominees has been decided well before the convention, there has been relatively little controversy on the floor of the conventions in recent years. The parties have turned to theatrics and celebrities in an effort to boost the audience watching the televised conventions. They have also shortened the proceedings on network television coverage to only a few hours in the evening. Even with these changes, audience share continued to drop in 2000.

caucuses, in part because delegates are required to pledge themselves to a specific presidential hopeful (in the Democratic party), or because one candidate has been able to amass a majority of delegates. And because of reforms encouraging delegates to stick with the person to whom they are pledged, there has been no room to maneuver at conventions. National party conventions used to be events of high excitement because they determined who would be the party nominee, but in every election since the Republican convention of 1948 and the Democratic convention of 1952, the party primaries have decided who would be the nominee.

As recently as 1988, Democratic and Republican national conventions were given gavel-to-gavel coverage by the major networks, meaning that from the beginning of the first night to the end of the fourth night, millions of people watched. Now the major networks leave comprehensive coverage to C-SPAN and CNN. National nominating conventions have ceased to dominate the national news, for the very good reason that they are no longer the place where candidates are selected.[32] The long-term trend of declining viewership and reduced hours of coverage has altered the parties' strategies. In 2000 the parties featured their most important speakers and highlighted their most important messages in the limited time given them by the networks.

Conventions follow standard rules, routines, and rituals. Usually the first day is devoted to a keynote address and other speeches touting the party and denouncing the opposition; the second day to committee reports, including party and convention rules and the party platform; the third day to presidential balloting; and the fourth to choosing the vice-presidential nominee and winding up with the presidential candidate's acceptance speech.[33]

Both party conventions in 2000 lacked drama. Gone were struggles over the adoption of the platform. For decades the parties have not fought over credentials—that is, over which delegates should be seated. The matter had been in dispute when southern states sent all-white delegations to the Democratic convention. The big news event of the 2000 conventions was Vice-President Gore's prolonged kiss with his wife Tipper before his acceptance speech.

THE PARTY PLATFORM   Delegates to the national party conventions decide upon the platform, a statement of party perspectives on public policy. Why does anyone care what is in the party platform? Critics have long pointed out that the party platform is binding on no one and is more likely to hurt than help a candidate. But presidential candidates as well as delegates take the platform seriously because it defines the direction a party wants to take. Also, despite the charge that the platform is ignored, most presidents make an effort to implement it.[34] Neither party had a platform fight in 2000.

THE VICE-PRESIDENTIAL NOMINEE   The choice of the vice-presidential nominee generates widespread attention. Rarely does a person actually "run" for the vice-presidential nomination because only the president's "vote" counts. But there is a good deal of maneuvering to capture that one vote. Sometimes the choice of a running mate is made at the convention—not a time conducive to careful and deliberate thought. More often the choice is made before the convention, and the announcement is timed to enhance media coverage and momentum going into the convention. The last time a presidential candidate left the choice of vice-president to the delegates was for the Democrats in 1956.

Traditionally the presidential nominee chooses a running mate who will "balance the ticket." Democratic presidential nominee Walter Mondale raised this tradition to a dramatic new height in 1984 by selecting a woman, Representative Geraldine A. Ferraro, to run with him. Mondale's bold decision was an effort to strengthen his appeal to women voters. But presidential candidates can also ignore the idea of a balanced ticket, as George W. Bush did when he chose another Texan from the oil industry to be his running mate. Dick Cheney moved his official residence to Wyoming and registered to vote there so that if the Bush-Cheney ticket won the popular vote in Texas, Republican Texas electors could vote for him, since the Constitution (Article II, Section 1) prohibits electors from voting for more than one person for president and vice-president from their own state.

THE VALUE OF CONVENTIONS   Why do the parties continue to have conventions if the nominee is known in advance and the vice-presidential nominee is the choice of one person? What role do conventions play in our system? For the parties, they are a time of "coming together" to endorse a party program and to build unity and enthusiasm for the fall campaign. For candidates as well as other party leaders, conventions are a chance to capture the national spotlight and further their political ambitions. For nominees, they are an opportunity to define themselves in positive ways. The potential is there to heal wounds festering from the primary campaign and move into the general election united, but the potential is not always achieved. Conventions can be potentially divisive, as the Republicans learned in 1964 when conservative Goldwater delegates loudly booed New York Governor Nelson Rockefeller, and as the Democrats learned in 1968 when the convention spotlighted divisions within the party over Vietnam as well as ugly battles between police and protesters near the convention hotels.

NOMINATION BY PETITION   There is a way to run for president of the United States that avoids the grueling process of primary elections and conventions—if you are rich enough or well known enough. John Anderson in 1980 and H. Ross Perot in 1992 met the various state petition requirements or paid the $500 filing fee in Louisiana and made it onto the ballot in all 50 states. In 2000, the petition process was as simple as submitting the signatures of 200 registered voters in Washington State, or as difficult as getting the signatures of 2 percent of voters who voted in the last election in North Carolina (52,000 signatures).[35] Patrick Buchanan, candidate of the Reform party, was able to get his name on the ballot in all but one state and the District of Columbia, and Ralph Nader, candidate of the Green party, in all but seven states.[36]

Stage 3: The General Election

The national party convention adjourns immediately after the presidential and vice-presidential candidates deliver their acceptance speeches to the delegates and the national television audience. Traditionally, the time between the conventions and Labor Day was a time for resting, binding up convention wounds, gearing up for action, and planning campaign strategy. In recent elections, however, the candidates have not paused after the convention but left the convention engaging in all-out campaigning.[37]

PRESIDENTIAL DEBATES   Televised presidential debates are a major feature of presidential elections. The 1960 debate between John Kennedy and Richard Nixon boosted Kennedy's campaign and elevated the role of television in national politics.[38] In 1976, President Gerald Ford debated Jimmy Carter and mistakenly said that each country in Eastern Europe "is independent, autonomous, it has its own territorial integrity, and none was under Soviet domination." That mistake damaged his credibility. Ronald Reagan's performance in the 1980 and 1984 debates confirmed the public view of him as decent, warm, and dignified. Bill Clinton's skirmishes with George Bush in 1992 and Bob Dole in 1996 showed him to be a skilled performer.

Each of the 2000 debates had a different format, one of which had voters asking George W. Bush and Al Gore questions. The debates did not result in large numbers of voters changing their minds about the candidates; rather, they reinforced voters' prior choices. Al Gore had the advantage of previous debate experience but was seen by critics and even some of his supporters as too aggressive in the first debate—asking for more time to answer charges and adopting a confrontational attitude. In the second debate he was more restrained, probably too much so. George W. Bush avoided any serious mistakes and met or exceeded expectations. As Tom Shales, media critic at *The Washington Post*, reported: George W. Bush "did not make any outrageous goofs, gaffes or bloopers and so the debate will go down as a plus for him."[39]

Since 1988, a nonpartisan Commission on Presidential Debates has sponsored and produced the presidential and vice-presidential debates. The commission includes representatives from such neutral groups as the League of Women Voters. Before the commission became involved, there was often a protracted debate about debates. No detail seemed too small to the candidate managers—whether the candidates will sit or stand, whether they will be able to ask each other questions,

Presidential debates give candidates an opportunity to show how quickly and accurately they can respond to questions and outline their goals. In the debates of the 2000 elections, many viewers felt that the vice-presidential candidates, Dick Cheney and Joseph Lieberman, were more effective than the presidential candidates.

whether they will be allowed to bring notes, and whether the questions will be posed by a single journalist or by a panel of reporters or by a sample of citizens. By negotiating in advance many of the contentious details and arranging for debate locations, the commission now facilitates the presidential and vice-presidential debates. In 2000, George W. Bush proposed alternative formats and locations, only to back down as it appeared he was avoiding debates.

Ralph Nader, the Green party candidate in 2000, charged that the commission had a bias in favor of the two major parties when he and Reform party candidate Pat Buchanan were excluded from the debates. But Nader and Buchanan failed to meet the Commission's criteria for inclusion of minor parties; neither had an average of 15 percent or higher in the five major polls used by the commission for this purpose. The other criteria for minor party candidate inclusion in debates are that the candidate be legally eligible and be on the ballot in enough states to be able to win at least 270 electoral votes.[40] In 1992 Ross Perot and his running mate, James Stockdale, had been included in the presidential and vice-presidential debates, which generated large viewing audiences, averaging more than 80 million for each debate. The issue of excluding minor party candidates remains contentious. Including them takes time away from the major party candidates, especially if two or more minor party candidates are invited. Including them may also reduce the likelihood of both major party candidates participating. But excluding them raises issues of fairness and free speech.

Although some critics are quick to express their dissatisfaction with presidential candidates for being so concerned with makeup and rehearsed answers, and although the debates have not significantly affected the election outcomes, they have provided important opportunities for candidates to distinguish themselves and for the public to weigh their qualifications. Candidates who do well in these debates are at a great advantage. They have to be quick on their feet, well rehearsed, and project a positive image. But these are not necessarily the qualities that make for a successful presidency.

Although each election is unique, politicians, pollsters, and political scientists have collected enough information to agree broadly on a number of basic factors they believe affect election outcomes. Whether the nation is prosperous probably has the most to do with who wins a presidential election, but, as we have noted, most voters vote on the basis of party and candidate appeal.[41] Who wins depends on voter turnout. The Democrats' advantage in number of people who identify themselves as Democrats is mitigated by the higher voter turnout among Republicans. Republicans also usually have better access to money, which means they can put on more television ads in more places and more often. In 2000, the Democrats achieved financial parity with the Republicans and more effectively targeted resources to key Senate races.[42]

MONEY IN AMERICAN ELECTIONS

Election campaigns cost money, and the methods of obtaining the money have long been controversial. Campaign money can come from a candidate's own wealth, political parties, interested individuals, or interest groups. Money is contributed to candidates for a variety of reasons, ranging from altruism to self-interest. Individuals or groups, in hopes of influencing the outcome of an election and subsequently influencing policy, give **interested money**. Concern about campaign finance stems from the possibility that candidates, in their pursuit of campaign funds, will decide it is more important to represent their contributors than their conscience or the voters. The potential corruption that results from politicians' dependence on interested money concerns many observers of American politics.

Scandals about money influencing policy are not new. In 1925, responding to the Teapot Dome scandal in which a cabinet member was convicted of accepting bribes, Congress passed the Corrupt Practices Act, which required disclosure of campaign funds but was "written in such a way as to exempt virtually all of them [members of Congress] from its provisions."[43]

interested money
Contributions by individuals or groups in hopes of influencing the outcome of an election and subsequently influencing policy.

THE SOFT MONEY LOOPHOLE IN JAPAN

The Japanese strategy to combat corruption and money politics has been to create some of the most stringent campaign regulations in the world:

- Door-to-door campaigning is banned.

- Candidates may not run campaign advertisements in the media although parties may.

- Each campaign may produce only two versions of its campaign brochure, and only a limited number may be distributed; the number varies according to the number of registered voters in a district.

- Campaign posters are allowed only on government-provided poster boards that are set up in several locations across a district during the campaign.

- Direct mailing of campaign literature is not allowed except for a specified number of government-provided campaign postcards.

- The number of campaign offices, employees, and vehicles is restricted by law.

These regulations should make it impossible for candidates to raise and spend large sums of money in a campaign, but Japanese candidates have found a giant loophole in these restrictions by avoiding "official" campaign activities. A candidate will go door-to-door or mail out literature to voters or put up posters *before* the official campaign period. In these precampaign activities, the candidates will be very careful never to mention the upcoming election, so their efforts are not covered by law.

Attempts to limit these activities have run into constitutional concerns. If a campaign has not begun and a person has not declared his or her candidacy, how can the Japanese government restrict the right of a citizen to hold meetings, discuss issues with people, mail information to people, or put up posters? In a similar manner, concern for free speech led to the soft money loophole in U.S. campaign restrictions.

The 1972 Watergate scandal—an illegal break-in of Democratic party headquarters by persons associated with the Nixon campaign to steal campaign documents and plant listening devices—led to discoveries by news reporters and congressional investigators that large amounts of money from corporations and individuals were "laundered" in secret bank accounts outside the country for political and campaign purposes. Nixon's 1972 campaign spent more than $60 million, more than twice what it had expended in 1968. Investigators discovered that wealthy individuals made large contributions to influence the outcome of the election or secure ambassadorships and administrative appointments.

In the early 1990s, Charles Keating and his failed Lincoln Savings and Loan spotlighted the possibility that undue influence comes with large contributions. Keating had asked five U.S. senators, all of whom had received substantial campaign contributions or other "perks" from him, to intervene on his behalf with federal bank regulators looking into his savings and loan business. These senators came to be called the Keating Five. One of the Senators was John McCain, who has since become a strong advocate of campaign finance reform.

The high costs of television advertising diminish the ability of challengers to mount visible campaigns, resulting in declining competition. Incumbents have a substantial advantage in raising interested money from wealthy individuals and political action committees (PACs). Hence it is not only the source of campaign money that is a problem but the pattern of unequal distribution as well.

During the 2000 presidential nomination battles, the Republican candidate John McCain and Democratic candidates Al Gore and Bill Bradley stressed campaign finance reform. McCain, more than any candidate, emphasized the role of large donors to both parties and the negative influences these individuals and groups have on the political process. Vice-President Gore inherited the negative publicity of the Clinton administration's fund-raising tactics, which included rewarding large donors with overnight stays in the White House and invitations to policy discussions. More incriminating, Gore had participated in a fund raiser at a Buddhist temple in 1996 at which illegal campaign contributions were made. This incident was fodder for ads against Gore by the Republican party in the general election. George W. Bush, after losing the New Hampshire primary, emphasized his own commitment to political reform with the slogan, "Reformer with Results"; still, he resisted endorsing any particular campaign finance reform agenda.

Efforts to Reform

Reformers have tried three basic strategies to prevent abuse in political contributions: (1) imposing limitations on giving, receiving, and spending political money; (2) requiring public disclosure of the sources and uses of political money; and (3) giving governmental subsidies to presidential candidates, campaigns, and parties. Recent campaign finance laws have tended to use all three strategies.

THE FEDERAL ELECTION CAMPAIGN ACT   In 1971 Congress passed two significant laws dealing with campaign funding. The Federal Election Campaign Act (FECA) limited amounts that candidates for federal office can spend on advertising, required the disclosure of the sources of campaign funds as well as how they are spent, and required political action committees to register with the government and report all major contributions and expenditures. This 1971 law also provided a checkoff that allowed taxpayers to contribute $1 to a fund to subsidize presidential campaigns by checking a box on their income tax form. The checkoff option is now $3.

In 1974 Congress passed and President Gerald Ford signed the most sweeping campaign reform measure in U.S. history. These amendments to the Federal Election Campaign Act established somewhat more realistic limits on contributions and spending, tightened disclosure, and provided for public financing of presidential campaigns.

The 1974 law was extensively amended after the 1976 *Buckley v Valeo* decision, which overturned several of its provisions on grounds that they violated the First Amendment.[44] The *Buckley* decision emphasized limitations on contributions and full and open disclosure of all fund-raising activities by candidates for federal office, as well as the system of public financing for presidential elections.[45] The Supreme Court made a distinction between campaign spending and campaign contributions, holding that the First Amendment protects spending; therefore, legislatures may not limit how much of their own money people spend on elections, but Congress may limit how much people contribute to somebody else's campaign. Later modifications of the law and court interpretations sought to encourage volunteer activities and party building by permitting national political parties, corporations, labor unions, and individuals to give unlimited amounts, called **soft money**, to state parties, provided the funds are used for party-building purposes.

The public subsidy of presidential candidates has started to break down. Until 2000, presidential candidates (except wealthy self-financed candidates) accepted the voluntary limitations that come with partial public financing of presidential campaigns. George W. Bush, who raised more than $125 million for his campaign,[46] declined federal matching funds in the 2000 primaries, but accepted the federal subsidy of $67.5 million for the general election and with it the limits on how much his campaign could spend. Whether future candidates will also pass up some federal funds depends on how well funded their opponents are and their own ability to raise money. Beyond the problem of candidates passing up the federal funds, the number of taxpayers checking the campaign subsidy on their income tax forms has been declining, although enough did so to cover all the costs of the 2000 elections.[47]

The Unsolved Problem of Soft Money

The most serious problem with the presidential campaign finance system is soft money—funds given to state and local parties by political parties, individuals, or political action committees ostensibly for party-building registration drives, mailings, and advertising, which do not specify a candidate by name. No limits are set on the amount of such contributions. The money is called "soft" because federal law does not limit how much individuals or groups can contribute or how much parties can spend. Although soft money is supposed to benefit only parties, it is used by the parties to influence the election of federal candidates. Both parties have made raising

The Federal Election Campaign Act (1971) and Amendments (1974)

- Establishes a Federal Election Commission appointed by the president with the advice and consent of the Senate to regulate the campaign financing of candidates for president, senator, and representative.

- Provides for public financing of presidential general election campaigns with funds from the income tax checkoff.

- Provides for partial public financing on a matching basis of presidential nominating campaigns.

- Provides for subsidies to the two national parties for their convention expenses and to any minor party that polled 5 percent of the total vote in the previous presidential election.

- Limits spending by candidates for presidential nominations (on a state-by-state basis and in total) and in the presidential general elections for those candidates who accept public funding.

- Limits the amounts that national parties may spend on presidential campaigns and on individual congressional and senatorial campaigns.

- Sets a limit of $1,000 on the amount that any individual can give to a candidate for the U.S. Senate or for the U.S. House of Representatives in the primary election; a limit of $1,000 per candidate in the general election; and a limit of $5,000 per candidate per election ($5,000 in primary and $5,000 in general election) for political action committees.

- Sets an overall limitation of $25,000 on the amount that any individual can donate to all candidates for federal office in an election cycle; no similar limitation applicable to political action committees.

- Sets no limit on the amount of their own money candidates can spend on their campaign.

- Sets no limit on the amount that individuals or groups can spend independently.

soft money
Money contributed to a state or local party for party-building purposes that does not have to be disclosed under federal law.

You Decide...

When Is an issue ad an election ad?

Political ads have many different purposes: some are about issues, attempting to persuade the audience to a point of view; others are about a candidate's qualifications; and still others are about both issues and candidates. But does the content of an advertisement indicate the ad's purpose?

Assume it is a few weeks before an election, and you are watching an ad on TV or listening to one on the radio. Ask yourself if what you are seeing or hearing is only about issues, or if it is about electing or defeating a candidate. Does it:

Show an image or likeness of a candidate?

Mention a candidate by name?

Mention an election?

Use words like "vote for," "vote against," "support...."?

Is it shown in the weeks before an election?

Defining characteristics like these are important because they can determine whether this is an "issue advertisement." As the current law states, only if an ad uses a candidate's name and words like "vote for" or "vote against" is it about electing or defeating a candidate and therefore subject to limitations or regulation.

soft money a high priority. Soft money spending has risen dramatically. All national party committees combined raised over $487 million of soft money in the 1999–2000 election cycle, up from $78 million in 1991–1992[48] (see Figure 9–4).

Soft money has brought back the large donors as major players in campaign finance. It has also strengthened the power of the national party committees, which allocate the money to state parties and indirectly to candidates. In 2000, national and congressional party committees spent nearly one-half billion dollars in soft money; Democratic party soft money spending pulled even with the Republicans. In the past, soft money had been more important in presidential than in congressional contests, but that changed in a dramatic way with the 1998 and 2000 congressional elections. The most dramatic growth in 2000 came among Senate Democrats, who raised only $372,000 in soft money in 1994 but raised $63 million in 1999–2000—a surge in spending that helped Senate Democrats pick up a net gain of four Senate seats, resulting in a 50 to 50 Senate. Figure 9–4 plots the surge in soft money funds for the four congressional campaign committees.

ISSUE ADVOCACY ADVERTISING   The 1996 election saw a surge in a campaign activity called **issue advocacy**. Money spent on issue advocacy ads is unlimited because it presumably deals with issues, not candidates. Issue ad spending in some U.S. House races has exceeded $1 million in recent elections; for example, in 2000, one group, the Alliance for Quality Nursing Home Care, spent more than $1 million on issue ads in the Delaware U.S. Senate race.[49] In the 1998 and 2000 elections, businesses, labor unions, health maintenance organizations, the Sierra Club, the League of Conservation Voters, the Business Roundtable, pro- and anti-gun groups, pro- and anti-abortion groups, and the pharmaceutical industry ran issue ads (see Table 9–1). These ads not only help the candidate interest groups prefer or punish the candidate they oppose; they also force candidates to discuss the interest group's agenda. While these ads do not specifically say to vote for or against a candidate, they do contain candidates' images and names.

The use of issue ads and the growth in soft money mean that competitive congressional elections are shifting from candidate-centered elections to party- and interest group-centered campaigns.[50] Soft money spending combined with interest group issue advocacy spending exceeded the candidate campaigns in radio and television advertising by a margin of 2 to 1 in 17 of the most competitive congressional races of 2000.[51] Parties and interest groups also spend large sums of money on mail

issue advocacy
Commercial advertising on radio and television advocating a particular position on an issue, paid for by interest groups and designed to influence voters' choices on election day.

independent expenditures
Money spent by individuals or groups not associated with candidates to elect or defeat candidates for office.

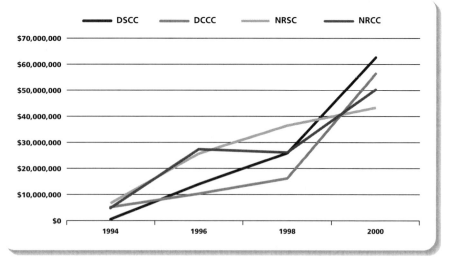

FIGURE 9–4 Congressional Campaign Committee Soft Money Spending, 1994–2000

SOURCE: Federal Election Commission, "Party Fundraising Escalates," press release, January 12, 2001, at fecweb1.fec.gov/press/011201partyfunds.htm.

and on the telephone. For example, in some congressional races in 2000, targeted voters received as many as 12 pieces of political mail per day as election day approached.[52]

One of the problems with issue ads is accountability. Since these interest groups are not required to disclose how much they spend or how they raise their money, voters have a hard time knowing the source of the funds. Ads by these groups also tend to be more negative. Often candidates get blamed for the attacks made by these groups because voters assume the ads are run by the candidates. Finally, because of the amounts of money involved and the negative tone of the communications, issue advocacy has reinforced cynicism and alienation among voters.

Some senators have proposed requiring disclosure of the identity of groups doing issue advertising in the 30 to 60 days before congressional and presidential elections; they define issue advertising as communication that mentions a candidate by name or shows the image or likeness of a candidate.

Defenders of issue ads point to recent ad campaigns that focused on legislation, like those mounted by tobacco companies in 1998 to defeat a tobacco tax in the Senate or ads run by insurance companies attacking the Clinton health care plan in 1994. Because issue advocacy ostensibly lacks a campaign or election referent, it is likely to be protected as free speech. Drawing a distinction between genuine issue advocacy and election issue advocacy is not easy, but election issue ads occur in the weeks before an election and frequently have the image of a candidate or mention the candidate by name.[53]

CANDIDATES' PERSONAL WEALTH   Campaign finance legislation cannot constitutionally restrict rich candidates—the Rockefellers, the Kennedys, the Perots—from giving heavily to their own campaigns. Big money makes a big difference, and wealthy candidates can afford to spend big money. In presidential politics, this advantage can be most meaningful in the period before the primaries begin. There may be no constitutional way to limit how much money people can spend on their own campaigns. The 2000 New Jersey U.S. Senate race set new records for a candidate spending personal wealth in an election. Wall Street investment banker John Corzine, a newcomer to elections, spent a total of $60 million, with $35 million of it spent in the primary alone.[54]

INDEPENDENT EXPENDITURES   Current finance laws do not constrain **independent expenditures** by groups or individuals who are separate from political candidates. This loophole has been permitted by the Supreme Court on free speech grounds. Groups sympathetic to, but independent of, candidates are allowed to raise and spend unlimited funds to help elect them or to defeat their opponents. For example, in 1984 Michael Goland, a Californian, spent $1,100,740 as an independent expenditure to defeat Illinois Senator Charles Percy.[55] As long as there is no collusion between the independent spender and the candidate, an individual or PAC can spend an unlimited amount of money for or against a candidate.

Issue ads have largely replaced independent expenditures in recent election cycles because interest groups can spend the same amount of money without having to disclose the activity. Some groups like the National Rifle Association and National Education Association continue to use independent expenditures, however, perhaps because they want to urge voters to "vote for" or "vote against" specific candidates, words you cannot include in an issue ad.

Consequences of Current Campaign Financing

The problems with federal election fund raising are easy to identify: dramatically escalating costs, a growing dependence on PAC money, decreasing visibility and competitiveness of challengers (especially in the House), the ability of

TABLE 9–1 **Top Ten Issue Advertisers, 2000** (in millions)	
Citizens for Better Medicare	$64
AFL-CIO	$45
Coalition to Protect America's Health Care	$30
National Rifle Association	$25
U.S. Chamber of Commerce	$15
Planned Parenthood Action Fund	$14
Business Roundtable	$13
Federation for American Immigration Reform	$12
NAACP National Voter Fund	$11
Americans for Job Security	$10

SOURCES: Data from David B. Magleby, ed., *Election Advocacy: Soft Money and Issue Advocacy in the 2000 Congressional Elections* (Center for the Study of Elections and Democracy, Brigham Young University, 2001); Erika Falk, "Issue Advocacy Advertising Through the Presidential Primary: 1999–2000 Election Cycle," Annenberg Public Policy Center, press release, September 20, 2000.

NOTE: The numbers estimate total spending: issue advocacy and express advocacy. However, a large proportion of the totals were issue advocacy.

Thinking It Through . . .

Based on a distinction in the *Buckley v Valeo* Supreme Court decision, communications that do not use words such as "vote for" or "vote against" are considered issue ads, which are not subject to the same disclosure rules as ads that are about electing or defeating a candidate. But in the context of an election, it is possible to convey a positive or negative election message without using these words. Some of these ads end by telling viewers to "Call" or "Write" the candidate to express support or opposition. But the real intent of the message is to get the audience to vote for or against a candidate.

Research on the types of ads run in election cycles have found that less than 10 percent were only about issues and not about candidates. Research also shows that people do not think it necessary to use words like "vote for" in order to convey an election message, but that even showing the candidate's image is enough to convey that the ad is about electing or defeating a candidate.

Opponents to limiting or prohibiting issue ads point out that Congress is often in session until a few days before an election, and interest groups need to be able to inform the public about important issues that are being considered. To limit issue ads during this period may stifle the free speech of groups with a more legislative than electoral agenda.

CAMPAIGN FINANCE REFORM

For several years Congress has considered campaign finance reform. However, due to a presidential veto, the lack of action by one house or the other, or the use of legislative obstructions, only minor changes have been enacted. Despite scandals involving the president and members of Congress that resulted in protracted legislative hearings and numerous editorials, Congress failed to pass changes in our campaign finance laws.

The most visible advocate of reform is Arizona Senator John McCain, who, ironically, was part of a scandal involving campaign contributions by Charles Keating, owner of a failed Savings and Loan. McCain made campaign finance reform a theme of his 2000 presidential campaign, forcing his rival, George W. Bush, to characterize himself as a "reformer with results." Although he lost the nomination to Bush, McCain continued to beat the campaign finance

reform drum and was successful in getting Senate leadership to schedule an early debate and vote on his bill, the McCain–Feingold–Cochran bill.

President Bush did not make campaign finance reform a high priority in his new administration. Bush's own proposal included what some saw as a "poison pill" for the bill, a requirement that union members must sign-off annually for their political contributions to their unions.

The 2000 elections resulted in a U.S. Senate more supportive of campaign finance reform and without enough votes for its opponents to sustain a filibuster. The result was passage of McCain-Feingold-Cochran by a vote of 59 to 41. The Senate version of the bill closely resembled versions of the legislation that had passed the House in 1998 and again in 1999.

Opponents of the legislation in the House sought to delay consideration of the bill. If the bill passed, opponents

In the opening weeks of the 2001 session, Senators John McCain and Russ Feingold kept up the fight for campaign finance reform that had failed to gain Senate approval in 1997 and 1998 but was successful in 2001.

hoped to force a conference committee that which would either kill the bill or force the Senate to reconsider and possibly reject it. President Bush was noticeably noncommital as to whether or not he would sign the Senate version of the bill.

---

wealthy individuals to fund their own campaigns, and the danger of large contributions altering election outcomes. These problems are exacerbated by soft money and issue advocacy, which have moved to the top of the agendas of campaign finance reformers.

RISING COSTS OF CAMPAIGNS   The American ideal that anyone—a person from humble beginnings or of modest wealth—should be able to run for public office is quickly becoming impossible. And rising costs mean incumbents spend more time raising funds and therefore less time legislating and representing their districts. Since the Federal Election Campaign Act became law in 1972, total expenditures by candidates for the House of Representatives have more than doubled after controlling for inflation, and they have risen even more in Senate elections (see Table 9–2). Television advertising is expensive, limiting the field of challengers to those who can spend more than a year raising money.

DECLINING COMPETITION   Unless something is done to help finance challengers, incumbents will continue to have the advantage in seeking reelection. Challengers in both parties are typically underfunded. House Democratic challengers averaged $168,650 in spending in 2000.[56] In today's expensive campaigns, candidates are invisible if they can spend only two or three hundred thousand dollars.

The high cost of campaigns dampens competition by discouraging individuals from running for office. Potential challengers look at the fund-raising advantages enjoyed by incumbents—at incumbents' campaign war chests, which sometimes

A candidate's personal fortune has played a big role in recent elections. Jon Corzine's $60 million investment won him the New Jersey seat in the U.S. Senate in 2000.

TABLE 9-2	Average Campaign Expenditures of Candidates for the House of Representatives, 1988–2000 General Election (1998 Dollars in Thousands)		
	Incumbent	Challenger	Open Seat
Republican			
1988	$563.8	$138.4	$1123.5
1990	496.5	138.2	1036.8
1992	617.7	219.3	727.5
1994	506.4	263.1	1111.8
1996	766.9	219.6	653.5
1998	668.9	245.1	709.2
2000	883.0	310.1	1200.0
Democrat			
1988	$493.6	$198.1	$616.0
1990	501.3	137.8	667.8
1992	702.6	186.8	560.2
1994	665.0	174.2	639.6
1996	593.7	307.9	652.5
1998	539.5	232.9	709.8
2000	735.7	454.0	1100.0

SOURCES: Federal Election Commission, "Congressional Fundraising and Spending Up Again in 1996," press release, April 14, 1997, p. 13; Federal Election Commission, "1998 Congressional Financial Activity Declines," press release, December 29, 1998, p. 5; ftp.fec.gov/fec.

have $1 million before the campaign even starts, and at the time it will take for them to raise enough money to launch a minimal campaign—and they decide to direct their energies elsewhere. Moreover, unlike incumbents, who are being paid while campaigning and fund raising, most challengers have to support themselves and their families for the duration of the campaign, which for the House and Senate is roughly two years.

INCREASING DEPENDENCE ON PACS AND WEALTHY DONORS   Where does the money come from to finance these expensive election campaigns? For most House incumbents the answer is political action committees (PACs), which we discussed in Chapter 6 as well. In 2000, for instance, 191 of the 408 incumbents seeking reelection raised more money from PACs than from individuals[57] (see Figure 9–5). Senators get a smaller percentage of their campaign funds from PACs, but because they spend so much more, they need to raise even more money from PACs than House incumbents do. Challengers receive little from PACs because PACs do not want to offend politicians in power.

To be sure, PACs and individuals give political money for many reasons. Most of them want certain laws to be passed or repealed, certain funds appropriated, or certain administrative decisions rendered. At a minimum, they want access to officeholders, a chance to talk with members before key votes.

Defenders of PACs point out that there is no demonstrable relationship between contributions and legislators' votes. But influence in the legislative process depends on access to staff and members of Congress, and most agree that campaign contributions give donors unusual access. PACs influence the legislative process in other ways as well. Their access helps them structure the legislative agenda with friendly legislators and influence the drafting of legislation or amendments to existing bills. These are all advantages that others do not have.

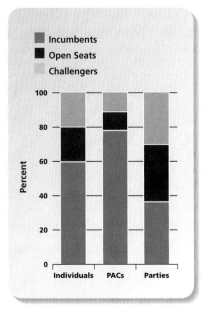

FIGURE 9–5 PAC Money Favors Incumbents

SOURCE: Federal Election Commission; ftp.fec.gov/fec.

A combination of party rules and state laws determines how we choose nominees for president. Reformers agree that the current process is flawed but disagree over which aspects require change.

Concern over how we choose presidents now centers on four issues: (1) the number, timing, and representativeness of presidential primaries; (2) the role of the Electoral College, including the possibility that a presidential election might be thrown into the House of Representatives;[58] (3) how we vote; and (4) campaign finance reform.

Reforming Presidential Primaries

Presidential primaries open the nominating process to more voters than do caucus or convention methods for selecting presidential candidates. Today the media play up the primary in every important state, and voters follow the races in other states as well as their own. In so doing, they can judge the candidates' political qualities: their abilities to organize campaigns, communicate through the media, stand up under pressure, avoid making mistakes (or recover if they do make them), adjust their appeals to shifting events and to different regions of the country, control their staffs as well as utilize them, and be decisive, articulate, resilient, humorous, informed, and ultimately successful in winning votes. In short, supporters claim, primaries test candidates on the very qualities they must exhibit in the presidency.[59]

Critics of primaries grant that more voters take part in primaries than in the caucus and convention methods of choosing delegates, but they question the quality of the participation. For one thing, supporters of the different candidates have no opportunity to deliberate together in public. Voters in caucuses can argue and persuade one another in small meetings; voters in primaries must depend largely on the news media and advertising for their information and basis for judgment. Voters in primaries tend to be more influenced by candidates' personalities and media skills than their positions on vital issues.[60]

Participation in primaries has been low in recent years (see Figure 9–6). In the 2000 primaries, turnout was generally under 18 percent of the voting-age population, and it declined as the primary season progressed and the field of candidates narrowed.[61] Low levels of turnout in primaries open the possibility that extreme groups will have a

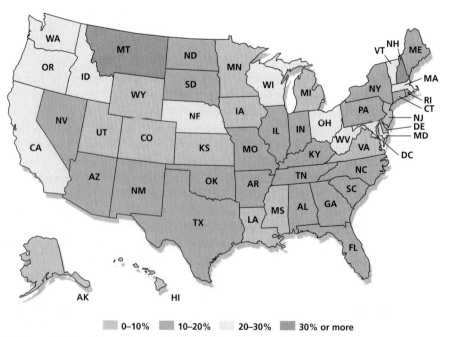

0–10%   10–20%   20–30%   30% or more

FIGURE 9–6 Voter Turnout in the 2000 Presidential Primaries

disproportionate say; the "selectorate" replaces the electorate. In addition, candidates are forced to appeal to highly motivated voters, usually from the conservative wing of the Republican party and the liberal wing of the Democratic party.

For many years the primary season was criticized for being too long.[62] Some states, by virtue of coming early in the process, had a disproportionate say in determining the nominee and therefore were more influential with presidents. Several states moved up their primary dates in 2000 so that 48 percent of the Republican and 37 percent of the Democratic delegates were selected by March 7.[63] Not surprisingly, Al Gore and George W. Bush had their nominations locked up by this date. States that came later in the process found the nominee had already been selected.

Finally, some critics question whether primaries test the qualities needed to be president. To win "the media game," candidates must be witty, resourceful, attractive, and articulate—not necessarily the most important qualities to be a good president. Thomas Jefferson, Abraham Lincoln, and Harry Truman were able presidents, but they did not have great "media appeal." Critics are disturbed by the gap between the qualities required to carry primary contests and the qualities needed to govern: to organize an administration, get support on issues, make hard decisions, and deal with congressional leaders, governors, and mayors.

Reforming the Nominating Process

What would the critics substitute for state presidential primaries? Some argue in favor of a *national presidential primary* that would take the form of a single nationwide election, probably held in May or September, or separate state primaries held in all the states on the same day. Supporters contend that a one-shot national presidential primary (though a runoff might be necessary) would be simple, direct, and representative. It would cut down the wear and tear on candidates, and it would attract a large turnout because of intensive media coverage. Opponents argue that such a reform would make the present system even worse. It would enhance the role of showmanship and gamesmanship; and, being enormously expensive, it would hurt the chances of candidates who lack strong financial backing.[64]

A more modest proposal is to hold *regional primaries*, possibly at two- or three-week intervals across the country. Regional primaries might bring more coherence to the process, encourage more emphasis on issues of regional concern, and also cut down on wear and tear. But such primaries would retain most of the disadvantages of the present system—especially the emphasis on money and media. Clearly, they would give an advantage to candidates from whatever region held the first primary, and this advantage would encourage regional candidates and might increase polarization among sections of the country.

A different proposal is to drastically reduce the number of presidential primaries and make more use of the caucus system. The turnout of voters in the Iowa caucuses in recent elections shows that participation can be high, and the time participants spent discussing candidates and issues shows that such participation can be thoughtful and informed. In caucus states, candidates are less dependent on the media and more dependent on convincing political activists. By centering delegate selection in party meetings, the caucus system would also, some say, enhance the role of the party.[65]

Still another idea—used by Colorado for nominations to state offices and by Utah for nominations to federal and state office—would turn the process around. Beginning in May, local caucuses and then state conventions would be held in every state. They would then send delegates—a certain percentage of whom would be unpledged to any presidential candidate—to the national party conventions, which would be held in the summer. The national conventions would select two or three candidates to compete in a national primary to be held in September. In this plan, voters registered by party would be allowed to vote for their party nominee in the September primaries.[66]

PEOPLE

It counts some votes as more important than others, according to the state in which they are cast.

THE ELECTORAL COLLEGE IS NOT FAIR

Lawrence D. Longley

Long before the curent controversy surrounding who won the 2000 presidential election, Americans have debated whether to abolish the Electoral College and what to replace it with. George W. Bush was the first candidate since Benjamin Harrison in 1888 to loose the popular vote but win office through the Electoral College. The failure of the popular vote winner to gain office in 2000 makes the debate over reform of the Electoral College a more salient issue.

Professor Lawrence D. Longley, in testimony before Congress, points out the unfair effects of the Electoral College:

The Electoral College means of presidential election is of great significance, even when it produces a clear decision. The Electoral College is not a neutral and fair counting device for tallying popular votes cast for President in the form of electoral votes. Instead, it counts some votes as more important than others, according to the state in which they are cast. As a result, these distortions of popular preferences greatly influence candidate strat-

egy: certain key states, their voters, parochial interests, political leaders, and unique local factions, are favored.

The Electoral College election of the President also discriminates among types of candidates. Independent or third-party contenders with a regional following have great opportunities for Electoral College significance, while independent or third-party candidates with broad-based but nationally distributed support may find themselves excluded from winning any Electoral College votes. Even without receiving electoral votes, however, such candidates can prove decisive in terms of swinging large blocs of electoral votes from one major party candidate to the other.

Finally, the Electoral College can reflect inaccurately the popular will because of the action of faithless electors—individual electors who vote differently in the electoral college from the expectations of those who elected them. ★

SOURCE: Statement of Lawrence D. Longley, Professor of Government at Lawrence University, before the U.S. Senate Committee on the Judiciary Subcommittee on the Constitution, July 21-22, 1992.

DEBATE

THE ELECTORAL COLLEGE FORMS A CONSENSUS

Senator Patrick Moynihan

It is easier to point out the limitations of the Electoral College than it is to come up with a process that does not also have significant problems. The most frequently proposed reform—eliminate the Electoral College and elect the popular vote winner—has the disadvantage of placing the entire country into a position where recounts might be necessary. Indeed, if the automatic recount provisions in most states had been in place in 2000, all ballots would have had to be recounted. As former Senator Patrick Moynihan articulated, there are other problems with proposed reforms as well:

> There is no fact more singular about our Constitution than its durability. . . No other large industrial . . . nation has anything like our experience of a sustained and stable government under a written constitution basically unchanged from its original construction. . . I would stress . . . the idea that the Founding Fathers had learned from history . . . the representation directly and indirectly of people and States. . . a principle that involved not just one majority, but in the most important sense, many majorities.
>
> Dr. Judith Best . . . has spoken at length . . . on the principle of concurrent majorities. . . She said, " . . . the principle of concurrent majority is, has been, and was intended to be the American idea of democracy because the size of the popular vote is not sufficient to maintain liberty." . . . The Electoral College requires the assembly of . . . concurrent majorities—in one part of the country and another part of the country, and yet another part, all defined in terms of several States. It has as its extraordinary ability the formation of consensus as between widely differing regions, political purposes and styles, and political agendas. It has as its purpose and function the narrowing of differences. . .
>
> . . . the proposal before us [direct election of the president], in the guise of perfecting an alleged weakness in the Constitution, proposes the most radical transformation in our constitutional system that has ever been considered. I remarked that the Founders devised our system with the idea of a network of concurrent majorities which would be required to exercise power. The fundamental thrust of this measure . . . would be to abolish that principle of concurrent majority. ★

It has as its purpose and function the narrowing of differences.

SOURCE: Senator Daniel Patrick Moynihan (D., NY) on the floor of the United States Senate, June 27, 1979; Judith A. Best, *The Choice of the People?* (Rowman & Littlefield Publishers, Inc., 1996), pp. 85-86; 151-159.

For further information about this debate, go to **www.prenhall.com/burns** *and click on the Debate Icon in Chapter 9.*

Reforming the Electoral College

The Florida ballot counting and recounting at the close of the 2000 election and the fact that the popular vote winner did not become president prompted a national debate on the Electoral College. The most frequently proposed reform of the Electoral College system is *direct popular election* of the president. Presidents would be elected directly by the voters, just as governors are, and the Electoral College and individual electors would be abolished. Such proposals usually provide that, if no candidate receives at least 40 percent of the total popular vote, a *runoff election* would be held between the two contenders with the most votes. Supporters argue that direct election would give every voter the same weight in the presidential balloting in accordance with the one-person, one-vote doctrine. Winners would take on more legitimacy because their victories would reflect the will of the voters.

Opponents contend that the plan would further undermine federalism, that it would encourage unrestrained majority rule and hence political extremism, and that it would hurt the smaller states, which would lose some of their present influence. Others fear that the plan would make presidential campaigns more remote from the voters; candidates might stress television and give up their forays into shopping centers and city malls.[67] Some also fear that the plan would increase the reliance of presidential campaigns on television.

From time to time, Congress considers proposals for a constitutional amendment to elect presidents directly. Such proposals, however, seldom get far because of the strong opposition of various interests that believe they may be disadvantaged by such a change, especially small states and minority groups whose role is enlarged by the Electoral College. Groups such as African Americans and farmers, for example, fear they might lose their swing vote power—their ability to make a difference in key states that may tip the Electoral College balance.

Another alternative to the Electoral College is sometimes called the National Bonus Plan. This plan adds to the current 538 Electoral College members another 102 electoral votes, to be awarded on a winner-takes-all basis to the candidate with the most votes, so long as that candidate received over 40 percent of the popular vote. This system would avoid elections being thrown into the House of Representatives and would help the popular vote winner take over the White House. The most serious liabilities of the plan are that it is complicated and requires a run-off election if there is no winner.

Finally, some states have already modified the Electoral College, adopting a district system in which the candidate who carries each congressional district gets that electoral vote, and the candidate who carries the state gets the state's two additional electoral votes. This quasi-proportional representation system has been used in Maine and Nebraska. It has the advantage of not shutting out a candidate who is strong in some areas of a state but not others, but otherwise it does not address the larger concerns with the Electoral College.

The failure of attempts to change the system of elections points to an important conclusion about procedural reform: Americans normally do not focus on procedures. Only after an Electoral College crisis like we experienced in 2000 is any significant change likely. As the crucial importance of ballot counts dragged on, citizens focused on actual problems with the electoral system, not on hypothetical problems discussed by political scientists and democratic theorists.

Reforming How We Vote

The 2000 presidential election ended with a month-long controversy over ballots and how to count them. While Florida became the focal point of national and international attention with its problems with punch-card ballots, dangling chads, voter confusion over ballot formats, and when to count or not count absentee ballots, such problems are common to most, if not all, states. As we noted earlier in this chapter, election administration is a state and local matter, and election law is constitutionally assigned to the individual states.

While technology could eliminate some of these problems by making electronic voting possible, the question of who would pay the costs of converting to new voting systems stands in the way of change. Improving election administration has not been high on the budget priorities of counties in Florida or most other states. Most observers agree that it will take a substantial infusion of money from the national government to fund new and improved voting systems.

As the country debates new voting systems, it is likely that state legislatures and Congress will debate permitting people to vote via the Internet. The argument will be that if people can make purchases over the Internet, why not let them vote electronically as well. Some states have experimented with "e-voting" on a small scale in presidential primaries in 2000. A shift to e-voting is in some respects an extension of the Oregon vote-by-mail experience since 1996. Yet critics worry that important elements of community and democracy are lost when people do not vote collectively at the schoolhouse or fire station. Another concern with e-voting is that it may encourage a proliferation of elections. If we can vote from home, why not vote on more things and more often? E-voting could foster a political culture of more and more ballot referenda.

CAMPAIGN FINANCING IN BRITAIN AND CANADA

U.S. election campaigns go on for months or even years and are very expensive. In contrast, Canadian general election campaigns are limited by law to about five weeks. Public opinion polls cannot be published during the last three days of a campaign, and the media are prohibited by law from reporting results from earlier time zones on the evening of the election in any district where voting is still taking place.

Expenditures are strictly limited for Canadian political parties and individual candidates. During the 1997 general election campaign to fill the 301 seats in the House of Commons, political parties that fielded candidates in all districts were limited by law to spending no more than approximately $8 million each for the entire election, and individual candidates could spend from about $35,000 to $45,000, depending on the number of voters per district. In return, media outlets were required to sell a certain amount of airtime to the parties, and national and regional television and radio networks had to donate some free airtime to these parties. If individual candidates received more than 15 percent of the vote in their districts, the government reimbursed 50 percent of their election-related expenses. Political parties receiving at least 2 percent of the national vote or at least 5 percent of the votes cast in electoral districts where they ran candidates were reimbursed 22.5 percent of their expenses.

In the June 1997 Canadian elections, 1,672 candidates ran for office, and 10 political parties received registered status. Total spending by the parliamentary candidates and political parties was approximately $70 million—much less than the $29 million spent by candidates in the United States seeking seats in the House of Representatives and the $128 million spent by candidates seeking seats in the Senate during the 1996 election campaign.

British general elections also offer an interesting contrast to elections in the United States. The election campaign lasts only three weeks. Candidates for the House of Commons, the most critical election in Britain, are allowed to raise and spend only $15,000. If they spend more, they are disqualified. Each candidate gets the same amount of free airtime, and each candidate is allowed one free election leaflet mailed to each voter in the constituency. About 75 percent of voters turn out, and about 95 percent of eligible voters are registered to vote. At the voting booth, the voter is handed a slip of paper with the names of three or four candidates for the House of Commons. No other offices or ballot questions are presented at the same time.

SOURCE: Adapted from Dudley Fishburn (a candidate for Parliament in 1992), "British Campaigning—How Civilized!" *The New York Times*, April 14, 1992, p. 25.

Reforming Campaign Finance

Although campaign finance reform is not a pressing concern to most citizens, large majorities of Americans think we need to reform the way we fund elections. The issues we have been discussing—soft money, issue advocacy, personal wealth, PAC contributions—are all examples of the need for reform. Why, then, has Congress been so slow to reform campaign finance? One reason is that the current members of Congress got elected with the current system, and they perceive the status quo to benefit them. Another reason is that the same interests who invest millions in funding campaigns also like things to stay as they are.

But campaign finance reform faces more fundamental problems as well. The courts and civil liberties groups have defined campaign money as political speech, and limitations on political speech face substantial constitutional hurdles. In a sense, the continuing debate about reforming presidential nominations, the Electoral College, how we vote, and how we fund elections can be taken as indications that elections and voting matter. The involvement of all the branches of government—legislative, executive, and judicial—in the outcome of the 2000 election and the nationwide interest in following the convoluted steps leading to the final decision reinforce the need to understand and take part in our democratic election procedures.

SUMMARY

1. American elections, even presidential elections, are largely governed by state law and administered by local election officials. Following the 2000 elections, governments at all levels have begun to look for ways to improve the system.

2. Our electoral system is based on winner-takes-all rules, with typically single-member-district or single-officeholder arrangements. These rules encourage a moderate, two-party system. That we have fixed and staggered terms of office adds predictability to our electoral system.

3. The Electoral College is the means by which presidents are actually elected. To win a state's electoral votes, a candidate must have a plurality of votes in that state. Except in two states, the winner takes all. Thus candidates cannot afford to lose the popular vote in the most populous states. The Electoral College also gives disproportionate power to the largest states and has the potential for defeat of the popular vote winner.

4. Many congressional, state, and local races are not seriously contested. The extent to which a campaign is likely to be hotly contested varies with the importance of the office and the chance a challenger has of winning. Senate races are more likely to be contested, though most incumbents win.

5. The race for the presidency actually takes place in three stages: winning enough delegate support in presidential primaries and caucuses to secure the nomination, campaigning at the national party convention, and mobilizing voters for a win in the Electoral College.

6. Even though presidential nominations today are usually decided weeks or months before the national party conventions, these conventions still have an important role in setting the parties' direction, unifying their ranks, and firing up enthusiasm. Speakers who are highlighted are positioned to pursue nominations in future years.

7. Because large campaign contributors are suspected of improperly influencing public officials, Congress has long sought to regulate political contributions. The main approaches to reform have been: (1) imposing limitations on giving, receiving, and spending political money; (2) requiring public disclosure of the sources and uses of political money; and (3) giving governmental subsidies to presidential candidates,

campaigns, and parties, including incentive arrangements. Present regulation includes all three approaches.

8. Loopholes in federal law—including soft money, issue advocacy, and independent expenditures—and rising costs of campaigns have led to declining competition for congressional seats and increasing dependence on PACs and wealthy donors.

9. The present presidential selection system is under criticism because of its length and expense, because of uncertainties and biases in the Electoral College, and because it seems to test candidates for media skills less needed in the White House than the ability to govern, including the capacity to form coalitions and make hard decisions.

10. Reform efforts center on presidential primaries and the Electoral College as well as on voting methods and campaign finance.

KEY TERMS

winner-takes-all 195
single-member district 195
proportional representation 195

Electoral College 195
safe seat 197
coattail effect 197

caucus 203
national party convention 203
interested money 207

soft money 209
issue advocacy 210
independent expenditures 210

FURTHER READING

R. MICHAEL ALVAREZ, *Information and Elections* (University of Michigan Press, 1998).

LARRY M. BARTELS, *Presidential Primaries and the Dynamics of Public Choice* (Princeton University Press, 1988).

LARRY M. BARTELS AND LYNN VAVRECK, EDS., *Campaign Reform: Insights and Evidence* (University of Michigan Press, 2000).

JUDITH A. BEST, *The Choice of the People? Debating the Electoral College* (Rowman and Littlefield, 1996).

EARL BLACK AND MERLE BLACK, *The Vital South: How Presidents Are Elected* (Harvard University Press, 1992).

ANDREW E. BUSH, *Horses in Midstream: U.S. Midterm Elections and Their Consequences, 1894–1998* (University of Pittsburgh Press, 2000).

ALAN EHRENHALT, *The United States of Ambition: Politicians, Power, and the Pursuit of Office* (Times Books, 1991).

THOMAS FERGUSON, *Golden Rule: The Investment Theory of Party Competition and the Logic of Money-Driven Political Systems* (University of Chicago Press, 1995).

LINDA L. FOWLER AND ROBERT D. McCLURE, *Political Ambition: Who Decides to Run for Congress* (Yale University Press, 1989).

THOMAS GAIS, *Improper Influence: Campaign Finance Law, Political Interest Groups, and the Problem of Equality* (University of Michigan Press, 1996).

PAUL GRONKE, *The Electorate, the Campaign, and the Office: A Unified Approach to Senate and House Elections* (University of Michigan Press, 2000).

PAUL S. HERRNSON, *Congressional Elections: Campaigning at Home and in Washington*, 3d ed. (Congressional Quarterly Press, 2000).

GARY C. JACOBSON, *The Politics of Congressional Elections*, 4th ed. (Longman, 1997).

MARION R. JUST, ANN N. CRIGLER, DEAN E. ALGER, TIMOTHY E. COOK, MONTAGUE KERN, AND DARREL M. WEST, *Crosstalk: Citizens, Candidates and the Media in a Presidential Campaign* (University of Chicago Press, 1996).

KIM F. KAHN AND PATRICK J. KENNEDY, *The Spectacle of U.S. Senate Campaigns* (Princeton University Press, 1999).

JOHN KESSEL, *Presidential Campaign Politics*, 4th ed. (Brooks Cole, 1992).

JONATHAN S. KRASNO, *Challengers, Competition, and Reelection: Comparing Senate and House Elections* (Yale University Press, 1994).

ROBERT D. LOEVY, *The Flawed Path to the Presidency, 1992: Unfairness and Inequality in the Presidential Selection Process* (State University of New York Press, 1994).

DAVID LUBLIN, *The Paradox of Representation: Racial Gerrymandering and Minority Interests in Congress* (Princeton University Press, 1997).

DAVID B. MAGLEBY AND CANDICE J. NELSON, *The Money Chase: Congressional Campaign Finance Reform* (Brookings Institution, 1990).

NELSON W. POLSBY AND AARON B. WILDAVSKY, *Presidential Elections: Contemporary Strategies of American Politics*, 9th ed. (Chatham House, 1995).

GERALD M. POMPER ET AL., *The Election of 1992* (Chatham House, 1993).

SAMUEL L. POPKIN, *The Reasoning Voter: Communication and Persuasion in Presidential Campaigns* (University of Chicago Press, 1991).

FRANK J. SORAUF, *Inside Campaign Finance: Myths and Realities* (Yale University Press, 1992).

JAMES A. THURBER AND CANDICE J. NELSON, EDS., *Campaign Warriors: Political Consultants in Elections* (Brookings Institution Press, 2000).

JAMES A. THURBER AND CANDICE J. NELSON, EDS., *Campaigns and Elections American Style* (Westview Press, 1995).

STEPHEN J. WAYNE, *The Road to the White House, 2000: The Politics of Presidential Elections* (St. Martin's Press, 2000).

See also *Public Opinion Quarterly, American Journal of Politics,* and *American Political Science Review.*

10

THE MEDIA AND AMERICAN POLITICS

E

LECTION NIGHT, NOVEMBER 7, 2000, SAW THE TELEVISION NETWORKS PROJECT AL GORE AS THE WINNER IN FLORIDA AT 7:50 P.M. (EASTERN STANDARD TIME), ONLY TO have that projection withdrawn. At 2:16 A.M. (Eastern Standard Time), Fox News projected George W. Bush as winning Florida and the presidency. Within minutes of Fox calling Florida for Bush, the other networks followed. The reality was that Florida was too close to call, and no network should have called the race. In the days and weeks after the election, the Voter News Service, which conducts exit polls for the broadcast networks and some newspapers, admitted that its Florida sample was flawed, that it underestimated the Florida absentee vote, and that it relied on incomplete actual vote totals.[1] The mistaken projections by the networks were embarrassing. Tom Brokaw of NBC said, "That's not 'an egg' on our faces; that's 'an omelette.'"[2]

Projecting Gore as having carried Florida before the polls had closed in western Florida prompted Republicans to charge that the networks had depressed turnout in this more Republican part of the state. Since the 1980 election, the networks generally followed the practice of not calling a state before the polls close in that state, and the embarrassment of the 2000 election night will likely reinforce that practice in the future.

Executives at Fox News, the first to call Florida for Bush, were on the defensive not only for their mistaken call, but because Governor Bush's cousin John Ellis was in charge of the analysts that called the state, placing him in a clear conflict of interest. Also troubling were reports that Mr. Ellis was on the phone with both Governor George W. Bush and Governor Jeb Bush throughout the evening, presumably sharing exit poll data with his cousins.

Election night projections were not the only media controversy in the 2000 elections. Republicans charged a clear media bias in favor of Democrats, especially Al Gore. Republican Representative Billy Tauzin, who chairs the House Commerce Subcommittee on Telecommunications, believed that election night coverage was biased toward Gore and suggested that networks were reluctant to call states for Bush in hopes that voters for Bush would be discouraged and not vote.[3]

The public had a different view of media bias in coverage of the 2000 presidential election; 65 percent said the media were fair in their treatment of Bush, while 74 percent gave the same response for Gore. Democrats and Republicans had similar views of fairness of the media toward Gore, but Republicans were far less likely than Democrats to say the media were fair toward Bush (48 percent for Republicans

CHAPTER MEDIA

POLITICS ONLINE
How to Be Your Own
News Filter
www.prenhall.com/burns

compared to 75 percent for Democrats). Democrats thought journalists favored Bush and Gore in roughly the same proportions, while Republicans overwhelmingly thought reporters favored Gore.[4]

Media coverage of the 2000 election and its aftermath in Florida demonstrated the public's tremendous appetite for instant news and analysis. Americans spend on average an hour a day consuming news. As people grow older, they devote even more time to the news.[5] Despite the fact that Americans have many news sources to choose from, people are quick to criticize the media. James Fallows, a journalist himself, begins his book on the media by saying: "Americans have never been truly fond of their press. Through the last decade, however, their disdain for the media establishment has reached new levels. Americans believe that the news media have become too arrogant, cynical, scandal-minded, and destructive."[6]

How often have you or your friends blamed the media for being biased, criticized the frenzy that surrounds a particular story, or denounced the "if it bleeds it leads" mentality of nightly television news? Yet the content and style of news coverage is driven by market research in which viewers and readers are asked what they want to see reported and how they want it presented. Advertising revenue is closely linked to the number of readers or viewers a media outlet has.

Media bashing has become something of a national pastime. People often blame the media for many of our ills—for increasing tension between the races, biased attacks upon public officials, sleaze and sensationalism—and for being more interested in making money than in conveying information. Many in the media even agree with these charges.[7] But complaints about the media may simply be a case of criticizing the messenger in order to avoid dealing with the message. Comments like, "It is the media's fault that we have lost our social values," or "The media's preoccupation with the private lives of politicians turns Americans off to politics," are overly broad assertions. Americans tend to blame far more problems on the media than they deserve.

THE INFLUENCE OF THE MEDIA ON POLITICS

The media, in particular the print media, have been called "the other government," "the fourth estate," and "the fourth branch of government."[8] Evidence that the media influence our culture and politics is plentiful. Before we can examine that influence, however, we must define some terms. The **mass media**—that is, newspapers and magazines, radio, television (broadcast, cable, and satellite), films, recordings, books, and electronic communication—are the means of communication that reach the mass public.[9] The **news media** are that part of the mass media that emphasizes the news, although the distinctions between entertainment and news are sometimes blurred. News programs often have entertainment value, and entertainment programs often convey the news. Programs in this latter category include TV newsmagazines such as *60 Minutes, 20/20, Dateline,* and talk shows with hosts like Larry King, Oprah Winfrey, Chris Matthews, and Geraldo Rivera.

By definition, the mass media disseminate messages to a large and often heterogeneous audience. Because they must have broad appeal, their messages are often simplified, stereotyped, and predictable. The mass media are big business and make money by appealing to large numbers of people. But do large audiences equal political clout? Two factors are important in answering this question: the media's pervasiveness and their role as a linking mechanism between politicians and government officials and the public.

Where do Americans get their news? Until 1960 most people got their news from newspapers. Today they rely primarily on television, although many people use several sources. Whenever there is a crisis—say the capture of Elian Gonzalez by immigration officials, or the impeachment of President Bill Clinton—or a major news event, such as the Florida presidential election recount controversy, many people are glued to their TV sets.

mass media
Means of communication that reach the mass public. The mass media include newspapers and magazines, radio, television (broadcast, cable, and satellite), films, recordings, books, and electronic communication.

news media
That part of the mass media that emphasizes the news.

November 1999, Elian Gonzales, his mother, and 11 others fled Cuba. All but Elian and two others died at sea. Controversy ensued about whether he should stay with his extended family in the U. S. or be returned to Cuba with his father. For days on end, audiences all over the world were watching the dramatic story of young Elian Gonzalez and his family unfold. Despite near-riots in Miami and international wrangling between Cuba and the United States, the boy was eventually allowed to return to Cuba with his father.

Today the Internet is becoming an increasingly important source of news for Americans, taking its place alongside print, radio, and television. The number of Americans going online for news is growing dramatically and promises to become even more important as candidates and issue advocates pay increasing attention to the Web as a way to get their messages to the voting public.[10]

The Pervasiveness of Television

Perhaps more than any other invention, television has changed the character of American politics. The average American watches 4.3 hours per day, and most homes have at least two sets.[11] While television is primarily an entertainment medium, most Americans use it for news as well. Most Americans watch some kind of television news network on a daily basis. Television provides instant news from around the country and the globe, permitting citizens and leaders alike to observe, firsthand, a refugee crisis in Indonesia or a hostage situation in Sierra Leone. This instant coverage increases the pressure on world leaders to respond quickly to crises, permits terrorists to gain widespread coverage of their actions, and elevates the role played by the president in both domestic and international politics.

Perhaps the single biggest change in American electoral politics in the last half century is that most voters now rely on television commercials for information about candidates and issues. Although candidate debates and speeches generate news coverage, the more pervasive battleground is radio and TV advertisements. As a result, electoral campaigns now focus on image and slogans rather than on substance. Successful candidates must be able to communicate with voters through this medium. To get their message across to TV audiences, politicians increasingly communicate with citizens through "sound bites"—10-to-45-second statements for the television or radio news—and 30-second political commercials.

Interest groups advocating one position or another—health care reform, trade agreements, affirmative action—also use paid advertising on television and radio to influence voters' choices on election day. These so-called **issue ads** permit groups to spend unlimited and undisclosed amounts of money so long as they do not explicitly call for the election or defeat of a candidate. Interest groups have mounted expensive advertising campaigns on health care reform and gun legislation in an

issue ad
Commercial advertising on radio and television advocating a particular position on an issue, paid for by interest groups and often designed to influence voters' choices on election day.

effort to sway votes in Congress, and in the weeks before recent general elections they have spent millions to influence votes. In referendum elections, advertising is the most important source of information in voter decision making.[12]

For several decades the network evening news programs on CBS, NBC, and ABC captured more than 90 percent of the audience for television news at set times in the morning and early evening hours. Over the last 15 years, with the rise of cable television and the advent of the Internet, prime-time viewership on the broadcast networks has declined to about 50 percent. The growth of around-the-clock cable news and information shows is one of the most important developments in recent years. More than half of the public are regular viewers of CNN, CNBC, MSNBC, or Fox News; and more than three in four regularly watch network prime-time news shows.[13]

Recent technological advances have created intense competition for advertising revenues and contributed to sweeping changes in the manner in which news is transmitted and received. Satellites, cable television, computers, and videocassette recorders (VCRs) make vast amounts of political information available 24 hours a day. These technologies eliminate the obstacles of time and distance and increase the volume of information that can be stored, retrieved, and viewed.

The Persistence of Radio

Television and the newer media have not displaced radio. On the contrary, radio continues to reach more American households than does television. Only one household in a hundred does not have a radio, compared with four in a hundred without a TV. Nine out of ten Americans listen to the radio every day.[14] Cars and radios seem to go together.

Americans get more than "the facts" from radio. They also get analysis and opinion from their favorite commentators and talk show hosts like conservatives Rush Limbaugh, Alan Keyes, Michael Reagan, and G. Gordon Liddy, or liberals like Mary Mason, Tom Leykis, or Mario Cuomo. These hosts have their own home pages on the World Wide Web and provide around-the-clock opinion on politics. Talk radio has been more closely identified with conservatives. Former House Speaker Newt Gingrich and other Republicans in the U.S. House of Representatives made widespread use of it. The popularity of the talk-show format has been applied as well to television. John McCain was a constant guest on many talk shows, as were Al Gore and George W. Bush during the election campaigns.

The Continuing Importance of Newspapers

Despite vigorous competition from the broadcast media, Americans still read newspapers. Daily newspaper circulation been declining to about 56 million nationwide—or about one copy for every four people—for the past 20 years.[15] Another indication of the print media's pervasiveness is the rise of nationwide newspapers. *The Wall Street Journal*, with a circulation of more than 1.7 million, has long acted as a national newspaper specializing in business and finance. *The Wall Street Journal* also boasts more than 400,000 subscribers to its online newspaper.[16] Other national newspapers with more general interests have also emerged. *USA Today*, created in 1982 by the Gannett Corporation, now has a circulation of more than 1.6 million. In addition, *The New York Times* has a national edition that is read by more than 1 million people. The circulation figures for newspapers mask a troubling decline in readership among younger persons. There is about a 30 percentage point differential in readership between the young and the old, with younger persons much less likely to read newspapers.[17] Unless this difference can be reversed or newspapers find a way to reinvent themselves through something like the Internet, they will decline in importance as their readers die off.

The World Wide Web

We have only begun to see the potential effect of the Internet on American politics. From its humble beginnings as a Pentagon research project in the 1970s, the Web has blossomed into an international phenomenon. There are now more than 1 billion documents on the Web,[18] and more than 15 million unique domains registered worldwide, including one for this book (**http://www.prenhall.com/burns**). The Web opens up resources for citizens in dramatic ways. One study found that nearly half of Americans go online to search for news on a particular topic; somewhat smaller proportions go online for updates on stock quotes and sports scores. Fewer people use the Internet as their primary source of news—29 percent.[19]

One application in electoral politics is candidate home pages where voters can learn about those seeking office or about ballot referenda. A second application of the Web is to mobilize citizens behind a candidate or cause. Minnesota Governor Jesse Ventura and presidential primary contender John McCain effectively used the Internet to get the word out to supporters about campaign events. The Internet is an inexpensive and efficient way to communicate with volunteers and will become an even larger component of campaigns in the future. Users of the Internet can also interact with other people or politicians about politics through electronic mail and chat rooms.

A third way the Internet is changing American politics is in fund raising. McCain's primary campaign demonstrated the usefulness of the Internet to raise contributions, collecting twice as much money over the Internet as Gore and Bush.[20] Once a candidate gains public recognition, as McCain did after his victory in the New Hampshire primary, it is possible to raise money quickly and inexpensively via the Internet.

Extensive use of computers by young children has left them vulnerable to sexual predators and commercial frauds, opening the issue of whether government regulation is needed. Parental supervision remains the best protection.

THE CHANGING ROLE OF AMERICAN NEWS MEDIA

Political Mouthpiece

At the time of the ratification of the Constitution, newspapers consisted of a single sheet, often printed irregularly by store owners to hawk their services or goods. Newspapers rarely lasted more than a year, due to delinquent subscribers and high costs.[21] But the framers understood the important role the press should play as a watchdog of politicians and government, and they included freedom of the press in the Bill of Rights.

The new nation's political leaders, such as Alexander Hamilton and Thomas Jefferson, recognized the need to keep voters informed. Political party organizations as we know them did not exist, but the active role of the press in supporting the Revolution had fostered a growing awareness of the political potential of newspapers. Hamilton recruited staunch Federalist John Fenno to edit and publish a newspaper in the new national capital of Philadelphia. Jefferson responded by attracting Philip Freneau, a talented writer and editor and a loyal Republican, to do the same for the Republicans. (Jefferson's Republicans later became the Democratic party.) The two papers became the nucleus of competing partisan newspaper networks throughout the nation.

Although the two newspapers competed in Philadelphia only several years, their lasting significance was as a model for future partisan newspapers. Federalist and Republican editors relied on each other for government news and editorials. The free mailing of newspapers granted by the U.S. Post Office allowed broader coverage.

The early American press served as a mouthpiece for political leaders. Its close connection with politicians and political parties offered the opportunity for financial stability, but at the cost of journalistic independence.

MEDIA IN JAPAN AND THE UNITED STATES: WATCHDOG OR LAPDOG?

A comparison of the media in Japan and the United States illustrates the strengths and weaknesses of both. In Japan the media are independently owned but work closely with one another in alliances, whereas in the United States media con-

glomerates include diverse businesses like General Electric or Disney. Compare this list of the six largest media outlets in Japan and the United States; for U.S. firms we also provide the business that owns the media outlet.

Japan*	United States
Asahi (newspaper)	General Electric (owns NBC and CNBC and, in partnership with Microsoft, MSNBC)
Yomiuri (newspaper)	
Tokyo Broadcasting	Dun and Bradstreet (owns *The Wall Street Journal*)
Shueisha (publishing house)	Westinghouse (owns CBS)
Nihon Television Broadcasting	Gannett (owns *USA Today*)
Nihon Keizai Newspaper	Walt Disney (owns ABC)
	Time Warner (owns TBS, CNN, TNT)

Although media firms are owned separately in Japan, this arrangement does not foster greater media independence, nor are the media in Japan more challenging and investigative than U.S. media. Rather, Japanese reporters are organized into reporter clubs that are affiliated with a specific government news source, and they gain all their information through that source. Japanese reporters know more about the inner workings of politics in their country than most investigative reporters in the United States know about the inner workings of our government. Yet Japanese reporters rarely print what they know, often reporting only the offi-

cial government line. As a result, whatever stories are printed are the same in each of Japan's newspapers. For these reasons, the Japanese media have earned a reputation for being a lapdog of the government rather than a watchdog. Despite the trend toward large corporations owning the major news providers in the United States, strong support for journalistic independence remains, and news reporting is driven by competition among news media to get the story.

*D. Eleanor Westney, "Mass Media as Business Organizations: A U.S.–Japanese Comparison," in *Media and Politics in Japan*, ed. Susan J. Pharr and Ellis S. Krauss (University of Hawaii Press, 1996), pp. 47–88.

Financial Independence

The Jacksonian era of the 1820s and 1830s was characterized by expansion of the right to vote to all white adult males through the elimination of property qualifications for voting. The press began to shift its appeal away from elite readers and toward large masses of less well educated and less politically interested readers. This popularization of the newspapers was reinforced by rising literacy rates that supported greater circulation for them. These two forces—increased political participation by the common people and the rise of literacy among Americans—began to alter the relationship between politicians and the press.

Some newspaper publishers began to experiment with a new way to finance their newspapers. They charged a penny a paper, paid on delivery, instead of the traditional annual subscription fee of $8 to $10, which was beyond the ability of most readers to pay. The "penny press," as it was called, expanded circulation and put more emphasis on advertising, enabling newspapers to become financially independent of the political parties.

The changing finances of newspapers also affected the definition of news. Before the penny press, all news was political—speeches, documents, editorials—directed at politically interested readers. The penny press reshaped the definition of news as it sought to appeal to less politically aware readers with human interest stories and reports on sports, crime, public trials, and social activities.

"Objective Journalism"

By the early decades of the twentieth century, many journalists began to argue that the press should be independent of the political parties. *New York Tribune* editor Whitelaw Reid eloquently expressed this sentiment: "Independent journalism! That is the watchword of the future in the profession. An end of concealments because it would hurt the party; an end of one-sided expositions . . . an end of assaults that are not believed fully just but must be made because the exigency of party warfare demands them."[22]

Journalists began to view their work as a profession and established professional associations with journals and codes of ethics. This professionalization of journalism reinforced the notion that journalists should be independent of partisan politics. Further strengthening the trend toward objectivity was the rise of the wire services, which were deliberately politically neutral to attract more customers.

The Impact of Broadcasting

Radio and television changed the media's role in politics by nationalizing and personalizing the news. Radio networks were created in the 1920s. Radio carried political speeches, campaign advertising, and coverage of political events such as national party conventions.[23] Radio provided a means to bypass the screening of editors and reporters, since politicians could speak directly to listeners. It also contributed to increased interest in national and international news, since activities outside a listener's local area could be heard as if one were actually there.

President Franklin Roosevelt used radio with a new effectiveness. Before 1933 most radio addresses were formal orations, but Roosevelt spoke to his audience on a personal level that showed how radio could be used as a one-to-one conversation. Roosevelt's "fireside chats" established a standard for presidential use of the broadcast media still followed today. When Roosevelt began speaking over the microphone, he would visualize the average citizen in front of him. "His face would smile and light up as though he were actually sitting on the front porch or in the parlor with them."[24]

Franklin D. Roosevelt was the first president to recognize the effectiveness of radio to reach the public. His fireside chats were the model for later presidents.

Television added a visual dimension, which contributed to rising audience interest in national events. By 1963 the then two largest networks expanded their evening news programs from 15 to 30 minutes. Today news broadcasting has expanded to the point where many local stations provide 90 minutes of local news every evening as well as a half-hour in the morning and at noon. Programs such as *60 Minutes*, *20/20*, and other news magazine shows are among the most popular in the prime-time evening hours.

The rise of cable television brought 24-hour news coverage. During the Clinton impeachment hearings and the 2000 Florida ballot-counting controversy, American cable news was watched at home and around the world for its instantaneous coverage. Other stations now provide coverage of Congress, the courts, and state and local governments.

Investigatory Journalism

Today news reporters do more than convey the news. They investigate it, and their investigations often have political consequences. Notable examples of influential investigatory reporters include Seymour Hersh of *The New York Times*, who exposed *The Pentagon Papers* on how the United States became involved in the Vietnam War; Robert Woodward and Carl Bernstein of *The Washington Post*, who played an important role in uncovering the Watergate conspiracy; Nina Totenberg of National Public Radio, whose reporting on sexual harassment charges against Clarence Thomas helped force the Senate Judiciary Committee to extend the hearings on his confirmation to the U.S. Supreme Court; and Michael Isikoff of *Newsweek*, who broke the story of Bill Clinton's alleged perjury involving sexual relations with Monica Lewinsky.

Media Conglomerates

Newspapers and television are big business. What happens if a few people corner the market on newspapers and television stations? Is the free flow of information to the public endangered? Is too much power to influence public opinion in the hands of too few people?

As in other sectors of the economy, media companies have merged with others and created large conglomerates. Radio networks and newspapers were among the first to purchase television stations when television was in its infancy. These mergers established cross-ownership patterns that persist in media ownership today. The Gannett Corporation, for example, owns 87 daily newspapers and 21 television stations and cable television systems—assets that provide news coverage to nearly 17 percent of the United States.[25] *The Chicago Tribune* substantially expanded its reach of newspapers and television stations in 2000 when it paid $6 billion for *Times/Mirror*, publisher of the *Los Angeles Times* and 10 other newspapers, 22 TV stations, 4 radio stations, and a growing online business.[26] The Federal Communications Commission (FCC) reinforced the trend toward media conglomeration by permitting one owner to control up to 30 AM and 30 FM radio stations. Previously, ownership was less concentrated, in part because the government was granting licenses to a finite number of stations.

Australian-born Rupert Murdoch owns dozens of U.S. television stations, magazines, publishing organizations, and movie studios.

Another concern has been the gobbling up of American communication assets by large corporations and foreign interests. Local firms used to own the local newspapers, radio, and television stations. Today large conglomerates, many of them foreign, have acquired ownership of many newspapers and broadcasting stations. The merger of the Disney organization with ABC/Capital Cities, approved early in 1996, cost Disney $19 billion but gave it control not only of the ABC television network but also ESPN, the cable sports station. Months later, the Westinghouse Company bought the CBS television network for $7.5 billion,[27] and CBS merged with Viacom in May 2000 at a cost estimated at $50 billion. Time Warner purchased Turner Broadcasting System in late 1996 for reportedly just under $7 billion,[28] and it, in turn, was purchased by America-OnLine (AOL) for $165 billion.[29] The foremost example of foreign involvement in our news media is Australian Rupert Murdoch, founder of the Fox network, who owns 22 television stations in the United States, the Family Channel, and 20th-Century Fox. Murdoch also owns HarperCollins and *TV Guide* magazine, which has the largest magazine circulation in America.

Media conglomerates with large financial resources now dominate the media business and have contributed to the control of news. Are a few media conglomerates likely to provide sufficient competition of ideas to support a democratic system?[30] And without them, can local populations scattered around the country, depending only on local media, find out what is happening in the nation's capital? Why not have government-owned media carry out educational and information functions, as they do in Great Britain and France?[31] The answer is that Americans continue to put great stock in the independence of the press and the news media and find centralized, government-owned media unacceptable.

When reporting national news, local outlets depend heavily on news that is gathered, edited, and distributed by national organizations like United Press International and Associated Press. As a result, some people contend that information these days is more diluted, homogenized, and moderated than it would be if the newspapers and broadcast stations were locally owned and the news was gathered and edited locally.[32]

Regulation of the Media

Regulation of the broadcast media has existed in some form since its inception. Because of the limited number of television and radio frequencies, government has overseen matters like licensing, financing, and even content. One such regulation required "fairness" in news programming.[33] As written into law and interpreted by the Federal Communications Commission, the **fairness doctrine** imposed an obligation on radio and television license holders to ensure that differing viewpoints were presented about controversial issues or persons. With the advent of cable television and the Reagan administration's antiregulatory campaign, much of the fairness doctrine was repealed in 1987 and the final remnants of it were repealed in 2000. Will broadcasters provide fair and balanced news coverage in the absence of regulation? Those who pushed for repeal think so.[34]

THE NEW MEDIATOR IN AMERICAN POLITICS

The pervasiveness of newspapers, magazines, radio, television, and the Web does not prove their political influence. But it does place those who determine what we read, hear, and see in a position to be influential because they can reach so much of the American public so quickly. With a large population scattered over a continent, both the reach and the speed of the modern media elevate the importance of those in charge of it.

Political parties and interest groups have long been political mediators that help organize the world of politics for the average citizen. Their role is less important today because the media now serve that function and political parties have largely lost control over the nominating process (see Chapters 7 and 9). Greater attention is

fairness doctrine
Doctrine interpreted by the Federal Communications Commission that imposed on radio and television licensees an obligation to ensure that different viewpoints were presented about controversial issues or persons; repealed in 1987.

now given to judging candidates not so much in terms of party affiliation and platform but in terms of character and competence. The press, not the parties, perform this evaluative function.

The news media have also taken over the role of "speaking for the people." Journalists report what "the people" want and think, and then they tell the people what politicians and policy makers are doing about it. Politicians realize how dependent they are on the media for getting their message out to voters, and they also know a hostile press can hurt them. Clearly, today's politicians have to spend much of their time cultivating the press.

The amount of television news devoted to politics has been declining and now constitutes less than one minute per thirty-minute broadcast. A major effort to get local television stations to devote a few minutes to candidate debate in their nightly local news ended up with stations averaging 45 seconds a night, or as one observer put it, just enough time for to "let candidates clear their throats."[35] In large urban areas it is rare for viewers to see stories about their member of Congress, in part because there are several congressional districts in that media market. Newspapers do a better job of covering politics, in part because they devote more attention to it. More broadly, the mediating role played by the media is limited by the declining political news content of broadcast media.

The Media and Public Opinion

Scholars, journalists, politicians, and political pundits have long debated the power of the media over public opinion. Do journalists and editors really shape opinions? Do they alter people's behavior? Can they even affect our core values? For a long time, analysts tended to play down the influence wielded by the media in American politics as compared with the influence wielded by political leaders. The impact of Franklin D. Roosevelt's fireside chats came to symbolize the power of the politician against that of the news editor. Roosevelt spoke directly to his listeners over the radio in a way and at a time of his own choosing, and no network official was able to block or influence that direct connection. President John Kennedy's use of the televised press conference represented a similar direct contact with the public. President Ronald Reagan was nicknamed the "Great Communicator" because of his ability to talk persuasively and often passionately about public policy issues with the people through television.

Broadcasters and journalists are now so important to the political process that elected officials and politicians spend considerable time trying to learn how to use them. Presidential events and "photo opportunities" are planned with the evening news and its format in mind.[36] Members of Congress use Capitol Hill recording studios to tape messages for local television and radio stations. White House press briefings are frequently included in the evening news. How government officials use the press, how the press uses government officials, and to what extent the press and television can and should be regulated are critical questions.

Factors That Limit Media Influence on Public Opinion

People are not just empty vessels into which politicians and journalists pour information and ideas. How people interpret political messages depends on a variety of factors: political socialization, selectivity, needs, and the individual's ability to recall and comprehend the message.

POLITICAL SOCIALIZATION   Although we would like to believe we consume the news with an open mind, the reality is that we employ a set of *filters*, screens that help us interpret and integrate information. When we watch television or read newspapers, magazines, and books, we bring with us values and attitudes that have been shaped by family, peers, school, and the groups to which we belong.[37] We develop our political attitudes, values, and beliefs through an education process that social scientists call **political socialization**. (See Chapters 4 and 8 for more detail on this

"Hey, do you want to be on the news tonight or not? This is a sound bite, not the Gettysburgh Address. Just say what you have to say, Senator, and get the hell off."

political socialization
The process by which we develop our political attitudes, values, and beliefs.

Should the government protect children from excessive violence and sex on TV?

The media are a powerful socializing agent. Many agree that there is too much violence and sex on television. Both candidates in the 2000 presidential race stressed the importance of taking action against the entertainment industry if it persists in marketing adult materials to children. The candidates did not specify what actions they would take, but presumably they would include legislation and prosecution.

The V-chip is a computer chip that can be installed in a television set to permit parents to restrict access to certain television programs. Some favor this type of system as a means of informing parents of the content of programs and permitting them to limit access to inappropriate programs. Others oppose such ratings systems and say the V-chip is a form of censorship. Shouldn't parents enforce their own standards by monitoring what their children watch? Will the V-chip exert any pressure on the television industry to clean up its act?

selective exposure

The process by which individuals screen out those messages that do not conform to their own biases.

selective perception

The process by which individuals perceive what they want to in media messages and disregard the rest.

---

process.) The media, particularly television, may influence our values and attitudes, but they are not as important as family in the formation of our political attitudes.[38] Moreover, face-to-face contacts with friends and business associates (*peer pressure*) often have far more impact than the impersonal television or newspaper. Strong identification with a party also acts as a powerful filter.[39] A conservative Republican from Arizona might watch the "liberal Eastern networks" night after night and year after year and complain about their biased news coverage while sticking to her own opinions. A liberal from New York will often complain about right-wing talk radio, even if he listens to it every night on the way home from work.

SELECTIVITY   People practice **selective exposure**—screening out those messages that do not conform to their own biases. They subscribe to newspapers or magazines that support their views. People also practice **selective perception**—perceiving what they want to in media messages and disregarding the rest.[40] One dramatic example was the differing reactions of Democrats and Republicans to reports of President Clinton's sexual relationship with Monica Lewinsky, a former White House intern, and the possibility that he encouraged her to lie under oath. In the first weeks after the story broke, Republicans were four times more likely than Democrats to believe that Clinton had been sexually involved with Lewinsky.[41] More than two-thirds of Republicans and Democrats agreed that Clinton committed perjury before the grand jury, but they had dramatically different opinions on whether Clinton should remain in office. Just over one-third of Republicans wanted Clinton to remain in office, while 63 percent of Independents and 87 percent of Democrats felt that Clinton should continue as president.[42] When Attorney General Janet Reno directed federal marshals and immigration authorities to use force to take Elian Gonzalez from his Miami relatives and turn him over to his father, Republicans talked about storm trooper tactics while Democrats talked about reuniting a child with his father.

NEEDS   People read newspapers, listen to the radio, or watch television for very different reasons—sometimes because they are bored, tired, or have nothing better to do, sometimes because they want information.[43] People who seek information and cultivate an interest in politics are affected by what they read and see differently from those who use media primarily for entertainment.[44] For those seeking entertainment, gossip about politicians' peccadilloes is more important than those politicians' opinions or votes. Members of the broader audience are also more likely to follow news that directly affects their lives, such as interest rate changes or the price of gasoline.[45]

RECALL AND COMPREHENSION   Still another limitation of media influence on public opinion is the extent to which the audience can recall the stories or comprehend their importance. Candidates and officials send out vast amounts of information designed to influence what people think and do, especially how they vote, but people forget or fail to comprehend much of it.[46] The fragmentary and rapid mode of presentation of television news contributes to the problem.

Given the abundance of information available about politics and government, it is not surprising that most people pick and choose which media source—television, radio, newspapers, cable, the Internet—they pay attention to and which news stories they consider important.[47] The best predictor of retention of news stories is political interest. People tend to fit today's news stories into their general assumptions or beliefs about government, politicians, or the media itself.

AUDIENCE FRAGMENTATION   With the growth of cable television and new media like the Internet, the influence of any one media source is weakened. Because people are scattered across a larger number of press outlets, and these outlets cover politics in varied ways, the impact of the press will be more disparate.

Are the Media Biased?

Americans tend to blame the media for lots of things. Conservatives complain "the media are too liberal." Speaking of the media, radio talk show host Rush Limbaugh argues, "They all just happen to believe the same way. . . . They are part of the same culture as Bill Clinton."[48] Liberals contend the mainstream press is controlled by the ruling class, and they charge that government propaganda distorts the facts. Conservatives say the press is too liberal in its selection of news covered and the interpretation of events. Liberals point to newspaper endorsements of Republican presidential candidates to support their claim that newspapers are biased toward conservative policies and candidates.

Newspapers, magazines, and television stations are business corporations concerned about profits. This means they work to boost circulation and ratings and must please their advertisers, sponsors, and stockholders. Do the preferences of advertisers or corporate owners show up in news reporting? Reporters and editors pride themselves on impartial reporting of the facts.[49] Yet some liberal critics contend that the media reflect a conservative bias not only in what they report but also in what they choose to ignore. Political scientist Michael Parenti states that journalists "rarely doubt their own objectivity even as they faithfully echo the established political vocabularies and the prevailing politico-economic orthodoxy."[50]

Newspapers and television management go to some lengths to insulate reporters from their advertising and business operations, in part to reduce criticism about favorable treatment of large advertisers or the corporate owners. When the management of *The Los Angeles Times* attempted to foster closer relations between the business and news divisions, it was criticized for insensitivity to this concern.[51] Another internal check on media bias is the fact that news coverage involves many reporters and a host of editors, all of whom have input into what is covered and how it is presented.

Some commentators have suggested that a possible bias flows from the fact that reporters and editors become too friendly with those they write about. David Broder of *The Washington Post* voices his concern about the confusion of roles by journalists who have served in government. According to Broder, a line should divide objective journalism from partisan politics, but many in the print and television media have crossed this line. Broder opposes the idea of journalists' becoming government officials and vice versa.[52] Others argue that journalists with previous government service have close working relationships with politicians and can give us a valuable perspective on government without losing their professional neutrality.

A frequent criticism is the media's alleged political bias, whether liberal or conservative. But to whom are these critics referring? To reporters, writers, editors, producers, or owners of TV and newspapers? Do they assume a journalist's personal politics will be translated into biased reporting? And does the public think so? Journalists are usually more liberal than the population as a whole; editors tend to be a bit more conservative than their reporters are; and media owners are more conservative still. Polling data demonstrate that slightly more than half the journalists classify themselves as liberals, compared with only about one-fourth of the general public (Table 10–1).[53] Elite journalists—those who work for national news media organizations—tend to share a similar culture: cosmopolitan, urban, upper class. Their approach to the events and issues they cover is governed by their common worldview, which may be derived from their professional training.[54] The result, some contend, is that elite journalists give greater weight to the side of issues that corresponds to their own version of reality.[55]

One bias of the media that does not have a particular partisan or ideological slant is the bias toward sensationalism. Scandals of all types happen to liberals and conservatives, Republicans and Democrats. Once the province of tabloids like *National Enquirer*, stories about scandal have become commonplace in mainstream media in recent years.

Thinking It Through . . .

The movement to have a ratings system for television programs gained enough support that all major television networks except NBC proposed their own rating system similar to that used for movies, in part to avoid one legislated by Congress. The ratings indicate if the program contains violence, sex, or language that might be objectionable.

Jack Valenti, president of the Motion Picture Association of America, argues that these ratings help parents make decisions. Valenti and others in the television industry say that to go further than their proposal would violate First Amendment rights.

The opposition says these ratings are insufficient because they do not give enough information about the programs, such as the degree of violence or the type of sexual material. Most parent and family groups want a more detailed system of ratings and description of program content.

Those who oppose such ratings systems contend that, once started, they can become a form of censorship. Moreover, they assert there is a lot of subjectivity in evaluating programs. What some may see as too violent or sexually explicit, others may not find objectionable. Then there is the added cost to equip televisions with V-chips and to employ people to rate the programs. Ultimately it will be advertisers who pay the costs of the ratings and consumers who pay for the V-chip.

The counterargument is that children learn what is acceptable behavior from the media, especially television. Critics point to an increasing incidence of violent and sexually explicit actions and language on TV. They contend the industry will not regulate itself. The V-chip, when combined with content disclosure and a detailed ratings system, would give parents control over this powerful socializing force.

You Decide . . .

How should the media report sex scandals?

Early in the 1992 presidential campaign, Bill Clinton's press coverage turned negative as reports circulated in the *Star*, a supermarket tabloid, that he and Gennifer Flowers, a former Arkansas state employee, had had a twelve-year-long extramarital affair. Clinton, with Mrs. Clinton by his side, denied the Flowers account in an interview on *60 Minutes*, a CBS-TV news program, on Superbowl Sunday. Because Flowers had been paid for her story by the *Star*, some people discounted the story. Others were doubtful that tabloid papers like the *Star* ever print anything close to the truth. Despite the existence of tapes that appeared to confirm the Flowers account, the press essentially dropped the story.

After winning the presidency, Clinton was dogged by a series of accusations of unwanted sexual advances toward Paula Jones and Kathleen Willey and of a consensual affair with Monica Lewinsky. In a transcript of his deposition in the Jones sexual harassment suit, Clinton admitted having an affair with Gennifer Flowers. This raised anew questions of how the media had reported the original accusations. Did the press handle those stories properly?

TABLE 10–1 The Politics of Journalists and the Public

	Washington-Based Reporters	Newspaper Editors (National)	Public
Party Identification			
Democrat	50%	31%	34%
Republican	4	14	28
Independent	37	39	25
Other	9	7	8
Self-Described Ideology			
Liberal	61	32	20
Moderate	30	35	34
Conservative	9	25	27

SOURCE: The Roper Center, *The Public Perspective*, October/November 1996, p. 8, based on a Media Studies Center/Roper Center survey of 1,200 persons conducted in September 1995.

Newspapers and television news often set a tone of dissatisfaction with the performance of the national government and cynicism about politics and politicians. A critical tone may be an inevitable element of the mindset of the press, but to whose benefit does that critical tone work? The media are accused of having an anti-incumbent bias, a generational bias, and a bias fostering continuing crises.[56] The question is not whether the press is biased, but whether a press bias—whatever the direction—seeps into the content of the news. The answer to that question is still not settled.

Public Opinion

The media shape public perceptions and knowledge. Television, with all its concreteness and drama, has an emotional impact that print cannot hope to match.[57] Television cuts across age groups, educational levels, social classes, and races. Newspapers provide more detail about the news and often contain contrasting points of view, at least on the editorial pages, that help inform the public. Two important influences of print and broadcast media are *agenda setting* and *issue framing*.

AGENDA SETTING   By calling public attention to certain issues, the media help to determine what topics will become the subject of public debate and legislation.[58] However, the agenda-setting function of the media is not uniformly pervasive. The audience and the nature of the issue limit it.[59]

According to former Vice-President Walter Mondale, "If I had to give up . . . the opportunity to get on the evening news or the veto power, . . . I'd throw the veto power away. [Television news] is the President's most indispensable power."[60] Ronald Reagan, more than any president before him, effectively used the media to set the nation's agenda. Reagan and his advisers carefully crafted the images and scenes of his presidency to fit television. Thus television became an "electronic throne."

ISSUE FRAMING   Politicians, like everybody else, try to frame issues to win arguments, and they try to influence the "spin" the media will give to their actions or issues. Examples abound. Those who opposed U.S. intervention in Bosnia tried to portray such action as another Vietnam. Opponents of permanent normal trade relations with China framed it as a human rights travesty. When Bill Clinton wanted to forestall a Republican tax cut, he framed the use of the budget surplus to rescue Social Security. Those who favor abortion define the issue as one of freedom of choice; those who oppose it define it as murder. In referendum campaigns, the side that wins the battle of interpreting what the referendum is about wins the election.[61]

THE MEDIA AND ELECTIONS

News coverage of campaigns and elections is greatest in presidential contests, decreases in statewide races for governor or senator, and decreases still further for other races. Generally, the more news attention given the campaign, the less likely voters are to be swayed by any one source. Hence, news coverage is likely to be more important in a city council contest than in an election for president or the Senate. In most city elections there are only one or two sources of information about what candidates say and stand for; for statewide and national contests, there are multiple sources.

Diversification of the news media also lessens the ability of any one medium to dominate politics. Newspaper publishers who were once seen as very important in state and local politics know that today politicians and their media advisers can communicate their message through television, radio, direct mail, videocassettes, the Internet, and cable television. Hence, there is now more competition among the various media, and politicians and candidates can get their message out regardless of what the editor of the state's largest newspaper may think.

How the Media Affect Elections

Candidates see the media as the means to communicate their message and win votes. The extensive use of television has made being "good on television" much more important, fostered a growth industry in political consulting, and made visibility the watchword in politics.

CHOICE OF CANDIDATES   Television greatly affects the public's idea of what traits are important in a candidate. A hundred years ago, successful candidates needed a strong pair of lungs; today it is a telegenic appearance, a pleasing voice, and no obvious physical impairments. Back in the 1930s, the press chose not to show Franklin Roosevelt in his wheelchair or using braces, whereas today the country knows every intimate detail of the president's health. The importance of the public's perception of these traits is evident in the ridicule often directed at candidates. In 2000, George W. Bush was lampooned for his inability to answer reporters' questions on foreign affairs, and Al Gore was the subject of jokes for following a consultant's advice to bring out the Alpha male side of his personality.

Although the media insist they pay attention to all candidates who have a chance to win, they also influence who gets such a chance. Consequently, candidates have to come up with creative ways to attract media attention. Paul Wellstone in his first Minnesota Senate campaign said in his advertisements that he did not have much money to pay for ads, so he would have to talk fast to cram what he had to say into fewer commercials. His witty commercial became a news event itself—it got Wellstone additional coverage, and Wellstone won.

In the 2000 elections, three U.S. Senate candidates in states bordering Canada organized bus trips to Canada for people to purchase prescription drugs at Canadian prices, which were sharply lower than in the United States. Montana Senate candidate Byron Schweitzer called his excursions "The Run for the Border" and generated substantial positive media coverage for his campaign through the tactic.[62]

CAMPAIGN EVENTS   Candidates schedule events—press conferences, interviews, "photo ops"—in settings that reinforce their verbal messages. Many events organized by campaigns fail to receive attention from reporters because of competing news stories and a sense that the events were staged primarily to generate news coverage. The absence of suspense or real news at the party presidential nominating conventions is one reason why the networks have dramatically cut back their coverage. In 1952 the average television set was tuned to the political conventions for 26 hours, or an average of more than three hours a night for the eight nights of convention coverage.[63] In 2000, in contrast, the major networks provided only one or two hours of prime-time coverage each evening. Political parties have sought, in vain, to regain audience interest by

"I'm still undecided—I like Leno's foreign policy, but Letterman makes a lot of sense on domestic issues."

Thinking It Through . . .

Some people dismiss reporting on sex scandals as prudish and unrelated to governing. Others, like Larry Sabato, a political scientist who has written on the media, disagree. Sabato says the press "didn't reveal what most of them knew then about Clinton and all the other women. If the press had done its job in '92, the country would not be facing this horrible dilemma in '98."*

The question of how to report sexual misbehavior by political candidates is unresolved. It is debatable whether such matters ought to be reported at all. Reporters appear to be looking for ways to avoid such stories. The public wants to know whether candidates meet high standards of personal conduct, but they react negatively to coverage that is too aggressive. Public reaction to the explicit details of the Starr report is instructive: 84 percent of the public wanted to know the conclusions of the investigation, but 70 percent felt that Congress should have omitted the details of the sexual encounters.**

*Larry J. Sabato, quoted in William Power, "News at Warp Speed," *National Journal*, January 31, 1998, p. 220.

**Frank Newport, "Initial Reaction Mixed on Delivery of Starr Report to Congress," Gallup Organization, September 12, 1998. See also www.gallup.com/poll_archives/980912.htm.

With the Internet, citizens now have the opportunity to interact with each other on a wide range of political topics. In this sense, the Internet is something like a town meeting, but without people leaving their homes or offices. In chat rooms on the World Wide Web, people express ideas and respond to each other's opinions. Examples of chat rooms include Abortion Chat, Democrat Chat, Environment Chat, Republican Chat, and Congress Chat. Most chat rooms offer group discussions in which anyone in the group can read and send messages, but some chat rooms also permit private messages to be sent.

As with town meetings, politicians can learn about public sentiment via the Web. They can participate in a chat room or read postings on the Internet in what is called Usenet. Reading messages posted on Usenet permits politicians to gauge public opinion and tap into particular segments of the population. But because those who use the Internet are not a representative sample of the general public, politicians should be wary not to generalize from the opinions expressed through this medium.

relying on "movie stars, entertainment routines, and professionally produced documentaries to spice up their conventions."[64]

TECHNOLOGY   Although the expense associated with media technology has contributed to the skyrocketing costs of campaigning, it also has made politics more accessible to more people. Thanks to satellites, candidates can conduct local television interviews without actually traveling to local studios. Specific voter groups can be targeted through cable television or low-power television stations that reach homogeneous neighborhoods and small towns. Videocassettes with messages from the candidates further extend the campaign's reach.[65] All serious candidates for Congress and governor in 2000 made themselves and their positions available through a home page on the World Wide Web.

Image Making

Attempts to spin the news and to portray candidates in the best possible light are not new. Presidential campaign sloganeering such as "Tippecanoe and Tyler Too" in 1840 and "Abe the Rail Splitter" in 1860 were used to convey the candidate's image. Radio, television, and the Web have expanded the ability to project images, and that expansion has in turn affected candidates' vote-getting strategies and their manner of communicating messages. Television is especially important because of the power of the visual image. But candidates recognize that their messages about issues are often ignored. The press tends to emphasize goofs and gossip or tensions among party leaders.

Media Consultants

Television has contributed to the rise of new players in campaign politics—*media consultants*, campaign professionals who provide candidates with advice and services on media relations, advertising strategy, and opinion polling.[66] For instance, a media consultant advised Al Gore on the colors and style of clothing he should wear, emphasizing earth tones and finding ways to convey his masculinity.[67]

A primary responsibility of a campaign media consultant is to present a positive image of the candidate and to reinforce negative images of the opponent. Some media consultants have been credited with propelling candidates to success. Dick Morris was seen as important to Clinton's resurgence after the 1994 congressional election defeats, until he had to resign from the campaign following a personal scandal. Republican consultants Mike Murphy and Stuart Stevens and Democratic consultants Rob Klain and Carter Eskew have acquired powerful reputations. But media consultants have also been blamed for the negativity of recent presidential campaigns.

Media consultants have taken over the role formerly played by party politicians. Before World War II, party professionals groomed candidates for office at all levels. Such leaders made their judgments about possible candidates on the basis of their chances of victory and observation of the candidates' performance under fire, decisiveness, conviction, political skill, and other leadership qualities. Party professionals advised candidates which party and interest group leaders to placate, which issues to stress, and which topics to avoid.

Today consultants coach candidates about television technique, appearance, and subject matter. Consultants report the results of *focus groups* (small sample groups of people who are asked questions about candidates and issues in a discussion setting) and *public opinion polls*, which in turn determine what the candidate says and does. Some critics allege that political consultants have become a new "political elite" who can virtually choose candidates by determining in advance which men and women have the right images, or at least images that can be restyled for the widest popularity.[68] But political consultants who specialize in media advertising and image making realize their own limitations in packaging candidates. As one media consultant put it, "It is a very hard job to turn a turkey into a movie star; you try instead to make people like the turkey."[69]

The Media and Voter Choice

As television has become increasingly important to politics, and as the political parties have been weakened with such reforms as primary elections, news coverage of candidates has taken on added significance. Although some critics think reporters pay too much attention to candidates' personality and background, others say character and personality are among the most important characteristics for readers and viewers to know about. What is not in dispute is the central role the news media play in our democratic process.

THE HORSE RACE   What voters know about candidates is based largely on what they see on television, read in newspapers, and hear on the radio. One criticism often heard is that voters do not get the kind of information about candidates and issues that would enable them to make an informed choice. Journalists are more likely to comment on a candidate's standing in the polls compared to other candidates—what is sometimes called the "horse race."[70] "Many stories focus on who is ahead, who is behind, who is going to win, and who is going to lose, rather than examining how and why the race is as it is."[71] Reporters focus on the tactics and strategy of campaigns because they perceive that the public is interested and influenced by such coverage.[72] The media's propensity to focus on the "game" of campaigns displaces coverage of issues.

NEGATIVE ADVERTISING   Political advertising has become increasingly negative in tone. A rule of thumb in the old politics was to ignore the charges of the opposition, thus according one's rival no importance or standing. That practice has changed as candidates today trade charges and countercharges.

WE THE PEOPLE

Profile of a Media Consultant

Dawn Laguens is a partner in the political consulting firm of Laguens Hamburger Stone. Dawn says her family believes she was destined for politics because the day she was christened in Arlington, Virginia, President Lyndon Johnson was attending church service there, and reporters captured a photo of the president with the new baby. Born in Washington, D.C., where her father was comptroller for the Department of Defense, she first became involved in politics in the fourth grade, where she started a student council in part to be sure playground rules were more fair to girls. She went on to be elected high school student body president and president of the student union at Louisiana State University. She later transferred to New Orleans University, where she ran a charitable foundation—the Vincent Memorial Legacy—which conducted outreach activities in the community and provided advocates for people with housing problems. Through her extracurricular activities, Dawn learned she preferred activism to academics, and she has not returned to college to complete her undergraduate degree.

One lesson she learned from her experience advocating for charity was that if you really want to make a difference, you need to be involved in politics. Her first work on a campaign was as deputy director of an unsuccessful mayoral candidacy in New Orleans. She went from there to a position as political director of the Coalition Against Racism and Nazism. David Duke, a white supremacist from Louisiana, was running for the U.S. Senate in 1990, and Laguens and the Coalition worked to defeat him. As part of that effort, she helped produce a commercial that won the Cleo award for best political ad in the nation that year.

Media consulting and campaign strategy became her passion. She is involved in all aspects of political communication, including message development, advertising production, and strategy. She has a wide range of clients and has developed a specialization in ballot initiative campaigns. In 2000 she managed media for Debbie Stabenow's successful bid for the U.S. Senate from Michigan. Other clients in recent years have included Planned Parenthood, organized labor, the gay community, the Nature Conservancy, and U.S. House candidates Dennis Moore and Tom Udall.

Laguens loves her work because it is always different, creative, and she can test her mettle against the bright minds working on the other side. In her spare time she and her partner are raising triplets.

Voters say they are turned off by the attack style of politics, but the widespread perception among campaign consultants is that negative campaigning works. This seeming inconsistency may be explained by some evidence suggesting campaigns that foster negative impressions of the candidates contribute to lower turnout.[73] Negative advertising may thus discourage some voters who would be inclined to support a candidate (called *vote suppression*), while reinforcing the inclination of committed supporters to come out to vote.

INFORMATION ABOUT ISSUES   In recent elections the media have experimented with a more issues-centered focus through what has been called *civic journalism*. With funding from charitable foundations, some newspapers have been identifying the concerns of community leaders and talking to ordinary voters, and then writing campaign stories from their point of view.[74] Some newspaper editors and reporters disagree with this approach; rather, they believe the media should respond to newsworthy events. Advocates of civic journalism counter that important concerns of the community are often overshadowed by news events like murders and violence.

MAKING A DECISION   Newspapers and television seem to have more influence in determining the outcome of primaries than of general elections,[75] probably because voters are less likely to know about the candidates and have fewer clues about how they stand in a primary. By the time of the November general election, however, party affiliation, incumbency, and other factors moderate the impact of media messages. The mass media are more likely to influence undecided voters who, in a close election, can determine who wins and who loses.

ELECTION NIGHT REPORTING   Does TV coverage on election night affect the outcome of elections? Election returns from the East come in three hours before the polls close on the West Coast. Because major networks often project the presidential winner well ahead of poll closings in western states, some western voters have been discouraged from voting. As a result, voter turnout in congressional and local elections has been affected. In a close presidential election, however, such early reporting may well stimulate turnout because voters know their vote could determine the outcome. In short, it is only in elections in which one candidate appears to be winning by a large margin that television reporting makes voters believe their vote is meaningless.[76]

THE MEDIA AND GOVERNANCE

The press rarely follows the policy process to its conclusion. Rather, it leaves the issue at the doorstep of public officials. By the time a political issue reaches the stages of policy formulation and implementation, the press has moved on to another issue. When policies are being formulated and implemented, decision makers are at their most impressionable, yet the press has little impact at this stage.[77]

Lack of press attention to how policies are implemented explains in part why we know less about how bureaucrats go about their business than we do about heated legislative debates or presidential scandals. Only in the case of a policy scandal, such as the lax security of nuclear secrets at Los Alamos, does the press take notice. "Most executives would be satisfied with a press strategy of no surprises. All their press officers need do to be doing their job is provide a rudimentary early warning system [for crises] and issue routine announcements."[78] But the assumption of most policy makers, even those handling classified national security information, is that their actions will leak out to the media sooner or later.

Some media critics contend a negative consequence of the media's approach to policy coverage is pressure on policy makers to resolve a problem immediately once it receives media focus. Foreign policy may be in particular danger from such quick responses:

> If an ominous foreign event is featured on TV news, the president and his advisers feel bound to make a response in time for the next evening news broadcast. . . . If he does not have a response ready by the late afternoon deadline, the evening news may report that the president's advisers are divided, that the president cannot make up his mind, or that while the president hesitates, his political opponents know exactly what to do.[79]

Political Institutions and the News Media

Presidents have become the stars of the media, particularly television, and have made the media their forum for setting the public agenda and achieving their legislative aims. Presidential news conferences command attention (see Table 10–2). Every public activity, both professional and personal, is potentially newsworthy; a presidential illness can become front-page news, as can presidential vacations and family pets. A president attempts to manipulate news coverage to his benefit. Speeches are used to set the national agenda or spur congressional action. Travel to foreign countries usually boosts popular support at home, thanks to the largely favorable news coverage. Better yet for the president, most coverage of the president—either at home or abroad—is favorable or at worst neutral.[80] President Clinton's trip to Israel during the height of the impeachment furor may have helped distract attention from his domestic problems, in both senses of that word.

Congress is more likely to get negative coverage than either the White House or Supreme Court. Congress is a fragmented body unable to act quickly.[81] Unlike the presidency, it lacks an ultimate spokesperson—a single individual who can speak for the whole institution.[82] Congress does not make it easy for the press to cover it. While the White House engages in the "care and feeding" of the press corps, Congress does not arrange its schedule to suit the media; floor debates, for example, often compete with committee hearings and press conferences.[83] Singularly dramatic actions rarely occur in Congress; the press, therefore, turns to the president to describe federal government activity on a day-to-day basis and treats Congress largely as a foil to the president. Most coverage of Congress is of its reaction to the initiatives of the president.[84]

The federal institution least dependent on the press is the Supreme Court, which does not rely on public communication for political support. Rather, it relies indirectly on public opinion for continued deference to and compliance with its decisions.[85] The Court has strong incentives to avoid the perception of manipulating the press, so it retains an image of aloofness from politics and public opinion. The justices' manipulation of press coverage of the Court is far more subtle and complex than that of the other two institutions.[86] For example, the complexity of the Supreme Court's decision in the Florida vote recounting case with multiple dissents and concurrences and with no press release or executive summary made broadcast reporting on the decision difficult.

The news media's greatest role may be at the local level. Most of us have multiple sources for finding out what is happening in Washington that act as a check on

TABLE 10–2 Presidential News Conferences with White House Correspondents

President	Average per Month	Total Number
Herbert Hoover (1929–33)	5.6	268
Franklin D. Roosevelt (1933–45)	6.9	998
Harry Truman (1945–53)	3.4	334
Dwight Eisenhower (1953–61)	2.0	193
John Kennedy (1961–63)	1.9	64
Lyndon Johnson (1963–69)	2.2	135
Richard Nixon (1969–74)	0.5	37
Gerald Ford (1974–77)	1.3	39
Jimmy Carter (1977–81)	0.8	59
Ronald Reagan (1981–89)	0.5	44
George Bush (1989–93)	3.0	142
Bill Clinton (1993–99)	2.0	192

SOURCE: *Weekly Compilation of Presidential Documents*, vol. 31, *Annual Index* (p. C12); Interview, White House Press Office, December 27, 2000.

the biases and limitations of reporters who cover national government and policy. But when it comes to finding out about the city council, the school board, or the local water district, most of us are dependent on the work of a single reporter. Consequently, the media's influence is much greater when there are fewer news sources.

Not all who think the media are powerful agree that their power is harmful. After all, they argue, the media perform a vital educational function. Almost 70 percent of the public think the press is a watchdog that keeps government leaders from doing bad things.[87] At the very least, the media have the power to mold the agenda of the day; at most, in the words of the late Theodore White, they have the power to "determine what people will talk and think about—an authority that in other nations is reserved for tyrants, priests, parties, and mandarins."[88]

POLITICS ONLINE

How To Be Your Own News Filter

We live in a time with more and more ways to learn what is happening around the world and in our community. Baseball fans used to turn to the sports pages of newspapers to get the box scores on games around the country; or people would turn to the weather page to learn what the forecast was for a city they were traveling to later in the week. Now there is no reason to wait until the newspaper arrives. You can learn the box scores on the Internet soon after the game ends, and the weather forecasts as rapidly.

The same principle applies to virtually all categories of news. Imagine getting only the news that interests you delivered every morning to your personal e-mail account. You can sign up for exactly that with most major newspaper websites, usually at no charge. Just look for the place to sign up for the e-mail newsletter. E-mail newsletters will be sent daily containing just the topics you like: entertainment, sports, business, lifestyles, and American politics. *USA Today* at: www.usatoday.com, *The New York Times* at: www.nytimes.com, *The Washington Post* at: www.washingtonpost.com, and *The Wall Street Journal* at: www.wsj.com all provide a form of e-mail headlines.

Not only in the print media can you act as your own gatekeeper, but you can also see or listen to only those reports that interest you in the broadcast media. Try going to major television media websites such as: www.msnbc.com, www.cbsnews.com, www.abcnews.com, www.cnn.com, and www.foxnews.com, or to radio websites like: www.npr.org. On these websites you can select which news reports you want to see or listen to, or even read them as text articles. Much like the newspaper sites, most of these sites also offer free headlines that can be e-mailed to your account. This is especially handy if you want to monitor a particular issue and cannot listen or watch the program in real time.

You can also make sure that your Web browser's home page shows only those topics, stories, articles, and headlines that interest you most—even your local weather. One place to do this is at: www.msn.com. You'll first need to create a free Passport account; then locate the places where you can click to change the content, layout, and even colors of your home page.

SUMMARY

1. The news media include newspapers, magazines, radio, television, films, recordings, books, and electronic communications, in all their forms. These means of communication have been called "the other government" and "the fourth branch of government."

2. The news media are a pervasive feature of American politics and generally help to define our culture. The rise of new communications technologies has made the media more influential throughout American society. The news media provide a "linking" function between politicians and government officials and the public.

3. Our modern news media emerged from a more partisan and less professional past. The autonomy of the media from political parties is one of the important changes. Now journalists strive for

objectivity and see themselves as important to the political process. They also engage in investigative journalism.

4. Broadcasting on radio and television has changed the news media, and most Americans use television and radio as primary news sources. The role of corporate ownership of media outlets, especially media conglomerates, raises questions about media competition and orientation.

5. The influence of the mass media over public opinion is significant yet not overwhelming. People may not pay much attention to the media or believe all they read or see or hear. They may be critical or suspicious of the media and hence resistant to it. People tend to "filter" the news in part through their political socialization, selectivity, needs, and ability to recall or comprehend the content of the news.

6. The media are criticized as biased both by conservatives (who charge that the media are too liberal) and by liberals (who claim that the media are captive of corporate interests and major advertisers). Little evidence exists of actual, deliberate bias in news reporting.

7. A major effect of mass media news is agenda setting—that is, determining what problems will become salient issues for people to form opinions about and to discuss. The media are also influential in defining issues for the general public.

8. Presidential campaigns are dominated by media coverage during both the pre- and post-convention stages. One effect of media influence is that most people seem more interested in the contest as a "game" or "horse race" than as an occasion for serious discussion of issues and candidates. Another effect has been the rise of image making and the media consultant.

9. The press serves as observer of and participant in politics as watchdog, agenda setter, and check on the abuse of power, but it rarely follows the policy process to its conclusion.

KEY TERMS

mass media 224

news media 224

issue ad 225

fairness doctrine 230

political socialization 231

selective exposure 232

selective perception 232

FURTHER READING

STEPHEN ANSOLABEHERE AND SHANTO IYENGAR, *Going Negative: How Attack Ads Shrink and Polarize the Electorate* (Free Press, 1996).

TIMOTHY COOK, *Governing with the News: The News Media as a Political Institution* (University of Chicago Press, 1998).

TIMOTHY E. COOK, *Making Laws and Making News: Press Strategies in the U.S. House of Representatives* (Brookings Institution, 1990).

TIMOTHY E. COOK, *Governing with the News: The News Media as a Political Institution* (University of Chicago Press, 1998).

RICHARD DAVIS, *The Web of Politics: The Internet's Impact on the American Political System* (Oxford University Press, 1999).

RICHARD DAVIS AND DIANA MARIE OWEN, *New Media and American Politics* (Oxford University Press, 1998).

JAMES FALLOWS, *Breaking the News: How the Media Undermine American Democracy* (Pantheon Books, 1996).

SUZANNE GARMENT, *Scandal: The Culture of Mistrust in American Politics* (Times Books, 1991).

DORIS A. GRABER, *Mass Media and American Politics*, 5th ed. (Congressional Quarterly Press, 1997).

DORIS A. GRABER, *Media Power in Politics*, 4th ed. (Congressional Quarterly Press, 2000).

LAWRENCE K. GROSSMAN, *The Electronic Republic: Reshaping Democracy in the Information Age* (Viking, 1995).

RODERICK P. HART, *Campaign Talk: Why Elections Are Good for Us* (Princeton University Press, 2000).

STEPHEN HESS, *Live from Capitol Hill: Studies of Congress and the Media* (Brookings Institution, 1991).

KATHLEEN HALL JAMIESON AND JOSEPH N. CAPPELLA, *Spiral of Cynicism: The Press and the Public Good* (Oxford University Press, 1997).

PHYLISS KANISS, *Making Local News* (University of Chicago Press, 1991).

HOWARD KURTZ, *Spin Cycle: Inside the Clinton Propaganda Machine* (Free Press, 1998).

PAUL J. LAVRAKAS AND MICHAEL W. TRAUGOTT, *Election Polls, The News Media and Democracy* (Chatham House, 2000).

PAUL J. LAVRAKAS AND MICHAEL W. TRAUGOTT, EDS., *Election Polls, The News Media and Democracy* (Chatham House, 2000).

S. ROBERT LICHTER, STANLEY ROTHMAN, AND LINDA S. LICHTER, *The Media Elite* (Adler and Adler, 1986).

JOHN ANTHONY MALTESE, *Spin Control: The White House Office of Communications and the Management of Presidential News* (University of North Carolina Press, 1992).

THOMAS E. PATTERSON, *OUT OF ORDER* (KNOPF, 1993).

MARTIN PLISSNER, *The Control Room: How Television Calls the Shots in Presidential Elections* (Free Press, 1999).

TOM ROSENSTEIL, *Strange Bedfellows: How Television and the Presidential Candidates Changed American Politics, 1992* (Hyperion, 1993).

LARRY J. SABATO AND S. ROBERT LICHTER, *Peepshow: Media and Politics in an Age of Scandal* (Rowman & Littlefield, 2000).

SIMON SEFATY, *The Media and Foreign Policy* (St. Martin's Press, 1990).

JAMES A. THURBER, CANDICE J. NELSON, AND DAVID A. DULIO, EDS., *Crowded Airwaves: Campaign Advertising in Elections* (Brookings Institution Press, 2000).

DARRELL M. WEST, *Air Wars: Television Advertising in Election Campaigns, 1952–1992* (Congressional Quarterly Press, 1993).

11

CONGRESS: THE PEOPLE'S BRANCH

T

THE UNITED STATES CONGRESS IS ONE OF THE MOST PRAISED YET MOST CRITICIZED POLITICAL INSTITUTIONS IN THE WORLD. IT IS PRAISED BECAUSE IT IS A REPRESENTATIVE and democratic institution. It is praised, too, because it is deliberative and open. And it is revered because many outstanding legislators have served in Congress and contributed greatly to the success of the American political experiment.

Yet Americans relentlessly criticize both Congress and its members. Citizens think members of Congress don't understand their needs and put the concerns of special interests ahead of those of their regular constituents. Sixty-two percent of participants in one national survey complained that "Congress creates more problems than it solves."[1] Congress is also criticized for being irrelevant, slow, and overly partisan.

Although most Americans profess a devotion to democracy, many have little or no appreciation of what it takes to make democracy work. "People do not wish to see uncertainty, conflicting options, long debate, competing interests, confusion, bargaining, and compromised, imperfect solutions," write political scientists John Hibbing and Elizabeth Theiss-Morse. Instead, they would like their government to perform its job quietly, efficiently, and without public bickering and gridlock. "In short," Hibbing and Theiss-Morse conclude, the American people "often seek a patently unrealistic form of democracy."[2]

Congress may be criticized, but it plays a key role in the American political system. Presidents cannot lead if they do not have a working relationship with both chambers of Congress. Congress controls decisions on budgets, taxes, trade policy, the shape of the federal bureaucracy, and appointments to the cabinet, the embassies, and the courts. A president has a certain amount of freedom in foreign policy, yet even here a president's policies will rarely be successful or properly implemented without support from Congress. For this reason President George Bush sought congressional support before the Persian Gulf War.

Because ours is a system of shared powers, Congress and the president are forced to work together while protecting their often-different policy positions. The pressure to compromise and consequently to appear inconsistent is often seen by the public and the media as a negative, when in fact it is a necessary result of divided public opinion.

In this chapter we examine the politics of representation and how Congress organizes itself to do its work of making laws and representing the people. We also look at

C H A P T E R M E·D I A

POLITICS ONLINE
What's Happening in Congress Today?
www.prenhall.com/burns

how this highly public, open, and political institution cannot avoid provoking conflicts that lead to sometimes bitter clashes with the White House and other rivals for influence in the shaping of American public policies.

CONGRESSIONAL ELECTIONS

The entire membership of the House of Representatives (435) is elected to two-year terms in even-numbered years. Elections for the six-year Senate terms are staggered, so that one-third of the Senate's 100 members are chosen every two years. Members of the House of Representatives must be 25 years old and have been citizens for seven years. Senators must be at least 30 years old and have been citizens for nine years. House and Senate candidates must live in the states in which they are elected.

Members of Congress are politicians who get their jobs by winning an election. Ironically, it is often good politics for them to deny they are politicians and to lead the charge against the institution they serve in. The willingness of "House members to stand and defend their own votes or voting record contrasts sharply with their disposition to run and hide when a defense of Congress might be called for," writes political scientist Richard F. Fenno, Jr. "Members of Congress run *for* Congress by running *against* Congress. The strategy is ubiquitous, addictive, cost-free, and foolproof. . . . In the short run, everybody plays and nearly everybody wins. Yet the institution bleeds from 435 separate cuts."[3]

The outcome of any congressional election depends on many factors. By far the most important is the nature of the state or district in which the candidate runs. The most common is a **safe seat**—one that is predictably won by one party or the other. Or it could be a competitive one, sometimes called a "swing district" in House races. Other factors affecting winning elections are personal appeal of the candidate, whether the opponent is an incumbent or a newcomer, local issues, campaign strategies, the fund-raising abilities of the candidate, and,

Freshmen House of Representatives of the 107th Congress, who took office in January 2001, on the steps of the U.S. Capitol for their "class" picture.

safe seat

An elected office that is predictably won by one party or the other, so reelection is almost taken for granted.

occasionally, national political tides, such as in the 1964, 1974, and 1994 elections.

Incumbents have traditionally enjoyed a great advantage over challengers, but incumbency isn't always an advantage. "Outsiders" like Ross Perot, Ralph Nader, Steve Forbes, and Rush Limbaugh have targeted "Washington insiders" and helped create a climate of antagonism toward Congress as an institution. Because of this climate, there have been repeated yet unsuccessful efforts in Congress to pass constitutional limits on congressional terms. But more than 90 percent of incumbents who run for reelection to Congress beat their challengers; more than 98 percent of House members were reelected in 2000, and 23 of 29 U.S. senators won reelection, for a success rate of almost 80 percent.

The Politics of Drawing House District Lines

Every state, according to the Constitution, has two U.S. senators; each senator represents his or her entire state. House of Representatives seats are distributed or apportioned among the states according to population. House districts have about 650,000 people in them.

The Constitution requires a national census every ten years. As a result of the 2000 census, Congress had to reallocate seats based on population shifts. New York and Pennsylvania lost two House seats, Ohio, Indiana, Illinois, Wisconsin, and Michigan all lost one seat. Florida, Georgia, Texas, and Arizona gained two seats. Colorado, Nevada, North Carolina and California gained one seat each.

Congress must provide for **reapportionment** of congressional seats among the states. Each state has the right to at least one seat; smaller population states such as Alaska, Wyoming, and Vermont have House seats with as many as 100,000 citizens less than a normal House seat elsewhere.

State legislators, or in some states **redistricting** commissions, draw the district lines for these House seats, although their proposals are subject to the approval or veto of the state's governor. In practice, in most states the party in control of the state legislature traditionally draws the district boundaries to enhance its own political fortunes.[4] This process is known as **gerrymandering**, after Governor Elbridge Gerry of Massachusetts, who, in 1811, reluctantly signed a redistricting bill that created a distinctly partisan district shaped like a salamander. Party-controlled gerrymandering explains why so many districts are "safe" for one party. However, if the partisanship is so biased that it makes it impossible for the other party to win, the legislature risks federal judicial objections. The U.S. Supreme Court has held that under certain circumstances, which it has never specified, excessive partisan gerrymandering might be unconstitutional.[5]

Indeed, the federal courts have insisted for years that state legislatures have to draw state and national legislative districts subject to both constitutional specifications and requirements of national laws. In *Baker v Carr* (1962), the U.S. Supreme Court held that voters do have *standing* (the right) to challenge how state legislatures allocate legislative seats, and that such questions should be considered by the federal courts.[6] Soon after the *Baker v. Carr* ruling, the Court announced that as far as U.S. House of Representatives seats are concerned, "As nearly as practicable one man's vote in congressional elections is to be worth as much as another's."[7]

Finally, although a state legislature can design its U.S. House of Representative districts to virtually guarantee the election of a member of a particular minority, it must be careful not to do so in a fashion that focuses *only* on racial considerations and ignores such matters as county lines and city boundaries.[8] Indeed, the Supreme

Why Do Incumbent Members of Congress Usually Win?

- They enjoy better name recognition, and to be known at all is generally to be known favorably. Challengers are almost always less well known.

- They enjoy free mailings (called the franking privilege) to every household in the state or district. These mailings—which often resemble campaign brochures—portray members as hardworking and influential.

- They have greater access to the media.

- They raise campaign money more easily than challengers, because lobbyists and political action committees (PACs) seek their ears and their favors. Also, many campaign contributors know that incumbents are more likely than challengers to get reelected, so they give to those they know will win. (PACs in recent elections have given as much as $8 out of every $10 to incumbents.)

- They usually have had more campaign experience, and they can claim to have had more experience in Congress and in Washington. And they usually are better campaigners.

- They have staffs to help with casework and constituency services for the folks back home.

- They take credit for federal money that gets allocated to their region.

- They are in a better position than challengers to take advantage of government research staffs, new government studies, and even classified information.

No one of these factors can guarantee a member's reelection, yet skillful use of them makes it difficult to unseat a healthy incumbent.

reapportionment
The assigning by Congress of congressional seats after each census. State legislatures reapportion state legislative districts.

redistricting
The redrawing of congressional and other legislative district lines following the census, to accommodate population shifts and keep districts as equal as possible in population.

gerrymandering
The drawing of election district boundaries to benefit a party, group, or incumbent.

The word "gerrymander" comes from the name of a governor of Massachusetts, Elbridge Gerry, and the salamander-shaped district that was created to favor his party in 1811.

Court has ruled that making race "the predominant factor," while ignoring traditional redistricting principles such as compactness, is unconstitutional.[9]

THE STRUCTURE AND POWERS OF CONGRESS

The most important feature of Congress is its **bicameralism**—that is, it is made up of two houses. Few other national legislatures are genuinely bicameral. Many have two houses, but one is usually ceremonial in practice. In the United States, the Senate and the House each have an absolute veto over the other's law making. Each chamber runs its own affairs, sets its own rules, and conducts its own investigations. The law-making role, however, is shared. Each must be seen as a separate institution, even though both houses reflect similar political forces and share common organizational patterns.

In other countries the "upper" house often has significantly fewer powers than the supposed "people's" house. For example, the French Senate (indirectly elected by local and regional officeholders) has full powers of debate and amendment, but the government can push through legislation blocked or amended in the Senate by obtaining a favorable vote in the lower house (the National Assembly).

In Germany, the upper house (Bundesrat) is composed of delegates named by the state governments. The size of the delegation is based on population, but each state's delegation casts its votes as a bloc in Bundesrat votes. The Bundesrat lacks the legislative powers of the lower house (Bundestag), but it does allow for the involvement of the states in legislation that affects them and their relationship to the federal government. The Bundesrat often plays a key political role, especially when its majority differs from the majority in the Bundestag.

The Consequences of Bicameralism

As James Madison explained in *The Federalist*, No. 51, the protection against giving too much power to the legislature "is to divide the legislature into different branches; and to render them, by different modes of election and different principles of action, as little connected with each other as the nature of their common functions, and their common dependence on the society will admit." (*The Federalist*, No. 51, is reprinted in the Appendix.)

The House of Representatives was expected to reflect the popular will of the average citizen, whereas the Senate was to provide for stability, continuity, and deliberation. The framers hoped the Senate would stem any rash populist impulses of the other chamber. Although the Seventeenth Amendment to the Constitution (1913), which provides for direct election of U.S. senators, altered the character of the Senate's membership, the two chambers still have differences (see Table 11–1). However, the two houses are more similar today in their membership and operations than they were two hundred or even one hundred years ago.

Defenders of bicameralism say it serves as a moderating influence on the partisanship or possible errors of either of the chambers. This constitutionally mandated structure also guarantees that many votes will be taken before a policy is finally approved. It provides more opportunities, too, for bargaining and allows legislators with different policy goals a role in the shaping of national laws.

The Senate is the only legislature in the United States where the principle of equal representation does not apply. As noted earlier, the number of senators from each state is not based on population. Because each state has two senators regardless of population, the Senate represents constituencies that are more rural, white, and conservative than would be the case if the one-person, one-vote norm applied to Senate elections.

Does it matter that California's 35 million (and growing!) people have the same two Senate votes as Wyoming's less than 500,000? Such disparities make the Senate the most malapportioned elected legislature in the democratic world, giving the advantage to citizens in the smaller as opposed to larger states. Frances Lee and

bicameralism
The principle of a two-house legislature.

TABLE 11-1 Differences Between the House of Representatives and the Senate

House of Representatives	Senate
Two-year term	Six-year term
435 members	100 members
Smaller constituencies	Larger constituencies
Fewer personal staff	More personal staff
Equal populations represented	States represented
Less flexible rules	More flexible rules
Limited debate	Extended debate
More policy specialists	Policy generalists
Less media coverage	More media coverage
Less prestige	More prestige
Less reliance on staff	More reliance on staff
More powerful committee leaders	More equal distribution of power
Very important committees	Less important committees
20 major committees	20 major committees
Nongermane amendments (riders) not allowed	Nongermane amendments (riders) allowed
Important Rules Committee	Special treaty ratification power
Some bills permit no floor amendments (closed rule)	Special "advice and consent" confirmation power
	Filibuster allowed

Bruce Oppenheimer conclude that the size of a state's population affects senator-constituent relationships, fund raising and elections, strategic behavior within the Senate, and ultimately policy decisions.[10] Retired U.S. Senator Daniel Patrick Moynihan (D.-N.Y.), who knew firsthand how citizens of larger states fared less well in U.S. Senate policy battles, predicted that "some time in the next century the United States is going to have to address the question of apportionment in the Senate."[11] That may be so, but the prospects for changing the one state/two U.S. senators constitutional rule are highly unlikely in the near future.

The Constitutional Separation of Powers

In Article I, the Constitution outlines the structure, powers, and responsibilities of Congress, giving it "All legislative Powers herein granted": the power to spend and tax in order to "provide for the common Defense and general Welfare of the United States"; the power to borrow money; the power to regulate commerce with foreign nations and among the states; the power to declare war, raise and support armies, and provide and maintain a navy; the power to establish post offices; and the power to set up the federal courts under the Supreme Court. As a final catchall, the Constitution gave Congress the right "to make all Laws which shall be necessary and proper for carrying into Execution" the powers set out. Several nonlegislative functions were also granted, such as participating in the process of constitutional amendment and impeachment (given to the House) and trying an impeached federal officer (given to the Senate).

The Constitution stipulates the grounds for impeachment that can lead to the removal from office of a president or vice president or other federal officers, including federal judges, are the commission of "High Crimes and Misdemeanors" (never clearly defined). The House sits to determine whether or not an official's actions reach the level of impeachable offenses, and if so, it can impeach by a majority vote. The Senate sits as a court to decide if the impeached official should be convicted, and whether the nature of the offense warrants removal from office. A two-thirds vote is

1. *Representation:* expressing the diversity and conflicting views of the regional, economic, social, racial, religious, and other interests in the United States.

2. *Law making:* enacting measures to help solve substantive problems.

3. *Consensus building:* the bargaining process by which these interests are reconciled.

4. *Overseeing the bureaucracy:* ensuring that laws and policies approved by Congress are faithfully carried out by the executive branch and accomplish what was intended.

5. *Policy clarification:* the identification and publicizing of issues.

6. *Investigating the operation of government agencies,* including the White House; this responsibility includes impeachment processes.

7. For the Senate, *confirming by a majority vote presidential appointees* and ratifying treaties by a two-thirds vote.

needed to convict; thus a minority of just 34 senators can reject a conviction or removal of an impeached official.

The Constitution confers additional responsibilities on the Senate. The Senate has the power to confirm many presidential nominations—sometimes as many as 500 key executive and judicial nominees a year. In a two-year session of Congress there may be more than 4,000 civilian nominations and 70,000 military nominations needing senatorial approval. Many of these nominations are approved in large blocks. The Senate must also play a crucial "advice and consent" role in treaty making—formal agreements between the United States and one or more countries. All treaties must be approved by a two-thirds vote in the Senate before they can be ratified by a U.S. president.

The House has some distinctive responsibilities, but they are not as important as those given to the Senate. For example, although all revenue bills must originate in the House, this practice does not give the House much advantage, because the Senate can freely amend spending bills, sometimes changing everything except the title.

The framers did not intend Congress to be all-powerful. They reserved certain authority for the states and for the people and gave other powers to the executive and judicial branches of the national government. As time passed, Congress has gained power in some respects and lost it in others. The power of Congress also changed with the president and the times.

As the role and authority of the national government have expanded, so have the policy-making and oversight responsibilities of Congress. Still, Congress has difficulty keeping pace with its great rival, the president. The president's national security responsibilities, preparation of the budget, media visibility, and agenda-setting influence have all enhanced the position of the presidency. The growth of executive authority may be part of a worldwide trend. Legislative bodies almost everywhere have become subordinate to the executive at all levels of government.

The House of Representatives

The organization and procedures in the House are different from those in the Senate, if only because the House is more than four times as large as the Senate. *How* things are done affects *what* is done. The House assigns different types of bills to different calendars. For instance, financial measures—tax or appropriations bills— are put on a special calendar for quicker action.

The House has other ways to speed up law making, including electronic voting. Ordinary rules may be suspended by a two-thirds vote, or immediate action may be taken by *unanimous consent* of the members on the floor. By sitting as the *committee of the whole*, the House is able to operate more informally and more quickly than under its regular rules. A *quorum* in the committee of the whole requires only 100 members, rather than a majority of the whole chamber, and voting is quicker and simpler. Members are limited in how long they can speak, and debate may be cut off simply by majority vote.

THE SPEAKER   The **Speaker** is the presiding officer in the House of Representatives.[12] The Constitution mandates that the House of Representatives shall choose its Speaker, yet it does not say anything about the duties or powers of the office. This officer is formally elected by the entire House yet is actually selected by the majority party. As the highest-ranking officer in Congress, the Speaker represents it on ceremonial occasions. Third in line of succession to the presidency (in case of death, resignation, or impeachment), the Speaker must keep the White House informed about his whereabouts.

The routine powers of the Speaker include recognizing members who wish to speak, ruling on questions of parliamentary procedure, and appointing members to

Speaker

The presiding officer in the House of Representatives, formally elected by the House but actually selected by the majority party.

temporary committees, not the major standing or regular committees. Revolts in 1910 by rank-and-file Progressives stripped Speakers of much of their previous power, including control over who served on which congressional committees. In general, the Speaker today directs business on the floor of the House. More significant, of course, is a Speaker's political and behind-the-scenes influence.

When the Republicans won control of the House in 1994, they elected representative Newt Gingrich (R.-Georgia) as Speaker. As the first Republican Speaker in 40 years, he was a novelty in Washington. "I had set out to do a very unusual job," said Gingrich, "which was part revolutionary, part national political figure, part Speaker, part intellectual."[13]

Gingrich established his authority—naming committee chairs, bypassing the seniority rule, reorganizing House committees, and reducing perks and committee staffs. He pushed through some of the legislation outlined in the Republican Contract with America. He delegated considerable power to fellow Republican leaders, yet claimed for himself the main role as spokesperson for major policy initiatives. He published books detailing his ideas about government and his party, and he cheerfully took on the White House and the national press.[14]

Following a volatile tenure and a two-year investigation, the House Ethics Committee found Gingrich had disregarded standards of conduct that applied to the use of tax-exempt funds. He had insisted there was little overlap between his partisan political activities and his supposedly nonpartisan educational endeavors. But the committee recommended, and the House of Representatives quickly passed, a reprimand of Gingrich and imposed a fine of $300,000 for misusing charitable deductions for political purposes and for misleading the House Ethics Committee. This was an unprecedented rebuke for a Speaker.

Gingrich retired both as Speaker and as a member of Congress following his party's poor showing in the midterm election of 1998. Republicans soon selected Illinois Representative J. Dennis Hastert as Speaker. Hastert, a former high school teacher and wrestling coach, had served for 6 years in the Illinois state legislature and 12 in the U.S. House of Representatives before becoming Speaker of the House. "It's a calling that I have not sought," said Hastert about the Speakership. "However, it is a duty that I cannot ignore."[15] Hastert displays a low-key, quiet self-confidence that has pleased most Republican House members. He concentrates on central issues on which Republicans can agree, aware that he is trying to lead a House with only a slender margin of majority control.[16] Speaker Hastert was reelected Speaker for the 107th House of Representatives; he even picked up a vote from a Democrat!

OTHER HOUSE OFFICERS   The Speaker is assisted by a **majority leader**, who helps plan party strategy, confers with other party leaders, and tries to keep members of the party in line. The minority party elects a **minority leader**, who usually steps into the Speakership when his or her party gains a majority in the House. (These positions are also sometimes called majority and minority floor leaders.) Assisting each floor leader are the party **whips**. (The term comes from the "whipper-in," who in fox hunts keeps the hounds bunched in a pack.) The whips serve as liaisons between the House leadership of each party and the rank-and-file. They inform members when important bills will come up for a vote, prepare summaries of the bills, do nose counts for the leadership, exert pressure (sometimes mild and sometimes heavy) on members to support the leadership, and try to ensure maximum attendance on the floor for critical votes.

At the beginning of the session and occasionally afterward, each party holds a **party caucus** of all its members (called a *conference* by Republicans) to elect party officers, approve committee assignments, elect committee leaders, discuss important legislation, and perhaps try to agree on party policy.

Republican Dennis Hastert, Speaker of the House of Representatives.

majority leader
The legislative leader selected by the majority party, who helps plan party strategy, confers with other party leaders, and tries to keep members of the party in line.

minority leader
The legislative leader selected by the minority party as spokesperson for the opposition.

whip
Party leader who is the liaison between the leadership and the rank-and-file in the legislature.

party caucus
Meeting of party members in a chamber of the legislature to select the party leadership in that chamber and to develop party policy. Called a *conference* by Republicans.

"Listen, pal! I didn't spend seen million bucks to get here so I could yield the floor to you."

closed rule

A procedural rule in the House of Representatives that prohibits any amendments to bills or provides that only members of the committee reporting the bill may offer amendments.

open rule

A procedural rule in the House of Representatives that permits floor amendments within the overall time allocated to the bill.

hold

A practice in the Senate whereby a senator temporarily blocks the consideration of a bill or nomination.

president pro tempore

Officer of the Senate selected by the majority party to act as chair in the absence of the vice-president.

filibuster

A practice in the Senate whereby a senator holds the floor and thereby delays proceedings and prevents a vote on a controversial issue.

cloture

Procedure for terminating debate, especially filibusters, in the Senate.

THE HOUSE RULES COMMITTEE   The House, unlike the Senate, has a Rules Committee that regulates the time of floor debate for each bill and sets limitations on floor amendments. By refusing to grant a *rule*, the committee can delay consideration of a bill. A **closed rule** prohibits amendments altogether or provides that only members of the committee reporting the bill may offer amendments; closed rules are usually reserved for tax and spending bills. An **open rule** permits debate within the overall time allocated to the bill.

From the New Deal era in the mid-1930s until the mid-1960s, the Rules Committee was dominated by a coalition of Republicans and conservative Democrats. Liberals denounced it as unrepresentative, unfair, and dictatorial. More recently, the Rules Committee membership has come to reflect the views of the general makeup of the majority party. The Rules Committee today is an arm of the leadership, and rather than block legislation, it offers a "dress rehearsal" on procedural issues, like time allotted for debate to those trying to press for new measures.

The Senate

The Senate has the same basic committee structure, elected party leadership, and decentralized power as the House, but because the Senate is a smaller body, its procedures are more informal, and it permits more time for debate. It is a more open, fluid, and decentralized body now than it was a generation or two ago. Indeed, it is often said that the Senate has one hundred separate power centers and is so splintered that the party leaders have difficulty arranging the day-to-day schedule.[17]

The Senate is individualistic. It has always operated under rules that vest great power in the individual senator. Extended debate allows senators to hold the floor as long as they wish unless a supermajority of 60 colleagues votes to end debate. "And, the Senate's permissive amending rules enable any senator to offer any and as many amendments as she pleases to almost any bill and those amendments need not even be germane [related to the measure]."[18]

In recent years, senators have used a practice called the **hold**. A hold is a procedure allowing any senator to block temporarily the consideration of either a legislative bill or a presidential nomination. Found nowhere in the Constitution or in Senate rules, the hold has "evolved as a courtesy for senators who could not be present when a vote was scheduled or who needed time to bone up on a subject before the floor debate began."[19] But over the past decade the hold has been expanded beyond its past purposes and is now often a tactic to kill a bill or nomination.

The president of the Senate (the vice-president of the United States) has little influence over Senate proceedings. A vice-president can vote only in case of a tie. The Senate elects a **president pro tempore**, usually the most senior member from the majority party, who acts as chair in the absence of the vice-president. Presiding over the Senate on most occasions is a thankless chore, so the president pro tempore regularly delegates this responsibility to junior members of the chamber's majority party.

The *Senate majority leader*—the elected leader of the majority party in the Senate—is an influential person within the Senate and sometimes nationally. The current majority leader, Senator Tom Daschle (D.-South Dakota), for example, has become a spokesperson for the Democratic party. As the Senate's power broker, the majority leader has the right to be the first senator heard on the floor. In consultation with the *Senate minority leader*, the majority leader determines the Senate's agenda and has much to say about committee assignments for members of the majority party. But the position confers less authority than the Speakership in the House, and its influence depends on the person's political and parliamentary skills and on the national political situation.[20] Senate majority leaders have to be persuaders and negotiators, not only working closely with the minority leader but also working with a number of powerful majority and minority senators as well as with the White House.

Party machinery in the Senate is somewhat similar to that of the House. There are party caucuses (conferences), majority and minority floor leaders, and party whips. Each party has a *policy committee*, composed of the leaders of the party, which is theoretically responsible for the party's overall legislative program. In the Senate the party policy committees assist the leadership in monitoring legislation and provide policy expertise. Unlike the House party committees, the Senate's party policy committees are formally provided for by law, and each has a regular staff and a budget. Although the Senate party policy committees have some influence on legislation, they have not asserted strong legislative leadership or managed to coordinate policy.

During the past 20 years the U.S. Senate has become more partisan than it had been previously. "Senators known for compromise, moderation and institutional loyalty," write political scientists Nicol Rae and Colton Campbell, "have been replaced with more ideological and partisan members who see the chamber as a place to enhance their party fortunes."[21] Partisanship in the Senate was vehement during the Bill Clinton impeachment proceedings and to a lesser extent in the confirmation battle of George W. Bush's nominee John Ashcroft as his attorney general.

Senator Trent Lott of Mississippi, Republican minority leader.

THE FILIBUSTER   A major difference between the Senate and the House is that debate is less limited in the Senate. A senator who gains the floor may go on talking until he or she relinquishes the right to talk voluntarily or through exhaustion. This right to unlimited debate may be used by a small group of senators to **filibuster**—that is, delay Senate proceedings by talking continually to postpone or prevent a vote.

At one time the filibuster was a favorite weapon of southern senators intent on blocking civil rights legislation. More recently the filibuster has been used for a wider range of issues. In 1993, Republicans used a filibuster to kill President Clinton's economic stimulus package and Democrats considered filibusters to derail the Ashcroft confirmation and parts of the Bush tax plan.

A filibuster, or the threat of a filibuster, is typically most potent at the end of a congressional session, when there is a fixed date for adjournment, because it could mean that many bills that have otherwise made it through the legislative process will die for lack of a floor vote. The knowledge that a bill might be subject to a filibuster is often enough to force a compromise satisfactory to its opponents. Sometimes the leaders, knowing that a filibuster will tie up the Senate and keep it from enacting other needed legislation, do not bring a controversial bill to the floor.

A filibuster can be defeated. Until 1917 the Senate could terminate a filibuster only if every member agreed. That year, however, the Senate adopted its first debate-ending rule, or **cloture**. Now, as long as the senators who are doing the talking stay on their feet, debate can be stopped only by a cloture vote. The rule of cloture specifies that two days after 16 members sign a petition, the question of curtailing debate must be put to a vote. If three-fifths of the total number of senators (60 of the 100 members) vote for cloture, no senator may speak on the measure under consideration for more than one hour. Then a final vote must be taken after no more than 30 hours of debate, including all delaying tactics, such as quorum calls and roll call votes on procedure.

There has been an increase in the use and threat of filibusters in recent years, and these tactics have often been used for partisan and parochial purposes. Indeed, senators usually anticipate a filibuster on controversial measures, and the threat is often sufficient to force the majority to compromise and modify its position.[22] Both parties have learned to use the filibuster when they are in the minority. The Senate has averaged a few dozen filibusters in recent years; nearly 50 cloture votes were held in 1999–2000.[23]

Tom Daschle from South Dakota, majority leader of the Senate, is the official spokesperson for the Democrats in the Senate.

THE POWER TO CONFIRM   The Constitution leaves the precise practices of the confirmation process somewhat ambiguous: "The President . . . shall nominate, and by and with the Advice and Consent of the Senate, shall appoint Ambassadors, other public Ministers and Consuls, Judges of the Supreme Court, all other officers of the United States."

The framers of the Constitution regarded the confirmation process—the Senate's "advice and consent" power—as an important check on executive power. Alexander Hamilton viewed it as a way for the Senate to prevent the appointment of "unfit characters."

As with other legislative business, the confirmation process starts in committees, with the relevant standing committee having jurisdiction. For example, the Judiciary Committee considers federal judges and Supreme Court nominees; the Foreign Relations Committee considers ambassadorial appointments. Nominees appear before the committee to answer questions, and they typically meet individually with key senators before the hearing.

Presidents have never enjoyed exclusive control over hiring and firing in the executive branch. The Senate jealously guards its right to confirm or reject or even delay major appointments; during the period of strong Congresses after the Civil War, presidents had to struggle to keep their power to appoint and dismiss. But for most of the past hundred years, presidents gained a reasonable amount of control over top appointments, in part because a growing number of people in and out of Congress believe that chief executives without compatible cabinet-level appointees of their choice cannot be held accountable. The Senate's advise and consent powers sometimes force presidents to make compromises, plainly constraining their ability to use the presidential appointment power.

The Senate's role in the confirmation process was never intended to prevent a president from taking political considerations into account when appointments are made, but rather to use the political judgment of senators as a safeguard against weak or ill-advised nominees. When the Senate was Democratic and the White House Republican, conservatives complained that the Senate was interfering with the executive power of the president by rejecting nominees because of their political beliefs. Yet when the Republicans controlled the Senate and the Democrats the White House, it was the liberals who made the same complaint.

In recent years the Senate has taken a tough stand on some presidential appointments and spent more time evaluating and screening presidential nominations. The Senate rejected several nominees of Presidents Ronald Reagan and George Bush, and Presidents Bill Clinton and George W. Bush had to withdraw nominees for attorney general, secretary of labor, and several other posts, including federal judgeships because of Senate opposition.

By a tradition called **senatorial courtesy**, a president confers with the senator or senators in his own political party from the state where an appointee is to work. Occasionally, too, a president has to take into account the views of a politically powerful senator in the opposition party. A nomination is less likely to secure Senate approval against the objection of these senators, especially if these senators are members of the president's party. Thus, for nearly all district court judgeships and a variety of other positions, senators can exercise what is, in fact, a veto that can be overridden only with difficulty. Further, it is usually exercised in secret and subject to little accountability. Since this form of patronage or influence is sufficiently important to senators it is likely to continue.

As noted earlier, a controversial practice has emerged in recent years that allows an individual senator to request of the Senate leadership that a hold be placed on a nomination. The hold is requested to permit that senator to meet with the nominee, to gain more information about the nominee, or similar purposes. Such holds have become more frequent and are used to delay an appointment, to extract concessions from the president or other senators, or sometimes even to kill a nomination. Presidents have protested this recent practice.

It is useful to note a distinction between *judicial* appointments, especially those to the Supreme Court, and *administration* appointments. The Senate plays a greater role in judicial appointments because federal judges serve for life and constitute an independent and vital branch of the government.[24] When it comes to cabinet-level

senatorial courtesy

Presidential custom of submitting the names of prospective appointees for approval to senators from the states in which the appointees are to work.

WOMEN IN THE U.S. SENATE SPEAK UP

The nine women members of the U.S. Senate in 2000 collaborated on a book about their experiences in the Senate. The six Democrats and three Republicans met for dinner every few weeks over a two-year period not to make deals but to lend support to one another by sharing experiences and discussing issues that mattered to them. They had to excel in what until very recently was considered an exclusive men's club.

They were nine individuals out of a group of one hundred making up the Senate. In the ordinary work of each day, they did not consider themselves "women senators," yet each of them appreciated that they bring a different perspective to issues facing the Senate.

Here are a few of their stories:

U.S. Senator Patty Murray (D.-Wash.)

I was told that I hadn't been in line long enough, that I didn't have the history, that I couldn't raise the money. Believe it or not, I was told many times that I was too short. I was actually advised to run as Pat Murray, so that people might think I was a man. And I said, "Wait a minute—I'm running because I'm a woman. I'm running because we need women." And they didn't want people to know I had young kids because their reaction, of course, would be "Oh, my God, how are you going to take care of your kids?" I said, "I'm running because I have young kids. We need policy makers who understand what women are going through so these policies work for women." I was angry. Imagine! They wanted me to trick voters into thinking I was a man. I said, "No way. If I get this job it's because I am a woman and I want people to know I'm a woman."

U.S. Senator Olympia Snowe (R.-Maine)

We certainly don't want to communicate that all of the women in the Senate are homogeneous, with the women sitting on one side and the men sitting on the other. That would be a pretty antiquated point of view, and that's not the case at all. Every one of us is different—in our political positions, our styles, our life experiences. However, women just come from a different place than men do in

Women senators pose before a book-signing for their book Nine and Counting: The Women of the Senate.

terms of being more relationship-oriented and more collaborative. In fact, many of the skills women develop in life actually work pretty well in this institution. When you think about it, maybe women are particularly well suited to the Senate, where collaboration is an essential ingredient in getting things done.

U.S. Senator Blanche Lincoln (D.-Ark.)

When Blanche Lincoln was first elected to Congress at the age of thirty-three,

she recalls, several older congressmen just couldn't get over it. "Why, I have granddaughters who are your age!" one of them exclaimed. Lincoln flashed a big smile, and replied, "I'll bet your granddaughters are glad I'm here."

SOURCE: *Nine and Counting: The Women of the Senate* (Morrow, 2000), pp. 45, 130, 191. © 2000 by Barbara Mikulski, Kay Bailey Hutchison, Dianne Feinstein, Barbara Boxer, Patty Murray, Olympia Snowe, Susan Collins, Mary Landrieu, Blanche L. Lincoln, with Catherine Whitney. Reprinted by permission of Harper Collins, Publishers, Inc.

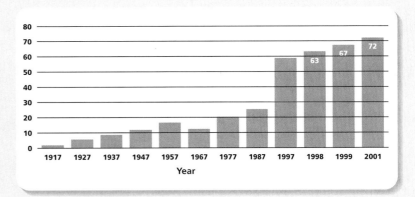

Number of Women in U.S. Congress

SOURCE: Rutgers University Center for the American Woman and Politics. Reprinted from *The Washington Post*, October 12, 1998, p. 10. Updated by the authors.

positions in the executive branch, it is assumed that a president ought to be able to choose those who will carry out the general views of the White House; in contrast, a president is not expected to enjoy partisan loyalty from those nominated to the bench.

THE JOB OF THE LEGISLATOR

The elegant U.S. Capitol building is the working center of our nation's legislative process. It is flanked by half a dozen House and Senate office buildings, the sprawling Library of Congress, and a number of other office buildings that help Congress do its work (Figure 11–1). Although staff size has been cut in recent years, members of Congress still employ about 16,000 staff aides who work in Washington, D.C., or in local district offices. Another 4,300 work for the General Accounting Office, the Congressional Research Service, the Congressional Budget Office, and other agencies under the direct control of Congress.[25] (We exclude for this count the Library of Congress and the U.S. Government Printing Office, which technically report to Congress, yet in fact serve the entire government as well as the general public.)

Congressional staffs grew enormously in the 1960s and 1970s. But in more recent years, critics and some elected officials called for major reductions in the number of both staffs and committees. As a result of cutbacks and certain reorganizations during the 1990s, staffs are about 10 percent smaller now than they were a decade ago.

Legislators as Representatives

Congress has a split personality. On the one hand, it is a *law-making institution* that writes laws and makes policy for the entire nation. In this capacity, all the members are expected to set aside their personal ambitions and perhaps even the concerns of their own constituencies. Yet Congress is also a *representative assembly*, made up of 535 elected officials who serve as links between their constituents and the national government. The dual roles of making laws and responding to constituents' demands force members to balance national concerns against the specific interests of their states or districts.

Members of Congress perceive their roles differently. Some believe they should serve as **delegates** from their districts. These legislators believe it is their duty to find out what "the folks back home" want and act accordingly. Other members see their role as that of **trustee**. Their constituents, they contend, did not send them to Congress to serve as mere robots or "errand-runners." They act and vote according to

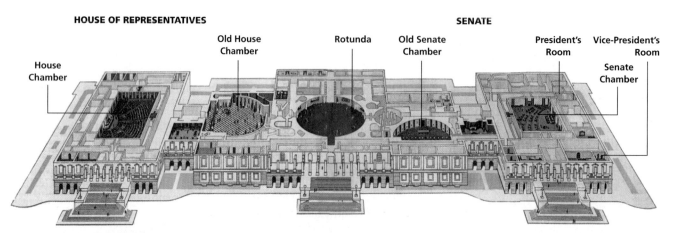

HOUSE OF REPRESENTATIVES   **SENATE**

House Chamber   Old House Chamber   Rotunda   Old Senate Chamber   President's Room   Vice-President's Room   Senate Chamber

FIGURE 11–1 The Capitol Building

their own view of what is best for their district or state as well as the nation. As one member explained, "I have a responsibility not only to follow [my constituents], but to inform them and lead them. I'm not going to betray my responsibility to my constituents. I owe them not only my industry but my judgment. That's why they sent me here."[26] In this view a legislature is a place for deliberation and learning, not a mere gathering of ambassadors from localities.

Most legislators shift back and forth between the delegate and trustee roles, depending on their perception of the public interest, their standing in the last and next elections, and the pressures of the moment. Most also view themselves more as free agents than as instructed delegates for their districts. And recent research suggests that they often are free, since about 50 percent of citizens are unaware of how their representatives voted on major legislation and often believe their representative voted in accord with constituent policy views. Still, nearly everyone in Congress spends a lot of time building constituency connections, mending political fences, reaching out to swing voters, and worrying about how a vote on a controversial issue will "play" back home.[27]

Legislators as Lawmakers

About 5,000 bills are introduced in the House every two years and sometimes as many as 3,000 in the Senate. Members of Congress cast as many as a thousand votes each year.[28] When they vote, members of Congress are influenced by their own philosophy and values, their perceptions of their constituents' interests, the views of their trusted colleagues and staff, their partisan ties, and party leaders, lobbyists, and the president.

POLICY AND PHILOSOPHICAL CONVICTIONS   Members are influenced by their ideological beliefs most of the time. Their experiences and their attitudes about the role of government shape their convictions and help explain a lot of the differences in voting patterns.[29] A liberal on social issues is also likely to be a liberal on tax and national security issues. On controversial issues such as Social Security reform, tax cuts, or defense spending, knowing the general philosophical leanings of individual members provides a helpful guide both to how they make up their minds and how they will vote.

VOTERS   Rarely does a legislator consistently and deliberately vote against the wishes of the people back home, but a paradox is evident here. Members of Congress sometimes think what they do and how they vote makes a lot of difference to voters back home. Yet the fact is most voters most of the time don't know how their member of Congress votes. In practice, most voters don't follow most issues that come before Congress. Most citizens don't even know the names of their senators and representative.[30] Aside from periodic polls, members hear most often from the **attentive public**—those who follow public affairs carefully—rather than the general public. Nearly 70 percent of constituents say they have not visited, faxed, phoned, e-mailed, or even written their members of Congress in the past four years.[31] Still, members of Congress are generally concerned about how they will explain their votes, especially around election day. Even if only a few voters are aware of their stand on a given issue, this group might make the difference between victory and defeat.

COLLEAGUES   Legislators are often influenced by the advice of their close friends in Congress. Their busy schedules and the great number of votes force them to depend on the advice of like-minded colleagues. In particular, they look to respected members of the committee who worked on a bill.[32] Legislators find out how their friends stand on an issue, listen to the party leadership's advice, and take into account the various committee reports. Sometimes, members are influenced to vote one way merely because they know a colleague is on the other side of the issue. For

delegate
A view of the role of legislators that holds that they should represent the views of their constituents even when personally holding different views.

trustee
A view of the role of legislators that holds that they should vote independently based on their judgment of the facts.

attentive public
Those who follow public affairs carefully.

Bill Bradley on What Influences a Senator's Decisions and Votes

"Every day, an effective Senator calculates the interaction of substance, procedure, and personality in his dealings with his fellow Senators. To have command of only one of these and not the other two dooms one to failure. The skillful Senators know what they're talking about and have mastered the substance of at least two or three subject areas. . . . The skillful Senators use procedures to further their goals. They don't let Senate leadership arrange their procedural lives. The skillful Senators are at home with their colleagues. . . .

Finally, the behavior of every Senator, be that Senator collegial or not, is affected by the quest for reelection. Senators running for reelection do not act normally. They justify an egregious legislative position or their sudden support of the other party's amendment or their participation in outrageous pandering to special interests as being absolutely necessary for reelection."

SOURCE: Bill Bradley, *Time Past, Time Present: A Memoir* (Knopf, 1996), pp. 88–89.

log rolling

Mutual aid and vote trading among legislators.

some legislators, the state delegation (senators and representatives from their home state) reinforces a common identity. Texas Democrats have long been a strong and cohesive delegation; other states, like California, have less cohesive state delegations.

A member may also vote with a colleague in the expectation that the colleague will later vote for a measure about which the member is concerned—called **log rolling**. Some vote trading takes place to build coalitions so that members can "bring home the bacon" to their constituents. Other vote trading reflects reciprocity in congressional relations or deference to colleagues' superior information or expertise.

CONGRESSIONAL STAFF   Representatives and senators used to be at a distinct disadvantage in dealing with the executive branch because they were overly dependent on information supplied by the White House or lobbyists. The complexity of the issues and increasingly demanding schedules created pressures for additional staff. Congress responded and gradually expanded its staffs, and this expansion has strengthened the role of Congress in the public policy process.

All members of Congress have personal staff members working for them both in their Washington and home-district offices. About one-third of the House of Representatives staff and one-fourth of the Senate staff are based back home. Local staff members help members of Congress communicate with the voters and provide constituency services and casework. (Helping people with a misplaced Social Security check or helping them qualify for veteran's benefits are examples of casework provided by congressional offices.) Much of the work done in district offices is akin to a continuous campaign effort: generating favorable publicity, arranging for local appearances and newspaper interviews, scheduling, and contacting important civic and business leaders in the region.

Members rely heavily on the advice of congressional staffers. Staff draft bills, do research, and are often involved in negotiating and coalition building. Staff specialists in policy areas sometimes deal on a day-to-day basis with their counterparts in the executive branch departments and with interest groups. With their direct access to the members of Congress they serve, these staff aides are often among the most influential people in Washington.

But we should not exaggerate the independent power base of staffers. They can be summarily fired at the whim of those they serve. Although they cannot be dismissed because of their race, sex, or national origin, they know that if they wander too far from the views of the one person who can fire them, they will quickly be called back into line. They are, however, asked to help raise money for their bosses.[33]

PARTY   Members generally vote with their party. Whether as a result of party pressure or natural affinity, on major bills there is a tendency for most Democrats to be arrayed against most Republicans. Partisan voting has been increasing in the House since the early 1970s and has intensified since the 1994 elections. Indeed, party-line voting has been greater in recent years than at any time in recent decades. Party differences are stronger over domestic, regulatory, and welfare reform measures than over foreign policy or civil liberty issues. Ninety-eight percent of House Republicans, for example, voted to impeach Bill Clinton in a historic vote in late 1998; 98 percent of House Democrats voted against impeachment.

Congressional redistricting has helped increase partisanship in congressional voting. "Advances in computer-driven mapping capabilities have made an art form of the old-fashioned gerrymandering that occurs where congressional districts are redrawn after each decennial census." Party operatives in the states can with great precision draw district lines to create relatively safe Democratic or Republican districts, "increasing the number of secure members answerable to only their own party's primary votes."[34]

As redistricting efforts in many states have ensured more safe seats, the House of Representatives has more members who are not inclined to compromise or be moderate. Consequently, House Republicans have become more politically conservative and House Democrats more confirmed liberals. The House is more politically partisan than the Senate not because of personalities but more due to these constitutional-political procedures.

Party leaders in both chambers do their best to get their members to vote together. Republican leaders claim cohesive voting is the only way Republicans can implement their party platform and satisfy the majorities who elected them in recent years. Senators are usually more independent, so party leaders in the Senate have a harder time encouraging party discipline than do leaders in the House.

The regional realignment in the American South has had the effect of diminishing the number of Democratic conservatives and strengthening Republican conservatives. There has been a similar decline of Republican moderates and a rise in more uniformly liberal Democratic districts.

In 2000, for example, on important party-unity legislation, that is, where the party leadership tried to rally its forces to vote with it, Republicans succeeded in holding an average of 88 percent of their conference in line in the House and 89 percent in the Senate. Democrats won party support in the House 82 percent of the time and in the Senate 88 percent of the time.[35] Republican moderates from the Northeast were most likely to split from their party ranks, while the few remaining conservative Democrats from the South are generally the most willing to side with the GOP when the parties lock horns.

Many forces—regional, local, ties of friendship—can override party influence. Members are sometimes influenced by ideological groups, ethnic caucuses, regional groupings, and even the class of colleagues with whom they were elected—for example, "the class of 1994." Ideological groups in Congress ranging from the Congressional Black Caucus to the more conservative Blue Dog Coalition of conservative Democrats or the even more conservative Family Concerns and New Federalists groups can also provide voting cues.[36]

INTEREST GROUPS   Interest groups, acting through their lobbyists and political action committees (PACs), make substantial contributions to congressional elections. These PACs give disproportionately to incumbents; at least 70 percent of PAC contributions went to incumbents in recent years.[37] In addition to their role as financiers of elections, interest groups are important participants in the legislative process because they provide information.

Interest groups not only watch and try to influence national legislators, but they also carefully watch one another. If a member of Congress tries to insert a "special interest" measure into an appropriations bill that is especially favorable to oil or education interests, for example, the odds are excellent that opposing interest groups are going to see this and exert their lobbying pressure to campaign for this measure's defeat. "The result is," says Senator Joe Lieberman of Connecticut, "that everyone on Capitol Hill is keeping a close eye on everyone else, creating a self-adjusting system of checks and balances."[38]

Interest groups can also be effective when they mobilize grass-roots activists and rally various constituencies to lobby their home state members of Congress. For example, higher education lobbying groups have effectively mobilized students and educators to write and call members of Congress on behalf of student aid and related provisions in various measures before the Congress.[39] And tobacco companies spent huge sums to fight taxes on cigarettes.

Most members of Congress deny the popular perception that interest groups "buy" their votes, yet political contributions certainly do influence the parties and help provide access to members of Congress. This is the way one prominent senator sees it:

In May of 2001 U.S. Senator Jim Jeffords of Vermont, a long term Republican in state and national political office, switched party affiliation and became an Independent. He did so because he believed the Republican Party had grown too conservative and was putting undo pressure on him to vote the party line. His critical shift out of the Republican Party turned control of the Senate over to the Democratic Party.

How to Kill a Bill

The complexity of the congressional system provides a tremendous built-in advantage for opponents of any measure. Multiple opportunities to kill a bill exist because of the dispersion of influence. At a dozen or more points a bill may be stopped or allowed to die (inaction is the same as killing a bill). Those who sponsor a bill must win at every step; opponents need to win only once. Whether good or bad, a proposal can be delayed or rejected by any one of the following:

1. The House subcommittee and its chair
2. The chair of the House standing committee
3. The House standing committee and its leaders
4. The House Rules Committee
5. The majority of the House
6. The Senate subcommittee and its chair
7. The Senate standing committee
8. The majority of the Senate
9. The floor leaders in both chambers
10. A few senators, in the case of a filibuster
11. The House-Senate conference committee, if the chambers disagree
12. The president (by veto)

In my experience I have found it to be not so much individual senators as the national parties and their congressional caucuses that become most dependent on special interest groups for money and grassroots support. They therefore advance the legislative priorities of some of the most ideological of those groups higher on their congressional agenda, which, in turn, further separates the parties and intensifies partisanship.[40]

THE PRESIDENT   Through effective use of their constitutional and political powers, presidents are usually partners with Congress in the legislative process. Members of Congress are invariably reluctant to admit that they are influenced by pressure from the White House. On domestic issues, legislators generally say they are more likely to be influenced by their own convictions or by their constituents than by what the White House wants. But presidents and their aides work hard to influence public opinion and to win members over to the president's point of view.

On key votes, presidents win needed majority support less than half the time. In his first term, Bill Clinton won an impressive 64 percent support from Congress on roll call votes on which he had taken a clear position.[41] However, he enjoyed much less success in his second term.

For a variety of reasons, especially because of the tendency of the nation to rally around the president in time of foreign crisis, presidents have more influence on how members of Congress vote on foreign policy or national security issues than on domestic policy.[42] Former president George Bush benefited from a bipartisan coalition that passed the resolution authorizing the use of military force in the Persian Gulf. President Clinton benefited from strong Republican support in Congress to help win approval for the various free trade agreements, even when large numbers in his own party opposed these measures.

THE LEGISLATIVE OBSTACLE COURSE

Congress operates under a system of multiple vetoes. The framers intentionally dispersed powers so they could not be accumulated by any would-be tyrant. Follow a bill through the legislative process, and you clearly see this dispersion of power (see Figure 11–2). The procedures and rules of the Senate differ somewhat from those of the House, but in each chamber power is fragmented and decentralized.

Every bill, including those drawn up in the executive branch, must be *introduced* in the House and the Senate by a member of that body. Bills are then *referred* by the leadership to the appropriate **standing committee**. A standing committee is one of the permanent working units established in the rules of the House and the Senate. Standing committees continue from one session to the next and are generally organized along policy lines (foreign policy, agriculture, and so forth). Their importance arises from the fact that most legislative measures are first considered in the appropriate standing committee or one of its relevant subcommittees. (See Table 11–2 for a list of both standing and select committees.)

Roughly 85 percent of the bills introduced in every two-year session of Congress die in committees for lack of support.[43] When bills have significant backing, a committee or subcommittee holds *hearings* to receive opinions. It then meets to *mark up* (discuss and amend) and vote on the bill. If the subcommittee and then the parent committee vote in favor of the bill, it is *reported*—that is, sent to the full chamber—where it is *debated* and *voted* on. In the House the bill must go first to the Rules Committee for a *rule* (specifying the length of debate and whether the bill may be amended).

In the Senate, it is not uncommon for legislators to attach **riders**—provisions that may have little relationship to the bill they are riding on. For

standing committee
A permanent committee established in a legislature, usually focusing on a policy area.

rider
A provision that may have little relationship to the bill it is attached to in order to secure its passage.

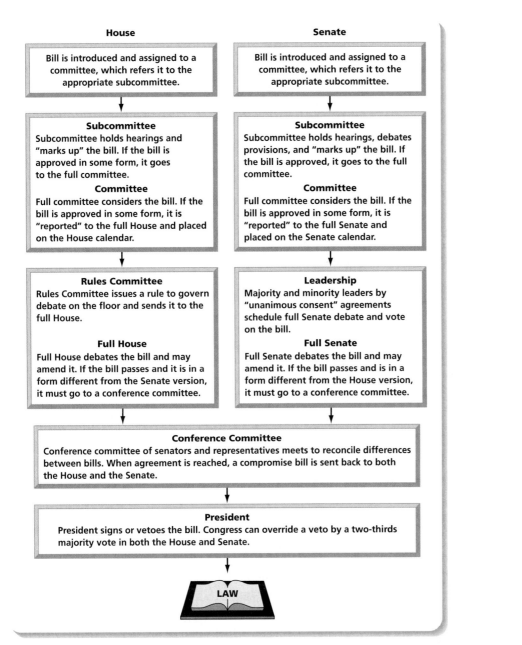

House	Senate
Bill is introduced and assigned to a committee, which refers it to the appropriate subcommittee.	**Bill is introduced and assigned to a committee, which refers it to the appropriate subcommittee.**

House

Subcommittee
Subcommittee holds hearings and "marks up" the bill. If the bill is approved in some form, it goes to the full committee.

Committee
Full committee considers the bill. If the bill is approved in some form, it is "reported" to the full House and placed on the House calendar.

Rules Committee
Rules Committee issues a rule to govern debate on the floor and sends it to the full House.

Full House
Full House debates the bill and may amend it. If the bill passes and it is in a form different from the Senate version, it must go to a conference committee.

Senate

Subcommittee
Subcommittee holds hearings, debates provisions, and "marks up" the bill. If the bill is approved, it goes to the full committee.

Committee
Full committee considers the bill. If the bill is approved in some form, it is "reported" to the full Senate and placed on the Senate calendar.

Leadership
Majority and minority leaders by "unanimous consent" agreements schedule full Senate debate and vote on the bill.

Full Senate
Full Senate debates the bill and may amend it. If the bill passes and is in a form different from the House version, it must go to a conference committee.

Conference Committee
Conference committee of senators and representatives meets to reconcile differences between bills. When agreement is reached, a compromise bill is sent back to both the House and the Senate.

President
President signs or vetoes the bill. Congress can override a veto by a two-thirds majority vote in both the House and Senate.

LAW

FIGURE 11–2 **How a Bill Becomes a Law**

example, riders that have little to do with spending money can be attached to appropriations bills. "In recent years, members of Congress have found the 'rider' to be a particularly helpful way of stripping from law various provisions that protect the environment."[44] The House of Representatives has stricter rules that require amendments to be relevant to the bill if they are allowed at all, but no such rule is enforced in the Senate. Senators use riders to force the president to accept legislation attached to a bill that was otherwise popular, because the president has either to accept the *entire* bill or to veto it. There has been an increase in the number of riders to appropriations bills in recent years. Republicans in both the House and Senate skirmished with President Clinton by adding riders concerning restrictions on abortion, on enforcement of environmental laws, and the right of nonprofit groups that receive federal grants to lobby.[45]

Except for tax bills, the House and Senate discuss bills simultaneously rather than waiting for one to act first. If only one chamber passes a bill at the end of that

TABLE 11–2 Congressional Standing and Select Committees

House	Senate	Joint Committees
Agriculture	Agriculture, Nutrition, and Forestry	Economics
Appropriations	Appropriations	Printing
Armed Services	Armed Services	Taxation
Budget	Banking, Housing, and Urban Affairs	On the Library
Education and the Workforce	Budget	
Energy and Commerce	Commerce, Science, and Transportation	
Financial Services	Energy and Natural Resources	
Government Reform	Environment and Public Works	
House Administration	Finance	
International Relations	Foreign Relations	
Judiciary	Governmental Affairs	
Resources	Health, Education, Labor, and Pensions	
Rules	Indian Affairs	
Science	Judiciary	
Select Intelligence	Rules and Administration	
Small Business	Select Ethics	
Standards of Official Conduct	Select Intelligence	
Transportation and Infrastructure	Small Business	
Veterans' Affairs	Special Aging	
Ways and Means	Veterans' Affairs	

congressional term, it dies. If both houses pass bills on the same subject but there are differences between the bills—and there often are—the two versions must go to a *conference committee* for *reconciliation*. If a bill does not make it through both chambers in identical form in the same Congress (two-year term), it must begin the entire process again in the next Congress.

When a bill has passed both houses in identical form, it then goes to the president, who may *sign* it into law or *veto* it. If Congress is in session and the president waits ten days (excluding Sundays), then the bill becomes law *without* his signature. If Congress has adjourned and the president waits ten days without signing the bill, it is then defeated by a **pocket veto**. Except for the pocket veto, when a bill is vetoed it is returned to the chamber of its origin by the president with a message explaining the reasons for the veto. Congress can vote to **override** the veto with a two-thirds vote in each chamber, but assembling such an extraordinary majority is often difficult.

Authorization and Appropriation

Congress legislates by a two-step process: first it *authorizes*; then it *appropriates*. After Congress and the president authorize a program by passing a law, Congress, with the president's concurrence, has to appropriate the funds by yet another measure to implement it. Appropriations are processed by the House and Senate Appropriations Committees and their subcommittees. For example, the 1998 Higher Education Act and its several titles reauthorized a variety of programs for a five-year period, including those for federal loans and grants for college students. The authorization act set the limits on the amount that students may borrow and the conditions under which they must pay back the loan. But the authorization is useless until Congress appropriates funds and the president signs the appropriations bill into law each year. Congress often appropriates less money than it has authorized.

pocket veto
A veto exercised by the president after Congress has adjourned; if the president takes no action for ten days, the bill does not become law and is not returned to Congress for a possible override.

override
An action taken by Congress to reverse a presidential veto that requires a two-thirds majority in each chamber.

The Importance of Compromise

Since it takes a majority vote in two chambers of Congress and the signature of the president before a bill becomes a law, sponsors of new legislation have to be willing to compromise. One tactical decision at the start is whether to push for action in the Senate first, in the House first, or in both simultaneously. For example, if it appears that the Senate is not likely to approve a bill, its sponsors may seek passage in the House and hope that a sizable victory there will spur the Senate into action. Another tactic concerns the committee that will consider a bill. Normally, referral to a committee is automatic, but sometimes sponsors have discretion. A bill that involves more than one jurisdiction can be written in such a way that it may go to a committee that will look more kindly on it.

Getting a bill through Congress requires that majorities and sometimes super-majorities be mobilized over and over again—in subcommittee, in committee, in chamber, and possibly again in chamber to override a presidential veto. These majorities shift and change, and they involve different legislators in different situations at different points in time. Thus coalitions must be built again and again.[46]

COMMITTEES: THE LITTLE LEGISLATURES

It is sometimes said Congress is a collection of committees that come together in a chamber every once in a while to approve one another's actions. There is much truth in this. Congress has long relied on committees to get its work done. Woodrow Wilson, a political scientist before he became president, expressed a similar thought: "Congress in session is Congress on display. Congress in committee is Congress at work."[47] More precisely, Congress in subcommittee is Congress at work, because the initial struggle over legislation takes place in subcommittees.[48]

Congress utilizes **joint committees** whose members are selected from both houses to oversee such institutions as the Library of Congress or to investigate issues

BELOW THE BELTWAY

Toles. © 1999. *Universal Press Syndicate.*

joint committee
Committee composed of members of both the House of Representatives and the Senate; such committees oversee the Library of Congress and conduct investigations.

like campaign finance reform. Committees organized to conduct investigations are called **select or special committees**.

The House of Representatives divides standing committees into three categories:

1. *Exclusive committees* include Appropriations, Ways and Means, and Rules; members who serve on one of these committees may not serve on any other standing committee.

2. *Major committees* include committees like Armed Services; members can serve on only one of these committees, but can add assignments to two nonmajor committees.

3. *Nonmajor committees*, such as Small Business, permit membership in two or three of these. House members rarely serve on more than three standing committees.

Occasionally a bill flies through a committee. More typically, however, it is kept in committee for a long while, and if and when it is reported back to the chamber, more often than not it has been amended considerably, sometimes beyond recognition. A committee reports out favorably only a small fraction of all the bills that come to it.

Although a bill can be forced to the floor of the House of Representatives through a **discharge petition** signed by a majority of the membership, legislators are reluctant to bypass committees. They regard committee members as experts in their fields. Sometimes, too, they are reluctant to risk the anger of committee leaders. And there is a strong sense of *reciprocity*: "You respect my committee's jurisdiction, and I will respect yours." Not surprisingly, few discharge petitions gain the necessary number of signatures.

While members of the House hold relatively few committee assignments, each senator normally serves on three standing committees and at least seven subcommittees. Among the most important Senate committees are Appropriations, Budget, Finance, and Foreign Relations.

Committees are not all alike. Some are powerful; others are less important. Because of the Senate's special role in foreign policy, for example, the Senate Foreign Relations Committee is usually more influential than the House Committee on International Relations. For the two Appropriations Committees, however, the reverse is true; the House Appropriations Committee plays a more significant role than the Senate Appropriations Committee, although these differences are less than they used to be.

Choosing Committee Members

Control and staffing of standing committees are partisan matters. The chair and a majority of each standing committee come from the majority party. The minority party is represented on each committee roughly in proportion to its membership in the entire chamber, except on some powerful committees on which the majority may want to enhance its position. Because Republicans and Democrats were evenly divided in the Senate after the 2000 elections 50 to 50, party leaders negotiated an equal split of membership on Senate committees. However, Republicans retained the committee chairmanships in recognition of Vice-President Dick Cheney providing the fifty-first vote in tie-breaking situations.

Getting on a politically advantageous committee is important to members of Congress. A representative from Kansas, for example, would rather serve on the Agriculture Committee than on the Banking and Financial Services Committee. Members usually stay on the same committees from one Congress to the next, although less senior members who have had less desirable assignments often seek better committees when places become available.

select or special committee
A congressional committee created for a specific purpose, sometimes to conduct an investigation.

discharge petition
Petition that, if signed by a majority of the members of the House of Representatives, will pry a bill from committee and bring it to the floor for consideration.

How are committee members chosen? In the House of Representatives, a Committee on Committees of the Republican membership allots places to Republican members. This committee is composed of one member from each state having Republican representation in the House; the member is generally the senior member of the state's delegation. Because each member has as many votes in the committee as there are Republicans in the delegation, the group is dominated by senior members from the large state delegations. On the Democratic side, assignment to committees is handled by the Steering and Policy Committee of the Democratic caucus in negotiation with senior Democrats from the state delegations.

In the Senate, veteran members also dominate the assignment process. Each party has a small Steering Committee that makes committee assignments. In making assignments, leaders are guided by various considerations: how talented and cooperative a member is, whether his or her region is already well represented on a committee, and whether the assignment will aid in reelecting the member. There sometimes are fierce battles within these committees, battles about liberal/conservative, rural/urban, environment/industry, and other differences.

One way Congress copes with its huge workload is that its committees and subcommittees are organized around subject matter specialties. This specialization allows members to develop technical expertise in specific areas and to recruit skilled staffs. Thus Congress is often able to challenge experts from the bureaucracy. Interest groups and lobbyists realize the great power a specific committee has in certain areas and focus their attention on its members. Similarly, members of executive departments are careful to cultivate the committee and subcommittee chairs and members of "their" committees.

How each chamber in Congress uses committees is critical in its role as a partner in policy making, both with the other house in Congress and with the executive branch. In recent years progress has been made in opening hearings to the public and improving the quality of committee staffs, but it is difficult to restructure committee jurisdictions so they do not overlap. Thus, a dozen different committees deal with energy, education, and the war on drugs. Efforts to make the committee system more efficient are often considered threats to the delicate balance of power within the chamber.

Seniority Rule

Forty years ago committee chairs determined the workload of committees, hired and fired staff, formed subcommittees, and assigned them jurisdictions, members, and aides. Chairs also managed the most important bills assigned to their committees. Since the mid-1970s, however, junior members have insisted they be given more authority. Subcommittee chairs also became more independent. In recent years there have also been moves to strengthen the powers of the party leaders and caucuses at the expense of the committee chairs.

Most chairs are selected on the basis of the **seniority rule**; the member of the majority party with the longest continuous service on the committee becomes chair upon the retirement of the current chair or a change in the party in control of Congress. The seniority rule gives power to representatives who come from safe districts where one party is dominant and a member can build up years of continuous service. Conversely, the seniority rule lessens the influence of states or districts where the two parties are more evenly matched and where there is more turnover.

Both Democrats and Republicans have occasionally passed over the most senior committee member in order to place someone with more energy or with

A 50/50 Split

Following the extraordinarily close outcome of the 2000 election, the Senate voted to grant Democrats and Republicans an equal number of seats on committees and an even share of the money to run the panels. . . .

Senator Trent Lott, the Republican leader, and Senator Tom Daschle, the Democratic leader, negotiated the proposal over several weeks and presented it to their respective parties, hailing it as a formula for bipartisanship.

A reluctant Republican conference signed off on the proposal after two days of discussion, realizing it was the best deal they could secure under the circumstances, Mr. Lott said.

"It's going to force us to work together more than we have in the past," Mr. Lott said. "No doubt. I don't think that's bad. I think this is a framework for bipartisanship."

. . . Neither party got everything it wanted, although Republicans were forced to bend the most. While Republicans retained control of the Senate because the Constitution gave the vice-president the right to break the votes, they were forced to share control of their committees, though they kept the chairmanships.

The resolution called for an equal division of committee assignments and an equal share of money between the two parties to run the committees, which meant Democrats could hire more policy experts and buy more computers. In the past, Republicans held a one-third advantage in staff, office space, and money.

SOURCE: Lizette Alvarez, "Senate to Divide Power and Money Equally in Panels," *The New York Times*, January 6, 2001, p. 1.

seniority rule
A legislative practice that assigns the chair of a committee or subcommittee to the member of the majority party with the longest continuous service on the committee.

How would you "reform" Congress?

Which of these proposed reforms do you think should be adopted to improve Congress?

Move to a European-style parliamentary system

Extend House terms to four years

Limit House and Senate tenure to 12 years

Provide for public financing of campaigns and ban campaign contributions

Permit only people who live in a district or state to contribute to candidates for Congress

Radically reduce the number of committees and subcommittees

Strengthen the power and resources of the party leaders

Reduce the size of congressional staffs

Abide by an agenda agreed to at the beginning of each session

Have shorter sessions for Congress so members can spend more time in their districts

a more compatible policy perspective in a committee chair position. Under Newt Gingrich's term as Speaker, a few aging committee chairs were replaced with members more allied with the Republican policy positions. It is not uncommon these days for a member of Congress to become chair of an important subcommittee after only one or two terms, and indeed such placement is the tradition in the Senate.

Still, the practice of elevating the senior member of a committee to serve as committee chair remains a general rule. It has long been respected in Congress for several reasons: it encourages members to stay on a committee; it encourages specialization and expertise; it also reduces the interpersonal politics that would arise if several members of a committee "ran" for election to become chair. However, one legacy from the Speaker Newt Gingrich era of the mid-1990s that remains is a Republican House rule that limits committee chairs to just three terms.[49] This limit brought about a lot of turnover and a fair amount of intraparty squabbles to decide who would become chair of certain key committees. Republicans departed from the seniority rule in several cases when they picked new committee chairs as the 107th Congress began in 2001.

Investigations and Oversight

The power to *investigate* is one of Congress's most important functions. Congress conducts investigations to determine if legislation is needed, to gather facts relevant to legislation, to assess the efficiency of executive agencies, to build public support, to expose corruption, and to enhance the image or reputation of its members.[50] Hearings by standing committees, their subcommittees, or special select committees are an important source of information and opinion. They provide an arena in which experts can submit their views.

Another important function of congressional hearings is the *oversight* function—the responsibility to question executive branch officials to see whether their agencies are complying with the wishes of the Congress and conducting their programs efficiently. Authorization committees regularly hold oversight hearings, and appropriations committees, exercising "the congressional power of the purse," often use appropriations hearings to communicate committee members' views about how agency officials should conduct their business. Cabinet members and agency heads have been known to dread the loaded questions of hostile members of Congress and to hate having to watch themselves on the evening news trying to explain why their agency made some mistakes.

Conference Committees

When the framers created a two-house national legislature, they anticipated the two chambers would represent sharply different interests. The Senate was to be a small chamber of persons elected indirectly by the state legislatures to hold long, overlapping terms. It was to be a chamber of deliberation, a gathering of wise leaders who would counsel and sanction a president. The House of Representatives, elected anew every two years, was to be a more direct reflection of the people.

The Senate did serve as a check on the House, especially in the late nineteenth and early twentieth centuries, when it was extremely conservative and something of a rich man's club. But today the House tends to be more conservative than the Senate. Executive departments and agencies, for instance, occasionally consider the Senate to be a court of appeals for appropriations that have been shot down by the House.

Given the differences between the House and the Senate, it is not surprising that the version of a bill passed by one chamber may differ substantially from the version passed by the other. Only if both houses pass an absolutely identical measure can

conference committee

Committee appointed by the presiding officers of each chamber to adjust differences on a particular bill passed by each but in different forms.

it become law. Most of the time one house accepts the language of the other, but about 10 to 12 percent of all bills passed, usually major ones, must be referred to a **conference committee**—a special committee of members from each chamber—that settles the differences between versions.[51] Both parties are represented, but the majority party has more members.

The proceedings of a conference committee are usually an elaborate bargaining process. When the revised bill is brought back to the two chambers, the conference report can be accepted or rejected (often with further negotiations ordered), but it cannot be amended. Conference members of each chamber must convince their colleagues that any concessions made to the other chamber were on unimportant points and that nothing basic to the original version of the bill was surrendered.

How much leeway does a conference committee have? Ordinarily members are expected to end up somewhere between the different versions. On matters for which there is no clear middle ground, members are sometimes accused of exceeding their instructions and producing an entirely new bill. For this reason, the conference committee has been called a "third house" of Congress and one of the most significant institutions within the Congress.[52]

Which chamber, House or Senate, wins more often in conference committees? On the surface it appears that the Senate's version wins more often, but this is partly because the Senate often acts on its legislation after the House. But by approving the initial bill first and thereby setting the agenda on an issue, the House often has more of an impact on the final outcome than the Senate.

CONGRESS: AN ASSESSMENT AND A VIEW ON REFORMS

Two hundred and fifteen years after its creation, Congress is a larger, more vital, and very different kind of institution from the one the framers envisioned. Yet most of its major functions remain the same, and their effective exercise is crucial to the health of our constitutional democracy. Even in the twenty-first century, we still look to Congress to make laws, raise revenues, represent citizens, investigate abuses of power, and oversee the executive branch.

Today most members must engage in continual electioneering to stay in office. Members appear driven by their desire to win reelection, so that much of what takes place in Congress seems mainly designed to promote reelection. These efforts usually pay off for members of Congress: most who want to get reelected do. At the same time, these efforts also pay off for our democracy. The concern of members with reelection fosters *accountability* and the desire to please the voters.

William Cohen, a popular Republican senator from Maine (and later secretary of defense in the Clinton administration), observed when he retired from the Senate that he admired Congress's deliberative process, yet he worried that too many checks and too much partisanship made it hard for Congress to get needed results:

> Our republic, we know, was designed to be slow-moving and deliberative. Our founding fathers were convinced that power had to be entrusted to someone, but that no one could be entirely trusted with power. They devised a brilliant system of checks and balances to prevent the tyranny of the many by the few. They constructed a perfect triangle of allocated and checked power. . . . There could be no rash action, no rush to judgment, no legislative mob rule, no unrestrained chief executive.
>
> The difficulty with this diffusion of power in today's cyberspace age is that everyone is in check, but no one is in charge. . . .
>
> But more than the constitutional separation of powers is leading to the unprecedented stalemate that exists today. There has been a breakdown in

Thinking It Through...

No reform is neutral in terms of effects. Some groups will benefit more than others from the passage of each reform proposal. Most reforms also have unanticipated consequences that may create more problems than they solve. Some would require amendments to our Constitution. Still, the search goes on for practical ways to improve Congress's ability to do the people's work.

Congress spent a lot of time in the 1990s trying to come up with procedural and fund-raising reforms, yet despite great public pressure to reform, Congress did little to alter its traditional ways.

civil debates and discourse. Enmity at times has become so intense that members of Congress have resorted to shoving matches outside the legislative chambers.[53]

How does such a Congress make any progress? In an institution where most members act as individual entrepreneurs and consider themselves leaders, the task of providing institutional leadership is increasingly difficult. With limited resources, and only sometimes aided by the president, congressional leaders are asked to bring together a diverse, fragmented, and independent institution. The congressional system acts only when majorities can be achieved. That the framers accomplished their original objective—creating a Congress that would not move with imprudent haste—has been generally well realized.

Americans often characterize Congress as a bickering, timid, ignorant, selfish, or narrow-minded body. Yet they also admire the stamina and civic responsibility of their own member of Congress. Individual members of Congress are almost always more popular than the institution. Typically, an individual member of Congress enjoys a 60–65 percent approval rating, whereas Congress as an institution fluctuates between a 35–50 percent approval rating by the general public, perhaps because people judge individual members primarily on how well they serve the interests of their states and districts and on their personal appeal.

Some of the criticism of Congress is justified. However, critics usually forget that our national legislature is particularly exposed, and some of our expectations of it are unrealistic. First, Congress does nearly all its work directly in the public eye, even more public now that it is televised live on C-SPAN. Unfortunate incidents—quarrels, name-calling, evasive actions, inaccurate statements, and ethical lapses—that might be hushed up in the executive or judicial branches are observed and duly reported by the media.

Second, Congress by its nature is controversial and argumentative. Its 535 members are found on both sides, sometimes on half a dozen sides, of every important question. Moreover, during the 1990s Congress raised taxes and cut services, closed military bases, reduced spending for welfare, the arts, and many research programs, shut down the government, and impeached a highly approved president—not a recipe for popularity!

Criticisms of Congress

CONGRESS IS INEFFICIENT   House and Senate procedures are, some charge, simply not suited to the needs of a modern information-age nation. Some of this criticism is exaggerated. Evaluating procedure and structure is difficult to separate from evaluating policy, about which everyone has an individual preference. Congress deals with an enormous number of complex measures. Many procedures expedite handling of bills, and the committee and subcommittee system is a reasonable device for hearing arguments and compiling information.

Still, the question of efficiency remains. Study groups inside and outside Congress have urged the chambers to reduce the number of committee assignments, establish better information systems, centralize more power in their leadership positions, and strengthen majority rule. Congress has done many of these things recently, yet the pace of legislation has not improved.

CONGRESS IS UNREPRESENTATIVE   The complaint is often made that Congress represents constituents' interests over the national interest. Defenders of Congress respond that representing their districts is precisely what Congress was designed to do. Legislators are described as being obsessed with staying in office—indeed, as concentrating solely on winning reelection—often at the expense of critical national issues such as Social Security, drug abuse, foreign policy, and trade.

Congress is supposed to reflect geographical and narrow interests, to register the diversity of the United States. In *The Federalist*, No. 57, James Madison wrote: "Who are to be the electors of the Federal Representatives? Not the rich more than the poor; not the learned more than the ignorant; not the haughty heirs of distinguished names more than the humble sons of obscure and unpropitious fortune."[54] Yet as the costs of campaigning increase, and as the majority of elected officials continue to come from the upper and upper-middle classes, we do have to ask whether ours is the open, representative, responsive, and responsible legislative system we can point to with pride as a model for those in other parts of the world who yearn for constitutional democracy. Can a Congress that has only 14 percent women and 7 percent African American membership truly represent our 51 percent female and 13 percent black populations?[55] That most members are the products of middle- and upper-middle-class families does not necessarily mean they are interested only in improving the position of that portion of the population. Affluent white males like Senators Edward Kennedy (D.-Mass.) and Jay Rockefeller (D.-W.Va.), for instance, are strong advocates of legislation to protect women, minorities, and the poor.[56]

WE THE PEOPLE

Profile of the 107th Congress, 2001–2003

	U.S. Senate (100)	U.S. House (435)
Republicans	49	221
Democrats	50	212
Independents	1	2
Sex		
Men	87	376
Women	13	59
Religion		
Catholic	24	125
Jewish	10	27
Protestant	53	251
Other	11	35
Average Age	60	54
Racial/Ethnic Minorities	3	63
Occupation		
Lawyers	53	156
Education	16	92
Business/Banking	24	159
Agriculture	6	25
Journalism	7	9
Engineering	0	9
Real Estate	4	24

SOURCE: *Congressional Quarterly Weekly*, January 20, 2001, pp. 180–181 (updated by authors May 29, 2001).

CONGRESS IS UNETHICAL   Some critics claim we have "the best Congress money can buy."[57] Many people—including U.S. Senator John McCain, who made this charge a central theme in his bid for the 2000 presidential nomination—allege that special interests and single-issue groups are stronger than ever, and that they are able to delay or block proceedings in Congress. The current system of financing congressional elections has been called a scandal because it forces members of Congress to beg for money from wealthy individuals and political action committees representing interest groups whose primary purpose is to seek support for pet legislation.

In response to occasional scandals, both houses passed ethics codes and created ethics subcommittees. These codes require public disclosure of income and property holdings by legislators, key aides, and spouses. They also ban most gifts of over $100 to a legislator, a staff member, or a legislator's family from a registered lobbyist, an organization with a political action committee, a foreign government, or a business with an interest in legislation before Congress. But valuable as these changes have been, they have apparently failed to improve the image of Congress.[58]

Defenders of Congress insist these charges are overstated. They say money would hardly influence the three dozen or more millionaires who are members of the Senate and the one hundred or so members of the House who are well-off financially. Defenders of Congress also point out that some members of Congress regularly turn down certain types of campaign contributions.

CONGRESS LACKS COLLECTIVE RESPONSIBILITY   Some critics see the main problem in Congress as the dispersion of power among committee and sub-committee leaders, elected party officials, factional leaders, informal caucus leaders, and other legislators. It is a "nobody's-in-charge" system. This dispersion of power means that to get things done, congressional leaders must bargain and negotiate. The result of this "brokering" system is that laws may be watered down, defeated, delayed, or written in vague language. According to some critics, too much leeway is given to unelected bureaucrats to develop the regulations that will implement the legislation. Accountability is confused, responsibility is eroded, and well-organized special interests that know how to work the system have an unfair advantage.

A Defense of Congress

Poking fun at Congress has been a national pastime for generations. Will Rogers told some of his best jokes at the expense of Congress, as Jay Leno and David Letterman do today. Cartoonists love Congress for its unfailing ability to put its worst foot forward. Even members of Congress, as noted earlier, often run against Congress when they are at home in their districts.

The challenge that confronted the framers—how to reconcile the need for executive energy with republican liberty—is still with us. The history of constitutional democracy has always been the search for limitations on absolute power and for techniques of sharing power. Our American style of constitutionalism and separation of powers often means a slow-moving and sometimes inefficient decision-making system. It means a system that often hinders rather than facilitates leadership, a system that invites contention, division, debate, delay, and political conflict. Critics call this gridlock or deadlock or even paralysis. Defenders of Congress prefer to call it the world's greatest deliberative body. They point out that the framers of the U.S. Constitution took great efforts to insulate policy-making processes from the momentary fancies of the people.

Newly elected presidents and members of Congress always arrive in Washington enthusiastically ready to enact the people's wishes. But they find that governing is invariably tougher and slower than they expected because government deals with complex issues about which there often is little consensus. Building policy majorities is hard because complex problems generate complex solutions, and the structure of Congress requires supermajorities to agree to serious changes. Thus the president's veto, the filibuster, the use of holds and legislative riders all make it harder to build a consensus for change. Not only is there often a lack of consensus in Congress, "there is a lack of consensus [on most major issues] among the public about what should be done."[59] And this makes it hard for legislators who are, after all, eager to please voters and remain in office.

Criticism of Congress—its alleged incompetence, its overresponsiveness to organized interests, its inefficiencies, its partisan character—are difficult to separate from the context of policy preferences and democratic procedures. Sometimes criticism tells us more about the critic than it does about the effectiveness of Congress. Constitutional democracy is not the most efficient form of government. Congress was never intended to act swiftly; it was not created to be a rubber stamp or even a cooperative partner for presidents. Its greatest strengths—its diversity and deliberative character—also weaken its position in dealing with the more centralized executive branch. Its members will rarely be fast on their feet. Not surprisingly, the 535 members, divided into two houses, two parties, dozens of committees, and nearly two hundred subcommittees, often have a difficult time arriving at a common strategy to collaborate with or to resist whoever is president.

POLITICS ONLINE

What's Happening in Congress Today?

When you visit Washington, D.C., be sure to visit the Capitol. The tour will give you a sense of the history of the building, and you will see and feel the bustle of lawmaking if Congress is in session. Also be sure to visit one of the office buildings to see committee rooms and an office of a representative or senator. If you do not have a chance to visit the Capitol, you can take a virtual tour of the building by going to the website for this book and Chapter 11 at: www.prenhall.com/burns.

One reason not to limit your tour of the Capitol to the two legislative chambers is that a lot of what happens in Congress happens in committees and subcommittees, and much of a legislator's time is spent meeting with constituents and supervising staff. To get a sample of what is going on in Congress at any given moment, you can check out any of three channels of C-SPAN, either on television or through the Internet at: www.cspan.org. If you miss an important hearing or floor speech, C-SPAN often replays the day's proceedings in the evening or on the weekend. The C-SPAN home page also provides an updated schedule of events.

You can also check on upcoming House and Senate schedules and find a vast amount on information on legislation and committees at the Thomas site: Thomas.loc.gov, maintained by the Library of Congress. The U.S. House of Representatives official home page: www.house.gov, and the U.S. Senate official home page: www.senate.gov, also offer a wide array of information and educational services, including schedules, votes, legislation, histories, and even ways to e-mail your own representative or senator.

SUMMARY

1. Congress plays a crucial role in our system of shared powers, controlling key decisions and constraining presidents. Yet, over time, Congress has lost some influence as the presidency has gained influence. In the last two decades, however, Congress has become more capable as a policy-making competitor for presidents. Redistricting and reapportionment have shaped a Congress that somewhat more accurately reflects the population.

2. The most distinctive feature of Congress is its bicameralism, which the framers intended as a moderating influence on partisanship and possible error. Each chamber

has a few distinctive functions. Their organizations and procedures also differ slightly, as do their political environments.

3. Congress performs these functions: representation, law making, consensus building, overseeing the bureaucracy, policy clarification, and investigating. The Senate also confirms or denies presidential appointments and participates in the ratification of treaties.

4. As a collective body, Congress must attempt to accomplish its tasks even as most of its members serve as delegates or trustees for their constituents. When they vote, members are influenced by

their philosophy and values, their perceptions of constituents' interests, and the views of trusted colleagues and staff, partisan ties and party leaders, lobbyists, and the president.

5. Congress does an excellent job of representing the values and views of most of their constituents. But they are cautious about enacting proposed measures by their own colleagues or the legislative agenda put forward by presidents. Most legislation dies for lack of majority support. In addition the legislative obstacle course sometimes involves filibusters, riders, holds, and an occasional override of a presidential veto.

6. Most of the work in Congress is done in committees and subcommittees. Congress has attempted in recent years to streamline its committee system and modify its methods of selecting committee chairs. Seniority practices are still generally followed, yet the threat of removal forces committee chairs to consult with younger members of the majority party. Subcommittees are important. They can prevent or delay legislation from being enacted. But there are numerous other stages where bills can be killed, making it easier to stop legislation than to enact it.

7. Members of Congress are motivated by the desire to win reelection, and much of what Congress does is in response to this motive. Members work hard to get favors for their districts, to serve the needs of constituents, and to maintain a high visibility in their districts or states. Incumbents have advantages that help explain their success at reelection: they have greater name recognition; they have large staffs; they are much better able to raise campaign money; and they have greater access to the media.

8. Individual members of Congress are more popular than the institution. Congress is criticized for being inefficient, unrepresentative, unethical, and lacking in collective responsibility. Yet criticisms of Congress are difficult to separate from the context of policy preference and democratic procedures. Congress's greatest strengths—its diversity and deliberative character—also contribute to its weaknesses.

KEY TERMS

safe seat 244
reapportionment 245
redistricting 245
gerrymandering 245
bicameralism 246
Speaker 248
majority leader 249
minority leader 249

whip 249
party caucus 249
closed rule 250
open rule 250
hold 250
president pro tempore 250
filibuster 250
cloture 250

senatorial courtesy 252
delegate 255
trustee 255
attentive public 255
log rolling 256
standing committee 258
rider 258
pocket veto 260

override 260
joint committee 261
select or special committee 262
discharge petition 262
seniority rule 263
conference committee 264

FURTHER READING

JOEL D. ABERBACH, *Keeping a Watchful Eye: The Politics of Congressional Oversight* (Brookings Institution, 1990).

SARAH A. BINDER AND STEVEN S. SMITH, *Politics or Principles? Filibustering in the United States Senate* (Brookings Institution, 1997).

BILL BRADLEY, *Time Present, Time Past: A Memoir* (Knopf, 1996).

DAVID W. BRADY AND CRAIG VOLDEN, *Revolving Gridlock: Politics and Policy from Carter to Clinton* (Westview Press, 1998).

ADAM CLYMER, *Edward M. Kennedy: A Biography* (William Morrow, 1999).

ROGER H. DAVIDSON AND WALTER J. OLESZEK, *Congress and Its Members*, 5th ed. (Congressional Quarterly Press, 1996).

CHRISTOPHER J. DEERING AND STEVEN S. SMITH, *Committees in Congress*, 3d ed. (Congressional Quarterly Press, 1997).

LAWRENCE C. DODD AND BRUCE J. OPPENHEIMER, EDS., *Congress Reconsidered*, 5th ed. (Congressional Quarterly Press, 1993).

RICHARD F. FENNO, JR., *Home Style: House Members in Their Districts* (Little, Brown, 1978).

RICHARD F. FENNO, JR., *Learning to Govern: An Institutional View of the 104th Congress* (Brookings Institution, 1997).

RICHARD F. FENNO, JR., *Senators on the Campaign Trail: The Politics of Representation* (University of Oklahoma Press, 1996).

MORRIS FIORINA, *Congress: Keystone of the Washington Establishment*, 2d ed. (Yale University Press, 1989).

PAUL HERRNSON, *Congressional Elections*, 3d ed. (Congressional Quarterly Press, 2000).

JOHN R. HIBBING AND ELIZABETH THEISS-MORSE, *Congress as Public Enemy: Public Attitudes Toward American Political Institutions* (Cambridge University Press, 1995).

GODFREY HODGSON, *The Gentleman from New York: Daniel Patrick Moynihan* (Houghton Mifflin, 2000).

LINDA KILLIAN, *The Freshmen: What Happened to the Republican Revolution?* (Westview Press, 1998).

FRANCES E. LEE AND BRUCE I. OPPENHEIMER, *Sizing Up the Senate: The Unequal Consequences of Equal Representation* (University of Chicago Press, 1999).

JOSEPH I. LIEBERMAN, *In Praise of Public Life* (Simon & Schuster, 2000).

TOM LOFTUS, *The Art of Legislative Politics* (Congressional Quarterly Press, 1994).

JANET M. MARTIN, *Lessons from the Hill: The Legislative Journey of an Education Program* (St. Martin's Press, 1993).

DAVID R. MAYHEW, *America's Congress: Actions in the Public Sphere, James Madison Through Newt Gingrich* (Yale University Press, 2000).

BARBARA MIKULSKI, KAY BAILEY HUTCHISON, ET AL., *Nine and Counting: The Women of the Senate* (William Morrow, 2000).

WALTER J. OLESZEK, *Congressional Procedures and the Policy Process*, 4th ed. (Congressional Quarterly Press, 1995).

Norman Ornstein, Thomas Mann, and Michael Malbin, *Vital Statistics on Congress, 1999–2000* (AEI Press, 2000).

Ronald M. Peters, Jr., ed., *The Speaker: Leadership in the U.S. House of Representatives* (Congressional Quarterly Press, 1995).

David E. Price, *The Congressional Experience: A View from the Hill* (Westview Press, 1993).

Nicole Rae and Colton Campbell, eds., *New Majority or Old Majority: The Impact of Republicans on Congress* (Rowman and Littlefield, 1999).

Warren B. Rudman, *Combat: Twelve Years in the U.S. Senate* (Random House, 1996).

Barbara Sinclair, *Unorthodox Lawmaking: New Legislative Processes in the U.S. Congress, 2nd ed.* (Congressional Quarterly Press, 2000).

Darvell M. West, *Patrick Kennedy: The Rise to Power* (Prentice Hall, 2001).

Students of Congress also should consult *Congressional Quarterly Weekly, National Journal, Roll Call,* and *The Hill.*

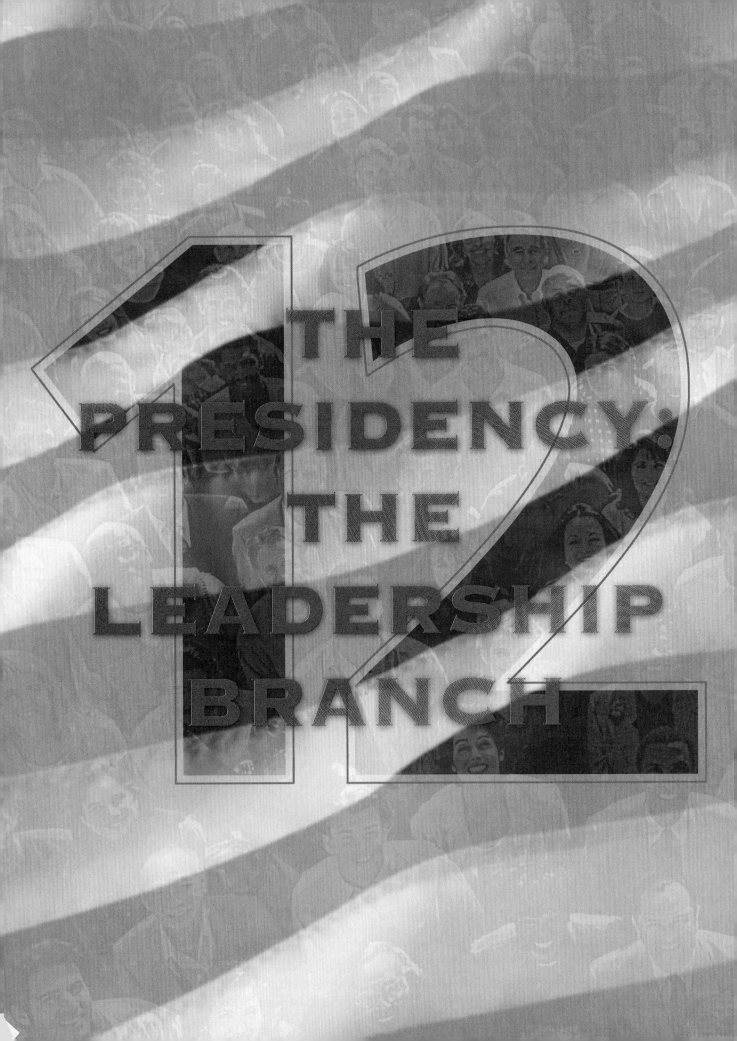

12

THE PRESIDENCY: THE LEADERSHIP BRANCH

AS HE TRAVELED SLOWLY UP THE EAST COAST FROM MOUNT VERNON TO NEW YORK (THE TEMPORARY SEAT OF GOVERNMENT) IN 1789, NEWLY ELECTED PRESIDENT George Washington was saluted with parades and fireworks. His whole trip was one long ovation, a celebration of the people's yearning for a strong individual who could provide continuity and leadership for the nation.

Yet Washington and his compatriots were of two minds about the power of the presidency. The framers both admired and feared centralized leadership. They realized the country needed a more effective national government, yet they were suspicious of the potential abuses of power, especially power vested in a single individual. Given what they had lived through in preceding decades, they had every right to these fears. Moreover, they hardly wanted to jeopardize the rights and liberties they had fought so hard to win in the Revolution.

Today, in the twenty-first century, we still have not resolved our ambivalence toward the presidency. Should a president be "above politics" and wait for a consensus to emerge from the people and Congress? Or should presidents be clearly political, leading the people and leading Congress? Should presidential powers be narrowly defined? Or should the presidency be granted broad authority to respond to national and international emergencies? Does the enlarged role of the presidency under today's circumstances undermine some of the fundamental checks and balances in our constitutional democracy? Should we be willing to overlook a president's personal failings if his performance of official duties meets with public approval? In this chapter we explore these questions as we look at the jobs we ask presidents to perform.

THE POLITICS OF SHARED POWERS

Original Intent

The framers of the Constitution created a presidency of limited powers. They wanted a presidential office that would steer clear of parties and factions, enforce the laws passed by Congress, handle communications with foreign governments, and help states put down disorders. They wanted a presidency strong enough to match Congress, yet not so strong it would overpower Congress.

CHAPTEROUTLINE

- The Politics of Shared Powers

- In Search of the Perfect President

- The Challenging Job of Being President

- The Vice-Presidency

- Keeping Presidents Accountable

- Presidential Greatness? How We Judge Them

CHAPTERMEDIA

POLITICS ONLINE
Want to Visit the West Wing?
www.prenhall.com/burns

The United States is among a very few democracies in which a strong presidential system has coincided with democratic rule. Elsewhere, democratic presidential regimes have often given way to authoritarian presidential rule.

Most democracies are based on the parliamentary system of government (as in Australia, Britain, and Israel) that confers full powers on a parliament, which then delegates executive powers to a handful of its members. These officials, the head of government (a prime minister or premier or chancellor), and cabinet ministers, make up what is known as "the Government." The Government serves only so long as it *maintains the confidence of a majority* in the lower house of parliament. If the parliament indicates its loss of support for the Government by a vote of censure, or a vote of no-confidence, or even by defeating a major piece of Government-sponsored legislation, the Government resigns, either to allow a new Government to be formed or to call for new parliamentary elections. In parliamentary systems, the head of state (usually a president elected by parliament but sometimes, as in Britain, a hereditary monarch) has only ceremonial responsibilities.

In the recent wave of democratizations, a number of countries have experimented with a mixed presidential-parliamentary system. Based on the French Fifth Republic (1958–present), the mixed system includes a popularly elected presidency that has extensive powers of its own, notably in foreign and defense matters, *and* a prime minister and cabinet accountable to the parliament. This mixed presidential-parliamentary system has been adopted in Russia, Poland, the Czech Republic, and several other new democracies.

There is a lively debate on which pattern of government—presidential, parliamentary, or the mixed presidential-parliamentary system—is most conducive to democracy. Some fear that powerful presidents are a source of authoritarianism. Others claim that a strong president is needed to give leadership and coherence to the often fragmented parliaments in newer democracies. Still others see the solution in some kind of hybrid.

It is true that historically most presidential regimes have given way to dictatorships. But in many of these cases, the causes for the failure of democracy were less with the specific institutions than with the attitudes and commitments of the people and their leaders. It is unlikely that any single set of institutions can create or perpetuate democratic government. The presence of democratic values is more important in building and maintaining democracy than the existence of a particular institutional arrangement.

They combined the ceremonial head of the nation with the chief executive of government. The term of office would be four years, and presidents would be indefinitely eligible to succeed themselves. (The two-term limit was added as the Twenty-second Amendment to the Constitution in 1951.)

Although independent from the legislature, presidents would still share considerable power with Congress. To enact government business, the separate branches would have to cooperate and consult with one another. A president's major appointments would have to be approved by the Senate; Congress could override the chief executive's veto by a two-thirds vote of each chamber, and the president could ratify treaties only with the advice and consent of two-thirds of the Senate. Appropriations would be initiated by Congress, not the president.

But even a president whose power was limited by a system of checks and balances worried many Americans in 1787. The framers deliberately outlined the powers of the president broadly. The president, they thought, should have discretionary power to act when other governmental branches failed to meet their responsibilities or to respond to the urgencies of the day. But Congress retained the right to impeach and remove a president if members of Congress believed a president had failed to abide by the Constitution.

Divided Powers

Our constitutional democracy was designed to be one of both shared powers and divided powers. The framers wanted disagreement as well as cooperation because they assumed that the checks and balances within the government would prevent the president and Congress from "ganging up" against the people's liberties. The framers actually made disagreement inevitable by providing that the president, Senate, and House of Representatives would be elected by different constituencies and for different lengths of service.

The United States is rare among major world powers because it is neither a parliamentary democracy nor a wholly executive-dominated government. Our Constitution plainly invites both Congress and president to set policy and govern the nation. Leadership and policy change are encouraged only when Congress and president, and sometimes these two and the courts, concur on the desirability of new directions.

A president and members of Congress are legitimate participants in a whole range of policy activities. Triumphs for a president acting alone in a system of separated powers are rare. "Whenever powers are shared, attention must be devoted to the other decision makers," writes political scientist Charles O. Jones. "How do they view the problem? What are their present commitments? On what basis will they compromise? The test in a separated system is not simply one of presidential success. It is rather one of achievement by the system, with presidents and members of Congress inextricably bonded and similarly judged."[1]

The politics of shared power has often been stormy, a subject we treat in detail in the next chapter. Making a separation of powers system work is never easy. A president is usually helped when majorities of his party are in control of Congress, which can join together what the framers separated. In recent decades, however, **divided government**, in which one party controls the executive branch and the other the legislative branch, has been the norm.

Democrat Bill Clinton served his last six years with a Congress controlled by Republicans. Republican George W. Bush won election in 2000 with a slim majority of Republicans in the House of Representatives and a U.S. Senate initially divided and soon controlled by a razor-thin Democratic majority. Thus, for all practical purposes, divided government endures, forcing presidents to govern from the center. President George W. Bush, like others before him, reached out to moderates in the other party for support, yet he, too, found that divided government inevitably encourages compromises and a certain amount of gridlock. More on this in the next chapter.

The Evolution of Presidential Influence

The formal powers the U.S. Constitution vests in a president have not been changed over the last two hundred years. But the influence of modern presidents is considerably greater today than it was two hundred years ago. The power and influence of any given president are partly the consequences of the incumbent's character and energy, combined with the needs of the time, the party balance in Congress, the values of the citizenry, and the challenges to our nation's survival. By and large, the history of presidential power is one of steady, if uneven, growth. Of the individuals who have filled the office, about one-third have enlarged its powers. Andrew Jackson, Abraham Lincoln, and both Roosevelts, for example, redefined both the institution and many of its powers by the way they set priorities and responded to crises.

In the evolution of executive power, Congress and the courts have sometimes been willing partners. In emergencies Congress often delegates discretion to the executive branch. In resolving complex problems, the legislature sometimes seems incapable of dealing with matters that are highly technical or that require immediate response and constant management. This weakness of Congress is not unique among legislative bodies. During the last two centuries, in all democracies and at all levels, power has drifted from legislators to executives. The English prime minister, the French president, governors of our states, and mayors of our cities all play more dominant roles than they did, generally speaking, a hundred years ago. This has been so in large part because people turn to executives to encourage a growing economy and press national interests in the international system.

Two centuries of national expansion and crises have increased the influence of the president beyond that specified by the Constitution. As we saw in Chapter 11, the complexity of Congress's decision-making procedures, its unwieldy numbers, and its constitutional responsibilities make it a more public, deliberative, and divided institution than the presidency. When crises occur, Congress traditionally holds debates and, almost as predictably, delegates authority to the president, charging the executive branch to take whatever actions are deemed necessary. Or Congress has allowed presidents to take charge, as was essentially what it did in the 1990s in response to presidential calls for U.S. involvement in Kuwait, Somalia, Haiti, Iraq, and Yugoslavia.

In the history of presidential–Supreme Court relations, the nation's highest court has generally favored an expansive interpretation of presidential power. The Court has on occasion halted a presidential action or ruled a presidential decision unconstitutional, but it has more frequently given legitimacy to the growth of presidential power.

divided government
Governance divided between the parties, especially when one holds the presidency and the other controls Congress.

Who Were the Best and Worst Presidents?

Several news organizations have published rankings of presidents by political historians and biographers. These lists often reveal as much about the professors and writers or the sponsoring organizations as the presidents, yet there is widespread agreement about the top five best and worst presidents. *The New York Times* and *Chicago Sun Times* published surveys that were almost identical in the mid-1990s. *The Wall Street Journal* published a ranking that relied on what it considered more balanced (that is, a survey with approximately equal number of experts on the left and right) than earlier surveys of presidential greatness. As a result Ronald Reagan and Dwight Eisenhower rose in their ranking, and Herbert Hoover and Calvin Coolidge escaped the bottom ten on its list.

New York Times/Chicago Sun Times Rankings (1996)

The Ten Best	The Ten Worst
1. Abraham Lincoln	1. Warren Harding
2. George Washington	2. James Buchanan
3. Franklin Roosevelt	3. Franklin Pierce
4. Thomas Jefferson	4. Ulysses Grant
5. Theodore Roosevelt	5. Andrew Johnson
6. Woodrow Wilson	6. Millard Fillmore
7. Harry Truman	7. Richard Nixon
8. Andrew Jackson	8. John Tyler
9. James Polk	9. Calvin Coolidge
10. Dwight Eisenhower	10. Herbert Hoover

SOURCES: Steve Neal, "Putting Presidents in Their Place," *Chicago Sun-Times*, November 19, 1995, pp. 30–31; Arthur M. Schlesinger, Jr., "The Ultimate Approval Rating," *The New York Times Magazine*, December 15, 1996, pp. 46–51.

The Wall Street Journal/Federalist Society Rankings (2000)

The Ten Best	The Ten Worst
1. George Washington	1. James Buchanan
2. Abraham Lincoln	2. Warren Harding
3. Franklin Roosevelt	3. Franklin Pierce
4. Thomas Jefferson	4. Andrew Johnson
5. Theodore Roosevelt	5. Millard Fillmore
6. Andrew Jackson	6. John Tyler
7. Harry Truman	7. Richard Nixon
8. Ronald Reagan	8. Ulysses Grant
9. Dwight Eisenhower	9. Zachary Taylor
10. James Polk	10. Jimmy Carter

SOURCE: James Lindgren and Steven Calabresi, "Ranking the Presidents," *The Wall Street Journal*, November 16, 2000, editorial page.

Several factors have strengthened the presidency in recent decades. The danger of war and the destructive potential of new weaponry plainly increased the president's influence. The cold war—with its enormous standing armies, nuclear weapons, and widespread intelligence and alliance operations—invited presidential leadership in national security matters. The post–cold war period has not reduced the need for presidential leadership, for the United States finds it still has extensive peacemaking, peacekeeping, and global economic leadership responsibilities.

Television has contributed to the growth of presidential influence. Previously, presidents had to rely on the press and party leaders in and out of Congress to get their message to the American people. With immediate access to vast television audiences, presidents can take their case directly to the people.

The growth of federal involvement in economic and social issues and the increasing complexity of public policies have increased presidential responsibility and contributed to the growth of agencies reporting directly to the White House. Problems not easily delegated to any one department often get pulled into the White House. When new programs involve several federal agencies, someone near the president is often asked to reconcile conflicts and set a consistent policy. White House aides, with some justification, claim the presidency is the only place in government where it is possible to establish and coordinate national priorities. Presidents set up central review and coordination units that help formulate new policies, settle jurisdictional disputes among departments, and provide access for the well-organized interest groups that want their views to be given weight in decision making.

Has there been a decline in the influence of presidents in recent years? Some people think so, pointing to diminished support for certain presidents in the wake of scandals, such as Watergate (Nixon), Iran-Contra (Reagan), and ethical problems in the Clinton presidency. The near impeachment of Richard Nixon and the impeachment of Bill Clinton are cited as decreasing respect for the presidency. The closeness of the 2000 presidential election and the sharp partisan divisions surrounding the Florida recount, plus the various court decisions in the 2000 presidential election, may also have limited the influence of George W. Bush. It is hard enough for a president to lead the nation, but it is harder still when he comes to the White House not having won the popular vote and after bitter disputes about voting irregularities and uncounted votes.

Still, it is generally agreed that events and forceful presidents over the last century have had the effect of magnifying the office and its potential influence. Presidential leadership in the cold war, in the Middle East, in the Balkans, and in international trade matters are all examples where presidents have played very significant policymaking roles.

The United States continues to struggle with the challenging paradox posed by some of the constitutional framers: If presidents have too much power, they could become arbitrary rulers and even tyrants; on the other hand, if presidents have too little power, they may be enfeebled and ineffective leaders.

There is little reason today to assume the role and impact of the American presidency will diminish in importance in coming decades. Not only does the president continue to be the primary focus of the nation's dreams and political aspirations; the nation's chief executive plays a central role as the nation's policy maker, party leader, chief administrator, and morale builder.[2]

Although we may dislike and even condemn individual presidents, public attitudes toward the institution of the presidency remain positive. We want to believe in our presidents; we want them to provide unifying leadership. Perhaps this is peculiarly the case in America, where we have no royal family, no established church, and no other common source of ceremonial leadership.

In Search of the Perfect President

The framers conceived their president in the image of George Washington, the man they expected would first occupy the office. Like Washington, the American chief executive is expected to be a wise, moderate, dignified, unifying leader of all the people. No one commanded the trust and respect that Washington did, and he was unanimously elected as the first president of the new Republic in 1789. George Washington knew the people needed to have confidence in their fledgling government, a sense of continuity with the past, and a time of calmness and stability free of emergencies and crises. He knew, too, that the new nation faced foreign dangers.

Today, if presidents take charge and try to run the country, they are often accused of being dictatorial and trying to impose their will on the nation. If they are not activist leaders, however, they are criticized for being weak or passive, and, even more likely, they are blamed for whatever happens to be wrong with the country. People who like what a president is doing are champions of presidential leadership; people who disapprove of what a president is doing point to the dangers of dictatorship.

Article II of the Constitution outlines the nature and scope of presidential power (see page 45 of this text). It responded to George Washington's calls for executive leadership. He was sensitive to the fine line between providing strong leadership and infringing on individual rights and liberties. He knew then—as every president after him has either known or learned—that Americans have a strong streak of antigovernment and even anti-authority sentiment.[3]

What kind of person does it take to perform this delicate balancing act? Our Constitution establishes only three qualifications for the office: a president must be at least 35 years of age, have lived in the United States for 14 years, and be a natural-born citizen. Yet the "unwritten presidential job description"—the one we carry around in our heads—says a president has to be many things to many people.

CHARACTER AND HONESTY   Voters often place as much emphasis on a presidential candidate's character and integrity as they do on a candidate's political philosophy and past experience. Such emphasis is not misguided. Presidents have enormous influence, especially in times of crisis. They recruit the people who run the executive departments and serve on our courts, and thus they have much to do with governmental performance and ethics. Hence it is important to weigh their character, allegiance to constitutional and democratic values, and ability to manage their emotions and turn them to constructive purposes.[4]

Concerns about presidential character are as old as the presidency itself. In 1800, for example, religious leaders denounced Thomas Jefferson from their pulpits as "godless," and in the 1820s Andrew Jackson was pilloried as a barbarian and adulterer.

The election of 1884 provides a fascinating case study of character in politics. In that election, Democratic candidate Grover Cleveland was charged with fathering a child out of wedlock. Cleveland took responsibility and agreed to pay for the child's upbringing. Not surprisingly, this became a hot issue for his opponent, James G. Blaine. The dilemma was that while Cleveland's private life raised doubts, he was responsible in his political and professional life. Blaine, on the other hand, had an "upright" private life yet was less well regarded for his political integrity. Voters elected Cleveland.

Bill Clinton had major character flaws, yet his political supporters hoped, sometimes in vain, that he would avoid reckless behavior and concentrate on the policy initiatives they favored. Clinton was impeached by the House of Representatives and nearly removed from office by the Senate for his moral weakness. What was remarkable was that an unusually large number of Americans (often 60 percent or more) continued to approve of Clinton's handling of the job of the presidency while decidedly disapproving of his personal behavior. Most people apparently judged Clinton on how well the economy did, on traditional "peace and prosperity" measures, and on his adroit political and communication skills rather than on his personal morals.

Still, Americans want presidents they can trust, individuals who have a basic respect for others as well as a commitment to serve the public interest. A sense of decency, integrity, and fair play will always be part of what is wanted in a president. Here, briefly, are some additional qualities Americans yearn for in an ideal president.

- *Courage:* Americans want a leader who takes firm stands on issues, is concerned about the average citizen, and places the country's interests ahead of politics. A president should have the intellectual courage to take risks and do what is right, even when it is not popular or easy; the willingness to serve all the people, not just those who bankrolled his candidacy; and the perseverance not to give up after initial legislative or political defeats.

- *Experience:* Americans want presidents who have proven competence in understanding complex policy issues. Presidents need to be skilled at bringing people together to solve intricate policy problems.

- *Political Savvy:* Presidents need an understanding of the role of politics in governing and the ability to be an effective politician working with people of all political viewpoints. The job requires recognition that coalition building is a central and constant part of the job.

- *A Sense of History and Constitutionalism:* Americans want a president to have a great respect for the U.S. Constitution and American values, exhibiting a solid grasp of how governments and markets work and how diplomacy and U.S. trade work.

- *Vision:* The ideal president should have ideas and programmatic plans to make the country stronger. We ask presidents to clarify options and help set the nation's policy agenda. A president must take positions on the compelling issues of the day—economic opportunity, civil rights, education, trade, nuclear proliferation, terrorism, equality, and so on. The president has to be a forest person, not one overwhelmed by the trees or leaves.

- *Listening and Teaching Skills:* Our best presidents both listen to us and lead us. They know that while a clear vision can excite us, it does not necessarily teach or rally us. We want presidents who give us a sense not only of who they are, but, more important, of who we are and what kind of nation we might become.

- *Communication Skills:* Ideas and wisdom are of little use if a president cannot motivate and rally the public and empower constituencies to act. Presidents have to develop impressive speaking and media management skills.

- *Morale-Building Skills:* The presidency is more than just a constitutional or political office; it has to help us navigate through crises and transitions and unify us when we experience national setbacks and tragedy. At their best, presidents remind us of our mutual obligations, shared beliefs, and the trust and caring that bind us together. Americans understandably yearn for presidents like George Washington and Abraham Lincoln, who can bring us together and challenge us to be better.

History conditions different cultures to expect different things of their national leaders. Doubtless in the United States we exaggerate the capacity for what even heroic presidents have done and can do to change the course of events.[5] Do we ask too much of our presidents? Sure we do. We want vision, character, competence, intelligence, honesty, stamina, inspiration, sound judgment, wisdom—and of course—someone who shares our political beliefs.

THE CHALLENGING JOB OF BEING PRESIDENT

The president has many responsibilities:

- To serve as chief executive of the federal bureaucracy
- To nominate and appoint key officials
- To implement and enforce laws
- To veto unwise bills
- To negotiate treaties
- To recognize foreign nations
- To serve as commander in chief
- To serve as chief of state
- To pardon or grant clemency
- To propose an annual budget
- To develop policies that promote peace and prosperity

All but the last two of these responsibilities are spelled out in the Constitution. Others are designated by laws enacted by Congress. But today a president is asked to perform additional roles not spelled out in the Constitution. We want the chief executive to be an international peacemaker as well as a national morale builder, a politician in chief as well as a commander in chief. We want the president to be the architect of a new world order, or at least a peaceful world order, who negotiates favorable trade pacts with major trading partners. In addition to the obvious leadership responsibilities a president has in foreign policy, economics, and domestic policy, a variety of broad functional kinds of leadership are expected of a president. These policy areas and functions permit us to develop a presidential job profile (see Table 12–1).

Presidents as Crisis Managers

"The President shall be Commander in Chief of the Army and Navy of the United States," reads Section 2 of Article II of the Constitution. Even though this is the first of the president's powers listed in the Constitution, the framers intended the military role to be a limited one—far less than a king's. Congress would declare war, making the rules for the army and navy, and control the funding of wars, yet it was

TABLE 12–1 A Presidential Job Description

	Examples of Policy Responsibilities		
	Foreign Policy	Economic Policy	Domestic Policy
Crisis management	Clinton's authorizing bombing of Iraq	FDR's handling of the Depression, 1930s	Initiating federal disaster relief
Symbolic and morale-building leadership	G.W. Bush's visit to Mexico to celebrate trade and friendship	Granting most-favored-nation status to China	Visiting flood and disaster victims
Recruitment of top officials	Selecting Joint Chiefs of Staff chair	Reappointing Alan Greenspan to head the Fed	Nominating Supreme Court justices
Priority setting and problem clarification	Working with United Nations on peacekeeping priorities	Outlining tax-cut or revenue-producing programs	Setting priorities in environmental protection and health care
Legislative and political coalition building	Negotiating with Congress on new members of NATO	Working out a tax cut with Congress	Clinton's efforts to pass health care reform
Program implementation, administration, and oversight	Hosting Middle East peace talks	Monitoring Internal Revenue Service performance	Appraising the impact of federal social programs

President Bill Clinton with Defense Secretary William Cohen and General Henry Shelton, chair of the Joint Chiefs of Staff.

important, the framers insisted, that the people's elected representative—the president—be in charge of the military.

This principle of *civilian control over the military* is a central element in our constitutional democracy.[6] It means all soldiers and sailors, from the newest recruit to every general and admiral, take their orders from and owe their allegiance to the one person elected by all the people. The professional military, no matter what their own personal political views and values, take their military orders from the president and his chief civilian agent, the secretary of defense.

When crises and national emergencies occur, Americans instinctively turn to the chief executive, who is expected to provide the appearance of a confident, "take-charge" executive with a steady hand at the helm. Public necessity forces presidents to do what Lincoln and Franklin Roosevelt did during the national emergencies of their day: provide the stability and continuity needed to protect the union and safeguard vital American interests.

The primary factor underlying this transformation in the president's function as commander in chief has been the changed role of the United States in the world, especially since World War II. In recent decades every president has argued for and won support for the use of U.S. troops overseas as part of the North Atlantic Treaty Organization (NATO) or the various United Nations peacekeeping forces. Nations grew dependent on our assistance, which often was spelled out in treaties, pacts, and diplomatic agreements. These commitments, plus the fear of nuclear war and the importance of deterrence, prompted Congress to give presidents great flexibility in making foreign policy.

Presidents are expected to be crisis managers in the domestic sphere as well. Whenever things go wrong, we demand presidential-level planning and problem solving. When terrorists attack U.S. citizens or U.S. naval vessels, people assume their president will retaliate or at least track down the terrorists. When a disastrous oil spill occurs, or a natural disaster happens, people expect the president to step in and assist. Even when there is little a president can do, the involvement by the chief executive signals that the government will do what it can and conveys empathy on the part of the president.

The Constitution delegates to Congress the authority to declare the legal state of war (with the consent of the president), but as commander in chief, the president often starts the actual fighting or initiates actions that lead to war. From George Washington's time until today, a president, by ordering troops into hostile areas, has often decided when and where Americans will fight and when they will not. When the president has political support for such actions, Congress has gone along. But, as we shall discuss in the next chapter, some members of Congress believe this power of the president to begin armed conflicts without prior congressional approval has been abused by recent presidents.

Presidents as Morale Builders

As chiefs of state, presidents are the symbolic equivalent of the British monarch—projecting a sense of national unity and serving as the country's chief ceremonial leader. The framers of the Constitution did not fully anticipate the symbolic and morale-building functions a president must perform. Certain magisterial functions, such as receiving ambassadors and granting pardons, were conferred. But over time the presidency has acquired enormous symbolic significance.

Presidents are the nation's number-one celebrities; almost anything they do is news. Presidents command attention merely by jogging, fishing, golfing, or going to church. By their actions they can arouse a sense of hope or despair, honor or dishonor.

The morale-building job of the president involves much more than just ceremonial cheerleading or quasi-chaplain duties. Presidential leadership, at its finest, radiates national self-confidence and helps unlock the possibility for good that exists in the nation. Our best leaders have been able to provide this special and often intangible element.

Presidents as Recruiters

Presidents make more than 4,000 appointments, including hundreds of federal judgeships and top positions in the military and diplomatic service. Recall, however, that many appointments require the approval of the Senate. Effective presidents shrewdly use their appointment powers not only to reward campaign supporters and enhance ties to Congress, but also to communicate priorities and policy directions. Moreover, the White House in recent decades has often placed campaign aides in key deputy positions to ensure loyalty to the White House.[7]

Besides identifying and recruiting them, the president must also try to keep the most talented of these officials in government as long as possible. Many able people come to top positions in the cabinet or subcabinet and stay for just two or three years. Among the reasons for these short terms is that top federal posts do not pay as much as similar positions in the private sector, and living in Washington is expensive.

Presidents have a lasting impact beyond their terms of office by their power to nominate federal judges. For example, President Dwight Eisenhower's nomination of Earl Warren to be chief justice of the United States was one of his most significant decisions in the area of domestic policy. Warren served for more than 15 years and presided over vast changes in civil rights and civil liberties. President Clinton nominated hundreds of federal judges, including Supreme Court justices Ruth Bader Ginsburg and Stephen Breyer, who are likely to have long-term effects. In a similar way, the selection of a secretary of state, a top economic adviser, a secretary of the treasury, a Federal Reserve Board member, or a top White House aide can have a substantial impact on long-term national policy. But Supreme Court appointments, because they are lifetime positions, overshadow almost all the others.

Various financial disclosure and conflict-of-interest requirements, imposed on presidential appointees as a result of the Ethics in Government Act of 1978, discourage some potential appointees from accepting government jobs. They must fill out many forms, and they must testify at sometimes complicated, time-consuming, confusing, and embarrassing congressional hearings. Media scrutiny of citizen-leaders called to government service has also become more intensive. Recruiters for recent presidents report they often have to go to their second or third choice before they find someone willing to accept an appointment.[8] A president must strengthen the

What Is the Pardon Power?

Article II, Section 2, of the U.S. Constitution provides that the president shall have the power to grant "Reprieves" and "Pardons" for offenses against the United States, except in cases of impeachment. This authority, the roots of which can be traced directly to the royal authority of the king of England, is probably the most imperial and often the most delicate power a president exercises. The pardon power is generally a tool of mercy, an instrument to correct miscarriages of justice and to restore full civil rights to those who have served their sentences and are expected to be law abiding.

The pardon power permits a president to be merciful, but it can also be used strategically when a pardon can restore peace and stability. George Washington used this power to help end the Whiskey Rebellion. Presidents Abraham Lincoln and Andrew Johnson used it to provide amnesty to Confederate leaders and soldiers. Presidents Gerald Ford and Jimmy Carter used it for Vietnam War draft evaders. President Ford also used it to pardon Richard Nixon, one of the most controversial exercises of the pardon power. Clinton, on his final day in office, pardoned his half-brother, one of his former business partners, one of his former cabinet members, and a fugitive commodities trader, Marc Rich, whose former wife was a big contributor to Clinton's campaigns and presidential library.

The Constitution leaves succession after the vice-president up to Congress. Thus this is the line of succession according to a law passed by Congress in 1947 and by the Twenty-fifth Amendment. However, the constitutional qualifications still apply. For example, if the secretary of state was born in a foreign country of parents who were not U.S. citizens, he or she would be bypassed in this line.

1. Vice-President
2. Speaker of the House of Representatives
3. Senate President Pro Tempore
4. Secretary of State
5. Secretary of the Treasury
6. Secretary of Defense
7. Attorney General
8. Secretary of the Interior
9. Secretary of Agriculture
10. Secretary of Commerce
11. Secretary of Labor
12. Secretary of Health and Human Services
13. Secretary of Housing and Urban Development
14. Secretary of Transportation
15. Secretary of Energy
16. Secretary of Education
17. Secretary of Veterans Affairs

hand of the ablest people working in the bureaucracy and promote them to higher positions at the senior reaches of the executive branch.[9]

Presidents as Priority and Agenda Setters

Presidents, by custom, have become responsible for proposing initiatives in foreign policy and economic growth and stability. This was not always the case. But beginning with Woodrow Wilson, and especially since the New Deal, a president has been expected to propose reforms to ensure domestic progress. New ideas are seized upon by a presidential candidate searching for campaign issues, and they are later refined and implemented by the executive office staff, by special presidential task forces, and by Congress.

NATIONAL SECURITY POLICY   The framers foresaw a special need for speed and unity in dealing with other nations. As a result, presidents generally have more leeway in foreign policy and military affairs than they have in domestic matters. The Constitution vests in a president command of the two major instruments of foreign policy—the diplomatic corps and the armed services. It also gives the chief executive responsibility for negotiating treaties and commitments with other nations, although the Senate must consent to treaty ratifications, and almost all international agreements require congressional action for their implementation.

Congress has granted presidents discretion in initiating foreign policies, for diplomacy frequently requires quick action. The Supreme Court has upheld strong presidential authority in this area. In *United States v Curtiss-Wright* (1936), the Court referred to the "exclusive power of the president as the sole organ of the federal government in the field of international relations—a power which does not require as a basis for its exercise an act of Congress, but which, of course, like every other governmental power, must be exercised in subordination to the applicable provisions of the Constitution."[10] These are sweeping and much-debated words.[11] Still, a determined Congress that knows what it wants does not lack power in foreign relations. Congress must authorize and appropriate the funds that back up the president's policies abroad.

President Clinton and Russian President Vladamir Putin sign the strategic Cooperation Initiative while attending the United Nations Millennium Summit on September 6, 2000.

ECONOMIC POLICY   Ever since the New Deal, presidents have been expected to promote policies to keep unemployment low, fight inflation, keep taxes down, and promote economic growth and prosperity. The Constitution did not specify these duties for the executive, yet presidents know that when the nation is not prosperous and jobs are scarce, they may suffer the fate of Herbert Hoover, who was denounced for his alleged inaction at the beginning of the Great Depression. The growth and complexity of economic problems since the Depression of the 1930s have placed more economic responsibility in the president's hands. The delicate balancing required to keep a modern economy operating means presidents must make key fiscal and budgetary policy decisions.[12] The presidential elections in 1980, 1992, and 1996 turned largely on the economy.

Although presidents sometimes get their economic advice elsewhere, their chief advisers on economic policy are the secretary of the treasury, the three members of the Council of Economic Advisers, and the director of the Office of Management and Budget. The chair of the Federal Reserve Board of Governors is also an influential, if independent, adviser on the economy.

DOMESTIC POLICY   A leader is one who knows where the followers are. Abraham Lincoln did not invent the antislavery movement. John Kennedy and Lyndon Johnson did not begin the civil rights movement. Bill Clinton was not the first leader to notice the unfairness of health care and welfare policies. Similarly, George W. Bush's campaign promises were shaped by public concern about prescription drug costs more than by him. But they all, in their respective times, became embroiled in these controversies, for a president cannot long ignore what divides or inspires a nation.

Presidents as Legislative and Political Coalition Builders

The Constitution provides that the president "shall from time to time give to the Congress information on the State of the Union, and recommend to their Consideration such Measures as he shall judge necessary and expedient." From the start, strong presidents have exploited this power. George Washington and John Adams went in person to Congress to deliver information and recommendations. Thomas Jefferson and many presidents after him sent written messages, but Woodrow Wilson restored the practice of delivering a personal, and often dramatic, message. (For these and related messages, see **www.whitehouse.gov**)

Less public, yet equally important, are the frequent written policy messages dispatched from the White House to the members of Congress on a range of public problems. These messages are important in defining the administration's position and in giving assistance to friendly legislators. Moreover, these messages are often accompanied by detailed drafts of legislation, which members of Congress sponsor with little or no change. These White House proposals, the products of bill-drafting experts on the president's staff or in the executive departments and agencies, may be strengthened or diluted by Congress, but many of the original provisions survive.

Presidents cannot escape political coalition building. As candidates, they made promises to the people and assembled an electoral coalition of supporters. To get things done and to get reelected, however, they must work with interest groups and people who have differing loyalties and responsibilities. Inevitably, presidents become embroiled in legislative, bureaucratic, and lobbying politics, and their approval ratings often suffer as a consequence.

Despite their formal powers, presidents can rarely command; they spend most of their time *persuading* people. The power to persuade is the president's chief resource, and that power comes through bargaining. Bargaining, in turn, comes primarily through getting others to believe it is in their self-interest to cooperate. Presidents and their aides spend a lot of time dispensing favors to various members of Congress from whom they are seeking votes and political support. Hence the skill of a president in communicating and winning others over is the necessary energizing factor in moving the institutions of the national government to action.

Presidents often clash with Congress, as we shall discuss in the next chapter, yet they cooperate and collaborate just as often, if not more so. Plainly, working with the Congress is a major part of the job of being president.

Presidents as Molders of Public Opinion

The press conference is an example of how a president can employ the machinery of communication to build legislative and political coalitions. Years ago press conferences were rather casual affairs. Franklin Roosevelt ran his get-togethers informally and was a master at withholding information as well as giving it. Under Harry Truman the conference became an institutionalized part of the presidential communications apparatus. John Kennedy authorized live telecasts of press conferences and used them frequently for direct communication with the people. Ronald Reagan and Bill Clinton effectively used five-minute Saturday afternoon radio chats to communicate their views, ask for support, and win Sunday morning media coverage.

Presidents regularly commission polls to find out how they are doing. They want to learn about the public's views, estimate the strength and direction of its thinking, and respond to it. Public opinion can be unstable and unpredictable. Richard Nixon's dramatic drop of nearly 40 percentage points in public opinion polls as a result of the Watergate scandal helped force his resignation. George Bush won solid public approval during and after the successful military efforts in the Persian Gulf in early 1991, yet his popular approval diminished sharply during the economic downturn that followed. Most presidents lose support the longer they are in office. Dissatisfaction sets in; interest groups grow impatient; unkept promises must be accounted for; and the president gets blamed for things that go wrong.

Bill Clinton surprisingly retained and even gained popularity the longer he was in office. Indeed, the more personal trouble Clinton got into, the more his public approval ratings went up—even after he was impeached by the U.S. House of Representatives. The Clinton years of "peace, prosperity, and moderation" kept his approval ratings high.[13] He also reinvented himself as a warrior against the Newt Gingrich–led Congress, yet he prudently collaborated, when necessary, on a number of Republican initiatives, such as welfare reform, balancing the budget, and crime prevention.

Bill Clinton had especially testy relations with the press and complained a lot about the media.[14] He used every available means to get his message out to the Amer-

Presidents Clinton, Bush, Reagan, Carter, and Ford and their wives attending the memorial service for former President Richard Nixon.

EVALUATING BILL CLINTON'S PRESIDENCY

An impressive 66 percent of the American people approved of the job Bill Clinton did at the end of his two terms. That was higher than Ronald Reagan's 63 percent or Dwight Eisenhower's 60 percent at the end of their two terms. Yet if Clinton won exceptionally high marks for his job as president, he won uncommonly low marks as a person or moral exemplar.*

Clinton's greatest successes were sustaining economic growth and job development, reducing the debt and creating a budget surplus, reforming the welfare system, keeping America out of war, and encouraging international trade through the North American Free Trade Agreement and other trade agreements. Polls of the American public concluded that his worst failings were his affair with Monica Lewinsky and the ensuing impeachment, setting the wrong moral tone for the country, his inability to win congressional approval for his health care reform package, and some unfortunate pardons at the end of his term.

In short, Bill Clinton, like FDR and Ronald Reagan before him, stirred

Bill Clinton expended considerable effort to bring about peace in the Middle East during his presidency, holding numerous summits and traveling to the area frequently. Here he meets with Israeli Prime Minister Ehud Barak and Palestinian leader Yasser Arafat, as well as UN Secretary General Kofi Annan and Egyptian President Hosni Mubarak, in October 2000, in an ultimately unsuccessful effort to end the bloodshed.

great passions, affirmatively and negatively. His place in history is hard to predict, but it is unlikely he will be judged either among the great or the worst presidents. Part of the verdict on his presidency will depend on what happens to our peace and prosperity in the next decade.

*Albert R. Hunt, "Clinton Ends His Tenure on High Note," *The Wall Street Journal*, December 14, 2000, p. A9.

---

ican public.[15] He was the first president to appear on MTV and, at least in his early years, he regularly turned up at town meetings and talk shows. He had to deal with the press in an era of "in your face journalism," where many of the old rules and courtesies about the separation of public and private life had disappeared, especially those having to do with marital and extramarital relations. We have to remember, however, that Thomas Jefferson, Abraham Lincoln, and Franklin Roosevelt were all vilified by the press and rarely shown much reverence in their lifetimes. Presidents, along with members of Congress, are always fair game for media critics.[16]

Presidents as Party Leaders

As chief of government, each president is called on to act as partisan political leader. Most presidents since Thomas Jefferson have been party leaders, and generally the more effective the president, the more use he has made of party support. Woodrow Wilson, the two Roosevelts, and Ronald Reagan fortified their executive and legislative influence by mobilizing support within their party. Reagan and Clinton were uncommonly effective fund raisers for their political parties.

Someone or something is needed to grease the wheels of government, which, if left to their own devices, grind slowly. A president who can use help from his party and galvanize a relatively cohesive party sometimes supplies the needed push to overcome gridlock. Yet presidents are often led by their party, or at least constrained by it, as much as they lead it; no president has ever wholly dominated his party.[17]

Presidents as Administrators

The Constitution charges the president to "take Care that the Laws be faithfully executed." Presidents, however, must delegate much of their administrative authority. Because their other responsibilities demand most of their attention, presidents are dependent on their subordinates. Theoretically, at least, orders flow down an administrative line: from president, to cabinet members, to bureau chiefs, to smaller offices. Like all top executives, a president is assisted by a staff who advise the chief executive. This *line and staff organization* is typical of every bureaucratic entity, whether it be the army, General Motors, or the United Nations.

THE WHITE HOUSE STAFF   Presidents have come to rely heavily on their personal staffs. Nowhere else—not in Congress, not in the cabinet, not in the party— can presidents find the loyalty and single-mindedness that often develops among their closest White House aides.[18] Cabinet heads, on the other hand, are often perceived as staunch advocates of their departments and the constituencies their departments serve. Presidents assume, however, that their aides will provide them with sound policy advice, but there are sometimes substantial costs to listening only to one's closest associates. The White House can usually be thought of as a palace court in which strong presidents create an environment that weeds out any assistant who persists in presenting irritating or opposing views.

The number of employees in the presidential entourage grew steadily from the early 1900s through the early 1990s. Today a White House staff of about 400 operates at a slight reduction from previous years. This staff makes up just one part of the Executive Office of the President.

The staff of the White House office can be categorized by their primary functions: (1) domestic policy; (2) economic policy; (3) national security or foreign policy; (4) administration and personnel matters (as well as personal paperwork and scheduling for the president); (5) congressional relations; and (6) public relations.

Presidential aides sometimes insist they are simply the eyes and ears of the president, that they make few important decisions, and that they never intrude between the chief executive and the heads of departments. But the inevitable emergence of a few strong White House advisers makes this traditional picture inaccurate.[19] Some White House aides, impatient with bureaucratic and congressional bottlenecks or even political sabotage, come to view the presidency as if it alone were the whole government.

THE INSTITUTIONALIZED EXECUTIVE OFFICE   Approved by Congress in 1939, the **Executive Office of the President** was the recommendation of Franklin Roosevelt's Committee on Administrative Management. The intention was to provide presidents with the help they obviously needed to carry out the growing responsibilities imposed by the Great Depression and by the enlarged role of government. The Executive Office of the President consists of the Office of Management and Budget, the Council of Economic Advisers, and several other staff units (see Figure 12–1).

The **Office of Management and Budget (OMB)** is the central presidential staff agency. Its director advises the president in detail about the hundreds of government agencies—how much money they should be allotted in the budget and what kind of job they are doing. OMB seeks to improve the planning, management, and statistical work of the agencies. It makes a special effort to see that each agency conforms to presidential policies in its dealings with Congress; each agency has to clear its policy recommendations to Congress through OMB first.[20]

Through the long budget preparation process, presidents use OMB as a way of conserving and centralizing their own influence. A budget is more than just a finan-

Executive Office of the President
The cluster of presidential staff agencies that help the president carry out his responsibilities. Currently the office includes the Office of Management and Budget, the Council of Economic Advisers, and several other units.

Office of Management and Budget
Presidential staff agency that serves as a clearinghouse for budgetary requests and management improvements.

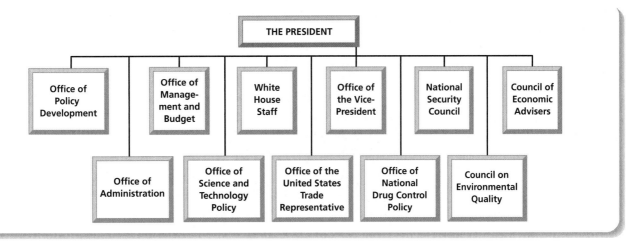

FIGURE 12–1 Executive Office of the President

SOURCE: *United States Government Manual, 2000/2001* (Government Printing Office, 2000), p.87.

cial plan, because it reflects power struggles and indicates national priorities (and wishful thinking). To the president, the budget is a means of control over administrators who may be trying to join ranks with other politicians or interest groups to thwart presidential priorities.

THE CABINET   It is hard to find a more unusual institution than the president's **cabinet**. The cabinet is not specifically mentioned by name in the Constitution, yet since George Washington's administration, every president has had one. Washington's consisted of his secretaries of state, treasury, and war, plus his attorney general.

Today the selection of cabinet members is the first major job for the president-elect. The cabinet consists of the president, the vice-president, the heads of the 14 executive departments, and a few others a president considers cabinet-level officials. The cabinet has always been a loosely designated body, and it is not always clear who belongs in it. In recent years, certain executive branch administrators and White House counselors have been accorded cabinet rank.

George W. Bush recruited a notably diverse cabinet that included several women, two African Americans, two Asian Americans, and other minorities. His key appointments at Defense, State, and Treasury had all served extensively in previous Republican administrations. One of his nominees, Linda Chavez, had to withdraw when a controversy developed over her having housed and employed an undocumented alien. Bush's attorney general appointment, former Missouri governor and U.S. senator John Ashcroft, won confirmation by a 58 to 42 vote after heated hearings and debates over some of his political beliefs and past votes.

Cabinet government as practiced in parliamentary systems—where the voice and the vote of the cabinet members count for a lot—simply does not exist in the United States.[21] In fact, an American president is not required by the Constitution to form a cabinet or to hold regular meetings. Presidents John Kennedy, Lyndon Johnson, and Richard Nixon all preferred small conferences with individuals specifically involved in a problem. Kennedy saw no reason to discuss defense department matters with his secretaries of agriculture and labor, and he thought cabinet meetings wasted valuable time. Both Jimmy Carter and Ronald Reagan tried to revive the cabinet, and both met often with their cabinets during their first two years. But the longer they remained in office, the less frequently they met with their cabinets as a whole. Bill Clinton, like those he followed, seldom called for full cabinet meetings, holding just 18 full cabinet meetings in his first term and even fewer during his second.[22]

Presidential advisers and the heads of various White House–based cabinet-level councils, such as the National Security Council and the Office of Management

cabinet
Advisory council for a president, consisting of the heads of the executive departments, the vice-president, and a few others the president considers cabinet-level officials.

The Cabinet

Vice-President

Secretary of State

Secretary of Treasury

Secretary of Defense

Attorney General

Secretary of Interior

Secretary of Agriculture

Secretary of Commerce

Secretary of Labor

Secretary of Health and Human Services

Secretary of Housing and Urban Development

Secretary of Transportation

Secretary of Energy

Secretary of Education

Secretary of Veterans Affairs

Chief of Staff at the White House

Director of the Office of Management and Budget

U.S. Trade Representative

Chair, Council of Economic Advisers

Administrator, Environmental Protection Agency

Counselor to the President

Note: Presidents can decide which posts, such as U. S. Trade Representative or UN ambassador, to include at cabinet level.

and Budget, have gained equal or even superior status to many cabinet secretaries. This shift occurred in part because these advisers are physically located in or next door to the White House (see Figure 12–2). Further, presidents are aware that some cabinet members adopt narrow "advocate" views: the Agriculture Department secretary is a strong advocate for the farmers; the Housing and Urban Development Department secretary is an ambassador for the housing industry and, to some extent, also for big city mayors; and so on through much of the cabinet, especially those preoccupied with domestic policy matters.

THE VICE-PRESIDENCY

Although the vice-presidency is now very much a part of the presidential establishment, it has been so for only a couple of generations. Until the 1950s, most vice-presidents served mainly as president of the Senate. Up to that time, the vice-president was at best a "fifth wheel" and at worst a political rival who sometimes connived against the president. The office was often dismissed as a joke. One reason for the vice-president's posture as an outsider was that presidential nominees usually chose running mates who were geographically, ideologically, demographically, and in other ways likely to "balance the ticket."

Ideally, a vice-president performs several tasks in addition to the ceremonial function of acting as president of the Senate. A vice-president gets to cast the tie-breaking vote if the Senate has a tie vote. The vice-president is also a member of the National Security Council.

The real test of the role of vice-president is whether he or she is fully integrated into the decision-making process in the White House. Inevitably all vice-presidents are "back-up equipment" in case something happens to the president. They can head up any number of councils, visit any number of countries, and still not be much involved in the day-to-day operations of the presidency. President Jimmy Carter included Walter Mondale in the daily processes of decision making in the White House; President Ronald Reagan sometimes included George Bush in a similar way; President Clinton used Al Gore as an important adviser and confidant on domestic as well as foreign policy matters and key appointments.

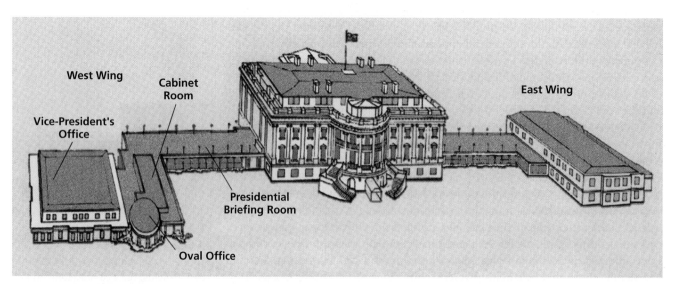

FIGURE 12–2 The White House

SOURCE: Adapted from *The Washington Post,* February 5, 1993, p. A23.

George W. Bush selected Dick Cheney for his vice-president in large part because Cheney's prior experience in Congress, in the White House, and in the cabinet brought credibility to the Bush campaign. His previous government positions would strengthen Bush's governing ability if the ticket won the White House. After the election Cheney headed up the presidential transition team, recruiting senior administrators and shaping the legislative agenda. Cheney became as important, if not more important, than any previous vice-president.

Vice-President Dick Cheney.

The vice-presidency has been significantly affected by two constitutional amendments. The Twenty-second Amendment, ratified in 1951, imposes a two-term limit on presidents; consequently, vice-presidents have a better chance of moving up to the Oval Office. The Twenty-fifth Amendment, ratified in 1967, confirms the practice of making the vice-president not an acting president, but president, in the event of the death of a president. Also of significance, this amendment outlines a procedure to determine whether an incumbent president is unable to discharge the powers and duties of the office and establishes procedures to fill a vacancy in the vice-presidency.[23] For a few hours in 1985, George Bush became the first "acting president" when President Reagan underwent a minor cancer operation.

The amendment also provides that in the event of a vacancy in the office of vice-president, the president nominates a vice-president, who takes office upon confirmation by a majority vote of both houses of Congress. This procedure generally ensures the appointment of a vice-president in whom the president has confidence. Thus vice-presidents who have to take over the presidency can be expected to reflect most of their predecessor's policies.

Although the sort of tensions between president and vice-president that existed in the past rarely affected Clinton and Gore or Bush and Cheney, tension between a president and a vice-president is natural. After all, except for the vice-president, everybody who works closely with a president can be fired. It is almost certain that vice-presidents will continue to have an undefined ad hoc set of assignments, subject more to the goodwill and mood of the president than to any fixed description.[24]

KEEPING PRESIDENTS ACCOUNTABLE

This nation has had great presidents, yet we have also had ineffective and flawed presidents. We have no foolproof way to guarantee that our presidents will possess the leadership skills and moral character the job requires.

Accountability refers to a president's responsiveness to the will of the majority and taking responsibility for one's actions. Accountability implies as well that important presidential decisions will be explained to the public to allow citizens to evaluate how well a president is handling the assignments of the office. Here are some of the ways presidents are constrained and held to account:

Reelection and Legacy

Presidents want to win reelection because reelection is a validation of their first term as well as an opportunity for them to continue to implement their agenda. To win reelection, a president has to win the approval of large numbers of attentive citizens. It is in this sense that elections hold a president to account after four years in office.

But even midterm congressional elections also serve as a check on presidents. For example, Lyndon Johnson, Gerald Ford, and Bill Clinton all suffered major losses in their party's ranks in the Congress in 1966, 1974, and 1994. These losses sent a stark message to the White House and affected how these presidents behaved. In Clinton's case, it had the effect of influencing him to move to the political center.

Every president also wants to leave a legacy that will be viewed positively by historians and later generations. Thus presidents usually are inclined to do what is right in hopes of being judged successful and effective.

Should presidents be limited to two terms in office?

Before he left office, former President Ronald Reagan called for the repeal of the Twenty-second Amendment to the Constitution, the one that limits a president to two terms. Why do you think he opposed the amendment? What additional reasons could be put forth to persuade people to repeal this relatively new (1951) provision in the Constitution? What are the best reasons for retaining the Twenty-second Amendment?

Congress and the President

The framers of the Constitution deliberately designed Congress as a formal check on the presidential exercise of power. Congress would be the primary lawmaker and even have the right to override a presidential veto. Congress could refuse to approve presidential nominees to the executive departments, to the courts, and to diplomatic posts. And Congress also was given that ultimate weapon—impeachment and conviction—to remove a president from office.

The Supreme Court and the President

The framers of the Constitution intended the Supreme Court to serve as a check on the potential abuses of power by presidents. The Court, they hoped, would comprise wise and well-educated statesmen who would strive to preserve the Constitution, especially from legislative and executive wrongdoing. Most of the framers believed the Supreme Court would work hand-in-hand with the executive. Some even viewed the courts as an executive department, involved in executing, interpreting, and applying the laws.

But presidents and the courts have had their share of clashes. In a good many instances, presidents have won these differences of opinion, yet the exceptions are notable:

Thomas Jefferson was told by the Supreme Court that he had acted wrongly in one of his military initiatives.

Abraham Lincoln was rebuffed for using military courts in areas outside the war zone where the Court said they were not justified.

Franklin Roosevelt saw several of his early New Deal initiatives struck down by the Court as unconstitutional.

Harry Truman was ordered by the Court to release steel mills from federal control.

Richard Nixon's policies were overturned by the Supreme Court or lower federal courts on dozens of occasions, most notably, of course, in the summer of 1974, when the Supreme Court directed him to release certain White House tape recordings for use in a criminal investigation.

The Court upheld Paula Jones's right to file a civil suit involving Bill Clinton's private behavior while he was still serving as president.

A Watchdog Media and the President

Ronald Reagan once walked away from one of his news conferences and, turning to an aide, blasted reporters, not realizing a microphone was picking up every word. John F. Kennedy canceled more than 50 White House subscriptions to the *New York Herald Tribune* because he was furious about the way the paper treated his administration. Bill Clinton complained about "gotcha journalism." George W. Bush, when running for the White House, referred over a live microphone to a prominent *New York Times* reporter as a "major league [epithet]." All recent presidents complain that the media misrepresent them and disproportionately report bad news.

Enjoying First Amendment rights in this country, reporters usually go about their business of analyzing and criticizing presidents with gusto. Scores of media representatives are stationed at the White House, and they travel everywhere the president goes, reporting on every move.

Presidents, of course, want their initiatives publicized and praised. But journalists and commentators believe they should provide a context in which presidential statements can be understood; hence they not only tell people what a president says, but often try to explain what the statement means. A free press is a basic check on presidents.

Most presidents have been patient and respected criticism as essential in a democracy. However, presidents and their aides engage in extensive public relations efforts aimed at winning admiration and support for the president and White House policies.[25] Out-of-town editors are invited in for special briefings, and extra effort is made to get the president out of Washington for meetings with local and regional media representatives, who are generally viewed as less critical than Washington-based media. White House media experts devise ways to get the president's point of view out to the public, to get the president on prime-time television, or to arrange for flattering photo opportunities.

No matter who is in the White House, presidents and the media will be in conflict. This ongoing struggle is inherent in a constitutional democracy. Exposés of campaign-contribution scandals and the Monica Lewinsky affair in the 1990s fortified the media's role in bringing these events to public attention. Further, because the media—especially television—are viewed as more trustworthy and believable than some other national institutions, most Americans, most of the time, believe what they hear and see on television. But the resources of the White House and the amount of free media coverage given presidents—especially communicators like Franklin Roosevelt, John Kennedy, and Ronald Reagan—provide an effective counterpoint to the media.

Public Opinion and Presidential Accountability

Presidents, in practice, are influenced by their anticipation not only of the next election but also of tomorrow's headlines and editorials, next week's public opinion polls, and next month's congressional hearings.

Presidents are subjected to a barrage of polls that judge their day-to-day or even minute-to-minute actions. In many ways, the time frame for presidential decision making and problem solving has been dramatically shortened. Issues cannot ripen, problems cannot be debated, discussed, and analyzed over several days. CNN-MSNBC-Fox television and website instant news analysis may indeed be holding presidents to instant accountability.

Although presidents on occasion have tried to govern without the benefit of public support, they have seldom succeeded. However, one of the more confusing aspects of presidential accountability is the way Americans find it convenient to blame the president for a whole range of problems, regardless of whether the problems were subject to presidential control. We generally withhold applause when a president's work is good, but we seldom fail to fault presidents when there are blunders.

As noted, most presidents lose public support over time. The decline in approval is in good measure a function of the understandable inability of a president to live up to the exaggerated buildup almost every president receives during the presidential honeymoon period (see Figure 12–3).

Political scientists are not exactly sure what people mean when they say they "approve" of a president's job performance. People respond to presidents at least as much through emotions as they do a rational understanding of the government's performance or a president's precise position on issues. But we do know that positive economic success helps a president's standing in the polls. Major nationally televised addresses also give a president a boost in public approval. Similarly, short successful wars and diplomatic breakthroughs at least temporarily improve a president's public approval. A president's favorable standing in the polls may help win congressional backing of White House policy measures; legislative victories, in turn, probably help enhance a president's standing in the polls.[26]

With the cold war era long over, a president's primary responsibility in the twenty-first century is to promote a successful domestic economy and productive trade relations. There will be occasional foreign policy tests, such as the U. S. intelligence-gathering plane that was forced down in China early in the Bush

Why Presidential Approval (in Polls) Usually Declines the Longer Presidents Are in Office

- Expectations that are raised in campaigns are dashed as time forecloses resources and options.

- Things that go wrong get blamed, rightly or wrongly, on presidents, whether or not presidents have the power to deal with these matters.

- Rising disapproval of incumbent presidents is often influenced by inflation and unemployment.

- Major negative events, such as the Vietnam War, Watergate scandal, or stock market declines, influence how people evaluate presidents.

- Press and media criticism accumulates over time and sharpens the public's dissatisfaction with a president. Perhaps, too, time in office simply wears out our welcome for a president.

Thinking It Through . . .

Reagan said the people should be able to reelect a president as many times as they want, just as they now reelect House and Senate members. He also hinted that the Twenty-second Amendment might weaken a president late in his second term by making him a lame duck, less powerful because everyone knows he will not be around in a year or so. Advocates of repeal also say we may sometimes need to keep a veteran president in office during a crisis period, much as we retained Franklin Roosevelt in 1940. Others say eight years may not be enough time to resolve certain major problems.

The Twenty-second Amendment is not only a limit on the incumbent but also on the electorate, the first since the ratification of the Constitution to restrict the power of the electorate rather than expand it. It is based, advocates of repeal suggest, on the assumption that the voters cannot be trusted.

Those who favor keeping the Twenty-second Amendment cite these reasons: First, the presidency is so powerful today that we need the Twenty-second Amendment as an additional check and balance against abuse of this power. Second, the amendment encourages both parties to seek out effective candidates to succeed to office and discourages dependence on a single ruler. Third, few leaders are likely to have the health, the intellectual energy, and the new ideas needed to perform the demanding responsibilities of the presidency beyond eight years in office. Finally, Americans have always believed in citizen-leaders rather than career politicians, and this amendment encourages this ideal.

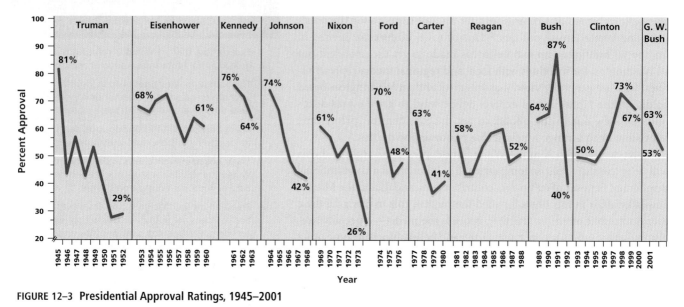

FIGURE 12–3 Presidential Approval Ratings, 1945–2001

Source: The Gallup Organization, www.gallup.org.

administration, but every recent president has found it imperative to create the impression that he has a plan for improving the economy. George W. Bush's father failed to do so, but the younger Bush's success or failure will likely be determined by his domestic rather than his foreign policies.

Ultimately no safeguard can hold a wayward president or a corrupt White House aide completely accountable. Our framers designed a constitutional system that does not depend on our finding angels to run the government. It assumes presidents, even good ones, need checks on their powers. James Madison's advice remains crucial: "A dependence on the people is, no doubt, the primary control of the government, but experience has taught mankind the necessity of auxiliary precautions" (see *The Federalist*, No. 51, in the Appendix of this book). Americans must vigilantly maintain the effectiveness of these "auxiliary precautions"—Congress, political parties, the courts, the press, the Bill of Rights, and concerned citizens' groups—to ensure a properly balanced and constitutional presidency.

PRESIDENTIAL GREATNESS? HOW WE JUDGE THEM

Most Americans judge contemporary presidents against the standard of the Mount Rushmore presidents. We want presidents who can summon us to live up to our shared ideals about liberty and freedom and who will pay close attention to our immediate needs.[27]

In sum, we use varying and sometimes unfair standards when we judge presidents. We expect a lot and leave little room for error. The opinions of historians differ from what the general public believes.

Historians and political scientists occasionally publish rankings of presidents. They rate presidents as outstanding, great, or near great on the basis of whether they brought about desirable changes and acted wisely to guide the nation through turbulent times. "We honor the great presidents of the past" wrote presidential historian Clinton Rossiter, "not for their strength but for the fact that they used it wisely to build a better America."[28]

One of the paradoxes of presidential greatness is that we yearn for the democratic "common person" and simultaneously for a leader who is uncommon, charismatic, visionary, and heroic. Political scientist Harold J. Laski once suggested, "He must have 'common opinions.' But it is equally important that he be an 'uncommon man.' The public must see themselves in him, but they must, at the same time, be confident that he is something bigger than themselves."[29]

The great presidents, often to the consternation of legal scholars and Congress, stretched the Constitution and *strengthened the presidency* to bring about change. Sometimes this is called the "doctrine of necessity"—doing what needs to be done. Thus those presidents considered "great" often were those who gave Congress the hardest time. They sometimes exercised powers that were thought to be solely or primarily congressional. Some of the presidents regularly challenged Congress and the Supreme Court as well.

What did the great presidents do? President Washington, more than any other person, converted the paper notions outlined in the Constitution into an enduring, practical governing process. With extraordinary character he set the precedents that balanced self-government and leadership, chief of state and chief executive, constitutionalism and statesmanship.

Thomas Jefferson, a genius in his generation, was a skilled organizer and a resourceful party leader and chief executive. He made mistakes, yet he adapted the presidency to the new realities of his day. His expansions of territory with the Louisiana Purchase, his sponsorship of the Lewis and Clark expedition, and similar bold ventures assures him a revered status among presidents.

President Lincoln is remembered for saving the union and is revered as the nation's foremost symbol of democracy and tenacious leadership in the nation's ultimate crisis. President Franklin Delano Roosevelt is viewed as guiding the nation through its worst economic crisis and for rallying the nation and the world to defeat Hitler's nazism.

These presidential accomplishments are part of the legend of America. Yet this heroic view of presidents raises a good many questions. If presidents alone were responsible for these and similar feats, it is little wonder that our expectations are so high concerning what current and future presidents should accomplish.

In fact, of course, a variety of people and institutions contributed to the achievements credited to past presidents. History seldom adequately honors the reformers and leaders who provided behind-the-scenes leadership. The best presidents surround themselves with talented advisers and administrators. Great leadership depends on situation, resources, opportunity, and on teams of leaders. Being at the right place at the right time also helps.

Many of the great presidents made mistakes, sometimes great mistakes. And the great presidents typically look better a few years later than they did while they were among the living. Harry Truman is a prime example of a presidential leader who was viewed as a lesser light while in office but was later recognized as great.

We learn a lot by those presidents we judge as failures. President Warren G. Harding was ranked near or at the bottom by experts because his administration was so corrupt; his loyalty to his friends was fatal. Others rank near the bottom because they lacked a compelling program, vision, political skill, or integrity. While Richard Nixon was respected for his foreign policy initiatives, especially for his recognition of the People's Republic of China, he is nonetheless viewed as one of the lesser presidents because he lied to the American public, plotted a cover-up of illegal and unconstitutional activities, resigned in disgrace, and, in the eyes of many, disgraced the dignity of the Oval Office. Bill Clinton will doubtless be judged a good political leader yet flawed in character.

First Lady: A Search for the Appropriate Role

Political spouses have often influenced their husbands or wives. Earlier presidential spouses—including Dolley Madison, Edith Wilson, and Eleanor Roosevelt—counseled and lobbied their presidential husbands. Every "first spouse" defines her responsibilities differently. Bess Truman and Pat Nixon chose to remain in the background. Lady Bird Johnson, Betty Ford, and Rosalynn Carter undertook projects of special interest to them. Hillary Rodham Clinton became an influential and important adviser to President Bill Clinton.

Hillary Clinton was as controversial as she was influential. Her role as an advocate of health care initiatives and women's rights attracted criticism as well as praise. Her role in the Whitewater real estate development and her alleged failure to answer specific questions about it caused additional concerns. She became the first First Lady to be subpoenaed to testify before a grand jury, and she, along with her husband, was questioned by a federal independent counsel.

Hillary Clinton was hailed as a first lady for our times and a model for contemporary women who choose to have both a career and a family. She was criticized in the press, satirized in the novel *Primary Colors*, and ridiculed by opposition politicians and pundits. She stood by her husband throughout the Monica Lewinsky scandal and energized Democratic opposition to her husband's impeachment. In 2000 she won election as a U.S. senator from New York.

The high-profile Hillary Clinton model of service as First Lady is unlikely to become the standard model. Laura Bush a former school librarian, prefers playing a lower profile role. One of her keen interests is promoting reading and celebrating books and authors. In Texas she founded an annual book festival for Texas public libraries. She is likely to sponsor similar programs as First Lady. And she has made it clear that she will not be involved in policy development. Unlike Hillary Clinton, she has an office in the east wing rather than the high-status west wing of the White House.

SUMMARY

1. The framers created a presidency with limited powers. To enact government business, the president must cooperate with Congress, but powers are divided among the branches, and the politics of shared power has often been stormy. In general, however, the role and influence of presidents have increased in the course of the nation's history.

2. The expansion of presidential influence has been a continual development during the past several decades. Crises, both foreign and economic, have enlarged these powers. When there is a need for decisive action, presidents are asked to supply it. Congress, of course, is traditionally expected to share in the formulation of national policy. Every president must learn anew the need to work closely with the members of Congress.

3. Every four years Americans search for a new president. We yearn for honest, experienced, effective presidents who will propose solutions to the nation's toughest problems. Doubtless we expect far more than is reasonable, but we inevitably want someone as good as Washington, Lincoln, and FDR.

4. Presidents must act as crisis-managing, morale-building, personnel-recruiting, priority-setting, coalition-building, public opinion-molding, party, and managerial leaders. No president can divide the job into tidy compartments. Ultimately, these responsibilities overlap.

5. The vice-presidency is now a part of the presidential establishment, and recent vice-presidents have been increasingly integrated into the White House decision-making process.

6. Presidential power is usually exercised for important and noble ends, yet it can also on occasion be abused. Presidents, however, are held to account by a variety of checks and balances, including elections and legacy, Congress, the court, the media, and public opinion.

7. Presidential greatness is something often talked about yet harder to define. But nearly everyone considers Lincoln, Washington, and Franklin Roosevelt as outstanding presidents. Presidents are viewed as great when they brought about desirable progress and guided the nation through crises.

KEY TERMS

divided government 275

Executive Office of the President 282

Office of Management and Budget 282

cabinet 287

FURTHER READING

DAVID GRAY ADLER AND LARRY N. GEORGE, EDS., *The Constitution and the Conduct of American Foreign Policy: Essays on Law and History* (University Press of Kansas, 1996).

PAUL BRACE AND BARBARA HINCKLEY, *Follow the Leader: Opinion Polls and the Modern Presidents* (Basic Books, 1992).

THOMAS E. CRONIN, ED., *Inventing the American Presidency* (University Press of Kansas, 1989).

THOMAS E. CRONIN AND MICHAEL A. GENOVESE, *The Paradoxes of the American Presidency* (Oxford University Press, 1998).

TERRY EASTLAND, *Energy in the Executive* (Free Press, 1992).

MICHAEL A. GENOVESE, *The Power of the American Presidency, 1989–2000* (Oxford University Press, 2000).

DAVID GERGEN, *Eyewitness to Power: The Essence of Leadership—Nixon to Clinton* (Simon & Schuster, 2000).

FRED GREENSTEIN, *The Presidential Difference* (Free Press, 2000).

ERWIN C. HARGROVE, *The President as Leader: Appealing to the Better Angels of Our Nature* (University Press of Kansas, 1998).

CHARLES O. JONES, *Passages to the Presidency, From Campaigning to Governing* (Brookings Institution, 1998).

MARK LANDY AND SIDNEY M. MILKIS, *Presidential Greatness* (University Press of Kansas, 2000).

LEONARD W. LEVY AND LOUIS FISHER, EDS., *Encyclopedia of the American Presidency* (Simon & Schuster, 1994).

JOHN A. MALTESE, *Spin Control: The White House Office of Communications and the Management of the Presidential News* (University of North Carolina Press, 1992).

SIDNEY M. MILKIS, *The President and the Parties: The Transformation of the American Party System Since the New Deal* (Oxford University Press, 1993).

SIDNEY M. MILKIS AND MICHAEL NELSON, *The American Presidency: Origins and Development, 1976–1998*, 3d ed. (Congressional Quarterly Books, 1999).

MICHAEL NELSON, ED., *The Presidency and the Political System*, 6th ed. (Congressional Quarterly Press, 2000).

RICHARD E. NEUSTADT, *Presidential Power and the Modern Presidents* (Free Press, 1991).

HUBERT S. PARMET, *George Bush: The Life of a Lone Star Yankee* (Scribner's, 1998).

BRADLEY H. PATTERSON, JR., *The White House Staff: Inside the West Wing and Beyond* (Brookings Institution, 2000).

JAMES P. PFIFFNER, *The Strategic Presidency: Hitting the Ground Running*, 2d ed. (University Press of Kansas, 1996).

GLENN A. PHELPS, *George Washington and American Constitutionalism* (University Press of Kansas, 1993).

LYN RAGSDALE, *Vital Statistics on the Presidency*, rev. ed. (Congressional Quarterly Press, 1998).

SHELLEY LYNNE TOMKINS, *Inside OMB: Politics and Process in the President's Budget Office* (M. E. Sharpe, 1998).

KENNETH T. WALSH, *Feeding the Beast: The White House Versus the Press* (Random House, 1996).

SHIRLEY ANNE WARSHAW, *Powersharing: White House–Cabinet Relations in the Modern Presidency* (State University of New York Press, 1996).

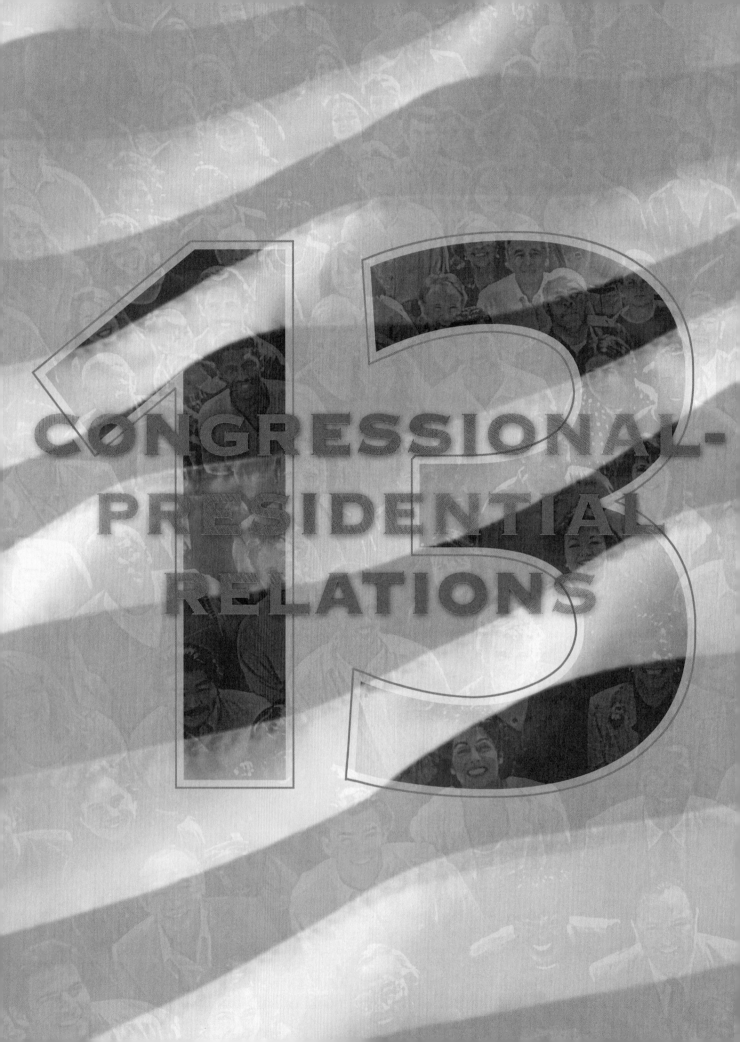

13

CONGRESSIONAL-PRESIDENTIAL RELATIONS

NEWLY ELECTED PRESIDENT GEORGE W. BUSH CAME TO THE WHITE HOUSE IN 2001 WITH DAUNTING CHALLENGES AND A "WEAK HAND." AS VETERAN *WASHINGTON Post* reporter David Broder noted, Bush enjoyed "No majority. No mandate. Not even broad agreement that he deserved the prize that fell into his hands when the Supreme Court, itself deeply divided, ordered the ballot recounts in Florida must halt."[1] This is hardly the way a president wants to launch a presidency.

Still, George W. Bush immediately set in motion legislative initiatives for a major tax cut, for increased spending on education and military pay, and for prescription drug coverage for Medicare recipients, among other things. He had campaigned on these issues, even though he understood that he might have to scale back some of his plans in order to win bipartisan support. But he understood, too, that the American people expect presidents to set the nation's policy agenda and that elections, even with unclear mandates, are part of the process of bringing about changes in public policy.

As soon as an election concludes, a president inevitably must try to win congressional support for his policies. This is never easy, even for presidents who have won decisive election victories. Members of the opposing party in Congress have their own agendas, and even members of the president's own party in Congress can pose a challenge to presidential plans. Such was the case in George W. Bush's first months in the White House, when Senator John McCain (R.-Ariz.) fought for campaign finance reform as a top priority—an issue the president did not especially support.

Tensions between Congress and presidents go back to the origins of American government. Alexander Hamilton, General George Washington's chief aide, complained about the deadlock rooted in the design of the Continental Congress more than 200 years ago. Yet it was the intention of the framers of the U.S. Constitution to create a government of sharply limited powers and separated institutions that would both share and compete for power. The framers saw the separation of powers not necessarily as a weakness but as a source of strength, and especially as a way to ensure deliberation and to prevent tyranny.

The popular assumption is that a president—as chief executive and commander in chief—essentially guides Congress in most of its law-making activity. But the reality is often different. The decentralized nature of Congress, the independent and entrepreneurial mode of legislators, and the institutional responsibilities and pride of Congress all conspire against presidential policy leadership.

CHAPTER MEDIA

POLITICS ONLINE
Are Limitations on Presidential War Powers Outdated?
www.prenhall.com/burns

POLISIM
Who's Got the Power?
www.prenhall.com/burns

Presidents are sometimes opposed by members of their own party, as George W. Bush was by Senator John McCain, his former opponent in the presidential campaign, on the matter of campaign finance reform.

Soon after a new president takes office—as both Bill Clinton and George W. Bush found out—members of Congress take the measure of the new White House occupant. Will the president reach out and try to cooperate with Congress? Will the president overreach and push too fast—as Clinton did with his health care proposal? Will the president be highly partisan or bipartisan? Will the president try to intimidate and coerce reluctant legislators? And how much can Congress exert its leadership?

Who should be in charge? The fact that responsibility and power are fragmented in our federal government often creates a fascinating blame game, with the president blaming Congress and Congress blaming the president. This happened between President Ronald Reagan and the Democrats in Congress in the 1980s and between Clinton and the Newt Gingrich–led Congress of the mid-1990s.

The success of Congress or the president is influenced by the partisan and ideological makeup of Congress, the popularity and skills of the president, the strength of the political parties, and the nature of various events that shape the politics of the times.

In this chapter we begin by looking at our complicated system of separate branches, which of necessity must find ways to work together. What did the framers intend? What has evolved over the years? Why do members of Congress often see things differently from the way presidents do? What are some of the ongoing controversies between the two branches? And what are some of the ways presidents try to win congressional support?

SEPARATE BUT EQUAL BRANCHES

The Constitution's writers saw Congress as the central, if not dominant, branch of government. Congress would have the power of the purse, in addition to extensive supervision of interstate and foreign commerce and the currency. Congress would also play a crucial role in military and foreign policy matters since only Congress could declare war and only the Senate could approve treaties. And Congress was granted the all-important power to make laws "which shall be necessary and proper" for carrying out its specified powers.

Presidents do not personally introduce legislation, but they are invited to give Congress information on the State of the Union and recommend measures they deem necessary for the good of the nation. Thus, in practice, presidents are invited to shape the nation's legislative agenda; it would be unthinkable for a president today not to submit an extensive legislative program to the Congress.

America's first presidents deferred to Congress on many issues, but gradually presidents began to play a more assertive role in the legislative process. A stronger executive gradually evolved to provide balance and leadership.

Congress was sometimes a willing participant in giving additional power to presidents. The rise in importance of the presidency in legislating did not, however, follow a clear linear path. Some of the more ambitious chief executives, such as Thomas Jefferson, used the newly formed political parties to exert influence in Congress. Others, such as Andrew Jackson, marshaled public opinion to gain influence with the Congress. Still others, such as Abraham Lincoln and Franklin Roosevelt, gained additional powers during national crises. In between these influence-aggrandizing presidents were less assertive or weaker chief executives. Thus, an institutional ebb and flow characterized the relationship between Congress and presidents. What was designed in many ways as a congressionally centered system evolved by the early twenty-first century into a system centered around the presidency.

But Congress can impose its will on presidents, as Ronald Reagan found out when Congress rejected his strongly argued plea for millions in military aid to Nicaragua rebels, and Bill Clinton discovered when Congress refused to enact his health care reform measures and when the Senate failed to ratify a Comprehensive Test Ban Treaty. Virtually every president has also faced setbacks in dealing with Congress on confirmation of nominees to the cabinet or the courts.

The separation of powers and divided government can be obstacles, yet they are not barriers to good public policy making. Indeed, a certain amount of delay and the need for compromise often make for better public policy. Presidents and Congress can legislate when the leaders of both institutions bargain and compromise. Although the Constitution distributes power and invites a continuous struggle between these rival branches, it also requires them to collaborate. And despite all the media attention highlighting their disagreements, these institutions usually do cooperate. Even when the relationship is highly partisan and hostile, bills get passed and become law, appointments are confirmed, budgets are enacted, and the government receives both the funding and the general direction it needs to get work done. This necessary cooperation generally takes place even when the White House and Congress are divided between the two major parties. And it is not a matter of one side winning and the other losing so much as a series of compromises between the two branches.

Most presidential budget requests eventually win approval, although Congress jealously guards its right to modify them, especially in certain areas such as defense and agriculture. Presidents, regardless of party, have about a fifty-fifty chance of getting their legislative proposals adopted by Congress. Whether this is a good thing or a bad thing depends on one's policy perspectives and partisan affiliation. Presidential scholar George Edwards, who carefully examined *major* legislative measures proposed by recent presidents, finds that less than 50 percent of these measures become law (see Figure 13–1). Thus, at least some of the time, presidents fail to win congressional backing even on their most cherished measures.[2]

"You've been around here longer than I have. What *are* 'congressional ethics'?"

WHY CONGRESS OFTEN VIEWS THINGS DIFFERENTLY

The framers divided legislative powers by creating two co-equal houses, which further magnified potential checks on a president's ability to lead. But the framers were worried, almost in equal measure, about ineffective government and the abuse of executive authority. Some additional factors encourage members of Congress to look at policy making and political decisions through lenses different from those of their counterparts down Pennsylvania Avenue at the White House.

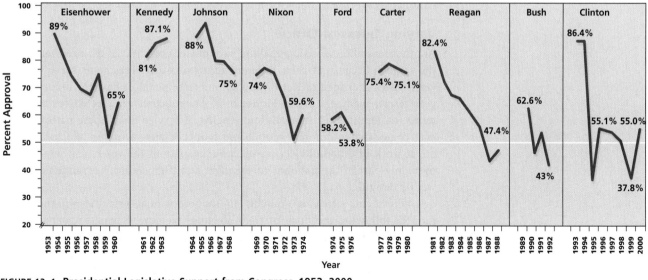

FIGURE 13–1 Presidential Legislative Support from Congress, 1953–2000

SOURCE: *Congressional Quarterly*, January 6, 2001, p. 52.

Note: Percentages represent average scores for both chambers of Congress.

Constitutional Ambiguities

Article I of the Constitution grants Congress "all legislative Powers" but limits those powers to those "herein granted." It then sets forth in some detail the powers vested in Congress. In contrast, Article II vests in the president "the executive Power" without limiting it to such powers as are "herein granted" and then proceeds to describe those powers in very general terms.

Is this difference in language between Articles I and II significant? Some scholars and most presidents have argued that a president is granted by Article II a general and undefined power to act to promote the well-being of the United States, subject only to precise constitutional limits. Therefore, they contend, a president is *not* limited to the specific powers spelled out in the Constitution, as is Congress, but has all the executive powers of the United States. Other scholars and many members of Congress say the president either has no such inherent power or has it only in extraordinary circumstances.[3]

Whatever the intent of the Constitution, the president has often exercised powers not expressly granted by it. These powers have been given a variety of names: *implied, inherent,* or *emergency powers.* For example, Bill Clinton ordered retaliatory bombings in Sudan and Afghanistan after U.S. embassies in Africa were bombed, and he did so without asking for congressional approval. Clinton also worked out a way to lend Mexico billions of dollars to stabilize its currency, even though Congress had essentially refused to do so. Actions like these prompt many in Congress to criticize presidents, even if they believe that in certain emergencies a president must act promptly without clear constitutional or statutory support.

Different Constituencies

Members of Congress represent state and local districts, and hence they reflect specific geographic, ethnic, and economic interests. James Madison and other framers of the Constitution anticipated that legislators would often be pressured by local and state interests to adopt a narrow or parochial view, as opposed to a national view, on certain policy issues, and presidents and their aides often think Madison was right. Members of Congress, of course, see sensitivity to state and local concerns as essential to their job as representatives and to their prospects for reelection. As a result, members of Congress—even those from a president's own party and own region—may look at problems and solutions somewhat differently from the way a president does, as a president represents, or at least is expected to represent, a national perspective.

Varying Terms of Office

Another reason the decision-making pace of Congress and of the president is not the same is because of their different terms of office. Presidents serve for four years with a chance of reelection to a second term; senators have the luxury of six-year terms; members of the House of Representatives are elected for two-year terms. Different constituencies and lengths of service make these national officials responsive to different moods and points of view. Different electoral forces are at work in different election years. A majority of the voters can win control over only part of the national government at a time, and this arrangement, too, was by design.

Presidents often act quickly to shape national priorities in their first months following the flush of their electoral victory, to win support for their agendas before a possible decline in public approval. Congress, on the other hand, usually moves more slowly "because it represents a vast array of local interests."[4] Another obvious difference in the speed of their two branches has to do with numbers: there is one president, but there are 435 members of the House and 100 senators.

Divided Government

Since 1952 there has been a split in partisan control of the presidency and Congress for most of the time. Republican Presidents Dwight Eisenhower, Ronald Reagan, George Bush, Gerald Ford, and Richard Nixon had to deal with Congresses that were most of the time under the control of Democrats. Only John Kennedy, Lyndon Johnson, and Jimmy Carter enjoyed majority control by their own party in Congress, and even they had considerable trouble getting support for their legislative programs.

Many people believe that presidents will generally enjoy more success in Congress when their party has clear control of both houses in Congress. "Unified party control is necessary, the argument goes, for ensuring that the two branches share common policy and electoral motivations," writes political scientist Sarah Blinder. "Under divided government, competing policy views and electoral incentives are sure to make legislative compromise unlikely."[5] Both parties seek a record that will enhance their election chances. This has been the case in recent decades, yet divided government is only one of many reasons that presidents fail to win the cooperation they would like to get from Congress.

Role of Political Parties

Most members of Congress finance their election campaigns with only minimal assistance from their national political party. They customarily respond to local conditions and run their campaigns independently of their party's presidential candidate or national platform. And changes in the electorate in recent years that enhance an incumbent's chances of reelection weaken the connection between the president and fellow partisans in Congress. Members of the president's party have typically run well ahead of their president in elections in their home districts, and thus they are less fearful of punishment for ignoring occasional party appeals for loyalty. They are more likely to go along with the president when a measure converges with their own political philosophy and is in the interest of their home district or state. And although parties have become vigorously partisan within Congress, especially in the House of Representatives, there are always several independent thinkers who will at times—sometimes crucial times for the White House—go their own way rather than cooperate with the White House, even when the president is a member of the same party.[6]

On the other hand, partisan affiliation is the most important predictor of how members of Congress vote. Congressional partisanship has been consistently strong on matters such as the Clinton impeachment and the John Ashcroft confirmation. Indeed, Clinton's problems with Congress often came about because the Republican party was so strong in his last several years that he had trouble winning support from them unless he proposed things the congressional Republicans wanted.

Fluctuating Public Support

In recent years Americans have generally held presidents in higher esteem than Congress as an institution—even after Bill Clinton was impeached—and this difference has consequences (see Figure 13–2). Greater prestige for the presidency can give the president a slight edge in battles with Congress.

Congress may be viewed by many people as slow or inefficient, in part because it has to represent local interests and respond to particular constituencies.[7] Yet when presidents decline in popularity, such as Nixon did after the Watergate scandal, or when a president loses moral authority, as Clinton did after the Lewinsky affair, Americans turn to Congress to hold the president and the presidency accountable.

The Need for Supermajorities

Although we have been taught that American government operates on the principle of majority rule, the reality is that the Senate's filibuster power, a president's veto authority, and the Senate's treaty approval responsibilities

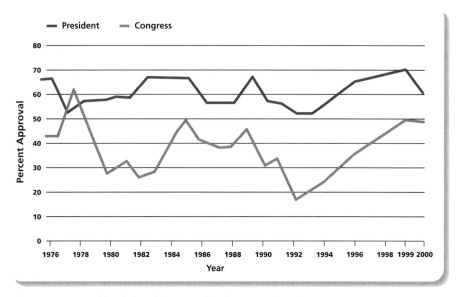

FIGURE 13–2 Presidential and Congressional Approval Ratings, 1976–2000

SOURCES: The Gallup Poll, CBS News/New York Times Poll, NBC News/Wall Street Journal Poll. Updated by the authors.

sometimes make *supermajorities* necessary. (At least 60 votes in the Senate are needed to end a filibuster; at least two-thirds of the senators present must concur on a proposed treaty; and a two-thirds supermajority vote in both the Senate and the House are needed to override a presidential veto of a proposed law.) The filibuster in the Senate has become more common in recent years. The filibuster effectively gives a veto to any 40 senators whose states may represent as little as 10 percent of the population, and whose views might not be especially centrist. Similarly, these realities make it harder for presidents to gain acceptance for their programs. They also cause members of Congress to be frustrated: "The harsh reality that new members discover is that developing supermajority coalitions around complex issues is difficult," write political scientists David W. Brady and Craig Volden. "Policy gridlock is the result of not being able to build such coalitions without violating the trust of the folks back home."[8]

In short, different constituencies, different powers, different time perspectives, and sometimes different parties help explain why members of Congress view their responsibilities and their political needs differently from the way presidents view theirs. The wonder sometimes is how they get along at all.

CONTROVERSY BETWEEN THE BRANCHES

The past few decades have been packed with political and legal controversies, ranging from the proper use of the war-making power to the intensely partisan politics when Bill Clinton was impeached. Some of these disputes were resolved in the courts, some were worked out between Congress and the administration, and others persist as disputes between the branches.

The War Power

Disputes have arisen over war powers because of seemingly contradictory passages in the Constitution, which states that Congress has the power to declare war, but it gives the president the ability to make war. Executive power is vested in the president, who shall be commander in chief of the army and navy.

James Madison and his colleagues recognized that the starting of a war or military hostility were the powers of a government most susceptible to abuse and the most dangerous. Abraham Lincoln, when he served in the U.S. Congress, aptly expressed the founders' intent when he wrote:

> The provision of the Constitution giving the war-making power to Congress was dictated, as I understand it, by the following reasons. Kings had always been involving and impoverishing their people in wars, pretending generally, if not always, that the good of the people was the object. This our convention understood to be the most oppressive of all kingly oppressions, and they resolved to so frame the Constitution that no one man should hold the power of bringing this oppression upon us.[9]

President Franklin D. Roosevelt signed the declaration of war against Japan on December 8, 1941, as leaders of Congress looked on. It was the last time a president of the United States signed a formal declaration of war.

The Constitution gives Congress, not the president, the authority to declare war. Yet in the last few decades, our presidents have sent troops or bombing missions into many nations, including Korea, Vietnam, Grenada, Panama, the Persian Gulf, and Yugoslavia, without asking Congress to declare war.

Presidents and other officials contend that presidents are better informed than Congress. Modern presidents need the flexibility and secrecy to respond quickly to military threats to the nation's security interests. One State Department official, in what many might call constitutional revisionism, described the president's war-making authority as: "The Constitution leaves to the President the judgment to determine whether the circumstances of a particular armed attack are so urgent and the potential consequences so threatening to the security of the U.S. that he should act without formally consulting the Congress."[10] And Madeleine Albright, Clinton's secretary of state, told members of Congress that the constitutional authority as commander in chief allows presidents "to use armed forces to protect our national interests."[11]

Some members of Congress and several scholars believe the actions of recent presidents in unilateral acts of executive war-making are in direct defiance of the war clause of the Constitution. They blame impatient and "imperial" presidents. "The absolutist pretensions of Bill Clinton which hearken to the swollen claims of the Stuart kings, have eviscerated the war power clause," writes political scientist David Gray Adler. "He has asserted the executive power to commence war at his pleasure, to determine its course and direction, and its intensity and duration."[12]

Others blame Congress for being passive and abdicating its constitutional authority to the presidency. Constitutional scholar Louis Fisher holds that Congress has repeatedly abdicated its fundamental war powers to the president. The framers knew what monarchy looked like and rejected it, writes Fisher. "Yet especially in matters of the war power, the United States is recreating a system of monarchy while it professes to champion democracy and the role of law abroad."[13] Fisher calls on members of Congress to reeducate themselves on their constitutional prerogatives.

In the aftermath of the Vietnam War, Congress tried to reassert its role and authority in the use of military force. In 1973 Congress enacted the War Power Resolution over Richard Nixon's veto. It declared that henceforth a president can commit the armed forces of the United States only: (1) after a declaration of war by Congress; (2) by specific statutory authorization; or (3) in a national emergency created by an attack on the United States or its armed forces. After committing the armed forces under the third circumstance, the president is required to report to

Congress within 48 hours. Unless Congress declares war, the troop commitment must be ended within 60 days.

This resolution signaled a new determination by Congress to take its prerogatives seriously, yet presidents have generally ignored it. And many leading scholars now believe this earnest and well-intentioned effort by Congress to reclaim its proper role actually gave away more authority than previous practices had already done. They say it was ill conceived and badly written, full of tortured ambiguity and self-contradiction. "The statute further subordinates Congress to presidential war initiatives and should be repealed in its entirety."[14]

Most observers believe the United States is best served when both president and Congress are fully engaged partners in foreign and defense policy making. Congressman Lee Hamilton sums up the virtues of joint action by these rival branches: "I believe that a partnership, characterized by creative tension between the president and the Congress, produces a foreign policy that better serves the American national interest—and better reflects the values of the American people—than policy produced by the President alone."[15]

Confirmation Politics

As noted in Chapter 11, the Constitution gives the Senate a crucial role in approving key presidential nominees, including members of his cabinet, senior military officials, and ambassadors. Senators normally defer to presidents, especially newly elected ones, on their choice for members in their cabinet. Standard differences in party ideology are not adequate reasons for blocking an appointment.

The Senate has rejected only nine proposed cabinet members (see Table 13–1) yet forced the withdrawal of others. Clinton saw three of his cabinet nominees withdraw because of Senate opposition. George W. Bush's first nominee for secretary of labor withdrew from the confirmation process even before Bush was sworn into office. The Senate has also rejected 28 of 145 nominees for the U.S. Supreme Court, and many more for the other courts.[16]

Bill Clinton faced a Republican-controlled Senate that used its "advice and consent" authority to deny or delay many of his nominations. Some senators insisted on an ideological veto over Clinton nominees, while others merely demanded a share of judicial patronage. Senator Orrin Hatch (R.-Utah) wrote that several of Clinton's

TABLE 13–1 Cabinet Nominees Rejected by the Senate

Nominee	Position	President	Date	Vote
Roger B. Taney	secretary of treasury	Jackson	1834	18–28
Caleb Cushing	secretary of treasury	Tyler	1843	19–27
Caleb Cushing	secretary of treasury	Tyler	1843	10–27
Caleb Cushing	secretary of treasury	Tyler	1843	2–29
David Henshaw	secretary of navy	Tyler	1844	6–34
James M. Porter	secretary of war	Tyler	1844	3–38
James S. Green	secretary of treasury	Tyler	1844	*
Henry Stanbery	attorney general	A. Johnson	1868	11–29
Charles B. Warren	attorney general	Coolidge	1925	39–41
Charles B. Warren	attorney general	Coolidge	1925	39–46
Lewis L. Strauss	secretary of commerce	Eisenhower	1959	46–49
John Tower	secretary of defense	Bush	1989	47–53

SOURCE: Senate Historical Office.

aNot recorded

nominees for federal court posts were not confirmed because Clinton failed to consult with the senators from states where the judgeships were located. "Senators from the states where the judgeship is located are the ones who usually exercise the power to oppose nominees, since they represent the citizens who will be subject to the decisions of that nominee."[17]

Some critics say the Senate has turned the process of confirming judges into a political sideshow for the political parties to curry favor with their more ideological supporters. Many Republicans trace this trend to the demonization of Judge Robert H. Bork by Senate Democrats in 1987, when they defeated his nomination (by Ronald Reagan) to the Supreme Court.

One former Reagan administration official says the confirmation process has become highly destructive because legislators are often guided more by what their campaign contributors want rather than by what they believe is right. "The confirmation process . . . is no longer controlled by the senators," says William Bradford Reynolds. "It is, for the most part, controlled by well-endowed constituency groups with their own special-interest agendas. Thus, the process has deteriorated into personal attacks, largely uncivil and underserved."[18]

While the Senate confirms the vast majority of presidential nominees for judicial or executive branch positions, there is considerable political bargaining and behind-the-scenes testiness. Political clashes induced by party polarization and divided government have led to a drawn-out confirmation process. Some of Clinton's federal court nominees had to wait three to four years before confirmation. And Clinton appointed judges who were more conservative than he might otherwise have appointed. He also had to trade appointments with prominent Republican senators to get their cooperation for some of his nominees.

Most people respect the notion that presidents elected by the entire nation deserve to have members of their cabinet who generally agree with them. Thus senators do not ordinarily object to nominees because of differences in party ideology. Yet a president's discretion is not unlimited. When George W. Bush nominated former U.S. Senator John Ashcroft to be attorney general, even though few people questioned his integrity and experience, there was strong opposition to him because of his positions on abortion and civil rights matters. Democrats sharply criticized his nomination and questioned him and other witnesses at length in the Ashcroft confirmation hearings. Nonetheless, he was confirmed by a vote of 58 to 42.

The confirmation provision in the Constitution has fulfilled most of the intentions of the framers. Unqualified nominees are usually, though not always, rejected. The process has sometimes deterred appointments of people who hold especially strident political views. The Senate's role in the confirmation process was never intended to eliminate politics but rather to use politics as a safeguard. Senators plainly, perhaps in recent years more than ever, use this process to make their political and policy views known to prospective confirmees as well as to the White House. And this is equally true for liberal senators such as Ted Kennedy or Joe Biden as it is for conservatives like Jesse Helms and Orrin Hatch.

On balance, the very existence of this sometimes contentious process deters presidents from appointing weak, questionable, radical, or "unfit characters." On the other hand, presidents who prepare and bargain well are still able to appoint talented people they want in important public service positions.

Executive Privilege

The presidential claim of **executive privilege** is yet another area of controversy between presidents and Congress. The Constitution does not authorize presidents to withhold information because Congress and the public need information to do their

A president's choices of cabinet members are usually approved without much difficulty, but George W. Bush's nomination of former Senator John Ashcroft for attorney general ran into considerable controversy because of some of Ashcroft's positions on racial matters and his vehement opposition to abortion. However, strong Republican support carried the confirmation by a vote of 58 to 42.

executive privilege
The right under certain conditions for a president to withhold or protect information related to national security.

President Richard Nixon held out vigorously against turning over tapes he had recorded of conversations in the Oval Office relating to Watergate. He claimed they were covered by executive privileges.

jobs. However, courts have recognized that presidents can keep secret some limited and narrowly defined kinds of information, especially information, which if released, would jeopardize national security.

One constitutional historian argues that executive privilege is a myth, without constitutional basis.[19] But presidents have in fact been withholding documents from Congress at least as far back as when President George Washington refused to share sensitive documents with a House committee studying an Indian massacre of federal troops. In this 1792 incident, Washington had the full support of his cabinet. Later he did share the information with Congress. But both then and later in his administration he set the precedent for the use of executive privilege to protect the public interest. Thomas Jefferson and the primary author of the Constitution, James Madison, also withheld information during their presidencies.

Most scholars, the courts, and even most members of Congress have long agreed that a president does have the implicit, if not constitutionally explicit, right to withhold information that could truly harm the nation's security. It was through the use of executive privilege, for example, that during World War II, the time and place of the Normandy Beach D-Day invasion were properly kept secret.

It was only in the Eisenhower administration of the 1950s that the term "executive privilege" began to be used, but it was the much more aggressive use of this claim by Richard Nixon that gave executive privilege its bad name.[20] In the Watergate scandal, President Nixon hid information to protect his administration from congressional and public scrutiny. He and his lawyers went so far as to claim that the decision to invoke executive privilege was not subject to review by Congress or the courts. And, in the famous Nixon tapes case of 1974, Nixon refused to turn over documents to congressional committees and to the judiciary.

The Supreme Court, speaking through Chief Justice Warren Burger, held Nixon's claims erroneous. The Court, in effect, said vital national security considerations could on occasion permit presidents to exercise executive privilege because the release of certain information would be damaging to the nation's security interests. But the court also ruled that national security was not being threatened, that this was a criminal case, and hence President Nixon had to yield his tapes (which helped doom his presidency). In this complicated decision, although the Supreme Court ruled against Nixon's claim, it did acknowledge for the first time the constitutionality of the executive privilege.[21] Yet it held that there is no absolute unreviewable executive privilege.

During the Clinton presidency, Congress requested a number of documents concerning U.S. foreign policy toward Haiti. The White House refused, claiming these documents contained sensitive national security information. Congress backed off, but was unhappy about the lack of cooperation in this and related incidents. The Clinton administration claimed executive privilege on at least a dozen occasions, often in cases related to various independent counsel investigations of Clinton or cabinet members.[22] Evidence plainly suggests that Clinton and his attorneys misused the claim of executive privilege, especially in their efforts to delay or undermine congressional and independent counsel investigations of the Monica Lewinsky affair.[23] Executive privilege cannot be asserted in either congressional or judicial proceedings when the issue is basically one of refusing to cooperate in investigations of personal wrongdoing.

Presidents and members of Congress will continue to differ over the way executive privilege is exercised. There is no way this matter can be settled once and for all. It is a matter that will be revisited in each administration, and invariably it will be tested by presidents and by the legislative branch. On occasion, courts will try to settle this ongoing dispute about the limits and conditions under which a president can invoke this well-established, if sometimes abused, presidential practice.

Executive Orders

Executive orders, though not provided for in the Constitution, have become a generally accepted presidential practice. Beginning with George Washington, presidents have issued more than 13,000 executive orders. These orders have been used to declare American neutrality in the war between France and England (1793), the internment of Japanese-Americans during World War II, and Bill Clinton's protection of large tracts of federal land as "national monuments" in Arizona, Colorado, Oregon, Utah, and Washington.

An **executive order** is a presidential directive that has the force of law. It can be challenged in the courts, and it can be overturned by subsequent presidents. Most executive orders are reasonable modifications or specific implementations of past legislation. But some presidential executive orders have antagonized members of Congress and led to charges that presidents were usurping the law-making functions assigned to Congress.

President Clinton, like presidents before him, made bold use of executive orders as a way to circumvent a Congress that often was unfriendly to certain of his initiatives. Reliance on executive orders is a strategy a president uses when traditional avenues are denied to the White House. Clinton used this power extensively (on more than 350 occasions),[24] strategically, and across many types of policy. He set a standard that George W. Bush and other successors will follow, especially when Congress is controlled by the opposition party.[25]

The president's power to shape public policy through executive orders has grown along with the expansion of other executive branch responsibilities. While some of these responsibilities have been delegated to presidents by Congress, presidents have also assertively assumed additional authority on their own. Courts can, but seldom do, strike down executive orders.

Members of Congress, especially in the opposition party, look suspiciously on presidents making policy decisions they think belong in the legislative process. The dispute is not resolved by the Constitution, which "avoids specifying precisely what decisions must be made under all current and future contingencies."[26]

Presidents, especially in modern times, rarely view their job as merely implementing laws as Congress passed them. Because the laws passed by Congress usually have not been written with all the details specified, considerable discretion is left to presidents and the agencies of the executive branch. And most presidents view themselves as an authority in their own right, not subordinates to Congress but co-equal with it.

Presidents have to exercise this power responsibly. "Should they go too far or fast, or move into the wrong areas at the wrong time, they would find that there are heavy political costs to be paid. . . . It is a matter of strategy. Presidents have to calculate . . . the costs as well as the benefits. . . . They have to pick their spots. But they will constantly be on the lookout, ready to move, and quite capable of moving if that is what they decide to do.[27]

Veto Politics

The Constitution provides that bills passed by the U.S. House of Representatives and Senate "shall be presented to the President of the United States," and the president can then approve the measure or **veto** it. If a bill is vetoed by a president, it can be enacted only if the veto is overridden, which requires a two-thirds vote in each chamber of Congress.

executive order
An order issued by a president or governor that has the force of law.

veto
Rejection of legislation by a president or governor .

Another variation of the veto is called the **pocket veto**. In the ordinary course of events, if a president does not sign or veto a bill within ten weekdays after receiving it, the bill becomes law without the president's signature. But if Congress adjourns within the ten days, the president—by taking no action—can kill the bill.

The crucial importance of the veto power lies in the difficulty of getting the required two-thirds majority to override the veto in both houses. Historically Congress has overridden less than 10 percent of presidents' regular vetoes (see Table 13–2). This obstacle means that presidents have a vital bargaining chip in the last stages of the legislating and the appropriating processes. Even the threat of a veto can frequently strengthen a president's hand in persuading and negotiating. Presidents merely indicate, either publicly or through their legislative aides, that bills under consideration by Congress will be turned back unless certain changes are made. More broadly, a president can use the threat of a veto against a bill Congress wants in exchange for other bills the president wants. Still, most of the time, the veto is essentially a negative weapon, more useful to presidents who want to block legislation than for a president who is pressing for programmatic changes.

Of course, a unified Congress that could repeatedly mobilize a two-thirds majority against a president could virtually take control of the law-making process. This has rarely been done in U.S. history, but such was the fate of President Andrew Johnson in the 1860s.[28]

Because the Constitution is fairly clear about the veto power, the regular use of it by presidents stirs little controversy. Franklin Roosevelt holds the record with 635 vetoes; Ronald Reagan vetoed 78 in his two terms; and Bill Clinton vetoed only 37 times in his eight years. In late 1999 President Clinton vetoed a Republican-backed appropriation bill and threatened to veto it again and again until Congress made major compromises with him. His use of the veto worked; Congress eventually went along on about two-thirds of the spending items that Clinton wanted. How often a president uses the veto power depends on factors like the composition of Congress and the extent to which the branches agree on policy.

The Item Veto

What did become controversial was the short life of the **item veto**. Ronald Reagan and other presidents had long sought to give the president the authority to strike specific items from the budget passed each year by Congress without having to veto the entire bill. Congress, in a surprising move that in effect delegated some of its power to the presidency, enacted the Line Item Veto Act, which President Clinton signed into law in 1996. Advocates of the item veto believed it would enable presidents to cut wasteful and ill-advised spending projects whose main purpose was to help an individual member of Congress win reelection. What was notable about the enactment of the item veto legislation was that a Congress controlled by Republicans actually voted to strengthen a Democratic president, Bill Clinton.

President Clinton exercised the item veto on ten occasions. But in mid-1998, the Supreme Court ruled, in a 6–3 decision, that Congress had improperly ceded to the president the power to rewrite legislation when it had passed the Line Item Veto Act. Supreme Court Justice Anthony Kennedy aptly summarized why the Court ruled as it did: "By increasing the power of the President beyond what the framers envisioned, the statue compromises the political liberty of our citizens, liberty which the separation of powers seeks to secure."[29]

Budget and Spending Politics

Battles over budgets and spending have been at the heart of national politics since the beginning of the Republic. The Constitution explicitly gives Congress the power to appropriate money; presidents are charged with implementing and administering the spending.

pocket veto
A veto exercised by the president after Congress has adjourned; if the president takes no action for ten weekdays, the bill does not become law and is not returned to Congress for a possible override.

item veto
Power of an executive to veto parts of legislation approved by a legislature. Most state governors have this power. It was granted by Congress to the president in 1996 but declared unconstitutional the next year by the U. S. Supreme Court.

TABLE 13-2 Presidential Vetoes, 1789–2001

President	Regular Vetoes	Pocket Vetoes	Total Vetoes	Overridden
Washington	2	0	2	0
J. Adams	0	0	0	0
Jefferson	0	0	0	0
Madison	5	2	7	0
Monroe	1	0	1	0
J. Q. Adams	0	0	0	0
Jackson	5	7	12	0
Van Buren	0	1	1	0
W. Harrison	0	0	0	0
Tyler	6	4	10	1
Polk	2	1	3	0
Taylor	0	0	0	0
Fillmore	0	0	0	0
Pierce	9	0	9	5
Buchanan	4	3	7	0
Lincoln	2	5	7	0
A. Johnson	21	8	29	15
Grant	45	*49	*94	4
Hayes	12	1	13	1
Garfield	0	0	0	0
Arthur	4	8	12	1
Cleveland (both terms)	346	238	584	7
B. Harrison	19	25	44	1
McKinley	6	36	42	0
T. Roosevelt	42	40	82	1
Taft	30	9	39	1
Wilson	33	11	44	6
Harding	5	1	6	0
Coolidge	20	30	50	4
Hoover	21	16	37	3
F. Roosevelt	372	263	635	9
Truman	180	70	250	12
Eisenhower	73	108	181	2
Kennedy	12	9	21	0
L. Johnson	16	14	30	0
Nixon	26	17	43	7
Ford	48	18	66	12
Carter	13	18	31	2
Reagan	39	39	78	9
Bush	29	17	44	1
Clinton	36	1	37	2
Total	1,484	1,069	2,551	106

SOURCE: U.S. Senate Historical Office, Senate Library, January 2001.

*Includes one pocket veto in which the bill was not placed before the president for signature.

Congress dominated the budget-making process until 1921, when it approved the Budget and Accounting Act of 1921. That act mandated that the president submit annual budgets to Congress, and it established a Bureau of the Budget that in 1970 became the Office of Management and Budget. Presidents have played an increasingly powerful role in shaping the federal budget.

President Nixon, however, overplayed his role when his White House developed legal theories that justified **impoundment**—not spending funds for purposes Congress had authorized—as an inherent constitutional power of the president. Impoundment had been used by presidents going back to George Washington. Actually, some impoundment can be justified to accommodate a change in events (if a war ends, for example), or to alter a managerial approach (for efficiency).

Nixon stretched the use of impoundment to new lengths. He claimed the Democratic Congress was authorizing too much spending that caused rising budget deficits. Congress responded that Nixon was using impoundment to set policy in explicit violation of the Constitution. Congress not only complained, it approved the 1974 Congressional Budget and Impoundment Control Act.

This act specified how a president could spend or refuse to spend monies approved by Congress. But it also set in motion years of wrangling between Congress and the White House about how best to estimate revenues and move toward balanced budgets.

In the Budget Act of 1974, Congress, among other things, restored greater budget authority. The act called for both the president and Congress to make budget forecasts with an eye toward achieving balanced budgets. But this proved a major challenge for Congress, where there is no chief executive like the president, so there could be no comparable (to the executive) powers for a congressional budget office. "Congress is inherently decentralized between two chambers, two parties, and various appropriation, authorization, and tax committees," writes Louis Fisher. "No amount of procedure tinkering can hide that reality."[30]

Congress tried again in 1985 to restructure the budget-making process by passing the Balanced Budget and Emergency Deficit Control Act. That legislation set a schedule for reducing the budget deficit to zero by 1991 and stipulated that both Congress and the White House had either to agree on a plan to meet each year's budget targets, or accept automatic budget cuts. In practice, however, Congress and presidents found ways to evade deficit targets.

Every budget cycle witnesses a new round of clashes between the branches. In recent years Congress has almost always failed to pass all of the appropriations bills by the beginning fo the fiscal year. Instead, the two branches have had to rely on *continuing resolutions*, extending the authority for government spending to a few days or months. This often led to confusion, constant bickering, and in 1995 to an especially bruising showdown between the Newt Gingrich-led Republican Congress and the Clinton Democratic White House. It resulted in two shutdowns of the federal government. "Having failed to agree on a new budget or on continuing resolutions to keep the government going in the meantime, the government ran out of money and federal workers locked the door of government offices around the country," writes Donald Kettl. "Even national parks, the Smithsonian Institution, and the Washington Monument were shuttered."[31] Despite these clashes, Congress voted to give the president greater budget power through the item veto.

George W. Bush came to the presidency when budgets were in balance and the country was enjoying impressive surpluses and thus should have a somewhat easier time working on budget matters with Congress. Yet the hard-to-control parts of the national budget continue to grow, and the two parties have strongly competing views about the size of tax cuts, whether defense spending should be increased, the role of the surplus to help finance Social Security and Medicare, and the timetable for paying down the national debt. Executive-legislative struggles over budget policy remain as a constant in the nation's capital.

A Closer Look

THE IMPEACHMENT OF BILL CLINTON

In all of our history only two presidents have been impeached—Andrew Johnson in 1868 and Bill Clinton in 1998. Richard Nixon was about to be impeached in 1974 when he abruptly resigned from office.

The Clinton impeachment hearings dramatized the House Judiciary Committee and its role in establishing whether an impeachment is justified. Nationally televised debates by the full House of Representatives were heated and partisan. Opinion polls showed the public solidly opposed to impeachment and removal from office, yet House Republicans remained unified in the effort to impeach. Two articles of impeachment were passed by the House of Representatives: for perjury before a federal grand jury (228 to 206) and for obstruction of justice (221 to 212). Most House Republicans voted for impeachment, and most House Democrats voted against the articles of impeachment. The matter was then turned over to the Senate.

The proceedings in the Senate were in marked contrast to the House deliberations. They were more formal, less heated, and in the end less partisan. Representatives from the House Judiciary Committee acted as the prosecutors, while lawyers for the president defended Bill Clinton. It would have taken a two-thirds majority, or 67 votes in the Senate, to convict Clinton, but only 45 senators voted to convict him on perjury charges; 10 Republicans defected to join 45 Democrats in

The House Judiciary Committee investigated charges that President Clinton had lied about his relationship to Monica Lewinsky to determine if they warranted impeachment. After long and angry argument between Republican and Democratic members, two articles of impeachment were passed by the House of Representatives, and the matter was turned over to the Senate for trial.

voting "not guilty." Fifty senators (all Republicans) voted to convict Clinton on the obstruction of justice charges, while 5 Republicans joined all 45 Democrats in voting "not guilty."

In the end it was the office of the presidency that saved the president. Republicans argued that when Clinton chose not to tell the truth, he put himself above the law and his oath of office. Democrats agreed that the president's conduct was wrong, boorish, indefensible, and even reprehensible, but they did not believe what Clinton did threatened the Republic. The president's legal team argued convincingly that Clinton's wrongdoings in the Monica Lewinsky affair were simply not fit subjects for impeachment. To remove a president on this basis, they

contended, would lower the impeachment bar too far and create an unhealthy precedent.

Some scholars believe this whole process was very damaging for the presidency and perhaps, too, for Congress. But most observers realized national institutions are resilient and fulfill their assigned responsibilities. Most people also believe that the Constitution prevailed.

One lesson of the Clinton impeachment process is that an impeachment conducted primarily along partisan lines is unlikely to succeed under our constitutional system of checks and balances. A second lesson is that impeachment was designed primarily for crimes against the state, against the system of government itself.

COALITION BUILDING

Our system of separation of powers and the nature of our party system ordinarily requires that presidents find common ground and build bipartisan coalitions if they want to get legislation approved by Congress. This is not an easy task in a country so large and divided and in a Congress that, as we have noted, is highly decentralized and designed more for deliberation than collaboration.

How to Win Friends and Influence Congress

- *Leadership meetings:* Inviting key leaders to the White House for exchange of ideas and "educational" efforts.

- *Bill-signing ceremonies:* Inviting supporters to the White House for official bill-signing celebrations.

- *Social events:* Inviting members to state dinners or celebrity or medal presentations.

- *Patronage:* Appointing the friends and political supporters of key members of Congress to various federal positions.

- *Campaign aid:* Rewarding a legislator with a presidential fund-raising appearance or a presidential visit during a campaign.

- *Constituency favors:* Providing presidential photographs, personal letters, White House tours, and souvenirs for a member's VIP constituents.

SOURCE: Cary R. Covington and Kedron Bardwell, "Helping Friends or Wooing Enemies? How Presidents Use Favors to Build Support in Congress." Paper presented at the American Political Science Association Annual Meeting, Boston, September 3–6, 1998, pp. 7–8.

Lessons from recent presidencies have led scholars to agree that presidents have to win the support of the American people in order to win the support of Congress. Political scientist George Edwards summarizes the realities:

1. Members of Congress are responsive to public opinion.

2. Public support is crucial to the president's success.

3. Presidents must not only earn public support with their performance in office but also must actively take their case to the people. Moreover, they must not only do it at reelection time but all the time.

4. Through the permanent campaign, the White House can persuade or even mobilize the public.32

Presidents use state of the union addresses, news conferences, and travel around the country in an effort to win political support for their programs. Presidents also spend considerable time meeting with reporters, editors, and publishers—both individually and in groups—trying to make the case for their legislative priorities. John Kennedy, Ronald Reagan, and Bill Clinton are considered to have been effective communicators. But careful analysis of their ability to sway the public suggests they were able to influence the public for only brief periods and usually on foreign policy matters or during short-term crises.[33]

All presidents face the challenge that it is hard to win the public's attention, and the public's attention span is generally short. While it is true that television has made presidents more important in terms of national visibility, it has not necessarily made them more popular or persuasive. Indeed, several retired presidents say one of their chief difficulties was trying to rouse the public's concern about major national issues.

Presidential efforts to rally public support for White House initiatives are inevitably aimed at building coalitions in Congress. A president's efforts at public relations are greatly helped, of course, if the president's party controls Congress. A president has almost twice as much likelihood of success of winning approval of significant White House–endorsed legislation with a like-minded partisan Congress than with the opposition party in control of Congress.[34]

But presidents must deal with the Congress they inherit. Presidents go to considerable lengths to reward their allies and to entice potential supporters to cross over and support at least some of the their legislative proposals. Sometimes this reaching out involves incorporating opponents' policy suggestions into the president's larger program. Sometimes a president will meet one-on-one with a key member and personally lobby the legislator.

White House aides are specifically assigned to build coalitions in both chambers of Congress. These aides spend a lot of time on Capitol Hill, talking with party and committee leaders and serving as ambassadors from the White House to various supporters and would-be supporters who could make the difference in whether a president's legislative program succeeds or fails.[35]

An ambitious agenda is difficult to pass in good times, but in a divided government, legislative victories are much harder to achieve. Clinton co-opted several Republican issues, such as welfare reform, crime measures, and deficit-reduction initiatives, and enjoyed success on these issues.

George W. Bush, who was narrowly elected and inherited a divided Congress, faced a challenge as he set about to build political coalitions in Congress. He had enjoyed success in his bipartisan efforts in Texas, where he had served as a popular governor for six years. During the election campaign he emphasized his abilities as a bipartisan uniter. But some of his campaign promises, like school vouchers and his opposition to abortion, invited partisan opposition.

THE CAPACITY TO LEAD

Writing about Franklin D. Roosevelt's relations with Congress in the 1930s, James MacGregor Burns wrote the following in his prize-winning political biography, *Roosevelt: The Lion and the Fox*. Nearly 50 years later, these observations are still true:

> The classic test of greatness in the White House has been the Chief Executive's capacity to lead Congress. Weak presidents have been those who had no program to offer, or whose proposals have been bled away in the endless twistings and windings of the legislative process. Strong presidents have been those who finessed or bulldozed their programs through Congress. . . .
>
> If Roosevelt had even stopped during these turbulent days [of his first term] to list his methods of dealing with Congress, the result might have looked something like this:

> 1. Full use of constitutional powers, such as the veto
>
> 2. Good timing
>
> 3. Drafting of measures in the executive branch
>
> 4. Almost constant pressure, adroitly applied
>
> 5. Careful handling of patronage
>
> 6. Face-to-face persuasiveness with legislative leaders
>
> 7. Appeal to the people.[36]

Congress can, of course, play a decisive role in setting and sometimes shaping the national policy agenda. It is difficult for an unwieldy plural institution to lead, yet Congress sometimes acts as a leadership institution as well as a representative institution. This happens when a party enjoys strong majorities in both chambers, when a president is vulnerable or is politically wounded (as Nixon was in 1973 and 1974), and when Congress has strong leaders, as when Lyndon Johnson served as Senate majority leader in the late Eisenhower years.

The discussions in the past few pages highlight most of the prominent areas where presidents and Congress regularly contest each other's authority. Does all this suggest that there is too much deadlock? Some reformers think so and call for major restructuring of the U.S. political system along parliamentary lines. But most political scientists defend the American system of congressional-presidential relations, saying despite the clashes and conflict, it generally reflects the cautious temperament of the American people. The system, these defenders say, was intended to have checks and balances—and tension in it. It is, moreover, especially well designed to protect the liberties of individuals and minorities, and it has succeeded in preventing authoritarianism. Most Americans, prize a certain amount of delay on presidential initiatives. The genius of the Congress, they add, is its continuing capacity for deliberation, debate, and reflection. What might appear as harmful delay to one person is an act of deliberation or conscientious review to another person. So it is with congressional-presidential relations. Which branch you want strengthened varies from time to time, often in direct relation to your partisan and policy values.

POLITICS ONLINE

Are Limitations on Presidential War Powers Outdated?

As this chapter has described, there is an enduring tension between Congress and the presidency over war powers. The dispute became acute during the Vietnam War, but it remains a continuing controversy today. Congress sought to limit presidential war powers with the War Powers Act. For the full text of the act, go to:

www.prenhall.com/burns.

The war powers issue is a question in political science about which a lot has been said and written. To explore this topic, a wide variety of resources is available from government documents, hearings, and legislative debate; go to:

www.fednet.net **or** www.thomas.loc.gov.

For books and journal articles, use the online search tools at your college library with access to periodical and book indexes. You can also access public opinion data and see if it changes during times of international crisis:

www.gallup.com, www.harrispollonline.com, **or** www.ropercenter.uconn.edu.

Another way to explore the topic is to review particular military conflicts and start to build a theory about when and why Congress objects to the deployment of military forces.

SUMMARY

1. The framers of the U.S. Constitution created a presidency that must win cooperation from Congress to get the work of government done. Lawmaking and policy-making powers are divided, and the politics of shared power has often been stormy. In general, however, Congress and presidents somehow find ways to collaborate and solve problems.

2. The relationship between a president and Congress is the most important one in the American political system, and while presidents spend great energy courting the media and appealing to the public, they do so in large part to gain support in the Congress. A president may not like it, but sustained cooperation from majorities in Congress is a necessity.

3. Several factors can cause conflict in our system of separated institutions sharing power. Among them are constitutional ambiguities, different constituencies,

varying terms of office, divided party control of the different branches, and fluctuating support of a president or the Congress.

4. The media has a way of exaggerating presidential tensions or disputes with Congress, yet there are clashes between the branches over presidential nominations, vetoes, budget proposals, military actions, or over the exercise of executive privilege and executive orders. These and other political realities are part of the continuing struggle that shapes presidential-congressional relations.

5. Presidential powers have increased over the past 60 years in good part because of grants of power by Congress to the presidency. Not surprisingly, many of these delegated powers have come in military and foreign policy areas and are due to the increased role of the U.S. in global affairs.

6. The framers created a presidency of limited powers, yet the role and lead-

ership responsibilities of presidents increased as a result of national security and economic emergencies throughout the past several generations and because of the nation's world leadership responsibilities in this era. Congress usually tries to assert itself and serve as a reasonable and responsible check on the exercise of presidential power. It is sometimes effective and sometimes less effective in this role; yet no president can ever take congressional support for granted, and presidents can always expect at least suspicion if not hostile actions from the opposition party in Congress.

7. Presidents spend considerable time trying to win both public and congressional support for their policy agenda. They hold press conferences, travel to key states, and engage in one-on-one lobbying as part of an overall effort to pass their priorities.

KEY TERMS

executive privilege 305   veto 307   pocket veto 308   item veto 308

executive order 307

FURTHER READING

DAVID GRAY ADLER AND MICHAEL A. GENOVESE, EDS., *The Presidency and the Law: The Clinton Legacy* (University Press of Kansas, 2002).

JON BOND AND RICHARD FLEISHER, EDS., *Polarized Politics: Congress and the President in a Partisan Era* (Congressional Quarterly Press, 2000).

DAVID BRADY AND CRAIG VOLDEN, *Revolving Gridlock: Politics and Policy from Carter to Clinton* (Westview Press, 1998).

JAMES MACGREGOR BURNS AND GEORGIA SORENSON, *Dead Center: Clinton-Gore Leadership and the Perils of Moderation* (Scribner's, 1999).

CHARLES M. CAMERON, *Veto Bargaining: Presidents and the Politics of Negative Power* (Cambridge University Press, 1999).

STEPHEN CARTER, *The Confirmation Mess: Cleaning Up the Federal Appointment Process* (Basic Books, 1994).

MORRIS FIORINA, *Divided Government*, 2d ed. (Allyn and Bacon, 1996).

LOUIS FISHER, *Congressional Abdication on War and Spending* (Texas A & M Press, 2000).

LOUIS FISHER, *The Politics of Shared Power: Congress and the Executive*, 4th ed. (Texas A & M Press, 1998).

CHARLES O. JONES, *The Presidency in a Separated System* (Brookings Institution, 1994).

DAVID MAYHEW, *Divided We Govern* (Yale University Press, 1991).

MARK PETERSON, *Legislating Together* (Harvard University Press, 1994).

RICHARD A. POSNER, *An Affair of State: The Investigation, Impeachment and Trial of President Clinton* (Harvard University Press, 1999).

MARK ROZELL, *Executive Privilege: The Dilemma of Secrecy and Democratic Accountability*, 2d ed. (University Press of Kansas, 2000).

ARTHUR M. SCHLESINGER, JR., *The Imperial Presidency* (Houghton Mifflin, 1972).

ROBERT J. SPITZER, *The Presidential Veto: Touchstone of the American Presidency* (State University of New York Press, 1988).

JAMES A. THURBER, ED., *Rivals for Power: Presidential-Congressional Relations* (Congressional Quarterly Press, 1996).

EMILY FIELD VAN TASSEL AND PAUL FINKELMAN, EDS., *Impeachable Offenses: A Documentary History from 1787 to the Present* (Congressional Quarterly Press, 1999).

See also *Legislative Studies Quarterly* and *Presidential Studies Quarterly*.

14

THE JUDICIARY: THE BALANCING BRANCH

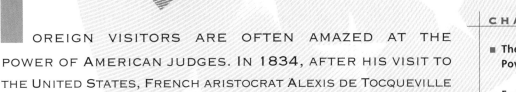

OREIGN VISITORS ARE OFTEN AMAZED AT THE POWER OF AMERICAN JUDGES. IN 1834, AFTER HIS VISIT TO THE UNITED STATES, FRENCH ARISTOCRAT ALEXIS DE TOCQUEVILLE wrote: "If I were asked where I place the American aristocracy, I should reply without hesitation . . . that it occupies the judicial bench and bar. . . . Scarcely any political question arises in the United States that is not resolved, sooner or later, into a judicial question."[1] A century later British political scientist Harold J. Laski observed, "The respect in which federal courts and, above all, the Supreme Court are held is hardly surpassed by the influence they exert on the life of the United States."[2]

Why do judges play such a central role in our political life? In 1803 Chief Justice John Marshall successfully claimed for judges the power of **judicial review**, that is, the power to authoritatively interpret the Constitution. Only a constitutional amendment or a later Supreme Court can modify the Court's doctrine. Justice Felix Frankfurter suggested tersely: "The Supreme Court is the Constitution."

Judges—and not just those on the Supreme Court—resolve disputes involving millions of dollars, decide conflicts among interests, supervise the criminal justice system, and make rules affecting the lives of millions of people. They not only settle legal conflicts, but they have, in some cases, become managers of schools, prisons, mental hospitals, and complex businesses. Sometimes they decide the details of how these institutions should be run. Still, the scope and nature of judicial power limit the role of judges.

THE SCOPE OF JUDICIAL POWER

The American judicial process rests on an **adversary system**. A court of law is a neutral arena in which two parties argue their differences and present their points of view before an impartial arbiter. The adversary system is based on the *fight theory*, that is, arguments over law and evidence, which may or may not arrive at the truth, aim at fairness in the judicial system.[3] The logic of the adversary system imposes formal restraints on the scope of judicial power.

Judicial power is essentially *passive*. Judges cannot instigate a case. Moreover, not all disputes are within the scope of judicial power. Judges decide only **justiciable disputes**—those that grow out of actual cases and are capable of settlement by legal methods. Judges do not use their power unless there is a real case or controversy. "It was never thought that . . . a party beaten in the legislature could transfer to the courts an inquiry

Statutory Law

Law that comes from authoritative and specific law-making sources, primarily legislatures but also including treaties and executive orders.

Common Law

Judge-made law that originated in England in the twelfth century, when royal judges traveled around the country settling disputes in each locality according to prevailing custom. The common law continues to develop according to the rule of *stare decisis*, which means "let the decision stand." This is the rule of precedent, which implies that a rule established by a court is to be followed in all similar cases.

Equity Law

Law used whenever common law remedies are inadequate. For example, if an injury done to property may do irreparable harm for which money damages cannot provide compensation, under equity a person may ask the judge to issue an injunction ordering the offending person not to take the threatened action. If the wrongdoer persists, he or she may be punished for contempt of court.

Constitutional Law

Statements interpreting the United States Constitution that have been given Supreme Court approval.

Admiralty and Maritime Law

Law applicable to cases concerning shipping and waterway commerce on the high seas and on the navigable waters of the United States.

Administrative Law

Law relating to the authority and procedures of administrative agencies as well as to the rules and regulations issued by those agencies.

Criminal Law

Law that defines crimes against the public order and provides for punishment. Government is responsible for enforcing criminal law, the great body of which is enacted by states and enforced by state officials in state courts. The criminal caseload of federal judges is growing.

Civil Law

Law that governs the relations between individuals and defines their legal rights. However, the government can also be a party to a civil action. Under the Sherman Antitrust Act, for example, the federal government may initiate civil as well as criminal action to prevent violations of the law.

---

as to the constitutionality of a legislative act."[4] In addition, litigants must have *standing to sue*; that is, they must have sustained or be in immediate danger of sustaining a direct and substantial injury. It is not enough merely for people to have a general interest in a subject or to believe that a law is unconstitutional.

Of increasing importance in recent years are **class action suits**, in which a small number of persons represent all other people similarly situated—a suit on behalf of all students in a university, for example, or all hospital patients, or all persons who smoke a particular brand of cigarettes. "Would-be class action litigants must show that they are proper representatives for the class of persons they seek to champion, that the types of issues they wish to raise are common to the class, and they must be able to demonstrate how a remedy can be formed that will meet the needs of the class."[5]

Courts cannot resolve all constitutional disputes. Some raise **political questions** that would require the use of methods and remedies not suitable for a court, and are better left to the other branches, or which are explicitly assigned by the Constitution to Congress or the president. Which of two competing state governments is the proper one? Which group of officials of a foreign nation should the United States recognize as the government of that nation?[6] These are political questions.

Do Judges Make Law?

"Do judges make law? 'Course they do. Made some myself," remarked Jeremiah Smith, judge of the New Hampshire Supreme Court.[7] Most judges are less candid. Judges obviously make law, but to admit it is somehow disturbing. Such statements do not conform to our notions of what judges should do.

Why do we think judges should not make law? Many people equate a judge's role with that of a referee in a prizefight. We expect referees to be impartial and disinterested, treating both parties as equals. We expect them to apply rules, not make them. Laws are not made, however, in the same way as the rules of a sport, and herein lies the answer to our question. Not only do judges make law, but they must. Legislatures make law by enacting statutes, but judges apply the statutes to concrete situations. Statutes are drawn in broad terms: drivers shall act with "reasonable care"; no one may make "excessive noise" in the vicinity of a hospital; employers must maintain "safe working conditions." Such broad terms must be used because legislators cannot know exactly what will happen in the future. Courts must judge their application in concrete cases.

These problems are intensified when judges are asked—as American judges are—to apply our more than 200-year-old Constitution. The Constitution is full of generalizations: "due process of law," "equal protection of the laws," "unreasonable searches and seizures," "Commerce . . . among the several States." Recourse to the intent of the framers or to the words of the Constitution may not help judges faced with cases involving electronic wiretaps, multinational corporations, the Web, or birth control.

Adherence to Precedent

Just because judges make policy, however, they are not free to do whatever they wish. They are subject to a variety of limits on what they decide—some imposed by the political system of which they are a part and some imposed by the legal profession. Among these constraints is the rule of *stare decisis*, the rule of precedent.

Stare decisis pervades our judicial system. Judges are expected to abide by previous decisions of their own courts and by rulings of superior courts. Although adherence to precedent is normal, the doctrine of *stare decisis* is not very restrictive.[8] Judges may distinguish between precedents because of differences in the context of cases, and many questions of law have conflicting precedents that can be used to support a decision for either party.

The doctrine of *stare decisis* is even less controlling in the field of constitutional law. Because the Constitution itself, rather than any one interpretation of it, is binding, the Court can *reverse* a previous decision it no longer wishes to follow, as it has done hundreds of times. Supreme Court justices are, therefore, not seriously restricted by *stare decisis*. As the first Justice John Marshall Harlan told a group of law students, "I want to say to you young gentlemen that if we don't like an act of Congress, we don't have too much trouble to find grounds for declaring it unconstitutional."[9] Since 1789 the Supreme Court has reversed 219 of its own decisions as well as overturned more than 159 acts of Congress, more than 956 pieces of state legislation and state constitutional provisions, and more than 112 city ordinances.[10]

FEDERAL JUSTICE

"The judicial Power of the United States," says Article III of the Constitution, "shall be vested in one supreme Court, and in such inferior Courts as the Congress may from time to time ordain and establish." Courts created to carry out this judicial power are called *Article III* or *constitutional courts*. Congress may also establish *Article I* or *legislative courts*—courts, for instance, to handle bankruptcies and veterans' appeals—to carry out the legislative powers the Constitution has granted to it. The main difference between a legislative and a constitutional court is that the judges of a legislative court need not be appointed to "hold their Offices during good Behavior" and may be assigned other than purely judicial duties, such as supervising tax collections.

The Constitution requires a Supreme Court. It is a necessity if the national government is to have the power to make and enforce laws that take precedence over those of the states. The lack of such a court to maintain national supremacy, ensure uniform interpretation of national legislation, and resolve conflicts among the states was one of the glaring defects of government under the Articles of Confederation.

Congress decides whether there will be other courts in addition to the Supreme Court. The First Congress divided the nation into circuits and created lower courts for each. That decision, though often supplemented, has never been seriously questioned. The Constitution also allows Congress to determine the size of the Supreme Court.

Federal Courts of General Jurisdiction

Today the hierarchy of federal courts of general jurisdiction consists of district courts, courts of appeals, and one Supreme Court (see Figure 14–1). In cases affecting ambassadors, other public ministers, and consuls, and in cases in which a state is a party, the Supreme Court has **original jurisdiction**, the authority of a court to hear a case "in the first instance." In all other cases, the Supreme Court has **appellate jurisdiction**—power to review decisions of other courts and agencies—except when Congress determines otherwise.

Although the Supreme Court and its justices receive most of the attention, the workhorses of the federal judiciary are the district courts within the states, in the District of Columbia, and in U.S. territories. Each state has at least one district court. Larger states have as many as the demands of judicial business and the pressure of politics require, although no state has more than four. There are 94 district courts in the 50 states, the District of Columbia, and the Commonwealth of Puerto Rico. Each has at least 2 judges but may have as many as 28. District judges normally sit separately and hold court by themselves, and hold office for life. District judges appoint

judicial review
The power to authoritatively interpret the Constitution.

adversary system
A judicial system in which a court of law is a neutral arena where two parties argue their differences.

justiciable dispute
A dispute growing out of an actual case or controversy and that is capable of settlement by legal methods.

class action suit
Lawsuit brought by an individual or a group of people on behalf of all those similarly situated.

political question
A dispute that requires knowledge of a nonlegal character, or the use of techniques not suitable for a court, or explicitly assigned by the Constitution to Congress or the president; judges refuse to answer constitutional questions that they declare are political.

stare decisis
The rule of precedent, whereby a rule or law contained in a judicial decision is commonly viewed as binding on judges whenever the same question is presented.

appellate jurisdiction
The authority of a court to review appeals of the decisions made by lower courts.

original jurisdiction
The authority of a court to hear a case "in the first instance."

Whether the Ninth Circuit should be split in two has been debated for years. It is the largest federal appellate court, with 28 circuit judges and 99 district judges. Geographically it is the size of Western Europe and contains 20 percent of the U.S. population. It reaches from Arizona, California, and Nevada to Idaho, Oregon, Montana, and Washington, and up to Alaska, as well as over to Hawaii and the Pacific territories. In addition, the Ninth Circuit has some of the most liberal judges, who often rule in conflict with the more conservative U.S. and California Supreme Courts. Is it too big to function properly?

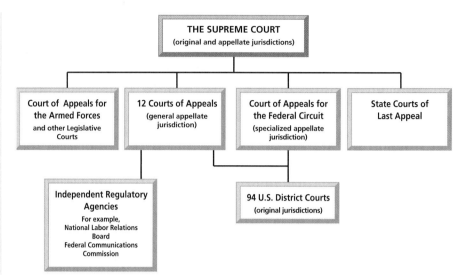

FIGURE 14–1 **The Structure of the Federal Courts**

grand jury

A jury of 12 to 23 persons who, in private, hear evidence presented by the government to determine whether persons shall be required to stand trial. If the jury believes there is sufficient evidence that a crime was committed, it issues an indictment.

petit jury

A jury of 6 to 12 persons who determine guilt or innocence in a civil or criminal action.

magistrate judge

An official who performs a variety of limited judicial duties.

court of appeals

A court with appellate jurisdiction that hears appeals from the decisions of lower courts.

habeas corpus

A court order requiring explanation to a judge why a prisoner is held in custody.

and are assisted by clerks, bailiffs, stenographers, law clerks, court reporters, probation officers, and magistrates.

District courts are the trial courts of original jurisdiction. They are the only federal courts that regularly employ **grand juries** (indicting) and **petit juries** (trial). When cases tried before district judges involve citizens of different states, judges apply the appropriate state laws. Otherwise, district judges are concerned with federal laws. For example, they decide cases involving crimes against the United States—suits under the national revenue, postal, patent, copyright, trademark, bankruptcy, and civil rights laws.[11]

Magistrate judges are increasingly important. After being screened by panels composed of residents of the judicial districts, full-time magistrates are appointed by the judges of the district court for eight-year renewable terms, part-time magistrates for four-year renewable terms. There are 429 full-time and 76 part-time federal magistrate judges.

Magistrates "look like a judge, act like a judge, and speak like a judge."[12] Most wear robes and since 1990 are called "Judge." They issue arrest warrants, hold hearings to determine whether arrested persons should be held for action by the grand jury, and, if so, set bail. They hear motions subject to varying kinds of review by their district judges. They preside over civil trials—jury and nonjury—with the consent of both parties, and over nonjury trials for petty offenses with the consent of the defendants. Under the supervision of the district judge, and with the consent of the accused, magistrates may preside over the selection of a jury for a felony trial.[13]

District judges are bound by the precedents of higher courts, but they have considerable discretion in applying them. Except for the few cases that may be taken directly to the Supreme Court, decisions of district courts are reviewable by a **court of appeals**. Courts of appeals are located geographically in 12 *judicial circuits*, (see Figure 14–2). A thirteenth appellate court is the Court of Appeals for the Federal Circuit, which is located in the District of Columbia and has national jurisdiction, though it deals primarily with appeals in patent, copyright, and international trade cases. Each circuit court of appeals consists of 6 to 28 permanent judgeships (179 in all). They normally hear cases in panels of three judges, but for especially important and controversial cases, all judges may be present; that is, they sit *en banc*. Although courts of appeals have only appellate jurisdiction, they are powerful policy makers. Less than 1 percent of their decisions are appealed to the Supreme Court. As the policy role of federal courts has become a prominent political issue, more attention has focused on these courts and the judges who serve on them.[14]

Some members of Congress have called for a term limit for members of the federal judiciary, perhaps for a nonrenewable term of 18 years. If such a limit were adopted, presidents could appoint one justice about every two years, but presidents, including one who served for two terms, could still not appoint a majority of the Supreme Court.[15] For more information about the federal judiciary, go to our website for a link (**www.prenhall.com/burns**), or go directly to the site for the Administrative Office of the U.S. Courts at **www.uscourts.gov**.

State and Federal Courts

In addition to federal courts, each state maintains a judiciary of its own, and many large municipalities have judicial systems as complex as those of the states. State courts primarily interpret and apply their state constitutions and law. Most litigation occurs in these courts. For more information on state courts as well as links to state court websites, go to our home page (**www.prenhall.com/burns**) or go directly to the National Council of State Courts at **www.ncsc.us/**.

The federal and state court systems are related, but they do not exist in a superior-inferior relationship. Except for the limited **habeas corpus** jurisdiction of the district courts (the power to release persons from custody if the judge is not satisfied that the person is being detained constitutionally), the Supreme Court is the only federal court that may review state court decisions, and only when there is a conflict with federal law.

Other than the original jurisdiction the Constitution vests directly in the Supreme Court, no federal court has any jurisdiction except that granted to it by an act of Congress. Congress also determines whether the judicial power of the United States will be exercised exclusively by federal courts or concurrently by both federal and state courts.

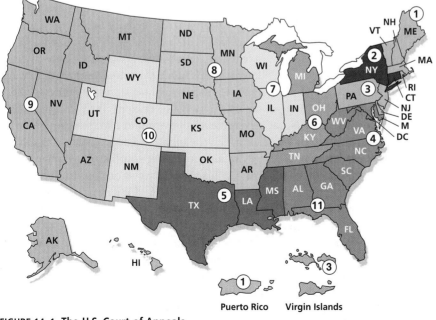

FIGURE 14–1 The U.S. Court of Appeals

SOURCE: *The Federal Register.*

Thinking It Through...

Republicans have tried to split the Ninth Circuit, isolating California and Nevada in one circuit and creating a new one for the other states. Logging, mining, and oil interests in the Pacific Northwest support the split because they view judges in California as too liberal and pro-environment.

The Senate voted to approve the split in 1997, but the House of Representatives did not. A commission selected by Chief Justice William H. Rehnquist studied the matter and recommended that the Ninth Circuit remain intact but divided into three geographic divisions. Although Chief Justice Rehnquist endorsed the report, there is still no consensus in Congress about what should be done.

Examples of Special Article III (Constitutional) Courts

In addition to courts of general jurisdiction, Congress has created constitutional courts with special jurisdiction:

United States Court of International Trade (formerly U.S. Customs Court)

Consists of nine judges who review rulings of customs collectors and conflicts arising under various tariff and trade laws.

Foreign Intelligence Surveillance Court

Composed of seven district court judges appointed by the chief justice. They serve on a regular rotation and meet in secret to hear requests from the Department of Justice acting on behalf of the National Security Agency, the Federal Bureau of Investigation, and other intelligence agencies that engage in electronic surveillance and physical searches of the homes and offices of foreign agents.

Examples of Article I (Legislative) Courts

United States Court of Claims

Consists of 16 judges appointed for 15-year terms who have jurisdiction over all property and contract damage suits against the United States.

United States Court of Appeals for the Armed Forces

Consists of five civilian judges appointed for 15 years each by the president with the consent of the Senate. This court, created by Congress under its grant of authority to make the rules and regulations for "land and naval forces," applies military law, which is separate from the body of law that governs the rest of the federal court system.

Bankruptcy Judges

Almost 300 judges appointed by the courts of appeals to serve as adjuncts to the federal district courts for terms of 14 years each. These judges handle bankruptcy matters subject to review by federal district judges.

United States Court of Veteran Appeals

Consists of two to six judges who hear appeals from certain administrative decisions of the Veterans Administration.

defendant

In a criminal action, the person or party accused of an offense.

plea bargain

Negotiations between a prosecutor and defendant aimed at getting the defendant to plead guilty for a lesser offense to avoid having to stand trial for a more serious offense.

Federal Lawyers

Judges decide cases; they do not prosecute persons. On the federal level, the job of prosecution falls to the Department of Justice: the attorney general, the solicitor general, the 94 U.S. attorneys, and some 1,200 assistant attorneys. The president, with the consent of the Senate, appoints a U.S. attorney for each district court. U.S. attorneys serve four-year terms but may be dismissed by the president at any time. These appointments are of great interest to senators, who exercise significant influence over the selection process. Because U.S. attorneys are almost always members of the president's political party, it is customary for them to resign if the opposition party wins the White House.

The attorney general, in consultation with the U.S. attorney in each district, appoints assistant attorneys. Some districts have only one; the largest, the Southern District of New York, has more than 65. These attorneys, working with the U.S. attorney and assisted by the Federal Bureau of Investigation and other federal law-enforcement agencies, begin proceedings against those alleged to have broken federal laws. They also represent the United States in civil suits.

Prosecutors and the Solicitor General

Prosecutors decide whether to charge an offense and which offense to charge. They have largely unreviewable discretion. "So long as the prosecutor has probable cause to believe that the accused committed an offense defined by statute, the decision whether or not to prosecute, and what charge to file or bring before a grand jury, generally rests entirely in his [or her] discretion."[16]

Prosecutors negotiate with the lawyers for **defendants** (those accused of an offense) and often work out a **plea bargain**, whereby defendants agree to plead guilty to a lesser offense to avoid having to stand trial and face a sentence for a more serious offense. Prosecutors make recommendations to judges about what sentences to impose.

Attorneys from the Department of Justice and from other federal agencies participate in more than half the cases on the Supreme Court's docket. Of special importance is the *solicitor general* (SG), who represents the federal government before the Supreme Court. (The SG appears before the Supreme Court in formal attire—dark vest, tails, and striped pants.) When the solicitor general petitions the Supreme Court and asks it to review an opinion of a lower court, the Court is likely to do so. "Overall, the government is involved in about two-thirds of all cases heard during a term, and the solicitor general's record of wins has been fairly consistent," winning about three-fourths of the time until the Clinton years, when the administration's views on constitutional interpretation clashed with those of the more conservative Supreme Court majority.[17] Moreover, no appeal may be taken on behalf of the United States to any appellate court without the approval of the solicitor general.

The solicitor general (sometimes called the "Tenth Justice") has traditionally been given considerable independence from the White House. But in recent decades that independence has been reduced. The Reagan and Bush administrations used the SG to try to persuade the justices to limit affirmative action and to restrict the right of women to have abortions.[18] The Clinton administration continued in the activist manner, although on the opposite side on many issues. (Briefs filed by the solicitor general may be found on the Web at **www.usdoj.gov/osg/briefs/search.html**.)

Federal Defense Lawyers

The federal government provides lawyers for poor defendants in criminal trials. District courts have some discretion in how they provide this assistance. Most districts use the traditional system of assigning a private attorney. About half the judicial districts, however, have opted to use the **public defender system**. Salaried public defenders operate under the general supervision of the Administrative Office of the United States Courts. The Judicial Conference of the United States has said the most important problem confronting the public defender program is lack of money.

The Legal Services Corporation (LSC) provides financial assistance to 323 organizations that furnish legal help to the poor in noncriminal legal matters. It is governed by an 11-member board of directors appointed by the president with the advice and consent of the senate. The corporation is the center of controversy. There are those (primarily Republicans) who would like to abolish it. They have barred it from filing class action suits; from representing prisoners, illegal aliens, and people being evicted from public housing for alleged drug activity; from litigating abortion or redistricting issues; and from challenging the legality of state or federal welfare laws. These restrictions extend not just to the use of federal funds but to the Legal Services Corporation's use of nonfederal money raised from private or state sources. The Legal Services Corporation is thus restricted to suing landlords, employers, husbands, or wives in traditional legal battles.

On the other side are those (primarily Democrats) who would fund the Legal Services Corporation more fully and would allow it to use class action suits to challenge the status quo. Some legal aid lawyers and organizations have challenged the restrictions on what it may do as unconstitutional.[19]

THE POLITICS OF JUDICIAL SELECTION

The selection of federal judges has always been a significant part of the political process. It makes a difference who serves on the federal courts. As the courts play an even more important role in the political process, and as more and more interests—African Americans and women, for example—participate in that process, judicial selection politics has come front and center on the political stage.

The president selects federal judges with the advice and consent of the Senate. Political reality imposes constraints on the president's discretion, so the selection of a federal judge is actually a complex bargaining process. The principal figures involved are the candidates, the president, and the "subpresidency for judicial selection"[20] consisting of key members of the Department of Justice, United States senators, the American Bar Association, party leaders, and, increasingly, interest groups. In addition, recent presidents have inserted the White House much more directly into the process than their predecessors did.

Department of Justice officials and key White House staff meet often to review proposed names. Before the White House submits names of nominees for the federal district courts to the Senate, the president observes the practice of **senatorial courtesy**—the presidential custom of submitting the names of prospective appointees for approval to senators from the states in which the appointees are to work. Even a senator from the opposition party is usually consulted. If negotiations are deadlocked between the senators or between the senators and the Department of Justice, a seat may stay vacant for years.[21] The custom of senatorial courtesy does not apply to Supreme Court appointments and is generally not observed in the selection of judges for the courts of appeals because these judges do not serve in any one senator's domain. This difference in selection politics means that district court judges often reflect values different from those of judges appointed to the courts of appeal or the Supreme Court.[22]

Factors Constraining Federal Judges

- The Constitution
- Precedent (*stare decisis*)
- Statutory law
- Legal thought as found in books and law reviews
- Opinions of other courts
- Interest groups
- Public opinion
- Media opinion
- Views of colleagues
- Views of law clerks
- Contemporary events and general social environment
- Traditions of the law
- Actions of the legislature, past and future
- Actions of executives, past and future
- Limitations of time and staffing

---

public defender system
Arrangement whereby public officials are hired to provide legal assistance to people accused of crimes who are unable to hire their own attorneys.

senatorial courtesy
The presidential custom of submitting the names of prospective appointees for approval to senators from the states in which the appointees are to work.

CONFIRMATION POLITICS

An examination of recent nomination battles highlights the interplay of party, race, gender, ideology, and judicial philosophy in the process of selecting and confirming a Supreme Court justice.

Robert Bork.

The Bork Battle

When Justice Lewis F. Powell, Jr., who cast the pivotal vote on such critical issues as affirmative action and abortion, announced his retirement as he neared 80 years of age at the end of the term in July 1987, President Reagan quickly nominated Judge Robert Bork, a member of the Court of Appeals for the District of Columbia and a noted jurist and legal scholar. Despite Bork's controversial writings on many current constitutional issues, his scholarly and legal qualifications made it appear initially that he would be confirmed. However, his nomination so offended women's and black organizations that they organized a campaign to block Bork's confirmation. After almost four months of national debate, 12 days of acrimonious questioning by the members of the Senate Judiciary Committee, and 23 hours of debate on the Senate floor, the Senate voted 58 to 42 against Bork's confirmation.

David Souter.

The Souter Solution

The political bruises resulting from the Bork confirmation proceedings were traumatic. Political pundits speculated that in the future, presidents would seek noncontroversial candidates for the Supreme Court. This prediction came true in 1990 with George Bush's nominee to replace William J. Brennan, Jr., leader of the liberal bloc on the Supreme Court. President Bush chose David Souter, a member of the New Hampshire Supreme Court. Educated at Harvard and Oxford, he had written no law articles, made practically no speeches, and lived the secluded life of a sitting judge. When he appeared before the Judiciary Committee, Souter steadfastly refused to answer any questions that might reveal his orientation on abortion and privacy issues, to the frustration of the Senate Democrats. He was confirmed by an overwhelming vote. He became one of the more liberal judges.

Clarence Thomas.

The Thomas Tangle

When Justice Thurgood Marshall retired in 1991, President Bush sent to the Senate the name of a controversial jurist,

Liberal interest groups, such as People for the American Way and Alliance for Justice, as well as conservative groups, such as the Heritage Foundation and a coalition of 260 conservative organizations and 35 talk show hosts called the Judicial Selection Monitoring Project, monitor potential judicial candidates. These organizations used to wait until after the president sent the name of a nominee to the Senate, but now they are active in the preliminaries, making known their views even before the names of nominees are released to the public or sent to the Senate Judiciary Committee.

The American Bar Association's Standing Committee on the Federal Judiciary once played a special role in evaluating candidates. Presidents were hesitant to sub-

Judge Clarence Thomas, then sitting on the Court of Appeals for the District of Columbia. Thomas is a conservative African American. Prior to his brief service on the Court of Appeals, he had served as chair of the Equal Employment Opportunity Commission (EEOC) and in the Office of Civil Rights. During five days of grueling questions about his constitutional views, Judge Thomas, as had his predecessor, refused to respond. The Senate Judiciary Committee narrowly recommended his confirmation.

Two days before the Senate was due to vote on his confirmation, documents leaked to the press revealed that a former associate of Judge Thomas, Anita Hill, had accused him of sexually harassing her when she worked for him

Ruth Bader Ginsburg.

in the Department of Education and the EEOC. Women's and liberal groups exploded in outrage. There followed three days of dramatic and emotion-charged hearings telecast to the nation in which Judge Thomas categorically denied the charges presented persuasively by his accuser. Panels of witnesses pro and con came forward to testify. Thomas was confirmed by the Senate 52 to 48, one of the closest confirmation votes for a Supreme Court justice.

The Clinton Choices

Almost as soon as President Bill Clinton took office, Justice Byron White announced he would leave the Court at the end of its 1992–93 term. It was clear that with this appointment, Clinton could arrest the Court's conservative drift and fulfill his campaign pledge to appoint justices committed to protect the right of privacy—that is, to preserve a woman's freedom to choose an abortion.

After several months of deliberation, including the embarrassingly public consideration of other candidates, President Clinton nominated Ruth Bader Ginsburg. Judge Ginsburg was a 13-year veteran of the Court of Appeals for the District of Columbia, to which President Carter had appointed her. On the Court of Appeals she had earned a reputation for fairness and moderation. She was readily confirmed by the Senate and took her seat for the opening of the 1993–94 term.

Clinton had a second opportunity when Harry A. Blackmun, at age 85,

announced his intention to leave the Court during the spring of 1994. Blackmun, best known for writing the opinion in *Roe v Wade*, was thought at first to be a judicial conservative, but by the time of his retirement, he had become the most liberal member of the Court. President Clinton nominated Stephen G. Breyer, chief judge of the First Circuit, a noncontroversial judicial moderate. Justice Breyer, a graduate of Stanford University, Oxford, and Harvard Law School, served as Supreme Court law clerk for Justice Arthur Goldberg and was a member of the faculty at Harvard Law School before being appointed by President Carter as a federal appeals court judge. After a cordial hearing before the Senate Judiciary Committee in July 1994, Breyer was easily confirmed by the Senate.

Stephen G. Breyer.

mit for Senate confirmation a candidate rated "not qualified" by the ABA. In recent years, conservative groups mounted an attack on the ABA's role, contending it reflects a liberal bias and gave low ratings to conservative nominees. In response to this criticism, Senator Orrin Hatch, current chair of the Judiciary Committee, announced that the ABA committee no longer has any special status and no longer is part of the official process. In March 2001, President George Bush announced that the ABA would no longer be asked to evaluate judicial candidates before nomination, but some Democratic senators said they could not vote on judicial nominees without first considering the ABA's views.[23]

TABLE 14–1 Party Affiliation of District Judges and Court of Appeals Judges Appointed by Presidents

President	Party	Appointees from Same Party
Roosevelt	Democrat	97%
Truman	Democrat	92
Eisenhower	Republican	95
Kennedy	Democrat	92
Johnson	Democrat	96
Nixon	Republican	93
Ford	Republican	81
Carter	Democrat	90
Reagan	Republican	94
Bush	Republican	89
Clinton	Democrat	88

Sources: Sheldon Goldman, "Judicial Selection Under Clinton: A Midterm Examination," *Judicature*, May/June 1995, p. 280; Sheldon Goldman and Elliot Slotnick, "Clinton's Second Term Judiciary: Selection Under Fire," *Judicature*, May/June 1999. See also the Alliance for Justice, Judicial Selection Project, at www.afj.org/jsp/home.html.

Senate: Advice and Consent

The normal presumption is that the president should be allowed considerable discretion in the selection of federal judges. Despite this presumption, the Senate takes seriously its responsibility in confirming judicial nominations, especially when the party controlling the Senate is different from that of the president, as has often been the case in recent years.

Until recently, most judicial appointments, especially those for the lower federal courts, were processed without much controversy. However, "now that lower court judges are more commonly viewed as political actors, there is increasing Senate scrutiny of these nominees."[24] The battle over judicial confirmations ordinarily takes place before the Senate Judiciary Committee. The Senate usually goes along with the recommendations of its Judiciary Committee without much debate, yet floor debates are not all that rare. Overall, the Senate has refused to confirm 29 of the 138 presidential nominations for Supreme Court justices.[25]

Prior to 1955, the common practice was for the Senate to look into candidates' qualifications and background but not to interview them in person. But in the last two decades, the committee has felt free to ask judicial nominees a wide range of questions, since their political orientation is a major factor in determining how they might vote on particular cases and controversies. Except for Robert Bork, nominated by President Ronald Reagan in 1987, most judicial nominees have steadfastly refused to answer questions that might reveal how they would decide a case. But Judge Bork had written so many articles, made so many speeches, and decided so many cases that he thought he had to clarify his constitutional views. His candor may well have contributed to the Senate's rejection of him and has scared off subsequent nominees from responding to similar questions.

The Role of Party, Race, and Gender

Presidents so seldom nominate judges from the opposing party (around 90 percent of judicial appointments since the time of Franklin Roosevelt have gone to candidates from the president's party) that partisan considerations are taken for granted, and partisan affiliation is rarely mentioned (see Table 14–1). Today more attention is paid to other characteristics, such as race and gender.[26]

President Jimmy Carter, who had no opportunity to make an appointment to the Supreme Court, selected more African Americans, Hispanics, and women for the lower federal courts than all other prior presidents combined—40 women, 37 African Americans, and 16 Hispanics. President Ronald Reagan, although the first to appoint a woman to the Supreme Court, appointed fewer minority members or women than did Carter, perhaps in part because fewer minorities and women could pass the Reagan administration's ideological screening.[27] Twenty percent of George Bush's appointees were women, 7 percent African Americans, and 4 percent Hispanics.[28]

Bill Clinton promised to appoint federal judges who would be more representative of the ethnic makeup of the United States. "There will not be an ideological blood test, like there was during the Reagan and Bush years, to see if the candidate is a moderate or liberal," said a prominent Democratic member of the Senate Judiciary Committee, "but there will be an insistence upon diversity." Clinton lived up to his pledge; he named more women and minorities to the bench than his predecessors had (Figure 14–3).

The Role of Ideology

Finding a party member is not enough; presidents want to pick the "right" kind of Republican or "our" kind of Democrat to serve as judges. By and large they have been able to achieve this goal. Judges picked by Republican presidents tend to be judicial conservatives (with the notable exception of President Dwight Eisenhower's appointments of Chief Justice Earl Warren and Justice William J. Brennan, Jr.). Judges picked by Demo-

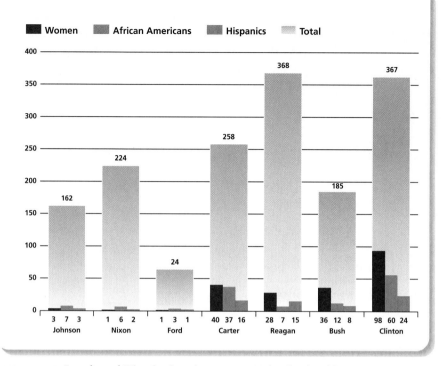

Women ■ **African Americans** ■ **Hispanics** ■ **Total** ▨

	Johnson	Nixon	Ford	Carter	Reagan	Bush	Clinton
	162	224	24	258	368	185	367
	3 7 3	1 6 2	1 3 1	40 37 16	28 7 15	36 12 8	98 60 24

FIGURE 14–3 Female and Minority Appointments to Federal Judgeships.

SOURCE: Sheldon Goldman and Elliot Slotnick, "Clinton's Second Term Judiciary: Selection Under Fire," *Judicature*, May/June 1999; updated from the Alliance for Justice, Judicial Selection Project (www.afg.org/jsp).

cratic presidents are more likely to be liberals. Both of these orientations are tempered by the fact that judges must go through a senatorial confirmation process that, during recent administrations, has been rigorous and driven by opposition to the White House.[29]

President Ronald Reagan's two terms made it possible for him to join Presidents Franklin D. Roosevelt and Dwight D. Eisenhower as the only presidents in the last century to appoint a majority of the federal bench. All told, Reagan appointed 368 lifetime judges. His administration acted carefully to nominate only those whose views about the role of the courts and constitutional issues were consistent with Reagan's own.[30] Not only were a large number of judicial conservatives appointed, but many of them—because they were comparatively young—will continue to have an effect on judicial policy well into the twenty-first century. But despite the care given to their selection, there is some evidence that the Reagan judges may not be that much more conservative than judges appointed by other Republican presidents.[31]

Because President Bush was less committed to conservatism than Reagan, conservative organizations—the Heritage Foundation, the Pacific Legal Foundation, and the Federalist Society—focused more attention on his judicial nominees. Bush appointed 148 district judges, 37 appellate judges, and 2 Supreme Court justices—David Souter and Clarence Thomas. It turned out that his appointees, with the exception of Justice Souter, were among the most conservative in recent history[32] and helped consolidate the Court's "turn to the right."

President Clinton gave Democratic senators "clear guidelines about the kind of judges he wants,"[33]—competent professionals who would bring diversity to the bench. But after the Republicans took control of the Senate in 1994, President Clinton instructed his advisers to consult closely with Republican Senator Orrin Hatch, chair of the Senate Judiciary Committee. Clinton abandoned or declined to nominate several judicial nominees opposed by conservative interest groups and had to reach compromises with Republican senators.

PEOPLE

Departing from the original intent of the Constitution undermines the legitimacy of the Court and leads to judicial legislation.

INTERPRETING THE CONSTITUTION: ORIGINAL INTENT

Justice Antonin Scalia

Justice Antonin Scalia, a staunch conservative, contends that departing from the original intent of the Constitution undermines the legitimacy of the Court and leads to judicial legislation.

The principal theoretical defect of non-originalism, in my view, is its incompatibility with the very principle that legitimizes judicial review of constitutionality. Nothing in the text of the Constitution confers upon the courts the power to inquire into, rather than passively assume, the constitutionality of federal statutes.

Justice Scalia maintains that originalism—holding to the original intent of the framers of the Constitution—is more compatible with the purpose of a constitution in a democracy:

A democratic society does not, by and large, need constitutional guarantees to insure that its laws will reflect "current values." Elections take care of that quite well. The purpose of constitutional guarantees—and in particular those constitutional guarantees of individual rights that are at the center of this controversy—is precisely to prevent the law from reflecting certain changes in original values that the society adopt-ing the Constitution thinks fundamentally undesirable. Or, more precisely, to require the society to devote to the subject the long and hard consideration required for a constitutional amendment before those particular values can be cast aside.

Originalism, according to Justice Scalia,

establishes a historical criterion that is conceptually quite separate from the preferences of the judge himself. And the principal defect of that approach—that historical research is always difficult and sometimes inconclusive—will, unlike nonoriginalism, lead to a more moderate rather than a more extreme result. The inevitable tendency of judges to think that the law is what they would like it to be will, I have no doubt, cause most errors in judicial historiography to be made in the direction of projecting upon the age of 1789 current, modern values—so that as applied, even as applied in the best of faith, originalism will (as the historical record shows) end up as something of a compromise. ★

SOURCE: Justice Antonin Scalia, "Originalism: The Lesser Evil," *University of Cincinnati Law Review* 55 (1989), p. 894.

DEBATE

A CONTEMPORARY RATIFICATION

Justice William Brennan, Jr.

Justice William J. Brennan, Jr., a leading liberal on the Court from 1956 to 1990, points out the problems with appealing to original intent:

> It is arrogant to pretend that from our vantage we can gauge accurately the intent of the Framers on application of principle to specific, contemporary questions. All too often, sources of potential enlightenment such as records of the ratification debates provide sparse or ambiguous evidence of the original intention. Typically, all that can be gleaned is that the Framers themselves did not agree about the application or meaning of particular constitutional provisions, and hid their differences in cloaks of generality. Indeed, it is far from clear whose intention is relevant—that of the drafters, the congressional disputants, or the ratifiers in the states?—or even whether the idea of original intention is a coherent way of thinking about a jointly drafted document drawing its authority from a general assent of the states. And apart from the problematic nature of the sources, our distance of two centuries cannot but work as a prism refracting all we perceive.

Justice Brennan maintains that constitutional interpretation is compatible with democratic governance:

> The view that all matters of substantive policy should be resolved through the majoritarian process has appeal under some circumstances, but I think it ultimately will not do. . . . Faith in democracy is one thing, blind faith quite another. Those who drafted the Constitution understood the difference. One cannot read the text without admitting that it embodies substantive value choices, it places certain values beyond the power of any legislature.
>
> We current Justices read the Constitution in the only way that we can: as twentieth-first century Americans. We look to the history of the time of framing and to the intervening history of interpretation. But the ultimate question must be: what do the words of the text mean in our time? For the genius of the Constitution rests not in any static meaning it might have had in a world that is dead and gone, but in the adaptability of its great principles to cope with current problems and current needs. ★

SOURCE: Justice William J. Brennan, Jr., "The Constitution of the United States: Contemporary Ratification." Lecture delivered at Georgetown University, October 12, 1985.

The ultimate question must be: what do the words of the text mean in our time?

For further information about this debate, go to **www.prenhall.com/burns** *and click on the Debate Icon in Chapter 14.*

By the end of his first term, Clinton had nominated and the Senate had confirmed 198 judges and 2 justices of the Supreme Court.[34] In his second term, Clinton faced increasing opposition from the Republican-controlled Senate, which slowed down confirmations to such an extent that Chief Justice Rehnquist, in his annual reports on the federal judiciary, scolded the Senate for jeopardizing the ability of the federal courts to do their work. Despite the slowdown in Senate confirmations, by the time Clinton left office he had named 367 of the approximate total of 800 federal judges, and appointed a large number of women and minorities.[35]

The Role of Judicial Philosophy

What about a candidate's judicial philosophy? Does a candidate believe that judges should interpret the Constitution to reflect what the framers intended and what its words literally say; that is, does the candidate believe in **judicial restraint**? Or does the candidate believe the Constitution should be adapted to reflect current conditions and philosophies; that is, does the candidate believe in **judicial activism**?

Throughout most of our history, federal courts have been more conservative than Congress, the White House, or state legislatures. Prior to 1937, judicial self-restraint was the battle cry of liberals who objected to judges interpreting the due process clauses of the Fifth and Fourteenth Amendments to strike down many laws passed to protect labor and women and to keep the national and state governments from regulating the economy. These judges broadly construed the words of the Constitution to prevent what they thought to be unreasonable regulations of property.

By the time of Richard Nixon, Ronald Reagan, and George Bush, however, the judicial shoe was on the other foot, and it was conservatives who were advocates of judicial self-restraint. What is needed, they argued, are judges who will let Congress, the president, and the state legislatures regulate or forbid abortions, adopt prayers for public schools, impose capital punishment, and not hinder law enforcement.

Still, it would be wrong to assume that judicial philosophy is nothing more than another way to argue about political ideology. Some conservatives, for example, favor judicial activism because they want current judges to reverse the last half-century of precedents on civil rights and to protect property rights from government regulation. Some liberals favor judicial restraint because they believe democratic self-governance will flourish when judges stay out of policy debates. Hence, the debate over the Supreme Court's role today is less about activism and restraint than it is about competing conceptions of the proper balance between government authority and individual rights, between the power of legislatures and that of courts.

Judicial Longevity and Presidential Tenure

Ideology and judicial philosophy affect not only presidents' nominations for the federal courts but also when sitting judges choose to retire. Because federal judges serve for life, they may be able to schedule their retirement to allow a president whose views they approve to nominate their successors. Chief Justice Roger B. Taney stayed on the bench long after his health began to fail to prevent President Abraham Lincoln from nominating a Republican. In 1929 Chief Justice William Howard Taft wrote: "I am older and slower and less acute and more confused. However, as long as things continue as they are, and I am able to answer in my place, I must stay on the court in order to prevent the Bolsheviki [Herbert Hoover, a conservative Republican, was in the White House] from getting control."[36]

Although Chief Justice Warren Burger denied that he retired in 1986 in order to permit President Ronald Reagan to replace him with a constitutional conservative, his retirement gave Reagan an opportunity to rejuvenate the conservative wing of the Court by promoting William H. Rehnquist to the chief justiceship. Reagan then picked another constitutional conservative, Antonin Scalia, to take the seat vacated by Rehnquist.[37] Liberal Supreme Court Justices William J. Brennan, Jr., and Thurgood Marshall held onto their seats well into their 80s, and many assumed

judicial restraint
Judicial philosophy proposing that judges should interpret the Constitution to reflect what the framers intended and what its words literally say.

judicial activism
Judicial philosophy proposing that judges should interpret the Constitution to reflect current conditions and values.

that they were doing so in the hope that they might be able to stay on the Court until a president more congenial to their views might be in the White House. They did not make it. Republican President Bush, rather than a Democrat, appointed their successors. It should be noted, however, that personal and institutional factors other than partisan concerns are the main reason justices retire.

Reforming the Selection Process?

The televised Bork and Thomas confirmation hearings aroused considerable criticism from both liberals and conservatives and created widespread complaints that "something is wrong with the process." Subsequently, a group of experts recommended that an attempt be made to constrain the partisan politics surrounding the confirmation process for Supreme Court justices. They proposed that "Supreme Court nominees should no longer be expected to appear as witnesses during the Senate Judiciary Committee's hearings on their confirmation" and that the Senate should return to the practice of judging nominees on their written record and on the testimony of legal experts.[38] A bipartisan commission on judicial selection from the Miller Center of Public Affairs at the University of Virginia recommended that the time between nominations and Senate confirmation be shortened.[39]

The politics of judicial selection may shock those who like to think judges are picked strictly on the basis of legal merit and without regard for ideology, party, gender, or race. But as a former Justice Department official observed, "When courts cease being an instrument for political change, then maybe the judges will stop being politically selected."[40] Moreover, as another scholar put it, "Supreme Court Justices have always been appointed for political reasons by politicians, and their confirmation process has always been dictated by politicians for political purposes." "In fact," he concluded, "not despite the politicization of the appointment and confirmation process, but because of it, the Supreme Court has endured as a flexible, viable force in the American democracy for over 200 years."[41]

CHANGING THE NUMBERS   One of the first actions of a political party after gaining control of the White House and Congress is often to increase the number of federal judgeships. With divided government, however, when one party controls Congress and the other holds the White House, a stalemate is likely to occur, and relatively few new judicial positions will be created. During Andrew Johnson's administration, Congress went so far as to reduce the size of the Supreme Court to prevent the president from filling two vacancies. After Johnson left the White House, Congress returned the Court to its former size to permit Ulysses S. Grant to fill the vacancies.

In 1937, President Franklin Roosevelt proposed an increase in the size of the Supreme Court by one additional justice for every member of the Court over the age of 70, up to a total of 15 members. Ostensibly, the proposal was aimed at making the Court more efficient. In fact, Roosevelt and his advisers were frustrated because the Court had declared much of the early New Deal legislation unconstitutional. Despite Roosevelt's popularity, his "court-packing scheme" aroused intense opposition. Roosevelt's proposals to change the Court's size failed. He lost the battle but won the war, as the Court began to sustain some important New Deal legislation.

CHANGING THE JURISDICTION   Congressional control over the structure and jurisdiction of federal courts has been used to influence the course of judicial policy making. Although unable to get rid of Federalist judges by impeachment, the Jeffersonians abolished the circuit courts created by the Federalist Congress just before they lost control. In 1869 radical Republicans in Congress altered the Supreme Court's appellate jurisdiction in order to snatch from the Court a case it was about to review involving the constitutionality of some Reconstruction legislation.[42]

Each year a number of bills are introduced in Congress to eliminate the jurisdiction of federal courts over cases relating to abortion, school prayer, and school busing, or to eliminate the appellate jurisdiction of the Supreme Court over such matters. These attacks on federal court jurisdiction spark debate about whether the Constitution gives Congress authority to take such actions. And Congress has not yet decided to do so, because it would amount to a fundamental shift in the relationship between Congress and the Supreme Court. As one scholar concluded: "History suggests the public has seen such attempts for precisely what they are, as attacks on judicial independence, and such attacks have been resisted."[43]

HOW THE SUPREME COURT OPERATES

The Supreme Court's term runs from the first Monday in October through the end of June. The justices listen to oral arguments for two weeks each month from October to April, and then adjourn for two weeks to consider the cases and to write opinions. By agreement, six justices must participate in each decision. Cases are decided by a majority vote. In the event of a tie vote, the decision of the lower court is sustained, although on rare occasions it may be reargued.

At 10:00 a.m. on the days when the Supreme Court sits, the eight associate justices and the chief justice, dressed in their robes (Chief Justice Rehnquist has four gold stripes on each sleeve of his robe),[44] file into the courtroom. As they take their seats—arranged according to seniority, with the chief justice in the center—the clerk of the Court introduces them as the "Honorable Chief Justice and Associate Justices of the Supreme Court of the United States." Those present in the courtroom, asked to stand when the justices enter, are seated, and counsel take their places along tables in front of the bench. The attorneys for the Department of Justice are at the right. The other attorneys are dressed conservatively; sport coats are not considered proper. Dress and ceremony are all part of the high ritual of the Court (see Figure 14–4).

1. Courtyards
2. Solicitor General's Office
3. Lawyers' Lounge
4. Marshall's Office
5. Main Hall
6. Court Room
7. Conference and Reception Rooms
8. Justices' Conference Room
9. Chief Justice's Chambers
10. Justices' Chambers

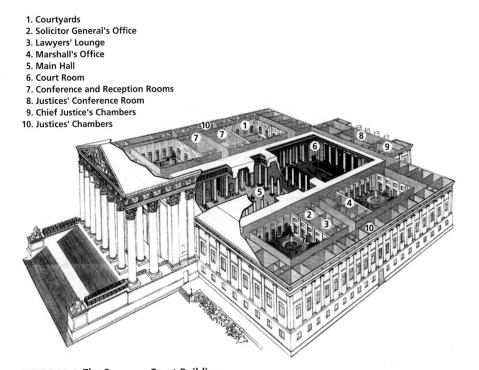

writ of *certiorari*
A formal writ used to bring a case before the Supreme Court.

FIGURE 14–4 **The Supreme Court Building**

Which Cases Reach the Supreme Court?

When citizens vow to take their cases to the highest court of the land even if it costs their last penny, they underestimate the difficulty of securing Supreme Court review and misunderstand the Court's role. The rules for appealing a case are established by the Supreme Court and Congress. Until 1988, the Supreme Court was obliged by law to review a large number of appeals. Today, however, almost all appeals come to the Court by means of a discretionary **writ of *certiorari***, a formal writ used to bring a case before the Court but which may simply be denied. Since the Supreme Court's docket is now largely discretionary, it has the power to set its own agenda and to decide which cases to decide. As a result, the justices decide fewer than 100 of the more than 8,000 cases appealed to them annually.[45] That is half the number of cases decided annually two decades ago.[46]

The crucial factor in determining whether the Supreme Court reviews a case is its importance to the operation of the governmental system as a whole. The Supreme Court will review a case only if the claim has broad public significance. For instance, the rulings among the courts of appeals may conflict; by deciding a case, the Supreme Court establishes which ruling is to be followed. Or a case may raise a constitutional issue on which a state supreme court has presented an interpretation with which the Court disagrees.

WE THE PEOPLE

Needed: Minority Clerks at the Court

A congressional hearing in 1999 on the Supreme Court's annual budget took a valuable detour as Justices Clarence Thomas and David Souter engaged in a lengthy colloquy with lawmakers about the Court's dismal record in recruiting and hiring minority law clerks.

Each of the nine justices personally selects up to four law clerks each term to help with screening appeals and drafting opinions. The 1999 crop of 34 clerks included only one minority member—a Hispanic woman—and for the second year running, the Court hired no African-American clerks. Of the 428 clerks hired over the years by the current justices, only 7 have been black, according to figures compiled by *USA Today*.

Chief Justice William Rehnquist has not hired even one African-American clerk in 27 years on the Court.

"There is not a person at the Court who would not want to change this," said Justice Thomas, the second African American to sit on the Court, responding to questioning by Democratic lawmakers. Justice Souter also expressed displeasure with the lopsided numbers and the perception they create. But other comments by the two justices suggested a reluctance to alter the clubby "feeder system" from top-tier law schools and judges that produces a nearly all-white coterie of high-caliber clerks.

SOURCE: Editorial, *The New York Times*, March 18, 1999, p. A24.

The Court grants cases based on the *rule of four*. If four justices are sufficiently interested in a petition for a writ of *certiorari*, it will be granted and the case brought forward for review. The justices' law clerks read the petitions and write a memorandum on each, recommending whether a review should be granted, and circulate it to all the justices except Justice John Paul Stevens, whose law clerks review the petitions for him, and he reads a few of them himself.[47]

Denial of a writ of *certiorari* does not mean that the justices agree with the decision of the lower court, nor does it establish precedent. Refusal to grant a review may indicate all kinds of possibilities. The justices may wish to avoid a political "hot potato," or the Court may be so divided on an issue that it is not yet prepared to take a stand.[48]

The Powers of the Chief Justice

The chief justice of the United States is appointed by the president upon confirmation by the Senate and holds tenure for life. This method of selecting the chief justice gives him (in our entire history they have all been men) greater visibility than if selected by rotation of fellow justices, as is the practice in the state supreme courts, or by seniority, as is the practice in the federal courts of appeals. But as Chief Justice Rehnquist said when he was still an associate justice, the chief deals not with "eight subordinates whom he may direct or instruct, but eight associates who, like him, have tenure during good behavior, and who are as independent as hogs on ice."[49]

The ability of the chief justice to influence the Court has varied considerably.[50] Chief Justice Charles Evans Hughes ran the conferences like a stern schoolmaster, keeping

Chief Justice William Hubbs Rehnquist presided at the Senate hearing on the impeachment of President Clinton.

The Committee on Long Range Planning of the Judicial Conference of the United States has studied the increasing caseload of federal courts and projects a continued growth in cases and a need for more judges:

Year	District Court Caseloads	Judges	Circuit Court Caseloads	Judges
1950	91,005	224	2,830	65
1960	87,421	245	3,899	68
1970	125,423	401	11,662	97
1980	196,757	516	23,200	132
1990	264,409	575	40,898	156
2000	386,200	940	84,800	430
2010	642,500	1,510	171,600	840
2020	1,109,000	2,530	325,100	1,580

SOURCE: Committee on Long Range Planning, Judicial Conference of the United States, *Proposed Long Range Plan for the Federal Courts* (Judicial Conference of the United States, 1995), pp. 14–15.

the justices on the point, moving the discussion along, and doing his best to work out compromises in order to achieve unanimous decisions, which carry greater weight. Chief Justice Harlan F. Stone, on the other hand, encouraged justices to state their own points of view and let the discussions wander. Chief Justice Warren Burger was not very successful in leading conferences. He devoted much of his time to judicial reform, speaking to bar associations and trying to build political support for modernizing the judicial process.

William H. Rehnquist had 15 years of Court experience prior to his elevation to chief justice. He "has not utilized his position as Chief Justice to shape the decisions of the Court."[51] But as the Reagan-Bush justices are still a majority, his constitutional views on federalism and affirmative action, formerly expressed in his dissenting opinions, are now becoming the opinions of the Court.[52]

"The Chief Justiceship does not guarantee leadership. It only offers its incumbent an opportunity to lead."[53] Yet the chief justice "sets the tone, controls the conference, assigns the most opinions, and usually, takes the most important, nation-changing decisions for himself. . . . The Chief Justice remains first among equals." Periods in Court history are often named after the chief justice, who is responsible for the institution's character."[54]

The Role of the Law Clerks

Beginning in the 1920s and 1930s, federal judges began hiring the best recent graduates of law schools to serve as clerks for a year or two. As the judicial work load increased, more law clerks have been appointed. Today each Supreme Court justice is entitled to four clerks. Clerks screen writs of *certiorari* and draft opinions for the justices. As the number of law clerks and computers has increased, so has the number of concurring and dissenting opinions. As a result, today's opinions are longer and have more footnotes and elaborate citations of cases and law review articles.

Amicus Curiae Briefs

Before a case is heard in open court, the justices receive printed *briefs* from each side, presenting legal arguments, historical background, and relevant precedents. In addition, the Supreme Court may receive briefs from *amici curiae* (literally, "friends of the court"), filed by individuals, organizations, or government agencies that have an interest in the case and claim they have information of value to the Court.

Often organizations file *amicus curiae* briefs before the Supreme Court grants a writ of *certiorari* in order to encourage the Supreme Court to review the case. Their doing so enhances the probability that the Court will take the case for review but has almost no influence on how the case is decided.[55] An *amicus* brief may help the justices by presenting arguments or facts that the parties to the case have not raised.

These briefs usually urge the Court to reach a particular decision. In *Webster v Reproductive Health Services*, dealing with a Missouri law regulating abortions and asking the Court to reverse *Roe v Wade*, 78 *amicus* briefs were filed.[56] In *United States v Lopez*, which challenged congressional authority to ban guns in and around schools, more than 40 parties filed a dozen *amicus* briefs. Ohio, New York, and the District of Columbia argued in favor of federal power, as did associations of police and school officials. On the other side were some conservative public interest firms, the National Governors Association, and the National League of Cities.[57]

The practice of filing *amicus curiae* briefs also guarantees that the Department of Justice is represented if a suit questions the constitutionality of an act of Congress or the executive branch. The solicitor general uses these briefs to bring to the Court's attention the views of the current administration.[58]

Oral Arguments

Formal oratory before the Supreme Court, once lasting for several days, is a thing of the past. As a rule, counsel for each side is now allowed only 30 minutes. Lawyers use a lectern with two lights: a white light flashes five minutes before time is up; when the red light goes on, the lawyer must stop, even in the middle of an "if."

amicus curiae
Literally, "friend of the court" brief, filed by an individual or organization to present arguments in addition to those presented by the immediate party to the case.

The entire procedure is informally formal. Sometimes, to the annoyance of attorneys, justices talk among themselves or consult briefs or books during oral arguments. Other times, if justices find a presentation particularly bad, they will tell the attorneys so. Justices freely interrupt the lawyers to ask questions and request additional information. In recent years, "the justices seem barely able to contain themselves, often interrupting the answer to one question with another query."[59] Hence, the 30-minute limit is problematic, especially when the solicitor general participates, since his 10 minutes come out of the time of the two parties before the Court.

If a lawyer is having a difficult time, the justices may try to help him or her out with a question. Occasionally, justices bounce arguments off a hapless attorney and at one another. Justice Antonin Scalia is a harsh questioner. "When Scalia prepares to ask a question, he doesn't just adjust himself in his chair to get closer to the microphone like the others; he looks like a vulture, zooming in for the kill. He strains way forward, pinches his eyebrows, and poses the question, like '. . . do you want us to believe?'"[60] Justice Ruth Bader Ginsburg is a particularly persistent questioner, frequently rivaling Justice Scalia in asking the most questions.[61] Justice Clarence Thomas almost never asks a question. Justice David Souter has a thick New England accent. He once asked an attorney during oral arguments in an affirmative action case, "What's the floor?" The attorney hemmed and hawed until, with a smile, Souter explained he meant, "What's the flaw?"[62] Oral arguments in landmark cases may be listened to on the Web by going to **www.oyez.nwu.edu.**

Behind the Curtains: The Conference

On Wednesday afternoons and Fridays the justices meet in private conference. They have heard the oral arguments and studied the briefs. Each brings to the meeting a red leather book in which the cases and the votes of the justices are recorded. These conferences are held in secret. They are usually a collegial but vigorous give-and-take.

The chief justice presides, usually opening the discussion by stating the facts, summarizing the questions of law, and suggesting how to dispose of each case. Each justice, in order of seniority, then gives his or her views and conclusions. Chief Justice Rehnquist tries to see to it that "everybody [speaks] once before the vote is taken."[63] Recently the justices have not bothered with formal votes because their votes are clear from their discussion of the case.[64]

Patrick Oliphant, Universal Press Syndicate.

opinion of the court

An opinion explaining the decision of the Supreme Court or any other appellate court.

dissenting opinion

An opinion disagreeing with the decision of the Court.

concurring opinion

An opinion that agrees with the decision of the Court but differs on the reasoning.

Opinions

As a general rule, Supreme Court opinions state the facts, present the issues, announce the decision, and, most important, explain the reasoning of the Court. These opinions are the Court's principal method of expressing its views to the world. Their primary function is to instruct judges of state and federal courts how to decide similar cases in the future.

Judicial opinions may also be directed at Congress or at the president. If the Court regrets that "in the absence of action by Congress, we have no choice but to . . ." or insists that "relief of the sort that petitioner demands can only come from the political branches of government," it is asking Congress to act.[65] Justices also use opinions to communicate with the public. A well-crafted opinion may increase support for a policy the Court favors.

ASSIGNING OPINIONS   When voting with the majority, the chief justice decides who will draft the **opinion of the Court**. When the chief justice is in the minority, the senior justice among the majority makes the assignment. The justice assigned to write the opinion must give persuasive reasons for the outcome, for no vote in conference is final until the opinion of the Court has been agreed to. Justices are free to change their minds if not persuaded by draft opinions.

Justices are free to write a **dissenting opinion** if they wish. Dissenting opinions are, in Chief Justice Charles Evans Hughes's words, "an appeal to the brooding spirit of the law, to the intelligence of a later day."[66] Dissenting opinions are quite common, as justices hope that some day these dissenting opinions will command a majority of the Court. If a justice agrees with the majority on how the case should be decided but differs on the reasoning, that justice may write a **concurring opinion**.

CIRCULATING DRAFTS   Writing the opinion of the Court is an exacting task. The document must win the support of at least four—even more, if possible—intelligent, strong-willed persons. Assisted by the law clerks, the assigned justice writes a draft and sends it to colleagues for comments. If the justice is lucky, the majority will accept the draft, perhaps with only minor changes. If the draft is not satisfactory to the other justices, it must be redrafted and recirculated until a majority reaches agreement.

The two weapons justices can use against their colleagues are their votes and the threat of writing dissenting opinions attacking the majority's opinion. Especially if the Court is closely divided, one justice may be in a position to demand that a certain point or argument be included in, or removed from, the opinion of the Court as the price of his or her vote. Sometimes such bargaining occurs even though the Court is not closely divided. An opinion writer who anticipates that a decision will invite critical public reaction may want a unanimous Court and therefore will compromise to achieve unanimity. For this reason, the Court delayed declaring school segregation unconstitutional, in *Brown v Board of Education*,[67] until unanimity was secured. The justices understood that any sign of dissension on the bench on this major social issue would be an invitation to evade the Court's ruling.

RELEASING OPINIONS TO THE PUBLIC   In the past, justices read their entire opinions from the bench on "Opinion Days." Now, they give only brief summaries of the decision and their opinions. Copies are immediately made available to reporters and the public and published in the official *United States Supreme Court*

Reports. Since April 2000, the Court makes its opinions available on its website: www.supremecourtus.gov.

After the Court Decides

Victory in the Supreme Court does not necessarily mean that winning parties get what they want. The Court does not implement its own decision but *remands*, that is, sends the case back to the lower court with instructions to act in accordance with its opinion. The lower court often has considerable leeway in interpreting the Court's mandate as it disposes of the case.

Decisions whose enforcement requires only the action of a federal agency usually become effective immediately. Thus, when the Supreme Court held that President Richard M. Nixon had to turn over confidential White House materials,[68] the president promptly complied.

The impact of a particular Supreme Court ruling on the behavior of those who are not immediate parties to a lawsuit is more uncertain. The most important rulings require a change in the behavior of thousands of administrative and elected officials. Sometimes Supreme Court pronouncements are simply ignored. For example, despite the Court's holding that it is unconstitutional for school boards to require students to pray within a school, some schools continue this practice.[69] And for years after the Supreme Court held public school segregation unconstitutional, many school districts remained segregated.[70]

The most difficult Supreme Court decisions to implement are those that require the cooperation of large numbers of officials. For example, a Supreme Court decision announcing a new standard for warrantless searches is not likely to have an impact on the way police make arrests for some time, since not many police officers subscribe to the *United States Supreme Court Reports.* The process is more complex. Local prosecutors, state attorneys general, chiefs of police, and state and federal trial court judges must all participate to give meaning to Supreme Court decisions. The Constitution may be what the Supreme Court says it is, but a Supreme Court opinion, for the moment at least, is what a trial judge or police officer or a prosecutor or a school board or a city council says it is.

"Do you ever have one of those days when *nothing* seems constitutional?"

The Wall Street Journal, August 3, 1998. By permission of Cartoon Features Syndicate.

JUDICIAL POWER IN A CONSTITUTIONAL DEMOCRACY

An independent judiciary is one of the hallmarks of a free society. As impartial dispensers of equal justice under the law, judges should not be dependent on the executive, the legislature, parties to a case, or the electorate. But judicial independence, essential to protect judges in their role as legal umpire, raises basic problems when a democratic society decides—as ours has—also to allow these same judges to make policy. Perhaps in no other society do the people resort to litigation as a means of making public policy as much as they do in the United States. For example, African American organizations turned to litigation to get relief from segregation practices in the 1930s and 1940s.

The involvement of courts in politics exposes the judiciary to political criticism. Throughout our history, the Supreme Court has been attacked for engaging in "judicial legislation." This is nothing new. Yet the active role of the federal courts on behalf of liberal causes since 1937 and Republican attacks on that role have returned these issues to the forefront of public debate.

Whereas in earlier times judges occasionally told public officials what they could *not* do, today they often tell them what they *must* do. For example, federal judges, responding to class action complaints, have told Congress, state legislatures, and local officials that they must provide attorneys for the poor, ensure adequate care for mental patients, modernize prisons, and even break up the telephone system. Often judges retain jurisdiction for years as they preside over the implementation of the decrees they have issued.[71] Judges have always been policy makers; that role is not a matter of choice but flows from the roles they play in deciding cases.

The Great Debate over the Proper Role of the Courts

Some people contend that the courts have a duty to protect the interests of the public. Defenders of this *activist* judicial role argue that if Congress, the White House, and the state legislatures are unwilling or unable to resolve pressing problems when people are denied justice and their constitutional rights, then the courts must address those problems. The Supreme Court, they say, should be "a leader in a vital national seminar that leads to the formulation of values for the American people."[72]

Critics of judicial activism contend that for the last half century the federal courts, in their zeal to protect people, became unhinged from their political moorings in the political and constitutional system. Even if courts make the "right" decisions, these critics argue, it is still not right for them to take over the legislative function of elected representatives. Courts should exercise self-restraint.

Others claim the debate between those who favor judicial activism and those who favor judicial restraint oversimplifies the choices. Judges, they argue, should take a leadership role in some areas but a restrained role in others. They stand with Chief Justice Harlan F. Stone, who argued that courts have a special duty to intervene: (1) whenever legislation restricts the political process by which decisions are made, or (2) whenever legislation restricts the rights of "discrete and insular minorities," and (3) when guarantees of the Bill of Rights are violated. In all other areas, the political process should be allowed to work, and judges should not set aside legislation or interfere with administrative agencies merely because they would prefer some other policy or even some other interpretation of the Constitution.[73]

The People and the Court

Whether judges are liberal or conservative, defer to legislatures or not, try to apply the Constitution as they think the framers intended or interpret it to conform to current values, there are linkages between what judges do and what the people want done. The linkages are not direct, and the people never speak with one mind, but these linkages are the heart of the matter.[74] In the first place, the president and the Senate are likely to appoint justices whose decisions reflect their values. Therefore, elections matter, because the perspectives of those who nominate and confirm the judges are reflected in the composition of courts. For instance, in 1992 the Supreme Court, by a 5 to 4 vote in *Planned Parenthood v Casey*, refused to overturn *Roe v Wade* and upheld its core holding—that the Constitution protects the right of a woman to an abortion—although upholding state regulations that do not "unduly burden" that right.[75] This close vote on abortion made it clear that the 2000 presidential election could determine whether that right would continue to be protected, depending on retirements from the bench and new appointments to the Court.

Scholars debate how public opinion influences what judges decide, whether it is direct or indirect through presidential selection and Senate confirmation of judges, but there is little question that there is a correlation between public opinion and judicial decisions.[76] Judicial opinions that reflect what the people want have the greatest survival value. When a new political coalition takes over the White House or Congress, the old regime may stay on in the federal courts. New electoral coalitions eventually take over the federal courts, and before long, new interpretations of the Constitution reflect the dominant political ideology.

Judges have neither armies nor police to execute their rulings. Although Congress cannot reverse Supreme Court decisions that relate to constitutional interpretations, and only six Supreme Court decisions have been reversed by formal constitutional amendment, the political system alters judicial policy in more subtle ways. Decisions are binding on the parties to a particular case, but the policies that result from judicial decisions are effective and durable only if they are supported by the electorate. To win a favorable Supreme Court decision is to win something of considerable political value.

"American courts are not all-powerful institutions."[77] If the Court's policies are too far out of step with the values of the country, the Court is likely to be reversed. In Chief Justice William H. Rehnquist's words, "No judge worthy of his salt would ever cast his vote in a particular case simply because he thought the majority of the public wanted him to vote that way, but that is quite a different thing from saying that no judge is ever influenced by the great tides of public opinion that run a country such as ours."[78]

"The people" speak in many ways and with many voices. The Supreme Court—and the other courts—represent and reflect the values of some of these people. Although the Court is not the defenseless institution portrayed by some commentators, and its decisions are as much shapers of public opinion as reflections of it, ultimately the power of the Court in a constitutional democracy rests on retaining the support of most of the people most of the time. The Court's power rests, as Chief Justice Edward White observed, "solely upon the approval of a free people,"[79] No better standard for determining the legitimacy of a governmental institution has been discovered.

POLITICS ONLINE

Oral Argument: How Good Are You at Thinking on Your Feet?

Not long after the Supreme Court heard oral arguments in the *Bush v. Gore* decision about the Florida vote count, the Court made available audiotapes of the proceedings. For many Americans, listening to the oral argument was a new experience. The Court had always been resistant to televising oral arguments, and releasing audio tapes so soon after an oral argument was unique. Television viewers who heard the oral argument while watching TV were able to see drawings of the participants and were told (in text) who was speaking.

For most viewers, the process of Supreme Court oral arguments was probably surprising. Unlike trial courts, there are no witnesses, only attorneys answering questions from the justices. Often the attorney is in mid-sentence when he is asked another question. Attorneys who argue before the Supreme Court clearly must be quick on their feet. They must try to answer questions directly because they do not know if they will get to say all they have prepared on any given question. They must also be respectful, even though they are frequently interrupted and challenged. Sometimes justices ask what appear to be friendly questions in an effort to structure the discussion and perhaps influence the later deliberations of the justices. Other times, the questions seem much more pointed.

To listen to the tape of the *Bush v. Gore* oral argument or many other oral argments, you can go to: http://oyez.nwu.edu. This site has abstracts and opinions from major court cases, plus oral arguments from selected cases. The site also has a virtual tour of the U.S. Supreme Court building and biographies of the current justices.

SUMMARY

1. The American judicial process is based on the adversary system. Judges in the United States play a more active role in the political process than they do in most other democracies. Federal courts are established by and receive their jurisdiction directly from Congress, which must decide the constitutional division of responsibilities among federal and state courts.

2. Federal judges apply federal, criminal, and civil law. Although bound by procedural requirements, including *stare decisis*, they can exercise discretion.

3. The Supreme Court has almost complete control over the cases it chooses to review as they come up from the state courts, the courts of appeals, and district courts. Its nine justices dispose of thousands of cases, but most of their time is concentrated on the fewer than 100 cases per year that establish guidelines for lower courts and the country.

4. A continuing concern of major importance is the reconciliation of the role of judges—especially those on the Supreme Court—as independent and fair dispensers of justice with their vital role as interpreters of the Constitution. This is an especially complex problem in our democracy because of the power of judicial review and the significant role courts play in making public policy.

5. The debate about how judges should interpret the Constitution is almost as old as the Republic. More than two hundred years after the Constitution was adopted, the argument between those who contend judges should interpret the document literally and those who believe they cannot, and should not, remains in the headlines.

6. Partisanship and ideology are important factors in the selection of federal judges, and these factors ensure a linkage between the courts and the rest of the political system, so that the views of the people are reflected, even if indirectly, in the work of the courts. In recent decades candidates for the presidency and the Senate have made judicial appointments an issue in their election campaigns.

KEY TERMS

judicial review 319
adversary system 319
justiciable dispute 319
class action suit 319
political question 319
stare decisis 319

appellate jurisdiction 319
original jurisdiction 319
grand jury 320
petit jury 320
magistrate judge 320
court of appeals 320

habeas corpus 320
defendant 322
plea bargain 322
public defender system 323
senatorial courtesy 323
judicial restraint 330

judicial activism 330
writ of *certiorari* 332
amicus curiae 334
opinion of the court 336
dissenting opinion 336
concurring opinion 336

FURTHER READING

HENRY J. AARON AND ROBERT D. REISCHAUER, EDS., *The Judiciary: Setting National Priorities: The 2000 Election and Beyond,* (Brookings Institution Press, 1999).

HENRY J. ABRAHAM, *The Judiciary: The Supreme Court in the Governmental Process,* 10th ed. (New York University Press, 1996).

HENRY J. ABRAHAM, *Justices, Presidents, and Senators: A History of U.S. Supreme Court Appointments from Washington to Clinton* (Rowman & Littlefield, 1999).

CORNELL CLAYTON AND HOWARD GILMAN, EDS. *Supreme Court Decision-Making: New Institutionalist Approaches* (University of Chicago Press, 1999).

CLARE CUSHMAN, *The Supreme Court Justices: Illustrated Biographies, 1789–1995,* 2d ed. (Congressional Quarterly Press, 1996).

LEE EPSTEIN AND JACK KNIGHT, *The Choices Justices Make* (C.Q. Press, 1998).

JERRY GOLDMAN, *The Supreme Court's Greatest Hits (A CD of 70 Hours of Oral Arguments)* (Northwestern University Press, 1999).

SHELDON GOLDMAN, *Picking Federal Judges: Lower Court Selection from Roosevelt Through Reagan* (Yale University Press, 1997).

KERMIT L. HALL, ED., *The Oxford Companion to the Supreme Court of the United States* (Oxford University Press, 1992).

PETER IRONS, *A People's History of the Supreme Court* (Viking, 1999).

EDWARD LAZARUS, *Closed Chambers: The First Eyewitness Account of the Epic Struggles Inside the Supreme Court* (Times Books, Random House, 1998).

PAUL C. LIGHT, *The New Public Service* (Brookings Institution Press, 1999).

CHARLES LOPEMAN, *The Activist Advocate: Policymaking in State Supreme Courts* (Praeger, 2000).

DAVID M. O'BRIEN, ED., *Judges on Judging: Views from the Bench* (Chatham House, 1997).

DAVID M. O'BRIEN, *Storm Center: The Supreme Court in American Politics,* 5th ed. (W. W. Norton, 2000).

J. W. PELTASON, *Federal Courts in the Political Process* (Doubleday, 1955).

TERRI JENNINGS PERETTI, *In Defense of a Political Court* (Princeton University Press, 1999).

GERALD N. ROSENBERG, *The Hollow Hope: Can Courts Bring About Social Change?* (University of Chicago Press, 1991).

C. K. ROWLAND AND ROBERT A. CARP, *Politics and Judgment in Federal District Courts* (University Press of Kansas, 1996).

PETER RUSSELL AND DAVID M. O'BRIEN, EDS., *Judicial Independence in the Age of Democracy: Critical Perspectives from Around the World* (University Press of Virginia, 2001).

ELLIOT E. SLOTNICK, Judicial Politics: *Readings from "Judicature,"* 2d ed. (American Judicature Society, 1999).

HARRY P. STUMPF, *American Judicial Politics,* 2d ed. (Prentice Hall, 1998).

DAVID ALISTAR YALOF, *Pursuit of Justices: Presidential Politics and the Selection of Supreme Court Nominees* (University of Chicago Press, 1999).

15

THE BUREAUCRACY: THE REAL POWER?

THe federal government is big. Even after major efforts in the 1990s to downsize and "reinvent" the federal bureaucracy, it employs nearly 2.7 million civilian federal workers and 1.4 million uniformed military personnel. The federal government will spend over $2 trillion in fiscal year 2002.[1] When Thomas Jefferson became president in 1801, the federal government employed just over 2,000 individuals, mostly postmasters, Indian commissioners, tax collectors, lighthouse keepers, and clerks. Our bureaucratic agencies, then and now, reflect how our political system has tried to identify our most important national goals and how policies are implemented.

Big bureaucracy today is a fact of life. But Americans have decidedly contradictory attitudes about the role of government. We like, even if we usually take for granted, the countless services government provides, such as postal delivery, national parks, food and drug inspections, federal emergency relief, and so on. Yet we dislike the idea of big government and wasteful bureaucracies. "Bureaucracy is inherently controlling. . . . Most of us do not like being controlled, even for the collective good. Even worse, bureaucracy strives. . . . to deliver even-handed treatment and to administer policies in a disinterested manner, showing no favoritism. But, of course, most of us think of other people as 'the rule' and ourselves as the exception."[2]

Some critics believe the federal bureaucracy is an overzealous guardian of the status quo and is too lazy or unimaginative to innovate or experiment. Others fear that a powerful national bureaucracy encourages a wasteful welfare state. Many people also think the federal bureaucracy is too large, too powerful, too unaccountable; 64 percent of respondents in a national survey complained that the federal government controls too much of our daily lives.[3]

Bureaucracy's chief characteristics are continuity, predictability, impartiality, standard operating procedures, and the inevitable "red tape." Large government bureaucracies are not characterized by flexibility, creativity, boldness, and innovation. Even when government agencies work well, and even when they are reasonably creative, we usually take them for granted rather than celebrate them.[4] It is as natural to rail against red tape as it is to complain about taxes and regulations.

In this chapter we explain who the bureaucrats are, examine the origins, functions, and realities of our national public bureaucracy, and explore how elected officials are trying to make the bureaucracy leaner, more responsive, and more accountable to the American people. It is important to ask whether our

CHAPTERMEDIA

POLITICS ONLINE
Want To Be a Bureaucrat?
www.prenhall.com/burns

PoliSim
*Balancing the Nation's
Checkbook*
www.prenhall.com/burns

bureaucracy and its methods are stifling innovation, productivity, and common sense.

BUREAUCRACY: A PERENNIAL POLITICAL ISSUE

Democrats and Republicans have been arguing over the proper role of government for more than a century, and especially since the New Deal programs of the 1930s. Bashing federal bureaucracies, especially the always unpopular Internal Revenue Service, is a great American pastime. Few of us have not been offended, irritated, or frustrated at one time or another in dealing with the Internal Revenue Service (IRS), the Immigration and Naturalization Service (INS), U.S. Custom agents, the Food and Drug Administration, or similar federal bureaucracies. No matter that these same agencies can also be a big help to us or serve the country well; we mainly remember the mistakes, delays, and hassles. As many as 2 million people, for example, are audited each year by the IRS. And despite the fact that most IRS agents do their job well and are fair-minded as they go after tax cheaters and tax evaders, there are well-documented instances of IRS intimidation and abuse.[5]

People believe that their lives are overregulated and the rules are numerous and unflexible. One critic writes that government "acts like some extraterrestrial power, not an institution that exists to serve us. Its actions have an arbitrary quality. It almost never deals with real-life problems in a way that reflects understanding of the situation."[6]

Democrats bragged at the end of the Clinton-Gore administration that they had reduced the number of federal workers by more than 300,000 and shrunk federal spending from 22 to 19 percent of the gross domestic product. Al Gore led bureaucracy reform efforts that were aimed at putting customers first, empowering federal workers to get more effective results, cutting red tape, and, in general, borrowing entrepreneurial ideas from the private sector about competition, choice, and reliance on the market.[7]

George W. Bush campaigned for the White House by charging that the federal bureaucracy was far too large, and that much of what the federal government was

bureaucrat
Career government employee.

bureaucracy
A professional corps of officials organized in a pyramidal hierarchy and functioning under impersonal, uniform rules and procedures.

spoils system
System of public employment based on rewarding party loyalists and friends.

Like these people waiting in line to mail packages, the public is often annoyed by bureaucratic rules.

doing should be done either by the private sector or local government. Bush promised to contract out to private companies or "faith-based" institutions—churches, synagogues, and charities—a lot of what federal bureaucrats did. He pledged also not to replace thousands of federal managers scheduled to retire during his presidency.[8]

Public opinion surveys regularly find that no matter who is president, most Americans are skeptical about whether they can trust the federal government to do what is right (see Table 15–1). With public moods like this, it is not surprising that candidates for office criticize federal bureaucrats.

THE FEDERAL BUREAUCRACY

Bureaucrats, or career government employees, work in the executive branch, in the 14 cabinet-level departments, and in the more than 50 independent agencies embracing about 2,000 bureaus, divisions, branches, offices, services, and other subunits of government. Five big agencies—the Departments of the Army, the Navy, and the Air Force (all three in the Department of Defense), the Department of Veterans Affairs, and the U.S. Postal Service—tower over the others in size. Most agencies are directly responsible to the president, yet some, like the Postal Service, are partly independent. Agencies exist by act of Congress; legislators can abolish them either by passing a new law or by withholding funds.

The terms "bureaucrat" and "bureaucracy" date from the early nineteenth century. Initially referring to a cloth covering the desks of French government officials in the eighteenth century, the term "bureau" came to be linked with the suffix "ocracy" signifying rule of government (as in "democracy" or "aristocracy"). **Bureaucracy**, as the term came to be used a century ago, referred to a rational, efficient method of organization. The term typically refers to the whole body of nonelected and nonappointed government officials in the executive branch who work for presidents and their political appointees. In this chapter we use the terms "bureaucracy" and "bureaucrat" in their neutral sense, although popular usage of these terms is typically negative.

Bureaucracies are public or private organizations that are large and hierarchical in structure, with each employee accountable to a superior through a chain of command. They provide each employee with a defined role or responsibility, base their decisions on impersonal rules, and hire and promote employees according to skills related to their jobs.[9] Bureaucracies in the modern sense came into being in government to provide predictability and efficiency and to minimize the arbitrary practices that so often characterized rule under dictatorial monarchs.

Bureaucracy in a large, complex society is virtually inevitable. Most of us will work in some public or private bureaucracy for part, if not most, of our careers. Public bureaucracies pose special challenges because they report to competing political institutions and must function within our constitutional democracy of shared powers and multiple checks and balances.

How Did the Bureaucracy Evolve?

From 1789 until about 1829, the federal service in this country was drawn from an upper-class, white male elite. In 1829 President Andrew Jackson called for greater participation by the middle and lower classes. He introduced what was labeled a **spoils system**, which his successors in office followed until well into the 1890s. This system, epitomized by the

Executive Branch Departments

- Department of State (1789)
- Department of the Treasury (1789)
- Department of Defense (1947, originally War, 1789)
- Department of Justice (1789)
- Department of the Interior (1849)
- Department of Agriculture (1862)
- Department of Commerce (1913, originally Commerce and Labor, 1903)
- Department of Labor (1913, originally Commerce and Labor, 1903)
- Department of Health and Human Services (1979, originally Health, Education and Welfare, 1953)
- Department of Housing and Urban Development (1965)
- Department of Transportation (1966)
- Department of Energy (1977)
- Department of Education (1979)
- Department of Veterans Affairs (1989)

Dates indicate when the department was established.

TABLE 15–1 Citizen Confidence in Federal Government

Q: "How much of the time do you think you can trust the government in Washington to do what is right: just about always, most of the time, or only some of the time?"

Just about always	4%
Most of the time	25
Only some of the time	63
Never	6
Not sure	2

SOURCE: Council for Excellence in Government, poll conducted by Peter Hart and Robert Teeter, May–June 1999. N=1214.

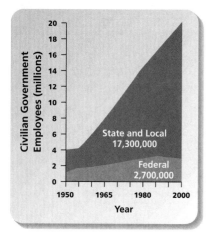

FIGURE 15–1 Civilian Government Employees, 1950–2000

SOURCE: Bureau of Labor Statistics, U.S. Department of Labor.

phrase "to the victor belong the spoils," operated on the theory that party loyalists should be rewarded and that government would be effective and responsive only if supporters of the president held most key federal posts. Besides, it was assumed that government should not be complicated; anybody should be able to do the job. With each new president came a full turnover in the federal service.

Later in the nineteenth century, however, a sharp reaction set in against the spoils system. In response to abuses such as bribery and poor performance, and most immediately to the assassination of President James Garfield in 1881 by a disappointed office seeker, Congress passed the Pendleton Act. It set up a limited **merit system** based on a testing program for evaluating candidates. Federal employees were to be selected and retained according to their "merit," not their party connections or loyalty. Federal service was placed under the control of a three-person bipartisan board called the Civil Service Commission, which functioned from 1883 to 1978.[10]

By the 1950s coverage under the merit system had grown from 10 percent of all federal employees, when it was first established, to about 90 percent. In 1978 the Civil Service Reform Act abolished the Civil Service Commission and split its functions between two new agencies. This split was made to eliminate the possible conflict of interest in an agency that recruits, hires, and promotes employees also being the same agency that passes judgment on employee grievances about fairness and discrimination.

Today the **Office of Personnel Management (OPM)** administers civil service laws, rules, and regulations (www.opm.gov). An independent Merit Systems Protection Board is charged with protecting the integrity of the federal merit system and the rights of federal employees. It conducts studies of the merit system, hears and decides charges of wrongdoing, considers employee appeals against adverse agency actions, and orders corrective and disciplinary actions against an agency executive or employee when appropriate (www.mspg.gov).

Who Are the Bureaucrats?

We are mainly interested here in the approximately 2.7 million civilians—including postal workers and excluding about 1.4 million in the military services—who make up the executive branch of the federal government (Figure 15–1). Certain facts about these people need to be emphasized:

1. Only about 15 percent of the career civilian employees work in the Washington area. The vast majority are scattered throughout the country and around the world.

2. More than 25 percent of the civilian employees work for the army, the navy, the air force, or some other defense agency; another 30 percent work for the U.S. Postal Service.

3. Welfare may consume a sizable portion of the U.S. budget, yet the federal bureaucracy that administers it is relatively small. Less than 10 percent of the bureaucrats work for welfare agencies such as the Social Security Administration or the Department of Veterans Affairs.

4. Bureaucrats are more broadly representative of the nation than are legislators or politically appointed executives in terms of social origin, education, religion, and other background factors.

5. Thousands of different personnel skills are represented in the federal government; however, most federal employees are white-collar workers: secretaries, clerks, lawyers, inspectors, engineers.

Most bureaucrats are honest professionals and experts at their business. Presidents, Congress, and other elected officials sometimes ignore the bureaucracy's advice at their peril. One example was provided by the Central Intelligence Agency's perceptive memoranda (many of them later published in the celebrated *Pentagon Papers*) warning that the Vietnam War as President Lyndon Johnson wanted to con-

merit system

A system in which selection and employment depend on demonstrated performance rather than political patronage.

Office of Personnel Management (OPM)

Agency that administers civil service laws, rules, and regulations.

duct it would be a failure. This was good advice. Yet the bureaucracy is not always right. John F. Kennedy may have been misled by government intelligence officials in the Bay of Pigs episode.

What Do Bureaucrats Do?

After Congress has passed and the president has signed a bill into law, it must be implemented. Implementation of legislation is the function of the executive branch, its bureaucracy, and, in some instances, state, county, and local governments.

More is involved in policy implementation than the mechanical translation of laws into practice. Indeed, it is during this stage that many key decisions are made. Legislation is often deliberately vague to conceal serious policy differences among supporters of a bill. Legislators frequently are more concerned with the symbolic potency of legislation than with its content. Thus Congress often sets general goals and passes the responsibility for interpretation on to the bureaucrats, who then have considerable latitude to translate general guidelines into specific directives. Bureaucrats are sometimes blamed for the confusion, yet they are merely trying to carry out ambiguous policies in a political atmosphere characterized by conflict and competition.

Consider the example of civil rights legislation. Often differences among women's groups, African American groups, Latino groups, employer groups, and trade unions are momentarily resolved and a bill becomes law. But after the bill has been enacted, the coalition that supported the bill falls apart, and conflicting pressures are felt by the agencies trying to implement the policies. Employers claim that the regulations are unrealistic and interfere with their rights; women's groups contend the agencies are failing to enforce the law vigorously enough; African American groups claim the agencies favor the women's groups but ignore African Americans. The more controversial the issue, the greater the chance of disputes, as powerful interest groups clash over a program and force bureaucrats to move cautiously.

The implementation process involves a long chain of decision points. At each point a public official or community leader can advance or delay the program. The more decision points a program needs to clear, the greater the chance of failure or delay. Special problems result if the successful implementation of a national program depends on the cooperation of state and local officials. One state or community may be eager to help; another may be opposed to a program and try to stop it.

A number of federal programs have failed to accomplish their desired goals because of problems in implementation. Sometimes these difficulties lead to the outright failure of a program, but more often they mean excessive delay, watered-down goals, or cost overruns. John Kennedy's economic reform programs in Latin America, Lyndon Johnson's Model Cities program, Richard Nixon's and Gerald Ford's crime control programs, the Reagan-Bush anti-drug crusade, and Bill Clinton's national service program all faced problems of implementation.

Like so much of politics, successful policy implementation cannot be guaranteed. It depends on the creation of effective routines, the ability to adjust to changing circumstances, the quality of the working relationship between agencies at various levels, the degree of conflict invoked by the policy, and its general level of public support.

How Is the Bureaucracy Organized?

FORMAL ORGANIZATION   The executive branch departments are headed by cabinet members called *secretaries* (except Justice, which is headed by the attorney general). Cabinet secretaries are directly responsible to the president. Although departments vary greatly in size, they have certain features in common. A *deputy* or an *undersecretary* takes part of the administrative load off the secretary's shoulders, and several assistant secretaries direct major programs. The secretaries have assistants who help them in planning, budget, personnel, legal services, public relations, and other staff functions.

The standard name for the largest subunit of a department is the **bureau**, sometimes called an office, administration, or service. Bureaus are the working units of the federal government. In contrast to the big departments, which often consist of a variety of agencies, bureaus usually have fairly definite and clear-cut duties, as their names show: the Bureau of the Census in the Commerce Department, the Forest Service in the Agriculture Department, the Social Security Administration in the Department of Health and Human Services, the United States Mint in the Treasury Department, the Bureau of Indian Affairs and the National Park Service in the Interior Department, and the Bureau of Prisons, Federal Bureau of Investigation, and Drug Enforcement Administration in the Justice Department.

Government corporations, such as the Corporation for Public Broadcasting and the Federal Deposit Insurance Corporation, are a cross between business corporations and regular government agencies. Government corporations were designed to make possible a freedom of action and flexibility not always found in the regular agencies. These corporations have been freed from certain regulations of the Office of Management and Budget and the comptroller general. They also have more leeway in using their own earnings. Still, because these corporations are a part of the government, the government retains some control over their activities.

Independent agencies are government entities that are not corporations and do not fall within cabinet departments. They consist of many types of organizations with differing degrees of independence. Many, however, are no more independent of the president and Congress than the cabinet departments. The huge General Services Administration (GSA), for example, which operates and maintains federal properties, is not represented in the cabinet, but its director is responsible to the White House and its actions are closely watched by Congress.

Another type of agency is the **independent regulatory board** or commission. Examples are the Securities and Exchange Commission and the Federal Reserve Board. Congress deliberately set up these boards to keep them somewhat free from White House influence; the president nominates their members and the Senate confirms them, but the president cannot fire them. Congress has protected their independence in several ways: the boards are headed by three or more commissioners with overlapping terms; they often have to be bipartisan in membership (that is, they must have some Democrats as well as some Republicans); and members are appointed for fixed terms in office, some for only 3 years but others for up to 14 years.

By assigning specific functions to each unit, placing an official at the head, and holding that official responsible for performance, formal bureaucracy allows for both specialization and coordination, permits ready communication, and in general makes a large and complex organization more manageable.

ASSISTANT SECRETARIES: A WEAK LINK   Although presidents can usually recruit people of prominence and influence as cabinet secretaries, they find it harder to hire outstanding people at the assistant secretary level. Assistant secretaries are supposed to infuse the views and values of the White House into the federal bureaucracy. These citizen policy makers serve as links between the people who elect the presidents and the civil servants.

Many people, however, are not willing to interrupt their professional or business careers to become assistant secretaries. Over the last three decades the position has become one of relatively low pay, little prestige in Washington, short tenure (people stay, on average, about two years in these posts), and high cost to one's family. As a result, presidents often fill these slots with relatively young people who, from the day they arrive in Washington, are looking for their next job. Assistant secretaries are forced to wear "kid gloves" with those they are supposed to regulate because it is from them that their next job is often likely to come. Others have strong ideological convictions but little experience in administration and congressional politics. Still others use the position as a transition to retirement.

bureau
The largest subunit of a government department or agency.

government corporation
Cross between a business corporation and a government agency, created to secure greater freedom of action and flexibility for a particular program.

independent agency
A government entity that is independent of the legislative, executive, and judicial branch.

independent regulatory board
An independent agency or commission with regulatory power whose independence is protected by Congress.

Most civil servants have virtually secure jobs. All they have to do to ignore assistant secretaries is to wait them out for a year or two. Moreover, in and around Washington, government workers constitute a powerful political group. Assistant secretaries who try to significantly alter the policy directions of those who are supposedly under their supervision rarely succeed.

THE SENIOR EXECUTIVE SERVICE The Civil Service Reform Act of 1978 created the Senior Executive Service. This pool of about 8,000 career officials (which can include up to 10 percent political appointees by an administration) can be filled without senatorial confirmation. The service was created to make senior career bureaucrats more responsive to the goals and policy preferences of the White House. This new service gave presidents greater flexibility in selecting, promoting, and rewarding with financial bonuses those in the top career service who are productive and responsive.

The Senior Executive Service has had mixed success. Government salaries haven't been competitive enough to attract or retain some people who would have been outstanding public servants. Yet recent presidents have shrewdly used this flexibility to their advantage to discipline the upper reaches of the executive branch. (For the website of the Senior Executive Service, see **www.gov/ses/**.)

THE OFFICE OF MANAGEMENT AND BUDGET Ever since Franklin Roosevelt strengthened the presidential staff, the budget bureau (currently called the **Office of Management and Budget**) has been a key resource. OMB's primary task is to prepare the president's annual budget. The budget is a major vehicle for shaping a president's policy priorities. It is the place and the process that determines which programs will get more funds, which will be cut, and which will remain the same. Departments and agencies fight to win larger chunks of the president's budget projections. OMB supervises the preparation of the budget and hence assists very directly in the formulation of policy. It evaluates the merits of the countless proposals and pleas that constantly pour into the White House.

OMB's staffers are career officials trained to evaluate ongoing projects and new spending requests. Its top officials are presidential appointees, and they are often among a president's most important advisers. They help make critical decisions not only about the budget but also about management practices, collaboration among government agencies, and legislative planning. OMB makes sure that both the departments and Congress are informed of the president's legislative preferences, and it plays an important role in expanding the policy and administrative options open to a president.

INFORMAL ORGANIZATION To study a formal organization is only to begin to understand how bureaucracy works, for we also need to understand the informal organization (see Figure 15–2). Bureaucrats differ in attitudes, motives, abilities, experiences, and political clout, and these differences matter. Leadership in an organization is exercised in a variety of places; some officials may have considerably more influence than others with the same formal status. Further, loyalties of officials cut across the formal aims of the agency.

Informal organization can have a significant effect on administration. A subordinate official in an agency may be especially close to the chief because they went to the same college, or because they play racquetball together, or because the subordinate knows how to ingratiate himself with the chief. A staff official may have tremendous influence not because of formal authority but because of experience, fairness, common sense, and personality. If an agency is headed by a chief who is weak or unimaginative, a vacuum may develop that encourages others to take over. Such informal organization and communication, cutting across regular channels, are inevitable in any organization—public or private, civilian or military.

Office of Management and Budget Presidential staff agency that serves as a clearinghouse for budgetary requests and management improvements.

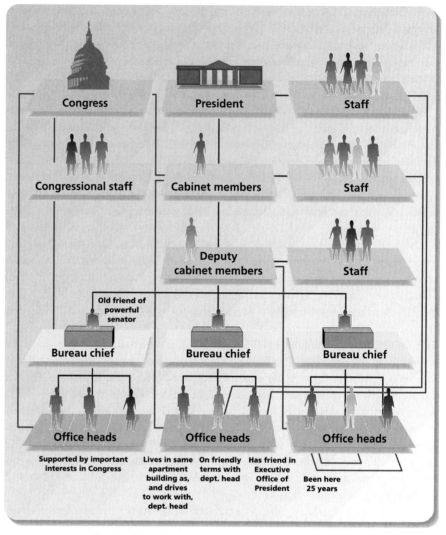

Congress

President

Staff

Congressional staff

Cabinet members

Staff

Deputy cabinet members

Staff

Old friend of powerful senator

Bureau chief

Bureau chief

Bureau chief

Office heads

Office heads

Office heads

Supported by important interests in Congress	Lives in same apartment building as, and drives to work with, dept. head	On friendly terms with dept. head	Has friend in Executive Office of President	Been here 25 years

FIGURE 15–2 Formal and Informal Lines of Communication within the Executive Branch

THE BUREAUCRACY IN ACTION

Hiring Practices and Employee Regulations

Senior government administrators work with the Office of Personnel Management in staffing their agencies. The OPM acts as a policy maker for recruiting, examining, and appointing government workers. It advertises for new employees, prepares and administers oral and written examinations throughout the country, and compiles a roster of names of those who pass the tests. The OPM delegates to the individual agencies the responsibility for hiring new personnel, subject to its standards. Individual agencies may promote people from within or transfer a civil servant from another agency in the government. If, however, they wish to consider an "outsider," they request the OPM to certify possible candidates from its roster of applicants. The OPM typically certifies the top three applicants who have applied for the opening, and the agency normally selects one of these. However, the agency can decide to make no appointment or to request other applicants if it thinks none of the three is qualified.

These procedures are intended to protect the merit principle and to meet agencies' needs for qualified personnel. In practice, the two objectives sometimes come into conflict. Trade-offs have to be made, particularly between central control by OPM and delegation of discretionary authority to the agencies. And sometimes the pursuit of both objectives is enfeebled by the introduction of additional and often incompatible objectives—the veteran preference system, for example.

THE HATCH ACT, OLD AND NEW   In 1939 Congress passed an Act to Prevent Pernicious Political Activities, usually called the **Hatch Act** after its chief sponsor, Senator Carl Hatch of New Mexico. The act was designed to neutralize the danger of a federal civil service being able to shape, if not dictate, the election of presidents and members of Congress. In essence, the Hatch Act permitted federal employees to vote in government elections, but not to take an active part in partisan politics. The Hatch Act also made it illegal to dismiss federal officials below cabinet and subcabinet rank for partisan reasons.[11]

In 1993 Congress, with the encouragement of the Clinton administration, overhauled the Hatch Act and made many forms of participation in partisan politics permissible. The revised Hatch Act still bars federal officials from running as candidates in partisan elections, but it does permit most federal civil servants to hold party positions and involve themselves in party fund raising and campaigning. This new law was welcomed by those who believed the old Hatch Act discouraged political participation by more than 2 million individuals who might otherwise be vigorous political activists.[12]

The new Hatch Act spells out many restrictions on federal bureaucrats; they cannot raise campaign funds in their agencies, and those who work in such highly sensitive federal agencies as the CIA, FBI, Secret Service, and certain divisions of the IRS are specifically barred from nearly all partisan activity. Those who work in the U.S. military have stricter rules regulating their political involvement. The rules for federal civilian employees specify that they:

May register and vote as they choose

May assist in voter registration

May express opinions about candidates and issues

May participate in campaigns as off-duty activities

May contribute money to political organizations or attend political fund-raising functions

May wear or display political badges, buttons, or stickers

May attend political rallies and meetings

May join political clubs or parties

May seek and hold positions in political parties

May campaign for or against referendum questions, constitutional amendments, and municipal ordinances

May not be candidates for public office in partisan elections

May not use official authority to interfere with or affect the results of an election

May not collect contributions or sell tickets to political fund-raising functions from subordinate employees

May not solicit funds or discourage the political activity of any person who has business before the employee's office

May not solicit funds or discourage political activity by any person who is the subject of an ongoing audit, investigation, or enforcement action.

GOVERNMENT EMPLOYEE UNIONS   Since 1962, federal civilian employees have had the right to form unions or associations that represent them in seeking to improve government personnel policies, and about one-third of them have joined such unions. Some of the more important unions representing federal employees

---

Principles of Bureaucratic Management

Followers of the noted German sociologist Max Weber contended that a properly run bureaucracy could be a model of efficiency based on rational and impartial management.* President Woodrow Wilson, when he was a Princeton University professor, adopted many of these views in his writings. Politics and public administration, he said, should be carefully separated. Leave politics to Congress and management to administrators who adhere to the laws passed by Congress.

According to the textbook model, bureaucrats should be closely controlled by established rules and regulations. Although this is not always true in practice, it is generally the case. Administrators are not free to make any rules they wish or to decide disputes any way they please. Several kinds of limitations exist:

1. The legislative power of Congress compels agencies to interpret and apply laws as Congress would wish. Congress can amend a law to make its intent clearer, conduct oversight hearings and investigations, or restrict appropriations.

2. Congress has closely regulated the procedures to be followed by regulatory agencies. Under the Administrative Procedures Act of 1946, agencies must publicize their procedures and organization, give advance information of proposed rules to interested persons, allow such persons to present written information and arguments, and allow parties appearing before the agency to be accompanied by counsel and to cross-examine witnesses.

3. Under certain conditions, final actions of agencies may be appealed to the courts.

4. Some federal agencies are created for the specific purpose of overseeing and limiting their fellow agencies. Examples are the Office of Management and Budget (OMB), which is supervised by the White House, and the General Accounting Office (GAO), which is supervised by Congress.

5. Administrators must keep in mind the demands of professional ethics, the advice and criticism of experts, and the attitudes of Congress, the president, interest groups, political parties, and citizens. In the long run, these informal safeguards may be the most important of all.

This textbook model remains influential because it reflects reality. Laws of Congress, although not the whole story, are an important part of the story. Federal agencies and career servants are creatures of the enabling laws under which they work.

*For an examination of Max Weber's ideas on bureaucracy, see Brian Fry, *Mastering Public Administration: From Max Weber to Dwight Waldo* (Chatham House, 1989).

Hatch Act
Federal statute barring federal employees from active participation in certain kinds of politics and protecting them from being fired on partisan grounds.

today are the American Federation of Government Employees, the National Treasury Employees Union, the National Association of Government Employees, and the National Federation of Federal Employees.

Unlike unions in the private sector, these groups lack the right to strike and are not able to bargain over pay and benefits. What can they do? They can attempt to negotiate better personnel policies and practices for federal workers; they can represent federal bureaucrats at grievance and disciplinary proceedings; and they can also lobby Congress on measures affecting personnel changes.

Challenges in Hiring and Retaining Civil Servants

As the twenty-first century began, it became increasingly clear that federal departments and agencies were having a hard time recruiting talented individuals, partly because of lower wages paid by government, as opposed to the private sector. There is a pay gap of 20–25 percent between comparable federal and private jobs.[13] Moreover, unlike the private sector, federal work rules provide few rewards for performance. And, of course, stock options are nonexistent in the federal government.

Political scientist Paul Light warns that the attractiveness of a federal job has lost some, if not much, of its past luster: "Sad to say, when young Americans are asked to picture themselves in public service careers, particularly at the federal level, they picture themselves in dreaded jobs, where seniority, not performance rules."[14]

Many federal civil servants consider leaving the government because of low pay. Some also find it hard to work for the government when politicians and the media are regularly criticizing their agencies. Another factor that may contribute to lowered morale in the bureaucracy is that innovative performance is more difficult because the federal government, as noted earlier, has an institutional bias in favor of continuity rather than change. Job security and caution are far more the hallmarks of federal bureaucracies than risk-taking and entrepreneurship. Still, talented career and appointed executives in the federal government have transformed programs such as the Federal Emergency Management Agency and the Department of Housing and Urban Development's Office of Community Planning.[15]

Efforts at Reform

A task force on reinventing government in the mid-1990s greatly trimmed the 10,000-page *Federal Personnel Manual*, which had specified everything down to the color of personnel folders. "We actually hauled it out to a dumpster in a wheelbarrow. The death of the manual gave agencies more freedom to tailor things to fit their own operations."[16]

Many federal agencies are changing how they hire people and go about their work. Innovation and customer service have become government priorities. Hierarchical organizations have become structurally somewhat flatter. Applicants can now use regular résumés instead of federal forms in applying for government jobs. A website (www.opm.gov) lets people find out what jobs are available, and applicants can apply by phone or fax for many jobs. And workers are being evaluated and rewarded with bonuses for how well their teams achieve measurable results.

The government has also tried to make the federal bureaucracy a more family-friendly workplace. The Family Leave Act passed in 1993 and other measures or experiments have encouraged job sharing, part-time work, alternative work schedules, telecommuting from home, and child and elder services.

Bureaucratic Realities

Career administrators are in a good position to know when a program is not operating properly and what action is needed. But one of the major complaints about bureaucrats is that they do not go out of their way to make things better. The problem is that many bureaucrats often learn by hard experience that they are more likely to get into trouble by attempting to improve or change programs than if they just do

iron triangle
A mutually supporting relationship among interest groups, congressional committees and subcommittees, and government agencies that share a common policy concern.

nothing. Hardening of administrative arteries is more likely, some critics say, than administrative aggressiveness.

Often the fiercest battles in Washington are not over principles or programs but over jurisdictional boundaries, personnel cuts, and fringe benefits. Career employees come to believe the expansion of their organization is vital to the public interest. They sometimes become more skillful at building political alliances to protect their own organization than at building political alliances to ensure their programs' effectiveness.

Career administrators usually try hard to be nonpartisan, yet they are inevitably involved in politics. Some of them have more bargaining and alliance-building skills than the elected and appointed officials to whom they report. In one sense, agency leaders are at the center of action in Washington. Over time, administrative agencies may come to resemble entrenched pressure groups in that they operate to advance their own interests. The FBI is a good example; it is always seeking more funds, new projects, and as much independence as possible from the Justice Department in which it is located.

The growth of federal programs from the 1930s through the 1970s brought an increase in the number of policy aides on Capitol Hill, of Washington law firms that specialize in assisting clients who are interested in policy development, and of lobbyists (some say at least 40,000) who work with Congress and the federal bureaucracy to advance various economic and professional interests.

Special interest groups that perceive real or potential harm to their interests cultivate the bureau chiefs and agency staffs who have jurisdiction over their programs. They also work closely with the committees and subcommittees of Congress that authorize, appropriate, and oversee programs run by these key bureaucracies. Recognizing the power of interest groups, bureau chiefs frequently recruit them as allies in pursuing common goals. What these bureau officials have in common with interest groups and their allies in Congress is a shared view that more money should be spent on federal programs run by the bureau in question. These alliances among bureaucrats, interest groups, and subcommittee members and their staffs on Capitol Hill are sometimes described as **iron triangles**.

The executive branch is not necessarily the smooth operating hierarchy it is made to appear on an organization chart. The president, cabinet members, and their politically appointed undersecretaries and assistant secretaries have their work cut out for them as they try to impose their will on the permanent civil service. Bureaucrats, with their strong allies in Congress and the interest groups, often resist change and direction from their appointed or elected political "superiors."[17] Some view these external relations as "administrative guerrilla warfare" and a serious roadblock to holding elected leaders accountable. Others view the clash over values as inevitable in a system that provides ample opportunities for such clashes. After all, the bureaucracy is merely one more forum for registering the many demands that people make upon government.

THE CASE OF BUREAU CHIEF GEORGE BROWN

The following case is fictional, yet based on actual experiences of typical bureaucrats. (Note that not only is our main character, George Brown, fictitious, but so are the Bureau of Erosion and the Department of Conservation. Other agencies mentioned do exist. This case illustrates some of the painful choices bureaucrats have to make.)

George Brown, age 47, is chief of the Bureau of Erosion in the Department of Conservation. A graduate of North Dakota State University, Brown is a career official in the federal service and a member of the Senior Executive Service. His appointment to the post was a result of both ability and luck. When his old bureau chief retired, the president wanted to bring in an erosion expert from Illinois, but influential members of Congress pressed for the selection of a recently "retired" (actually he was defeated

THE JAPANESE BUREAUCRACY

In Japan the most prestigious job a college student can aspire to is not a doctor, lawyer, corporate executive, or even a politician. It is to become a top-level member of the national bureaucracy. One recent college graduate who passed the entrance exam for Japan's Ministry of Foreign Affairs (the equivalent of the U.S. State Department) was featured in his local newspaper and received congratulatory messages from his governor and national politicians from his home province.

A comparison of television news programs in Japan and the United States found that 26 percent of the news stories in Japan were about the bureaucracy, whereas only 2 percent in the United States were about the bureaucracy. The most news stories in the United States were about the president (25 percent); in Japan the prime minister was the subject of only 7 percent of news stories.

The popularity of a top-level bureaucratic job is also shown by the recruitment patterns of bureaucrats. More than 50 percent of all of Japan's top bureaucrats graduated from Japan's best university, Tokyo University, with the most difficult major, an undergraduate degree in law. When Japan's second-best university, Kyoto University, is included, fully three-fourths of all Japan's high-level bureaucrats came from these two universities. In Japan, only the best and brightest students go on to elite careers in the national bureaucracy.

SOURCE: Ellis S. Krauss, "Portraying the State: NHK Television News and Politics," in *Media and Politics in Japan*, ed. Susan J. Pharr and Ellis S. Krauss (University of Hawaii Press, 1996).

in the last election!) member of the House of Representatives from a farm state. After deadlock and delay, Brown, then a division head in the Bureau of Erosion, was promoted to bureau chief as a compromise.

Early in March of Brown's second year in his new post, his boss, the secretary of conservation, summoned him and the other bureau heads to an important conference and informed them that he had just attended a cabinet meeting in which the president had called on each department to make at least a 10 percent cut in spending in the coming fiscal year. The president, the secretary reported, was responding to popular demands for federal fiscal restraint.

Brown quickly calculated what this cutback would mean for his agency. For several years the Bureau of Erosion had been spending about $1.7 billion a year to help farmers protect their farmland. Could it get along on about $1.53 billion, and where could savings be made? Returning to his office, Brown called a meeting of his personnel, budget, and management officials. After hours of discussion, it was agreed that savings could be effected only by decreasing the scope of the program, a step that would involve terminating about 400 of the bureau's employees. Brown asked his subordinates to prepare a list of employees who were the least useful to the bureau. He would decide which to drop after checking with the affected members of Congress.

A few weeks later Brown presented a $1.6 billion budget to Conservation Secretary Jones, who approved it and passed it along to the White House. The president then went over the figures with the director of the Office of Management and Budget, and a few weeks later the White House submitted the budget for the whole executive department to Congress.

Meanwhile Brown was running into trouble. News of the proposed budget cut had leaked to the bureau's personnel in the field. Nobody knew who would be dropped, and some employees were already looking around for other positions. Morale fell. Hearing of the cut, farmers' representatives in Washington notified local farm organizations throughout the country. Soon Brown began to receive letters demanding certain services be maintained. Members of the farm bloc in Congress were also becoming restless.

Shortly after the president's budget went to Congress, Representative Jim Smith of Kansas asked Brown to meet with him. Smith was chair of the Subcommittee on Agriculture of the influential House Appropriations Committee. Smith said his fellow subcommittee members, both Democratic and Republican, all agreed the Erosion Bureau's budget must not be cut. The farmers needed even more than the usual $1.7 billion because of severe flood conditions in some sections of the country. He warned that farmers would really be outraged if the program was reduced. Members of Congress from agricultural states, Smith went on, were under tremendous pressure. Leaders of farm groups in Washington were mobilizing farmers everywhere. Besides, Smith said, the president was unfair in cutting down on the farm program; he did not understand agricultural problems, and he failed to recognize that programs designed to increase agricultural output were the best way to reduce the trade imbalance. Let the cuts in federal programs be made elsewhere.

Smith then came to the point. Brown, he said, must vigorously oppose the budget cut. Hearings on appropriations would begin in a few days, and Brown as bureau chief would, of course, testify. At that time he must insist that the cuts would hurt the bureau and undermine its whole program. Brown would not have to volunteer this statement, Smith said. He could just respond to leading questions put by committee members. Brown's testimony, Smith thought, would help clinch the argument against the cut because the committee would respect the judgment of the administrator closest to the problem. Other bureaucrats were fighting to save their appropriations. Obviously, said Smith, they are counting on public reaction to get them exemptions from the 10 percent cutback, and Brown would be foolish not to do the same.

Brown was in an embarrassing position. He had submitted his estimates to the secretary of conservation and to the president, and it was his duty to back them up. The rules of the game demanded, moreover, that agency heads defend budget estimates submitted to Congress, whatever their personal feelings might be. The president had appointed Brown to his position and had a right to expect loyalty. On the other hand, Brown was on the spot with his own agency. His employees all expected their chief to look out for them. Brown had developed cordial relations with his staff, and he squirmed at the thought of having to let more than a thousand employees go. What would they think when they heard him defend the cut? More important, he needed to maintain friendly relations with the farmers, the farm organizations, and the farm bloc in Congress. Finally, Brown was committed to the work of his department. He grasped its true importance, whereas the president's budget advisers did not. And he knew that his pet project—aid to poverty-stricken areas in Appalachia—would probably be sacrificed because it was not supported by a powerful constituency.

Brown turned for advice to an old friend in the Office of Management and Budget. This friend urged him to defend the president's budget. He appealed to Brown's professional pride as an administrator and career public servant. He reminded him that the chief executive must have control of the budget and that agency heads must subordinate their interests to the executive program. He said the only way to balance the budget would be for all agencies to make program cuts. As for the employees to be dropped—well, that was part of the game. Some of them might be able to get jobs in other government agencies; civil service would protect their status. Anyway, they would understand Brown's position. In a parting shot he mentioned that the president had Brown in mind for bigger things.

The next day Brown had lunch with a North Dakota senator, wise and experienced in Washington ways, who had helped him get his start in government. The senator was sympathetic. But there was no doubt about what Brown should do, the senator said. He should follow Representative Smith's plan, of course, being as diplomatic as possible about it. That way he would protect his position with those who would be most important in the long run.

"After all," the senator said, "presidents come and go, parties rise and fall, but Smith and the other members of Congress will be here a long time, and so will the farm organizations. They can do a lot for you in future years. And remember one other thing," the senator concluded. "These people are the elected representatives of the people. Constitutionally, Congress has the power to spend money as it sees fit. Why should you object if they want to spend an extra $78 or $80 million?"

Brown realized his dilemma was worse than ever. The arguments on both sides were persuasive. He felt hopelessly divided in his loyalties and responsibilities. The president expected one thing of him; Congress expected another. As a professional administrator, he felt obliged to side with the president. As head of a bureau, however, he wanted to protect his team and his programs. His future? Whatever decision he made, he was bound to antagonize important people and interests.

Privatization is the process of contracting public services to private organizations. Examples of privatization include the contracting out by the Air Force of the building of fighter planes and the contracting out by several state governments of the construction and operation of prisons. The National Aeronautics and Space Administration contracts out most of the manufacturing of its space vehicles.

Private or nonprofit firms handle a vast array of services, from repairing ships to delivering meals-on-wheels to the home-bound elderly. Some people contend that our public schools might be more effectively operated by private firms. Advocates of privatization claim it would reduce costs and provide better service than reliance on the federal and state bureaucracies.

"Think of it. Presidents come and go, but WE go on forever!"

Berry's World. Reproduced by permission of Newspaper Enterprise Association, Inc.

After much soul searching, Brown decided the issue involved more than loyalties, ambitions, and programs. Ultimately it boiled down to two questions: First, to whom was he, Brown, legally and administratively responsible? Formally, of course, he was responsible to the chief executive who appointed him, who was accountable to the people. Brown knew, too, that he was accountable to Congress, which after all has the power over all fiscal matters. Second, which course of action did he think was better for the welfare of all the people? Looking at the question this way, he believed the president was right in asking for fiscal restraint. As a taxpayer and consumer himself, Brown recognized the need to balance the budget and reduce the national debt. To be sure, Congress must make the final decision. Yet to make the decision, Congress had to act on the advice of the administration, and the administration should speak with one voice for the majority of the people, or it should not be speaking out at all.

With mixed feelings, Brown decided to support the president. Being a seasoned alliance builder, however, he hedged his bets. He came out strongly for the president's budget, yet at the same time he sent friendly members of Congress some questions to be asked of him in congressional hearings so he could explain the impact of the cutbacks. He also circulated to some of these same members of Congress an analysis of the impact of personnel and funding cuts in their states and districts.

BUREAUCRATIC ACCOUNTABILITY

Should bureaucrats be accountable to the president, the cabinet, the majority in Congress, or the people who elected the president? Plainly, most Americans would like the bureaucracy to be responsive to them as taxpaying customers. In general terms, they would say the bureaucracy should be responsive to the public interest. But defining the public interest is the crucial problem. The president and the House and the Senate and the committees of Congress all claim to speak on behalf of the public interest.

To whom bureaucrats should be accountable is an inherently political question. Accountability to the White House, for example, depends in large measure on the supporters' partisanship toward the president. Republicans, not surprisingly, favor strong presidential control over the bureaucracy when Republicans occupy the White House, as do Democrats when their party wins the White House.

To the President

Modern presidents invariably contend the president should be in charge, for the chief executive is responsive to the broadest constituency. A president, it is argued, must see that popular needs and expectations are converted into administrative action. When the nation elects a conservative president who favors cutbacks in federal programs and less governmental intervention in the economy, his policies must be carried out by the bureaucracy. The voters' wishes can be translated into action only if the bureaucrats support presidential policies.

Yet, as we have seen, under the American system of checks and balances the party winning a presidential election does not acquire total control of the national government. Under our Constitution, the president is not even the undisputed master of the executive structure. Presidents come into an ongoing system over which they have little control and within which they have little leeway to make the bureaucracy responsive. Still, some presidential control over the bureaucracy may be exercised through the president's powers of appointment, reorganization, and budgeting. More specifically, a president can attempt to control the bureaucracy by appointing or promoting sympathetic personnel, mobilizing public opinion and congressional pressure, changing the administrative apparatus, influencing budget decisions, using extensive personal persuasion, and if all else fails, shifting a bureaucracy's assignment to another department or agency (although this shift requires tacit if not explicit congressional approval).[18]

Presidents appoint about 4,000 people to top positions within the executive branch; however, many of these are confidential assistants or special aides to cabinet officers who require Senate confirmation and are not exclusively a president's choice. Some critics suggest that a president's hand could be strengthened if the chief executive were able to make two or three times as many political appointments.

To Congress

Congress has a number of ways to exercise control over the bureaucracy: by establishing agencies, formulating budgets, appropriating funds, confirming personnel, authorizing new programs or new shifts in direction, conducting investigations and hearings, reorganizing authority, and rebuking officials.

The foundation of this bureaucratic power is legal authority. A bureaucrat's information and expertise augment this legal authority. Ordinarily, bureaucrats know more than anyone else about their programs and the consequences of what they are doing. Recognizing this, Congress often requests agency heads to frame policy proposals and to provide estimates for the costs of what they propose. Agency heads respond because they know if they fail to provide accurate information, Congress has ways of reducing agency funds.

Most constituents, especially businesspeople, turn to their members of Congress for help as they battle federal red tape. Members of Congress earn political credit by interceding in federal agencies on behalf of their constituents. Still, Congress is under fire, at least in some quarters, for encouraging the growth of federal spending and allowing the bureaucracy to become too independent. Members of Congress, so this reasoning goes, profit from the growth and complexity of the federal government.

The brutal fact is that only a small minority of our 535 members of Congress would trade the present bureaucratic structure for one which was an efficient, effective agent of the general interest—the political payoffs of the latter are lower than those of the former. Congressional talk of inefficient, irresponsible, out-of-control bureaucracy is typically just that—talk—and when it is not, it usually refers to agencies under the jurisdiction of other legislators' committees. Congress can abolish or reorganize an agency. Congress can limit or expand an agency's jurisdiction, or allow its authority to lapse entirely. Congress can slash an agency's appropriations.

Congress called upon Attorney General Janet Reno and FBI Director Louis Freeh to explain why the Justice Department had not investigated fund-raising irregularities by President Clinton and the Democrats in the 1996 presidential campaign.

Thinking It Through . . .

Critics of privatization point to the cost overruns and waste in the procurement of weapons systems as failures of privatization. According to David Osborne and Ted Gaebler, privatization is one answer, but not *the* answer:

Services can be contracted out or turned over to the private sector. But governance cannot. We can privatize discrete [governmental programs], but not the overall process of governance. If we did, we would have no mechanism by which to make collective decisions, no way to set the rules of the marketplace, no means to enforce rules of behavior. We would lose all sense of equity and altruism: services that could not generate a profit, whether housing for the homeless or health care for the poor, would barely exist. . . .

Business does some things better than government, but government does some things better than business. The public sector tends to be better, for instance, at policy management, regulation, ensuring equity, preventing discrimination or exploitation, ensuring continuity and stability of services, and ensuring social cohesion. . . . Business tends to do better at performing economic tasks, innovating, replicating successful experiments, adapting to rapid change, abandoning unsuccessful or obsolete activities, and performing complex or technical tasks.[*]

Would we be better off if the U.S. Postal Service were turned over to private firms? A business executive who served as postmaster general, Anthony Frank, says no. He praises the Postal Service for its high on-time delivery and points out that all Americans, no matter where they live, get essentially the same service at the same price. "If you privatize it," Frank pointed out, "the cost would go up for a lot of Americans." Frank added that it is anywhere from 10 to 100 percent more expensive in most industrial nations, and they seldom have overnight service.[**]

[*]David Osborne and Ted Gaebler, *Reinventing Government: How the Entrepreneurial Spirit Is Transforming the Public Sector* (Addison-Wesley, 1992), pp. 45–46. See also Charles Haddad, "Private Prisons Don't Work," *Business Week*, September 11, 2000, pp. 95–98.

[**]Anthony Frank, quoted in an interview in *USA Today*, January 8, 1992, p. 7A.

Congress can investigate. Congress can do all these things, but individual congressmen generally find reasons not to do so.[19]

Congress, it is charged, anxious whenever possible to avoid conflict, adopts such sweeping legislation and delegates so much authority to the bureaucracy that bureaucrats, in effect, have become the nation's lawmakers. Congress could pass laws with precise wording, but it would get too bogged down in details to complete its work.

It is not Congress as a whole that shares direction over the bureaucracy with the president. More accurately, individual members and committees specialize in the appropriations and oversight processes. They oversee policies of a particular cluster of agencies—often the agencies serving constituents in their own districts. Some legislators stake out a claim over specific areas. Members of Congress, who see presidents come and go, come to think they know more about particular agencies than the president does (and often they do). Some congressional leaders prefer to seal off "their" agencies from presidential direction and maintain their influence over public policy. Sometimes their power is institutionalized; the Army Corps of Engineers, for example, is given authority by law to plan public works and report to Congress without going through the president.

Whose Bureaucracy Is This, Anyway?

Both presidents and members of Congress strive to exercise control over the bureaucracy, and interest groups and court rulings also influence the way the bureaucracy operates. For their part, career bureaucrats say they are responsive to the laws and statutes they work under and to their own standards of professionalism and responsibility. The search for improved means of ensuring bureaucratic accountability is never ending. Experiments with countless reforms—reorganization, deregulating the public service, sunset practices, selective privatization, budgetary planning, and oversight hearings—also continue.

It is increasingly clear, moreover, that virtually all national bureaucracies are more responsive today than once was the case. Even organizations such as the FBI or the Corps of Engineers are now more accountable to Congress and the White House, and ultimately to the American people. "Thanks to Freedom of Information statutes and other 'sunshine' legislation, [the bureaucracy] has become less selective, and the weakening of iron triangles has made it much more responsive to broad constituencies and much less the creature of its own clients."[20]

WHAT THE PUBLIC THINKS OF BUREAUCRATS AND THE BUREAUCRACY

Big bureaucracy in the abstract is unpopular. It engages in many activities that most people find offensive, like taxing, inspecting, or regulating. Big bureaucracy is sometimes defined as that part of the government people dislike.

As individuals, civil servants are appreciated, but as a class they are not. Citizens who have dealings with federal employees on a face-to-face basis say they are pleased by employees' performance. Three-quarters of the public who have dealings with federal bureaucrats find them "helpful" and say bureaucrats treated them "fairly."[21] In contrast to scorn for bureaucrats and bureaucracy in general, Americans seem to approve the conduct of individual federal employees—Postal Service delivery persons, forest rangers, Veterans Affairs Department officials, or county field agents who help with the local 4-H programs. They also admire astronauts, marines, FBI agents, and Coast Guard officers, all of whom are also federal employees.

Red Tape and Waste

Americans are skeptical of, if not cynical about, big government. They equate bigness with remoteness, incompetence, and unresponsiveness. They also assume that the bigger government gets, the less efficient it is, and the more it wastes. Perhaps the most criticized aspect of the federal bureaucracy is that career public employees seem to enjoy the closest thing to job security; they are almost as secure in their jobs as if they were confirmed for life as members of the Supreme Court.

A central problem with the bureaucracy, critics say, is that we have failed to subject it to the control and discipline alleged to operate in the private sector. Despite the talk about numerous federal programs being eliminated or downsized, most federal agencies survive. The tests of efficiency and cost effectiveness that are the basic standards of business are much less important in decisions about which federal programs will survive. Outdated and ineffective programs endure because both Republicans and Democrats have forged coalitions of convenience based on a desire to deliver favors and protect programs located in their particular districts.

Congress throughout the 1990s took steps to downsize federal agencies. It abolished the Interstate Commerce Commission; it called for the gradual privatization of Amtrak; and it scaled back the Environmental Protection Agency, the Bureau of Mines, the Bureau of Indian Affairs, and several scientific advisory boards and projects. Many Republicans in Congress wanted to end support for public broadcasting, saying that *Sesame Street*, *Car Talk*, and *Wall Street Week* would all be picked up by the networks and that today's abundance of cable television channels makes publicly subsidized broadcasting no longer necessary.[22]

A few years ago there was a Republican crusade to dismantle the Departments of Energy, Commerce, Housing and Urban Development, and Education. "But even as they claimed a mandate to end 'big government,' these Republicans discovered that voter sentiment about closing down agencies typically ranged from apathy to uneasiness to outright opposition."[23] Moreover, various interest groups came to the defense of these departments. For example, a coalition of major corporations—including AT&T, IBM, Boeing, General Electric, and Motorola—supported the Commerce Department and its trade promotion and industrial research operations.[24]

In the 2000 election, Republicans avoided the issue of closing down federal departments and stressed instead that we should rely less on the federal government and more on the private sector and "faith-based" institutions such as churches.

Two Cheers for Bureaucracy

Recent efforts by some state and local government levels have made their bureaucracies more entrepreneurial. The cities of St. Paul, Minnesota, and Indianapolis, Indiana, and the states of Florida and Massachusetts have introduced various market incentives, rewards, and public-private partnerships that encourage efficiency and responsiveness.[25] They have shown that competition and incentives can prudently be built into various government monopolies so that bureaucracies become more responsive to their customers.

In the private sector, if you are displeased with the service provided by a company such as AT&T, you can switch to MCI or Sprint, and this is now happening to some government services. It used to be that you could use only the U.S. Postal Service to deliver your messages, whether you liked the service or not. Now numerous delivery services compete with the postal service; fax and e-mail have become popular means of communication. (It should be noted that the postal service is getting better—credit this to the competition.)

A comparison of the performance of the U.S. bureaucracy with most bureaucracies in the world suggests we should be grateful for the service we get from our

Among its proposed reforms of the bureaucracy, Congress wanted to end support of public broadcasting, claiming that programs like Sesame Street *could support themselves on commercial television. The public, however, disagreed, and Big Bird, the Grouch, and other childhood favorites still receive government subsidies.*

public employees. The U.S. Postal Service provides a good example. Although it is sometimes criticized as being a dinosaur, it is more efficient and less costly than comparable services around the world. Another example is the United States tax system; although it is constantly cursed and has been properly chided for its abuses of power, it is the most effective and efficient such system in the world.

POLITICS ONLINE

Want To Be a Bureaucrat?

Close to 90,000 different agencies exist in federal, state, and local government. You may wonder what all these agencies do and why they employ so many people. The Internet provides excellent resources for understanding these questions. The website for this text has prepared an Interactive graphic that will allow you to match some government agencies with what they do. This graphic is located at: www.amgovtplace.com/interactivegraphics/bureaucracy.html.

In addition, each agency or department usually has its own website. A complete listing of federal agencies can be found at:
www.lib.lsu.edu/gov/fedgovall.html. The site contains links to each agencies' home page.

Most of these agencies are constantly looking for interns and full-time employees. It is estimated that over 25,000 government positions are open on any given day. From research to law enforcement, the government employs people in virtually every field. For detailed information on federal employment opportunities, go to the Office of Personnel Management site at:
www.opm.gov or to the federal employment search engine at:
www.fedworld.gov/jobs/jobsearch.html.

State and local jobs are also available and information about them can be found at city and state home pages. Information on accessing these sites will be available in later chapters.

SUMMARY

1. Bureaucracy's chief characteristics are continuity, predictability, impartiality, standard operating procedures, and the inevitable "red tape." Our bureaucratic agencies reflect how our political system has tried to identify our most important national goals and how policies are implemented.

2. We often condemn bureaucracy and bureaucrats, yet we continue to turn to them to solve our toughest problems and to render more and better services. In the last decade there have been major efforts to overhaul and improve the workings of the federal bureaucracy. Despite numerous initiatives to streamline the government, eliminate waste, and make government more like an effective business, critics continue to call for less bureaucracy and more reforms.

3. Most of the 2.8 million civilian employees of the federal government serve under a merit system that protects their independence of politics. They work in one of the 14 cabinet departments as well as government corporations, independent agencies, and independent regulatory boards or commissions. A major responsibility is policy implementation.

4. The federal government's Office of Personnel Management sets policy for recruiting and evaluating federal workers. Various restrictions exist on federal workers that prevent them from running for political office or political party fund-raising activities. The federal bureaucracy general prizes continuity, stability, and following the rules more than risk-taking or innovation.

5. The American bureaucracy has at least two immediate bosses: Congress and the president. It must pay considerable attention as well to the courts and their rulings and, of course, to well-organized interest groups and public opinion. In many ways the bureaucracy is a semi-independent force—a fourth branch of government—in American politics.

6. Debates and controversy over big government and big bureaucracy, and over how to reorganize and eliminate waste in them, continue. Compared with many other nations and their centralized bureaucracies, the hand of bureaucracy rests more gently and less oppressively on Americans than on citizens elsewhere. Efforts to make the bureaucracy more responsive are enduring struggles in a constitutional democracy.

KEY TERMS

bureaucrat 344
bureaucracy 344
spoils system 344
merit system 346

Office of Personnel Management (OPM) 346
bureau 348
government corporation 348

independent agency 348
independent regulatory board 348

Office of Management and Budget 349
Hatch Act 351
iron triangle 352

FURTHER READING

JOEL D. ABERBACH, *Keeping a Watchful Eye: The Politics of Congressional Oversight* (Brookings Institution, 1990).

DAN BAUM, *Smoke and Mirrors: The War on Drugs and the Politics of Failure* (Little, Brown, 1996).

BARRY BOZEMAN, *Bureaucracy and Red Tape* (Prentice Hall, 2000).

SHELLEY L. DAVIS, *Unbridled Power: Inside the Secret Culture of the IRS* (Harper Business, 1997).

JOHN J. DIIULIO, JR., ED., *Deregulating the Public Service: Can Government Be Improved?* (Brookings Institution, 1994).

JOHN J. DIIULIO, JR., GERALD GARVEY, AND DONALD F. KETTL, *Improving Government Performance: An Owner's Manual* (Brookings Institution, 1993).

JOHN D. DONAHUE, ED., *Making Washington Work: Tales of Innovation in the Federal Government* (Brookings Institution, 1999).

JAMES W. FESLER AND DONALD F. KETTL, *The Politics of the Administrative Process* (Chatham House, 1991).

CHARLES T. GOODSELL, *The Case for Bureaucracy*, 3d ed. (Chatham House, 1994).

AL GORE, *The Best Kept Secrets in Government: How the Clinton Administration Is Reinventing the Way Washington Works* (Random House, 1996).

AL GORE, *Creating a Government That Works Better and Costs Less: The Report of the National Performance Review* (Plume-Penguin, 1993).

PHILIP K. HOWARD, *The Death of Common Sense: How Law Is Suffocating America* (Random House, 1994).

RONALD N. JOHNSON AND GARY D. LIBECAP, *The Federal Civil Service System and the Problem of Bureaucracy* (University of Chicago Press, 1994).

HERBERT KAUFMAN, *The Administrative Behavior of Federal Bureau Chiefs* (Brookings Institution, 1981).

DONALD F. KETTL, *Reinventing Government: A Fifth Year Report Card* (Brookings Institution, 1998).

ANDREW KOHUT, ED., *Deconstructing Distrust: How Americans View Government* (Pew Research Center for the People and the Press, 1998).

PAUL C. LIGHT, *The New Public Service* (Brookings Institution, 1999).

PAUL C. LIGHT, *Thickening Government: Federal Hierarchy and the Diffusion of Accountability* (Brookings Institution, 1995).

PAUL C. LIGHT, *The Tides of Reform: Making Government Work, 1945–1995* (Yale University Press, 1997).

DAVID OSBORNE AND TED GAEBLER, *Reinventing Government: How the Entrepreneurial Spirit Is Transforming the Public Sector* (Addison-Wesley, 1992).

DAVID OSBORNE AND PETER PLASTRIK, *Banishing Bureaucracy: The Five Strategies for Reinventing Government* (Addison-Wesley, 1997).

JAMES Q. WILSON, *Bureaucracy: What Government Agencies Do and Why They Do It* (Basic Books, 1989).

Four useful journals are *Journal of Policy Analysis and Management, National Journal, Public Administration Review,* and *Government Executive.*

16

FIRST AMENDMENT FREEDOMS

"**C**ONGRESS SHALL MAKE NO LAW," DECLARES
THE FIRST AMENDMENT, "RESPECTING AN ESTABLISHMENT
OF RELIGION, OR PROHIBITING THE FREE EXERCISE THEREOF,
or abridging the freedom of speech, or of the press, or the right of the people peaceably
to assemble, and to petition the Government for a redress of grievances." In this one sentence our Constitution lays down the fundamental principles of a free society: freedom
of conscience and freedom of expression. These freedoms are essential to our individual
self-determination and to our collective self-governance—to government by the people.

Yet these freedoms were not constitutionally guaranteed until the addition in 1791
of the first ten amendments, the Bill of Rights. For that reason, we begin this chapter by
discussing the rights in the original Constitution and in the Bill of Rights as applied to
both the national and state governments before turning to the "first freedoms" of religion, speech, press, and assembly.

RIGHTS IN THE ORIGINAL CONSTITUTION

Even though most of the framers did not think a Bill of Rights was necessary, they
considered certain rights important enough to be spelled out in the Constitution.
These rights included the writ of *habeas corpus* and protection against *ex post facto* laws
and bills of attainder.

Foremost among constitutional rights is the **writ of *habeas corpus***. Literally
meaning "produce the body," this writ is a court order directing any official having a
person in custody to produce the prisoner in court and explain why the prisoner is
being held. As originally used, the writ was merely a judicial inquiry to determine
whether a person in custody was being held as the result of the action of a court with
proper jurisdiction. But over the years it developed into a remedy for any illegal confinement. People being held can appeal to a judge, usually through an attorney, stating
why they believe they are held unlawfully and should be released. The judge then orders
the jailer or a lower court to show cause why the writ should not be issued. If a judge
finds a petitioner is detained unlawfully, the judge may order the prisoner's immediate
release. Although state judges lack jurisdiction to issue writs of *habeas corpus* to find
out why federal authorities are holding persons, federal district judges may do so to
find out if state and local officials are holding people in violation of the Constitution
or national laws.

CHAPTER MEDIA

POLITICS ONLINE

*Surf Watch: Pornography on
the Internet*
www.prenhall.com/burns

At the outset it is helpful to clarify certain terms—liberties, rights, freedoms, and privileges—that are often used interchangeably in discussions of rights and freedoms. We offer these definitions:

Civil liberties: The freedoms of all persons that are constitutionally protected against governmental restraint; the freedoms of conscience, religion, and expression, for example, which are secured by the First Amendment. These civil liberties are also protected by the due process and equal protection clauses of the Fifth and Fourteenth Amendments.

Civil rights: The constitutional rights of all persons, not just citizens, to due process and the equal protection of the laws; the constitutional right not to be discriminated against by governments because of race, ethnic background, religion, or gender. These civil rights are protected by the due process and equal protection clauses of the Fifth and Fourteenth Amendments and by the civil rights laws of national and state governments.

Rights of persons accused of crimes: The rights of all persons, guilty as well as innocent, to protection from abusive use by the government of the power to prosecute and punish persons accused of violating criminal laws. These rights are secured by the Fourth, Fifth, Sixth, Eighth, and Fourteenth Amendments.

Political rights: The rights of citizens to participate in the process of governance flowing from the right to vote. These rights are secured by the Fourteenth, Fifteenth, Nineteenth, and Twenty-third Amendments.

Legal privileges: Privileges granted by governments to which we have no constitutional right and which may be subject to conditions or restrictions; for example, the right to welfare benefits or to a driver's license. But once such privileges are granted, we may have a legal right to them, and they cannot be denied except for "reasonable reasons" and by appropriate procedures.

Common law: Judge-made law based on the interpretation and application of legal principles—the principle of freedom of speech, for example. Australia, England, and the United States are *common law* countries, in contrast with *civil law* countries on the European Continent.

Civil law: It evolved from Roman law and is based on codes that are strictly applied by judges. The term *civil law* also refers to law that applies to disputes between individuals and the government that carry no criminal penalties.

writ of *habeas corpus*

A court order requiring explanation to a judge why a prisoner is held in custody.

ex post facto law

Retroactive criminal law that works to the disadvantage of an individual; forbidden in the Constitution.

In recent years, the use of the writ of *habeas corpus* by federal courts to review convictions by state courts has been widely criticized. Some people believe the writ has been abused by state prisoners to get an endless and expensive round of reviews, which sometimes lead to convictions being set aside by a federal judge after the matter has been reviewed by two or more state courts. Partly because of concerns about maintaining the principles of federalism, and partly because of the growing caseloads of federal courts, the Supreme Court and Congress have severely restricted the *habeas corpus* discretion of federal judges. The Antiterrorism and Effective Death Penalty Act of 1996, for example, restricts the number of times a person may be granted a *habeas corpus* review, stops appeals for most *habeas* petitions at the level of the U.S. Court of Appeals, and calls for deference by federal judges to the decisions of state judges unless they are clearly "unreasonable."[1]

An ***ex post facto* law** is a retroactive criminal law making a particular act a crime that was not a crime when an individual committed it, or increasing punishment for a crime after the crime was committed, or lessening the proof necessary to convict for a crime after it was committed. This constitutional prohibition does not prevent the retroactive application of laws that work to the benefit of an accused person—a law decreasing punishment, for example—or prevent the retroactive application of civil law, such as an increase in income tax rates applied to income already earned.

Bills of attainder are legislative acts inflicting punishment, including deprivation of property, without a trial on named individuals or members of a specified group. For example, Congress enacted a bill of attainder when it accused three federal employees of being disloyal in an appropriations bill and fired them.

THE BILL OF RIGHTS AND THE STATES

Although it was the framers who wrote the Constitution, in a sense it was the American people who drafted our basic charter of rights. As we saw in Chapter 1, the Constitution drawn up in Philadelphia included guarantees of a few basic rights, but it lacked a specific bill of rights similar to those in most state constitutions. The Federalists argued that the Constitution established a limited government that would not threaten individual freedoms, and therefore a bill of rights was unnecessary. The Anti-Federalists were not persuaded, and the omission aroused widespread suspicion. As a result, in order to persuade delegates to the state ratification conventions to vote for the Constitution, the Federalists promised to correct this deficiency. In its first session, the new Congress made good on that promise by proposing 12 amendments, 10 of which were ratified and became part of the Constitution.[2]

Note that the Bill of Rights literally *applies only to the national government*, not state governments.[3] Why not the states? The framers were confident that states could control their own state officials, and most state constitutions already had bills of rights. It was the new and distant central government the people feared. As it turned out, those fears were largely misdirected. The national government has generally shown less tendency to curtail civil liberties than have state and local governments.

When the Fourteenth Amendment, which does apply to the states, was adopted in 1868, supporters contended that its **due process clause**—which states that no person shall be deprived of life, liberty, or property without due process of law—limits states in precisely the same way the Bill of Rights limits the national government. At least, they argued, freedom of speech is protected by the Fourteenth Amendment. But for decades the Supreme Court refused to interpret the Fourteenth Amendment in this way. Then in *Gitlow v New York* (1925), the Court announced that it assumed "that freedom of speech and of the press—which are protected by the First Amendment from abridgment by Congress—are among the fundamental personal rights and 'liberties' protected by the due process clause of the Fourteenth Amendment from impairment by the States."[4]

Gitlow v New York was a revolutionary decision. For the first time, the U.S. Constitution protected freedom of speech from abridgment by state and local governments. In the 1930s and continuing at an accelerated pace during the 1960s, through the **selective incorporation** of provision after provision of the Bill of Rights into the due process clause, the Supreme Court applied various rights to the states.[5] Today the Fourteenth Amendment imposes on the states all the provisions of the Bill of Rights except those of the Second and Third Amendments, the Fifth Amendment provision for indictment by a grand jury, the Seventh Amendment right to a jury trial in civil cases, and the Ninth and Tenth Amendments (see Table 16–1).

BRITAIN ACQUIRES PROTECTION FOR FREEDOM OF EXPRESSION

After hundreds of years without constitutional guarantees for freedom of expression, the European Convention on Human Rights became the law of the land for Great Britain on October 2, 2000. The convention defines and puts on paper certain human rights—freedom of expression, the right to a fair trial, privacy, among other rights—for the first time in Britain. British courts now increasingly look to the European Convention and how it has been interpreted and applied by courts on the continent.

For further discussion, see Donald W. Jackson, *The United Kingdom Confronts the European Convention on Human Rights* (University of Florida Press, 1997); also Alec Stone Sweet, *Governing with Judges: Constitutional Politics in Europe* (Oxford University Press, 2000).

TABLE 16–1 Selective Incorporation and the Application of the Bill of Rights to the States

Right	Amendment	Year
Public use and just compensation for the taking of private property by the government	5	1897
Freedom of speech	1	1925
Freedom of the press	1	1931
Fair trial	6	1932
Freedom of religion	1	1934
Freedom of assembly	1	1937
Free exercise of religion	1	1940
Separation of religion and government	1	1947
Right to a public trial	6	1948
Right against unreasonable searches and seizures	4	1949
Freedom of association	1	1958
Exclusionary rule	4	1961
Ban against cruel and unusual punishment	8	1962
Right to counsel in felony cases	6	1963
Right against self-incrimination	5	1964
Right to confront witness	6	1965
Right of privacy	1,3,4,5,9	1965
Right to impartial jury	6	1966
Right to a speedy trial and to compulsory process for obtaining witnesses	6	1967
Right to jury trial in nonpetty cases	6	1968
Right against double jeopardy	5	1969

bill of attainder
Legislative act inflicting punishment, including deprivation of property, without a trial, on named individuals or members of a specific group.

due process clause
Clause in the Fifth Amendment limiting the power of the national government; similar to clause in the Fourteenth Amendment prohibiting state governments from depriving any person of life, liberty, or property without due process of law.

selective incorporation
The process by which provisions of the Bill of Rights are brought within the scope of the Fourteenth Amendment and so applied to state and local governments.

1. Writ of *habeas corpus*

2. No bills of attainder

3. No *ex post facto* laws

4. No titles of nobility

5. Trial by jury in national courts

6. Protection for citizens as they move from one state to another, including the right to travel

7. Protection against using crime of treason to restrict other activities; limitation on punishment for treason

8. Guarantee that each state has a republican form of government

9. No religious test oaths as a condition for holding a federal office.

Selective incorporation of most provisions of the Bill of Rights into the Fourteenth Amendment is probably the most important constitutional development since the writing of the Constitution. It has profoundly altered the relationship between the national government and the states. It made the federal courts, under the guidance of the Supreme Court of the United States, the most important protectors of our liberties.

Recently, however, there has been a renewal of interest in state constitutions as independent sources of additional protection for civil liberties and civil rights.[6] Advocates of what has come to be called *new judicial federalism* contend that the U.S. Constitution should set minimum but not maximum standards to protect our rights. State bills of rights sometimes provide more protection of rights—the rights to equal education and personal privacy, for instance—than does the national Bill of Rights or the Supreme Court's rulings on its guarantees. Despite the revival of interest in state bills of rights, the U.S. Supreme Court and the national Bill of Rights remain the dominant protectors of civil liberties and civil rights.

FREEDOM OF RELIGION

The first words of the First Amendment are emphatic and brief: "Congress shall make no law respecting an *establishment* of religion, or prohibiting the *free exercise* thereof." Note there are *two* religion clauses: the establishment clause and the exercise clause. The Supreme Court has struggled to reconcile these two clauses, both of which are cast in absolute terms, and either of which, if expanded to a logical extreme, would clash with the other. Does a state scholarship for blind students given to a college student who decides to attend a college to become a minister violate the establishment clause by indirectly aiding religion? Or would denying the scholarship violate the student's free exercise of religion? The Supreme Court has held that giving such benefits does not violate the establishment clause.[7]

The Establishment Clause

In writing what has come to be called the **establishment clause**, the framers were reacting to the English system, wherein the Crown was the head not only of the government but also of the established church—the Church of England—and public officials were required to take an oath to support the established church as a condition of holding office. The establishment clause goes beyond merely separating government from religion by forbidding the establishment of a religion. It is designed to prevent three evils: government sponsorship of religion, government financial support of religion, and government involvement in religious matters. However, the clause does not prevent governments from "accommodating" religious needs. To what extent and under which conditions governments may accommodate these needs are at the heart of much of the debate in the Supreme Court and the country over interpreting the clause.

Controversies over the establishment clause are not easy to resolve. They stir deep feelings and frequently divide the justices among themselves. The prevailing interpretation stems from the decision in *Everson v Board of Education* (1947) that the establishment clause creates a "wall of separation" between church and state and prohibits any law or governmental action designed to specifically benefit any religion, even if all religions are treated the same.[8] That decision, though, was decided by a bare majority and upheld state support for transportation of children to private religious schools as a "child benefit."

The separation of church and state was further elaborated in *Lemon v Kurtzman* (1971), which laid down a three-part test: (1) a law must have a secular legislative purpose; (2) it must neither advance nor inhibit religion; and (3) it

establishment clause

Clause in the First Amendment that states that Congress shall make no law respecting an establishment of religion. It has been interpreted by the Supreme Court to forbid governmental support of any or all religions.

must avoid "excessive government entanglement with religion."[9] This so-called *Lemon* test is often, but not always, used because the justices remain divided over how much separation between government and religion is required by the First Amendment.

Another test, championed by Justice Sandra Day O'Connor, is the *endorsement test.* Justice O'Connor believes that the establishment clause forbids governmental practices that a reasonable observer would view as endorsing religion, even if there is no coercion.[10] The endorsement test has been honed in a series of decisions as the Court struggled with the question of whether governments may allow religious symbols to be displayed on, in, or near public properties and in public places. For example, the Court concluded that when a nativity scene was displayed in a shopping district together with Santa's house and other secular and religious symbols of the Christmas season, there was little danger that a reasonable person would conclude that the city was endorsing religion.[11] But the Constitution does not permit a city government to display the nativity scene on the steps of the city hall, because, in this context, the city gives the impression that it is endorsing the display's religious message.[12]

The Court's three most conservative justices—Chief Justice William Rehnquist and Justices Antonin Scalia and Clarence Thomas—support a *nonpreferentialist test.*[13] They believe the Constitution prohibits favoritism toward any particular religion but does not prohibit government aid to *all* religions. In their view, government may accommodate religious activities and even give nonpreferential support to religious organizations, so long as individuals are not legally coerced into participating in religious activities, and religious activities are not singled out for favorable treatment.

By contrast, the more liberal justices—Justices David H. Souter, John Paul Stevens, Ruth Bader Ginsburg, and Stephen Breyer—usually maintain that there should be *strict separation* between religion and the state.[14] They generally hold that even indirect aid for religion, such as scholarships or teaching materials and aids for students attending private religious schools, crosses the line separating the government from religion.

Applying these generalizations, we find that the establishment clause forbids states—including state universities, colleges, and school districts—from introducing

Prayer Before School Football Games

The school prayer issue occasioned a spirited argument at the Supreme Court during which a majority of the justices expressed reluctance to permit organized prayer at public high school football games. Such prayers almost inevitably give official endorsement to religious beliefs that may offend some students and parents.

The case started when a Mormon family and a Roman Catholic family sued a small school district in Texas, objecting to the Christian prayers offered by chaplains at school events. Since then, the district has modified its policies to have a student chosen in a schoolwide election offer a pregame invocation or message of his or her own choosing. The district is trying to persuade the court that prayer led by such an "independent speaker" creates no constitutional problem—unlike clergy-led prayer at graduation, which the court outlawed in a decision eight years ago.

It proved a difficult sell. Six justices suggested that using an elected student surrogate to deliver the prayer could not mask the school's role in organizing the religious worship or overcome the risk of indirect coercion inherent in prayer exercises in elementary and secondary schools.

SOURCE: *Santa Fe Independent School District v Doe*, 120 S. Ct. 2266 (2000).

Court cases have sought to prohibit prayers before football games because they coerce students of all faiths to participate in a school-sponsored religious ceremony.

A Closer Look

AID FOR CHILDREN ATTENDING PAROCHIAL SCHOOLS

A troublesome area concerning the separation of church and state involves attempts by many states to provide financial assistance to students who attend parochial schools. The Supreme Court has tried to draw a line between permissible tax-provided aid to schoolchildren and impermissible aid to religion.

At the college level the problems are relatively simple. Tax funds may be used to construct buildings and operate educational programs at church-related schools, as long as the money is not spent directly on buildings used for religious purposes or on teaching religious subjects. Even if students choose to attend religious schools and become ministers, government aid to these students is permissible, because such aid has a secular purpose. Its effect on religion is the result of individual choice "and it does not confer any message of state endorsement of religion."[*]

At the elementary and secondary levels, however, the constitutional problems become more complicated. Here the secular and religious parts of institutions and instruction are much more closely interwoven. Also, students are younger and more susceptible to indoctrination, so the chances are greater that aid to church-operated schools might become aid to religion.

Despite the constitutional obstacles, some states have provided tax credits or deductions for those who send their children to private, largely church-affiliated schools. Such deductions or credits available *only* to parents of children attending nonpublic schools are unconstitutional, but allowing tax-paying parents to deduct or take a credit from their state income taxes for what they paid for tuition and other costs to send their children to school—public or private—is constitutional, even if most of the benefit goes to those who send their children to private religious schools.[**]

The Supreme Court has also approved using tax funds to provide students who attend primary and secondary church-operated schools (except those that deny admission because of race or religion) with textbooks, standardized tests, lunches, transportation to and from school, and diagnostic services for speech and hearing problems. For example, the Court upheld the assignment of a sign-language interpreter, paid for by public funds, to accompany a deaf child to a parochial school on the ground that this is aid to the student, not to a religion.[***] And the Court recently upheld programs that provide tax-supported teachers to teach remedial and enrichment classes to dis-

advantaged students, as well as programs providing computers in both public and parochial schools.[****]

Tax funds may *not* be used in religious schools to pay teachers' salaries, purchase equipment, produce teacher-prepared tests, repair facilities, or transport students on field trips. School authorities may not permit religious instructors to come into public school buildings during the school day to provide *religious* instruction, even on a voluntary basis.

A hot controversy remains whether states may use tax money to give parents vouchers for the tuition of children to attend schools of their choice, including religious schools. Cleveland, Milwaukee, and Florida have experimented with vouchers, but their programs have been challenged in the courts. Opponents argue that such voucher programs violate the establishment clause, while supporters counter that they do not, and to deny the use of vouchers for attending religious schools violates the free exercise clause. The Supreme Court has yet to rule on the matter.

[*]*Witters v Washington Department of Services for the Blind*, 474 US 481 (1986).

[**]*Mueller v Allen*, 463 US 388 (1983).

[***]*Zobrest v Catalina Foothills School District*, 515 US 1 (1993).

[****]*Agostini v Felton*, 521 US 74 (1997); *Mitchell v Helms*, 120 S.Ct. 2530 (2000).

---

devotional exercises into the public school curriculum, including school graduations and pre–football game events.[15] However, the Supreme Court has not, as some people assume, entirely prohibited prayer in public schools. It is not unconstitutional for students to pray in a school building. What is unconstitutional is sponsorship or encouragement of prayer *by public school authorities*.[16] Devotional reading of the Bible, recitation of the Lord's Prayer, and posting of the Ten Commandments on the walls of classrooms in public schools are also prohibited by the Constitution. A state may not forbid the teaching of evolution or require the teaching of "creation science"—the belief that human life did not evolve but rather was created by a single act of God.[17]

Tax exemptions for church properties, similar to those granted other nonprofit institutions, are constitutional. State legislatures and Congress may also hire chaplains to open each day's legislative session—a practice that has continued without interruption since the first session of Congress. But if done in a public school, this practice would be unconstitutional. Apparently, the difference is that legislators, as adults, are not "susceptible to religious indoctrination or peer pressure."[18] Also, as the joke goes, legislators need the prayer more.

The Free Exercise Clause

The right to hold any or no religious belief is one of our few absolute rights. The **free exercise clause** affirms that no government has authority to compel us to accept any creed or to deny us any right because of our beliefs or lack of them. Requiring religious oaths as a condition of public employment or as a prerequisite to running for public office is unconstitutional. In fact, the original Constitution states: "No religious Test shall ever be required as a Qualification to any Office or public Trust under the United States" (Article VI).

Although carefully protected, the right to practice a religion has had less protection than the right to hold particular beliefs. Prior to 1990 the Supreme Court carefully scrutinized laws allegedly infringing on religious practices and insisted that the government provide some compelling governmental interest to justify actions that might infringe upon somebody's religion: In other words, the First Amendment was thought to throw "a mantle of protection" around religious practices, and the burden was on the government to justify interfering with them in the least restrictive way.

Then, in *Employment Division v Smith* (1990), the Rehnquist Court significantly altered the interpretation of the free exercise clause by discarding the compelling governmental interest test for overriding the interests of religious minorities.[19] As long as a law is generally applicable and does not single out and ban religious practices, the law may be applied to conduct even if it burdens a particular religious practice.

The ruling in *Employment Division v Smith* was controversial and led Congress to enact the Religious Freedom Restoration Act of 1993 (RFRA), which aimed to override the *Smith* decision and to restore the earlier test prohibiting the government—federal, state, or local—from limiting a person's exercise of religion unless the government demonstrates a compelling interest that is advanced by the least restrictive means. Congress asserted its power to pass RFRA because the Fourteenth Amendment gives it the authority to enforce rights secured by that amendment, including the right to free exercise of religion.

However, when the Catholic archbishop of San Antonio was denied a building permit in 1997 to enlarge a church in Boerne, Texas, because the remodeling did not comply with the city's historical preservation plan, he claimed that the city's denial of a building permit interfered with religious freedom as protected by the Religious Freedom Restoration Act. The Supreme Court then ruled RFRA to be unconstitutional because Congress was attempting to define—rather than enforce or remedy—constitutional rights and thereby was assuming the role of the courts, which contradicted "vital principles necessary to maintain separation of powers and the federal balance."[20]

Tensions between the establishment and free exercise clauses have recently become more prominent. On the one hand, the University of Virginia denied a Christian student group funds to pay for the printing of its newspaper, *Wide Awake*, because it interpreted the establishment clause to forbid allocating student fee money to a newspaper that "primarily promotes a belief in or about a deity." The students argued that the university deprived them of their freedom of speech, including religious speech, and the Supreme Court agreed with the students.[21] On the other hand, some Christian students at the University of Wisconsin objected to the use of mandatory student activity fees for funding groups they deemed offensive and contrary to their religious beliefs. They argued that they should be exempt from paying that portion of their fees, but the Supreme Court rejected their claim.[22]

Reverend Anthony Cummins, pastor of St. Peter the Apostle Church, in front of his church in Boerne, Texas, after a battle with city officials who denied the church permission to build an addition to the historic structure.

free exercise clause
Clause in the First Amendment that states that Congress shall make no law prohibiting the free exercise of religion. Children may pray in public schools, provided that the prayer is not authorized, organized, or endorsed by the school authorities.

You Decide . . .

Should the Bill of Rights be amended to prohibit flag burning?

The American flag arouses patriotic emotions in Americans, many of whom fought and saw friends die under that banner. It is understandable that they would be angry to see that flag burned by protesters. Do you think the Constitution should be amended to give Congress the right to prohibit desecration of the American flag? Or would a constitutional amendment to prohibit flag burning be an unconstitutional violation of free speech?

bad tendency test
Interpretation of the First Amendment that would permit legislatures to forbid speech that has a tendency to cause people to engage in illegal action.

clear and present danger test
Interpretation of the First Amendment that holds government cannot punish a person for speech unless the speech presents a clear and present danger that it will lead to illegal acts. To shout "Fire!" falsely in a crowded theater is Justice Oliver Wendell Holmes's famous example.

preferred position doctrine
Interpretation of the First Amendment that holds that freedom of expression is so essential to the operation of a democracy that judges should give it special protection and should almost never allow governments to punish persons for what they say, only for what they do.

nonprotected speech
Libel, obscenity, fighting words, and commercial speech, which are not entitled in all circumstances to constitutional protection.

FREE SPEECH AND FREE PEOPLE

Government by the people is based on every person's right to speak freely, to organize in groups, to question the decisions of the government, and to campaign openly against them. Only through free and uncensored expression of opinion can government be kept responsive to the electorate and political power transferred peacefully. Elections, separation of powers, and constitutional guarantees are meaningless unless all persons have the right to speak frankly and to hear and judge for themselves the worth of what others have to say. As Justice Oliver Wendell Holmes observed, "The best test of truth is the power of the thought to get itself accepted in the competition of the market. . . . That at any rate is the theory of our Constitution. It is an experiment, as all life is an experiment."[23]

Free speech is not simply the personal right of individuals to have their say; it is also the right of the rest of us to hear them. John Stuart Mill, whose *Essay on Liberty* (1859) is the classic defense of free speech, put it this way:

> The peculiar evil of silencing the expression of opinion, is that it is robbing the human race. . . . If the opinion is right, they are deprived of the opportunity of exchanging error for truth; if wrong, they lose what is almost as great a benefit, the clearer perception and livelier impression of truth, produced by its collision with error.[24]

Americans overwhelming support the principle of freedom of expression in general. Yet some who say they believe in free speech draw the line at ideas they consider dangerous, or when speech is directed at them or is critical of their race, religion, or ethnic origin. But what is a dangerous idea? Who decides? In the realm of political ideas, who can find an objective, eternally valid standard of right? The search for truth involves the possibility—even the inevitability—of error. The search cannot go on unless it proceeds freely in the minds and speech of all. This means, in the words of Justice Robert Jackson, "Freedom to differ is not limited to things that do not matter much. That would be a mere shadow of freedom. The test of its substance is the right to differ as to things that touch the heart of the existing order."[25]

Even though the First Amendment explicitly denies Congress the power to pass any law abridging freedom of speech, the amendment has never been interpreted in absolute terms. Like almost all rights, the freedoms of speech and of the press are limited. In discussing the constitutional power of government to regulate speech, it is useful to distinguish among *belief*, *speech*, and *action*.

At one extreme is the right to *believe* as we wish. Despite occasional deviations in practice, the traditional American view is that government should not punish a person for beliefs or interfere in any way with the freedom of conscience. At the other extreme is *action*, which is usually subject to governmental restraint. As has been said, "The right to swing your arm ends where the other person's nose begins."

Speech stands somewhere between belief and action. It is not an absolute right, as is belief, but neither is it as exposed to governmental restraint, as is action. Some kinds of speech—libel, obscenity, fighting words, and commercial speech—are not entitled in all circumstances to constitutional protection. Many problems arise in distinguishing between what does and does not fit into the categories of nonprotected speech. People disagree, and it usually falls upon the courts to decide and to defend the free speech of individual and minority dissenters.

The Act of Judging: Line-Drawing

Plainly, questions of free speech require that judges weigh a variety of factors: What was said? Where was it said? How was it said? Which level of government is attempting to regulate the speech—a city council speaking for a few people, or the Congress speaking for many? (The Supreme Court is much more deferential to acts of Congress than to those of a city council or state legislature.) How is the government attempting to regulate the speech—by prior restraint (censorship) or by punishment after the speech? Why is the government doing so—to preserve the public peace or to prevent criticism of those in power? These and scores of other considerations are involved in the never-ending process of determining what the First Amendment permits and what it forbids.

Historic Constitutional Tests

It is useful to start with the three constitutional tests developed in the first part of the twentieth century: the bad tendency test, the clear and present danger test, and the preferred position doctrine. Although they are no longer applied, they provide a background for the current judicial approach to governmental regulation of speech and to the courts' expanding protection for free speech.

THE BAD TENDENCY TEST   This test was rooted in the English common law. According to the **bad tendency test**, judges presumed it was reasonable to forbid speech that has a tendency to corrupt society or cause people to engage in illegal action. The test was abandoned because it swept too broadly and ran "contrary to the fundamental premises underlying the First Amendment as the guardian of our democracy."[26] Some legislators still appear to hold this position today, and it also seems to be the view of some college students, who want to see their institution punish student colleagues or faculty who express "hateful" or "offensive" ideas.

THE CLEAR AND PRESENT DANGER TEST   This is perhaps the most famous test. The **clear and present danger test** was formulated by Justice Oliver Wendell Holmes, Jr., in *Schenck v United States* (1919), as an alternative to the bad tendency test. In the words of Justice Holmes: "The question in every case is whether the words are used in circumstances and are of such a nature as to create a clear and present danger that they will bring about substantive evils that Congress has a right to prevent."[27] A government should not be allowed to interfere with speech unless it can prove, ultimately to a skeptical judiciary, that the particular speech in question presents an immediate danger—for example, speech leading to a riot, the destruction of property, or the corruption of an election.

Supporters of the clear and present danger test concede speech is not an absolute right. Yet they believe free speech to be so fundamental to the operations of a constitutional democracy that no government should be allowed to restrict speech unless it can demonstrate a close connection between the speech and an imminent lawless action. To shout "Fire!" falsely in a crowded theater is the most famous example of unprotected speech.

THE PREFERRED POSITION DOCTRINE   This was advanced in the 1940s when the Court applied all of the guarantees of the First Amendment to the states. The **preferred position doctrine** came close to the position that freedom of expression—that is, the use of words and pictures—should rarely, if ever, be curtailed. This interpretation of the First Amendment gives these freedoms, especially freedom of speech and of conscience, a preferred position in our constitutional hierarchy. Judges have a special duty to protect these freedoms and should be most skeptical about laws trespassing on them. Once that judicial responsibility was established, judges had to draw lines between nonprotected and protected speech, as well as between speech and nonspeech.

NONPROTECTED AND PROTECTED SPEECH

Today, the Supreme Court holds that only four narrow categories of speech—*libel, obscenity, fighting words,* and *commercial speech*—are **nonprotected speech** because they lack social redeeming value and are not essential to democratic deliberations and self-governance.

The fact that nonprotected speech does not receive First Amendment protection does not mean that the constitutional issues relating to these kinds of speech are

Police arrest Scott Tyler of Chicago after he set fire to an American flag on the steps of the Capitol building in Washington. The Supreme Court ruled that freedom of speech even covers "symbolic speech" like burning the U.S. flag.

Thinking It Through . . .

On June 21, 1989 the Supreme Court, in *Texas v Johnson*, decided by a 5 to 4 vote that the First Amendment protects the act of burning the flag as freedom of expression. President George Bush denounced the decision and called for a constitutional amendment that would nullify it. Congress responded by passing a federal law that would make it a crime to burn or to deface the flag—whatever one's purposes or intent. In June 1990 the Supreme Court declared that law unconstitutional in *United States v Eichman.*

A Flag Amendment to the Constitution would give Congress the power to prohibit flag desecration. Public opinion polls show strong support for it. Forty-nine state legislatures have already indicated they would ratify such an amendment, far more than the 36 needed. A Senate majority has several times voted in favor of such an amendment, but has fallen short of the two-thirds majority needed to pass a constitutional amendment.

Before you decide, you might want to read the opinions of the Supreme Court justices in *Texas v Johnson*, 491 US 397 (1989) and *United States v Eichman*, 496 US 310 (1990). You may listen to the oral arguments in these cases by going to the Oyez website at www.oyez.nwu.edu.

Hustler *publisher Larry Flynt agrees to a plea bargain in which obscenity charges were dropped and a fine imposed if Flynt removed X-rated videos from a downtown store.*

simple. How we prove *libel*, how we define *obscenity*, how we determine which words are *fighting words*, and how much *commercial* speech may be regulated remain hotly contested issues.

Libel

At one time newspaper publishers and editors had to take considerable care about what they wrote for fear they might be prosecuted for **libel**—written defamation or false statements—by the government or sued by individuals. Today, through a progressive elevation of constitutional standards, it has become more difficult to win a libel suit against a newspaper or magazine.

Seditious libel—defaming, criticizing, and advocating the overthrow of government—was once subject to criminal penalties but no longer is. Seditious libel was rooted in the common law of England, which has no First Amendment. In 1798, only seven years after the First Amendment had been ratified, Congress enacted the first national law aimed against **sedition**, the Sedition Act of 1798. Those were perilous times for the young Republic, for war with France seemed imminent. The Federalists, in control of both Congress and the presidency, persuaded themselves that national safety required some suppression of speech. But popular reaction to the Sedition Act helped defeat the Federalists in the elections of 1800, and the Sedition Act expired in 1801. The Federalists had failed to grasp the democratic idea that a person may criticize the government, oppose its policies, and work for the removal of those in power, but still be loyal to the nation. They also failed to grasp the distinction between *seditious speech* and *seditious action*—conspiring to commit and engaging in violence against the government, which can be prosecuted and punished.

Another attempt to limit political criticism of the government was the Smith Act of 1940. That law forbid advocating the overthrow of the government, distributing material advocating the overthrow of government by violence, and organizing any group having such purposes. In 1951, during the cold war, the Supreme Court agreed that the Smith Act could be applied to the leaders of the Communist party who had been charged with conspiring to advocate the violent overthrow of the government.[28]

Since then, however, the Court has substantially modified constitutional doctrine, giving all political speech First Amendment protection. In *The New York Times v Sullivan* (1964), seditious libel was declared unconstitutional.[29] Now, neither Congress nor any government may outlaw mere advocacy of the abstract doctrine of violent overthrow of government: "The essential distinction is that those to whom the advocacy is addressed must be urged to do something now or in the future, rather than merely to believe in something."[30] Moreover, advocacy of the use of force may not be forbidden "except where such advocacy is directed to inciting or producing imminent lawless action and is likely to incite or produce such action."[31]

In the landmark ruling in *The New York Times v Sullivan* and subsequent cases, the Supreme Court established guidelines for libel cases and severely limited state power to award monetary damages in libel suits brought by public officials against critics of official conduct. Neither public officials nor public figures can collect damages for comments made about them unless they can prove with "convincing clarity" the comments were made with "actual malice." *Actual malice* means not merely that the defendant made false statements but that the "statements were made with a knowing or reckless disregard for the truth."[32]

Public figures cannot collect damages even when subject to outrageous, clearly inaccurate parodies and cartoons. Such was the case when *Hustler* magazine printed a parody of the Reverend Jerry Falwell; the Court held parodies and cartoons cannot reasonably be understood as describing actual facts or actual events.[33] Nor does the mere fact that a public figure is quoted as saying something that he or she did *not* say amount to a libel, unless the alteration in what the person said was made deliberately, with knowledge of its falsity, and "results in material change."[34]

libel
Written defamation of another person. Especially in the case of public officials and public figures, the constitutional tests designed to restrict libel actions are very rigid.

sedition
Attempting to overthrow the government by force or to interrupt its activities by violence.

Constitutional standards for libel charges brought by private persons are not as rigid as those for public officials and figures. State laws may permit private persons to collect damages without having to prove actual malice if they can prove the statements made about them are false and were negligently published.[35]

Obscenity and Pornography

Obscene publications are not entitled to constitutional protection, but members of the Supreme Court, like everybody else, have great difficulty in defining obscenity. As Justice Potter Stewart put it, "I know it when I see it."[36] Or, as the second Justice John Marshall Harlan explained, "One man's vulgarity is another man's lyric."[37]

In *Miller v California* (1973), the Court finally agreed on a constitutional definition of **obscenity**. A work may be considered legally obscene provided: (1) the average person, applying contemporary standards of the particular community, would find that the work, taken as a whole, appeals to a prurient interest in sex; (2) the work depicts or describes in a patently offensive way sexual conduct specifically defined by the applicable law or authoritatively construed; and (3) the work, taken as a whole, lacks serious literary, artistic, political, or scientific value.[38]

Pornography used to be merely a synonym for obscenity. The *Miller* standard has meant that only hard-core pornography is constitutionally unprotected. X-rated movies and adult theaters that fall short of the constitutional definition of obscenity are entitled to some constitutional protection, but less protection than political speech, and they are subject to greater government regulation. Cities may, as New York City has done, also regulate where adult theaters may be located by zoning laws,[39] and they may ban totally nude dancing in adult nightclubs.[40] Under narrowly drawn statutes, state and local governments can also ban the sale of "adult" magazines to minors, even if such materials would not be considered legally obscene if sold to adults.

The Court has also held that *child pornography*—sexually explicit materials either about minors or aimed at them—is not protected by the First Amendment.[41] Just as the government may protect minors, so apparently may it protect members of the armed forces. The Supreme Court left standing a ruling of a lower court upholding an act of Congress forbidding the sale or rental on military property of magazines or videos whose "dominant theme" is to portray nudity "in a lascivious way."[42]

Pressure for regulating pornography came primarily from political conservatives and religious fundamentalists concerned that it undermines moral standards. More recently, some feminists have joined them, arguing that pornography is degrading and perpetuates sexual discrimination and violence. They argue that just as sexually explicit materials about minors are not entitled to First Amendment protection, so should there be no protection for pornographic materials. They contend that pornography promotes sexual abuse of individual women and maintains the social subordination of women as a class. Some feminists define pornographic materials more broadly than the Court has and would include sexually explicit pictures or words that depict women as sexual objects enjoying pain and humiliation or that present abuse of women as a sexual stimulus for men.[43]

Not all feminists favor antipornography ordinances, yet those who do have been joined by social conservatives, and thus a new battle over pornography continues to be fought. For this new antipornography coalition to be successful, a substantial alteration in constitutional doctrine will be required. Unlike the Canadian Supreme Court, which redefined obscenity to include materials that degrade women,[44] the U.S. Supreme Court does not appear willing to substantially change current doctrine.

obscenity
Quality or state of a work that, taken as a whole, appeals to a prurient interest in sex by depicting sexual conduct in a patently offensive way and that lacks serious literary, artistic, political, or scientific value.

You Decide...

Hate speech on campus

Recent incidents of blatantly offensive signs and comments on college campuses have led to cases challenging so-called "hate codes." That speech may be insulting or racially offensive or sexist does not mean that it lacks constitutional protection. As the Supreme Court has repeatedly said, "If there is a bedrock principle underlying the First Amendment, it is that the Government may not prohibit the expression of an idea simply because society finds the idea offensive or disagreeable."* Do you think students should be punished for insulting or vicious remarks about minorities on campus?

United States v Eichman, 496 US 310 (1990).

fighting words
Words that by their very nature inflict injury upon those to whom they are addressed or cause acts of violence by them.

commercial speech
Advertisements and commercials for products and services that receive less First Amendment protection, primarily false and misleading ads.

prior restraint
Restraint or censorship imposed before a speech is made or a newspaper published, usually presumed to be unconstitutional.

Fighting Words

Fighting words were held to be constitutionally unprotected because "their very utterance may inflict injury or tend to incite an immediate breach of peace."[45] That the words are abusive, offensive, and insulting, or that they create anger, alarm, or resentment is not sufficient. Thus, a four-letter word worn on a sweatshirt was not judged to be a fighting word in the constitutional sense, even though it was offensive and angered some people.[46] In recent years, the Court has overturned convictions for uttering fighting words and struck down laws that criminalized "hate speech"—insulting racial, ethnic, and gender slurs.[47]

Commercial Speech

Commercial speech—such as advertisements and commercials—was held to be unprotected because it was deemed to have lesser value than political speech. But in recent years the Court has reconsidered and extended more protection to commercial speech, as it has to fighting words. In *44 Liquormart, Inc. v Rhode* Island (1996), for instance, the Court struck down a law forbidding the advertising of the price of alcoholic drinks.[48] It now appears that states may only forbid and punish false and misleading advertising, along with advertising the sale of anything illegal—for example, narcotics. Although the Supreme Court has not specifically removed it from the nonprotected category, the Court has so interpreted the First, Fifth, and Fourteenth Amendments to provide considerable constitutional protection for commercial speech.

Protected Speech

Apart from these four categories of nonprotected speech, all other expression is constitutionally protected, and courts strictly scrutinize government regulation of such speech. The Supreme Court uses the following doctrines to measure the limits of governmental power to regulate speech.

PRIOR RESTRAINT   Of all the forms of governmental interference with expression, judges are most suspicious of those that impose **prior restraint**—censorship before publication. Prior restraints include governmental review and approval before a speech can be made, before a motion picture can be shown, or before a newspaper can be published. Most prior restraints are unconstitutional, as the Court has said: "Any system of prior restraints of expression comes to this Court bearing a heavy presumption against its constitutional validity."[49] About the only prior restraints approved by the Court relate to military and security matters, but also to high school authorities' control over the style and content of student newspapers.[50] Student newspapers at colleges and universities receive the same protections as other newspapers, because they are independent and financially separate from the college or university.

VOID FOR VAGUENESS   Laws must not be so vague that people do not know whether their speech would violate the law and, thus, are afraid to exercise protected freedoms. Laws must not allow those who administer them so much discretion that they may discriminate against those whose views they dislike. For these reasons, the Court strikes down laws under the void for vagueness doctrine.

LEAST DRASTIC MEANS   Even for an important purpose, a legislature may not pass a law that impinges on First Amendment freedoms if other, least drastic means are available. To illustrate, a state may protect the public from unscrupulous lawyers, but it may not do so by forbidding attorneys from advertising their fees for simple services. The state could adopt other ways to protect the public from such lawyers that do not impinge on their freedom of speech; it could, for example, provide for the disbarment of lawyers who mislead their clients.

CONTENT AND VIEWPOINT NEUTRALITY   Laws concerning the time, place, or manner of speech that regulate some kinds of speech but not others, or that regulate speech expressing some views but not others, are much more likely to be struck down than those that are content-neutral or viewpoint-neutral; that is, laws that apply to *all* kinds of speech and to *all* views. For example, the Constitution does not prohibit laws forbidding the posting of handbills on telephone poles. Yet laws prohibiting only religious handbills or handbills advocating racism or sexism would, in all probability, be declared unconstitutional because they would relate to the kind of handbills or what is being said, rather than applying to all handbills regardless of what they say.

The lack of viewpoint neutrality was the grounds for the Court striking down a St. Paul, Minnesota, ordinance that prohibited the display of a symbol that would arouse anger on the basis of race, color, creed, religion, or gender. The ordinance was not considered viewpoint-neutral because it did not forbid displays that might arouse anger for other reasons, for example, because of political affiliation.[51]

FREEDOM OF THE PRESS

Courts have carefully protected the press's right to publish information, no matter how journalists get it. But some reporters, editors, and others argue that this is not enough. They insist that the First Amendment gives them the right to ignore legal requests and to withhold information. They also contend that the First Amendment gives them a *right of access*, a right to go wherever they need to go to get information.

Does the Press Have the Right to Withhold Information?

Although most reporters have challenged the right of public officials to withhold information, they claim the right to do so themselves, including the right to keep information from grand juries and legislative investigating committees. Without this right to withhold information, reporters insist they cannot assure their sources of confidentiality, and they will not be able to get the information they need to keep the public informed.

The Supreme Court has, however, refused to acknowledge that reporters, and presumably scholars, have a constitutional right to ignore legal requests such as subpoenas and withhold information from governmental bodies.[52] It is up to Congress and the states to provide such privileges for news reporters, and many states have passed so-called *press shield laws* providing some protection for reporters from state court subpoenas.

Does the Press Have the Right to Know?

The press has argued that if reporters are excluded from places where public business is conducted or are denied access to information in government files, they are not able to perform their historic function of keeping the public informed. In similar fashion, some reporters argue that they may enter facilities such as food markets, child care centers, and homes for the mentally ill, even using false identities, to expose racial discrimination, employment discrimination, and financial frauds. The Supreme Court, however, has refused to acknowledge a *constitutional right of the press to know*, although it did concede that there is a First Amendment right for the press, along with the public, to be present at criminal trials.[53]

Although they have no constitutional obligation to do so, many states have adopted *sunshine laws* requiring government agencies to open their meetings to the public and the press. Congress requires most federal executive agencies to open hearings and meetings of advisory groups to the public, and most congressional committee meetings are open to the public. Federal and state courtroom trials are

Thinking It Through...

The speech of faculty and staff at universities and colleges, public or private, is protected by the Constitution from regulation by the government. As state agencies, public universities and colleges are subject to the restrictions of the Constitution. Nonetheless, as an employer a public university has some leeway in regulating the speech of its employees, more leeway than it has in regulating the speech of its students—especially student speech outside of the classroom or away from residence halls. The administration has some discretion—in fact, under federal laws, some obligation—to control racially or sexually harassing speech by faculty and staff. In its role of landlord for residence halls, universities and colleges have the authority to impose reasonable time, place, and manner regulations. As institutions of higher learning, they have the responsibility to overcome bigotry and stereotyping.

Private universities and colleges are not subject to constitutional limitations on how they may regulate the speech of their students. However, private universities that receive federal funds may find that their freedom to punish the use of offensive speech by students is limited by federal laws and regulations. Federal and state laws regulating the responsibilities of employers to provide a workplace free from sexual harassment also apply to universities, both private and public.

also open, but judicial conferences, in which the judges discuss how to decide the cases, are not.

Congress has authorized the president to establish a classification system to keep some public documents and governmental files secret, and it is a crime for any person to divulge such classified information. So far, however, although they have been threatened, no newspapers have been prosecuted for doing so.

The Freedom of Information Act (FOIA) of 1966 as amended liberalized access to nonclassified federal government records. This act makes the records of federal executive agencies available subject to certain exceptions, such as private financial transactions, personnel records, criminal investigation files, interoffice memoranda, and letters used in internal decision making. If federal agencies fail to move promptly on requests for information, applicants are entitled to speedy judicial hearings. The burden is on an agency to explain its refusal to supply material, and if the judge decides the government has improperly withheld information, the government has to pay the legal fees. Since the inception of FOIA, more than 250,000 people have requested information, and more than 90 percent of these requests have been granted.

President Bill Clinton issued an executive order calling for automatic declassification of almost all government documents after 25 years. Any person who wants access to documents that are not declassified can appeal to an Interagency Security Classification Appeals panel, which has a record of ruling in favor of releasing documents. The Electronic Freedom of Information Act of 1996 requires most federal agencies to put their files online and to establish an index of all their records. The National Aeronautics and Space Administration (NASA) has done the most of the federal agencies (see **www.firstgov.com**). One of the most frequent requests to NASA's Electronic Reading Room is for documents relating to unidentified flying objects (UFOs).

Free Press versus Fair Trials

When newspapers and television report in vivid detail the facts of a crime, interview prosecutors and police, question witnesses, and hold press conferences for defendants and their attorneys—as in the O. J. Simpson murder and Oklahoma City bombing cases—they may so inflame the public that finding a panel of impartial jurors and conducting a fair trial is difficult. In England, strict rules determine what the media may report, and judges do not hesitate to punish newspapers that comment on pending criminal proceedings. In the United States, in contrast, free comment is protected. Yet the Supreme Court has not been indifferent to protecting persons on trial from inflammatory publicity. Its remedies have been to order new trials or to instruct judges to impose sanctions on prosecutors and police, not on reporters.

Federal rules of criminal procedure forbid radio or photographic coverage of criminal cases in federal courts, but most states permit televising courtroom proceedings, and court TV programs have become very popular.

OTHER MEDIA AND COMMUNICATIONS

When the First Amendment was written, freedom of "the press" referred to leaflets, newspapers, and books. Today the amendment protects other media as well—the mails, motion pictures, billboards, radio, television, cable, telephones, fax machines, and the Internet. Because each form of communication entails special problems, each needs a different degree of protection.

The Mails

More than 80 years ago, Justice Oliver Wendell Holmes, Jr., wrote in dissent: "The United States may give up the Post Office when it sees fit, but while it carries it on, the use of the mails is almost as much a part of free speech as is the right to use our tongues."[54] In 1965 the Court adopted Holmes's view by striking down an act that had directed the postmaster general to detain foreign mailings of "communist political propaganda" and to deliver these materials only upon the addressee's request.[55] The Court has also set aside federal laws authorizing postal authorities to exclude from the mails materials they consider obscene.

Although government censorship of mail is unconstitutional, household censorship is not. The Court has sustained a law giving householders the right to ask the postmaster to order mailers to delete their names from certain mailing lists and to refrain from sending any advertisements that they believe to be "erotically arousing or sexually provocative."[56] Moreover, Congress may forbid—and has forbidden—the use of mailboxes for any materials except those sent through the United States mails.

Handbills, Sound Trucks, and Billboards

Religious and political pamphlets, leaflets, and handbills have been historic weapons in the defense of liberty, and their distribution is constitutionally protected. So, too, is the use of their contemporary counterparts—sound trucks and billboards. A state cannot restrain the distribution of leaflets merely to keep its streets clean,[57] but it may impose reasonable restrictions on their distribution so long as they are neutrally enforced, without regard to the content of the expression.

Motion Pictures and Plays

Prior censorship of films to prevent the showing of obscenity is not necessarily unconstitutional; however, laws calling for submission of films to a government review board are constitutional only if there is a prompt judicial hearing. The burden is on the government to prove to the court that the particular film in question is obscene. Prior censorship of films by review boards used to be common in some places. Live performances, such as plays and revues, are also entitled to constitutional protection.[58]

Broadcast and Cable Communications

Television remains an important means of distributing news and appealing for votes, though the Web has been gaining in popularity. Yet of all the mass media, broadcasting receives the least First Amendment protection. Congress has established a system of commercial broadcasting, supplemented by the Corporation for Public Broadcasting, which provides funds for public radio and television. The Federal Communications Commission (FCC) regulates the entire system by granting licenses and making regulations for their use.

The First Amendment would prevent censorship if the FCC tried to impose it. The First Amendment does not, however, prevent the FCC from imposing sanctions on stations that broadcast filthy words, even though such indecencies are not legally obscene.[59] The FCC did precisely that when it fined Infinity Broadcasting for indecent remarks by "shock jock" Howard Stern. Nor does the First Amendment prevent the FCC from refusing to renew a license if, in its opinion, a broadcaster does not serve the public interest.

The Supreme Court allowed more governmental regulation of broadcasters than of newspaper and magazine publishers because there were a limited number of airwaves. However, technological changes such as cable television, videotapes, and satellite broadcasting have opened up new means of communication and brought competition to the electronic media. Recognizing these changes, Congress passed the Telecommunications Act of 1996, allowing telephone companies, broadcasters, and cable TV stations to compete with one another. In adopting the act, Congress did not abandon all government regulation of the airways. On the contrary, the act calls for many new regulations, for example requiring that all new television sets sold in the United States be equipped with V-chips that allow viewers to block programs containing violent or sexual material.

At a press conference, Howard Stern defends his use of raunchy language and subject matter that led to the FCC fining the Infinity Broadcasting network.

The Court has upheld a congressional requirement that cable television stations must carry the signals of local broadcast television stations.[60] The Court has also held that Congress may authorize cable operators to refuse access to leased channels for "patently offensive" programs. The Court, however, struck down congressional requirements that if a cable operator allows such offensive programming, it must be blocked and unscrambled through special devices. In *United States v Playboy Entertainment Group* (2000), the Court underscored the greater protection for cable than for broadcast television. Whereas broadcast television may be required to provide programming for children and not air violence at certain times, the Court held that such rules do not apply to cable television because unwanted programming can be blocked at the household.[61]

Telecommunications and the Internet

More than 30 million Americans log on to the Internet to buy books, clothing, jewelry, airplane tickets, stocks, and bonds. Because the Internet has become a commercial marketplace and a major channel for communication, Congress is struggling with issues raised by cyberspace communication: Should the national government preempt state taxation? Do existing laws against copyright piracy apply to the Web? Should there be national regulation of junk e-mail, or can state laws take care of the problem? Should Congress try to protect the privacy of those who use the Web? (For more information about privacy and developments on the Web, go to the Electronic Privacy Information Center at **www.epic.org**.)

As Congress and the state legislatures begin to deal with these and other new problems, legislators and judges will have to apply traditional constitutional principles to new technologies and means of communication. The Court distinguishes between a limited ban on indecent messages on radio and broadcast television and those on telephones, cable television, and the Internet. Radio and broadcast messages are readily available to children and can intrude into the privacy of the home without prior warning. By contrast, telephone messages may be blocked, and access by minors is more readily restricted.[62] In its first ruling on First Amendment protection for the Internet, *Reno v American Civil Liberties Union* (1997), the Court struck down provisions of the Communications Decency Act of 1996 that had made it a crime to send obscene or indecent messages to anyone under 18 years of age. The Court emphasized the unique character of the Internet, holding that it is less intrusive than radio and broadcast television.[63]

FREEDOM OF ASSEMBLY

In the fall of 1998, Khallid Abdul Muhammad, a known racist and anti-Semite, organized a "Million Youth March" in New York City. Mayor Rudolph Giuliani denied a permit for the march on grounds that it would be a "hate march." A federal appeals court upheld a lower court ruling that denial of the permit was unconstitutional; however, the three-judge panel placed restrictions on the event, limiting its duration to four hours and scaling it back to a six-block area. The march proceeded, surrounded by police in riot gear who broke up the demonstration after Muhammad delivered a vitriolic speech against police, Jews, and city officials.[64]

It took judicial authorities to defend the rights of these unpopular speakers and marchers, but it is not always the "bad guys" whose rights have to be protected by the courts. It also took judicial intervention in the 1960s to preserve for Martin Luther King, Jr., and for those who marched with him, the right to demonstrate in the streets of southern cities on behalf of civil rights for African Americans.

Such incidents present a classic free speech problem. It is almost always easier, and certainly politically more prudent, to maintain order by curbing public demonstrations of unpopular groups. On the other hand, if police did not have the right to order groups to disperse, public order would be at the mercy of those who resort to street demonstrations to create tensions and provoke street battles.

New York City police in riot gear formed a human wall in front of the Million Youth March and charged the stage after Khallid Abdul Muhammad, organizer of the rally, urged the audience to riot and kill.

Public Forums and Time, Place, and Manner Regulations

The Constitution protects the right to speak, but it does not give people the right to communicate their views to everyone, every place, at every time they wish. No one has the right to block traffic or to hold parades or make speeches in public streets or on public sidewalks whenever he or she wishes. Governments may not censor what can be said, but they can make *reasonable time, place,* and *manner* regulations for protests or parades. The Supreme Court has divided public property into three categories: public forums, limited public forums, and nonpublic forums. The extent to which governments may limit access depends on the kind of forum involved.

Public forums are public places historically associated with the free exercise of expressive activities, such as streets, sidewalks, and parks. Courts look closely at time, place, and manner regulations that apply to these traditional public forums to ensure that they are being applied evenhandedly and that action is not taken because of what is being said rather than how and where or by whom it is being said.[65]

Other kinds of public property, such as rooms in a city hall or after-hour use of school buildings, may be designated as *limited public forums*, available for assembly and speech for limited purposes, a limited amount of time, and even for a limited class of speakers (such as only students, only teachers, or only employees), provided the distinctions between those allowed access and those not allowed access are not biased.

Nonpublic forums include public facilities such as libraries, courthouses, prisons, schools, swimming pools, and government offices that are open to the public but are not public forums. As long as people use such facilities within the normal bounds of conduct, they may not be constitutionally restrained from doing so. However, people may be excluded from such places as a government office or a school if they engage in activities for which the facilities were not created. They have no right to interfere with programs or try to take over a building—especially facilities such as a university president's office—in order to stage a political protest.

Does the right of peaceful assembly include the right to violate a law nonviolently but deliberately? We have no precise answer, but in general, **civil disobedience**, even if peaceful, is not a protected right. When Dr. Martin Luther King, Jr., and his followers refused to comply with a state court's injunction forbidding them to parade in Birmingham without first securing a permit, the Supreme Court sustained their conviction, even though there was serious doubt about the constitutionality of the injunction and the ordinance on which it was based.[66]

More recently, the First Amendment right of anti-abortion protesters to picket in front of abortion clinics has come into conflict with a woman's right to go to an abortion clinic. Protesters have often massed in front of clinics, shouting at employ-

civil disobedience
Action in which people refuse to obey the law or comply with the orders of public officials as a means of expressing their opposition to the government or some of its laws.

ees and patrons and blocking entrances to the clinic. The Supreme Court has struck down provisions that prohibit protesters from peacefully, even if assertively, expressing their views. But the Court has upheld injunctions that keep anti-abortion protesters outside of a reasonable buffer zone around abortion clinics and also upheld injunctions that were issued because of prior unlawful conduct by the protesters. The proper constitutional test for such injunctions is "whether the challenged provisions . . . burden no more speech than necessary to serve a significant government interest," such as public safety or the right of women to go into such a clinic.[67]

The combination of written guarantees for rights and freedoms and their judicial enforcement is one of the basic features of our government and political system. As Supreme Court Justice Robert H. Jackson wrote:

> The very purpose of a Bill of Rights was to withdraw certain subjects from the vicissitudes of political controversy, to place them beyond the reach of majorities and officials and to establish them as legal principles to be applied by the courts. One's right to life, liberty, and property, to free speech, a free press, freedom of worship and assembly, and other fundamental rights may not be submitted to vote: they depend on the outcome of no elections.[68]

The connection between constitutional limitations and judicial enforcement is an example of the "auxiliary precautions" James Madison believed were necessary to prevent arbitrary governmental action. Citizens in other free nations rely on elections and political checks to protect their rights; in the United States we also appeal to judges when we fear our freedoms are in danger.

POLITICS ONLINE

Surf Watch: Pornography on the Internet

Should government regulate the content of Internet communications that include indecent words or pictures that children can access with the click of a mouse? In 1996 Congress passed the Communications Decency Act, which made it illegal to send "indecent" or "patently offensive" words or pictures online where they can be found by children. In defending the act before the Supreme Court, the Justice Department contended: "The Internet threatens to give every child a free pass to the equivalent of every adult bookstore and every adult video store in the country." But the American Civil Liberties Union countered that "the government cannot reduce the adult population to reading or viewing only what is appropriate for children."

During oral arguments, it appeared that the justices were uncertain whether Internet speech is most like speech on a street corner or in a park, communication over the telephone, or some type of publication. To read how the Court resolved this contentious issue, log onto www.prenhall.com/burns and view the case of *Reno v American Civil Liberties Union*, and also access the Communications Decency Act of 1996.

More recently, in an effort to keep pornography out of public schools, Congress passed the "Children's Internet Protection Act." This legislation mandates that schools using federal money for computer services must make use of a government-created filter device designed to block pornographic material. For more information log onto: www.cybertelecom.org/cda/cipatext.htm

For different perspectives on these issues, check out the American Civil Liberties Union at: www.aclu.org and the American Center for Law and Justice at: www.aclj.org.

SUMMARY

1. The Constitution protects our right to seek a writ of *habeas corpus* and forbids *ex post facto* laws and bills of attainder.

2. First Amendment freedoms—freedom of religion, freedom from the establishment of religion, freedom of speech, freedom of the press, freedom of assembly and association—are at the heart of a healthy constitutional democracy.

3. Since World War I, the Supreme Court has become the primary branch of government for giving meaning to these constitutional restraints. And since 1925 these constitutional limits have been applied not only to Congress but to all governmental agencies—national, state, and local.

4. The First Amendment forbids the establishment of religion and also guarantees the free exercise of religion. These two freedoms, however, are often in conflict with each other and represent conflicting notions of what is in the public interest.

5. The Supreme Court holds that there are four categories of nonprotected speech—libel, obscenity, fighting words, and commercial speech. All other speech is protected under the First Amendment, and government may regulate that speech only when it has a compelling reason and does so in a content-neutral way.

6. Over the years, the Supreme Court has taken a practical approach to First Amendment freedoms. It has refused to make them absolute rights above any kind of governmental regulation, direct or indirect, or to say that they must be preserved at whatever price. But the justices have recognized that a constitutional democracy tampers with these freedoms at great peril. They have insisted upon compelling justification before permitting these rights to be limited. How compelling the justification is, in a free society, will always remain an open question.

KEY TERMS

writ of *habeas corpus* 364
ex post facto law 364
bill of attainder 365
due process clause 365
selective incorporation 365

establishment clause 366
free exercise clause 369
bad tendency test 370
clear and present danger
    test 370

preferred position doctrine 370
nonprotected speech 370
libel 372
sedition 372
obscenity 372

fighting words 374
commercial speech 374
prior restraint 374
civil disobedience 379

FURTHER READING

JAMES MACGREGOR BURNS AND STEWART BURNS, *A People's Charter: The Pursuit of Rights in America* (Knopf, 1991).

T. BARTON CARTER, *The First Amendment and the Fifth Estate: Regulation of Electronic Mass Media*, 4th ed. (Foundation Press, 1996).

JESSE CHOPER, *Securing Religious Liberty: Principles for Judicial Interpretation of Religion Clauses* (University of Chicago Press, 1995).

EDWARD J. CLEARY, *Beyond the Burning Cross: A Landmark Case of Race, Censorship, and the First Amendment* (Random House, 1995).

STEPHEN M. FELDMAN, ED., *Law and Religion: A Critical Anthology* (New York University Press, 2000).

MIKE GODWIN, *Cyber Rights: Defending Free Speech in the Digital Age* (Times Books, 1998).

KENT GREENAWALT, *Fighting Words: Individuals, Communities, and Liberties of Speech* (Princeton University Press, 1995).

NAT HENTOFF, *Living the Bill of Rights: How to Be an Authentic American* (HarperCollins, 1998).

LEONARD W. LEVY, *Emergence of a Free Press* (Oxford University Press, 1985).

LEONARD W. LEVY, *The Establishment Clause: Religion and the First Amendment* (Macmillan, 1986).

ANTHONY LEWIS, *Make No Law: The Sullivan Case and the First Amendment* (Random House, 1991).

CATHARINE A. MACKINNON, *Only Words* (Harvard University Press, 1993).

ALEXANDER MEIKLEJOHN, *Political Freedom: The Constitutional Powers of the People* (Harper & Row, 1965).

JOHN STUART MILL, *Essay on Liberty* (1859), in *The English Philosophers from Bacon to Mill*, ed. Arthur Burtt (Random House, 1939), pp. 949–1041.

JOHN T. NOONAN, JR., *The Lustre of Our Country: The American Experience of Religious Freedom* (University of California Press, 1998).

J. W. PELTASON AND SUE DAVIS, *Understanding the Constitution*, 15th ed. (Harcourt College Division, 2000).

FRANK S. RAVITCH, *School Prayer and Discrimination: The Civil Rights of Religious Minorities and Dissenters* (Northwestern University Press, 1999).

NADINE STROSSEN, *Defending Pornography: Free Speech, Sex, and the Fight for Women's Rights* (Scribner's, 1995).

17

RIGHTS TO LIFE, LIBERTY, AND PROPERTY

I N COUNTRIES AROUND THE WORLD, MEN AND WOMEN ARE REBELLING AGAINST THE POLICE STATES UNDER WHICH THEY LIVE, AGAINST GOVERNMENTS IN WHICH the police are unrestrained in how they go about finding and punishing so-called "enemies of the people." In the United States we sometimes get impatient about the time-consuming steps that must be followed before criminals are taken off the streets, and about the endless rounds of appeals and reviews available to those charged with crimes. But we need to remember how fortunate we are to live in a society that values *due process*—established rules and regulations that restrain those in government who exercise power. Such procedures are not available to citizens in Iraq, China, and much of Africa and South America, as well as elsewhere in the world.

Public officials in the United States do have great power. Under certain conditions they can seize our property, put us in jail, and—in extreme circumstances—even take our lives. The framers of our Constitution recognized that it is necessary—but dangerous—to give power to those who govern. It is so dangerous that to keep our officials from becoming tyrants, we do not depend on the ballot box alone. Because political power can threaten our liberty, we parcel it out in small chunks and surround it with restraints. No single official can decide to take our lives, liberty, or property. Officials must act according to the rules. If they act outside the scope of their authority or contrary to the law, they can be restrained, dismissed, or punished. These rights to due process are the precious rights of all who live under the American flag—rich or poor, young or old, black or white, man or woman, alien or citizen.

In this chapter we look at the rights of all persons to due process, but before we do, let us look at the rights that flow from citizenship.

CITIZENSHIP RIGHTS

E very nation has rules that determine nationality and define who is a member of, owes allegiance to, and is a subject of the nation. But in a constitutional democracy, citizenship is an *office* and, like other offices, it carries with it certain powers and responsibilities. How citizenship is acquired and retained is therefore a matter of considerable importance.

CHAPTER MEDIA

POLITICS ONLINE
Are Your E-Mail Messages Private?
www.prenhall.com/burns

An applicant for naturalization must:

1. Be over age 18.

2. Be lawfully admitted to the United States for permanent residence and have resided in the United States for at least five years and in the state for at least six months.

3. File a petition of naturalization with a clerk of a court of record (federal or state) verified by two witnesses.

4. Be able to read, write, and speak English.

5. Possess a good moral character.

6. Understand and demonstrate an attachment to the history, principles, and form of government of the United States.

7. Demonstrate that he or she is well disposed toward the good order and happiness of the country.

8. Demonstrate that he or she does not now believe in, nor within the last ten years has ever believed in, advocated, or belonged to an organization that supports opposition to organized government, overthrow of government by violence, or the doctrines of world communism or any other form of totalitarianism.

For more information about immigration and naturalization, go to the website of the Federation for American Immigration Reform, at www.fairus.org/04118604.htm.

How Citizenship Is Acquired and Lost

The basic right of citizenship was not given constitutional protection until 1868, when the Fourteenth Amendment was adopted; prior to that, each state determined citizenship. The Fourteenth Amendment states: "All persons born or naturalized in the United States, and subject to the jurisdiction thereof, are citizens of the United States and of the State wherein they reside." This means that all persons born in the United States, except children born to foreign ambassadors and ministers, are citizens of this country regardless of the citizenship of their parents. (Congress has defined the United States for this purpose to include Puerto Rico, Guam, the Northern Marianas, and the Virgin Islands.) A child born to an American citizen living abroad or who has an American citizen as a grandparent is an American citizen if either the parent or grandparent has lived in the United States for at least five years, including two of which were after age 14. Although the Fourteenth Amendment does not make Native Americans citizens of the United States and of the states in which they live, Congress did so in 1924.

NATURALIZATION   Citizenship may also be acquired by **naturalization**, a legal action conferring citizenship upon an alien. Congress determines naturalization requirements. Today, with minor exceptions, nonenemy aliens over age 18 who have been lawfully admitted for permanent residence and who have resided in the United States for at least five years and in the state for at least six months are eligible for naturalization. Any state or federal court in the United States or the Immigration and Naturalization Service (INS) can grant citizenship. The INS, with the help of the Federal Bureau of Investigation (FBI), makes the necessary investigations.

Any person denied citizenship after a hearing before an immigration officer may appeal to a federal district judge. Citizenship is granted if the judge is satisfied that the applicant has met all the requirements after reviewing the FBI check that no disqualifying felony conviction has been found. The applicant

naturalization
A legal action conferring citizenship upon an alien.

Proud naturalized citizens are sworn in at an emotional ceremony.

renounces allegiance to his or her former country, swears to support and defend the Constitution and laws of the United States against all enemies, and promises to bear arms on behalf of the United States when required to do so by law. Those whose religious beliefs prevent them from bearing arms are allowed to take an oath swearing that, if called to duty, they will serve in the armed forces as noncombatants or will perform work of national importance under civilian direction. The court or INS then grants a certificate of naturalization.

Naturalized citizenship may be revoked by court order if the government can prove citizenship was secured by deception. But citizenship cannot be taken from people because of what they have done—for example, for committing certain crimes, voting in foreign elections, or serving in foreign armies. In addition, citizenship, however acquired, may be renounced voluntarily. Even so, the government must prove that the citizen "not only voluntarily committed the expatriating act prescribed in the statute, but also intended to relinquish his citizenship."[1]

DUAL CITIZENSHIP   Because each nation has complete authority to decide for itself the definition of nationality, it is possible for a person to be considered a citizen by two or more nations. **Dual citizenship** is not unusual, especially for people from nations that do not recognize the right of individuals to renounce their citizenship, called the **right of expatriation**. (One of the issues of the War of 1812 was that England did not recognize sailors born in England as having abandoned their English citizenship on becoming naturalized American citizens.) Children born abroad to American citizens may also be citizens of the nation in which they were born. Children born in the United States of parents from a foreign nation may also be citizens of their parents' country.

Among the nations that allow dual citizenship are Canada, Mexico, France, and the United Kingdom. One expert estimates that, based on the number of American children born to foreign-born parents, the number of Americans eligible to hold citizenship in another country grows by at least 500,000 a year.[2] Moreover, with more than 7 million Mexican-born immigrants in the United States and their American-born children now becoming eligible to apply for Mexican citizenship, the number of dual citizens in the United States is on the rise. Dual citizenship carries negative as well as positive consequences; for example, a person with dual citizenship may be subject to national service obligations and taxes in both countries.

Rights of American Citizens

An American becomes a citizen of one of our states merely by residing in that state. *Residence* as understood in the Fourteenth Amendment means the place one calls home. The legal status of residence should not be confused with the fact of physical presence. A person may be living in Washington, D.C., but be a citizen of California—that is, consider California home and vote in that state.

Most of our most important rights flow from *state* citizenship. In the *Slaughter-House Cases* (1873), the Supreme Court carefully distinguished between the privileges of United States citizens and those of state citizens. It held that the only privileges of national citizenship are those that "owe their existence to the Federal Government, its National Character, its Constitution, or its laws." These privileges have never been completely specified, but they include the right to use the navigable waters of the United States and to protection on the high seas, to assemble peacefully and petition for redress of grievances, to vote if qualified to do so under state laws and have one's vote counted properly, as well as to travel throughout the United States.

THE RIGHT TO LIVE AND TRAVEL IN THE UNITED STATES   This right, which is not subject to any congressional limitation, is perhaps the most precious aspect of American citizenship. Aliens have no such right. They may be stopped on the high seas or at the borders and turned away if they fail to meet the terms and conditions

dual citizenship
Citizenship in two or more nations.

right of expatriation
Right of individuals to renounce their citizenship.

An estimated 2.3 to 2.4 million undocumented aliens—mostly from Mexico and other nations in Central and South America and a few from Canada and Poland—illegally cross our borders, not because they fear political persecution but because they see greater economic opportunity in the United States. Even though most undocumented immigrants from Mexico return to Mexico after only two years and well over half return within 10 years, undocumented aliens present a big political problem.

stipulated by the Congress for admission. Today millions of people around the world yearn to come and live in the United States, but only American citizens have a constitutionally guaranteed right to do so.

THE RIGHT TO TRAVEL ABROAD   The right to international travel can be regulated within the bounds of due process. Under current law it is unlawful for citizens to leave or enter the United States without a valid passport (except as otherwise provided by the president, as has been done for travel to Mexico, Canada, and parts of the Caribbean).

Rights of Aliens

During periods of hostility toward aliens, the protections of citizenship are even more precious. True, the Constitution protects many rights of *all persons*, not just of American citizens; for example, neither Congress nor the states can deny to aliens the right of freedom of religion or the right of freedom of speech. Nor can any government deprive any person, alien or citizen, of the due process of the law or equal protection under the laws.

However, Congress may deny or limit welfare and many other kinds of benefits to aliens. Congress has denied most federally assisted benefits to illegal immigrants and has permitted states to deny them many other benefits, making an exception only for emergency medical care, disaster relief, and some nutrition programs. While states have considerable discretion over what benefits they give to aliens, the Supreme Court has held that states cannot constitutionally exclude children of undocumented aliens from the public schools or charge their parents tuition.[3]

Admission to the United States

President Franklin Roosevelt, reminding us of our heritage as a haven for people fleeing religious and political persecution, opened his address to a convention of the Daughters of the American Revolution with the salutation, "Fellow immigrants and revolutionaries." Some Americans, however, are concerned that admitting so many people from abroad will dilute American traditions and values. Throughout our history debates have flared among those wishing to open our borders and those wishing to close them.

Immigrants arriving at Ellis Island in 1900 came with high hopes but few material possessions.

property rights
The rights of an individual to own, use, rent, invest in, buy, and sell property.

Aliens do not have a constitutional right to enter the United States. Congress has wide discretion in setting the numbers, terms, and conditions under which aliens can enter and stay in the United States. The Immigration Act of 1965, as amended in 1990 and 1996, sets an annual ceiling of 675,000 for nonrefugee aliens allowed to come here as permanent residents, but when refugees and other exempt categories are added, more than 800,000 people enter the United States each year. The law also sets an annual limit on immigrants from any single country. Preference is given for family reunification and to people who have special skills or who are needed to fill jobs for which U.S. workers are not available. Another provision allows for the admission of "millionaire immigrants" who are willing and able to invest a substantial sum to create or support a business in the United States that will provide jobs for Americans. There have been few takers for admission under this provision. There is also a "diversity" category to provide visas for 55,000 immigrants from 34 countries, whether or not they have relatives living in the United States. These visas are drawn annually by lottery from a pool of qualified applicants.

In addition to regularly admitted aliens, in recent years more than 100,000 political refugees have been admitted. *Political refugees* are people who have well-founded fears of persecution in their own countries based on their race, religion, nationality, social class, or political opinion. People admitted as political refugees can apply to become permanent residents after one year. The attorney general, acting through the Immigration and Naturalization Service, may also grant *asylum* to applicants who have well-founded fears of persecution in the country to which they would be returned, based on their race, religion, nationality, membership in a particular social group, or political opinion. It is not enough, however, that applicants face the same terrible conditions that all other citizens of their country face, or that they wish to escape bad economic conditions. They must show specific danger of persecution.

The Immigration and Naturalization Service may turn back at the border persons seeking asylum when it considers their requests insubstantial, or even hold them in detention camps. The president may order the Coast Guard—as both former President George Bush and Bill Clinton did with respect to Haitian and Cuban refugees—to stop people on the high seas before they enter the territorial waters of the United States and return them to the country from which they have fled without determining whether they qualify as refugees.[4] Nonetheless, many people are still willing to risk great danger to get here and suffer detention once they arrive, just for the chance of being granted asylum.

Once in the United States, aliens are subject to the full range of obligations, including the payment of taxes. Aliens are counted in the census for the purpose of apportioning seats in the U.S. House of Representatives. Legally admitted aliens may be deported for a variety of reasons—for example, conviction of crimes involving immoral acts, turpitude, incitement of terrorist activity, illegal voting in elections, and conviction of domestic violence.

PROPERTY RIGHTS

Constitutional Protection of Property

Property does not have rights. People do. People have the right to own, use, rent, invest in, buy, and sell property. Historically, the close connection between liberty and ownership of property, between property and power, has been emphasized in American political thinking and American political institutions. A major purpose of the framers of the Constitution was to establish a government strong enough to protect people's rights to use and enjoy their property. At the same time, the framers wanted to limit government so it could not endanger that right. As a result, the framers included in the Constitution a variety of clauses protecting **property rights**.

Thinking It Through . . .

The inability to keep illegal aliens out of the country is not a question of constitutional power, for Congress has complete power over the admission of aliens. Rather, the problems are political and practical. Although Congress has authorized an increase in the number of border patrol guards and funded additional fencing of the California-Mexican border, there are thousands of miles of borders. Moreover, it is difficult to track down undocumented aliens once inside the United States and then expel them in a fashion consistent with the practices and policies of a free society.

Congress faces conflicting pressures: from Hispanic groups concerned that making it illegal to hire undocumented workers will make employers hesitate to hire any Hispanics; from employers who do not want to keep costly records and investigate the legal status of everybody they hire; from employers of farm workers who want to be sure they will have enough laborers to pick seasonal crops; from American workers who do not want undocumented workers being used to keep wages low; and from city and local governmental officials who have to find the funds to provide social services for undocumented aliens.

The United States government tends to consider immigration policy a purely internal matter. In California and some other states there are strong anti-immigration pressures. Immigration policy clearly affects our relations with other nations, most especially with Mexico, as the lengthy negotiations over the North American Free Trade Agreement (NAFTA) demonstrated. Although we view immigration policy as a matter of national sovereignty, Mexicans see it as a matter that directly affects them and have advocated "open borders."

Of special concern to the framers were the efforts of some state legislatures to protect debtors at the expense of their creditors by issuing paper currency and setting aside private contracts. To prevent these practices, the legal tender and contract clauses in the Constitution forbid states from making anything except gold or silver legal tender for the payment of debts and from passing any "Law impairing the Obligation of Contracts."

The **contract clause** (Article I, Section 10) was designed to prevent states from extending the period during which debtors could meet their payments or otherwise get out of contractual obligations. The framers had in mind an ordinary contract between private persons. However, beginning with Chief Justice John Marshall (1801–35), the Supreme Court expanded the coverage of the clause to prevent states from taking away privileges previously conferred on corporations. In effect, the contract clause was used to protect property and to maintain the status quo at the expense of a state's power.

In the late nineteenth century, however, the Supreme Court gradually began to restrict the coverage of the contract clause and to subject contracts to what in constitutional law are known as **police powers**—the powers of states to protect the public health, safety, welfare, and morals of their residents. By 1934 the Supreme Court actually held that even contracts between individuals—the very ones the contract clause was intended to protect—could be modified by state law to avert social and economic catastrophe.[5] Although the contract clause is still invoked occasionally to challenge state regulation of property, it is no longer a significant limitation on governmental power.

What Happens When the Government Takes Our Property?

Both the national and state governments have the power of **eminent domain**—the power to take private property for public use—but the owner must be fairly compensated. This limitation, contained in the Fifth Amendment, was the first provision of the Bill of Rights to be enforced as a limitation on state governments as well as on the national government.[6]

What constitutes a "taking" for purposes of eminent domain? Ordinarily, but not always, the taking must be direct, and a person must lose title and control over the property. Sometimes, especially in recent years, the courts have found that a governmental taking has gone "too far," and the government must pay compensation to its owners, even when title is left in the hands of the owners.[7] These are called **regulatory takings**. Thus, if a government creates landing and takeoff paths for airplanes over property adjacent to an airport, making the land no longer suitable for its prior use (say, raising chickens), compensation is warranted.

"Just compensation" is not always easy to define. When there is a dispute over compensation, the courts make the final resolution based on the rule that "the owner is entitled to receive what a willing buyer would pay in cash to a willing seller at the time of the taking."[8] An owner is not entitled to compensation for the personal value of an old, broken-down house that is loved dearly—just the value of the old, broken-down house.

DUE PROCESS RIGHTS

Perhaps the most difficult parts of the Constitution to understand are the clauses in the Fifth and Fourteenth Amendments forbidding the national and state governments to deny any person life, liberty, or property without due process of law. Cases involving these clauses have resulted in hundreds of Supreme Court decisions. Even so, it is impossible to explain *due process* precisely. In fact, the Supreme Court has refused to give due process a precise definition and has emphasized that "due process, unlike some legal rules, is not a technical conception with a fixed content unrelated to time, place and circumstances."[9] We define **due process** as rules and regulations that restrain those in government who exercise power. There are, however, basically two kinds of due process: procedural and substantive.

contract clause
Clause of the Constitution that was originally intended to forbid state governments to modify contracts made between individuals; for a while interpreted to forbid state governments from adversely affecting property rights; no longer interpreted so broadly and no longer constrains state governments from exercising their police powers.

police powers
Inherent powers of state governments to pass laws to protect the public health, safety, and welfare; the national government has no directly granted police powers, but through other delegated powers accomplishes the same goals.

eminent domain
Power of a government to take private property for public use; the U.S. Constitution gives national and state governments this power and requires them to provide just compensation for property so taken.

regulatory taking
Government regulation of property so extensive that government is deemed to have taken the property by the power of eminent domain, for which it must compensate the property owners.

due process
Established rules and regulations that restrain those in government who exercise power.

Procedural Due Process

Traditionally, **procedural due process** refers not to the law itself but to the *way in which a law is applied*. To paraphrase Daniel Webster's famous definition, the due process of law requires a procedure that hears before it condemns, proceeds upon inquiry, and renders judgment only after a trial or some kind of hearing. Originally, procedural due process was limited to criminal prosecutions, but it now applies to most kinds of governmental proceedings. It is required, for instance, in juvenile hearings, disbarment proceedings, proceedings to determine eligibility for welfare payments, revocation of drivers' licenses, and disciplinary proceedings in state universities and public schools.

A law may also violate the procedural due process requirement if it is too vague or if it creates an improper presumption of guilt. A vague statute fails to provide adequate warning and does not contain sufficient guidelines for law enforcement officials, juries, and courts.

The liberty that is protected by due process includes "the right of the individual to contract, to engage in any of the common occupations of life, to acquire useful knowledge, to marry, to establish a home and bring up children, to worship God according to the dictates of his own conscience, and generally to enjoy those common law privileges long recognized as essential to the orderly pursuit of happiness by free men."[10] The property protected by due process includes a variety of rights that may be conferred by state law, such as certain kinds of licenses, protection from being fired from some jobs except for just cause (for example, incompetence) and according to certain procedures, as well as protection from deprivation of certain pension rights.

Substantive Due Process

Procedural due process places limits on *how* governmental power may be exercised; **substantive due process** places limits on *what* a government may do. Procedural due process mainly limits the executive and judicial branches because they apply the law and review its application; substantive due process mainly limits the legislative branch because it enacts laws. Substantive due process means that an "unreasonable" law, even if properly passed and properly applied, is unconstitutional. It means that there are certain things governments *should not be allowed to do.*

Before 1937, substantive due process was used primarily to protect the right of employers to make contracts with employees freely, without government interference. During this period the Supreme Court was dominated by conservative jurists who considered almost all social welfare legislation unreasonable. They used the due process clause to strike down laws setting maximum hours of labor, establishing minimum wages, regulating prices, and forbidding employers to fire workers because they joined a union.

Since 1937 the Supreme Court has largely refused to apply the doctrine of substantive due process in reviewing laws regulating business enterprises and economic interests. The Court now believes that deciding what constitutes reasonable regulation of business and commercial life is a legislative, not a judicial, responsibility. As long as the justices find a conceivable connection between a law regulating business and the promotion of the public welfare, the Supreme Court will not interfere with laws passed by Congress or state legislatures.

This does not mean, however, that the Court has abandoned substantive due process. On the contrary, substantive due process has taken on new life as a protector of civil liberties, most especially the right of privacy. Substantive due process has deep roots in concepts of natural law and a long history in the American constitutional tradition. For most Americans most of the time, it is not enough merely to say that a law reflects the wishes of the popular or legislative majority. We also want our laws to be just, and we continue to rely heavily on judges to decide what is just.

procedural due process
Constitutional requirement that governments proceed by proper methods; places limits on how governmental power may be exercised.

substantive due process
Constitutional requirement that governments act reasonably and that the substance of the laws themselves be fair and reasonable; places limits on what a government may do.

The battle over abortion has been fought in the courts and on the streets, and has been a key issue in recent presidential elections. Republicans anticipate that George W. Bush will appoint justices to the Supreme Court who will reverse Roe v Wade.

PRIVACY RIGHTS

The most important extension of substantive due process in recent decades has been its expansion to protect the right of privacy, especially marital privacy. Although there is no mention of the right of privacy in the Constitution, in *Griswold v Connecticut* (1965) the Supreme Court pulled together elements of the First, Third, Fourth, Fifth, Ninth, and Fourteenth Amendments to recognize that personal privacy is one of the rights protected by the Constitution.[11]

There are three aspects of this right: (1) the right to be free from governmental surveillance and intrusion, especially in marital matters; (2) the right not to have private affairs made public by the government; and (3) the right to be free in thought and belief from governmental regulations.[12]

Abortion Rights

The most controversial aspect of constitutional protection of privacy relates to the extent of state power to regulate abortions. In *Roe v Wade* (1973) the Supreme Court ruled: (1) during the first trimester of a woman's pregnancy, it is an unreasonable and therefore unconstitutional interference with her liberty and privacy rights for a state to set any limits on her choice to have an abortion or on her doctor's medical judgments about how to carry it out; (2) during the second trimester, the state's interest in protecting the health of women becomes compelling, and a state may make a reasonable regulation about how, where, and when abortions may be performed; and (3) during the third trimester, when the life of the fetus outside the womb becomes viable, the state's interest in protecting the unborn child is so important that the state can prohibit abortions altogether, except when necessary to preserve the life or health of the mother.[13]

The *Roe* decision led to decades of heated public debate and attempts by Presidents Ronald Reagan and George Bush to select Supreme Court justices who might be expected to reverse it. Nonetheless, *Roe v Wade* was reaffirmed in *Planned Parenthood v. Casey* (1992). A bitterly divided Rehnquist Court, by a five-person majority (O'Connor, Kennedy, Souter, Blackmun, and Stevens), upheld the view that the due process clauses of the Constitution protect a woman's liberty to choose an abortion prior to viability. The Court, however, held that the right to have an abortion prior to viability may be subject to state regulation that does not "unduly burden" it. In other words, states may make "reasonable regulations" on how a woman exercises her right to an abortion so long as they do not prohibit any woman from making the ultimate decision on whether to terminate a pregnancy before viability.[14]

Applying the *undue burden* test, the Court has held, on the one hand, that states can prohibit the use of state funds and facilities for performing abortions; states may make a minor's right to an abortion conditional on her first notifying at least one parent or a judge; and states may require women to sign an informed consent form and to wait 24 hours before having an abortion. On the other hand, a state may not condition a woman's right to an abortion on her first notifying her husband. The Court also struck down Nebraska's ban on "partial birth" abortions in *Stenberg v Carhart* (2000), because it completely forbid one kind of medical procedure and provided no exception for when a woman's life is at stake and thus imposed an "undue burden" on women.[15]

Sexual Orientation Rights

Although there is general agreement on how much constitutional protection is provided for marital privacy, in *Bowers v Hardwick* (1986) the Supreme Court refused to extend such protection to relations between homosexuals.[16] By a 5 to 4 vote, the Court refused to declare unconstitutional a Georgia law that made consensual sodomy a crime. That homosexual sodomy occurs in the privacy of the home, said the majority, does not matter. But a number of state supreme courts, including that in Georgia, found greater privacy protection in their state constitutions than the U.S.

Supreme Court found in the U.S. Constitution. In 1999 the Vermont state supreme court held that same-sex couples must be given the same benefits and protections as married couples.[17]

In *Boy Scouts of America v Dale* (2000), again by a 5 to 6 vote, the Supreme Court held that a New Jersey public accommodations law could not be applied to keep the Boy Scouts from excluding gays from being Scout leaders.[18] The Court majority concluded that the Boy Scouts are a private association, and as such they have a right to exclude people whose beliefs and conduct are inconsistent with the Scouts' views and mission.

The U.S. Supreme Court, in *Romer v Evans* (1996), struck down an initiative amending the Colorado constitution that prohibited all legislative, executive, or judicial action designed to protect homosexuals at any level of state or local government. This provision violated the equal protection clause because it lacked a rational basis and simply represented a prejudice toward a particular group of people. Justice Antonin Scalia in dissent accused the Court of taking sides in "the cultural wars through an act not of judicial judgment but of political will."[19]

Because of the strong emotions on both sides of this issue, the right of privacy as an element of substantive due process is one of the developing edges of constitutional law, one about which people both on and off the Court have strong disagreements. How the Supreme Court handles privacy issues has become front-page news.

RIGHTS OF PERSONS ACCUSED OF CRIMES

Despite what you sometimes see in television police dramas, law enforcement officers have no general right to break down doors and invade homes. They are not supposed to search people except under certain conditions, and they have no right to arrest them except under certain circumstances. They also may not compel confessions, and they must respect other procedural guarantees aimed at ensuring fairness and the rights of the accused. Persons accused of crimes are guaranteed these and other rights under the Fourth, Fifth, Sixth, Eighth, and Fourteenth Amendments.

Freedom from Unreasonable Searches and Seizures

According to the Fourth Amendment, "The right of the people to be secure in their persons, houses, papers, and effects, against unreasonable searches and seizures, shall not be violated, and no Warrants shall issue, but upon probable cause, supported by Oath or affirmation, and particularly describing the place to be searched, and the persons or things to be seized."

Protection from unreasonable searches and seizures requires police, if they have time, to obtain a valid **search warrant**, issued by a magistrate after the police indicate under oath that they have *probable cause* to justify its issuance. Magistrates must perform this function in a neutral and detached manner and not serve merely as rubber stamps for the police. The warrant must specifically describe: (1) what place is to be searched, and (2) what things are to be seized. *General search warrants*—warrants that authorize police to search a particular place or person without limitation—are unconstitutional. A search warrant is usually needed to search a person in any place he or she has an "expectation of privacy that society is prepared to recognize as reasonable," for example, in a hotel room, in a rented home, in a friend's apartment.[20] In short, the Fourth Amendment protects people, not places, from unreasonable governmental intrusions.[21]

Police may make reasonable *warrantless searches* in *public places* if and the officers have probable cause, or at least a reasonable suspicion, that the persons in question have committed or are about to commit crimes. No later than two days after

search warrant
A warrant issued by a magistrate that authorizes the police to search a particular place or person, specifying the place to be searched and the objects to be seized.

When police fired 41 bullets into an unarmed black man, protests erupted in the Bronx, New York neighborhood.

Police may detain and search cars and their passengers if they have probable cause to believe the passengers may be involved in criminal activity.

making such an arrest, the police must take the arrested person to a magistrate so that the magistrate—not just the police—can decide whether probable cause existed to justify the warrantless arrest.[22] Probable cause, however, does not, except in extreme emergencies, justify a warrantless arrest of people in their own homes.

Under the common law, police officers apprehending a fleeing suspected felon can use weapons that might result in the felon's serious injury, even death. But the Fourth Amendment places substantial limits on the use of what is called *deadly force*. It is unconstitutional to shoot at an apparently unarmed, fleeing, suspected felon unless the officer has probable cause to believe that the suspect poses a significant threat of death or serious injury to the officer or others. Also, when feasible, the officer must first warn the suspect: "Halt or I'll shoot."

Not every time the police stop a person to ask questions or to seek that person's consent to a search is there a seizure or detention requiring probable cause or a warrant. If the police just ask questions or even seek consent to search an individual's person or possessions in a noncoercive atmosphere, there is no detention. "So long as a reasonable person would feel free 'to disregard the police and go about his business,' the encounter is consensual and no reasonable suspicion is required." But if the person refuses to answer questions or consent to a search, and the police, by either physical force or a show of authority, restrain the movement of the person, even though there is no arrest, the Fourth Amendment comes into play.[23] For example, if police approach people in airports and request identification, this act by itself does not constitute a detention. The same is true if police ask bus passengers for consent to search their luggage for drugs. But if the police do more, especially after consent is refused, then their actions require them to have some objective justification for the search beyond mere suspicion.

The Supreme Court also upheld, in *Terry v Ohio* (1968), a *stop and frisk* exception to searches of individuals, when officers have reason to believe they are armed and dangerous, or have committed or are about to commit a criminal offense. The so-called *Terry* search is limited to a quick pat-down to check for weapons that might be used to assault the arresting officer, to check for contraband, to determine identity, or to maintain briefly the status quo while obtaining more information.[24] If an officer stops and frisks a suspect to look for weapons and finds criminal evidence that might justify an arrest, then the officer can make a full search.[25] Police and border guards may also conduct *border* searches—searches of persons and the goods they bring with them at border crossings.[26] The border search exception also permits officials to open mail entering the country if they have "reasonable cause" to suspect it contains merchandise imported in violation of the law.[27]

There are several other exceptions to the general rule against warrantless searches and seizures of what is found by police and customs officials. The most important are:

The Plain-View Exception: The plain-view exception permits officers to seize evidence without a warrant if: (1) they are lawfully in a position from which the evidence can be viewed; (2) it is immediately apparent to them that the items they observe are evidence of a crime or are contraband; and (3) they have probable cause to believe—a reasonable suspicion will not do—that the evidence uncovered is contraband or evidence of a crime.[28]

Exigent Circumstances: Searches are permissible when officers do not have time to secure a warrant before evidence is destroyed, or a criminal escapes capture, or when there is need "to protect or preserve life or avoid serious injury." An example is that fire fighters and police may enter a burning building without a warrant and may remain there for a reasonable time to investigate the cause of the blaze after the fire has been extinguished. However, after the fire has been put out, the emergency is not to be used as an excuse to make an exhaustive, warrantless search for evidence.

The Automobile Exception: If officers have probable cause to believe that an automobile is being used to commit a crime, even a traffic offense, or that it contains persons who have committed crimes, or that it contains evidence of crimes, they may stop the automobile, detain the persons found therein, and search them and any containers or packages found inside the car.[29] Once an automobile has been lawfully detained, the police officers may order the driver and passengers to get out of the car without violating the Fourth Amendment.[30]

Foreign Agents: Although never directly sustained by the Supreme Court, Congress has endorsed the presidential claim that a president can authorize warrantless wiretaps and physical searches of agents of foreign countries. Congress created a special Foreign Intelligence Surveillance Court to approve such requests; this court, consisting of seven federal district judges, meets in secret.[31]

In addition, various administrative searches by nonpolice government agents, such as teachers and health officials, do not require search warrants. Rules governing the conduct of such administrative searches are more lenient than are those for searches by police investigating crimes. Administrative searches conducted without grounds for suspicion of particular individuals have been upheld in certain limited circumstances.[32]

One recent troublesome area relates to compulsory, random drug testing. The Supreme Court has upheld the constitutionality of blood and urine tests of rail employees involved in train accidents, of federal employees, and of high school students engaged in interscholastic athletic competitions. But it struck down a Georgia law requiring candidates for designated state offices to certify that they had taken a drug test and that the test result was negative, because Georgia failed to show why this invasion of personal privacy was necessary.[33]

THE EXCLUSIONARY RULE   In *Mapp v Ohio* (1961), the Supreme Court adopted a rule excluding from a criminal trial evidence that the police obtained unconstitutionally or illegally.[34] This **exclusionary rule** was adopted to prevent police misconduct. Critics of the exclusionary rule question why criminals should go free just because of police misconduct or ineptness,[35] but the Supreme Court has refused to abandon the rule. It has made some exceptions to it, however, such as cases in which police relied in "good faith" on a search warrant that subsequently turned out to be defective or granted improperly.[36]

THE RIGHT TO REMAIN SILENT   During the seventeenth century, certain special courts in England forced confessions from religious dissenters. The British privilege against self-incrimination developed in response to these practices. Because they were familiar with this history, the framers of our Bill of Rights included in the Fifth Amendment the provision that persons shall not be compelled to testify against themselves in criminal prosecutions. This protection against self-incrimination is designed to strengthen the fundamental principle that no person has an obligation to prove innocence. Rather, the burden is on the government to prove guilt.

The privilege against self-incrimination applies literally only in criminal prosecutions. But it has always been interpreted to protect any person subject to questioning by any agency of government, such as a congressional committee. It is not enough, however, to contend that answers might be embarrassing or might lead to loss of a job or even to civil suits; persons must have a reasonable fear that their answers might support a criminal prosecution against them.

Sometimes authorities would rather have information from witnesses than prosecute them. Congress has established procedures so that prosecutors and congressional committees may secure a grant of **immunity** for such a witness. When immunity has been granted, a witness no longer has a constitutional right to refuse to testify, and the government cannot use the information derived directly from the

Use of metal detectors and locker searches at schools does not require search warrants and other protections applied to police searches.

exclusionary rule
Requirement that evidence unconstitutionally or illegally obtained be excluded from a criminal trial.

immunity
Protection granted by prosecutors to witnesses in exchange for giving up their constitutional right not to testify against themselves.

"The court finds itself on the horns of a dilemma. On the one hand, wiretap evidence is inadmissible, and on the other hand, I'm dying to hear it."

compelled testimony in any subsequent prosecution, though the witness may still be prosecuted for crimes on the basis of other evidence.

THE MIRANDA WARNING   Police questioning of suspects is a key procedure in solving crimes. Roughly 90 percent of all criminal convictions result from guilty pleas and never reach a full trial. Police questioning, however, can easily be abused. Police officers sometimes forget or ignore the constitutional rights of suspects, especially those who are frightened and ignorant. Unauthorized detention and lengthy interrogation to wring confessions from suspects, common practice in police states, were not unknown in the United States.

Federal and state laws require police officers to take people they have arrested before a magistrate promptly so that the magistrate may inform them of their constitutional rights and allow them to get in touch with friends and seek legal advice. Despite these requirements, police were often tempted to quiz suspects first, trying to get them to confess before a magistrate informed them of their constitutional right to remain silent.

To put an end to such practices, the Supreme Court, in *Miranda v Arizona* (1966), announced that no conviction could stand if evidence introduced at the trial had been obtained by the police during "custodial interrogation" unless suspects were notified that they have a right to remain silent and to have an attorney present during questioning by police, as well as have a lawyer appointed to represent them if they cannot afford to hire their own attorney.[37] If suspects answer questions in the absence of an attorney, the burden is on prosecutors to demonstrate that suspects knowingly and intelligently gave up their rights to remain silent. Failure to comply with these requirements leads to reversal of a conviction, even if other evidence is sufficient to establish guilt.

Critics of the *Miranda* decision believe the Supreme Court severely limited the ability of the police to bring criminals to justice. Over the years, the Court has modified the original ruling by allowing evidence obtained contrary to the *Miranda* guidelines to be used to attack the credibility of defendants who offer testimony at their trial that conflicts with their statements to the police. Congress tried to get around *Miranda* in the Crime Control and Safe Streets Act of 1968 by allowing confessions made in violation of *Miranda* to be used as evidence in federal courts. But in a decision handed down in June 2000, the Court reaffirmed the constitutionality of the *Miranda* doctrine. In an opinion by Chief Justice William H. Rehnquist, the Court held that the *Miranda* warning is not merely a rule of evidence to enforce the constitutional guarantee, but is itself constitutionally required and applies in both state and federal courts.[38]

Fair Trial Procedures

Many people consider the rights of persons accused of a crime to be less important than other rights. But, as Justice Felix Frankfurter observed, "The history of liberty has largely been the history of observance of procedural safeguards." Further, these safeguards have frequently "been forged in controversies involving not very nice people."[39] Nonetheless, they guarantee that all persons accused of crimes will have the right to representation by counsel and to a fair trial by an impartial jury.

THE RIGHT TO COUNSEL   If after questioning by police the suspect is arrested and charged with a crime, the Supreme Court has ruled that the accused has a constitutional right to counsel at every stage of the criminal proceedings—preliminary hearings, bail hearings, trial, sentencing, and first appeal.

INDICTMENT   Except for members of the armed forces, the national government cannot require anyone to stand trial for a serious crime except on the basis of a grand jury indictment; states are not required to use grand juries, and those that do not, vest

The Miranda warning is read to a suspect by a police officer to inform him of his rights, such as the right to remain silent and the right to have an attorney present.

prosecutors with the power to seek indictments. A **grand jury** is concerned not with a person's guilt or innocence but merely with whether there is enough evidence to warrant a trial. The grand jury has wide-ranging investigatory powers and "is to inquire into all information that might bear on its investigations until it is satisfied that it has identified an offense or satisfied itself that none has occurred."[40] The strict rules that govern jury proceedings do not apply. The grand jury may admit hearsay evidence, and the exclusionary rule to enforce the Fourth Amendment does not apply. If a majority of the grand jurors agree that a trial is justified, they return what is known as a true bill, or **indictment**.

The Constitution guarantees the accused *the right to be informed of the nature and cause of the accusation* so that he or she can prepare a defense. After indictment for an offense, prosecutors and the attorney for the accused usually discuss the possibility of a **plea bargain**—that is, the defendant pleads guilty to a lesser offense that carries a shorter prison sentence. Prosecutors, faced with more cases than they can handle, like plea bargains because they save the expense and time of going to trial. Likewise, defendants are often willing to "cop a plea" for a lesser offense to avoid the risk of more serious punishment.

When defendants plead guilty, they are usually forever prevented from raising objections to their conviction. That is why, before accepting guilty pleas, the judge questions defendants to be sure their attorneys have explained the alternatives and they know what they are doing.

THE TRIAL   After indictment and preliminary hearings that determine bail and what evidence will be used as evidence against the accused, the Constitution guarantees a *speedy and public trial*. Do not, however, take the word "speedy" too literally. Defendants are given time to prepare their defense and, in fact, often ask for delays, because delay often works to their advantage. In contrast, if the government denies the accused a speedy trial, not only is the conviction reversed but the case must also be dismissed outright.

Under the Sixth Amendment, the accused has a right to trial before a **petit jury** selected from the state and district in which the alleged crime was committed. Although federal law requires juries of 12 members, the Supreme Court has held that states may try defendants before juries consisting of at least 6 persons. Conviction in federal courts must be by unanimous vote, but the Court has ruled that state courts may render guilty verdicts by nonunanimous juries, provided such juries consist of 6 or more persons.[41]

An *impartial jury*, one that meets the requirements of due process and equal protection, consists of persons who represent a fair cross-section of the community. Although defendants are not entitled to juries on which there must be members of their own race, sex, religion, or national origin, government prosecutors cannot strike people from juries because of race or gender, and neither can defense attorneys use what are called *peremptory challenges* to keep people off juries because of race, ethnic origin, or sex.[42]

During the trial, the defendant has a right to obtain witnesses in his favor and to have the judge subpoena witnesses to appear at the trial and testify. Both the accused and witnesses may refuse to testify on the grounds that their testimony would tend to incriminate them. If they testify, the prosecution has the right to cross-examine them, just as the accused has the right to confront and to cross-examine witnesses.

Sentencing and Punishment

At the conclusion of the trial, the jury recommends a verdict of guilty or not guilty. If the accused is found guilty, the judge then hands down the sentence. The Eighth Amendment forbids the levying of excessive fines and the inflicting of cruel and unusual punishment.

The Miranda Warning

In *Miranda v Arizona* (1966), the Supreme Court held that before questioning criminal suspects, the police must warn them that:

1. They have a right to remain silent.
2. Anything they say may and will be used against them in a court of law.
3. They have the right to presence of a lawyer during police questioning.
4. If they cannot afford an attorney, one will be appointed for them.
5. They have a right to terminate police questioning at any point.

grand jury
A jury of 12 to 23 persons who, in private, hear evidence presented by the government to determine whether persons shall be required to stand trial; if the jury believes there is sufficient evidence that a crime was committed, it issues an indictment.

indictment
A formal charge issued by a grand jury against an individual for a specified crime; also called a *true bill*.

plea bargain
Negotiations between prosecutor and defendant aimed at getting the defendant to plead guilty in return for the prosecutor's agreeing to reduce the seriousness of the crime for which the defendant will be charged.

petit jury
A jury of 6 to 12 persons that determines guilt or innocence in a civil or criminal action.

Cruel and Unusual Punishment

The Eighth Amendment ban against cruel and unusual punishment limits government in three ways:

1. It limits the kinds and methods of punishment that may be imposed, prohibiting, for example, torture, intentional denial of medical care, inhumane conditions, unnecessary or wanton inflicting of pain, and deliberate indifference to medical and other needs of prisoners.*

2. It prohibits punishments grossly disproportionate to the severity of the crime. However, the Supreme Court has been reluctant to review legislative prescriptions of terms of punishment, and successful challenges to the severity of punishments have been extremely rare.**

3. It limits the power of the government to decide what can be made a criminal offense. For example, the mere act of being a chronic alcoholic may not be made a crime because alcoholism is an illness. However, being drunk in public may be a criminal offense.

*Hudson v McMillian, 503 US 1 (1992); Farmer v Brennan, 511 US 825 (1994).

**Hutto v Davis, 454 US 370 (1982); Solem v Helm, 463 US 277 (1983).

In federal courts, judges follow the sentencing guidelines set down by the United States Sentencing Commission. Such sentences are not considered cruel and unusual. Many states have also established guidelines for sentencing by state courts.

THREE STRIKES AND YOU'RE OUT   Although the crime rate has actually been going down in the past few years, public concern about crime still remains high. At the national and state level, presidents, governors, and legislators vie with one another to show their toughness on crime. Virginia, Washington, and a number of other states have *three strikes and you're out* laws, requiring lifetime sentences without the possibility of parole for those convicted of three felonies. In some states, the felonies have to be for violent crimes; in others any three felonies will do. Scholars are skeptical that "three strikes and you're out" laws will reduce the crime rate. Moreover, constructing more jails to take care of aging felons will certainly require great expenditures of public funds.

APPEALS AND DOUBLE JEOPARDY   After trial, conviction, and sentencing, defendants may appeal their convictions if they claim they have been denied some constitutional right or denied the due process and equal protection of the law. The Fifth Amendment also provides that no person shall be "subject for the same offense to be twice put in jeopardy of life or limb." **Double jeopardy** does not prevent punishment by the national and the state governments for the same offense or for successive prosecutions for the same crime by two states. Nor does the double jeopardy clause forbid civil prosecutions, even after acquittal in a criminal trial for the same conduct.[43]

THE DEATH PENALTY   Capital punishment remains controversial. Japan and the United States are the only two industrialized countries to retain the death penalty. The 15 members of the European Union outlawed capital punishment, and courts in South Africa, Hungary, and other Central and East European countries have declared it unconstitutional and a denial of human dignity.

After a ten-year moratorium on executions in the late 1960s and early 1970s, the U.S. Supreme Court ruled the death penalty is not necessarily cruel and unusual punishment if it is imposed for conviction of crimes that resulted in a victim's death, if the procedures used by the courts "ensure that death sentences are not meted out wantonly or freakishly," and if these processes "confer on the sentencer sufficient discretion to take account of the character and record of the individual offender and the circumstances of the particular offense to ensure that death is the appropriate punishment in a specific case."[44]

In the 1990s, the Rehnquist Court made it easier to impose death sentences, cut back on appeals, and carry out executions. More states also added the death penalty (there are now 38), and the national government increased the number of crimes for which the death penalty may be imposed. As a result, the number of persons on death row increased dramatically. Since capital punishment was reinstated in 1976, more than 600 people have been executed nationwide, and more than 3,600 are on death row. As the number of executions has increased, however, concerns have also grown about the fairness of how capital punishment is imposed.

HOW JUST IS OUR SYSTEM OF JUSTICE?

double jeopardy
Trial or punishment for the same crime by the same government; forbidden by the Constitution.

What are the major criticisms of the American system of justice? How have they been answered? How accurate are TV shows and movies that highlight criminals going free and innocent people being imprisoned? Do they accurately reflect how our system of justice works?

Too Many Loopholes?

Some observers argue that by overprotecting criminals and placing too much of a burden on the criminal justice system not to make any mistakes, we delay justice, encourage disrespect for the law, and allow guilty persons to go unpunished. Justice should be swift and certain without being arbitrary. But under our procedures, criminals may go unpunished because: (1) the police decide not to arrest them; (2) the prosecutor decides not to prosecute them; (3) the grand jury decides not to indict them; (4) the judge decides not to hold them for trial; (5) the jury decides not to convict them; (6) the appeals court decides to reverse the conviction; (7) the judge decides to release them on a *habeas corpus* writ; or (8) the president or governor decides to pardon, reprieve, or parole them if convicted. As a result, the public never knows whom to hold responsible when laws are not enforced. The police blame prosecutors, prosecutors blame the police, and they all blame the juries and judges.

Others take a different view and point out that there is more to justice than simply securing convictions. All the steps in the administration of criminal laws have been developed over centuries of trial and error, and each step has been constructed to protect ordinary persons from particular abuses by those in power. History warns against entrusting the instruments of criminal law enforcement to a single officer. For this reason, responsibility is vested in many officials.

Too Unreliable?

Critics who say that our system of justice is unreliable often point to trial by jury as the chief source of trouble. No other country relies as heavily on trial by jury as does the United States. Jury trials are also time-consuming and costly. Trial by jury, critics argue, leads to a theatrical combat between lawyers who base their appeals on the prejudices and sentiments of the jurors. "Mr. Prejudice and Miss Sympathy are the names of witnesses whose testimony is never recorded, but must nevertheless be reckoned with in trials by jury."[45]

The jury system allows for what is called *jury nullification*, in which jurors ignore their instructions to consider only the evidence presented in court, and, by voting for acquittal, express their displeasure with the law or the actions of prosecutors or police. Jury nullification has a long history. In colonial times juries refused to convict colonists of political crimes against the king as a way to protest British rule. Before the Civil War, northern juries refused to convict people for helping runaway slaves. Before the 1970s, white southern juries sometimes refused to convict police for brutality against blacks.

Responding to growing public disenchantment with juries after a raft of unpopular verdicts, states have been rewriting the rules for the jury system. These changes include making it more difficult for people to be excused from jury service, allowing for nonunanimous decisions, limiting how long jurors can be sequestered, and exerting more control by judges over lawyer's statements to jurors in order to prevent appeals to jurors' emotions.

Defenders of the jury system reply that trial by jury provides a check by nonprofessionals on the actions of judges and prosecutors. There is no evidence that juries are unreliable; on the contrary, decisions of juries do not significantly differ from those of judges.[46] Moreover, the jury system helps to educate citizens and enables them to participate in the application of their country's laws.

Too Discriminatory?

During the last several decades, the Supreme Court has worked particularly hard to enforce the ideal of equal justice under the law. Persons accused of a crime who cannot afford attorneys must be furnished them at government expense. If transcripts are required for appeals, such transcripts must be made available to those who cannot afford to purchase them. If appeals are permitted, the government must provide attorneys for at least one appeal of the decision of the trial court. Poor people cannot be

THE DEATH PENALTY ON TRIAL

As the number of death row inmates and executions has grown, debate over the fairness and permissibility of capital punishment has become widespread. The American Bar Association called for a halt to executions because the death penalty is administered in ways that deny fundamental due process and the equal protection of law. Christian televangelist Pat Robinson joined the ABA and Catholic bishops in calling for a moratorium on executions. Illinois Republican Governor George Ryan declared a moratorium on executions in his state because more death row inmates were released from prison in recent years who had been wrongly convicted than were executed. Other prominent Republicans and Democrats also began questioning the system of imposing the death penalty.

The debate about the fairness of capital punishment was sparked by the increasing number of inmates who have been released because new DNA evidence proved their innocence—often after spending a decade or more on death row. DNA evidence is useful, however, only in cases of rape or murder when blood or tissue samples remain. A recent poll found that 92 percent of Americans say prison inmates convicted before the technology was available should be given the opportunity to submit to DNA tests now. For more information, go to Gallup's website: www.gallup.com/index.html.

This debate has refocused the controversy by drawing into question the fairness of the entire process of capital punishment. Critics point out the seemingly randomness in imposing capital punishment. Public prosecutors seek the death penalty in less than 5 percent of all murder cases. Defendants often agree to plea bargains in return for life sentences. When murder trials are held, some juries refuse to impose death sentences. And of those sentenced to death, some receive clemency or are pardoned.

A study of more than 4,500 capital cases released in June 2000 found that more than two-thirds of all death sentences are overturned. Why? The primary reasons are that defense lawyers were incompetent,

Illinois governor George Ryan called a halt to executions in his state because of mishandling and inadequate defense of accused individuals who were later discovered to be innocent.

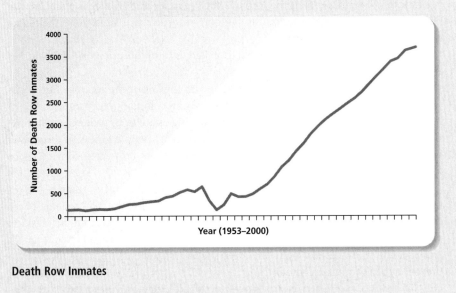

Death Row Inmates

imprisoned because of inability to pay a fine. Nor, once sentenced, can poor people be kept in jail beyond the term of the sentence because they cannot afford to pay a fine. Even for civil proceedings—divorce proceedings, for example—fees cannot be imposed that deny poor people their fundamental rights, such as the right to obtain a divorce.

Unfair to Minorities?

One of the more acute problems of our society is the tension between the police and the African American and Hispanic communities congregated in the ghettos and barrios of our large cities. Many members of minorities do not believe they have

Rubin "Hurricane" Carter was a boxer who was wrongly convicted of a murder in 1967 and spent 21 years on death row before he was exonerated and released.

important evidence was overlooked by police, witnesses lied, and prosecutors sometimes withheld evidence from the defense.

Besides the apparent randomness in who is sentenced to death and later executed, racial discrimination in the imposition of capital punishment is a major concern. Blacks who murder whites are much more likely to receive death sentences than whites who murder blacks or blacks who kill blacks. The American public generally supports the death penalty, though support slipped in 2000 to 66 percent, the lowest point since 1978. Some people are morally opposed to capital punishment because of its finality; others maintain that it should be inflicted on those who commit heinous murders,

and still others insist that it is too arbitrary and randomly imposed—or as Justice Potter Stewart put it, "Death sentences are cruel and unusual in the same way that being struck by lightening is cruel and unusual."

SOURCES: "A Life or Death Gamble," *Newsweek*, May 29, 2000, pp. 22–27; Barry Scheck, Peter Neufeld, and Jim Dwyer, *Actual Innocence: Five Days to Execution, and Other Dispatches from the Wrongly Convicted* (Doubleday, 2000); Harry Weinstein, "Death Penalty Is Overturned in Most Cases," *The Los Angeles Times*, June 20, 2000, p. A1; reporting James S. Liebman, "A Broken System: Error Rates in Capital Cases, 1973–1995." See *McCleskey v Kemp*, 481 US 279 (1987); Walter Berns, *For Capital Punishment: Crime and Morality of the Death Penalty* (Basic Books, 1979); Justice Potter Stewart, concurring in *Furman v Georgia*, 408 US 238 (1972); Charles L. Black, Jr., *Capital Punishment: The Inevitability of Caprice and Mistake* (W.W. Norton, 1974).

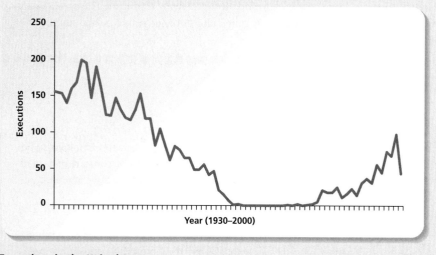

SOURCE: U.S. Department of Justice, Bureau of Criminal Justice Statistics and the Death Penalty Information Center. For more information go to Death Penalty Information Center at www.deathpenaltyinfo.org.

Executions in the United States

equal protection under the law. "Whether the stated belief is well founded or not is," as one political scientist observed, "at least partly beside the point. The existence of the belief is damaging enough."[47]

Some blacks consider the police to be enforcers of white law. Studies proving prejudice on the part of some white police officers and examples of rough, if not brutal, police treatment of blacks are ample evidence to support this viewpoint. One study in California found that "the rate of unfounded arrest was four times higher for African Americans than Anglos. Latino rates were double those of Anglos."[48] Police use of **racial profiling** also concerns blacks, Hispanics, and whites.[49]

racial profiling
Police target racial minorities as potential suspects of criminal activities.

In recent decades action has been taken to recruit more African Americans, Hispanics, and women as police officers, including appointment to command posts. In larger cities there are now oversight boards including civilians to which complaints about police misconduct can be brought. **Community policing** is also being substituted in some cities for the traditional police procedures. Police departments work with churches and other local community groups and take police out of patrol cars to walk the beat and work in neighborhoods. Community policing, when combined with working with community organizations to sponsor crime-prevention programs, appears not only to reduce crime but to improve minorities' confidence in the police.[50]

THE SUPREME COURT AND CIVIL LIBERTIES

Clearly, judges play a major role in enforcing constitutional guarantees. Such reliance on judicial protection of our civil liberties focuses public attention on the Supreme Court. Yet only a small number of controversies are actually carried to the Supreme Court, and a Supreme Court decision is not the end of the judicial process. Lower-court judges as well as police, superintendents of schools, local prosecutors, school boards, state legislatures, and thousands of others clarify the Court's doctrines.

Moreover, the Supreme Court can do little unless its decisions over time reflect a national consensus. As Supreme Court Justice Robert H. Jackson (on the Court 1941–54) observed:

> It is my belief that the attitude of a society and of its organized political forces, rather than its legal machinery, is the controlling force in the character of free institutions. Any court that undertakes by its legal processes to enforce civil liberties needs the support of an enlightened and vigorous public opinion.[51]

Thus, the Bill of Rights—and the other procedural and substantive liberties of our Constitution—cannot rest on a foundation merely of tradition. The preservation of these rights depends on wide, continuing, and knowledgeable public support.

community policing
Recent programs to move police from patrol cars into neighborhoods, where they walk the beat and work with churches and other community groups to reduce crime and improve relations with minorities.

POLITICS ONLINE

Are Your E-mail Messages Private?

The e-mail message you send or receive at work or at school may not be private. Employers and some educational institutions assert their right to periodically monitor the content of e-mail run through their servers or addresses. For information on the current e-mail privacy policy and how employers and universities can monitor your e-mail go to:
www.nolo.com/encyclopedia/articles/ilaw/email_privacy.html.

You should not assume that because you have deleted e-mail messages from your computer at work or at school, that these messages cannot be read by others; these messages are probably backed up on the institutional mainframe computer. One alternative to ensure your e-mail is private is to send personal messages on your own account.

You may have received unsolicited messages from business, travel, or other websites. Most likely these companies bought your address from a company you patronized. Businesses are free to buy and sell your address unless you indicate that you do not want your address shared. In this sense, the sale and resale of e-mail lists is like the sale of conventional mailing lists. For many e-mail users, unsolicited use of their e-mail address is annoying. To limit this annoyance, be sure to check the box that specified that you do not want to give your address out (if such an option exists). Many e-mail servers like Yahoo and Hotmail offer a "block sender" option. Check this option on your next junk mail message, and the server will block that company from sending you mail in the future.

For an interesting example of an internet privacy case, read: **www.prenticehall.burns/com** for this chapter, or check the websites of groups concerned about Internet privacy like: **www.eff.org/CAF**, and go to their academic freedom home page.

SUMMARY

1. One of the basic distinctions between a free society and a police state is that in a free society there are effective restraints on the way public officials, especially law enforcement officials, perform their duties. In the United States the courts enforce these constitutional restraints.

2. The Constitution protects the acquisition and retention of citizenship. It protects the basic liberties of citizens as well as aliens.

3. The Constitution protects our property from arbitrary governmental interference, although debates about which interferences are reasonable and which are arbitrary are not easily settled.

4. The Constitution imposes limits not only on the procedures government must follow but also on the ends it may pursue. Some actions are out of bounds no matter what procedures are followed. Legislatures have the primary role in determining what is reasonable and what is unreasonable. However, the Supreme Court continues to exercise its own independent and final review of legislative determinations of reasonableness, especially on matters affecting civil liberties and civil rights.

5. The Supreme Court has pulled together elements from the First, Fourth, Fifth, Ninth, and Fourteenth Amendments to recognize a constitutionally protected right to personal privacy, especially with regard to marital privacy, including the right of a woman to choose an abortion.

6. The framers knew from their own experiences that in their zeal to maintain power and to enforce the laws, public officials are often tempted to infringe on the rights of those accused of crimes. To prevent such abuse, the Bill of Rights requires federal officials to follow detailed procedures in making searches and arrests and in bringing people to trial.

7. The Supreme Court continues to play a prominent role in developing public policy to protect the rights of the accused, to ensure that the innocent are not punished, and to guarantee that the public is protected against those who break the laws. The Court's decisions influence what the public believes and how police officers and others involved in the administration of justice behave. But the Court alone cannot guarantee fairness in the administration of justice.

KEY TERMS

naturalization 384
dual citizenship 385
right of expatriation 385
property rights 386
contract clause 388
police powers 388

eminent domain 388
regulatory taking 388
due process 388
procedural due process 389
substantive due process 389

search warrant 391
exclusionary rule 393
immunity 393
grand jury 395
indictment 395

plea bargain 395
petit jury 395
double jeopardy 396
racial profiling 399
community policing 400

FURTHER READING

JEFFREY ABRAMSON, *We, The Jury: The Jury System and the Ideal of Democracy* (Basic Books, 1994).

LIVA BAKER, *Miranda: Crime, Law and Politics* (Atheneum, 1983).

DAVID COLE, *No Equal Justice: Race and Class in the American Criminal Justice System* (New Press, 1999).

GEORGE P. FLETHER, *Basic Concepts of Criminal Law* (Oxford University Press, 1998).

DAVID J. GARROW, *Liberty and Sexuality: The Right to Privacy and the Making of Roe v. Wade* (Macmillan Publishing Co., 1994).

KENNETH KARST, *Law's Promise, Law's Expression: Visions of Power in the Politics of Race, Gender, and Religion* (Yale University Press, 1993).

RANDALL KENNEDY, *Race, Crime, and the Law* (Pantheon, 1997).

ANTHONY LEWIS, *Gideon's Trumpet* (Random House, 1964).

JOHN R. LOTT, JR., *More Guns, Less Crime: Understanding Crime and Gun Control Laws* (University of Chicago Press, 2000).

DAVID M. O'BRIEN, *Constitutional Law and Politics*, Vol. 2, *Civil Rights and Civil Liberties*, 4th ed. (W.W. Norton, 2000).

J. W. PELTASON AND SUE DAVIS, *Understanding the Constitution*, 15th ed. (Harcourt College Division, 2000).

BARRY SCHECK, PETER NEUFELD, AND JIM DWYER, *Actual Innocence: Five Days to Execution, and Other Dispatches from the Wrongly Convicted* (Doubleday, 2000).

JUDITH N. SHKLAR, *American Citizenship: The Quest for Inclusion* (Harvard University Press, 1991).

MELVIN UROFSKY, *Lethal Judgments: Assisted Suicide and American Law* (University Press of Kentucky, 2000).

U.S. COMMISSION ON IMMIGRATION REFORM, *Report to Congress: Executive Summary: Becoming an American, Immigration and Immigrant Policy* (U.S. Commission on Immigration Reform, 1997).

WELSH S. WHITE, *The Death Penalty in the Nineties* (University of Michigan Press, 1991).

ROBERT V. WOLF and AUSTIN SARAT, EDS., *The Jury System* (Chelsea House, 1998).

18

EQUAL RIGHTS UNDER THE LAW

C ONSIDER AGAIN THE RINGING WORDS OF THE DECLARATION OF INDEPENDENCE: "WE HOLD THESE TRUTHS TO BE SELF-EVIDENT, THAT ALL MEN ARE CREATED equal, that they are endowed by their Creator with certain unalienable Rights, that among these are Life, Liberty, and the pursuit of Happiness." In this one sentence the Declaration affirmed the precious rights of *equality* and *liberty* and appeared to rate equality at least on a par with liberty. Although the Declaration does not specify equality of white, Christian, or Anglo-Saxon men (at that time "all men" meant white, property-owning Anglo-Saxon men), it has taken more than two hundred years for that definition to be expanded to include all races, all religions, and all women. This creed of individual dignity and equality is older than our Declaration of Independence; its roots go back into the teachings of Judaism and Christianity.

What about the Constitution? What does that historic document say about the framers' attitude toward liberty and equality? Although you will not find any reference to equality (the word never appears in the Constitution or in the Bill of Rights), we know the framers believed that all men—at least all white men—were equally entitled to life, liberty, and the pursuit of happiness. But like the Declaration, the Constitution referred only to "men" or "him," not to women, and none of its lofty sentiments applied to slaves, who enjoyed neither liberty nor equality.

The framers resolved their ambiguity about what kind of equality and for whom by creating a system of government designed to protect what they called *natural rights.* (Today we speak of *human rights*, but the idea is the same.) By **natural rights** the framers meant that every person has an equal right to protection against arbitrary treatment, an equal right to the liberties guaranteed by the Bill of Rights. These rights do not depend on citizenship; they are not granted by governments. They are the rights of *all people.*

The terms *civil liberties* and *civil rights* are often used interchangeably to refer to rights that are protected by the constitutional systems of constitutional democracies. *Civil liberties* is sometimes used more narrowly to refer to freedom of conscience, religion, and expression. *Civil rights* is used to refer to the right not to be discriminated against because of race, religion, gender, ethnic origin, or sexual orientation. Our Constitution provides two ways of protecting civil rights: first, it ensures that *government officials do not discriminate* against us; second, it grants national and state governments the power to *protect* these civil rights against interference *by private individuals.*

CHAPTER MEDIA

POLITICS ONLINE
Reparations for Slaves?
www.prenhall.com/burns

POLISIM
Travel the Civil Rights Timeline
www.prenhall.com/burns

This chapter is concerned with both the protection of our rights from abuse *by government* and the protection *through government* of our right to be free from abuse by our *fellow citizens*. In this chapter we focus on the struggles of African Americans, women, Hispanics, Asian Americans, and Native Americans to secure the basic civil rights to the vote, to an education, to a job, and to a place to live on equal terms with their fellow citizens.

EQUALITY AND EQUAL RIGHTS

Americans are committed to equality. *Equality*, however, is an elusive term. The concept for which there is the greatest consensus and is most clearly written into the Constitution is that everybody should have *equality of opportunity* regardless of race, ethnic origin, religion, and, in recent years, gender and sexual orientation. Ensuring this equality of opportunity has led to the historic struggle for civil rights in this country.

A variation of the concept of equal opportunity is *equality of starting conditions*. There is not much equal opportunity if one person is born into a well-to-do family, lives in a safe suburb, is well fed, and receives a good education, while another is born into a poor, broken family, lives in an inner-city neighborhood, and attends inferior schools. Thus, it is argued, if we are to have equality of opportunity in a meaningful sense, we must provide opportunities for the disadvantaged through federal programs such as Head Start, which provides children from poor families with preschool experiences that prepare them for elementary school.

Empowering people so they share equal starting conditions can be accomplished by ensuring that individuals are not placed at a disadvantage because of prejudice or poverty. Traditional emphasis has been upon *individual* achievement, but such action sometimes shades into a concept of *equality between groups*. When large disparities in wealth and advantage exist between groups—as between blacks and whites or between women and men—equality becomes a highly divisive political issue. The disadvantaged tend to emphasize economic and social factors that exclude them from the mainstream. They champion programs like **affirmative action**, which are designed to provide special help to people based upon their group memberships. Those who are advantaged, however, often act to maintain the status quo and downplay socioeconomic disparities. As a result, whether such programs promote or deny equality remains one of the most controversial current debates.

Finally, equality can also mean *equality of results*. One perennial debate, especially among college students, is whether social justice and genuine equality can exist in a nation in which some people have so much and others have so little, and where the gap between them grows ever wider. Socialists and others call for a more equal distribution of wealth, yet such a view has had little support in the United States. There is considerable support for guaranteeing a minimum floor—a "safety net"—below which no one should be allowed to fall, but many people fear that insistence on equality of results would undermine equality of opportunity. The American view is not that everybody should have the same amount of material goods, but that, whatever a person's economic status for the moment, he or she should be able to expect that things will get better, and that hard work and risk-taking will be rewarded.

THE QUEST FOR EQUAL JUSTICE

To put into perspective the court decisions, laws, and other governmental actions relating to civil rights for women and minorities, we review here the political history and social contexts in which these constitutional issues were raised. Constitutional questions do not involve only court decisions, laws, and constitutional amendments; they encompass the entire social, economic, and political system.

natural rights
Rights of all people to dignity and worth.

affirmative action
Remedial action designed to overcome the effects of past discrimination against minorities and women.

Although the struggles of all groups are interwoven, they are not identical, so we deal briefly and separately with each.

White versus Black

Americans had a painful confrontation with the problem of race before, during, and after the Civil War. As a result of the northern victory, the Thirteenth, Fourteenth, and Fifteenth Amendments became part of the Constitution. During Reconstruction, Congress passed a series of civil rights laws to implement these amendments and established programs to provide educational and social services for the freed slaves. But the Supreme Court struck down many of these laws, and it was not until the 1960s that progress was again made toward ensuring African Americans their civil rights.

SEGREGATION AND WHITE SUPREMACY   Before Reconstruction programs had any significant effect, however, the white southern political leadership was restored to power, and by 1877 Reconstruction was ended. Northern political leaders abandoned African Americans to their fate at the hands of their former white masters; presidents no longer concerned themselves with the enforcement of civil rights laws; and Congress enacted no new ones. The Supreme Court either declared old laws unconstitutional or interpreted them so narrowly that they were ineffective. The Court also gave such a limited construction to the Thirteenth, Fourteenth, and Fifteenth Amendments that they failed to accomplish their intended purpose of protecting the rights of African Americans.

White supremacy was unchallenged in the South, where most African Americans lived. They were kept from voting; they were forced to accept menial jobs; and they were denied educational opportunities. African Americans were being lynched on an average of one every four days, and few whites raised a voice in protest.

During World War I, African Americans began to migrate to northern cities to seek jobs in war factories. Their relocation was accelerated in the 1930s by the depression and in the 1940s by World War II. Although discrimination continued, there were more jobs and more social gains. As migration of African Americans out of the rural South into southern and northern cities shifted the racial composition of cities, the African American vote became important in national elections. These changes created an African American middle class opposed to segregation as a symbol of servitude and a cause of inequality. By the middle of the twentieth century, urban African Americans were active and politically powerful citizens. There was a growing demand for the abolition of color barriers.

THE NATIONAL GOVERNMENT RESPONDS   In the 1930s, African Americans began resorting to lawsuits to challenge the doctrine of segregation. After World War II, this civil rights litigation began to have an impact. In the years that followed, the Supreme Court, beginning with *Brown v Board of Education* (1954), outlawed all forms of government-imposed segregation and struck down most of the devices that had been used by state and local authorities to keep African Americans from voting.

Presidents Harry S. Truman and Dwight D. Eisenhower used their executive authority to fight segregation in the armed services and the federal bureaucracy. They directed the Department of Justice to enforce whatever civil rights laws were available, but Congress still held back. In the late 1950s, an emerging national consensus in favor of governmental action to protect civil rights plus the political clout of African Americans in the northern states began to have some influence on Congress. In 1957 Congress overrode a southern filibuster in the Senate and enacted the first federal civil rights laws since Reconstruction.

A TURNING POINT   Even after the Supreme Court declared government-imposed racial segregation unconstitutional, most African Americans were still kept from voting. Many legal barriers in the path of equal rights had fallen, yet most African Americans

Martin Luther King, Jr.

"Five score years ago, a great American in whose symbolic shadow we stand signed the Emancipation Proclamation. This momentous decree came as a great beacon light of hope to millions of Negro slaves who had been seared in the flames of withering injustice. It came as a joyous daybreak to end the long night of captivity. But one hundred years later, we must face the tragic fact that the Negro is still not free. One hundred years later, the life of the Negro is still sadly crippled by the manacles of segregation and the chains of discrimination. One hundred years later, the Negro lives on a lonely island of poverty in the midst of a vast ocean of material prosperity. One hundred years later, the Negro is still languishing in the corners of American society and finds himself an exile in his own land. So we have come here today to dramatize an appalling condition. . . .

I have a dream that one day this nation will rise up and live out the true meaning of its creed: 'We hold these truths to be self-evident, that all men are created equal.'

I have a dream that one day on the red hills of Georgia the sons of former slaves and the sons of former slave owners will be able to sit down together at the table of brotherhood.

I have a dream that one day even the state of Mississippi, a desert state sweltering with the heat of injustice and oppression, will be transformed into an oasis of freedom and justice.

I have a dream that my four little children will one day live in a nation where they will not be judged by the color of their skin but by the content of their character."

SOURCE: Martin Luther King, Jr., address at the Lincoln Memorial, August 28, 1963. To listen to the speech, go to our website (www.prenhall.com/burns) or to the History and Politics Out Loud website at www.hpol.org, or go directly to database.library.nwu.edu/scripts/webobjects.exe/hpol.woa/wa/displayclip?wosid=v3600pn400fa200p7clipid=72.

still could not buy houses where they wanted, secure the jobs they needed, find educational opportunities for their children, or eat in a restaurant or walk freely on the streets of "white neighborhoods."

But times were changing. What had once been thought of as a "southern problem" was finally being recognized as a national challenge. A massive social, economic, and political movement began to supplement the struggles in the courtrooms. It began in Montgomery, Alabama, on December 1, 1955, when Rosa Parks refused to give up a seat in the front of a bus and was removed from the bus. The black community responded by boycotting city buses.

The boycott worked. It also produced a charismatic national civil rights leader, the Reverend Martin Luther King, Jr. Through his doctrine of nonviolent resistance, Dr. King gave a new dimension to the struggle. By the early 1960s, new organizational resources came into existence in almost every city to support and sponsor sit-ins, freedom rides, live-ins, and other nonviolent demonstrations. These measures were often met with violence, and some state and local governments failed to protect the victims or to prosecute those responsible for the violence.[1]

The forces of social discontent exploded in the summer of 1963. The explosion started with a demonstration in Birmingham, Alabama, which was countered with fire hoses, police dogs, and mass arrests. It ended in a march in Washington, D.C., where at least 250,000 people heard Dr. King and other civil rights leaders speak, and countless millions watched them on television. By the time the summer was over, there was hardly a city, North or South, that had not had demonstrations, protests, or sit-ins. Some also had violence.

This direct action had some effect. Many cities enacted civil rights ordinances, more schools were desegregated, and President John Kennedy urged Congress to enact a comprehensive civil rights bill. Late in 1963, the nation's grief over the assassination of President Kennedy, who had become identified with civil rights goals, added political fuel to the drive for decisive federal action to protect civil rights.[2] President Lyndon Johnson made civil rights legislation his highest priority, and on July 2, 1964, after months of debate, he signed into law the Civil Rights Act of 1964.[3]

TWO SOCIETIES? By the early 1970s the legal phase of the civil rights movement had come to a close, but as things got better, discontent grew. Millions of impoverished African Americans demonstrated growing impatience with the discrimination that remained. This volatile situation gave way to racial violence and disorders. In 1965 a brutal riot took place in Watts, a section of Los Angeles. In 1966 and 1967 the disorders increased in scope and intensity. The Detroit riot in July 1967, the worst such disturbance up to that time in modern American history, made clear the deep divisions between the races and the urgency of taking corrective action.[4]

THE KERNER COMMISSION President Johnson appointed a special Advisory Commission on Civil Disorders to investigate the origins of the riots and to recommend measures to prevent such disasters in the future. When the commission (called the Kerner Commission after its chair, Illinois Governor Otto Kerner) issued its report, it said in stark, clear language: "What white Americans have never fully understood—but what the Negro can never forget—is that white society is deeply implicated in the ghetto. White institutions created it, white institutions maintain it, and white society condones it." The basic conclusion of the commission was: "Our nation is moving toward two societies, one black, one white—separate and unequal" and that "only a commitment to national action on an unprecedented scale" could change this trend.[5]

The commission made sweeping recommendations on jobs, education, housing, and the welfare system. But other events diverted attention from these recommendations: the Vietnam War; Watergate; the elections of Ronald Reagan and George Bush, who were reluctant to take governmental actions to enforce civil rights; and a growing skepticism about the effectiveness of governmental action generally.

The Clinton administration was more sympathetic toward the use of governmental power to deal with issues of inequality than its immediate predecessors, but because of budgetary constraints and Republican opposition to "big government" programs, it was largely unable to promote any major initiatives directly aimed at the problems of the inner cities.

Women's Rights

The struggle for equal rights for women was intertwined with the battle to secure equal rights for African Americans. The Seneca Falls Women's Rights Convention (1848), which launched the women's movement, involved men and women who actively campaigned to abolish slavery. But as the Civil War approached, women were urged to abandon their cause and devote their energies to getting rid of slavery.[6] The Civil War brought the women's movement to a halt, and the temperance movement to prohibit the sale of liquor diverted attention away from women's rights as well. The Fourteenth and Fifteenth Amendments did not advance voting rights for women, even as they guaranteed that right to freed male slaves.

By the turn of the century, however, a vigorous campaign was under way for **women's suffrage**—the right to vote. The first victories came in western states, where Wyoming led the way. As a territory, Wyoming had given women the right to vote. When members of Congress in Washington grumbled about this "petticoat provision," the Wyoming legislators replied they would stay out of the Union one hundred years rather than come in without women's suffrage. Congress gave in and admitted

Fire fighters in Birmingham, Alabama, turned their hoses full blast on civil rights demonstrators in the 1960s. At times the water came with such force, even on children, that it literally tore the bark off fully grown trees.

Rosa Parks's decision not to give up her seat on the bus in Montgomery, Alabama, sparked a boycott by African Americans who, for more than a year, refused to ride the segregated city buses.

women's suffrage
The right of women to vote.

The Supreme Court has interpreted Title VII of the Civil Rights Act of 1964 to impose on employers an obligation to provide a workplace environment that does not subject any employee to sexual harassment. Sexual harassment comes in two forms: (1) "quid pro quo," in which an employer makes it a condition of employment (hiring, promotion, etc.) that a person provide sexual favors; and (2) situations in which an employee experiences discrimination because of being forced to work in a "hostile environment." A hostile environment is defined as a workplace "permeated" with intimidation, ridicule, and insult that is severe or pervasive.

Sexual harassment was brought to national attention by accusations made against Justice Clarence Thomas by Anita Hill at the time of his Senate confirmation, by the lawsuit brought by Paula Jones against President Bill Clinton for allegedly seeking sexual favors when he was governor of Arkansas and she was an employee, and by Kathleen Willey, who contended that President Clinton groped her.

In the Paula Jones case, the judge dismissed the charge on the grounds that, even if what Ms. Jones said was true, there was no evidence that she had been deprived of her constitutional or legal rights, nor had she suffered any job discrimination. However, this was a case that would not die, and Ms. Jones and her lawyers appealed the decision. After prolonged negotiations over money, in November 1998 President Clinton agreed to pay $850,000 to settle the claim of sexual harassment, and Ms. Jones dropped her demand that he apologize.

Susan B. Anthony and Elizabeth Cady Stanton were the two most influential leaders of the women's suffrage movement in the nineteenth century.

Wyoming to the Union. By the end of World War I, more than half the states had granted women the right to vote in some or all elections.

To many suffragists this state-by-state approach seemed slow and uncertain. They wanted a decisive victory—a constitutional amendment that would force all states to allow qualified women to vote. Finally, in 1919, Congress proposed the Nineteenth Amendment. Opposition to granting voting rights to women was intertwined with opposition to granting voting rights to African Americans. Many southerners opposed the amendment because it gave Congress enforcement power, which might bring federal officials to investigate elections to ensure that the amendment was being obeyed—an interference that might call attention to how blacks were being kept from voting.

With the ratification of the Nineteenth Amendment in 1920, women won the right to vote, but they were still denied equal pay and equal rights, and they suffered numerous legal disabilities imposed by both national and state laws. In the 1970s and 1980s the unsuccessful struggle to secure the adoption of the Equal Rights Amendment occupied much of the attention of the women's movement, but there are now other goals, and the political clout of women is mobilized behind issues that range from equal pay to world peace, sexual harassment, abortion rights, and election to office.[7]

Hispanics

The struggle for civil rights has not been limited to women and African Americans. Each new wave of immigrants has been considered suspect by those who arrived earlier—all the more so if its members were not white or English speaking. Formal barriers of law and informal barriers of custom combined to deny equal rights. But as groups established themselves—first economically, then politically—most of these barriers were swept away, and constitutionally guaranteed rights were asserted.

As we discussed in Chapter 5, most Hispanics—many of whose ancestors have been Americans for generations—are bilingual, speaking English as well as Spanish. However, because English may not be their first language, it has been difficult for some Hispanics to establish themselves educationally or to advance into the ranks of executives and professionals. Although not as visible as African Americans, Hispanics have suffered the same kinds of discrimination in employment, education, and accommodations.

Hispanic political clout has been unrealized because of internal political differences and because many Hispanics are not citizens or registered to vote. However, after California adopted Proposition 187 in 1994, which denied medical, educational, and social services to illegal immigrants, and Congress amended the federal welfare laws to curtail benefits to noncitizens, many immigrants rushed to become naturalized. In the 2000 election both George W. Bush and Al Gore campaigned vigorously among Hispanics, and more voted in 2000 than in 1996, with big increases in California and Texas.

Asian Americans

The term "Asian American" describes approximately 10 million individuals from many different countries and many different ethnic backgrounds. Most do not think of themselves as "Asians" but as Americans of Chinese, Japanese, Vietnamese, Cambodian, Korean, or other specific ancestry. They live chiefly in the western states, but there has been a rapid increase in Asian Americans in New York and Texas.

Although Asian Americans are often considered a "model minority" because of their general success in education and business, the U.S. Civil Rights

Commission found that "Asian-Americans do face widespread prejudice, discrimination and barriers to equal opportunity" and that racially motivated violence against them "occurs with disturbing frequency."[8]

CHINESE AMERICANS   The Chinese were the first Asians to come to the United States. Beginning in 1847, when young male peasants came here to get away from poverty and to work in mines, on railroads, and on farms, the Chinese encountered economic and cultural fears of the white majority, who did not understand them or their culture. In response, the Chinese seldom tried to assimilate but instead gravitated to "Chinatowns." Discriminatory immigration and naturalization restrictions, imposed beginning in 1882, were strengthened in later years and were not removed until the end of World War II.

Since that time, the Chinese have moved into the mainstream of American society, and they are beginning to run for and win local political offices. In 1996 Gary Locke, a Democrat and a graduate of Yale and Boston University Law School, was elected governor of Washington, the first Chinese American to become governor of a continental state.

In the war hysteria following the outbreak of World War II, Japanese Americans were rounded up and transported to internment camps.

JAPANESE AMERICANS   The Japanese first migrated to Hawaii in the 1860s and then to California in the 1880s. Most Japanese immigrants remained in the West Coast states. By the beginning of the twentieth century, they faced overt hostility. In 1905 labor leaders organized the Japanese and Korean Exclusion League, and in 1906 the San Francisco Board of Education excluded all Chinese, Japanese, and Korean children from neighborhood schools. Some western states passed laws denying the right to own land to aliens who were ineligible to become citizens—meaning aliens of Asian ancestry.

During World War II, anti-Japanese hysteria provoked the internment of West Coast Japanese—most of whom were loyal American citizens guilty of no crimes—in prison camps in California, Colorado, and some other states. During this time the property of Japanese Americans was often sold at confiscatory rates, and many lost their businesses, jobs, and incomes. Following the war, the exclusionary acts were repealed. In 1988 President Ronald Reagan signed a law providing $20,000 restitution to each of the approximately 60,000 surviving World War II internees.

OTHER ASIAN AMERICANS   Like other Asian Americans, Koreans faced overt discrimination in jobs and housing, but a Korean middle class has been growing, with many becoming teachers, doctors, and lawyers. Many others operate small family businesses such as dry cleaners, florist shops, service stations, and small grocery stores, often in inner cities.[9] As prosperous small businesspeople, they are often the target of the anger of the poor people whose neighborhoods they serve. Many Korean stores in African American neighborhoods were destroyed in the 1992 Los Angeles riots.

When Filipinos first came to the United States in the early part of this century, they were considered American nationals because the United States owned the Philippine Islands, their native country. Nonetheless, they were denied their rights to full citizenship and faced discrimination and even violence, including anti-Filipino riots in the state of Washington in 1928 and later in California, where nearly one-third of the approximately 1.5 million Filipinos live.[10] Their economic status has improved, but their influence in politics remains as small as their numbers.

The newest Asian arrivals consist of more than a million refugees from Vietnam, Laos, and Cambodia, who first came to the United States in 1975 and settled mostly in California. Although this group included middle-class people who left during the fall of Saigon following the end of the Vietnam War, it also consisted of large numbers of "boat people" who came to our shores without any financial resources. In a relatively short time, most established themselves economically. Although they are starting to have political influence, some remain socially and economically segregated.

Native Americans

Almost half of the more than 2 million Native Americans live on or near a *reservation*—a tract of land given to the tribal nations by treaty—and are enrolled as members of one of the 550 federally recognized tribes, including 226 groups in Alaska.[11] About 200 different Native American languages are spoken.

Native Americans speak of their tribes as "nations," yet they are not possessed of the full attributes of sovereignty. Rather, they are a separate people with power to regulate their own internal affairs, subject to congressional supervision. States are precluded from regulating or taxing the tribes or extending the jurisdiction of their courts over the tribes unless authorized to do so by Congress.[12] In recent years Congress has stepped in to mediate growing tensions between Indian tribes who used their sovereignty over reservations to operate gambling casinos and the states in which these reservations are located.

By acts of Congress, Native Americans are citizens of the United States and of the states in which they live. They have the right to vote. Native Americans living off reservations and working in the general community pay taxes just as everybody else; off reservations they have the same rights as any other Americans. If they are enrolled members of a recognized tribe, they are entitled to certain benefits created by law and by treaty. The Bureau of Indian Affairs of the Department of the Interior administers these benefits.

During the period of assimilation that began in 1887 and lasted until 1934, tribal governments were weak, some reservations were dissolved, and more than 100 tribes had their relationship with the federal government severed.[13] The civil rights movement of the 1960s created a more favorable climate for the concerns of Native Americans. Their goals were to reassert treaty rights and secure greater autonomy for the tribes. Under the leadership of the Native American Rights Fund (NARF), more Indian law cases were brought in the last several decades than at any time in our history.[14]

As a result of the militancy of Native American leaders and a greater national consciousness of the concerns of minorities, most Americans are now aware that many Native Americans live in poverty. Native Americans "are in far worse health than the rest of the population, dying earlier and suffering disproportionately from alcoholism, accidents, diabetes, and pneumonia."[15] Although in recent years the rest of the United States has enjoyed less than 4 percent unemployment, many reservations continue to experience 50–60 percent unemployment. Some reservations lack adequate health care facilities, educational opportunities, decent hous-

Sioux Indians took part in a 220-mile March of Memory to mark the 100th anniversary of the Battle of Wounded Knee, when U.S. troops opened fire and killed 200 men, women, and children.

ing, and jobs. Congress has started to compensate Native Americans for past injustices and to provide more opportunities for the development of tribal economic independence, and judges are showing greater vigilance in the enforcement of Indian treaty rights.

In 1986 Ben Nighthorse Campbell became the first Native American to be elected to Congress. He was elected as a Democrat from Colorado but became a Republican after being elected to the Senate in 1992.

EQUAL PROTECTION OF THE LAWS: WHAT DOES IT MEAN?

The **equal protection clause** of the Fourteenth Amendment declares that no state (including any subdivision thereof) shall "deny to any person within its jurisdiction the equal protection of the laws." Although there is no parallel clause explicitly limiting the national government, the Fifth Amendment's **due process clause**, which states that no person shall "be deprived of life, liberty, or property, without due process of law," has been interpreted to impose the same restraints on the national government as the equal protection clause imposes on the states.

The equal protection clause applies only to the *actions of governments*, not to those of private individuals. If a discriminatory action is performed by a private person, it does not violate the Constitution, although it may violate federal and state laws. The equal protection clause does not, however, prevent governments from creating various classifications of people in its laws. What the Constitution forbids is *unreasonable* classifications. In general, a classification is unreasonable when there is no relation between the classes it creates and permissible governmental goals. A law prohibiting redheads from voting, for example, would be unreasonable. On the other hand, laws denying persons under 18 the right to vote, to marry without the permission of their parents, or to apply for a license to drive a car appear to be reasonable (at least to most persons over 18).

Constitutional Classifications and Tests

One of the most troublesome constitutional questions is how to distinguish between constitutional and unconstitutional classifications. The Supreme Court uses three tests for this purpose: (1) the *rational basis* test, (2) the *strict scrutiny* test, and (3) the *heightened scrutiny* test.

THE RATIONAL BASIS TEST   The traditional test to determine whether a law complies with the equal protection requirement places the burden of proof on those attacking the law. They must show that the law has no rational or legitimate governmental goals. For example, the Supreme Court has held that a state might deny unemployment benefits to those who attend day school but make them available to those who attend night school. This classification of schools meets the rational basis test since it is reasonable to assume that students who go to school during the day are less likely to be available for employment than are those who go to school after work.[16]

SUSPECT CLASSIFICATIONS AND STRICT SCRUTINY   When a law is subject to strict scrutiny, the courts must be persuaded that there is both a "compelling public interest" to justify such a classification and no less restrictive way to accomplish this compelling purpose. The Court applies the strict scrutiny test to suspect classifications. A *suspect classification* is a class of people deliberately subjected to such unequal treatment in the past, or relegated by society to a position of such political powerlessness as to require extraordinary judicial protection.[17]

Classifications based on race or national origin are always suspect. It does not make any difference if the laws are designed for supposedly benign purposes—that

equal protection clause
Clause in the Constitution that forbids any state to deny to any person within its jurisdiction the equal protection of the laws. By interpretation, the Fifth Amendment imposes the same Limitation on the national government. This clause is the major constitutional restraint on the power of governments to discriminate against persons because of race, national origin, or sex.

due process clause
Clauses in the Fifth and Fourteenth Amendments stating that the national (Fifth) and state (Fourteenth) governments shall not deprive any person of life, liberty, or property without due process of law.

is, to help persons of a particular race or national origin. For example, the Supreme Court has held that laws that give preference for public employment based on race are subject to strict scrutiny.

QUASI-SUSPECT CLASSIFICATIONS AND HEIGHTENED SCRUTINY   To sustain a law under this test, the burden is on the government to show that its classification serves "important governmental objectives." Classifications based on gender are subject to heightened scrutiny. Not until 1971 was any classification based on gender declared unconstitutional. Before that time, many laws provided special protection for women—such as a Michigan law forbidding any woman other than the wife or daughter of a tavern owner to serve as barmaid. As Justice William J. Brennan, Jr., wrote for the Court : "There can be no doubt that our nation has had a long and unfortunate history of sex discrimination. Traditionally such discrimination was rationalized by an attitude of 'romantic paternalism' which in practical effect put women, not on a pedestal, but in a cage."[18]

Today the Court's view is that treating women differently from men (or vice versa) is forbidden when supported by no more substantial justification than "the role-typing society has long imposed upon women."[19] If the government's objective is "to protect members of one sex because they are presumed to suffer from an inherent handicap or to be innately inferior," that objective is illegitimate.[20] The Supreme Court has struck down most laws brought before it that were alleged to discriminate against women.

POVERTY AND AGE   Just as racial minorities and women are entitled to special constitutional protection, it is argued, so too should the poor and the elderly be. But the Supreme Court rejected the argument "that financial need alone identifies a suspect class for purposes of equal protection analysis."[21] However, state supreme courts in Texas, Ohio, and elsewhere have ruled that unequal funding for public schools as a result of "rich" districts spending more per pupil than "poor" districts violates their state constitutional provisions for free and equal education.

Age is not a suspect class. Many laws commonly make distinctions based on age: to obtain a driver's license, to marry without parental consent, to attend schools, to buy alcohol, and so on. Many governmental institutions have age-specific programs: for senior citizens, for adult students, for midcareer persons. The Supreme Court has repeatedly refused to make age a suspect classification requiring extra judicial protection. "States may discriminate," as Justice Sandra Day O'Connor observed, "on the basis of age without offending the Fourteenth Amendment if the age classification in question is rationally related to a legitimate state interest."[22]

Congress, however, responding to "gray power," frequently treats age as a protected category. Congress has made it illegal for most employers to discriminate on the basis of old age. Except for a few exempt occupations, employers may not impose mandatory retirement requirements. Congress also attempted to extend the protections against age discrimination to cover state employees, but the Supreme Court ruled that Congress lacks the constitutional authority to open the federal courts to suits by state employees for alleged age discrimination. State employees are limited to recovering monetary damages under state laws in state courts.[23]

FUNDAMENTAL RIGHTS AND STRICT SCRUTINY   The Court also strictly scrutinizes laws impinging on *fundamental rights*. What makes a right fundamental in the constitutional sense? It is not the importance or the significance of the right that makes it fundamental, but whether it is explicitly or implicitly *guaranteed by the Constitution*. Under this test, the rights to travel and to vote have been held to be fundamental, as well as First Amendment rights such as the right to associate for the advancement of political beliefs. Rights to an education, to housing, or to welfare benefits have not been held fundamental. Important as these rights may be, there are no constitutional provisions specifically protecting them from governmental regulation.

Proving Discrimination

Does the fact that a law or a regulation has a differential effect—what has come to be known as *disparate impact*—on persons of a different race or sex by itself establish that the law is unconstitutional? In one of its most important decisions, *Washington v Davis* (1976), the Supreme Court said no.[24] "An unwavering line of cases" from the Supreme Court "hold that a violation of the Equal Protection Clause requires state action motivated by discriminatory intent; the disproportionate effects of state action are not sufficient to establish such a violation."[25] Or, as the Court said in another case: "The Fourteenth Amendment guarantees equal laws, not equal results."[26]

What do these rulings on disparate impact mean in practical terms? They mean, for example, that even when city ordinances permit only single-family residences and thus make low-cost housing projects impossible, they are not unconstitutional—even if their effect is to keep minorities from moving into the city—unless it can be shown that they were adopted with the *intent* to discriminate against minorities. Another example: preference for veterans in public employment does not violate the equal protection clause, even though its effect is to keep many women from getting jobs; the distinction between veterans and nonveterans was not adopted deliberately to create a sex barrier.

What is constitutional can nonetheless be illegal. For example, state laws creating legislative districts with no intent to discriminate against African Americans, but which in effect dilute their voting power, are not unconstitutional. But in the Voting Rights Act of 1965, Congress made voting requirements illegal if they do, in fact, dilute the voting power of African Americans, even if they were adopted with no such intention. The Voting Rights Act of 1965 tests the legality of state voting laws and practices by their *effects* rather than by the *intentions* of those who passed them.

VOTING RIGHTS

Under our Constitution, it is the states, not the federal government, that regulate elections and voting qualifications. However, Article I, Section 4, gives Congress the power to supersede state regulations as to the "Times, Places and Manner" of elections for representatives and senators. Congress has used this authority, along with its authority under Article II, Section 2, to set the date for selection of electors, to set age qualifications and residency requirements to vote in national elections, to establish a uniform day for all states to hold elections for members of Congress and presidential electors, and to give American citizens who reside outside the United States the right to vote for members of Congress and presidential electors in the states in which they previously lived.

Limitations on the states' power to set voting qualifications are contained in the Fourteenth Amendment (forbidding qualifications that have no reasonable relation to the ability to vote), the Fifteenth Amendment (forbidding qualifications based on race), the Nineteenth Amendment (forbidding qualifications based on sex), and the Twenty-sixth Amendment (forbidding states to deny citizens 18 years of age or older the right to vote on account of age). These amendments also empower Congress to enact the laws necessary to enforce their provisions.

Protecting Voting Rights

In the 1940s the Supreme Court began to strike down one after another of the devices that had been used to keep African Americans from voting. In *Smith v Allwright* (1944) the Court declared the **white primary** (a primary operated by the Democratic party that, in the then one-party South, was where public officials were actually chosen) unconstitutional.[27] In 1960 it held that **racial gerrymandering**—the drawing of election districts to ensure that African Americans would be a minority in all districts—was contrary to

white primary
Primary operated by the Democratic party in southern states that, before Republicans gained strength in the "one-party South," essentially constituted an election; ruled unconstitutional in *Smith v Allwright* (1944).

racial gerrymandering
The drawing of election districts so as to ensure that members of a certain race are always a minority in the district; ruled unconstitutional in *Gomillion v Lightfoot* (1960).

poll tax

Payment required as a condition for voting; prohibited for national elections by the Twenty-fourth Amendment (1964) and ruled unconstitutional for all elections in *Harper v Virginia Board of Election* (1966).

literacy test

Literacy requirement imposed by some states as a condition of voting, generally used to disqualify blacks from voting in the South; now illegal.

the Fifteenth Amendment.[28] In 1964 the Twenty-fourth Amendment eliminated the **poll tax**—payment required as a condition for voting—in presidential and congressional elections. In 1966 the Court held that the Fourteenth Amendment forbade the poll tax as a condition in any election.[29]

In many southern areas, **literacy tests** were used to discriminate against African Americans. Some states required applicants to demonstrate that they understood the national and state constitutions and, furthermore, that they were persons of good character. Although poor whites often avoided registering out of fear of embarrassment from failing a literacy test, the tests were more often used to discriminate against African Americans.[30] Whites were often asked simple questions; blacks were asked questions that would baffle a Supreme Court justice. "In the 1960s southern registrars were observed testing black applicants on such matters as the number of bubbles in a soap bar, the news contained in a copy of the Peking Daily, the meaning of obscure passages in state constitutions, and the definition of terms such as *habeas corpus*."[31] In Louisiana, 49,603 illiterate white voters were able to persuade election officials they could understand the Constitution, but only two illiterate black voters were able to do so.

Those wishing to deny African Americans the right to vote were forced to rely on registration requirements. On the surface such requirements appeared to be perfectly proper, but it was the way they were administered that kept African Americans from the polls. White election officers confronted African Americans trying to register while white police stood guard; white judges heard appeals of decisions made by registration officials. Officials often seized on the smallest error in an application form as an excuse to disqualify a black voter. In one parish in Louisiana, after four white voters challenged the registration of some black voters on the grounds that those voters had made an "error in spilling" (*sic*) in their applications, registration officials struck 1,300 out of approximately 1,500 black voters from the rolls.[32]

The Voting Rights Act of 1965

For two decades after World War II, under the leadership of the Supreme Court, many limitations on voting were declared unconstitutional, but this approach still did not open the voting booth to African Americans. Finally Congress acted. The Civil Rights Act of 1964 had hardly been enacted when events in Selma Alabama, dramatized the inadequacy of depending on the courts to prevent racial barriers in polling places. Led by Martin Luther King, Jr., a voter registration drive in Selma, produced arrests, marches on the state capital, and the murder of two civil rights workers. Still there was no dent in the color bar at the polls. Responding to events in Selma, President Lyndon Johnson made a dramatic address to Congress and the nation calling for federal action to ensure that no person would be deprived of the right to vote in any election for any office because of color or race. Congress responded with the Voting Rights Act of 1965.

Section 2 of the Voting Rights Act prohibits voting qualifications or standards that result in a denial of the right of any citizen to vote on account of race and color. Section 5 requires that states that had a history of denying African Americans or Hispanic citizens the right to vote must clear with the Department of Justice changes in voting practice or laws that might dilute the voting power of these groups.[33] What precisely constitutes "dilution" and how it is to be measured are the subject of much litigation. Examples include changes in the location of polling places; changes in candidacy requirements and qualifications; changes in filing deadlines; changes from ward to at-large elections; changes in boundary lines of voting districts; and changes that affect the creation or abolition of an elective office and imposition by state political parties of fees for delegates to nominating conventions.[34]

Following the 1990 census, the Department of Justice pressured southern state legislatures to draw as many districts as possible in which minorities would constitute a majority of the electorate. Most of these districts tended to be Democratic, leaving the other congressional districts in these states heavily white and Republican. The lower federal courts sustained the Department of Justice's interpretation. As a result, there was a considerable increase in the number of congressional districts represented by minorities and Republicans.

The Supreme Court, however, in a series of cases beginning with *Shaw v Reno* (1993), announced that although it was a legitimate goal for state legislatures to take race into account when they drew electoral districts in order to increase the voting strength of minorities, they could not make race the sole or predominant reason for drawing district lines. The Department of Justice, said the Supreme Court, was wrong in forcing states to create as many **majority-minority districts** as possible. A test case involved the North Carolina legislature's creation of a majority-minority district 160 miles long and in some places only an interstate highway wide. "If you drove down the interstate," said one legislator about this district, "with both car doors open, you'd kill most of the people in the district." North Carolina's reapportionment scheme, the Supreme Court declared, was so "irrational on its face that it can be understood only as an effort to segregate voters into separate voting districts because of their race." To comply with the Voting Rights Act, the Supreme Court explained, states must provide for districts roughly proportional to the minority voters' respective shares in the voting-age population.[35]

Since then the Court has expanded *Shaw* by clarifying that it was not meant to suggest that a "district must be bizarre on its face before there is a constitutional violation." Legislatures may be aware of racial considerations when they draw district lines, but when race becomes the overriding motive, the state violates the equal protection clause.[36] As a result, many southern states have had to redraw legislative districts. However, even when African-American incumbents ran in these newly drawn districts with majority white electors, they were reelected.[37]

Thurgood Marshall (center), George C. E. Hayes (left), and James Nabrit, Jr., (right) argued and won Brown v Board of Education of Topeka *before the Supreme Court in 1954.*

EDUCATION RIGHTS

Until the Supreme Court struck down such laws in the 1950s, southern states had made it illegal for whites and blacks to ride in the same train cars, attend the same theaters, go to the same schools, be born in the same hospitals, or be buried in the same cemeteries. **Jim Crow laws**, as they came to be called, blanketed southern life. How could these laws stand in the face of the equal protection clause? This was the question raised in *Plessy v Ferguson* (1896).

In the *Plessy* decision, the Supreme Court endorsed the view that governmentally imposed racial segregation in public transportation, and presumably in public education, did not necessarily constitute discrimination if "equal" accommodations were provided for the members of both races[38]—but the "equal" part of the formula was meaningless. African Americans were segregated in unequal facilities and lacked the political power to protest effectively. The passage of time did not lessen the inequalities. Beginning in the late 1930s, African Americans started to file lawsuits challenging the doctrine. They cited facts to show that in practice, separate but equal always resulted in discrimination against African Americans.

The End of Separate but Equal: *Brown v Board of Education*

At first the Supreme Court was not willing to upset the separate but equal doctrine, but in *Brown v Board of Education of Topeka* (1954), the Court finally reversed the *Plessy* doctrine as it applied to public schools by holding that "separate but equal" is a contradiction in terms. *Segregation is itself discrimination.*[39] A year later the Court ordered school boards to proceed with "all deliberate speed to desegregate public schools at the earliest practical date."[40]

majority-minority district
A congressional district created to include a majority of minority voters; ruled constitutional so long as race is not the main factor in redistricting.

Jim Crow laws
State laws formerly pervasive throughout the South requiring public facilities and accommodations to be segregated by race; ruled unconstitutional.

Residents of the Charlestown section of Boston took part in a "March Against Forced Busing" in May 1976.

But many school districts moved very slowly, and in the 1960s Congress and the president joined even more directly in the battle against school segregation. Title VI of the Civil Rights Act of 1964, as subsequently amended, stipulated that federal dollars under any grant program or project must be withdrawn from an entire school or institution of higher education that discriminates "on the ground of race, color, or national origin" gender, age, or disability in "any program or activity receiving federal financial assistance."

From Segregation to Desegregation—But Not Yet to Integration

School districts that had operated two kinds of schools, one for whites and one for African Americans, now had an obligation to develop plans and programs to move from segregation to integration. For such school districts, desegregation would not be enough; they would have a duty to bring about integration. If they failed to do so on their own initiative, federal judges would supervise the school districts to ensure that they were doing what was necessary and proper to overcome the evils of segregation.

But since most whites and most African Americans continued to live in separate neighborhoods, merely removing legal barriers to school integration did not by itself integrate the schools. To overcome this residential clustering by race, some federal courts mandated busing across neighborhoods, moving white students to once predominantly black schools and vice versa. Busing students was not popular and fostered widespread protest in many cities.

The Supreme Court sustained busing only if it was to remedy the consequences of *officially* sanctioned, that is, **de jure segregation**. The Court refused to permit federal judges to order busing to overcome the effects of **de facto segregation**, segregation that arises as a result of social and economic conditions such as housing patterns.

Since *Brown v Board of Education*, the federal government has intervened in more than 500 school desegregation cases. However, there has been no such judicial action for northern schools that have de facto segregation. As a result, many southern cities now have more integrated schools than do large northern cities. Both in the North and South, many school districts in central cities today are predominantly African American or Hispanic. This segregated pattern of schools is partly the result of "white flight" to the suburbs in the 1970s and 1980s and the transfer of white students to private schools to escape court-ordered busing. In more recent years it is also due to higher birth rates and immigration among African Americans and Hispanics.[41]

After a period of vigorous federal court supervision of school desegregation programs, the Supreme Court has started to restrict the role of federal judges.[42] It has instructed some of them to restore control of a school system to the state and local authorities and to release districts from any busing obligations once a judge concludes that the authorities "have done everything practicable to overcome the past consequences of segregation."[43]

Political support for busing and for other efforts to integrate the schools is fading.[44] Many school districts have eliminated mandatory busing, with the result, according to one expert, that we may get "to a level of segregation we haven't seen since before the civil rights movement."[45] Some African American leaders, while still supporting desegregation efforts, are now more concerned about improving the quality of inner-city schools than desegregating them.

RIGHTS OF ASSOCIATION, ACCOMMODATIONS, JOBS, AND HOMES

Association

As we have noted, the Fifth and Fourteenth Amendments apply only to governmental action, not to private discriminatory conduct. As Justice William O. Douglas said, our Constitution creates "a zone of privacy which precludes govern-

de jure segregation
Laws that made it a crime for black or white people to go to school together, or to be served together in public places, or to sit together in public transportation.

de facto segregation
Segregation that comes about because of economic or social conditions or results from individual choices.

commerce clause
The clause (Article I) in the Constitution that gives Congress the power to regulate commerce among the states, with other nations, and with the Indian tribes. This clause provides the constitutional basis for most national regulations of our economy, as well as for much civil rights legislation.

ment from interfering with private clubs or groups. The associational rights which our system honors permit all-white, all-black, all-brown, and all-yellow clubs to be established. They also permit all-Catholic, all-Jewish, or all-agnostic clubs. . . . Government may not tell a man or a woman who his or her associates must be. The individual may be as selective as he desires."[46]

Families, churches, or private groups organized for political, religious, cultural, or social purposes are constitutionally different from large associations organized along other lines. The Supreme Court, for example, has upheld the application of laws forbidding sex or racial discrimination by organizations such as the Jaycees, the Rotary Club, and large (in this case more than 400 members) private eating clubs. Such associations and clubs are not small intimate groups. Nor were they able to demonstrate that allowing women or minorities to become members would change the content or impact of their purposes.[47] In *Boy Scouts of America v Dale* (2000), however, the Court held that the Boy Scouts may exclude homosexuals because of the association's overall mission.[48]

Accommodations

In 1883 the Supreme Court had declared unconstitutional an act of Congress that made it a federal offense for any operator of a public conveyance, hotel, or theater to deny accommodations to any person because of race or color on the grounds that the Fourteenth Amendment does not give Congress such authority.[49] Since the 1960s, however, the constitutional authority of Congress to legislate against discrimination by private individuals is no longer an issue because the Court has broadly construed the **commerce clause**—which gives Congress the power to regulate interstate and foreign commerce—to justify action against discriminatory conduct by individuals. Congress has also used its power to tax and spend to prevent not only racial discrimination but also discrimination based on ethnic origin, sex, disability, and age.

WE THE PEOPLE

Native Americans and Welfare Reform

"The 1996 welfare reform legislation, with its stricter work and job training requirements, is affecting Native American college enrollment, curriculum, and student services, according to a recent survey. The reservations on which most of the colleges are located have relatively high numbers of welfare recipients. . . . Given these needs, many states and tribes are turning to the colleges to provide remedial education and job training to reservation residents.

To examine the changes that have occurred since the welfare reform legislation was passed, the American Indian Higher Education Consortium (AIHEC) surveyed all 30 tribal colleges in the United States in spring 1998. . . .

The most obvious effects of the welfare reform provisions are on college enrollments. On the one hand, welfare recipients may get pushed out of higher education and into jobs; on the other, the new requirements may drive recipients who lack basic skills into basic adult education, GED, and vocational training programs.

Of the 18 colleges that responded, 11 colleges (61 percent) have seen enrollment changes that they believe are attributable to welfare reform. The reported shifts are varied: four of the colleges mentioned increases in enroll-

ment: three felt the enrollment changes have been mixed; one college said enrollment has declined; one college believed the students were getting younger; and two did not mention the direction of the enrollment changes. . . .

In addition to educating welfare recipients, the colleges are actively involved in helping them complete their transition into the labor force. For example, virtually all of the responding colleges (16, or 89 percent) work with local welfare agencies to coordinate their activities. Furthermore, seven of the colleges currently offer placement services for their students and graduates; two are planning to do so in the future; and two assist their students informally. These efforts continue despite an acute lack of available jobs.

According to recent Department of Commerce data, the average unemployment rate on reservations with tribal colleges is 28 percent and may be higher than 40 percent on some reservations. Some of the tribal colleges are following the paths of their students after graduation; 13 of the colleges said they currently track the employment or enrollment status of their graduates."

SOURCE: Alisa F. Cunningham, "Survey Reports Tribal Colleges' Response to Welfare Reform," *Tribal College Journal: Journal of American Indian Higher Education* (Winter 1998–99), p. 36.

TITLE II: PLACES OF PUBLIC ACCOMMODATION   For the first time since Reconstruction, the Civil Rights Act of 1964 authorized the massive use of federal authority to combat privately imposed racial discrimination. Title II makes it a federal offense to discriminate against any customer or patron in a place of public accommodation because of race, color, religion, or national origin. It applies to any inn, hotel, motel, or lodging establishment (except establishments with fewer than five rooms and occupied by the proprietor—in other words, small boardinghouses); to any restaurant or gasoline station that serves interstate travelers or serves food or products that have moved in interstate commerce; and to any movie house, theater, concert hall, sports arena, or other place of entertainment that customarily presents films, performances, athletic teams, or other sources of entertainment that are moved in interstate commerce. Within a few months after its adoption, the Supreme Court sustained the constitutionality of Title II.[50] As a result, public establishments, including those in the South, opened their doors to all customers.

TITLE VII: EMPLOYMENT   Title VII of the 1964 Civil Rights Act made it illegal for any employer or trade union in any industry affecting interstate commerce and employing 15 or more people (and, since 1972, any state or local agency such as a school or university) to discriminate in employment practices against any person because of race, color, national origin, religion, or sex. Employers have an obligation to create workplaces that avoid abusive environments. Related legislation made it illegal to discriminate against those with physical handicaps, veterans, or persons over 40.

There are a few exceptions. Religious institutions such as parochial schools may use religious standards. Age, sex, or handicap may be considered where occupational qualifications are absolutely necessary to the normal operation of a particular business or enterprise—for example, hiring only women to work in women's locker rooms.

The Equal Employment Opportunity Commission (EEOC) was created to enforce Title VII. The commission works together with state authorities to try to bring about compliance with the act and may seek judicial enforcement of complaints against private employers. The attorney general prosecutes Title VII violations by public agencies. Not only do aggrieved persons have a right to sue for damages for themselves, but also they can do so for other persons similarly situated in a **class action suit**. The vigor with which the EEOC and the attorney general have acted has varied over the years, depending on the commitment of the president in office and the willingness of Congress to provide an adequate budget for the EEOC.[51]

Title VII was supplemented by a 1965 presidential executive order requiring all contractors doing work for the federal government, including universities, to adopt and implement affirmative action programs to correct "underutilization" of women and minorities. Such programs may not establish racial or ethnic quotas for minorities or women, but they may require contractors to establish timetables and goals; to follow open recruitment procedures; to keep records of applicants by race, sex, and national origin; and to explain why their labor force does not reflect the same proportion of persons within the appropriate labor market pools. Failure of contractors to file and implement an approved affirmative action plan may lead to loss of federal contracts or grants.

THE FAIR HOUSING ACT AND AMENDMENTS, 1968 AND 1988   Housing is the last frontier of the civil rights crusade, the area in which progress is slowest and genuine change most remote.

> Segregated housing contributes mightily to a vicious circle that also includes educational and employment discrimination. . . . Because of poor schools for many minorities, they cannot find well-paying jobs. Without such jobs they often cannot afford to live in nicer neighborhoods with decent housing. And because of their location in less desirable communities, good educational systems are less likely to be available.[52]

In 1948 the Supreme Court made **racial or religious restrictive covenants** (a provision in a deed to real property restricting its sale) legally unenforceable.[53] The 1968 Fair Housing Act forbids discrimination in housing, excluding from its protection so-called "Mrs. Murphy boarding houses," housing owned by private individuals who own no more than three houses; dwellings that have no more than four

class action suit
Lawsuit brought by an individual or a group of people on behalf of all those similarly situated.

racial or religious restrictive covenants
A provision in a deed to real property excluding its sale to persons of a particular race or religion. Judicial enforcement of such deeds is unconstitutional.

separate living units in which the owner maintains a residence; and religious organizations and private clubs housing their own members on a noncommercial basis. For all other housing, the act forbids owners to refuse to sell or rent to any person because of race, color, religion, national origin, sex, or physical handicap or because a person has children. Discrimination in housing also covers efforts to deny loans to minorities.

The Department of Justice has filed hundreds of cases, especially those involving large apartment complexes, yet African Americans and Hispanics continue to face discrimination in housing. Realtors continue to steer African Americans and Hispanics toward neighborhoods that are not predominantly white, to require larger rental deposits from minorities than from whites, and to even refuse outright to sell or rent to minorities.[54] Yet less than 1 percent of these discriminatory actions are complained about because they are so subtle that victims are often unaware that they are being discriminated against. However, the number of discrimination complaints received by the Department of Housing and Urban Development and local and state agencies has been increasing as the result of more aggressive enforcement.

Voluntary segregation obviously exists. "It's a fact of life that blacks like to live in black neighborhoods and whites like to live in white neighborhoods," according to Daniel Mitchell, who added, "Real estate agents generally like to bring customers to places they will like and where the agent can make a sale."[55] Whatever the reasons, housing segregation persists.

Allan Bakke, who challenged the constitutionality of the University of California's affirmative action program.

AFFIRMATIVE ACTION: IS IT CONSTITUTIONAL?

When white majorities were using governmental power to discriminate against African Americans, civil rights advocates cited with approval the famous words of the first Justice John Marshall Harlan: "Our Constitution is color-blind and neither knows nor tolerates class among citizens."[56] But by the 1960s there was a new set of constitutional and national policy debates. Many people began to assert that government neutrality is not enough. If governments and universities and employers stopped discriminating yet changed nothing else, those previously discriminated against would still be kept from equal participation in American life. Because they had been so disadvantaged by past discrimination, they suffered disabilities not shared by white males in the competition for openings in medical schools, for skilled jobs, or for their share of government grants and contracts.

Remedies to overcome the consequences of past discrimination against African Americans, Hispanics, Native Americans, and women are known as *affirmative action* by those who support them, but they are regarded as *reverse discrimination* by those who oppose them. The Supreme Court's first major statement on the constitutionality of affirmative action programs came in a celebrated case relating to university admissions. Allan Bakke—a white male and a top student at Minnesota and Stanford Universities, as well as a Vietnam War veteran—applied both in 1973 and 1974 to the medical school of the University of California at Davis. In each of those years the school admitted 100 new students, 84 in a general admissions program and 16 in a special admissions program created for minorities who had previously been underrepresented. Bakke's application was rejected each year while students with lower grade-point averages, test scores, and interview ratings were admitted under the special admissions program. After his second rejection, Bakke brought suit in federal court claiming he had been excluded because of his race, contrary to requirements of the Constitution and Title VI of the Civil Rights Act of 1964.

In *University of California Regents v Bakke* (1978), the Supreme Court ruled the California plan unconstitutional.[57] But the Court also declared that affirmative action programs are not necessarily unconstitutional. In order to achieve a diversified student body, a state university may properly take race and ethnic background into account as one of several factors in choosing students. The problem with the

PEOPLE

Affirmative action does not mean admitting or hiring unqualified or less meritorious candidates.

IN DEFENSE OF AFFIRMATIVE ACTION

Theodore M. Shaw[*]

The goal of affirmative action is to break the cycle of discrimination and to enlarge opportunity for everyone. It is a moderate, effective remedy for exclusion, to achieve equality which is real and not illusory. As Justice Harry Blackmun has eloquently stated, "In order to get beyond racism, we must first take racism (and sexism) into account."

Affirmative action is not a single, rigid concept, but rather a mosaic of actions designed to eliminate artificial barriers and to allow merit to shine through. The particular affirmative measures utilized will vary in different circumstances, flexibly addressing the problem at hand.

Affirmative action does not mean admitting or hiring unqualified or less meritorious candidates. However, it may mean refining our definitions of merit. Affirmative action recognizes that we have not achieved the ideal of either merit selection or a colorblind and genderblind society. In addition to invidious discrimination based on race, ethnicity, and gender, our employment and contracting systems have always relied upon such non-merit-related criteria as nepotism, cronyism, and the "old boy network."

Affirmative action produces benefits for the entire community and nation. For example, as women have entered the medical profession and the United States Congress, more attention has been focused on crucial health needs of all women, such as breast cancer research.

Businesses have found that affirmative action is good for the bottom line. Productivity is improved in many instances, and a work force that reflects the diversity of the markets they serve allows businesses to compete more effectively. The Business Roundtable and the National Association of Manufacturers have repeatedly endorsed affirmative action.

We believe that there ought to be more opportunity for all poor and working-class people, who have been hurt by structural changes in our economy even while governmental and social policies much of the last 15 years have been tilted in favor of the rich, with the result that the wealthiest of Americans have become richer while the middle class has shrunk, and millions of people joined the ranks of the impoverished.★

SOURCE: U.S. Congress, House of Representatives, Subcommittee on Employer-Employee Relations of the Committee on Economic and Educational Opportunities, 104th Cong., 1st Sess., *Hearings on Affirmative Action in Employment* (Government Printing Office, 1995), pp. 167–86.

DEBATE

TOWARD ENDING PREFERENCES IN EDUCATION AND EMPLOYMENT

Brian W. Jones*

I maintain that government-imposed preferential policies based upon race and gender, whether in the employment or education context, have outlived their usefulness, so to speak, and presently do a great deal more social harm than good. While 30 years ago such policies may have been an important tool for breaking down the systemic barriers to black entry into the economic mainstream, they have today, I think, reached the point of diminishing returns. . . .

The cost of preference policies can be measured in terms of: (1) the social discord created between preferred and nonpreferred groups, and among the preferred groups; (2) the opportunity cost of mismatched minority talent and capital; (3) the economic cost to employers of complying with affirmative action mandates; (4) the injury done to innocents; and (5) the damage done to the constitutional ideal of equality.

Despite their significant social and economic cost, race and gender preferences in America are today justified essentially on two grounds: (1) the remediation of disadvantage caused by past discrimination; and (2) the desire to promote diversity.

Remediation of disadvantage was in fact the original moral claim of the proponents of affirmative action. . . . However, that justification today contains insuperable flaws. First, preferen-

tial policies today tend to benefit the least disadvantaged among and within preferred groups. Middle-class white women are now the primary beneficiaries of preferences, largely due to their relatively high level of education and cultural advantage.

The second justification for preferential policies is the notion of diversity. By diversifying the ranks of our employees, the theory goes, we will breed transracial familiarity and, consequently, harmoniously dynamic workplaces.

The anecdotal evidence suggests that both of these theories have been woefully inaccurate. Race relations in contexts where preference is writ large—college campuses and municipal employment, for example—have often become toxic as a result of increasing racial antagonism.

A truly constructive civil rights policy in America should focus on constructive efforts to confront the real underlying problems of performance in some of America's most distressed communities. A truly affirmative civil rights policy must concern itself with the hard work of improving the performance of disadvantaged individuals. ★

I maintain that government-imposed preferential policies based upon race and gender, whether in the employment or education context, have outlived their usefulness.

SOURCE: U.S. Congress, Senate, Committee on Labor and Human Resources, 104th Cong., 1st Sess., *Hearings on Affirmative Action and the Office of Federal Contract Compliance* (Government Printing Office, 1995), pp. 77–82.

For further information about this debate, go to **www.prenhall.com/burns** *and click on the Debate Icon in Chapter 18.*

California plan was it created a quota—a category of admissions from which whites were excluded solely because of race.

After *Bakke*: Refinements and Uncertainty

Following *Bakke* in the 1980s, the Court dealt with a variety of affirmative action programs, sustaining most but not all of them. As the justices continued to disagree on the application of the equal protection clause, opposition to such programs became more heated.

In *Richmond v Croson* (1989) the Rehnquist Court struck down a regulation by the city of Richmond requiring nonminority city contractors to subcontract at least 30 percent of the dollar amount of their contracts to one or more minority business enterprises. Writing for the Court, Justice Sandra Day O'Connor called into question the validity of most government affirmative action plans and stated, "Race-sensitive remedial measures are to be justified only after a strong basis in evidence has established that remedial action is necessary to overcome the consequences of past discriminatory action."[58]

Since *Croson*, a bare majority of the Court has rejected the view that racial classifications, whether benign or hostile, should ever be subject to less than strict scrutiny by either the national or state and local governments.[59] And as we have noted, the Rehnquist Court is similarly opposed to the use of race as the sole criterion in the drawing of electoral district lines.[60]

The Court declined to review a decision by the Court of Appeals for the Fifth Circuit in *Hopwood v Texas* (1996), striking down the University of Texas law school's affirmative action plan for admission of students.[61] That decision, along with some other lower court rulings, called into question the holding in *Bakke* that race may be used as one factor in university admissions in order to achieve a diverse student body.

Thus, until matters are clarified by the Supreme Court, as far as the United States Constitution is concerned, race—and presumably gender—may no longer be considered as a factor for admission to public universities and colleges in the Fifth Circuit (Texas, Louisiana, and Mississippi), but may be considered in the rest of the nation. It is nonetheless clear that the Supreme Court is closely scrutinizing programs that provide a preference based on race or ethnic origin or gender.

California's Proposition 209 and Other Plans

In July 1995, the Regents of the University of California voted to eliminate race or gender as factors in employment, purchasing, contracting, or admissions at the University of California. Then in November 1996, Californians voted overwhelmingly for Proposition 209 to amend the state constitution to forbid state agencies—including schools, colleges, and universities—to discriminate against or grant preferential treatment to any individual or group on the basis of race, sex, color, ethnicity, or national origin in public employment, public education, or public contracting, except where necessary to comply with a federal requirement.

Although Proposition 209 clearly forbids universities and other state agencies to take race and gender into account, it does not appear to make unconstitutional state-supported outreach programs designed to recruit more women and minorities to become scientists and engineers, nor does it prevent state universities from continuing outreach programs aimed at schools with large minority enrollments. In fact, due to such outreach programs, 17.6 percent of the students admitted in the 2000–2001 academic year into the University of California came from "underrepresented groups"—African Americans, Native Americans, and Hispanics. Although that was a drop from the 18.8 percent admitted in the last year before racial preferences were eliminated, it was less than predicted.[62]

Opponents of affirmative action had hoped that the adoption of Proposition 209 in California would start a national movement to restrict or eliminate affirmative action programs, and some federal programs designed to give women- and minority-owned businesses greater access to federal contracts were cut back. Under pressure from the Office of Civil Rights, some universities stopped offering scholarships based solely on race or ethnicity.[63] But Congress has not moved to limit other federal affirmative action programs.

In the state of Washington, Initiative 200, almost identical to California's Proposition 209, called for abolishing preferential treatment in hiring and contracting. It received 58 percent of the popular vote, despite the fact that Governor Gary Locke and leading businesses outspent their opponents 3 to 1. Heartened by that victory, opponents of affirmative action moved toward putting the question before voters in other states, including Nebraska and Michigan.

California, Washington, Texas, Florida, and some other states have abandoned affirmative action programs and adopted the strategy of automatic admissions for a certain percentage of all high school graduates as a means of maintaining diversity in colleges and expanding educational opportunities for minorities. California offers admission to the top 4 percent of high school graduates, Texas offers admission to the top 10 percent, and Florida to the top 20 percent of every high school graduating class.

Public support for affirmative action as measured in public opinion polls varies by race, social class, education, and life experience, but close inspection suggests that "whites and blacks are not separated by unbridgeable gaps on affirmative action issues, at least not insofar as college admissions decisions are concerned."[64] People's responses seem to depend to a significant degree on how the survey question is put. If the question asked is something like, "Are you in favor of abolishing preferences in hiring or college admissions based on race or gender?" most people say yes. But if the question is something like, "Do you favor affirmative action programs to increase the number of minorities in colleges or in jobs?" there is general support for such programs.

Clearly the debate over the merits and constitutionality of affirmative action is not over. There are more decisions to come as the courts—and the nation—debate whether affirmative action is a vital tool to overcome decades of discrimination that needs to be "amended not ended." Or, as the proponents of Proposition 209 contend, has affirmative action served its purpose, so that government-mandated preference for any person based on race or gender is always unfair and unjust to those not given the preference and demeaning to those to whom it is offered?

EQUAL RIGHTS TODAY

Today legal barriers have been lowered, if not removed, by civil rights legislation, executive orders, and judicial decisions. Important as these victories are, "They were victories largely for the middle class—those who could travel, entertain in restaurants, and stay in hotels. Those victories did not change life conditions for the mass of blacks who are still poor."[65]

More than a generation after the Kerner Commission issued its report, life for inner-city minorities is worse. As prosperous middle-class African Americans have moved out of the inner city, the remaining *underclass*, as they are coming to be called, has become even more isolated from the rest of the nation.[66] Children are growing up on streets where drug abuse and crime are everyday events. They live in "separate and deteriorating societies, with separate economies, diverging family structures and basic institutions, and even growing linguistic separation within the core ghettos. The scale of their isolation by race, class, and economic situation is much greater than it was in the 1960s, impoverishment, joblessness, educational inequality, and housing insufficiency even more severe."[67]

One of the difficulties is that, as conditions have become better for many African Americans and Hispanics, the less fortunate see them as getting worse; however, most Americans see conditions for minorities as improving. "Both perceptions will be correct.

And the fact that both are correct in arriving at opposite perceptions of what is going on will itself lead to further misunderstanding."[68]

Despite the lack of improvement in social conditions, the push for integration has lessened:

> In fact, power on both sides of the color line is based to some extent on acceptance of segregation. On the black side of the color line, it is advantageous to keep African Americans within black electoral areas and keep black-controlled resources within black institutions; integrationist policies are often viewed as posing larger threats than they actually do. On the white side of the line . . . some residents in outlying suburbs see critical advantages in their almost all-white and all middle-class status.[69]

Some contend that attention should be paid to the plight of the underclass and that, instead of focusing on issues of race, what is needed is a policy of providing jobs and improving education.[70] Others say there has to be a revival of the civil rights crusade, a restoration of vigorous civil rights enforcement, job training, and, above all, an attack on residential segregation.[71]

POLITICS ONLINE

Reparations for Slaves?

Whether or not the U.S. government should pay reparations to the descendants of slaves is a new and controversial issue in race relations. Civil rights and class action lawyers, including Harvard Law School Professor Charles J. Ogletree, are preparing this case. Reparations considered in the past included victims of nuclear fallout in the Mountain West, and Japanese-Americans who were interred during World War II.

The scope of a reparations program for U.S. slavery would be large and costly. Arguments for the reparations include an admission by the government that it was wrong to tolerate slavery, and restitution for the economic losses incurred by the slaves and their descendants. Arguments against reparations include the cost of the program and the reinforcement of racial classifications and thinking. For views both in favor and against reparation, visit: **www.true-blue.org/page8.html.**

The reparations issue became more controversial when David Horowitz, a conservative journalist, attempted to place an ad in college newspapers around the country titled "10 Reasons Why Reparations for Blacks Is a Bad Idea for Blacks—and Racist Too." To read the ad, go to: **www.frontpagemag.com/horowitznotepad/2001/hn01-02.htm.** Some school newspapers, like the *Harvard Crimson*, refused to run the ad. At colleges where the ad was run, protesters destroyed copies of the newspaper and demanded apologies. To read more about this controversy, go to: **www.newsmax.com/archives/articles/2001/3/7/221937.shtml.**

The reparations issue taps into strongly held views about race, slavery, and equal opportunity. As this episode illustrates, the feelings about this issue are so intense that it is even difficult to debate.

SUMMARY

1. Americans are committed to equality, an elusive term, with most support for equality of opportunity, some for equality of starting conditions, and some for equality of results.

2. Progress in securing civil rights for African Americans was a long time in coming. After the Civil War the national government briefly tried to secure some measure of protection for the freed slaves and to enforce the Thirteenth, Fourteenth, and Fifteenth Amendments and the civil rights laws passed to implement them. But when federal troops withdrew from the South in 1877, the national government withdrew from the field and blacks were left to their own resources. Not for nearly a century did the national government take action to prevent racial segregation and discrimination against blacks.

3. The crusade for women's rights was born partly out of the struggle to abolish slavery. Similarly, the modern women's movement learned and gained power from the civil rights movements of the 1950s and early 1960s. The fate of these two social movements has long been intertwined.

Women secured the right to vote in the Nineteenth Amendment.

4. Concern for equal rights under the law continues today for African Americans and women. Hispanics, Asian Americans, and Native Americans have also experienced discrimination.

5. The Supreme Court uses a three-tiered approach to evaluate the constitutionality of laws challenged as violating the equal protection clause. Laws touching economic concerns are sustained if they are rationally related to the accomplishment of a legitimate government goal. Laws that classify people because of sex or illegitimacy are subject by the courts to heightened scrutiny and are sustained only if they serve important governmental objectives. Strict scrutiny is used to review laws that touch fundamental rights or classify people because of race or ethnic origin. Such laws will be sustained only if the government can show a compelling public purpose.

6. A series of constitutional amendments, Supreme Court decisions, and laws passed by Congress have now secured the right to vote to all Americans, age 18 and over. Following the Voting Rights Act of 1965, the Justice Department can oversee practices in locales with a history of discrimination. Recent Supreme Court decisions have refined the lengths to which legislatures can go, or are obliged to go, in creating minority-majority districts.

7. *Brown v Board of Education of Topeka* (1954) struck down the "separate but equal" doctrine that had justified segregated schools in the South, but school districts responded slowly. The Supreme Court demanded compliance, and some federal courts mandated busing children across neighborhoods to comply. Still, full integration has proved elusive, as "white flight" has made many inner cities, and their schools, predominantly black or Hispanic.

8. Discrimination in public accommodations was outlawed by the Civil Rights Act of 1964. This act also provided for equal employment opportunity. The Fair Housing Act of 1968 and its 1988 amendments forbid discrimination in housing.

9. The desirability and constitutionality of affirmative action programs that provide special benefits to those members of groups subjected to past discrimination divide the nation and the Supreme Court. Remedial programs tailored to overcome specific instances of past discrimination are likely to pass the Supreme Court's suspicion of race, national origin, and sex classifications. However, the courts must still clarify constitutional issues concerning preferential treatment in school admissions and hiring practices.

KEY TERMS

natural rights 404
affirmative action 404
women's suffrage 407
equal protection clause 411
due process clause 411

white primary 413
racial gerrymandering 413
poll tax 414
literacy test 414
majority-minority district 415

Jim Crow laws 415
de jure segregation 416
de facto segregation 416
commerce clause 416
class action suit 418

racial or religious restrictive covenants 418

FURTHER READING

BARBARA R. BERGMAN, *In Defense of Affirmative Action* (Basic Books, 1996).

WILLIAM G. BOWEN and DEREK BOK, *The Shape of the River: Long-Term Consequences of Considering Race in College and University Admissions* (Princeton University Press, 1998).

TAYLOR BRANCH, *Parting the Waters: America in the King Years, 1954–1963* (Simon & Schuster, 1988).

TAYLOR BRANCH, *Pillar of Fire: America in the King Years, 1963–65* (Simon & Schuster, 1998).

KEITH J. BYBELL, *Mistaken Identity: The Supreme Court and the Politics of Minority Representation* (Princeton University Press, 1998).

DAVID DENT, *In Search of Black America: Discovering the African-American Dream* (Simon & Schuster, 2000).

JANET DEWART, ED., *The State of Black America* (National Urban League, published annually).

WILLIAM N. ESKRIDGE, JR., *Gaylaw: Challenging the Apartheid of the Closet* (Harvard University Press, 2000).

BERNARD GROFMAN, ED., *Legacies of the 1964 Civil Rights Act* (University Press of Virginia, 2000).

ANDREW HACKER, *Two Nations: Black and White, Separate, Hostile, Unequal* (Charles Scribner's Sons, 1992).

RANDALL KENNEDY, *Race, Crime, and the Law* (Pantheon, 1997).

PHILIP A. KLINKER AND ROGERS M. SMITH, *The Unsteady March: The Rise and Decline of Racial Equality in America* (University of Chicago Press, 2000).

RICHARD KLUGER, *Simple Justice: The History of Brown v Board of Education* (Knopf, 1976).

GARY ORFIELD, SUSAN E. EATON, AND THE HARVARD PROJECT ON SCHOOL DESEGREGATION, *Dismantling Desegregation: The Quiet Reversal of Brown v Board of Education* (New Press, 1996).

J. W. PELTASON, *Fifty-eight Lonely Men: Southern Federal Judges and School Desegregation* (University of Illinois Press, 1971).

MICHAEL J. PERRY, *We the People: The Fourteenth Amendment and the Supreme Court* (Oxford University Press, 1999).

RUTH ROSEN, *The World Split Open: How the Modern Women's Movement Changed America* (Viking, 2000).

GIRARDEAU A. SPANN, *The Law of Affirmative Action: Twenty-five Years of Supreme Court Decisions on Race and Remedies* (New York University Press, 1999).

ROBERTO SURO, *Strangers Among Us: How Latino Immigration Is Transforming America* (Knopf, 1998).

STEPHEN THERNSTROM AND ABIGAIL THERNSTROM, *America in Black and White* (Simon & Schuster, 1997).

19

THE DEMOCRATIC FAITH

AMERICA'S FOUNDING GENERATION FOUGHT AN
EIGHT-YEAR REVOLUTION TO SECURE THEIR RIGHTS AND
LIBERTY. THEN THEY FACED THE CHALLENGE OF CREATING A
government, first at the Constitutional Convention in 1787 and later in the first
Congress, writing a Constitution, and drafting a Bill of Rights that would protect
the rights to life, liberty, and self-government for themselves and for those who
would come later. But they knew, as we also know, that passive allegiance to ideals
and rights is never enough. Every generation must see itself as having a duty to
nurture these ideals by actively renewing the community and nation of which it
is a part.

The framers knew about the rise and decline of ancient Athens. They were
familiar with Pericles and his famed funeral oration in which he said that the person who takes no part in public affairs is a useless person, a good-for-nothing. The
city's business, as Pericles and many Athenians saw it, was everyone's business.
Athens had flourished as an example of what a civilized city might be, but it
foundered when greed, self-centeredness, and smugness set in. As time went on, the
Athenians wanted security more than they wanted liberty; they wanted comfort
more than they wanted freedom. In the end they lost it all—security, comfort, and
freedom. "Responsibility was the price every man must pay for freedom. It was to be
had on no other terms."[1]

If we are to be responsible citizens of the United States in the truest meaning of
the term, our dreams must transcend personal ambition and the accumulation of
material goods. Our country needs citizens who understand that our well-being is tied
to the well-being of our neighbors, community, and country.

The theme in this last chapter is simple: elected leadership and constitutional structures and protections are important, yet an active, committed citizenry is equally important. Freedom and obligation go together. Liberty and duty
go together. The answer to a nation's problems lies not in producing a perfect constitution or a few larger-than-life leaders. The answer lies in encouraging a nation
of citizen-leaders who will, above and beyond their professional and private ambitions, care about the common concerns of the Republic and strive to make
democracy work.

THE CASE FOR GOVERNMENT BY THE PEOPLE

More people today live under conditions of political freedom rather than under authoritarian governments than at any previous time. Throughout history, most people lived in societies in which a small group at the top have imposed their will on the others. Authoritarian governments justify their actions by saying people are too weak to govern themselves; they need to be ruled. Thus, neither in Castro's Cuba nor in the military regime of North Korea, neither in the People's Republic of China nor in Saudi Arabia, do ordinary people have a voice in the type of decisions we Americans routinely make: Who should be admitted into college, or serve in the military? Who should be allowed to immigrate into the country? How much money should be spent for schools, economic development initiatives, health care, or environmental protection?

The essence of our Constitution is that it both grants power to and withholds power from government. Fearing national weakness and popular disorder, the framers wanted to limit the powers of the national government to what it might need to carry out its responsibilities, such as maintaining national defense. They also wanted to limit state governments in order to keep them from interfering with civil rights and property rights. Valuing above all the principle of individual liberty, the framers wanted to protect the people from too much government. They wanted a limited government—yet one that would work. The solution was to divide up the power of the national government, to make it ultimately responsive, if only indirectly, to the voters.

Most Americans want a government that is efficient and effective but also promotes social justice. We want to maintain our commitment to liberty and freedom. We want a government that acts for the majority yet also protects minorities. We want to safeguard our nation and our streets in a world full of change and violence. We want to protect the rights of the poor, the elderly, and minorities. Do we expect too much from our elected officials and public servants? Of course we do!

Constitutional democracy is a system of checks and balances. It balances values against competing values. Government must balance individual liberties against the collective security and needs of society. The question always is: Which rights of which people are to be protected by what means and at what price to individuals and to the whole society?

PARTICIPATION AND REPRESENTATION

No political problem is more complicated than working out the proper relationship between voters and elected officials. It is not just a simple issue of being sure that elected officials do what the voters want them to do. Every individual has a host of conflicting desires, fears, hopes, and expectations, and no government can represent them all. But even if millions of voters could be represented in their many interests, the question of how they would be represented would remain. Through direct representation, such as a traditional New England town meeting or ballot initiatives and referenda? Through economic or professional associations, such as labor unions or political action committees? Through a coalition of minority groups? All these and other alternatives can be defended as proper forms of representation in a constitutional democracy. Yet all also have limitations.

Some propose to bypass this thorny problem of representation by vastly increasing the role of direct popular participation in decision making. What many people regard as the most perfect form of democracy would exist when every person

This participant in a Black Voter Awareness Rally urges citizens to accept responsibility for perpetuating democracy.

has a full and equal opportunity to participate in all decisions and in all processes of influence, persuasion, and discussion that bear on those decisions. Direct participation in decision making, its advocates contend, will serve two major purposes. It will enhance the dignity, self-respect, and understanding of individuals by giving them responsibility for the decisions that shape their lives. And it will act as a safeguard against undemocratic and antidemocratic forms of government and prevent the replacement of democracy by dictatorship or tyranny. This idea rests on a theory of self-protection that says interests can be represented, furthered, and defended best by those they concern directly.

New technologies present ways in which governments can appeal directly to voters, and voters can speak directly to public officials. We now have voting by mail in Oregon and other places, and some people advocate voting on the Internet. Digital town halls may be next. Some applaud these developments; others are appalled by them.

The average American citizen has access to an abundance of information about public affairs: the number of cable television news programs has increased enormously in recent years; talk radio regularly airs diverse views on every political controversy; newspapers and magazines do a fine job of covering national politics, although they do less well at covering state and local public affairs. In half the states, people can vote on many citizen-initiated ballot issues. We also have polls nearly every day on nearly every subject, fascinating technologies that encourage interactive video conferencing, and groups who advocate electronic town meetings.

But we still need institutions such as elected legislatures, which can take the time to digest complicated information and conduct impartial hearings to hear competing points of view. The average citizen rarely has the time or experience to digest all the available information. We are only now beginning to learn how to harness our new electronic technologies to infuse more deliberation into our leadership and public policy making programs.

Experience with many forms of participatory democracy also suggests its limitations as a form of decision making. In an age of rapidly growing population, increasingly complex economic and social systems, and enormously wide-ranging decision-making units of government, direct participation can work only in small communities or at the neighborhood level. As a practical matter, people simply cannot put in endless hours taking part in every decision that affects their lives.

Participatory democracy can still play an important role in smaller units—in neighborhood associations, local party committees, and the like. And perhaps the idea of participation could be greatly extended, for example, to greater influence of workers in the running of factories and corporations. But we must distinguish between democracy as direct participation and as citizen participation. One course of action would be to enlarge the role of participation in representation—that is, to broaden the power of all people to take part in choosing their representatives in larger units of government. This brings us back to the hard questions of indirect representation.

If we must have representatives, who shall represent whom? By electing representatives in a multitude of districts, it is possible to build into representative institutions—the U.S. Congress, for example—most minority interests and attitudes. In the United States we generally have election processes in which only the candidate with the most votes wins. But there are other ways. For example, one way widely used in European nations is proportional representation—a system in which each party running receives the proportion of legislative seats corresponding to its proportion of votes.

Representation can also be influenced by whether there is only one party, or two, or several. Ours is a generally strong two-party system that knits local constituencies into coalitions that can elect and sustain national majorities.

To Protect the Dissenter

". . . we have devised a variety of ways to protect the dissenter. Our civil liberties are a part of that system, and so are Robert's Rules of Order, and grievance procedures, and the commonly held view that we should hear both sides of an argument. In short, we have a tradition, a set of attitudes and specific social arrangements designed to ensure that points of view at odds with prevailing doctrine will not be rejected out of hand.

But why be so considerate of dissent and criticism? To answer this question is to state one of the strongest tenets of our political philosophy. We do not expect organizations or societies to be above criticism, nor do we trust the men who run them to be adequately self-critical. We believe that even those aspects of society that are healthy today may deteriorate tomorrow. We believe that power wielded justly today may be wielded corruptly tomorrow. We know that from the ranks of the critics come cranks and troublemakers, but from the same ranks come the saviors and innovators. And since the spirit that welcomes nonconformity is a fragile thing, we have not depended on that spirit alone. We have devised explicit legal and constitutional arrangements to protect the dissenter."

SOURCE: John W. Gardner, *Self-Renewal*, rev. ed. (Norton, 1981), pp. 71–72.

Proud to Be a Politician

Must a politician gain public office by denouncing the profession? From the tone of many recent congressional races, it would appear that this is a growing trend. Journalist Charles McDowell of the *Richmond Times-Dispatch* noted this trend on the PBS series *The Lawmakers* and suggested that such a tactic "demeans an honorable and essential profession—that of the politician." McDowell proposed that every member of Congress be required to take the following oath:

I affirm that I am a politician. That I am willing to associate with other known politicians. That I have no moral reservations about committing acts of politics. Under the Constitution, I insist that politicians have as much right to indulge in politics as preachers, single-issue zealots, generals, bird-watchers, labor leaders, big business lobbyists, and all other truth-givers.

I confess that, as a politician, I participate in negotiation, compromise, and tradeoffs in order to achieve something that seems reasonable to a majority. And, although I try to be guided by principle, I confess that I often find people of principle on the other side, too.

So help me God.

Which is better: elected officials who represent coalitions of minorities, or officials who represent a relatively clear-cut majority and have little or no obligation to the minority? The answer depends on what you expect from government. A system that represents coalitions of minorities usually reflects the trading, competition, and compromising that must take place in order to reach agreement among the various groups. Such a government has been called *broker rule;* elected officials act essentially as a go-between, as a mediator among organized groups that have definite policy goals. Under broker rule, leaders cannot get too far ahead of the groups; they must tack back and forth, shifting in response to changing group pressures. Instead of acting for a united popular majority with a fairly definite program, either liberal or conservative, the government tries to satisfy all major interests by giving them a voice in decisions and sometimes a veto over actions. In the pushing and hauling of political groups, the government is continually involved in delicate balancing acts.

Some critics point out that fair representation has not been achieved in the American system. They point to the extent of nonvoting and other forms of nonparticipation in politics; the fact that low-income persons are less well organized than upper-income persons; the bias of strong organized groups toward the status quo; the domination of television and the press by a few corporations; and the virtual monopoly of party politics by the two major parties, which do not always offer the voters meaningful alternatives. Critics are concerned that our system of government builds in procedures designed to curtail legislative majorities—for example, the filibuster in the Senate or the power of the Supreme Court to declare laws unconstitutional. Critics also point to the many mistakes made by voters and election machines in the 2000 Florida elections as yet another weakness of our democratic system.

Such charges may be exaggerated, yet they cannot be denied. Those who believe governments should be more directly responsive to political majorities can point to steady improvement in recent years. There have been changes in election laws to simplify voter registration, expand and improve voting procedures, and enforce one-person, one-vote standards. Pressure has been building to limit the ability of rich people and well-financed interests to influence elections. Pressure has also been building to streamline voting systems and pass campaign reform measures. And some progress has been made in Congress to strengthen majority rule.

By this point, you undoubtedly appreciate that democracy has to mean much more than popular government and unchecked majority rule. A democracy needs competing politicians with differing views about the public interest. A vital democracy, living and growing, places its faith in the voters, faith that they will elect not just people who will mirror their views but leaders who will exercise their best judgment—"faith that the people will not condemn those whose devotion to principle leads them to unpopular courses, but will reward courage, respect honor, and ultimately recognize right."[2]

The Role of the Politician

Americans today have decidedly mixed views about elected officials. They realize that at their best politicians are skillful at compromising, mediating, negotiating, brokering—and that governing often requires these qualities. But they also suspect politicians of being ambitious, conniving, unprincipled, opportunistic, and corrupt. Compared to people in other professions, Americans hold politicians in low esteem.

Still, we often find that individual officeholders are bright, hardworking, and friendly (even though we may suspect they are simply trying to get our vote). And our liking sometimes turns into reverence after these same politicians die. George

Washington, Abraham Lincoln, Dwight D. Eisenhower, and John F. Kennedy are acclaimed today. Harry Truman liked to joke that a statesman is merely a politician who has been dead for about ten years.

Of course, we must put the problem in perspective. In all democracies the public probably expects too much from politicians. Further, people naturally dislike those who wield power. Public officeholders, after all, tax us, regulate us, and conscript us. We dislike political compromisers and ambitious opportunists—even though we may need such people to get things done.

Politics is a necessity. Politics is a vital and—at critical times—a noble leadership activity. Politicians are essential for running the American Republic, whose fragmented powers require them to mediate among factions, build coalitions, and compromise among and within branches of government to produce policy and action.

Leadership for a Constitutional Democracy

Even though one of the most universal cravings of our time is a hunger for creative and compelling leadership, defining leadership is a challenge in itself. Leadership can be understood only in the context of both leaders and followers. A leader without followers is a contradiction in terms. Leadership is also situational and contextual; a person is often effective in only one kind of situation. Leadership is not necessarily transferable. James Madison, for example, was a brilliant political and constitutional theorist; he was also a superb politician. Still, he was not a brilliant president. The leadership required to lead a marine platoon up a hill in battle is different from the leadership needed to change racist or sexist attitudes in city governments. The leadership required of a campaign manager differs from that required of a candidate. Leaders of thought are not always effective as leaders of action.

Although leaders are often skilled managers, they need more than just managerial skills. Managers are concerned with doing things the right way; leaders are concerned with doing the right thing. Managers are concerned with efficiency and process, especially routines and standard operating procedures. Leaders, on the other hand, concentrate on goals, purposes, and a vision of the future.

Some leaders have indispensable qualities of contagious self-confidence, unwarranted optimism, and dogged idealism that attract and mobilize others to undertake tasks they never dreamed they could accomplish. In short, they empower others and enable many of their followers to become leaders in their own right. Most of the significant breakthroughs in our nation, as well as in our communities, have been made or shaped by people who, while seeing all the complexities and obstacles ahead of them, believed in themselves and in their purposes so much that they refused to be overwhelmed and paralyzed by self-doubts. They were willing to gamble, to take risks, to look at things in a fresh way, and often to invent new rules.[3]

Leaders recognize the fundamental—unexpressed as well as expressed—wants and needs of potential followers. By bringing followers to a fuller consciousness of their needs, they help convert their hopes and aspirations into practical demands on other leaders, especially leaders in government. A leader in a democracy consults and listens while educating followers and attempting to renew the goals of an organization.

RECONCILING DEMOCRACY AND LEADERSHIP

Americans are fond of saying, "It is all politics, you know." This greatly oversimplified insight is offered as profound. More important, it is intended as a negative judgment, as if things somehow would be improved if we did not have politics and politicians.

But politics is the lifeblood of democracy, and without politics there is no freedom. To conclude that politicians are interested in winning elections is about as profound as to conclude that businesspeople are interested in profits. Of course they are! We do not expect our economy to operate because the shoe store owner is motivated

- To solve problems and promote the American Dream

- To advance fresh ideas and approaches

- To "throw some rascal out" whose views they dislike

- To gain a voice in policy making

- To serve as a party spokesperson

- To acquire political influence and a platform from which to influence public opinion

- To gain prominence and power

- To satisfy ego needs

- To gain opportunities to learn, grow, travel, and meet all kinds of people

- To be "where the action is"—involved in the thick of government and political life—campaigning, debating, drafting laws, reconciling diverse views, and making the system responsive

only by a desire to see that people have dry, warm feet. Rather, we harness the store owner's desire to make a living as a way to see to it that the largest number of people get the shoes they want at the lowest possible price. So also we harness the elected official's desire for reelection as the way to ensure that elected officials do what most of the voters want them to do. It is the politician's need to serve and please the voters that is the indispensable link in making democracy work.[4]

One of our major political challenges is to reconcile democracy and leadership. In the past we often have held a view of leaders as all powerful. Yet a nation of subservient followers can never be a democratic one. A democratic nation requires educated, skeptical, caring, engaged, and conscientious citizen-leaders. It also requires citizen leaders who will recognize when change is needed and have the courage to bring about necessary reforms and progress.[5]

Such democratic citizen-leaders appreciate that power wielded justly today may be wielded corruptly tomorrow. Democratic citizen-leaders are moved to protest when they know a policy is wrong or when the rights of other citizens are diminished. Such leaders appreciate that criticism of official error is not unpatriotic criticism of our country. Citizen-leaders recognize as well that democracy rests solidly upon a realistic view of human nature. Our capacity for justice, as theologian and philosopher Reinhold Niebuhr observed, makes democracy possible. But our "inclination to injustice makes democracy necessary."[6]

Democratic politics is the forum for excellence and responsibility, where, by acting together, citizens become free. In this sense, politics is not a necessary evil; it is a realistic good. It is the preoccupation of free people, and its existence is a test of freedom.[7]

Leadership thought of as an engagement among equals can empower people and enlarge their opinions, choices, and freedoms. The answer for our Republic lies not in producing a handful of great, charismatic, Mount Rushmore leaders, but in educating a citizenry who can boast that we are no longer in need of superheroes because we have become a nation of citizens who believe that each of us can make a difference, and that all of us should regularly try.[8]

Leaders will always be needed. However, our system of government is, in many ways, designed to prevent strong and decisive action, lest too much political power be placed in the hands of too few people. Thus, while we have emphasized the role of leadership in constitutional democracies in these last few pages, the potential for abuse is checked not only by an involved citizenry but also by the very structure of our constitutional system—separation of powers, checks and balances, federalism, bicameral legislatures, and the rule of law.

The ultimate test of a democratic system is the legal existence of an officially recognized opposition. A cardinal characteristic of a constitutional democracy is that it not only recognizes the need for the free organization of opposing views but positively encourages this organization. Freedom for political expression and dissent is basic—even freedom for nonsense to be spoken so that good sense not yet recognized gets a chance to be heard.[9]

THE DEMOCRATIC FAITH

Crucial to the democratic faith is the belief that a constitutional democracy cherishes the free play of ideas. Only where the safety valve of public discussion is available and where almost any policy is subject to perpetual questioning and challenge can there be the assurance that both minority and majority rights will be served. To be afraid of public debate is to be afraid of self-government. "Rulers always have and always will find it dangerous to their security to permit people to think, believe, talk, write, assemble, and particularly to criticize the government as they please," said former Supreme Court Justice William J. Brennan, "but the language of the First Amendment indicates the framers weighed the risk involved in such freedoms and deliberately chose to stake this government's security and life upon preserving liberty to discuss public affairs intact and untouched by government."[10]

Your authors hold with Thomas Jefferson that there is nothing in the country so radically wrong that it cannot be cured by good newspapers, sound schoolmasters, and a critical reading of history. Inform and educate the citizenry, and a major hurdle is overcome. Jefferson had boundless faith in education. He believed people are rationally endowed by nature with an innate sense of justice; the average person has only to be informed to act wisely. In the long run, said Jefferson, only an educated and enlightened democracy can hope to endure.

Education is one of the best predictors of voting, participation in politics, and knowledge of public affairs. People may not be equally involved or equally willing to invest in democracy, but the attentive public—frequently those like yourself who have gone to college—has the willingness and self-confidence to see government and politics as necessary and important. An educated public has an understanding of how government works, how individuals can influence decision makers, and how to elect like-minded people.

Recent years have sadly witnessed an increase in racial and ethnic tensions in the United States. These tensions sometimes encourage separation and antagonism toward the larger and more dominant culture. When carried to the extreme, these tensions promote various ethnicity cults that exaggerate differences, intensify resentments, and drive deep wedges between nationalities and races. "The genius of America" writes historian Arthur M. Schlesinger, Jr., "lies in its capacity to forge a single nation from peoples of remarkably diverse racial, religious, and ethnic origins." Schlesinger acknowledges that our government and society have been more open to some than to others, "but it is more open to all today than it was yesterday and it is likely to be even more open tomorrow than today."[11]

We are a restless, dissatisfied, and searching people. We are often our own toughest critics. Our political system is far from perfect, but it still is an open system. People *can* fight city hall. People who disagree with policies in the nation can band together and be heard. We know only too well that the American Dream is never fully attained. It must always be pursued.

Millions of Americans visit the great monuments in our nation's capital each year. They are always impressed by the memorials to Washington, Jefferson, Lincoln, Franklin D. Roosevelt, and the Vietnam and Korean War veterans; they are awed by the beauty of the Capitol, the Supreme Court, and the White House. The strength of the nation, however, resides not in these official buildings and monuments but in the hearts, minds, and behavior of citizens. If we lose faith, stop caring, stop participating, and stop believing in the possibilities of self-government, the monuments "will be meaningless piles of stone, and the venture that began with the Declaration of Independence, the venture familiarly known as America will be as lifeless as the stone."[12]

The future of democracy in America will be shaped by those citizens who care about preserving and extending our political rights and freedoms. Our individual liberties will never be assured unless there are people willing to take responsibility for the progress of the whole community, people willing to exercise their determination and democratic faith. Carved in granite on one of the long corridors in a building on the Harvard University campus are these words of American poet Archibald MacLeish: "How shall freedom be defended? By arms when it is attacked by arms, by truth when it is attacked by lies, by democratic faith when it is attacked by authoritarian dogma. Always, in the final act, by determination and faith."

Why People Shy Away from Running for Office

- Invasion of privacy
- Less time to spend with families or favorite pastimes
- Less income than in many business or professional occupations
- Exposure to partisan and media criticism
- Involvement in many things most people would rather not do—like marching in countless parades, attending county fairs, and going to endless political dinners, banquets, and service club meetings
- Fear that one may have to compromise principles because of the complexity of our adversarial system
- Expense of campaigning
- Aversion to conflict, divisiveness, and ambition
- Concern that the constitutional structure and party system make it nearly impossible to exercise meaningful leadership

APPENDIX

THE DECLARATION OF INDEPENDENCE

Drafted mainly by Thomas Jefferson, this document adopted by the Second Continental Congress, and signed by John Hancock and fifty-five others, outlined the rights of man and the rights to rebellion and self-government. It declared the independence of the colonies from Great Britain, justified rebellion, and listed the grievances against George the III and his government. What is memorable about this famous document is not only that it declared the birth of a new nation, but that it set forth, with eloquence, our basic philosophy of liberty and representative democracy.

IN CONGRESS, JULY 4, 1776
(The unanimous Declaration of the Thirteen United States of America)

Preamble
When, in the course of human events, it becomes necessary for one people to dissolve the political bands which have connected them with another, and to assume, among the powers of the earth, the separate and equal station to which the laws of nature and of nature's God entitle them, a decent respect to the opinions of mankind requires that they should declare the causes which impel them to the separation.

New Principles of Government

We hold these truths to be self-evident; that all men are created equal, that they are endowed by their Creator with certain unalienable rights, that among these are life, liberty, and the pursuit of happiness.

That, to secure these rights, governments are instituted among men, deriving their just powers from the consent of the governed.

That whenever any form of government becomes destructive of these ends, it is the right of the people to alter or to abolish it, and to institute new government, laying its foundation on such principles, and organizing its powers in such form, as to them shall seem most likely to effect their safety and happiness. Prudence, indeed will dictate that governments long established should not be changed for light and transient causes; and accordingly all experience hath shown that mankind are more disposed to suffer while evils are sufferable, than to right themselves by abolishing the forms to which they are accustomed. But when a long train of abuses and usurpations, pursuing invariably the same object, evinces a design to reduce them under absolute despotism, it is their right, it is their duty, to throw off such government, and to provide new guards for their future security.

Reasons for Separation

Such has been the patient sufferance of these colonies; and such is now the necessity which constrains them to alter their former systems of government. The history of the present king of Great Britain is a history of repeated injuries and usurpations, all having in direct object the establishment of an absolute tyranny over these states. To prove this, let facts be submitted to a candid world.

He has refused his assent to laws, the most wholesome and necessary for the public good.

He has forbidden his governors to pass laws of immediate and pressing importance unless suspended in their operation till his assent should be obtained; and when so suspended, he has utterly neglected to attend to them.

He has refused to pass other laws for the accommodation of large districts of people, unless those people would relinquish the right of representation in the legislature, a right inestimable to them, and formidable to tyrants only.

He has called together legislative bodies at places unusual, uncomfortable, and distant for the depository of their public records, for the sole purpose of fatiguing them into compliance with his measures.

He has dissolved representative houses repeatedly, for opposing, with manly firmness, his invasions on the rights of people.

He has refused, for a long time after such dissolutions, to cause others to be elected; whereby the legislative powers incapable of annihilation, have returned to the people at large for their exercise; the state remaining, in the meantime, exposed to all the dangers of invasion from without and convulsions within.

He has endeavored to prevent the population of these states; for that purpose obstructing the laws of naturalization of foreigners, refusing to pass others to encourage their migration hither, and raising the conditions of new appropriations of lands.

He has obstructed the administration of justice, by refusing his assent to laws for establishing judiciary powers.

He has made judges dependent on his will alone for the tenure of their offices, and the amount and payment of their salaries.

He has erected a multitude of new offices, and sent hither swarms of officers to harass our people and eat out their substance.

He has kept among us, in times of peace, standing armies, without the consent of our legislature.

He has affected to render the military independent of, and superior to, the civil power.

He has combined with others to subject us to jurisdiction foreign to our constitution and unacknowledged by our laws, giving his assent to their acts of pretended legislation:

For quartering large bodies of armed troops among us;

For protecting them, by a mock trial, from punishment for any murders which they should commit on the inhabitants of these states;

For cutting off our trade with all parts of the world;

For imposing taxes on us without our consent;

For depriving us, in many cases, of the benefits of trial by jury;

For transporting us beyond seas, to be tried for pretended offenses;

For abolishing the free system of English laws in a neighboring province, establishing therein an arbitrary government, and enlarging its boundaries, so as to render it at once an example and fit instrument for introducing the same absolute rule into these colonies;

For taking away our charters, abolishing our most valuable laws, and altering, fundamentally, the forms of our governments;

For suspending our own legislatures, and declaring themselves invented with power to legislate for us in all cases whatsoever.

He has abdicated government here, by declaring us out of his protection and waging war against us.

He has plundered our seas, ravaged our coasts, burned our towns, and destroyed the lives of our people.

He is at this time transporting large armies of foreign mercenaries to complete the works of death, desolation, and tyranny already begun with circumstances of cruelty and perfidy scarcely paralleled in the most barbarous ages and totally unworthy of the head of a civilized nation.

He has constrained our fellow-citizens, taken captive on the high seas, to bear arms against their country, to become the executioners of their friends and brethren, or to fall themselves by their hands.

He has excited domestic insurrections among us, and has endeavored to bring on the inhabitants of our frontiers the merciless Indian savages, whose known rule of warfare is an undistinguished destruction of all ages, sexes, and conditions.

In every stage of these oppressions we have petitioned for redress in the most humble terms; our repeated petitions have been answered only by repeated injury. A prince whose character is thus marked by every act which may define a tyrant is unfit to be the ruler of a free people.

Nor have we been wanting in attention to our British brethren. We have warned them, from time to time, of attempts by their legislature to extend an unwarrantable jurisdiction over us. We have reminded them of the circumstances of our emigration and settlement here. We have appealed to their native justice and magnanimity; and we have conjured them, by the ties of our common kindred, to disavow these usurpations, which would inevitably interrupt our connections and correspondence. They, too, have been deaf to the voice of justice and of consanguinity. We must, therefore, acquiesce in the necessity which denounces our separation, and hold them, as we hold the rest of mankind, enemies in war, in peace, friends.

We, therefore, the representatives of the United States of America, in General Congress assembled, appealing to the Supreme Judge of the world for the rectitude of our intentions, do, in the name and by authority of the good people of these colonies, solemnly publish and declare, that these united colonies are, and of right ought to be, free and independent states; that they are absolved from all allegiance to the British crown, and that all political connection between them and the state of Great Britain is, and ought to be, totally dissolved; and that, as free and independent states, they have full power to levy war, conclude peace, contract alliances, establish commerce, and do all other acts and things which independent states may of a right do. And, for the support of this declaration, with a firm reliance on the protection of Divine Providence, we mutually pledge to each other our lives, our fortunes, and our sacred honor.

THE FEDERALIST, NO. 10, JAMES MADISON

The Federalist, No. 10, *written by James Madison soon after the Constitutional Convention, was prepared as one of several dozen newspaper essays aimed at persuading New Yorkers to ratify the proposed constitution. One of the most important basic documents in American political history, it outlines the need for and the general principles of a democratic republic. It also provides a political and economic analysis of the realities of interest group or faction politics.*

To the People of the State of New York: Among the numerous advantages promised by a well-constructed union, none deserves to be more accurately developed than its tendency to break and control the violence of faction. The friend of popular governments, never finds himself so much alarmed for their character and fate, as when he contemplates their propensity of this dangerous vice. He will not fail, therefore, to set a due value on any plan which, without violating the principles to which he is attached, provides a proper cure for it. The instability, injustice, and confusion introduced into the public councils, have, in truth, been the mortal diseases under which popular governments have everywhere perished; as they continue to be the favorite and fruitful topics from which the adversaries to liberty derive their most specious declamations. The valuable improvements made by the American constitutions on the popular models, both ancient and modern, cannot certainly be too much admired; but it would be an unwarrantable partiality, to contend that they have as effectually obviated the danger on this side, as was wished and expected. Complaints are everywhere heard from our most considerate and virtuous citizens, equally the friends of public and private faith, and of public and personal liberty, that our governments are too unstable; that the public good is disregarded in the conflicts of rival parties; and that measures are too often decided, not according to the rules of justice, and the rights of the minor party, but by the superior force of an interested and overbearing majority. However anxiously we may wish that these complaints had no foundation, the evidence of known facts will not permit us to deny that they are in some degree true. It will be found, indeed, on a candid review of our situation, that some of the distresses under which we labor have been erroneously charged on the operations of our governments; but it will be found, at the same time, that other causes will not alone account for many of our heaviest misfortunes; and, particularly, for that prevailing and increasing distrust of public engagements, and alarm for private rights, which are echoed from one end of the continent to the other. These must be chiefly, if not wholly, effects of the unsteadiness and injustice, with which a factious spirit has tainted our public administrations.

By a faction, I understand a number of citizens, whether amounting to a majority of the whole, who are united and actuated by some common impulse of passion, or of interest, adverse to the rights of other citizens, or to the permanent and aggregate interests of the community.

There are two methods of curing the mischiefs of faction: the one, by removing its causes; the other, by controlling its effects.

There are again two methods of removing the causes of faction: the one, by destroying the liberty which is essential to its existence; the other, by giving to every citizen the same opinions, the same passions, and the same interests.

It could never be more truly said, than of the first remedy, that it was worse than the disease. Liberty is to faction what air is to fire, an aliment without which it instantly expires. But it could not be a less folly to abolish liberty, which is essential to political life, because it nourishes faction, than it would be to wish the annihilation of air, which is essential to animal life, because it imparts to fire its destructive agency.

The second expedient is as impracticable, as the first would be unwise. As long as the reason of man continues fallible, and he is at liberty to exercise it, different opinions will be formed. As long as the connection subsists between his reason and his self-love, his opinions and his passions will have a reciprocal influence on each other; and the former will be objects to which the latter will attach themselves. The diversity in the faculties of men, from which the rights of property originate, is not less an insuperable obstacle to an uniformity of interests. The protection of these faculties is the first object of government. From the protection of different and unequal faculties of acquiring property, the possession of different degrees and kinds of property immediately results; and from the influence of these on the sentiments and views of the respective proprietors, ensues a division of the society into different interests and parties.

The latent causes of faction are thus sown in the nature of man; and we see them everywhere brought into different degrees of activity, according to the different circumstances of civil society. A zeal for different opinions concerning religion, concerning government, and many other points, as well of speculation as of practice; an attachment to different leaders ambitiously contending for preeminence and power; or to persons of other descriptions whose fortunes have been interesting to the human passions, have, in turn, divided mankind into parties, inflamed them with mutual animosity, and rendered them much more disposed to vex and oppress each other, than to cooperate for their common good. So strong is this propensity of mankind, to fall into mutual animosities, that where no substantial occasion presents itself, the most frivolous and

fanciful distinctions have been sufficient to kindle their unfriendly passions and excite their most violent conflicts. But the most common and durable source of factions, has been the various and unequal distribution of property. Those who hold, and those who are without property, have ever formed distinct interests in society. Those who are creditors, and those who are debtors, fall under a like discrimination. A landed interest, a manufacturing interest, a mercantile interest, a moneyed interest, with many lesser interests, grow up of necessity in civilized nations, and divide them into different classes, actuated by different sentiments and views. The regulation of these various and interfering interests forms the principal task of modern legislation, and involves the spirit of the party and faction in the necessary and ordinary operations of the government.

No man is allowed to be a judge in his own cause; because his interest will certainly bias his judgment, and, not improbably, corrupt his integrity. With equal, nay, with greater reason, a body of men are unfit to be both judges and parties at the same time; yet what are many of the most important acts of legislation, but so many judicial determinations, not indeed concerning the right of single persons, but concerning the rights of large bodies of citizens? And what are the different classes of legislators, but advocates and parties to the causes which they determine? Is a law proposed concerning private debts? It is a questions to which the creditors are parties on one side, and the debtors on the other. Justice ought to hold the balance between them. Yet the parties are, and must be, themselves the judges; and the most numerous party, or, in other words, the most powerful faction, must be expected to prevail. Shall domestic manufacturers be encouraged, and in what degree, by restrictions on foreign manufacturers? Are questions which would be differently decided by the landed and the manufacturing classes; and probably by neither with a sole regard to justice and the public good. The apportionment of taxes, on the various descriptions of property, is an act which seems to require the most exact impartiality; yet there is, perhaps, no legislative act, in which greater opportunity and temptation are given to a predominant party to trample on the rules of justice. Every shilling, with which they overburden the inferior number, is a shilling saved to their own pockets.

It is in vain to say, that enlightened statesmen will be able to adjust these clashing interests, and render them all sub-

servient to the public good. Enlightened statesmen will not always be at the helm, nor, in many cases, can such an adjustment be made at all, without taking into view indirect and remote considerations, which will rarely prevail over the immediate interest which one party may find in disregarding the rights of another, or the good of the whole.

The inference to which we are brought is, that the causes of faction cannot be removed; and that relief is only to be sought in the means of controlling its effects.

If a faction consists of less than a majority, relief is supplied by the republican principle, which enables the majority to defeat its sinister views, by regular vote. It may clog the administration, it may convulse the society; but it will be unable to execute and mask its violence under the forms of the Constitution. When a majority is included in a faction, the form of popular government, on the other hand, enables it to sacrifice to its ruling passion or interest, both the public good and the rights of other citizens. To secure the public good, and private rights, against the danger of such a faction, and at the same time to preserve the spirit and the form of popular government, is then the great object to which our inquiries are directed. Let me add, that it is the great desideratum, by which alone this form of government can be rescued from the opprobrium under which it has so long laboured, and be recommended to the esteem and adoption of mankind.

By what means is this object attainable? Evidently by one of two only. Either the existence of the same passion or interest in a majority, at the same time, must be prevented; or the majority, having such coexistent passion or interest, must be rendered, by their number and local situation, unable to concert and carry into effect schemes of oppression. If the impulse and the opportunity be suffered to coincide, we well know that neither moral nor religious motives can be relied on as an adequate control. They are not found to be such on the injustice and violence of individuals, and lose their efficacy in proportion to the number combined together; that is, in proportion as their efficacy becomes needful.

From this view of the subject, it may be concluded, that a pure democracy, by which I mean a society consisting of a small number of citizens, who assemble and administer the government in person, can admit of no cure for the mischiefs of faction. A common passion or interest will, in almost every case, be felt by a majority of the whole; a communication and concert, results from the form of government itself; and there is nothing to check the inducements to sacrifice the weaker party, or an obnoxious individual. Hence, it is, that such democracies have ever been spectacles of turbulence and contention; have ever been found incompatible with personal security, or the rights of property; and have in general been as short in their lives, as they have been violent in their deaths. Theoretic politicians, who have patronized this species of government, have erroneously supposed, that by reducing mankind to a perfect equality in their political rights, they would, at the same time be perfectly equalized and assimilated in their possessions, in their opinions, and their passions.

A republic, by which I mean a government in which the scheme of representation takes place, opens a different prospect, and promises the cure for which we are seeking. Let us examine the points in which it varies from pure democracy, and we shall comprehend both the nature of the cure and the efficacy which it must derive from the union.

The two great points of difference, between a democracy and a republic, are, first, the delegation of the government, in the latter, to a small number of citizens, elected by the rest; secondly, the greater number of citizens, and greater sphere of country, over which the latter may be extended.

The effect of the first difference is, on the one hand, to refine and enlarge the public views, by passing them through the medium of a chosen body of citizens, whose wisdom may best discern the true interest of their country, and whose patriotism and love of justice, will be least likely to sacrifice it to temporary or partial considerations. Under such a regulation, it may well happen, that the public voice, pronounced by the representatives of the people, will be more consonant to the public good, than if pronounced by the people themselves, convened for the purpose. On the other hand the effect may be inverted. Men of factious tempers, of local prejudices, or of sinister designs, may by intrigue, by corruption, or by other means, first obtain the suffrages, and then betray the interest of the people. The question resulting is, whether small or extensive republics are most favourable to the election of proper guardians of the public weal; and it is clearly decided in favour of the latter by two obvious considerations.

In the first place, it is to be remarked that, however small the republic may be, the representatives must be raised to a certain number, in order to guard against the cabals of a few; and that however large it may be, they must be limited to a certain number, in order to guard against the confusion of a multitude. Hence, the number of representatives in the two cases not being in proportion to that of the constituents, and being proportionally greatest in the small republic, it follows, that if the proportion of fit characters be not less in the large than in the small republic, the former will present a greater option, and consequently a greater probability of a fit choice.

In the next place, as each representative will be chosen by a greater number of citizens in the large than in the small republic, it will be more difficult for unworthy candidates to practice with success the vicious arts, by which elections are too often carried; and the suffrages of the people being more free, will be more likely to centre in men who possess the most attractive merit, and the most diffusive and established characters.

It must be confessed, that in this, as in most other cases, there is a mean, on both sides of which inconveniences will be found to lie. By enlarging too much the number of electors, you render the representatives too little acquainted with all their local circumstances and lesser interests; as by reducing it too much, you render him unduly attached to these, and too little fit to comprehend and pursue great and national objects. The federal constitution forms a happy combination in this respect; the great and aggregate interests being referred to the national, the local and particular to the state legislatures.

The other point of difference is, the greater number of citizens, and extent of territory, which may be brought within the compass of republican, than of democratic government; and it is this circumstance principally which renders factious combinations less to be dreaded in the former, than in the latter. The smaller the society, the fewer probably will be the distinct parties and interests composing it; the fewer the distinct parties and interests, the more frequently will a majority be found of the same party; and the smaller the number of individuals composing a majority, and the smaller the compass within which they are placed, the more easily will they concert and execute their plans of oppression. Extend the sphere, and you take in a greater variety of parties and interests; you make it less probable that a majority of the whole will have a common motive to invade the rights of other citizens; or if such a common motive exists, it will be more difficult for all who feel it to discover their own strength, and to act in unison with each other. Besides other impediments, it may be remarked, that where there is a consciousness of unjust or dishonourable purposes, communication is always checked by distrust, in proportion to the number whose concurrence is necessary.

Hence, it clearly appears, that the same advantage, which a republic has over a democracy, in controlling the effects of faction, is enjoyed by a large over a small republic—is enjoyed by the union over the states composing it. Does this advantage consist in the substitution of representatives, whose enlightened views and virtuous sentiments render them superior to local prejudices, and to schemes of injustice? It will not be denied that the representation of the union will be most likely to possess these requisite endowments. Does it consist in the greater security afforded by a greater variety of parties, against the event of any one party being able to outnumber and oppress the rest? In an equal degree does the increased variety of parties, comprised within the union, increase the security? Does it, in fine, consist in the greater obstacles opposed to the concert and accomplishment of the secret wishes of an unjust and interested majority? Here, again, the extent of the union gives it the most palpable advantage.

The influence of factious leaders may kindle a flame within their particular states, but will be unable to spread a general conflagration through the other states; a religious sect may degenerate into a political faction in a part of the confederacy; but the variety of sects dispersed over the entire face of it, must secure the national councils against any danger from that source: a rage for paper money, for an abolition of debts, for an equal division of property, or for any other improper or wicked project, will be less apt to pervade the whole body of the union than a particular member of it; in the same proportion as such a malady is more likely to taint a particular county or district, than an entire state.

In the extent and proper structure of the union, therefore, we behold a republican remedy for the diseases most incident to republican government. And according to the degree of pleasure and pride we feel in being republicans, ought to be our zeal in cherishing the spirit, and supporting the character of federalists.

THE FEDERALIST, NO. 51, JAMES MADISON

The Federalist, No. 51, also written by Madison, is a classic statement in defense of separation of powers and republican processes. Its fourth paragraph is especially famous and is frequently quoted by students of government.

To what expedient, then, shall we finally resort, for maintaining in practice the necessary partition of power among the several departments as laid down in the Constitution? The only answer that can be given is that as all these exterior provisions are found to be inadequate the defect must be supplied, by so contriving the interior structure of the government as that its several constituent parts may, by their mutual relations, be the means of keeping each other in their proper places. Without presuming to undertake a full development of this important idea I will hazard a few general observations which may perhaps place it in a clearer light, and enable us to form a more correct judgment of the principles and structure of the government planned by the convention.

In order to lay a due foundation for that separate and distinct exercise of the different powers of government, which to a certain extent is admitted on all hands to be essential to the preservation of liberty, it is evident that each department should have a will of its own; and consequently should be so constituted that the members of each should have as little agency as possible in the appointment of the members of the others. Were this principle rigorously adhered to, it would require that all the appointments for the supreme executive, legislative, and judiciary magistracies should be drawn from the same fountain of authority, the people, through channels having no communication whatever with one another. Perhaps such a plan of constructing the several departments would be less difficult in practice than it may in contemplation appear. Some difficulties, however, and some additional expense would attend the execution of it. Some deviations, therefore, from the principle must be admitted. In the constitution of the judiciary department in particular, it might be inexpedient to insist rigorously on the principle: first, because peculiar qualifications being essential in the members, the primary consideration ought to be to select that mode of choice which best secures these qualifications; second, because the permanent tenure by which the appointments are held in that department must soon destroy all sense of dependence on the authority conferring them.

It is equally evident that the members of each department should be as little dependent as possible on those of the others for the emoluments annexed to their offices. Were the executive magistrate, or the judges, not independent of the legislature in this particular, their independence in every other would be merely nominal.

But the great security against a gradual concentration of the several powers in the same department consists in giving to those who administer each department the necessary constitutional means and personal motives to resist encroachments of the others. The provision for defense must in this, as in all other cases, be made commensurate to the danger of attack. Ambition must be made to counteract ambition. The interest of the man must be connected with the constitutional rights of the place. It may be a reflection on human nature that such devices should be necessary to control the abuses of government. But what is government itself but the greatest of all reflections on human nature? If men were angels, no government would be necessary. If angels were to govern men, neither external nor internal controls on government would be necessary. In framing a government which is to be administered by men over men, the great difficulty lies in this: you must first enable the government to control the governed; and in the next place oblige it to control itself. A dependence on the people is, no doubt, the primary control on the government; but experience has taught mankind the necessity of auxiliary precautions.

This policy of supplying, by opposite and rival interests, the defect of better motives, might be traced through the whole system of human affairs, private as well as public. We see it particularly displayed in all the subordinate distributions of power, where the constant aim is to divide and arrange the several offices in such a manner as that each may be a check on the other—that the private interest of every individual may be a sentinel over the public rights. These inventions of prudence cannot be less requisite in the distribution of the supreme powers of the State.

But it is not possible to give to each department an equal power of self-defense. In republican government, the legislative authority necessarily predominates. The remedy for this inconveniency is to divide the legislature into different branches; and to render them, by modes of election and different principles of action, as little connected with each other as the nature of their common functions and their common dependence on the society will admit. It may even be necessary to guard against dangerous encroachments by still further precautions. As the weight of the legislative authority requires that it should be thus divided, the weakness of the executive may require, on the other hand, that it should be fortified. An absolute negative on the legislature appears, at first view, to be the natural defense with which the executive magistrate should be armed. But perhaps it would be neither altogether safe nor alone sufficient. On ordinary occasions it might not be exerted with the requisite firmness, and on extraordinary occasions it might be perfidiously abused. May not this defect of an absolute negative be supplied by some qualified connection between this weaker department and the weaker branch of the stronger department, by which the latter may be led to support the constitutional rights of the former, without being too much detached from the rights of its own department?

If the principles on which these observations are founded be just, as I persuade myself they are, and they be applied as a criterion to the several State constitutions, and to the federal Constitution, it will be found that if the latter does not perfectly correspond with them, the former are infinitely less able to bear such a test.

There are, moreover, two considerations particularly applicable to the federal system of America, which place that system in a very interesting point of view.

First. In a single republic, all the power surrendered by the people is submitted to the administration of a single government; and the usurpations are guarded against by a division of the government into distinct and separate departments. In the compound republic of America, the power surrendered by the people is first divided between two distinct governments, and then the portion allotted to each subdivided among distinct and separate departments. Hence a double security arises to the rights of the people. The different governments will control each other, at the same time that each will be controlled by itself.

Second. It is of great importance in a republic not only to guard the society against the oppression of its rulers, but to guard one part of the society against the injustice of the other part. Different interests necessarily exist in different classes of citizens. If a majority be united by a common interest, the rights of the minority will be insecure. There are but two methods of providing against this evil: the one by creating a will in the community independent of the majority—that is, of the society itself; the other, by comprehending in the society so many separate descriptions of citizens as will render an unjust combination of a majority of the whole very improbable, if not impracticable. The first method prevails in all governments possessing an hereditary or self-appointed authority. This, at best, is but a precarious security; because a power independent of the society may as well espouse the unjust views of the major as the rightful interests of the minor party, and may possibly be turned against both parties. The second method will be exemplified in the federal republic of the United States. Whilst all authority in it will be derived from and dependent on the society, the society itself will be broken into so many parts, interests and classes of citizens, that the rights of individuals, or of the minority, will be in little danger from interested combinations of the majority. In a free government the security for civil rights must be the same as that for religious rights. It consists in the one case in the multiplicity of interests, and in the other in the multiplicity of sects. The degree of security in both cases will depend on the number of interests and sects; and this may be presumed to depend on the extent of country and number of people comprehended under the same government. This view of the subject must particularly recommend a proper federal system to all the sincere and considerate friends of republican government, since it shows that in exact proportion as the territory of the Union may be formed into more circumscribed Confederacies, or States, oppressive combinations of a majority will be facilitated; the best security, under the republican forms, for the rights of every class of citizen, will be diminished; and consequently the stability and independence of some member of the government, the only other security, must be proportionally increased. Justice is the end of government. It is the end of civil society. It ever has been and ever will be pursued until it be obtained, or until liberty be lost in the pursuit. In a society under the forms of which the stronger faction can readily unite and oppress the weaker, anarchy may as truly be said to reign as in a state of nature, where the weaker individual is not secured against the violence of the stronger; and as, in the latter state, even the stronger individuals are prompted, by the uncertainty of their condition, to submit to a government which may protect the weak as well as themselves; so, in the former state, will the more powerful factions or parties be gradually induced, by a like motive, to wish for a government which will protect all parties, the weaker as well as the more powerful. It can be little doubted that if the State of Rhode Island was separated from the Confederacy and left to itself, the insecurity of rights under the popular form of government within such narrow limits would be displayed by such reiterated oppressions of factious majorities that some power altogether independent of the people would soon be called for by the voice of the very factions whose misrule had proved the necessity to it. In the extended republic of the United States, and among the great variety of interests, parties, and sects which it embraces, a coalition of a majority of the whole society could seldom take place on any other principles than those of justice and the general good; whilst there being thus less danger to a minor from the will of a major party, there must be less pretext, also, to provide for the security of the former, by introducing into the government a will not dependent on the latter, or, in other words, a will independent of the society itself. It is no less certain that it is important, notwithstanding the contrary opinions which have been entertained that the larger the society, provided it lie within a practicable sphere, the more duly capable it will be of self-government. And happily for the *republican cause*, the practicable sphere may be carried to a very great extent by a judicious modification and mixture of the *federal principle*.

THE FEDERALIST, NO. 78, ALEXANDER HAMILTON

The Federalist, *No. 78, written by Alexander Hamilton, explains and praises the provisions for the judiciary in the newly drafted Constitution. Notice especially how Hamilton asserts that the courts have a key responsibility in determining the meaning of the Constitution as fundamental law. Hamilton is outlining here the doctrine of judicial review as we now know it.*

We proceed now to an examination of the judiciary department of the proposed government.

In unfolding the defects of the existing Confederation, the utility and necessity of a federal judicature have been clearly pointed out. It is the less necessary to recapitulate the considerations there urged as the propriety of the institution in the abstract is not disputed; the only questions which have been raised being relative to the manner of constituting it, and to its extent. To these points, therefore, our observations shall be confined.

The manner of constituting it seems to embrace these several objects: 1st. The mode of appointing the judges. 2nd. The tenure by which they are to hold their places. 3rd. The partition of the judiciary authority between different courts and their relations to each other.

First. As to the mode of appointing the judges: this is the same with that of appointing the officers of the Union in general and has been so fully discussed in the two last numbers that nothing can be said here which would not be useless repetition.

Second. As to the tenure by which the judges are to hold their places: this chiefly concerns their duration in office, the provisions for their support, the precautions for their responsibility.

According to the plan of the convention, all judges who may be appointed by the United States are to hold their offices *during good behavior*, which is conformable to the most approved of the State constitutions, and among the rest, to that of this State. Its propriety having been drawn into question by the adversaries of that plan is no light symptom of the rage for objection which disorders their imaginations and judgments. The standard of good behavior for the continuance in office of the judicial magistracy is certainly one of the most valuable of the modern improvements in the practice of government. In a monarchy it is an excellent barrier to the despotism of the prince; in a republic it is a no less excellent barrier to the encroachments and oppressions of the representative body. And it is the best expedient which can be devised in any government to secure a steady, upright, and impartial administration of the laws.

Whoever attentively considers the different departments of power must perceive that, in a government in which they are separated from each other, the judiciary, from the nature of its functions, will always be the least dangerous to the political rights of the Constitution; because it will be least in a capacity to annoy or injure them. The executive not only dispenses the honors but holds the sword of the community. The legislature not only commands the purse but prescribes the rules by which the duties and rights of every citizen are to be regulated. The judiciary, on the contrary, has no influence over either the sword or the purse; no direction either of the strength or of the wealth of the society, and can take no active resolution whatever. It may truly be said to have neither FORCE NOR WILL but merely judgment; and must ultimately depend upon the aid of the executive arm even for the efficacy of its judgments.

This simple view of the matter suggests several important consequences. It proves incontestably that the judiciary is beyond comparison the weakest of the three departments of power; that it can never attack with success either of the other two; and that all possible care is requisite to enable it to defend itself against their attacks. It equally proves that though individual oppression may now and then proceed from the courts of justice, the general liberty of the people can never be endangered from that quarter; I mean so long as the judiciary remains truly distinct from both the legislature and the executive. For I agree that "there is no liberty if the power of judging be not separated from the legislative and executive powers." And it proves, in the last place, that as liberty can have nothing to fear from the judiciary alone, but would have everything to fear from its union with either of the other departments, that as all the effects of such a union must ensue from a dependence of the former on the latter, notwithstanding a nominal and apparent separation; that as, from the natural feebleness of the judiciary, it is in continual jeopardy of being overpowered, awed, or influenced by its co-ordinate branches; and that as nothing can contribute so much to its firmness and independence as permanency in office, this quality may therefore be justly regarded as an indispensable ingredient in its constitution, and, in a great measure, as the citadel for the public justice and the public security.

The complete independence of the courts of justice is peculiarly essential in a limited Constitution. By a limited Constitution, I understand one which contains certain specified exceptions to the legislative authority; such, for instance, as that it shall pass no bills of attainder, no *ex post facto laws*, and the like. Limitations of this kind can be preserved in practice no other way than through the medium of courts of justice, whose duty it must be to declare all acts contrary to the manifest tenor of the Constitution void. Without this, all the reservations of particular rights or privileges would amount to nothing.

Some perplexity respecting the rights of the courts to pronounce legislative acts void, because contrary to the Constitution, has arisen from an imagination that the doctrine would imply a superiority to the judiciary to the legislative power. It is urged that the authority which can declare the acts of another void must necessarily be superior to the one whose acts may be declared void. As this doctrine is of great importance in all the American constitutions, a brief discussion of the grounds on which it rests cannot be unacceptable.

There is no position which depends on clearer principles than that every act of a delegated authority, contrary to the tenor of the commission under which it is exercised, is void. No legislative act, therefore, contrary to the Constitution, can be valid. To deny this would be to affirm that the deputy is greater than his principal; that the servant is above his master; that the representatives of the people are superior to the people themselves; that men acting by virtue of powers do not authorize, but what they forbid.

If it be said that the legislative body are themselves the constitutional judges of their own powers and that the construction they put upon them is conclusive upon the other departments it may be answered that this cannot be the natural presumption where it is not to be collected from any particular provisions in the Constitution. It is not otherwise to be supposed that the Constitution could intend to enable the representatives of the people to substitute their *will* to that of their constituents. It is far more rational to suppose that the courts were designed to be an intermediate body between the people and the legislature in order, among other things, to keep the latter within the limits assigned to their authority. The interpretation of the laws is the proper and peculiar province of the courts. A constitution is, in fact, and must be regarded by the judges as, a fundamental law. It therefore belongs to them to ascertain its meaning as well as the meaning of any particular act proceeding from the legislative body. If there should happen to be an irreconcilable variance between the two, that which has the superior obligation and validity ought, of course, to be preferred; or, in other words, the Constitution ought to be preferred to the statute, the intention of the people to the intention of their agents.

Nor does this conclusion by any means suppose a superiority of the judicial to the legislative power. It only supposes that the power of the people is superior to both, and that where the will of the legislature, declared in its statutes, stands in opposition to that of the people, declared in the Constitution, the judges ought to be governed by the latter rather than the former. They ought to regulate their decisions by the fundamental laws rather than by those which are not fundamental.

This exercise of judicial discretion in determining between two contradictory laws is exemplified in a familiar instance. It not uncommonly happens that there are two statutes existing at one time, clashing in whole or in part with each other and neither of them containing any repealing clause or expression. In such a case, it is the province of the courts to liquidate and fix their meaning and operation. So far as they can, by any fair construction, be reconciled to each other, reason and law conspire to dictate that this should be done; where this is impracticable, it becomes a matter of necessity to give effect to one in exclusion of the other. The rule which has obtained in the courts for determining their relative validity is that the last in order of time shall be preferred to the first. But this is a mere rule of construction, not derived from any positive law but from the nature and reason of the thing. It is a rule not enjoined upon the courts by legislative provision but adopted by themselves, as consonant to truth and propriety, for the direction of their conduct as interpreters of the law. They thought it reasonable that between the interfering acts of an equal authority that which was the last indication of its will should have the preference.

But in regard to the interfering acts of a superior and subordinate authority of an original and derivative power, the nature and reason of the thing indicates the converse of that rule as proper to be followed. They teach us that the prior act of a superior ought to be preferred to the subsequent act of an inferior and subordinate authority; and that accordingly, whenever a particular statute contravenes the Constitution, it will be the duty of the judicial tribunals to adhere to the latter and disregard the former.

It can be of no weight to say that the courts, on the pretense of a repugnancy, may substitute their own pleasure to the constitutional intentions of the legislature. This might as well happen in the case of two contradictory statutes; or it might as well happen in every adjudication upon any single statute. The courts must declare the sense of the law; and if they should be disposed to exercise WILL instead of JUDGMENT, the consequence would equally be the substitution of their pleasure to that of the legislative body. The observation, if it prove anything, would prove that there ought to be no judges distinct from that body.

If, then, the courts of justice are to be considered as the bulwarks of a limited Constitution against legislative encroachments, this consideration will afford a strong argument for the permanent tenure of judicial offices, since nothing will contribute so much as this to that independent spirit in the judges which must be essential to the faithful performance of so arduous a duty.

This independence of the judges is equally requisite to guard the Constitution and the rights of individuals from the effects of those ill humors which the arts of designing men, or the influence of particular conjunctures, sometimes disseminate among the people themselves, and which, though they speedily give place to better information, and more deliberate reflection, have a tendency, in the meantime, to occasion dangerous innovations in the government, and serious oppressions of the minor party in the community. Though I trust the friends of the proposed Constitution will never concur with its enemies in questioning that fundamental principal of Republican government which admits the right of the people to alter or abolish the established Constitution whenever they find it inconsistent with their happiness; yet it is not to be inferred from this principle that the representatives of the people, whenever a momentary inclination happens to lay hold of a majority of their constituents incompatible with the provisions in the existing Constitution would, on that account, be justifiable in a violation of those provisions; or that the courts would be under a greater obligation to connive at infractions in this shape than when they had proceeded wholly from the cabals of the representative body. Until the people have, by some solemn and authoritative act, annulled or changed the established form, it is binding

upon themselves collectively, as well as individually; and no presumption, or even knowledge of their sentiments, can warrant their representatives in a departure from it prior to such an act. But it is easy to see that it would require an uncommon portion of fortitude in the judges to do their duty as faithful guardians of the Constitution, where legislative invasions of it had been instigated by the major voice of the community.

But it is not with a view to infractions of the Constitution only that the independence of the judges may be an essential safeguard against the effects of occasional ill humors in the society. These sometimes extend no farther than to the injury of the private rights of particular classes of citizens, by unjust and partial laws. Here also the firmness of the judicial magistracy is of vast importance in mitigating the severity and confining the operation of such laws. It not only serves to moderate the immediate mischiefs of those which may have been passed but it operates as a check upon the legislative body in passing them; who, perceiving that obstacles to the success of iniquitous intention are to be expected from the scruples of the courts, are in a manner compelled, by the very motives of the injustice they mediate, to qualify their attempts. This is a circumstance calculated to have more influence upon the character of our governments than but a few may be aware of. The benefits of the integrity and moderation of the judiciary have already been felt in more States than one; and though they may have displeased those whose sinister expectations they may have disappointed, they must have commanded the esteem and applause of all the virtuous and disinterested. Considerate men of every description ought to prize whatever will tend to beget or fortify that temper in the courts; as no man can be sure that he may not be tomorrow the victim of a spirit of injustice, by which he may be a gainer today. And every man must now feel that the inevitable tendency of such a spirit is to sap the foundations of public and private confidence and to introduce in its stead universal distrust and distress.

That inflexible and uniform adherence to the rights of the Constitution, and of individuals, which we perceive to be indispensable in the courts of justice, can certainly not be expected from judges who hold their offices by a temporary commission. Periodical appointments, however regulated, or by whomsoever made, would, in some way or other, be fatal to their necessary independence. If the power of making them was committed either to the executive or legislature there would be danger of an improper complaisance to the branch which possessed

it; if to both, there would be an unwillingness to hazard the displeasure of either; if to the people, or to persons chosen by them for the special purpose, there would be too great a disposition to consult popularity to justify a reliance that nothing would be consulted by the Constitution and the laws.

There is yet a further and a weighty reason for the permanency of the judicial offices which is deducible from the nature of the qualifications they require. It has been frequently remarked with great propriety that a voluminous code of laws is one of the inconveniences necessarily connected with the advantages of a free government. To avoid an arbitrary discretion in the courts, it is indispensable that they should be bound down by strict rules and precedents which serve to define and point out their duty in every particular case that comes before them; and it will readily be conceived from the variety of controversies which grow out of the folly and wickedness of mankind that the records of those precedents must unavoidably swell to a very considerable bulk and must demand long and laborious study to acquire a competent knowledge of them. Hence it is that there can be but few men in the society who will have sufficient skill in the laws to qualify them for the stations of judges. And making the proper deductions for the ordinary depravity of human nature, the number must be still smaller of those who unite the requisite integrity with the requisite knowledge. These considerations apprise us that the government can have no great option between fit characters; and that a temporary duration in office which would naturally discourage such characters from quitting a lucrative line of practice to accept a seat on the bench would have a tendency to throw the administration of justice into hands less able and less well qualified to conduct it with utility and dignity. In the present circumstances of this country and in those in which it is likely to be for a long time to come, the disadvantages on this score would be greater than they may at first sight appear; but it must be confessed that they are far inferior to those which present themselves under the other aspects of the subject.

Upon the whole, there can be no room to doubt that the convention acted wisely in copying from the models of those constitutions which have established *good behavior* as the tenure of their judicial offices in point of duration, and that so far from being blamable on this account, their plan would have been inexcusably defective if it had wanted this important feature of good government. The experience of Great Britain affords an illustrious comment on the excellence of the institution.

Presidential Election Results 1789–2000

Year	Candidates	Party	Popular Vote	Electoral Vote
1789	George Washington			69
	John Adams			34
	Others			35
1793	George Washington			132
	John Adams			77
	George Clinton			50
	Others			5
1796	John Adams	Federalist		71
	Thomas Jefferson	Democratic-Republican		68
	Thomas Pinckney	Federalist		59
	Aaron Burr	Democratic-Republican		30
	Others			48
1800	Thomas Jefferson	Democratic-Republican		73
	Aaron Burr	Democratic-Republican		73
	John Adams	Federalist		65
	Charles C. Pinckney	Federalist		64
1804	Thomas Jefferson	Democratic-Republican		162
	Charles C. Pinckney	Federalist		14
1808	James Madison	Democratic-Republican		122
	Charles C. Pinckney	Federalist		47
	George Clinton	Independent-Republican		6
1812	James Madison	Democratic-Republican		128
	DeWitt Clinton	Federalist		89
1816	James Monroe	Democratic-Republican		183
	Rufus King	Federalist		34
1820	James Monroe	Democratic-Republican		231
	John Quincy Adams	Independent-Republican		1
1824	John Quincy Adams	Democratic-Republican	108,740(30.5%)	84
	Andrew Jackson	Democratic-Republican	153,544(43.1%)	99
	Henry Clay	Democratic-Republican	47,136(13.2%)	37
	William H. Crawford	Democratic-Republican	46,618(13.1%)	41
1828	Andrew Jackson	Democratic	647,231(56.0%)	178
	John Quincy Adams	National Republican	509,097(44.0%)	83
1832	Andrew Jackson	Democratic	687,502(55.0%)	219
	Henry Clay	National Republican	530,189(42.4%)	49
	William Wirt	Anti-Masonic		7
	John Floyd	National Republican	33,108(2.6%)	11
1836	Martin Van Buren	Democratic	761,549(50.9%)	170
	William H. Harrison	Whig	549,567(36.7%)	73
	Hugh L. White	Whig	145,396(9.7%)	26
	Daniel Webster	Whig	41,287(2.7%)	14
1840	William H. Harrison	Whig	1,275,017(53.1%)	234
	Martin Van Buren	Democratic	1,128,702(46.9%)	60
1844	James K. Polk	Democratic	1,337,243(49.6%)	170
	Henry Clay	Whig	1,299,068(48.1%)	105
	James G. Birney	Liberty	63,300(2.3%)	
1848	Zachary Taylor	Whig	1,360,101(47.4%)	163
	Lewis Cass	Democratic	1,220,544(42.5%)	127
	Martin Van Buren	Free Soil	291,163(10.1%)	
1852	Franklin Pierce	Democratic	1,601,474(50.9%)	254
	Winfield Scott	Whig	1,386,578(44.1%)	42
1856	James Buchanan	Democratic	1,838,169(45.4%)	174
	John C. Fremont	Republican	1,335,264(33.0%)	114
	Millard Fillmore	American	874,534(21.6%)	8
1860	Abraham Lincoln	Republican	1,865,593(39.8%)	180
	Stephen A. Douglas	Democratic	1,381,713(29.5%)	12
	John C. Breckinridge	Democratic	848,356(18.1%)	72
	John Bell	Constitutional Union	592,906(12.6%)	79
1864	Abraham Lincoln	Republican	2,206,938(55.0%)	212
	George B. McClellan	Democratic	1,803,787(45.0%)	21
1868	Ulysses S. Grant	Republican	3,013,421(52.7%)	214
	Horatio Seymour	Democratic	2,706,829(47.3%)	80
1872	Ulysses S. Grant	Republican	3,596,745(55.6%)	286
	Horace Greeley	Democratic	2,843,446(43.9%)	66
1876	Rutherford B. Hayes	Republican	4,036,571(48.0%)	185
	Samuel J. Tilden	Democratic	4,284,020(51.0%)	184
1880	James A. Garfield	Republican	4,449,053(48.3%)	214
	Winfield S. Hancock	Democratic	4,442,035(48.2%)	155
	James B. Weaver	Greenback-Labor	308,578(3.4%)	
1884	Grover Cleveland	Democratic	4,874,986(48.5%)	219
	James G. Blaine	Republican	4,851,931(48.2%)	182
	Benjamin F. Butler	Greenback-Labor	175,370(1.8%)	
1888	Benjamin Harrison	Republican	5,444,337(47.8%)	233
	Grover Cleveland	Democratic	5,540,050(48.6%)	168

Presidential Election Results 1789–2000

Year	Candidates	Party	Popular Vote	Electoral Vote
1892	Grover Cleveland	Democratic	5,554,414(46.0%)	277
	Benjamin Harrison	Republican	5,190,802(43.0%)	145
	James B. Weaver	Peoples	1,027,329(8.5%)	22
1896	William McKinley	Republican	7,035,638(50.8%)	271
	William J. Bryan	Democratic; Populist	6,467,946(46.7%)	176
1900	William McKinley	Republican	7,219,530(51.7%)	292
	William J. Bryan	Democratic; Populist	6,356,734(45.5%)	155
1904	Theodore Roosevelt	Republican	7,628,834(56.4%)	336
	Alton B. Parker	Democrat	5,084,401(37.6%)	140
	Eugene V. Debs	Socialist	402,460(3.0%)	0
1908	William H. Taft	Republican	7,679,006(51.6%)	321
	William J. Bryan	Democratic	6,409,106(43.1%)	162
	Eugene V. Debs	Socialist	420,820(2.8%)	0
1912	Woodrow Wilson	Democratic	6,286,820(41.8%)	435
	Theodore Roosevelt	Progressive	4,126,020(27.4%)	88
	William H. Taft	Republican	3,483,922(23.2%)	8
	Eugene V. Debs	Socialist	897,011(6.0%)	0
1916	Woodrow Wilson	Democratic	9,129,606(49.3%)	277
	Charles E. Hughes	Republican	8,538,211(46.1%)	254
1920	Warren G. Harding	Republican	16,152,200(61.0%)	404
	James M. Cox	Democratic	9,147,353(34.6%)	127
	Eugene V. Debs	Socialist	919,799(3.5%)	0
1924	Calvin Coolidge	Republican	15,725,016(54.1%)	382
	John W. Davis	Democratic	8,385,586(28.8%)	136
	Robert M. La Follette	Progressive	4,822,856(16.6%)	13
1928	Herbert C. Hoover	Republican	21,392,190(58.2%)	444
	Alfred E. Smith	Democratic	15,016,443(40.8%)	87
1932	Franklin D. Roosevelt	Democratic	22,809,638(57.3%)	472
	Herbert C. Hoover	Republican	15,758,901(39.6%)	59
	Norman Thomas	Socialist	881,951(2.2%)	0
1936	Franklin D. Roosevelt	Democratic	27,751,612(60.7%)	523
	Alfred M. Landon	Republican	16,681,913(36.4%)	8
	William Lemke	Union	891,858(1.9%)	0
1940	Franklin D. Roosevelt	Democratic	27,243,466(54.7%)	449
	Wendell L. Wilkie	Republican	22,304,755(44.8%)	82
1944	Franklin D. Roosevelt	Democratic	25,602,505(52.8%)	432
	Thomas E. Dewey	Republican	22,006,278(44.5%)	99
1948	Harry S. Truman	Democratic	24,105,812(49.5%)	303
	Thomas E. Dewey	Republican	21,970,065(45.1%)	189
	J. Strom Thurmond	States' Rights	1,169,063(2.4%)	39
	Henry A. Wallace	Progressive	1,157,172(2.4%)	0
1952	Dwight D. Eisenhower	Republican	33,936,234(55.2%)	442
	Adlai E. Stevenson	Democratic	27,314,992(44.5%)	89
1956	Dwight D. Eisenhower	Republican	35,590,472(57.4%)	457
	Adlai E. Stevenson	Democratic	26,022,752(42.0%)	73
1960	John F. Kennedy	Democratic	34,227,096(49.9%)	303
	Richard M. Nixon	Republican	34,108,546(49.6%)	219
1964	Lyndon B Johnson	Democratic	43,126,233(61.1%)	486
	Barry Goldwater	Republican	27,174,989(38.5%)	52
1968	Richard M. Nixon	Republican	31,783,783(43.4%)	301
	Hubert H. Humphrey	Democratic	31,271,839(42.7%)	191
	George C. Wallace	American Independent	9,899,557(13.5%)	46
1972	Richard M. Nixon	Republican	46,632,189(61.3%)	520
	George McGovern	Democratic	28,422,015(37.3%)	17
1976	Jimmy Carter	Democratic	40,828,587(50.1%)	297
	Gerald R. Ford	Republican	39,147,613(48.0%)	240
1980	Ronald Reagan	Republican	42,941,145(51.0%)	489
	Jimmy Carter	Democratic	34,663,037(41.0%)	49
	John B. Anderson	Independent	5,551,551(6.6%)	0
1984	Ronald Reagan	Republican	53,428,357(59%)	525
	Walter F. Mondale	Democratic	36,930,923(41%)	13
1988	George Bush	Republican	48,881,011(53%)	426
	Michael Dukakis	Democratic	41,828,350(46%)	111
1992	Bill Clinton	Democratic	38,394,210(43%)	370
	George Bush	Republican	33,974,386(38%)	168
	H. Ross Perot	Independent	16,573,465(19%)	0
1996	Bill Clinton	Democratic	45,628,667(49%)	379
	Bob Dole	Republican	37,869,435(41%)	159
	H. Ross Perot	Reform	7,874,283(8%)	0
2000	George W. Bush	Republican	50,456,169(48%)	271
	Al Gore	Democrat	50,996,116(48%)	266
	Ralph Nader	Green	2,767,176(3%)	0

GLOSSARY

adversary system A judicial system in which the court of law is a neutral arena where two parties argue their differences.

advisory opinion An opinion unrelated to a particular case that gives a court's view about a constitutional or legal issue.

affirmative action Remedial action designed to overcome the effects of past discrimination against minorities and women.

amendatory veto The power of governors in a few states to return a bill to the legislature with suggested language changes, conditions, or amendments. Legislators then decide either to accept the governor's recommendations or to pass the bill in its original form over the veto.

American Dream The widespread belief that individual initiative and hard work can bring economic success and that the United States is a land of opportunity.

amicus curiae brief Literally, "friend of the court" brief, this document is filed, with permission of the court, by an individual or organization to present arguments in addition to those presented by the immediate parties to the case.

Annapolis Convention A convention held in September 1786 to consider problems of trade and navigation, attended by five states and important because it issued the call to Congress and the states for what became the Constitutional Convention.

Antifederalists Opponents of ratification of the Constitution and of a strong central government generally.

antitrust legislation Federal laws (starting with the Sherman Act of 1890) that try to prevent monopolies from dominating an industry and restraining trade.

antitrust regulation Federal laws and regulations that try to prevent one or a few businesses from dominating a particular market through monopoly or restraint of trade.

appellate jurisdiction The authority of a court to review a decision of a lower court.

Articles of Confederation The first constitution of the American states, drafted in 1777, ratified in 1781, and replaced by the present Constitution in 1789.

assigned council system Arrangement whereby attorneys are provided for persons accused of crime who are unable to hire their own attorneys. The judge assigns a member of the bar to provide counsel to a particular defendant.

attentive public Those who follow public affairs carefully.

Australian ballot A secret ballot printed by the state.

bad tendency doctrine Interpretation of the First Amendment that would permit legislatures to forbid speech that has a tendency to cause people to engage in illegal action.

bicameral legislature A two-house legislature.

bicameralism The principle of a two-house legislature.

bill of attainder Legislative act inflicting punishment, including deprivation of property, without trial on named individuals or members of a specified group.

binding arbitration A collective bargaining situation in which both parties agree to adhere to the decision of an arbitrator.

bipartisanship A policy that emphasizes a united front and cooperation between the major political parties, especially on sensitive foreign policy issues.

blanket primary A primary open to all voters, who may vote for candidates from any party for each office.

bundling A tactic of political action committees whereby they collect contributions from like-minded individuals (each limited to $2,000) and present them to a candidate or political party as a "bundle," thus increasing their influence.

bureau The largest subunit of a government department or agency.

bureaucracy A professional corps of officials organized in a pyramidal hierarchy and functioning under impersonal, uniform rules and procedures.

bureaucrat Career government employee.

cabinet Loosely designated advisory body for the president, consisting of the heads of the executive departments, the vice-president, and a few others the president considers cabinet-level officials.

capitalism An economic system characterized by private property, competitive markets, economic incentives, and limited government involvement in the production and pricing of goods and services.

caucus Meeting of local party members to choose party officials and/or candidates for public office and to decide the platform.

caucus (legislative) Meeting of the members of a party in a legislative chamber to select party leadership and discuss party policy. Called a conference by Republicans.

centralists Those who favor national action over action at the state and local levels.

charter A city "constitution" that outlines the structure of city government, defines the authority of the various officials, and provides for their selection.

charter school A publicly funded alternative to standard public schools in some states, initiated when individuals or groups receive charters; charter schools must meet state standards.

checks and balances Constitutional grant of powers that enables each of the three branches of government to stop some acts of the others and therefore ensure that no branch can dominate.

civil disobedience Deliberate refusal to obey a law or requirement one believes is unjust in the hopes of calling forth public pressure to change it.

civil liberties Rights of freedom of conscience, religion, and expression.

civil rights Rights protecting against discrimination because of race, religion, gender, ethnic origin, or sexual orientation.

class action suit Lawsuit brought by an individual or a group of people on behalf of all those similarly situated.

clear and present danger doctrine Interpretation of the First Amendment that holds government cannot interfere with speech unless the speech presents a clear and present danger that it will lead to acts that are evil or illegal. To shout "Fire!" falsely in a crowded theater was Justice Oliver Wendell Holmes's famous example.

closed primary A primary in which only persons registered in the party holding the primary may vote.

closed rule A procedural rule in the House of Representatives that prohibits any amendments to bills or provides that only members of the committee reporting the bill may offer amendments.

closed shop A company with a labor agreement whereby union membership is a condition of employment.

cloture Procedure for terminating debate, especially filibusters, in the Senate.

coattail effect The boost candidates of the same party as the president receive in a presidential election from the president's popularity.

collective bargaining Method whereby representatives of the union and employer determine wages, hours, and other conditions of employment through direct negotiation.

commerce clause The clause of the Constitution giving Congress the power to regulate all business activities that cross state lines or affect more than one state, and also prohibiting states from unduly burdening or discriminating against the business activities of other nations or states.

commercial speech Advertisements and commercials for products and services that receive less First Amendment protection, primarily false and misleading ads.

community policing Recent programs to move police from patrol cars into neighborhoods, where they walk the beat and work with churches and other community groups to reduce crime and improve relations with minorities.

comptroller general Head of the General Accounting Office, appointed by the president with the approval of the Senate for a 15-year term.

concurrent powers Powers the Constitution gives to both the national and state governments, such as the power to levy taxes.

concurrent resolution A resolution passed in the same form by both houses of Congress that expresses the "sense" of Congress on some question. It is not sent to the president and does not have the force of law.

concurring opinion An opinion that agrees with the majority in a Supreme Court ruling but differs on the reasoning.

confederation A constitutional arrangement in which sovereign nations or states, by compact, create a central government but carefully limit its power and do not give it direct authority over individuals.

conference committee Committee appointed by the presiding officers of each chamber to adjust differences on a particular bill passed by each but in different forms.

Congressional Budget Office (CBO) An agency of Congress that analyzes presidential budget recommendations and estimates the costs of proposed legislation.

Connecticut Compromise Compromise agreement by states at the Constitutional Convention for a bicameral legislature with a lower house in which representation would be based on population, and upper house in which each state would have two senators.

conservatism A belief that limited government ensures order, competitive markets, and personal opportunity.

Constitutional Convention The convention in Philadelphia, May 25–September 17, 1787, that framed the Constitution of the United States.

constitutional democracy A government that enforces recognized limits on those who govern and allows the voice of the people to be heard through free and fair elections.

constitutional home rule State constitutional authorization for local governments to conduct their own affairs.

constitutional initiative petition A device that permits voters to place specific amendments to a state constitution on the ballot by petition.

constitutionalism The set of arrangements and processes—checks and balances, federalism, separation of powers, rule of law, due process, and a bill of rights—that disperses and limits the power of government officials. Constitutionalism provides for the granting as well as restraining of powers and seeks to ensure that a government's leaders and representatives are accountable to the citizens.

contract clause Clause of the Constitution that was originally intended to prohibit laws that adversely affect the value of property and to maintain the status quo at the expense of the power of the states to guard the public welfare; it now allows states to make reasonable modifications of contracts to protect public health and safety.

council-manager plan Form of local government in which the city council hires a professional administrator to manage city affairs; also known as the city-manager plan.

court of appeals A court with appellate jurisdiction, which hears appeals from the decisions of lower courts.

cross-cutting cleavages Divisions within society that make groups more heterogeneous or different.

crossover voting A member of one party voting for a candidate of another party.

de facto segregation Segregation that arises as a result of social practices, such as housing patterns.

de jure segregation Segregation sanctioned by law.

dealignment Dramatic change in the composition of the electorate or its partisan preferences that points to a rejection of both major parties and a rise in the number of Independents.

debt The accumulated total of federal deficits, minus surpluses, over the years.

decentralists Those who favor state or local action rather than national action.

defendant In a criminal action, the person or party accused of an offense.

deficit The difference between the revenues raised from sources of income other than borrowing and the expenditure of government, including paying the interest on past borrowing.

delegate A view of the role of a member of Congress which holds that legislators should represent the views of constituents even when personally holding different views.

demagogue Leader who gains power by appealing to the emotions and prejudices of the masses.

democracy Government by the people, either directly or indirectly, with free and frequent elections.

democratic consensus Widespread agreement on fundamental principles of democratic governance and the values that undergird them.

demographics The study of the characteristics of populations.

deregulation A policy promoting cutbacks in the amount of federal regulation in specific areas of economic activity.

devolution revolution The effort to slow the growth of the federal government by returning many functions to the states.

direct democracy Government in which citizens come together to discuss and pass laws and select rulers.

direct primary Election open to all members of the party in which voters choose the persons who will be the party's nominees in the general election.

discharge petition Petition that, if signed by a majority of the members of the House of Representatives, will pry a bill from committee and bring it to the floor for consideration.

disclosure A requirement that candidates specify where the money came from to finance their campaign.

dissenting opinion An opinion that conflicts with the majority in a Supreme Court ruling.

divided government Governance divided between the parties, as when one controls the executive branch and the other the legislative branch.

double jeopardy Trial or punishment for the same crime by the same government; forbidden by the Constitution.

dual citizenship Citizenship in two or more nations.

due process Established rules and regulations that restrain those in government who exercise power.

due process clause Clauses in the Fifth and Fourteenth Amendments stating that the national (Fifth) and state (Fourteenth) governments shall not deprive any person of life, liberty, or property without due process of law.

economic sanction A denial of export, import, or financial relations with a target country in an effort to change that nation's policies.

Electoral College The electoral system used in electing the president and vice-president, in which voters vote for electors pledged to cast their ballots for a particular candidate.

eminent domain Power of a government to take private property for public use; the U.S. Constitution gives national and state governments this power and requires them to provide just compensation for property so taken.

enterprise zone Inner-city areas designated as offering tax incentives to companies that invest in plants there and provide job training for the unemployed.

entitlement program Programs such as Social Security, Medicare, and unemployment insurance that provide a specified set of benefits as a matter of right to all who meet the criteria established by law.

environmental impact statement A statement required by federal law from all agencies for any project using federal funds that assesses the potential effect of the new construction or development on the environment. Many states also require these statements.

environmentalism An ideology that is dominated by concern for the environment but also promotes grass-roots democracy, social justice, equal opportunity, nonviolence, respect for diversity, and feminism.

equal protection clause Clause in the Constitution that forbids any state to deny to any person within its jurisdiction the equal protection of the laws. By interpretation, the Fifth Amendment imposes the same limitation on the national government. This clause is the major constitutional restraint on the power of governments to discriminate against persons because of race, national origin, or sex.

establishment clause Clause in the First Amendment that states that Congress shall make no law respecting an establishment of religion. It has been interpreted by the Supreme Court to forbid governmental support to any or all religions.

ethnicity A social division based on national origin, religion, language, and often race.

ethnocentrism Selective perception based on individual background, attitudes, and biases that leads one to believe in the superiority of one's nation or ethnic group.

ex post facto law Retroactive criminal law that works to the disadvantage of an individual; forbidden in the Constitution.

excise tax Consumer tax on a specific kind of merchandise, such as tobacco.

exclusionary rule Requirement that evidence unconstitutionally or illegally obtained be excluded from criminal trial.

Executive Office of the President The cluster of presidential staff agencies that help the president carry out his responsibilities. Currently the office includes the Office of Management and Budget, the Council of Economic Advisers, and several other units.

executive order A directive issued by presidents or governors that has the force of law.

executive privilege A long-recognized doctrine with some constitutional standing that permits a president to withhold sensitive documents and information from Congress and the courts.

express powers Powers specifically granted to one of the branches of the national government by the Constitution.

extradition Legal process whereby an alleged criminal offender is surrendered by the officials of one state to officials of the state in which the crime is alleged to have been committed.

faction A term used by James Madison and other founders of this country to refer to political parties as well as what we now call special interests or interest groups.

fairness doctrine Doctrine interpreted by the Federal Communications Commission that imposed on radio and television licensees an obligation to ensure that differing viewpoints were presented on controversial issues or persons; repealed in 1987.

federal mandate A requirement imposed by the federal government as a condition of receipt of federal funds.

Federal Register Official document published every weekday that lists new and proposed regulations of executive departments and regulatory agencies.

Federal Reserve System The public-private banking regulatory system created by Congress in 1913 to establish banking practices and regulate currency in circulation and the amount of credit available. It is comprised of 12 regional banks, and its major responsibilities are supervised by a seven-member presidentially appointed Federal Reserve Board of Governors in Washington, D.C.

federalism Constitutional arrangement whereby power is distributed between a central government and subdivisional governments, called states in the United States. The national and the subdivisional governments both exercise direct authority over individuals.

Federalists Supporters of ratification of the Constitution whose position promoting a strong central government was later voiced in the Federalist party.

fee for service System of health care payment in which patients can choose their own physician, whose bills are then covered by insurance companies.

felony A serious crime, the penalty for which can range from death to imprisonment in a penitentiary for more than a year.

fighting words Words that by their very nature inflict injury upon those to whom they are addressed or cause acts of violence by them.

filibuster A procedural practice in the Senate whereby a senator holds the floor and thereby delays proceedings and prevents a vote on a controversial issue.

fiscal policy Government policy that attempts to manage the economy by controlling taxing and spending.

free exercise clause Clause in the First Amendment that states that Congress shall make no law prohibiting the free exercise of religion.

free rider An individual who does not join an interest group representing his or her interests, yet receives the benefit of the influence the group achieves.

full faith and credit clause Clause in the Constitution requiring each state to recognize the civil judgments rendered by the courts of the other states and to accept their public records and acts as valid documents.

gender gap The difference between the political opinions or political behavior of men and women.

General Accounting Office (GAO) An independent investigative arm of Congress established in 1921 to check on receipt and disbursement of public funds and review the performance of government agencies.

General Agreement on Tariffs and Trade (GATT) An international trade organization with 125 members, including the United States, that seeks to encourage free trade by lowering tariffs and other trade restrictions.

general property tax Tax levied by local and some state governments on real property or personal, tangible property, the major portion of which is on the estimated value of one's home and land.

gerrymandering The drawing of legislative district boundaries to benefit a party, group, or incumbent.

government corporation Cross between a business corporation and a government agency; created to secure greater freedom of action and flexibility for a particular program.

grand jury A jury of 12 to 23 persons who, in private, hear evidence presented by the government to determine whether persons shall be required to stand trial. If the jury believes there is sufficient evidence that a crime was committed, it issues an indictment.

gross domestic product (GDP) An estimate of the total output of all economic activity in the nation, including goods and services.

habeas corpus See Writ of *habeas corpus*.

Hatch Act Federal statute barring federal employees from active participation in certain kinds of politics and protecting them from being fired on partisan grounds.

health maintenance organization (HMO) Alternative means of health care in which people or their employers are charged a set amount and the HMO provides health care and covers hospital costs.

hold A procedural practice in the Senate whereby a senator temporarily blocks the consideration of a bill or nomination.

honeymoon A period at the beginning of a new president's term in which the president enjoys generally positive relations with the press and Congress, usually lasting about six months.

ideology One's basic beliefs about political values and the role of government.

immunity An exemption from prosecution for a particular crime in return for testimony pertaining to the case.

impeachment Formal accusation against a public official and the first step in removal from office.

implied powers Powers inferred from express powers that allow Congress to carry out its functions.

impoundment Presidential refusal to allow an agency to spend funds authorized and appropriated by Congress.

independent agency A government entity that is independent of the legislative, executive, and judicial branch.

independent expenditures Money spent by groups or individuals not associated with candidates to elect or defeat candidates for office.

independent regulatory agency A government agency that exists outside the three branches of government and is responsible for enforcing particular statutes. Generally a regulatory agency has quasi-legislative and quasi-judicial functions as well as executive powers.

independent regulatory board An independent agency with regulatory power whose independence is protected by Congress. Some are independent regulatory commissions.

indictment A formal written statement from a grand jury charging an individual with an offense.

inflation A rise in the general price level (and decrease in dollar value) owing to an increase in the volume of money and credit in relation to available goods.

information affidavit Certification by a public prosecutor that there is evidence to justify bringing named individuals to trial.

inherent powers Those powers of the national government in the field of foreign affairs that the Supreme Court has declared do not depend upon constitutional grants but rather grow out of the very existence of the national government.

initiative Procedure whereby a certain number of voters may, by petition, propose a law or constitutional amendment and have it submitted to the voters.

initiative petition A device that permits voters to place specific amendments to a state constitution on the ballot by petition.

interest group A collection of people who share some common interest or attitude and seek to influence government for specific ends. Interest groups usually work within the framework of government and employ tactics such as lobbying to achieve their goals.

interested money Financial contributions by individuals or groups in the hopes of influencing the outcome of an election and subsequently influencing policy.

interlocking directorate A corporation in which an officer or director sits on the board of a competitor, with the effect of restraining trade.

interstate compact An agreement among two or more states. The Constitution requires that most such agreements be approved by Congress.

iron triangle A mutually supporting relationship among interest groups, congressional committees and subcommittees, and government agencies that share a common policy concern.

issue advertising Commercial advertising on radio and television advocating a particular position on an issue, paid for by interest groups and designed to influence voters' choices on election day.

issue advocacy Promoting a particular position on an issue, often funded by interest groups and designed to influence voters' choices on election day.

item veto Authority of the president or governor of a state to veto parts of a legislative bill without having to veto the entire bill. Also known as the line-item veto.

Jim Crow laws State laws formerly pervasive throughout the South requiring public facilities and accommodations to be segregated by race; ruled unconstitutional.

joint committee Committee composed of members of both the House of Representatives and the Senate; such committees oversee the Library of Congress and conduct investigations.

judiciable dispute A dispute that grows out of an actual case and is capable of settlement by legal methods.

judicial activism Judicial philosophy proposing that judges should interpret the Constitution to reflect current conditions and values.

judicial interpretation A method whereby judges can modify a constitutional provision's restrictive force by a narrow interpretation of its meaning.

judicial restraint Judicial philosophy proposing that judges should interpret the Constitution to reflect what the framers intended and what its words literally say.

judicial review The power of a court to refuse to enforce a law or a government regulation that in the opinion of the judges conflicts with the Constitution, or, in a state court, that conflicts with the state constitution.

Keynesian economics Economic theory based on the principles of John Maynard Keynes stating that government spending should increase during business slumps and be curbed during booms.

labor injunction A court order forbidding specific individuals or groups from performing certain acts (such as striking) that the court considers harmful to the rights and property of an employer or community.

laissez-faire economics Theory that opposes governmental interference in the economy beyond what is necessary to protect life and property.

libel Written defamation of another person. In the case of public officials and public figures, the constitutional tests designed to restrict libel actions are very rigid.

liberalism A belief in the positive uses of government to bring about justice and equality of opportunity.

libertarianism An ideology that cherishes individual liberty and insists on a sharply limited government, promoting a free-market economy, a noninterventionist foreign policy, and an absence of regulation in the moral and social sphere.

literacy test Literacy requirement imposed by some states as a condition of voting; generally used to disqualify blacks from voting in the South; now illegal.

lobby To attempt to influence public officials, especially legislators, and the policies they enact.

lobbying Activities aimed at influencing public officials, especially legislators, and the policies they enact.

lobbyist A person who is employed by and acts for an organized interest group or corporation to try to influence policy decisions and positions in the executive and legislative branches.

log rolling Mutual aid and vote trading among legislators.

magistrate judge An official appointed for renewable terms who performs a variety of limited judicial duties.

majority The candidate or party that wins more than half the votes cast to win an election.

majority leader The legislative leader selected by the majority party who helps plan party strategy, confers with other party leaders, and tries to keep members of the party in line.

majority rule Governance according to the expressed preferences of the majority.

majority-minority district A congressional district created to include a substantial number of minority voters.

malapportionment Legislative districts of unequal populations.

manifest destiny A notion held by nineteenth-century Americans that the United States was destined to rule the continent from the Atlantic to the Pacific oceans.

mass media Means of communication that reach the mass public. The mass media include newspapers and magazines, radio, television (broadcast, cable, and satellite), films, recordings, books, and electronic communication.

mayor-council charter The oldest and most common form of city government; consisting of either a weak mayor and a city council or a strong mayor and council.

Medicaid Federal program that provides medical benefits for low-income persons.

medical savings account Alternative means of health care in which individuals make tax-deductible contributions to a special account that can be saved from year to year and used to pay for medical expenses.

Medicare National health insurance program for the elderly and disabled.

merit system A system of public employment in which selection and promotion depend on demonstrated performance rather than political patronage.

minor party A small political party that rises and falls with a charismatic candidate or, if composed of ideologues on the right or left, usually persists over time.

minority leader The legislative leader selected by the minority party as spokesperson for the opposition.

misdemeanor A less serious violation of state and local laws.

Missouri Plan A system for selecting judges that combines features of the appointive and elective methods. The governor selects judges from lists presented by panels of lawyers and laypersons, and at the end of their term the judges may run against their own record in retention elections.

monetarism A theory that government should control the money supply to encourage economic growth and restrain inflation.

monetary policy Government policy that attempts to manage the economy by controlling the money supply and thus interest rates.

monopoly Domination of an industry by a single company; also the company that dominates.

movement A large body of people interested in a common issue, idea, or concern that is of continuing significance and who are willing to take action on that issue. Movements seek to change attitudes or institutions, not only policies.

national party convention The national meeting of delegates elected in primaries, caucuses, or state conventions who assemble once every four years to nominate candidates for president and vice-president, ratify the party platform, elect officers, and adopt rules.

national supremacy Constitutional doctrine that whenever conflict occurs between the constitutionally authorized actions of the national government and those of a state or local government, the actions of the national government take priority.

natural law God's or nature's law that defines right from wrong and is higher than human law.

natural rights The rights of all citizens to dignity and worth; also called human rights.

naturalization A legal action conferring citizenship upon an alien.

necessary and proper clause Clause of the Constitution setting forth the implied powers of Congress. It states that Congress, in addition to its express powers, has the power to make all laws necessary and proper for carrying out all powers vested by the Constitution in the national government.

New Jersey Plan Proposal at the Constitutional Convention made by William Paterson of New Jersey for a central government with a single-house legislature in which each state would be represented equally.

new judicial federalism The practice of some state courts of using the bill of rights in their state constitutions to provide more protection for some rights than is provided by the Supreme Court's interpretation of the Bill of Rights in the Constitution.

news media That part of the mass media that emphasizes the news.

nonpartisan election A local or judicial election in which candidates are not selected or endorsed by political parties.

nonprotected speech Libel, obscenity, fighting words, and commercial speech, which are not entitled in all circumstances to constitutional protection.

North American Free Trade Agreement (NAFTA) Agreement signed by the United States, Canada, and Mexico in 1992 to form the largest free-trade zone in the world.

obscenity Quality or state of a work that taken as a whole appeals to a prurient interest in sex by depicting sexual conduct as specifically defined by legislation or judicial interpretation in a patently offensive way and that lacks serious literary, artistic, political, or scientific value.

office block ballot Method of voting in which all candidates are listed under the office for which they are running.

Office of Management and Budget (OMB) Presidential staff agency that serves as a clearinghouse for budgetary requests and management improvements for government agencies.

Office of Personnel Management Agency that administers civil service laws, rules, and regulations.

one-party state A state in which one party wins all or nearly all the offices and the other party receives only a small proportion of the popular vote.

open primary A primary in which any voter, regardless of party, may vote.

open rule A procedural rule in the House of Representatives that permits floor amendments within the overall time allocated to the bill.

open shop A company with a labor agreement whereby union membership cannot be required as a condition of employment.

opinion of the court An opinion explaining the decision of the Supreme Court or any other appellate court.

original jurisdiction The authority of a trial court to hear a case "in the first instance."

outsourcing The contracting out to the private sector of services that are typically provided by government; also called privatization.

override An action taken by Congress to reverse a presidential veto that requires a two-thirds majority in each chamber.

party column ballot Type of ballot that encourages party-line voting by listing all a party's candidates in a column under the party name. Also called Indiana ballot.

party convention A meeting of party delegates to pass on matters of policy and in some cases to select party candidates for public office.

party identification An informal and subjective affiliation with a political party that most people acquire in childhood.

party platform The official statement of party policy.

party registration The act of declaring party affiliation; in some states required when one registers to vote.

patronage Dispensing government jobs to persons who belong to the winning political party.

permanent normal trade relations status (PTNR) Trade status granted as part of an international trade policy that gives a nation the same favorable trade concessions and tariffs that the best trading partners receive.

petit jury A jury of 6 to 12 persons that determines guilt or innocence in a civil or criminal action.

plea bargain An agreement between a prosecutor and defendant aimed at getting the defendant to plead guilty to a lesser offense to avoid having to stand trial for a more serious offense.

plurality A candidate or party wins the most votes cast, not necessarily more than half.

pocket veto A veto exercised by the president after Congress has adjourned; if the president takes no action for ten days, the bill does not become law and is not returned to Congress for a possible override.

police powers Inherent powers of state governments to protect the public health, safety, welfare, and morals; in the United States, the states, but not the national government, have these powers.

political action committee (PAC) The political arm of an interest group that is legally entitled to raise funds on a voluntary basis from members, stockholders, or employees in order to contribute funds to favored candidates or political parties.

political culture The widely shared beliefs, values, and norms concerning the relationship of citizens to government and to one another.

political party An organization that seeks political power by electing people to office so that its positions and philosophy become public policy.

political predisposition A characteristic of individuals that is predictive of political behavior.

political question A dispute that requires knowledge of a nonlegal character, or the use of techniques not suitable for a court, or explicitly assigned by the Constitution to Congress or the president; judges refuse to answer constitutional questions that they declare are political.

political socialization The process by which we develop our political attitudes, values, and beliefs.

poll tax Payment required as a condition for voting; prohibited for national elections by the Twenty-fourth Amendment (1964) and ruled unconstitutional for all elections in *Harper v Virginia Board of Elections* (1966).

popular consent The idea that a just government must derive its powers from the consent of the people it governs.

popular sovereignty A belief that ultimate power resides in the people.

pork-barrel legislation Government benefits or programs that may help the economy of a member of Congress's district.

preemption The right of a federal law or regulation to preclude enforcement of a state or local law or regulation.

preferred position doctrine Interpretation of the First Amendment that gives freedom of expression a preferred position in the constitutional hierarchy as it is essential to the political process.

president pro tempore Officer of the Senate selected by the majority party to act as chair in the absence of the vice-president.

prior restraint Restraint or censorship imposed before a speech is made or a newspaper published; usually presumed to be unconstitutional.

privatization The process of contracting public services to private organizations.

procedural due process Constitutional requirement that governments proceed by proper methods; places limits on how governmental power may be exercised.

progressive tax A tax graduated so that people with higher incomes pay a larger fraction of their income than people with lower incomes.

property rights The rights of an individual to own, use, rent, invest in, buy, and sell property.

proportional representation An election system in which each party running receives the proportion of legislative seats corresponding to its proportion of the vote.

protectionism Policy of erecting trade barriers to protect domestic industry.

public defender system Arrangement whereby public officials are hired to provide legal assistance to those persons accused of crimes who are unable to hire their own attorneys.

public opinion The distribution of individual preferences or evaluations of a given issue, candidate, or institution within a population.

race A grouping of human beings with common characteristics presumed to be transmitted genetically.

racial gerrymandering The drawing of election districts so as to ensure that members of a certain race are a minority in the district; ruled unconstitutional in *Gomillion v Lightfoot* (1960).

racial or religious restrictive covenants A provision in a deed to real property excluding its sale to persons of a particular race or religion; judicial enforcement of such deeds is unconstitutional.

racial profiling Police target racial minorities as potential suspects of criminal activities.

realigning election An election that proves to be a turning point, redefining the agenda of politics and the alignment of voters within parties during periods of historic change in the economy and society.

reapportionment The assigning by Congress of congressional seats after each census. State legislators reapportion state legislative districts.

recall Procedure for submitting to popular vote the removal of officials from office before the end of their term.

recidivist A repeat offender.

reconciliation Process by which Congress, by a budget resolution, sets ceilings on what appropriations subcommittees can appropriate.

redistributive policies Governmental tax programs that shift wealth or benefits from one segment of the population to another, often from the rich to the poor.

redistricting The redrawing of congressional and other legislative district lines following the census, to accommodate population shifts and keep districts as equal as possible in population.

reduction veto The power of governors in a few states to reduce a particular appropriation.

referendum Procedure for submitting to popular vote measures passed by the legislature or proposed amendments to a state's constitution.

regressive tax A tax whereby people with lower incomes pay a higher fraction of their income than people with lower incomes. In other words, a regressive tax is one that weighs most heavily on those least able to pay.

regulation The attempt by government to control the behavior of corporations, other governments, or citizens through altering the natural workings of the open market to achieve some desired goal.

regulatory taking Government regulation of property so extensive that government is deemed to have taken the property and thus exercised the power of eminent domain, for which it must compensate the property owners.

reinforcing cleavages Divisions within society that reinforce one another, making groups more homogeneous or similar.

representative democracy Government that derives its powers indirectly from the people, who elect those who will govern; also called a republic.

responsibility contract A welfare strategy adopted by some states in which recipients sign a written agreement specifying their responsibilities and outlining a plan for obtaining work and achieving self-sufficiency.

revenue sharing Program from 1972 to 1987 whereby federal funds were provided to state and local governments to be spent largely at the discretion of the receiving governments, subject to few and very general conditions.

revision commission A state commission that recommends changes in the state constitution for action by the legislature and vote by the voters.

revolving door The employment cycle in which individuals work, in turn, for governmental agencies regulating interests and then for the interest groups or businesses with the same policy concern.

rider A provision that may have little relationship to the bill it is attached to in order to secure its passage.

right of expatriation Right of an individual to choose his or her own nationality.

safe seat An elected office, usually in a legislature, that is predictably won by one party or the other, so reelection is almost taken for granted.

sales tax General tax on sales transactions, sometimes exempting food and drugs; the most important source of revenue for states.

search warrant A warrant issued by a magistrate that authorizes the police to search a particular place or person, specifying the place to be searched and the objects to be seized.

sedition Attempting to overthrow the government by force or to interrupt its activities by violence.

select or special committee A congressional committee created for a specific purpose, sometimes to conduct an investigation.

selective exposure The process by which individuals screen out those messages that do not conform to their own biases.

selective incorporation The process by which provisions of the Bill of Rights were bought within the scope of the Fourteenth Amendment and so applied to state and local governments.

selective perception The process by which individuals perceive what they want to in media messages and disregard the rest.

senatorial courtesy Presidential custom of submitting the names of prospective appointees for approval to senators from the states in which the appointees are to work.

seniority rule A legislative practice that assigns the chair of a committee or subcommittee to the member of the majority party with the longest continuous service on the committee.

separation of powers Constitutional division of powers among the legislative, executive, and judicial branches, with the legislative branch making law, the executive applying and enforcing the law, and the judiciary interpreting the law.

severance tax A tax on the privilege of "severing" such natural resources as coal, oil, timber, and gas from the land.

Shays' Rebellion Rebellion by farmers in western Massachusetts in 1786–87, protesting mortgage foreclosures, led by Daniel Shays, and important because it highlighted the need for a strong national government just as the call for a Constitutional Convention went out.

single-member district An electoral district in which in any given election the voters choose one representative or official.

social capital Participation in voluntary associations that reinforce democratic and civic habits of discussion, compromise, and respect for differences.

Social Security A combination of entitlement programs, paid for by employer and employee taxes, that includes retirement benefits, health insurance, and support for disabled workers and the children of deceased or disabled workers.

social stratification   Divisions in a community among socioeconomic groups or classes.

socialism   An economic and governmental system based on public ownership of the means of production and exchange.

socioeconomic status (SES)   A division of population based on occupation, income, and education.

soft money   Money contributed to a state or local political party for party-building purposes that does not have to be disclosed under federal law.

Speaker   The presiding officer in the House of Representatives; formally elected by the House but actually selected by the majority party.

split ticket   Voting for some of one party's candidates and some from another party.

spoils system   System of public employment based on rewarding party loyalists.

standing committee   A permanent committee established in a legislature, usually focusing on a policy area.

stare decisis   The rule of precedent, whereby a rule or law contained in a judicial decision is commonly viewed as binding on judges whenever the same question is presented.

statism   The idea that the rights of the state (meaning nation) are supreme over the rights of the individual.

straight ticket   Voting for all of one party's candidates.

strong mayor-council   Form of local government in which the voters directly elect the city council and the mayor, who enjoys almost total administrative authority and appoints the department heads.

substantive due process   Constitutional requirement that governments act reasonably and that the substance of the laws themselves be fair and reasonable; places limits on what a government may do.

tariff   Tax levied on imports to help protect a nation's industries, labor, or farmers from foreign competition. It can also be used merely to raise additional revenue.

tax expenditure   Loss of tax revenue due to federal tax laws that provide special tax incentives or benefits to individuals or businesses.

The Federalist   Series of essays promoting ratification of the Constitution, written by Alexander Hamilton, John Jay, and James Madison in 1787 and 1788.

theocracy   Government by religious leaders, who claim divine guidance.

three-fifths compromise   Compromise agreement between northern and southern states at the Constitutional Convention in which the slave population would be counted at three-fifths for determining direct taxation and representation in the House of Representatives.

tort law   Law relating to noncontractual injuries to person, reputation, or property.

trade deficit   An imbalance in international trade in which the value of imports exceeds the value of exports.

trust   A monopoly that controls goods and services, often in combinations that reduce competition.

trustee   A view of the role of a member of Congress that holds that legislators are elected to think and vote independently for the general welfare, and not as their constituents direct.

turnout   The proportion of the voting-age public that votes.

two-party state   A state in which the two major parties alternate in winning majorities.

unicameral legislature   A one-house legislature.

union shop   A company in which new employees must join a union within a stated time period.

unitary system   A constitutional arrangement in which power is concentrated in a central government; also called a unitary government.

user fee   Fees charged directly to individuals who use certain public services on the basis of service consumed; also called a user charge.

value-added tax (VAT)   A tax on increased value of a product at each stage of production and distribution (rather than a sales tax just at the point of sale), commonly used by governments in Europe to raise revenues.

veto   Rejection by a president or governor of legislation passed by a legislature.

Virginia Plan   Proposal at the Constitutional Convention made by the Virginia delegation for a strong central government with a bicameral legislature, the lower house to be elected by the voters and the upper chosen by the lower.

voter registration   System designed to reduce voter fraud by limiting voting to those who have established eligibility by submitting the proper form.

voucher   A school reform program whereby a set amount of money is provided by government to parents for their use in paying for their child's education, in a public or private school of their choice.

weak mayor-council   Form of local government in which the members of the city council select the mayor, who then shares power with other elected or appointed boards and commissions.

whip   Party leader who is the liaison between the leadership and the rank-and-file in the legislature.

white primary   Primary operated by the Democratic party in southern states that, before Republicans gained strength in the "one-party South," essentially constituted an election; ruled unconstitutional in *Smith v Allwright* (1944).

winner-take-all   An election system in which the candidate with the most votes wins.

women's suffrage   The right of women to vote.

workfare   A welfare strategy adopted by some states that gives able-bodied adults who do not have preschool-aged children the opportunity to learn job skills that can lead to employment.

World Trade Organization (WTO)   International organization derived from the General Agreement on Tariffs and Trade (GATT) it promotes free trade around the world.

writ of *certiorari*   A formal writ used to bring a case before the Supreme Court.

writ of *habeas corpus*   Court order directing any official having a person in custody to produce the prisoner in court and explain to the judge why the prisoner is being held.

writ of *mandamus*   Court order directing an official to perform an official duty.

yellow-dog contract   Contract by an anti-union employer that forces new workers to promise they will not join a union as a condition of employment.

NOTES

CHAPTER 1

1. See Jackie Calmes, "State of the Union: Ambivalence," *The Wall Street Journal*, December 14, 2000, p. 12.
2. Garry Wills, *A Necessary Evil: A History of American Distrust of Government* (Simon & Schuster, 1999), pp. 306–7.
3. John W. Gardner, speech to the White House Fellows Association, Corcoran Gallery of Art, Washington, D.C., October 1, 1999.
4. Robert H. Jackson, *West Virginia State Board of Education v Barnette*, 319 US 624 (1943).
5. Robert Dahl, *On Democracy* (Yale University Press, 1998), p. 145.
6. Harold Stanley and Richard Niemi, *Vital Statistics on American Politics, 1999–2000* (Congressional Quarterly Press, 2000), pp. 25–29.
7. For a major theoretical work on the principle of majority rule, see Robert A. Dahl, *Democracy and Its Critics* (Yale University Press, 1989).
8. Seymour Martin Lipset, "The Social Requisites of Democracy Revisited," *American Sociological Review* 59 (1994), pp. 1–22.
9. For a discussion of the importance for democracy of such overlapping group memberships, see David Truman's seminal work, *The Governmental Process*, 2d ed. (Knopf, 1971).
10. See Robert D. Putnam, *Bowling Alone: The Collapse and Revival of American Community* (Simon & Schuster, 2000), p. 19. See also Pippa Norris, ed., *Critical Citizens: Global Support for Democratic Governance* (Oxford University, 1999), and for a somewhat different point of view, Everett Carll Ladd, *The Ladd Report* (Free Press, 1999).
11. Michael Schudson, *The Good Citizen: A History of American Civic Life* (Harvard University Press, 1998), p. 296.
12. Quoted in D. W. Miller, "Perhaps We Are Bowling Alone, But Does It Really Matter?" *Chronicle of Higher Education*, July 16, 1999, p. A17.
13. Joyce Appleby, "The American Heritage: The Heirs and the Disinherited," *Journal of American History* (December 1987), p. 808.
14. Richard L. Hillard, "Liberalism, Civic Humanism and the American Revolutionary Bill of Rights, 1775–1790," paper presented at the annual meeting of the Organization of American Historians, Reno, Nevada, 1988.
15. Quoted in Charles L. Mee, Jr., *The Genius of the People* (Harper & Row, 1987), p. 51.
16. Seymour Martin Lipset, "George Washington and the Founding of Democracy," *Journal of Democracy* (October 1998), p. 31.
17. See the essays in Thomas E. Cronin, ed., *Inventing the American Presidency* (University Press of Kansas, 1989). See also Richard J. Ellis, ed., *Founding the American Presidency* (Rowman and Littlefield, 1999).
18. Charles A. Beard and Mary R. Beard, *A Basic History of the United States* (New Home Library, 1944), p. 136.
19. See Herbert J. Storing, ed., abridgment by Murray Dry, *The Anti-Federalist: Writings by the Opponents of the Constitution* (University of Chicago Press, 1985).
20. On the role of the promised bill of rights amendments in the ratification of the Constitution, see Leonard W. Levy, *Constitutional Opinions* (Oxford University Press, 1986), chap. 6.

CHAPTER 2

1. Max Lerner, *Ideas for the Ice Age* (Viking, 1941), pp. 241–42. See also *The American Public's Knowledge of the U.S. Constitution: A National Survey of Public Awareness and Personal Opinion* (Hearst Corporation, 1987).
2. Sanford Levinson, *Constitutional Faith* (Princeton University Press, 1988), pp. 9–52.
3. Richard Morin, "We Love It—What We Know of It," *The Washington Post National Weekly Edition*, September 22, 1997, p. 35.
4. Thomas Jefferson, quoted in Alpheus T. Mason, *The Supreme Court: Palladium of Freedom* (University of Michigan Press, 1962), p. 10.
5. James Madison, *The Federalist*, No. 47, ed. Clinton Rossiter (Mentor Books), p. 301.
6. James L. Sundquist, "Needed: A Political Theory for the New Era of Coalition Government in the United States," *Political Science Quarterly* (Winter 1988–89), pp. 613–35; Robert A. Godwin and Art Kaufman, eds., *Separation of Powers: Does It Still Work?* (AEI Press, 1986).
7. Charles O. Jones, "The Separate Presidency," in Anthony King, ed., *The New American Political System*, 2d ed. (AEI Press, 1990), p. 3.
8. Morris P. Fiorina, "An Era of Divided Government," *Political Science Quarterly* 107, no. 3 (1992), p. 407.
9. David R. Mayhew, *Divided We Govern: Party Control, Lawmaking, and Investigations, 1946–1990* (Yale University Press, 1991), p. 4. See also James A. Thurber, ed., *Divided Democracy: Presidents and Congress in Cooperation and Conflict* (Congressional Quarterly, 1991).
10. Charles O. Jones, *Separate But Equal Branches: Congress and the Presidency* (Chatham House, 1995).
11. Robert C. Vipond, *Liberty and Community: Canadian Federalism and the Failure of the Constitution* (State University of New York Press, 1991), p. 192.
12. Alec Stone, "Governing with Judges: The New Constitutionalism," in Jack Hayward and Edward C. Page, eds. *Governing the New Europe* (Polity Press, 1995), pp. 286–313; Donald P. Kommers, "The Federal Constitutional Court in the German Political System," *Comparative Political Studies* 26 (January 1994), pp. 470–91; Martin J. Shapiro, "The European Court of Justice," in Alberta M. Sbrdagia, ed., *Euro-Politics*, (Brookings Institution, 1992); Martin J. Shapiro and Alec Stone, "The New Constitutional Politics," *Comparative Political Studies* 26 (January 1994), pp. 397–420; Alec Stone, *The Birth of Judicial Politics in France* (Oxford University Press, 1993).
13. *Marbury v Madison*, 1 Cranch 137 (1803).
14. Dumas Malone, *Jefferson the President: First Term, 1801–1805* (Little, Brown, 1970), p. 145.
15. J. W. Peltason, *Federal Courts in the Political Process* (Random House, 1955).
16. See Eleanore Bushnell, *Crimes, Follies, and Misfortunes: The Federal Impeachment Trials* (University of Illinois Press, 1992); Michael J. Gerhardt, *The Federal Impeachment Process: A Constitutional and Historical Analysis* (Princeton University Press, 1996).
17. Richard E. Neustadt, *Presidential Power* (Free Press, 1990), pp. 180–81.
18. Ronald L. Goldfarb, "The 11,000th Amendment: There's a Rush to Amend the Constitution, and It Shows No Signs of Letting Up," *The Washington Post National Weekly Edition*, November 25–December 1, 1996, p. 22.
19. See Committee on the Constitutional System, *A Bicentennial Analysis of the American Political Structure: Report and Recommendations of the Committee on the Constitutional System* (1987), for recommendations of a committee co-chaired by Senator Nancy L. Kassebaum, C. Douglas Dillon, and Lloyd Cutler. For critical comments, see Mark P. Petracca, "To Right What the Constitution Has Wrought or To Wrong What Is Right," paper presented at annual meeting of the American Political Science Association, Washington, D.C., 1988.
20. Ann Stuart Diamond, "A Convention for Proposing Amendments: The Constitution's Other Method," *Publius* (Summer 1981), pp. 113–46; Wilbur Edel, "Amending the Constitution by Convention: Myths and Realities," *State Government* 55 (1982), pp. 51–56.

21. Russell L. Caplan, *Constitutional Brinksmanship: Amending the Constitution by National Convention* (Oxford University Press, 1988), p. x. See also David E. Kyvig, *Explicit and Authentic Acts: Amending the U.S. Constitution, 1776–1995* (University Press of Kansas, 1996), p. 440.

22. Samuel S. Freedman and Pamela J. Naughton, *ERA: May a State Change Its Vote?* (Wayne State University Press, 1979).

23. Kyvig, *Explicit and Authentic Acts*, p. 286; *Dillon v Gloss*, 256 US 368 (1921).

24. Gregory A. Caldeira, "Constitutional Change in America: Dynamics of Ratification Under Article V," *Publius* (Fall 1985), p. 29.

25. Mark R. Daniels, Robert Darcy, and Joseph W. Westphal, "The ERA Won—At Least in the Opinion Polls," *PS: Political Science and Politics* (Fall 1982), p. 583.

26. Ibid.

27. Janet K. Boles, *The Politics of the Equal Rights Amendment: Conflict and Decision-Making Powers* (Longman, 1979), p. 4.

28. Gilbert Y. Steiner, *Constitutional Inequality: The Political Fortunes of the Equal Rights Amendment* (Brookings Institution, 1985), p. 64. See also Mary Frances Berry, *Why the ERA Failed: Politics, Women's Rights, and the Amending Process of the Constitution* (Indiana University Press, 1986).

CHAPTER 3

1. For background, see Samuel H. Beer, *To Make a Nation: The Rediscovery of American Federalism* (Harvard University Press, 1993).

2. The term "devolution revolution" was coined by Richard P. Nathan in testimony before the Senate Finance Committee, as quoted by Daniel Patrick Moynihan, "The Devolution Revolution," *The New York Times*, August 6, 1995, p. B15.

3. See Michael Burgess, *Federalism and the European Union: Building of Europe, 1950–2000* (Routledge, 2000).

4. *United States v Lopez*, 514 US 549 (1995).

5. *Alden v Maine*, 119 S.Ct. 2240 (1999); *Kimel v Florida Board of Regents*, 120 S.Ct. 631 (2000); and *Vermont Agency of Natural Resources v United States ex rel. Stevens*, 120 S.Ct. 1858 (2000).

6. *Saenz v Roe*, 119 S.Ct. 1518 (1999). See also Roderick M. Hills, Jr., "Poverty, Residency, and Federalism: States' Duty of Impartiality Toward Newcomers," in Dennis J. Hutchinson, David A. Strauss, and Geoffrey R. Stone, eds., *The Supreme Court Review—1999* (University of Chicago Press, 2000), pp. 277–336.

7. *Reno v Condon*, 120 S.Ct. 666 (2000).

8. Martha Derthick, "American Federalism: Half-Full or Half-Empty," *Brookings Review* (Winter 2000), pp. 24–27.

9. William H. Stewart, *Concepts of Federalism* (Center for the Study of Federalism and University Press of America, 1984). See also Edward L. Rubin and Malcolm Feeley, "Federalism: Some Notes on a National Neurosis," *UCLA Law Review* 41 (April 1994), pp. 903–52.

10. Morton Grodzins, "The Federal System," in *Goals for Americans: The Report of the President's Commission on National Goals* (Columbia University Press, 1960).

11. Thomas R. Dye, *American Federalism: Competition Among Governments* (Lexington Books, 1990), pp. 13–17.

12. Michael D. Reagan and John G. Sanzone, *The New Federalism* (Oxford University Press, 1981), p. 175.

13. Gregory S. Mahler, *Comparative Politics: An Institutional and Cross-National Approach* (Prentice-Hall, 2000), p. 31.

14. Frederick K. Lister, *The European Union, the United Nations and the Revival of Confederal Governance* (Greenwood Press, 1996).

15. William H. Riker, *The Development of American Federalism* (Academic Publishers, 1987), pp. 14–15. Riker contends that not only does federalism not guarantee freedom but that the framers of our federal system, as well as those of other nations, were not animated by considerations of safeguarding freedom but by practical considerations of preserving unity.

16. The Court, however, ruled in several recent cases that Congress exceeded its power to regulate interstate commerce. See *Printz v Mack*, 117 S.Ct. 2365 (1997); *United States v Lopez*, 514 US 549 (1995); *New York v United States*, 505 US 144 (1992); and *United States v Morrison*, 120 S.Ct. 1740 (2000).

17. *Heart of Atlanta Motel v United States*, 379 US 241 (1964).

18. See *United States v Morrison*, 120 S.Ct. 1740 (2000), striking down the Violence Against Women Act, and discussed later in this chapter.

19. *New York v United States*, 505 US 144 (1992); *Printz v United States*, 117 S.Ct. 2365 (1997).

20. *Seminole Tribe of Florida v Florida*, 517 US 44 (1996); *Alden v Maine*, 119 S.Ct. 2240 (1999); and *Kimel v Florida Board of Regents*, 120 S.Ct. 631 (2000).

21. *California v Superior Courts of California*, 482 US 400 (1987).

22. David C. Nice, "State Participation in Interstate Compacts," *Publius* 17 (Spring 1987), p. 70. See also Council of State Governments, *Interstate Compacts and Agencies* (1995), for a list of compacts by subject and by state with brief description.

23. *McCulloch v Maryland*, 4 Wheaton 316 (1819).

24. Joseph F. Zimmerman, "Federal Preemption Under Reagan's New Federalism," *Publius* 21 (Winter 1991), pp. 7–28.

25. Oliver Wendell Holmes, Jr., *Collected Legal Papers* (Harcourt, 1920), pp. 295–96.

26. *U.S. Term Limits, Inc. v Thornton*, 514 US 779 (1995).

27. *Garcia v San Antonio Metro*, 469 US 528 (1985).

28. See, e.g., *United States v Lopez*, 514 US 549 (1995). Also see Richard A. Brisbin, Jr., "The Reconstitution of American Federalism? The Rehnquist Court and Federal-State Relations, 1991–1997," *Publius* (Winter 1998), pp. 189–217.

29. *U.S. Term Limits v Thornton*, 514 US 779 (1995).

30. *Seminole Tribe of Florida v Florida*, 517 US 44 (1996).

31. *Alden v Maine*, 119 S.Ct. 2240 (1999); *Kimel v Florida Board of Regents*, 120 S.Ct. 631 (2000); and *Vermont Agency of Natural Resources v United States ex rel. Stevens*, 120 S.Ct. 1858 (2000).

32. George Will, "A Revival of Federalism?" *Newsweek*, May 29, 2000, p. 78.

33. See *Jones v United States*, 120 S.Ct. 2236 (2000).

34. *United States v Morrison*, 120 S.Ct. 1740 (2000).

35. John E. Chubb, "The Political Economy of Federalism," *American Political Science Review* 79 (December 1985), p. 1005.

36. Paul E. Peterson, *The Price of Federalism* (Brookings Institution, 1995), p. 127.

37. Donald F. Kettl, *The Regulation of American Federalism* (Johns Hopkins University Press, 1987), pp. 154–55.

38. See Paul J. Posner, *The Politics of Unfunded Mandates: Whither Federalism?* (Georgetown University Press, 1998).

39. Advisory Commission on Intergovernmental Relations, *Restoring Confidence and Competence* (ACIR, 1981), p. 30.

40. Cynthia Cates Colella, "The Creation, Care and Feeding of the Leviathan: Who and What Makes Government Grow," *Intergovernmental Perspective* (Fall 1979), p. 9.

41. Aaron Wildavsky, "Bare Bones: Putting Flesh on the Skeleton of American Federalism," in Advisory Commission on Intergovernmental Relations, *The Future of Federalism in the 1980s* (ACIR, 1981), p. 79.

42. Peterson, *Price of Federalism*, p. 182.

43. "GOP Confounds Expectations, Expands Federal Authority," *Congressional Quarterly Weekly Report*, November 2, 1996, p. 3117.

44. Eliza Newlin Carney, "Power Grab," *National Journal*, April 11, 1998, p. 798. See also Joshua Wolf Shenk, "Washington's Counter-Devolutionaries," *U.S. News and World Report*, November 24, 1997, p. 34.

45. Luther Gulick, "Reorganization of the States," *Civil Engineering* (August 1933), pp. 420–21.

46. David E. Osborne, *Laboratories of Democracy* (Harvard Business School Press, 1988), p. 363.

47. Dye, *American Federalism*, p. 199.

48. Edward Felsenthal, "Firms Ask Congress to Pass Uniform Rules," *The Wall Street Journal*, May 10, 1993, p. B4.

49. John J. DiIulio, Jr., and Donald F. Kettl, *Fine Print: The Contract with America, Devolution, and the Administrative Realities of American Federalism* (Brookings Institution, 1995), p. 60.

CHAPTER 4

1. Robert D. Putnam, "Bowling Alone: America's Declining Social Capital," *Journal of Democracy* 6, no. 1 (January 1995), pp. 65–78. See also Robert D. Putnam, *Bowling Alone: The Collapse and Revival of American Community* (Simon & Schuster, 2000).
2. Clinton Rossiter, *Conservatism in America* (Vintage, 1962), p. 72.
3. See Ronald Dworkin, *Taking Rights Seriously* (Harvard University Press, 1977).
4. *Marbury v Madison*, 1 Cranch 137 (1803).
5. For an analysis of one aspect of the underclass, see Paul M. Sniderman and Michael Hagen, *Race and Inequality: A Study in American Values* (Chatham House, 1985).
6. When adjusted using the consumer price index (CPI), the percent of households earning over $75,000 a year has risen from 9.0 percent in 1970 to 18.4 percent in 1997. U.S. Bureau of the Census, *Statistical Abstract of the United States, 1999* (Government Printing Office, 1999), table 742.
7. Bernard Bailyn, *The Ideological Origins of the American Revolution* (Harvard University Press, 1967).
8. Robert A. Dahl, "Liberal Democracy in the United States," in *A Prospect of Liberal Democracy*, ed. William Livingston (University of Texas Press, 1979), p. 64.
9. Ibid., pp. 59–60.
10. Franklin D. Roosevelt, State of the Union Address, January 11, 1944, *The Public Papers of the President of the United States, 1944* (Government Printing Office, 1962), pp. 371–94.
11. Harry S Truman, State of the Union Address, 1949, *The Public Papers of the President of the United States, 1949* (Government Printing Office, 1964), pp. 1–7.
12. E. J. Dionne, Jr., *They Only Look Dead: Why Progressives Will Dominate the Next Political Era* (Simon & Schuster, 1996), p. 13.
13. David Brooks, "Need a Map? The Right," *The Washington Post*, October 31, 1999, p. B1.
14. Warren B. Rudman, *Combat: Twelve Years in the U.S. Senate* (Random House, 1996), p. 270.
15. David B. Magleby, "Issue Advocacy in the 2000 Presidential Primaries," in David B. Magleby, ed., *Getting Inside the Outside Campaign* (Center for the Study of Elections and Democracy, Brigham Young University, 2000), p.13. Also at www.byu.edu/outsidemoney.
16. Kathleen Day, *S & L Hell: The People and the Politics Behind the $1 Trillion Savings and Loan Scandal* (W.W. Norton & Co., 1993).
17. Sylvia Nasar, "Even Among the Well-Off, the Rich Get Richer," *The New York Times*, March 5, 1992, p. A1.
18. Irving Howe, *Socialism and America* (Harcourt, 1985); Michael Harrington, *Socialism: Past and Future* (Arcade, 1989).
19. Daniel Yergin and Joseph Stainslaw, *The Commanding Heights: The Battle Between Government and the Marketplace That is Remaking the Modern World* (Simon & Schuster, 1998).
20. www.gp.org/fullplatform.htm
21. Charles Murray, *What It Means to Be a Libertarian* (Broadway Books, 1997); see their 2000 platform at www.lp.org/issues/campplat
22. Center for Political Studies, University of Michigan, *American National Election Study, 1990: Post-Election Survey* (April 1991).
23. Michael Kranish, "Discord Replaced by Desire to Win," *The Boston Globe,* July 31, 2000, p. A10.
24. Nat Hentoff, "Liberal Trimmers of the First Amendment," *The Washington Post,* January 17, 1998, p. A25.
25. Dinesh D'Sousa, *Illiberal Education: The Politics of Race and Sex on Campus* (Free Press, 1991), p. 313.

CHAPTER 5

1. George W. Bush Campaign, "Governor Bush Proposes 6-Month Standard for All Immigration Applications," press release, July 5, 2000, at the Annual Conference of the National Council of La Raza, San Diego, Calif., at www.georgewbush.com/News.asp?FormMode=NR&Search=1&ID=829, August 15, 2000.
2. Albert Einstein, quoted in Laurence J. Peter, *Peter's Quotations* (William Morrow, 1977), p. 358.
3. Alexis de Tocqueville, *Democracy in America*, ed. J. P. Mayer, trans. George Lawrence (Doubleday and Company, 1969), p. 278.
4. *Handbook of International Statistics* (Central Intelligence Agency, Directorate of Intelligence, February 1999), Table 41: "Big Seven: Exports by Commodities," pp. 52–53.
5. U.S. Bureau of the Census, *Statistical Abstract of the United States, 1999* (Government Printing Office, 1999), p. 300.
6. V. O. Key, Jr., *Politics, Parties, and Pressure Groups*, 5th ed. (Thomas Y. Crowell, 1964), p. 232.
7. Earl Black and Merle Black, *The Vital South: How Presidents Are Elected* (Harvard University Press, 1992), p. 4.
8. Joseph A. Pika and Richard A. Watson, *The Presidential Contest*, 5th ed. (Congressional Quarterly Press, 1996), pp. 80–81.
9. www. census.gov/population/cen2000/tab01.pdf./
10. Robert S. Erikson, Gerald C. Wright, and John P. McIver, *Statehouse Democracy: Public Opinion and Policy in the American States* (Cambridge University Press, 1993).
11. U.S. Bureau of the Census, *Statistical Abstract of the United States, 1997* (Government Printing Office, 1997), p. 28.
12. Holly Idelson, "Count Adds Seats in Eight States," *Congressional Quarterly Weekly Report* 48 (December 29, 1999), p. 4240.
13. *Statistical Abstract, 1999*, p. 40.
14. Ibid., p. 46.
15. U.S. Bureau of the Census, www.census.gov/population/socdemo/race/black/tabs99/tab16.txt.
16. Kevin M. Pollard, "America's Racial and Ethnic Minorities," *Population Bulletin*, September 1999.
17. *Statistical Abstract, 1999*, p. 48.
18. Ibid., p. 34.
19. Robert D. Ballard, "Introduction: Lure of the New South," *In Search of the New South: The Black Urban Experience in the 1970s and 1980s*, ed. Robert D. Ballard (University of Alabama Press, 1989), p. 5; *Statistical Abstract, 1999*, p. 34.
20. U.S. Bureau of the Census, www.census.gov/hhes/income/histinc/f05.html, August 2000.
21. *Statistical Abstract, 1999*, p. 484.
22. Joseph Dalker and Bernadette D. Proctor, U.S. Census Bureau, Current Population Reports, *"Poverty in the United States, 1999,"* September 2000 (www.census.gov/hhes/www/povty99.html).
23. *Statistical Abstract, 1999*, p. 475.
24. U.S. Bureau of the Census, www.census.gov/hhes/www/wealth/wlth93f.html.
25. U.S. Bureau of the Census, *Household Wealth and Asset Ownership, 1991*, Current Population Reports P-70, no. 34 (Government Printing Office, 1991), table H.
26. Ibid., p. 169.
27. Ibid., p. 191.
28. Ibid., p. 23.
29. Mark R. Levy and Michael S. Karmer, *The Ethnic Factor: How America's Minorities Decide Elections* (Simon & Schuster, 1973). See also Mark Stern, "Democratic Presidency and Voting Rights," in *Blacks in Southern Politics*, ed. Lawrence W. Mooreland, Robert P. Steed, and Todd A. Baker (Praeger, 1987), pp. 50–51.
30. David Bositis, *Blacks and the 1992 Republican National Convention* (Joint Center for Political and Economic Studies, 1992), p. 5; "Portrait of the Electorate," *The New York Times*, November 10, 1996, p. 16.
31. *Statistical Abstract, 1999*, p. 39.
32. See Frank R. Parker, *Black Votes Count: Political Empowerment in Mississippi After 1965* (University of North Carolina Press, 1990).
33. "Number of Black Elected Officials in the United States, by State and Office, January 1998," Joint Center for Political and Economic Studies, at www.jointcenter.org/databank/graphs/98_beo.pdf.
34. Ibid.
35. Rodolfo O. de la Garza, Louis DeSipio, F. Chris Garcia, John Garcia, and Angelo Falcon, *Latino Voices: Mexican, Puerto Rican, and Cuban Perspectives on American Politics* (Westview Press, 1992), p. 14.
36. Todd S. Purdum, "Shift in the Mix Alters the Face of California," *The New York Times*, July 4, 2000, p. A1.
37. *Statistical Abstract, 1999*, p. 54.

38. de la Garza et al., *Latino Voices*, p. 14.
39. *Statistical Abstract, 1999*, p. 38.
40. U.S. Bureau of the Census, *The Foreign-Born Population in the United States, March 1999*. Issued August 2000 (www.census.gov/prod/2000pubs/p20–519.pdf), p. 1.
41. *Statistical Abstract, 1999*, p. 169.
42. *Statistical Abstract, 1999*, p. 10.
43. Martha Farnsworth Riche, "America's Diversity and Growth: Signpost for the 21st Century," *Population Bulletin*, January 2000.
44. James West Davidson, William E. Gienapp, Christine Leigh Heyrman, Mark H. Lytle, and Michael B. Stoff, *Nation of Nations* (McGraw-Hill, 1990), pp. 833–34.
45. G. Thomas Edwards, *Sowing Good Seeds: The Northwest Suffrage Campaigns of Susan B. Anthony* (Oregon Historical Society Press, 1990), p. 136.
46. Paul Kleppner, *Continuity and Change in Electoral Politics, 1893–1928* (Greenwood Press, 1987), p. 172.
47. Margaret C. Trevor, "Political Socialization, Party Identification, and the Gender Gap," *Public Opinion Quarterly* 63 (Spring 1999), p. 62.
48. Diane L. Fowlkes, "Feminist Theory: Reconstructing Research and Teaching About American Politics and Government," *News for Teachers of Political Science* (Winter 1987), pp. 6–9. See also Sally Helgesen, *Everyday Revolutionaries: Working Women and the Transformation of American Life* (Doubleday, 1998); Karen Lehrman, *The Lipstick Proviso: Women, Sex and Power in the Real World* (Anchor Books and Doubleday, 1997); Tanya Melich, *The Republican War Against Women: An Insider's Report from Behind the Lines: Updated Edition* (Bantam Books, 1998); and Virginia Valian, *Why So Slow? The Advancement of Women* (MIT Press, 1998).
49. Barbara C. Burrell, *A Woman's Place Is in the House: Campaigning for Congress in the Feminist Era* (University of Michigan Press, 1994).
50. Marjorie Connelly, "The Election; Who Voted: A Portrait of American Politics, 1976–2000," *The New York Times*, November 12, 2000, p. D4.
51. Arlie Russell Hochschild, "There's No Place Like Work," *The New York Times*, April 20, 1997, p. 51.
52. Alexis Simendinger, "Why Issues Matter," *National Journal*, April 1, 2000, based on data from a Pew Center Poll conducted March 15–19, 2000.
53. *Statistical Abstract, 1999*, p. 481.
54. June O'Neill and Solomon Polachek, "Why the Gender Gap in Wages Narrowed in the 1980's," *Journal of Labor Economics* 11 (1993), pp. 225–29.
55. Jeffrey Schmalz, "Survey Stirs Debate on Number of Gay Men in U.S.," *The New York Times*, April 16, 1993, p. A20.
56. Tamar Lewin, "So, Now We Know What Americans Do in Bed. So?" *The New York Times*, October 9, 1994, sec. 4, p. 3.
57. Adam Clymer, "Senate Expands Hate Crimes Law to Include Gays," *The New York Times*, June 21, 2000, p. A1.
58. *Boy Scouts of America and Monmouth Council et al. v James Dale*, 120 S. Ct. 2446 (2000).
59. *Statistical Abstract, 1999*, p. 111.
60. Ibid., p. 110.
61. www.icpsr.umich.edu/GSS99/codebook/pework.htm.
62. For a discussion of the Holocaust, see Leni Yahil, *The Holocaust: The Fate of European Jewry* (Oxford University Press, 1990).
63. Stephen C. LeSuer, *The 1838 Mormon War in Missouri* (University of Missouri Press, 1987), pp. 151–53.
64. John Conway, "An Adapted Organic Tradition," *Daedalus* 117 (Fall 1988), p. 382. For an extended comparison of the impact of religion on politics in the United States and Canada, see Seymour Martin Lipset, *Continental Divide: The Values and Institutions of the United States and Canada* (Routledge, 1990), pp. 74–89.
65. Robert N. Bellah, *Beyond Belief: Essays on Religion in a Post-Traditional World* (University of California Press, 1991), pp. 168–90.
66. National Opinion Research Center, General Social Survey, 1972–94.
67. William H. Flanigan and Nancy H. Zingale, *Political Behavior of the American Electorate*, 9th ed. (Congressional Quarterly Press, 1998), p. 118.
68. *Statistical Abstract, 1997*, p. 69.
69. www.cnn.com/ELECTION/2000/results.
70. Ibid.
71. Lyman A. Kellstedt and John C. Green, "Is There a Culture War: Religion and the 1996 Election," paper presented at the American Political Science Association Annual Meeting, Washington, D.C., 1997, at www.wheaton.edu\polsci\kellstedt.
72. Telephone survey of 113,000 households in the 48 contiguous states, April 1989–April 1990, Graduate School of the City University of New York.
73. Organization for Economic Cooperation and Development (OECD), *National Accounts*, vol. 1, *Main Aggregates, 1960–89* (OECD, 1991), p. 145.
74. Raymond E. Wolfinger, Fred I. Greenstein, and Martin Shapiro, *Dynamics of American Politics*, 2d ed. (Prentice Hall, 1980), p. 19.
75. Thomas Jefferson, "Autobiography," in *The Life and Selected Writings of Thomas Jefferson*, ed. Adrienne Koch and William Peden (Modern Library, 1944), p. 38.
76. U.S. Department of Education, *Digest of Education Statistics, 1997* (Government Printing Office, 1997), p. 324.
77. Harold W. Stanley and Richard G. Niemi, *Vital Statistics on American Politics 1999–2000* (Congressional Quarterly Press, 2000), p. 115.
78. Stanley Fischer, "Symposium on the Slowdown in Productivity Growth," *Journal of Economic Perspectives* 2 (Fall 1988), pp. 3–7.
79. U.S. Bureau of the Census: www.census.gov/hhes/poverty/threshld/thresh99.html.
80. *Statistical Abstract, 1999*, p. 486.
81. Ibid., p. 487.
82. W. Michael Cox and Richard Alm, "Why Decry the Wealth Gap?" *The New York Times*, January 24, 2000, p. A24.
83. U.S. Bureau of the Census: www.census.gov/hhes/income/incineq/p60tb3.html.
84. *Statistical Abstract, 1999*, p. 459. "Real" means that inflation has already been taken into account.
85. Daniel Bell, *The Coming of Post-Industrial Society: A Venture in Social Forecasting* (Basic Books, 1973), p. xviii.
86. *Statistical Abstract, 1999*, pp. 424–34.
87. Ibid., p. 460.
88. Ibid., p. 428.
89. Mattei Dogan and Dominique Pelassy, *How to Compare Nations: Strategies in Comparative Politics*, 2d ed. (Chatham House, 1990), p. 47.
90. Responses for subjective social class vary somewhat with wording of the question. The data on Great Britain are from the *Index to International Public Opinion, 1991–92* (Greenwood Press, 1992), p. 462.
91. Lipset, *Continental Divide*, p. 170.
92. www.bls.gov/csx/1999/Aggregate/age.pdf.
93. *Statistical Abstract, 1999*, p. 484.
94. U.S. Bureau of the Census: www.census.gov/population/socdemo/voting/history/vot23/txt, May 1998.
95. www.cnn.com/election/2000/results/index.epolls.html.
96. Seymour Martin Lipset, *Political Man* (Doubleday, 1963), pp. 283–86.
97. Thomas Jefferson to P. S. du Pont de Nemours, April 24, 1816, *The Writings of Thomas Jefferson*, ed. Paul L. Ford (G. P. Putnam's Sons, 1899), 10:25.
98. *Statistical Abstract, 1999*, p. 163.
99. Ibid., p. 170.
100. Ibid., p. 169.
101. Herbert McClosky and John Zaller, *The American Ethos: Public Attitudes Toward Capitalism and Democracy* (Harvard University Press, 1984), p. 261.
102. John Gunther, *Inside U.S.A.* (Harper & Brothers, 1947), p. 911.
103. Carl N. Degler, *Out of Our Past: The Forces That Shaped Modern America*, 3d ed. (Harper & Row, 1984), p. 322.

CHAPTER 6

1. Richard M. Stevenson, "The 2000 Campaign: The Tactics—Wealthy Texan Bought Anti McCain Ads," *The New York Times*, March 4, 2000, p. A1.
2. David Rogers, "Lobbyist Funded Mailing That Hurt McCain Campaign," *The Wall Street Journal*, July 11, 2000, p. A28.
3. See David B. Magleby, "Getting Inside the Outside Campaign: Issue Advocacy in the 2000 Presidential Primaries," report released at the National Press Club, Washington, D.C., July 17, 2000, www.byu.edu/outsidemoney.

4. James Parks, "COPE Endorsements, 1968–1992," AFL-CIO, Department of Information, personal communication, January 6, 1994.

5. U.S. Bureau of the Census, *Statistical Abstract of the United States, 1997* (Government Printing Office, 1997), pp. 398, 400.

6. James MacGregor Burns and Stewart Burns, *A People's Charter: The Pursuit of Rights in America* (Knopf, 1991).

7. William R. Donohue, *The Politics of the American Civil Liberties Union* (Transaction, 1985).

8. See NEA home page: www.nea.org/index.html.

9. Robert Salisbury, "Interest Representation: The Dominance of Institutions," *American Political Science Review* 78 (March 1984), p. 66.

10. V. O. Key, Jr., *Public Opinion and American Democracy* (Knopf, 1961), pp. 504–507.

11. R. Kenneth Godwin, *One Billion Dollars of Influence: The Direct Marketing of Politics* (Chatham House, 1988).

12. Lucius J. Barker, "Third Parties in Litigation: A Systemic View of the Judicial Function," *Journal of Politics* 29 (February 1967), pp. 41–69; Jethro K. Lieberman, *Litigious Society*, rev. ed. (Basic Books, 1983).

13. Gregory A. Calderia and John R. Wright, "Organized Interests and Agenda Setting in the U.S. Supreme Court," *American Political Science Review* 82 (December 1988), pp. 1109–27. See also Gregory A. Calderia and John R. Wright, "Amici Curiae before the Supreme Court: Who Participates, When, and How Much?" *Journal of Politics* 52 (August 1990), pp. 782–806.

14. Karen O'Connor, *Women's Organizations' Use of the Courts* (Lexington Books, 1980).

15. Steven Preston Brown, "Restoring Faith: The New Christian Right, Religious Liberty and the Courts" (University of Virginia, May 1998), Ph.D. diss.

16. Lee Epstein and C. K. Rowland, "Debunking the Myth of Interest Group Invincibility in the Courts," *American Political Science Review* 85 (March 1991), pp. 205–17.

17. For a discussion of the 1998 New Mexico race, see Lonna Rae Atkeson and Anthony C. Coveny, "The 1998 New Mexico Third Congressional District Race," in David B. Magleby, ed., *Outside Money: Soft Money and Issue Advocacy in the 1998 Congressional Elections* (Rowman & Littlefield, 2000), pp. 135–52.

18. Ethan Bronner, *Battle for Justice: How the Bork Nomination Shook America* (Norton, 1989), pp. 50–55.

19. David Mayhew, *Congress: The Electoral Connection* (Yale University Press, 1974), p. 45.

20. John R. Wright, "Contributions, Lobbying, and Committee Voting in the U.S. House of Representatives," *American Political Science Review* 84 (June 1990), pp. 417–38.

21. For evidence of the impact of PAC expenditures on legislative committee behavior and legislative involvement generally, see Richard L. Hall and Frank W. Wayman, "Buying Time: Moneyed Interests and the Mobilization of Bias in Congressional Committees," *American Political Science Review* 84 (September 1990), pp. 797–820.

22. Edwin M. Epstein, "Business and Labor Under the Federal Election Campaign Act of 1971," in Michael J. Malbin, ed., *Parties, Interest Groups, and Campaign Finance Laws* (American Enterprise Institute for Public Policy Research, 1980), p. 112. See also Gary Jacobson, *Money in Congressional Elections* (Yale University Press, 1980).

23. Senator Charles C. Mathias, statement in *The New York Times*, February 27, 1986, p. A31.

24. Brody Mullins and Charlie Mitchell, "Soft Money Unleashed," *National Journal*, February 7, 2001, pp. 500–501.

25. Amy Dockster, "Nice PAC You've Got Here . . . A Pity If Anything Should Happen to It: How Politicians Shake Down the Special Interests," *Washington Monthly*, January 27, 1987, p. 24, quoted in Margaret Cates Nugent and John R. Johannes, eds., *Money, Elections, and Democracy: Reforming Congressional Campaign Finance* (Westview Press, 1990), p. 1.

26. Hall and Wayman, "Buying Time," pp. 797–820. A different study of the House Ways and Means Committee found campaign contributions to be part of the representatives' policy decisions, but even more important was the number of lobbying contacts. See Wright, "Contributions, Lobbying, and Committee Voting," pp. 417–38.

27. Ronald Reagan, "Remarks to Administration Officials on Domestic Policy," December 13, 1988, *Weekly Compilation of Presidential Documents*, vol. 24 (December 1988), pp. 1615–20.

28. Sylvia Tesh, "In Support of Single-Interest Politics," *Political Science Quarterly* 99 (Spring 1984), pp. 27–44.

29. Report and Recommendations of the California Commission on Campaign Financing, *The New Gold Rush: Financing California's Legislative Campaigns* (Center for Responsive Government, 1985), pp. 177–97. For a study of state lobby regulation, see Cynthia Opheim, "Explaining the Differences in State Lobby Regulation," *Western Political Quarterly* 44 (June 1991), pp. 405–21.

30. Adam Clymer, "Congress Sends Lobbying Overhaul to Clinton," *The New York Times*, December 16, 1995, sec. 1, p. 36.

31. David B. Magleby and Candice J. Nelson, *The Money Chase: Congressional Campaign Finance Reform* (Brookings Institution, 1990), pp. 72–97.

32. Factors that predict the formation of PACs include company size and the degree of regulation for corporations. See Craig Humphries, "Corporations, PACs and the Strategic Link Between Contributions and Lobbying Activities," *Western Political Quarterly* 44 (June 1991), pp. 353–72.

33. Harold W. Stanley and Richard G. Niemi, *Vital Statistics on American Politics* (Congressional Quarterly Press, 2000), p. 100.

34. ftp.fec.gov/fed.

35. Greg Hitt, "Democrats Move Ahead in Soft-Money Race," *The Wall Street Journal*, August 17, 2000, p. A24.

36. www.opensecrets.org/industries/indus.asp?Ind+H04.

37. Marianne Holt, "Stealth PAC's Revealed: Interest Group Profiles." Press release from the Center for Public Integrity, February 5, 2001.

38. David B. Magleby, ed., *Election Advocacy: Soft Money and Issue Advocacy in the 2000 Congressional Elections* (Center for the Study of Elections and Democracy, 2001) at www.byu.edu/outsidemoney.

CHAPTER 7

1. John E. Mueller, "Choosing Among 133 Candidates," *Public Opinion Quarterly* 34 (Fall 1970), pp. 395–402.

2. E. E. Schattschneider, *Party Government* (Holt, Rinehart and Winston, 1942), p. 1.

3. See Scott Mainwaring, "Party Systems in the Third Wave," *Journal of Democracy* (July 1998), pp. 67–81.

4. Joseph A. Schlesinger, *Political Parties and the Winning of Office* (University of Michigan Press, 1994).

5. Lizette Alvarez, "Senate to Divide Power and Money Equally in Panels," *The New York Times*, January 6, 2001, p. A1.

6. See David B. Magleby, ed., *Outside Money: Soft Money and Issue Advocacy in the 1998 Congressional Elections* (Rowman & Littlefield, 2000).

7. Nick Anderson and Jonathan Peterson, "China Trade Vote: House OK's China Trade Bill," *Los Angeles Times*, May 25, 2000, p. A1.

8. David W. Brady and Craig Volden, *Revolving Gridlock: Politics and Policy from Carter to Clinton* (Westview Press, 1998); James A. Thurber, ed., *Divided Democracy: Cooperation and Conflict Between the Presi-dent and Congress* (CQ Press, 1991); James A. Thurber, ed., *Rivals for Power: Presidential-Congressional Relations* (CQ Press, 1996); Charles O. Jones, *Separate But Equal Branches: Congress and the Presidency* (Chatham House, 1995), chaps. 5, 6; Jon R. Bond and Richard Fleisher, *The President in the Legislative Arena* (University of Chicago Press, 1990).

9. *California Democratic Party et al. v Jones*, 120 S.Ct. 2402 (2000).

10. Arthur Sanders and David Redlawsk, "Money and the Iowa Caucuses," in *Getting Inside the Outside Campaign*, ed. David Magleby (Center for the Study of Elections and Democracy, 2000), pp. 20–29.

11. *The Book of the States, 1998–1999* (Council of State Governments, 1998), pp. 159–60.

12. www.cnn.com/ELECTIONS/2000/results, November 27, 2000.

13. William H. Riker, "The Two-Party System and Duverger's Law: An Essay on the History of Political Science," *American Political Science Review* 76 (December 1982), pp. 753–66. For a classic analysis, see Schattschneider, *Party Government*.

14. See Paul S. Herrnson and John C. Green, eds., *Multiparty Politics in America* (Rowman and Littlefield, 1997); J. David Gillespie, *Politics at the Periphery: Third Parties in Two-Party America* (University of South Carolina Press, 1993).

15. Steven J. Rosenstone, Roy L. Behr, and Edward H. Lazarus, *Third Parties in America: Citizen Response to Major Party Failure*, 2d ed. (Princeton University Press, 1996). See also Xandra Kayden and Eddie Mahe, Jr., *The Party Goes On: The Persistence of the Two Party System in the United States* (Basic Books, 1985), pp. 143–44.

16. On the impact of third parties, see Howard R. Penniman, "Presidential Third Parties and the Modern American Two-Party System," in William J. Crotty, ed., *The Party Symbol* (W. H. Freeman, 1980), pp. 101–17. See also Frank Smallwood, *The Other Candidates: Third Parties in Presidential Elections* (University Press of New England, 1983).

17. Benjamin Franklin, George Washington, and Thomas Jefferson, quoted in Richard Hofstadter, *The Idea of a Party System* (University of California Press, 1969), pp. 2, 123.

18. For concise histories of the two parties, see two studies by Robert A. Rutland, *The Democrats: From Jefferson to Clinton* (University of Missouri Press, 1996), and *The Republicans: From Lincoln to Bush* (University of Missouri Press, 1996).

19. See V. O. Key, "A Theory of Critical Elections," *Journal of Politics* 17 (February 1955), pp. 3–18; Walter Dean Burnham, *Critical Elections and the Mainsprings of American Politics* (Norton, 1970), pp. 1–10; and E. E. Schattschneider, *The Semisovereign People: A Realist's View of Democracy in America* (Holt, Rinehart and Winston, 1975), pp. 78–80.

20. William E. Gienapp, *The Origins of the Republican Party, 1852–1856* (Oxford University Press, 1987).

21. David W. Brady, "Elections, Congress and Public Policy Changes: 1886–1960," in Bruce A. Campbell and Richard Trilling, eds., *Realignment in American Politics: Toward a Theory* (Texas University Press, 1980), p. 188.

22. Gerald Pomper, "Classification of Presidential Elections," *Journal of Politics* 29 (1967), p. 538.

23. www.cnn.com/ELECTION/2000/results/index.epolls.htm.

24. Federal Election Commission, "15-Month Summary on Political Party Finances," June 8, 1998 (www.fec.gov/press/pty1598.htm).

25. Paul Allen Beck, *Party Politics in America*, 8th ed. (Longman, 1997), chap. 2.

26. See L. Sandy Maisel, *From Obscurity to Oblivion: Running in the Congressional Primary*, rev. ed. (University of Tennessee Press, 1986).

27. The early Republican efforts and advantages over the Democrats are well documented in Thomas B. Edsall, *The New Politics of Inequality* (Norton, 1984); Gary C. Jacobson, "The Republican Advantage in Campaign Finances," in John E. Chubb and Paul E. Peterson, eds., *New Direction in American Politics* (Washington, D.C.: Brookings Institution, 1985), p. 6.

28. John F. Bibby, *Politics, Parties, and Elections in America*, 3d ed. (Nelson-Hall, 1996). For further data on these roles, see Cornelius P. Cotter, James L. Gibson, John F. Bibby, and Robert J. Huckshorn, *Party Organizations in American Politics* (Praeger, 1984).

29. See James L. Gibson, Cornelius P. Cotter, John F. Bibby, and Robert J. Huckshorn, "Assessing Party Organizational Strength," *American Journal of Political Science* 27 (May 1983), pp. 193–222; Cotter et al., *Party Organizations in American Politics*.

30. Paul S. Herrnson, *Party Campaigning in the 1980s: Have the National Parties Made a Comeback as Key Players in Congressional Elections?* (Harvard University Press, 1988), p. 122.

31. Jonathan S. Krasno and Daniel E. Seltz, *Buying Time: Television Advertising in the 1998 Congressional Elections*, report of a grant funded by the Pew Charitable Trusts (1998).

32. On the influence of local parties, see Kayden and Mahe, *Party Goes On*. See also John C. Green and Daniel M. Shea, eds., *The State of the Parties: The Changing Role of Contemporary Parties*, 2d ed. (Rowman and Littlefield, 1996), which presents their recent case studies of parties at the local level.

33. Bob Nash, director, White House Office of Personnel, interview with David Magleby, October 26, 1998. A listing of many of these positions is presented in *Policy and Supporting Positions* (Government Printing Office, November 9, 1988). For a general discussion of this topic, see G. Calvin Mackenzie, "Partisan Presidential Leadership: The President's Appointees," in Maisel, ed., *Parties Respond* pp. 316–37.

34. *Marbury v Madison* I Cranch 137 (1803).

35. See Angus Campbell, Philip E. Converse, Warren E. Miller, and Donald E. Stokes, *The American Voter* (Wiley, 1960); Norman A. Nie, Sidney Verba, and John R. Petrocik, *The Changing American Voter*, enlarged ed. (Harvard University Press, 1979); Warren E. Miller and J. Merrill Shanks, *The New American Voter* (Harvard University Press, 1996).

36. "At the Races: A Weekly Review of Campaign 2000," *National Journal* 39 (September 2000), p. 2991.

37. Campbell et al., *American Voter*, pp. 121–28.

38. Keith et al., *Myth of the Independent Voter*.

39. See Byron E. Shafer, *The End of Realignment: Interpreting American Electoral Eras* (University of Wisconsin Press, 1991).

40. Hedrick Smith, *The Power Game: How Washington Works* (Random House, 1988), p. 671.

41. Nine percent of all voters were Pure Independents in 1956 and 1960. Keith et al., *Myth of the Independent Voter*, p. 51. In 1992 the same percent were Pure Independents. *1992 American National Election Study*, Center for Political Studies, University of Michigan.

42. For the "optimistic view," see Ralph M. Goldman, *Search for Consensus: The Story of the Democratic Party* (Temple University Press, 1979), pp. 366–73; Kayden and Mahe, *Party Goes On*; Larry Sabato, *The Party's Just Begun: Shaping Political Parties in America's Future* (Scott, Foresman, 1988); Joseph A. Schlesinger, "The New American Political Party," *American Political Science Review* 79 (December 1985), pp. 1152–69; David E. Price, *Bringing Back the Parties* (Congressional Quarterly Press, 1984).

43. "Party Unity Background," *Congressional Quarterly Weekly Report* 57 (December 1999), p. 2993.

44. Ibid.

45. Barbara Sinclair, "Evolution or Revolution?" in *Parties Respond*, ed. Maisel, pp. 263–85.

46. Herrnson, *Party Campaigning in the 1980s*, pp. 80–81.

CHAPTER 8

1. David B. Magleby, ed., *Election Advocacy: Soft Money and Issue Advocacy in the 2000 Congressional Elections* (Brigham Young University, Center for the Study of Elections and Democracy, 2001), monograph presented at the National Press Club, Washington, D.C., February 5, 2000, available at www.byu.edu/outsidemoney/2000general.

2. See Todd Donovan, "Campaign Spending and Activity in the 2000 Washington 2nd Congressional District Race," in David B. Magleby, ed., *Election Advocacy*, pp. 261–76. See also Drew Linzer and David Menefee-Libey, "Campaign Spending and Activity in the 2000 California Twenty-Seventh Congressional District Race," in ibid., pp. 132–47.

3. www.gallup.com/poll/releases/pr001107.asp.

4. www.cnn.com/ELECTION/2000/results/index.html.

5. Robert Coles, *The Moral Life of Children* (Atlantic Monthly Press, 1986); Robert Coles, *The Political Life of Children* (Atlantic Monthly Press, 1986).

6. Coles, *Political Life of Children*, pp. 59–60.

7. Pamela Johnston Conover, "The Influence of Group Identifications on Political Perception and Evaluation," *Journal of Politics* 46 (August 1984), pp. 760–85; Henry E. Brady and Paul M. Sniderman, "Attitude Attribution: A Group Basis for Political Reasoning," *American Political Science Review* 79 (December 1985), pp. 1061–78.

8. Shawn W. Rosenberg, "Sociology, Psychology, and the Study of Political Behavior: The Case of the Research on Political Socialization," *Journal of Politics* 47 (May 1985), pp. 715–31.

9. Russell J. Dalton, "Reassessing Parental Socialization: Indicator Unreliability Versus Generational Transfer," *American Political Science Review* 74 (June 1980), pp. 421–31.

10. Suzanne Koprince Sebert, M. Kent Jennings, and Richard G. Niemi, "The Political Texture of Peer Groups," in M. Kent Jennings and Richard G. Niemi, *The Political Character of Adolescence* (Princeton University Press, 1974), p. 246.

11. Edgar Litt, "Civic Education Norms and Political Indoctrination," *American Sociological Review* 28 (February 1963), pp. 69–75. See also Elizabeth Leonie Simpson, *Democracy's Stepchildren* (Jossey-Bass, 1971); Jennings and Niemi, *Political Character of Adolescence*; Stanley Allen Renshon,

"Personality and Family Dynamics in the Political Socialization Process," *American Journal of Political Science* 19 (February 1975), pp. 63–80; Frances Fitzgerald, *America Revised* (Atlantic–Little, Brown, 1979).

12. Kenneth Feldman and Theodore M. Newcomb, *The Impact of College on Students*, vol. 2 (Jossey-Bass, 1969), pp. 16–24, 49–56.

13. Everett C. Ladd and John Benson, "The Growth of News Polls in American Politics," in Thomas Mann and Gary Orren, eds., *Media Polls in American Politics* (Washington, D.C.: Brookings Institution, 1992), pp. 19–31.

14. Benjamin I. Page and Robert Y. Shapiro, *The Rational Public: Fifty Years of Trends in Americans' Policy Preferences* (University of Chicago Press, 1992), p. 237.

15. George J. Church, "What in the World Are We Doing?" *Time*, October 18, 1993, p. 42.

16. David Mayhew, *Congress: The Electoral Connection* (Yale University Press, 1974); Richard F. Fenno, Jr., *Home Style: House Members in Their Districts* (Little, Brown, 1978).

17. Robert S. Erikson and Kent L. Tedin, *American Public Opinion: Its Origins, Content and Impact*, 5th ed. (Allyn and Bacon, 1995), p. 279.

18. Thomas E. Mann and Raymond E. Wolfinger, "Candidates and Parties in Congressional Elections," *American Political Science Review* 74 (September 1980), pp. 617–40.

19. Erikson and Tedin, *American Public Opinion*, p. 304.

20. Neil S. Newhouse and Christine L. Matthews, "NAFTA Revisited: Most Americans Just Weren't Deeply Engaged," *Public Perspective* 5 (January/February 1994), pp. 31–32.

21. Center for Political Studies, *American National Election Studies, 1960–90* (University of Michigan, 1990).

22. www.umich.edu/~nes/nesguide/gd-index.htm and interview by Christopher Rees with Ian Stirton, Federal Election Commission Clearinghouse on Election Administration, March 5, 2001.

23. Frank R. Parker, *Black Votes Count: Political Empowerment in Mississippi After 1965* (University of North Carolina Press, 1990), p. 3.

24. Bernard Grofman and Lisa Handley, "The Impact of the Voting Rights Act on Black Representation in Southern State Legislatures," *Legislative Studies Quarterly* 16 (February 1991), pp. 111–28.

25. G. Bingham Powell, Jr., "American Voter Turnout in Comparative Perspective," *American Political Science Review* 80 (March 1986), p. 38.

26. Raymond E. Wolfinger and Steven J. Rosenstone, "The Effect of Registration Laws on Voter Turnout," *American Political Science Review* 72 (March 1978), p. 24.

27. Raymond E. Wolfinger and Steven J. Rosenstone, *Who Votes?* (Yale University Press, 1980), pp. 78, 88.

28. www.fec.gov/votregis/nvrasum.htm. See also www.essential.org/human_serve.html.

29. See Raymond E. Wolfinger and Ben Highton, "Estimating the Effects of the National Voter Registration Act of 1993," *Political Behavior* (June 1998), pp. 79–104; Raymond E. Wolfinger and Jonathan Hoffman, "Registering and Voting with Motor Voter," *PS: Political Science and Politics* (March 2001), pp. 85–92.

30. "Voter Turnout Drops in 1998 Primaries," *The New York Times*, June 30, 1998, p. A18.

31. For a discussion of the differences in the turnout between presidential and midterm elections, see James E. Campbell, "The Presidential Surge and Its Midterm Decline in Congressional Elections, 1868–1988," *Journal of Politics* 53 (May 1991), pp. 477–87.

32. David E. Rosenbaum, "Democrats Keep Solid Hold on Congress," *The New York Times*, November 9, 1988, p. A24; Louis V. Gerstner, "Next Time, Let Us Boldly Vote As No Democracy Has Before," *USA Today*, November 16, 1998, p. A15; for 2000, see www.cnn.com/2000/ALLPOLITICS/stories/12/19/election.turnout.ap.

33. Paula Ries and Anne J. Stone, eds., *The American Women, 1992–93: A Status Report* (Women's Research and Education Institute, 1992), p. 415.

34. Congressional Research Service, "Voter Turnout in the Presidential Election of 1992: The States," January 26, 1993, pp. 4–5. See also Powell, "American Voter Turnout," pp. 17–43.

35. Wolfinger and Rosenstone, *Who Votes?* p. 102.

36. Howard W. Stanley and Richard G. Niemi, *Vital Statistics on Politics, 1999–2000* (Congressional Quarterly Press, 2000), pp. 120–21; and www.cnn.com/ELECTION/2000/results/index.my.html.

37. See Angus Campbell, Philip E. Converse, Warren E. Miller, and Donald E. Stokes, *The American Voter* (Wiley, 1960). This volume is a founda-tion of modern voting analysis despite much new evidence and reinter-pretation. See also Norman H. Nie, Sidney Verba, and John R. Petrocik, *The Changing American Voter* (Harvard University Press, 1976); Ruy A. Teixeira, *Why Americans Don't Vote: Turnout Decline in the United States, 1960–1984* (Greenwood, 1987).

38. David E. Rosenbaum, "Democrats Keep Solid Hold in Congress," *The New York Times*, November 9, 1988, p. A24.

39. Austin Ranney, "Nonvoting Is Not a Social Disease," *Public Opinion*, October/November 1983, pp. 16–19.

40. Thomas Byrne Edsall, *The New Politics of Inequality* (W. W. Norton, 1984), p. 181.

41. Frances Fox Piven and Richard A. Cloward, "Prospects for Voter Registration Reform: A Report on the Experiences of the Human SERVE Campaign," *PS: Political Science and Politics* 18 (Summer 1985), pp. 582–92.

42. Wolfinger and Rosenstone, *Who Votes?* p. 109.

43. E. E. Schattschneider, *The Semisovereign People* (Dryden Press, 1975), p. 96.

44. Stephen Earl Bennett and David Resnick, "The Implications of Non-voting for Democracy in the United States," *American Journal of Political Science* 84 (August 1990), pp. 771–802.

45. Bruce E. Keith, David B. Magleby, Candice J. Nelson, Elizabeth Orr, Mark C. Westlye, and Raymond E. Wolfinger, *The Myth of the Independent Voter* (University of California Press, 1992), pp. 60–75; 2001 American National Election Study, Center for Political Studies, University of Michigan, Ann Arbor.

46. Martin P. Wattenberg, *The Rise of Candidate Centered Politics: Presidential Elections of the 1980s* (Harvard University Press, 1991), p. 1.

47. Barry Goldwater, quoted in Theodore H. White, *The Making of the President, 1964* (Athenaeum Publishers, 1965), p. 217.

48. William H. Flanigan and Nancy H. Zingale, *Political Behavior of the American Electorate*, 8th ed. (Congressional Quarterly Press, 1994), p. 173.

49. Kevin Sack, "The 2000 Campaign: The Democrats; Gore Surrogates Bluntly Question Bush's Competence," *The New York Times*, October 20, 2000, p. A27.

50. See Alton Mitchell, "The 2000 Campaign: The Credibility Issue; A Sustained G.O.P. Push to Mock Gore's Image," *The New York Times*, October 15, 2000, pp. 1–28; Melinda Henneberger, "The 2000 Campaign: The Gun Lobby; Rallying Voters and Relishing a Leading Role," *The New York Times*, November 3, 2000, p. A25.

51. www.cnn.com/ELECTION/2000/results/index.epolls.html.

52. J. Merrill Shanks and Warren E. Miller, "Policy Direction and Performance Evaluation: Complementary Explanations of the Reagan Elections," *British Journal of Political Science* 20 (1990), pp. 143–235; Warren E. Miller and J. Merrill Shanks, "Policy Direction and Performance Evaluation: Comparing George Bush's Victory with Those of Ronald Reagan in 1980 and 1984," paper presented at the American Political Science Association Annual Meeting, Atlanta, August 31–September 2, 1989.

53. Amihai Glazer, "The Strategy of Candidate Ambiguity," *American Political Science Review* 84 (March 1990), pp. 237–41.

54. Robert S. Erikson and David W. Romero, "Candidate Equilibrium and the Behavioral Model of the Vote," *American Political Science Review* 84 (December 1990), p. 1122.

55. Morris P. Fiorina, *Retrospective Voting in American National Elections* (Yale University Press, 1981).

56. www.cnn.com/ELECTION/2000/results/index.epolls.html.

57. Gerald H. Kramer, "Short-Term Fluctuations in U.S. Voting Behavior, 1896–1964," *American Political Science Review* 65 (March 1971), pp. 131–43. See also Edward R. Tufte, "Determinants of the Outcomes of Midterm Congressional Elections," *American Political Science Review* 69 (September 1975), pp. 812–26.

58. John R. Hibbing and John R. Alford, "The Educational Impact of Economic Conditions: Who Is Held Responsible?" *American Journal of Political Science* 25 (August 1981), pp. 423–39; Morris P. Fiorina, "Who Is Held Responsible? Further Evidence on the Hibbing-Alford Thesis," *American Journal of Political Science* (February 1983), pp. 158–64.

59. Robert M. Stein, "Economic Voting for Governor and U.S. Senator: The Electoral Consequences of Federalism," *Journal of Politics* 52 (February 1990), pp. 29–53.

CHAPTER 9

1. *1994 Census of Governments* (Government Printing Office, 1995), vol. 1, no. 2, p. 1.

2. Washington voters enacted term limits in 1992 after defeating them in 1991.

3. In the 1992 and 1994 National Election Studies, 77–78 percent of Americans favored term limits. Center for Political Studies, University of Michigan.

4. *U.S. Term Limits Inc. v Thornton*, 514 U. S. 799 (1995).

5. For an insightful examination of electoral rules, see Bernard Grofman and Arend Lijphart, eds., *Electoral Laws and Their Political Consequences* (Agathon Press, 1986).

6. Arend Lijphart, "The Political Consequences of Electoral Laws, 1945–85," *American Political Science Review* 84 (June 1990), pp. 481–95.

7. One of Al Gore's electors abstained, reducing his vote from 267 to 266. www.cnn.com/2001/ALLPOLITICS/stories/01/06/electoral.vote/index.html.

8. Dany M. Adkison and Christopher Elliott, "The Electoral College: A Misunderstood Institution," *PS: Political Science and Politics* 30 (March 1997), pp. 77–80.

9. George Rabinowitz and Stuart Elaine MacDonald, "The Power of the States in U.S. Presidential Elections," *American Political Science Review* 80 (March 1986), pp. 65–87.

10. See, as examples, David Mayhew, *Congress: The Electoral Connection* (Yale University Press, 1974); Richard F. Fenno, Jr., *Home Style: House Members in Their Districts* (Little, Brown, 1978); James E. Campbell, "The Return of Incumbents: The Nature of Incumbency Advantage," *Western Political Quarterly* 36 (September 1983), pp. 434–44.

11. Gary King and Andrew Gelman, "Systemic Consequences of Incumbency Advantage in U.S. House Elections," *American Journal of Political Science* 35 (February 1991), pp. 110–37.

12. See Gary C. Jacobson, *The Politics of Congressional Elections*, 4th ed. (Longman, 1997), chap. 6; Alan I. Abramowitz, "Economic Conditions, Presidential Popularity, and Voting Behavior in Midterm Congressional Elections," *Journal of Politics* (February 1985), p. 130.

13. See Edward R. Tufte, *Political Control of the Economy* (Princeton University Press, 1978); see also his "Determinants of the Outcomes of Midterm Congressional Elections," *American Political Science Review* 69 (1975), pp. 812–26. For a more recent discussion of the same subject, see Jacobson, *Politics of Congressional Elections*, pp. 123–78.

14. Alan I. Abramowitz and Jeffrey A. Segal, "Determinants of the Outcomes of U.S. Senate Elections," *Journal of Politics* 48 (1986), pp. 433–39.

15. This includes the postelection switch of Alabama Senator Richard Shelby to the Republican party.

16. Linda L. Fowler and Robert D. McClure, *Political Ambition: Who Decides to Run for Congress* (Yale University Press, 1989); David T. Canon, "Political Conditions and Experienced Challengers in Congressional Elections, 1972–1984," paper presented at the American Political Science Association Annual Meeting, New Orleans, August 29–September 1, 1985.

17. Keith Krehbiel and John R. Wright, "The Incumbency Effect in Congressional Elections: A Test of Two Explanations," *American Journal of Political Science* 27 (February 1983), p. 140.

18. Roll Call, "Roll Call Casualty List," *Roll Call Politics*, November 5, 1998, p. 15; "Senate, House, Gubernatorial Results," *Congressional Quarterly Weekly Report*, November 11, 2000, pp. 2694–2703.

19. "Financial Activity of Senate and House General Election Campaigns," Federal Election Commission: ftp.fec.gov/fec.

20. D. Cover, "One Good Term Deserves Another: The Advantages of Incumbency in Congressional Elections," *American Journal of Political Science* 21 (August 1977), pp. 523–42; Morris P. Fiorina, *Congress: Keystone of the Washington Establishment* (Yale University Press, 1978); Mayhew, *Congress*, pp. 52–53.

21. Mayhew, *Congress*, p. 61; Richard F. Fenno, Jr., *Congressmen in Committees* (Little, Brown, 1973); Steven S. Smith and Christopher J. Deering, *Committees in Congress*, 3d ed. (Congressional Quarterly Press, 1997).

22. Candice J. Nelson, "Campaign Finance in Presidential and Congressional Elections," *Political Science Teacher* (Summer 1988), p. 6.

23. Jonathan S. Krasno, *Challengers, Competition, and Reelection: Comparing Senate and House Elections* (Yale University Press, 1994).

24. Alan I. Abramowitz, "Explaining Senate Election Outcomes," *American Political Science Review* 82 (June 1988), pp. 385–403.

25. David B. Magleby, "More Bang for the Buck: Campaign Spending in Small State U.S. Senate Elections," paper presented at the Western Political Science Association Annual Meeting, Salt Lake City, March 30–April 1, 1989.

26. The Green Papers, "2000 Primary and Caucus Results," at www.thegreenpapers.com/PCC/Tabul.html.

27. Paul T. David and James W. Caesar, *Proportional Representation in Presidential Nominating Politics* (University Press of Virginia, 1980).

28. For a discussion of the 1996 primary rules, see Rhodes Cook, "GOP's Rules Favor Dole, If He Doesn't Stumble," *Congressional Quarterly Weekly Report*, January 27, 1996, pp. 228–31.

29. The descriptions of these types of primaries are drawn from James W. Davis, *Presidential Primaries*, rev. ed. (Greenwood Press, 1984), chap. 3. See pp. 56–63 for specifics on each state (and Puerto Rico). This material is used with the permission of the publisher.

30. *The Book of the States, 2000–2001* (Council of State Governments, 2000), pp. 164–65.

31. David B. Magleby, *Getting Inside the Outside Campaign: Issue Advocacy in the 2000 Presidential Primaries* (Center for the Study of Elections and Democracy, Brigham Young University, 2000).

32. The viewership of conventions has declined as the amount of time devoted to conventions dropped. In 1988, Democrats averaged 27.1 million viewers and Republicans 24.5 million. By 1996 viewership for the Democrats was 18 million viewers on average and Republicans averaged 16.6 million viewers. See John Carmody, "The TV Column," *The Washington Post*, September 2, 1996, p. D4. In 2000, Democrats only averaged 20.6 million viewers and Republicans 19.2 million. See Don Aucoin, "Democrats Hold TV Ratings Edge," *The Boston Globe*, August 19, 2000, p. F3.

33. Stephen J. Wayne, *The Road to the White House, 2000: The Politics of Presidential Elections* (St. Martin's Press, 2000), chap. 5.

34. Jeff Fishel, *Presidents and Promises* (Congressional Quarterly Press, 1984).

35. CNN, "Burden of Proof," August 9, 2000.

36. www.ballot_access.org/2000/status.html.

37. Jules Witcover uses the image of a marathon to describe the 1976 presidential campaign in *Marathon: The Pursuit of the Presidency, 1972–1976* (Viking, 1977).

38. Sidney Kraus, *The Great Debates: Kennedy vs Nixon, 1960* (Indiana University Press, 1962). See also Myles Martel, *Political Campaign Debates* (Longman, 1983).

39. Tom Shales, "Round 1: Candidates with Their Hats, But Not Their Hearts, in the Ring," *The Washington Post*, October 4, 2000, p. C1.

40. www.debates.org/pages/history.html.

41. Robert S. Erikson, "Economic Conditions and the Presidential Vote," *American Political Science Review* 83 (June 1989), pp. 567–75. Class-based voting has also become more important. See Robert S. Erikson, Thomas O. Lancaster, and David W. Romers, "Group Components of the Presidential Vote, 1952–1984," *Journal of Politics* 51 (May 1989), pp. 337–46.

42. David B. Magleby, ed., *Election Advocacy: Soft Money and Issue Advocacy in the 2000 Congressional Elections* (Center for the Study of Elections and Democracy, Brigham Young University, 2001) www.byu.edu/outsidemoney/2000general.

43. David B. Magleby and Candice J. Nelson, *The Money Chase: Congressional Campaign Finance Reform* (Brookings Institution, 1990), pp. 13–14.

44. *Buckley v Valeo*, 424 US 1 (1976).

45. For a discussion of recent legislation, see Herbert E. Alexander and Monica Bauer, *Financing the 1988 Election* (Westview, 1991); Frank J. Sorauf, *Money in American Elections* (Scott, Foresman, 1988).

46. Including federal funding, Federal Election Commission reports show that George W. Bush raised just over $193 million. "2000 Presidential Race: Total Raised and Spent," Center for Responsive Politics, 2001, at www.opensecrets.org/2000elect/index/AllCands.htm, February 12, 2001.

47. Federal Election Commission, Public Disclosure Office, interview by author, January 9, 2001.

48. Beth Donovan, "Parties Turned Soft Money Law into Hard and Fast Spending," *Congressional Quarterly Weekly Report*, May 15, 1993, pp. 1196–97; David E. Rosenbaum, "In Political Money Game, the Year of Big Loopholes," *The New York Times*, December 26, 1996, p. A1 fecwebl.fec.gov/press/01120/partyfunds.htm.

49. See Joseph Pika, "Campaign Spending and Activity in the 2000 Delaware U.S. Senate Race," in Magleby, ed., *Election Advocacy*, pp. 51–61.

50. Ibid.

51. Ibid.

52. Ibid.

53. See David B. Magleby, *Dictum Without Data: The Myth of Issue Advocacy and Party Building* (Center for the Study of Elections and Democracy, Brigham Young University, 2000), available on the web at www.byu.edu/outsidemoney/dictum.

54. Rick Hampson, "Former Banker Was Big Spender," *USA Today*, November 9, 2000, p. A9.

55. Sorauf, *Money in American Elections*, pp. 64–65.

56. Federal Election Commission, "Congressional Financial Activity Soars for 2000," press release, January 9, 2001.

57. Federal Election Commission: ftp.fec.gov/fec.

58. See Robert Hunter, ed., *Electing the President: A Program for Reform, Final Report of the Commission on National Election* (Center for Strategic and International Studies, 1986); James L. Sundquist, *Constitutional Reform* (Brookings Institution, 1986); Edward N. Kearny, "Presidential Nominations and Representative Democracy: Proposals for Change," *Presidential Studies Quarterly* 14 (Summer 1984), pp. 348–56.

59. Barbara Norrander and Greg W. Smith, "Type of Contest, Candidate Strategy, and Turnout in Presidential Primaries," *American Politics Quarterly* 13 (January 1985), p. 28.

60. John G. Geer, "Voting in Presidential Primaries," paper presented at the American Political Science Association Annual Meeting, Washington, D.C., September 1984. See also Albert R. Hunt, "The Media and Presidential Campaigns," in A. James Reichley, ed., *Elections American Style* (Brookings Institution, 1987), pp. 52–74.

61. Ben White, "After Drama Left the Primaries, Voter Turnout Fell Dramatically," *The Washington Post*, September 1, 2000, p. A5.

62. George S. McGovern, "Considerations on Our Political Processes," *Presidential Studies Quarterly* 14 (Summer 1984), pp. 341–47.

63. Mark Sandalow, "Gore, Bush Sweep Six Southern Primaries–Nominations Cinched," *The San Francisco Chronicle*, March 15, 2000, p. A1.

64. *A National Agenda for the Eighties*, Report of the President's Commission for a National Agenda for the Eighties (Government Printing Office, 1980), p. 97, proposes holding only four presidential primaries, scheduled about one month apart.

65. Nelson Polsby, *Consequences of Party Reform* (Oxford University Press, 1983), p. 118.

66. Thomas E. Cronin and Robert Loevy, "The Case for a National Primary Convention Plan," *Public Opinion*, December 1982/January 1983, pp. 50–53.

67. Neal R. Peirce and Lawrence Longley, *The People's President: The Electoral College in American History and the Direct-Vote Alternative*, 2d ed. (Yale University Press, 1981), describes and advocates the direct-vote alternative. Nelson W. Polsby and Aaron B. Wildavsky, *Presidential Elections: Contemporary Strategies of American Politics*, 9th ed. (Chatham House, 1995), favors the present system.

CHAPTER 10

1. Howard Kurtz, "Errors Plagued Election Night Polling Service: VNS Report Also Faults Networks in Florida Blunder," *The Washington Post*, December 22, 2000, p. A1.

2. Marvin Kalb, "Financial Pressure Doomed Networks on Election Night," *Deseret News*, December 3, 2000, p. AA7.

3. www.cnn.com/2000/ALLPOLITICS/stories/11/16/tauzin.networks/index.htm.

4. Pew Research Center for the People and the Press, "Media Seen as Fair, But Tilting to Gore," press release, October 15, 2000.

5. Pew Research Center for the People and the Press, "Internet News Takes Off," press release, June 8, 1998, p. 1.

6. James Fallows, *Breaking the News: How the Media Undermine American Democracy* (Pantheon Books, 1996), p. 3.

7. Paul Starobin, "Heeding the Call," *National Journal*, November 30, 1996, pp. 2584–89.

8. William Rivers, *The Other Government* (Universe Books, 1982); Douglas Cater, *The Fourth Branch of Government* (Houghton Mifflin, 1959); Dom Bonafede, "The Washington Press: An Interpreter or a Participant in Policy Making?" *National Journal*, April 24, 1982, pp. 716–21; Michael Ledeen, "Learning to Say 'No' to the Press," *Public Interest* 73 (Fall 1983), p. 113.

9. Leslie G. Moeller, "The Big Four: Mass Media Actualities and Expectations," in *Beyond Media: New Approaches to Mass Communication*, ed. Richard W. Budd and Brent D. Ruben (Transaction Books, 1988), p. 15.

10. Andrew Kohut, "Internet Users Are on the Rise; But Public Affairs Interest Isn't," *Columbia Journalism Review*, January/February 2000, p. 68. One service that e-mails customized news and reminders to subscribers is infobeat.com.

11. U. S. Bureau of the Census, *Statistical Abstract of the United States, 1999* (Government Printing Office, 1999) Tables 910, 920.

12. David B. Magleby, "Direct Legislation in the American States," in David Butler and Austin Ranney, eds., *Referendums Around the World: The Growing Use of Direct Democracy* (AEI Press, 1994), pp. 218–57.

13. "Media and Evaluation," *The Gallup Organization 2000*, at www.gallup.com/poll/indicators/indmedia2.asp.

14. See Ray Hiebert, Donald Ungarait, and Thomas Bohn, *Mass Media VI* (Longman, 1991), chap. 11.

15. U. S. Bureau of the Census, *Statistical Abstract of the United States, 2000* (Government Printing Office, 2000) Table 932.

16. James Flanigan, "Newspapers Aren't Dying, They're Just Turning a Page," *Los Angeles Times*, March 19, 2000, p. C1.

17. Darrell West, *The Rise and Fall of the Media Establishment* (Bedford/St. Martin's Press, 2001).

18. Inktomi, press release, "Web Surpasses One Billion Documents," at www.inktomi.com/new/press/billion.html, January 18, 2000.

19. Kohut, "Internet Users Are on the Rise," p. 68.

20. J. Scott Orr, Newhouse News Service, "Internet Becomes New Source of Untapped Campaign Cash," *The Times-Picayune*, April 5, 2000, p. A10.

21. See Robert A. Rutland, *Newsmongers: Journalism in the Life of the Nation, 1690–1972* (Dial Press, 1973).

22. Quoted in Frank Luther Mott, *American Journalism*, 3d ed. (Macmillan, 1962), p. 412.

23. During the 1930s, more than one thousand speeches were made by members of Congress on one network alone. See Edward W. Chester, *Radio, Television and American Politics* (Sheed and Ward, 1969), p. 62.

24. Frances Perkins, quoted in James MacGregor Burns, *Roosevelt: The Lion and the Fox* (Harcourt Brace, 1956), p. 205.

25. www.gannett.com/map/gan/007.htm.

26. "California; Southland Focus; Tribune Gets Antitrust Approval in *Times* Deal," *The Los Angeles Times*, April 7, 2000, p. C2.

27. Stephanie Storm, "Mergers for Year Approach Record," *The New York Times*, October 31, 1996, p. A1.

28. Geraldine Fabrikant, "The Media Business," *The New York Times*, October 11, 1996, p. D2.

29. Saul Hansell, "Media Megadeal: The Overview," *The New York Times*, January 11, 2000, p. A1.

30. Ben H. Bagdikian, *The Media Monopoly* (Beacon Press, 1983).

31. See Doris A. Graber, *Mass Media and American Politics*, 5th ed. (Congressional Quarterly Press, 1997); Gina M. Garramone and Charles K. Atkin, "Mass Communication and Political Socialization: Specifying the Effects," *Public Opinion Quarterly* 50 (Spring 1986), pp. 76–86.

32. Shanto Iyengar and Donald R. Kinder, *News That Matters* (University of Chicago Press, 1987).

33. Steven J. Simmons, *The Fairness Doctrine and the Media* (University of California Press, 1978).

34. *Christian Science Monitor*, October 17, 2000, p. 10.

35. Alliance for Better Campaigns, *The Political Standard*, Vol. 4, no. 1, p. 6.

36. Harvey G. Zeidenstein, "News Media Perception of White House News Management," *Presidential Studies Quarterly* 24 (Summer 1984), pp. 391–98.

37. See, for example, Jack Dennis, "Preadult Learning of Political Independence: Media and Family Communications Effects," *Communication Research* 13 (July 1987), pp. 401–33; Olive Stevens, *Children Talking Politics* (Martin Robertson, 1982).

38. Elihu Katz and Paul Lazarsfeld, *Personal Influence: The Part Played by People in the Flow of Mass Communications* (Free Press, 1955).

39. See the classic, Angus Campbell, Philip E. Converse, Warren E. Miller, and Donald E. Stokes, *The American Voter* (Wiley, 1960).

40. See other classic works: Paul Lazarsfeld, Bernard Berelson, and Hazel Gaudet, *The People's Choice: How the Voter Makes Up His Mind in a Presidential Campaign*, 3d ed. (Columbia University Press, 1968); Bernard

Berelson, Paul Lazarsfeld, and William McPhee, *Voting: A Study of Opinion Formation in a Presidential Campaign* (University of Chicago Press, 1954).

41. Pew Research Center for the People and the Press, "Scandal Reporting Faulted for Bias and Inaccuracy: Popular Policies and Unpopular Press Lift Clinton Ratings," press release, February 6, 1998, p. 6.

42. www.gallup.com/poll-archives/980926.htm.

43. Stuart Oskamp, ed., *Television as a Social Issue* (Sage Publications, 1988); James W. Carey, ed., *Media, Myths, and Narratives: Television and the Press* (Sage Publications, 1988).

44. Doris A. Graber, *Processing the News: How People Tame the Information Tide*, 2d ed. (Longman, 1988), pp. 107–13.

45. Times Mirror Center for the People and the Press, "Times Mirror News Interest Index," press releases, January 16 and February 28, 1992.

46. John K. Robinson and Mark R. Levy, eds., *The Main Source: Learning from Television News* (Sage Publications, 1986).

47. Graber, *Processing the News*, p. 115.

48. Rush Limbaugh, *See, I Told You So* (Pocket Books, 1993), p. 326.

49. See Nelson Polsby, *Consequences of Party Reform* (Oxford University Press, 1983), pp. 142–46. See also Stanley Rothman and S. Robert Lichter, "Media and Business Elites: Two Classes in Conflict!" *Public Interest* 69 (Fall 1982), pp. 119–25.

50. Michael Parenti, *Inventing Reality: The Politics of the Mass Media* (St. Martin's Press, 1986), p. 35.

51. Rick Lyman, "Multimedia Deal: The History; 2 Commanding Publishers, 2 Powerful Empires," *The New York Times*, March 14, 2000, p. C16.

52. David Broder, "Beware of the 'Insider' Syndrome: Why Newsmakers and News Reporters Shouldn't Get Too Cozy," *The Washington Post*, December 4, 1988, p. A21; see also Broder, "Thin-Skinned Journalists," *The Washington Post*, January 11, 1989, p. A21.

53. Robert Lichter, "Consistently Liberal: But Does It Matter?" *Forbes Media Critic* 4 (Fall 1996), pp. 26–39. These data are essentially the same as data reported a decade earlier. See David Shaw, "The Times Poll: Public and Press—Two Viewpoints," *Los Angeles Times*, August 11, 1985, pt. 1, p. 1.

54. Daniel P. Moynihan, "The Presidency and the Press," *Commentary* 51 (March 1971), p. 43.

55. S. Robert Lichter, Stanley Rothman, and Linda S. Lichter, *The Media Elite* (Adler and Adler, 1986).

56. See Thomas Patterson, *Out of Order* (Knopf, 1993); Paul Weaver, *News and the Culture of Lying* (Free Press, 1993); Anthony Munro, "Yet Another Conspiracy Theory," *Columbia Journalism Review* 33 (November 1994), p. 71.

57. Among others researching this topic, see Doris A. Graber, "Say It with Pictures: The Impact of Audio-Visual News on Public Opinion Formation," paper presented at the Midwest Political Science Association Annual Meeting, Chicago, April 1987; Benjamin I. Page, Robert Y. Shapiro, and Glenn R. Dempsey, "What Moves Public Opinion?" *American Political Science Review* 76 (March 1987), pp. 23–43.

58. Shanto Iyengar, Mark D. Peters, and Donald R. Kinder, "Experimental Demonstrations of the 'Not-So-Minimal' Consequences of Television News Programs," *American Political Science Review* 76 (December 1982), pp. 848–58.

59. Ibid.; Maxwell E. McCombs and Donald L. Shaw, "The Agenda-Setting Function of the Mass Media," *Public Opinion Quarterly* 36 (1972), pp. 176–87; Maxwell E. McCombs and Sheldon Gilbert, "News Influence on Our Pictures of the World," in Jennings Bryant and Dolf Gillman, eds., *Perspectives on Media Effects* (Lawrence Erlbaum, 1986), pp. 1–15; Iyengar and Kinder, *News That Matters*.

60. Quoted in Robinson and Sheehan, *Over the Wire and on TV*, p. xiii.

61. David B. Magleby, *Direct Legislation: Voting on Ballot Propositions in the United States* (Johns Hopkins University Press, 1984).

62. Peter Marks, "Costly Prescriptions: One Issue That Fits All," *The New York Times*, October 1, 2000, p. A22.

63. Paul T. David, Ralph M. Goldman, and Richard C. Bain, *The Politics of the National Party Conventions* (Brookings Institution, 1960), pp. 300–301.

64. Richard Davis, *The Press and American Politics: The New Mediator*, 2d ed. (Prentice Hall, 1996), p. 279.

65. Frank I. Lutz, *Candidates, Consultants, and Campaigns* (Basil Blackwell, 1988), chap. 7.

66. Larry J. Sabato, *The Rise of Political Consultants* (Basic Books, 1981).

67. Tina Cassidy, "Tipper Marches to Own Beat on Campaign Trail," *The Boston Globe*, July 11, 2000, p. C1.

68. See, in general, ibid.; James David Barber, *The Pulse of Politics: Electing Presidents in the Media Age* (Norton, 1980); Fred Barnes, "The Myth of Political Consultants," *New Republic*, June 16, 1986, p. 16.

69. Quoted in Sabato, *Rise of Political Consultants*, p. 144.

70. Thomas E. Patterson, *The Mass Media Election: How Americans Choose Their President* (Praeger, 1980), chap. 12.

71. John H. Aldrich, *Before the Convention* (University of Chicago Press, 1980), p. 65. This book is a study of candidates' choices and strategies. See also Patterson, *Mass Media Election*.

72. John Foley et al., *Nominating a President: The Process and the Press* (Praeger, 1980), p. 39. For the press's treatment of incumbents, see James Glen Stovall, "Incumbency and News Coverage of the 1980 Presidential Election Campaign," *Western Political Quarterly* 37 (December 1984), p. 621.

73. Priscilla Southwell, "Voter Turnout in the 1986 Congressional Elections: The Media as Demobilizer?" *American Politics Quarterly* 19 (January 1991), pp. 96–108.

74. William Glaberson, "A New Press Role: Solving Problems," *The New York Times*, October 3, 1994, p. D6.

75. Patterson, *Mass Media Election*, pp. 115–17.

76. Raymond Wolfinger and Peter Linguiti, "Tuning In and Tuning Out," *Public Opinion* 4 (February/March 1981), pp. 56–60.

77. Lewis Wolfson, *The Untapped Power of the Press* (Praeger, 1985), p. 79.

78. Stephen Hess, *The Government/Press Connection* (Brookings Institution, 1984), p. 106.

79. Lloyd Cutler, "Foreign Policy on Deadline," *Foreign Policy* 56 (Fall 1984), p. 114.

80. Michael B. Grossman and Martha Joynt Kumar, *Portraying the President* (Johns Hopkins University Press, 1981), pp. 255–63; Fredric T. Smoller, *The Six O'Clock Presidency: A Theory of Presidential Press Relations in the Age of Television* (Praeger, 1990), pp. 31–49.

81. Michael J. Robinson and Kevin R. Appel, "Network News Coverage of Congress," *Political Science Quarterly* 94 (Fall 1979), pp. 407–18; Charles Tidmarch and John C. Pitney, Jr., "Covering Congress," *Polity* 17 (Spring 1984), pp. 463–83.

82. Susan Heilmann Miller, "News Coverage of Congress: The Search for the Ultimate Spokesperson," *Journalism Quarterly* 54 (Autumn 1977), pp. 459–65.

83. See Stephen Hess, *Live from Capitol Hill: Studies of Congress and the Media* (Brookings Institution, 1991), pp. 102–10.

84. Richard Davis, "Whither the Congress and the Supreme Court? The Television News Portrayal of American National Government," *Television Quarterly* 22 (1987), pp. 55–63.

85. For a discussion of the Supreme Court and public opinion, see Thomas R. Marshall, *Public Opinion and the Supreme Court* (Unwin Hyman, 1989); Gregory Caldiera, "Neither the Purse nor the Sword: Dynamics of Public Confidence in the Supreme Court," *American Political Science Review* 80 (December 1986), pp. 1209–28.

86. For a discussion of the relationship between the Supreme Court and the press, see Richard Davis, "Lifting the Shroud: News Media Portrayal of the U.S. Supreme Court," *Communications and the Law* 9 (October 1987), pp. 43–58; Elliot E. Slotnick, "Media Coverage of Supreme Court Decision Making: Problems and Prospects," *Judicature*, October/November 1991, pp. 128–42.

87. Times Mirror Center, "Campaign '92," January 16, 1992.

88. Quoted in Herbert Schmertz, "The Making of the Presidency," *Presidential Studies Quarterly* 16 (Winter 1986), p. 25.

CHAPTER 11

1. From a poll by Opinion Dynamics, Inc., for Fox News Channel, cited in *National Journal*, September 20, 1998, p. 1856.

2. John R. Hibbing and Elizabeth Theiss-Morse, *Congress as Public Enemy: Public Attitudes Toward American Political Institutions* (Cambridge University Press, 1995), p. 147.

3. Richard F. Fenno, Jr., *Home Style: House Members in Their Districts* (Little, Brown, 1978), p. 168.

4. For an examination of this practice, see Michael Lyons and Peter F. Galderisi, "Incumbency, Reapportionment, and U.S. House Redistricting," *Political Research Quarterly* (December 1995), pp. 857–71.

5. *Davis v Bandemer*, 478 US 109 (1986).

6. *Baker v Carr*, 369 US 186 (1962).

7. See *Wesberry v Sanders*, 376 US 1 (1964).

8. *Shaw v Reno*, 509 US 630 (1993).

9. *Miller v Johnson*, 512 US 622 (1995); *Bush v Vera*, 517 US 952 (1996).

10. Frances E. Lee and Bruce I. Oppenheimer, *Sizing Up the Senate: The Unequal Consequences of Equal Representation* (University of Chicago Press, 1999).

11. Daniel Patrick Moynihan, introduction to Monica Friar and Herman Leonard, *The Federal Budget and the States: Fiscal Year 1994* (Kennedy School of Government, 1994).

12. For a brief discussion of the speakership in the 1990s, see Barbara Sinclair, "House Majority Party Leadership in an Era of Legislative Constraint," in Roger H. Davidson, ed., *The Postreform Congress* (St. Martin's Press, 1992), pp. 91–111. See also Ronald M. Peters, Jr., ed., *The Speaker: Leadership in the U.S. House of Representatives* (Congressional Quarterly Press, 1995).

13. Quoted in Adam Clymer, "Firebrand Who Got Singed Says Being Speaker Suffices," *The New York Times*, January 22, 1996, p. 1.

14. Newt Gingrich, *To Renew America* (HarperCollins, 1995) and *Lessons Learned the Hard Way* (HarperCollins, 1998).

15. Quoted in Greg Hitt, "Hastert Is Tapped as House Speaker to Fill Vacuum Created by Livingston," *The Wall Street Journal*, December 21, 1998, p. A20.

16. Richard E. Cohen and David Baumann, "Speaking Up for Hastert," *National Journal*, November 13, 1999, pp. 3298–3303.

17. For insightful memoirs by three recently retired U.S. Senators, see Bill Bradley, *Time Present, Time Past: A Memoir* (Knopf, 1996); Warren B. Rudman, *Combat: Twelve Years in the U.S. Senate* (Random House, 1996); and Alan K. Simpson, *Right in the Old Kazoo: A Lifetime of Scrapping with the Press* (Morrow, 1997). See also the reflections of Joseph I. Lieberman, *In Praise of Public Life* (Simon and Schuster, 2000), and Adam Clymer, *Edward M. Kennedy: A Biography* (William Morrow, 1999).

18. Barbara Sinclair, "Unorthodox Lawmaking in the Individualist Senate," *Extensions: A Journal of the Carl Albert Congressional Research and Studies Center* (Fall 1997), p. 11. See also Sinclair, *Unorthodox Lawmaking: New Legislative Processes in the U.S. Congress* (Congressional Quarterly Press, 1997), chap. 3.

19. Norman J. Ornstein, "Prima Donna Senate," *The New York Times*, September 4, 1997, p. A17. See also Carroll J. Doherty, "Senate Caught in the Grip of Its Own 'Holds' System," *Congressional Quarterly Weekly Report*, August 15, 1998, pp. 2241–43.

20. For an insightful set of essays on Senate leadership, see Richard A. Baker and Roger H. Davidson, eds., *First Among Equals: Outstanding Senate Leaders of the Twentieth Century* (Congressional Quarterly Press, 1991).

21. Nicol Rae and Colton Campbell, "The Changing Role of Political Parties in the U.S. Senate in the 104th and 105th Congresses," paper presented at the American Political Science Association Annual Meeting, Boston, September 3–6, 1998, p. 21.

22. Sarah A. Binder and Steven S. Smith, *Politics or Principles? Filibustering in the United States Senate* (Brookings Institution, 1997).

23. David Baumann, "The Collapse of the Senate," *National Journal*, June 3, 2000, p. 1759.

24. For a criticism of recent confirmation hearings and various reform proposals, see Stephen L. Carter, *The Confirmation Mess: Cleaning Up the Federal Appointments Process* (Basic Books, 1994). See also G. Calvin Mackenzie and Robert Shogan, eds., *Obstacle Course: The Report of the Twentieth Century Fund Task Force on the Presidential Appointment Process* (Twentieth Century Fund Press, 1996).

25. Norman Ornstein, Thomas Mann, and Michael Malbin, *Vital Statistics on Congress, 1999–2000* (AEI Press, 2000), p. 129.

26. Robert C. Byrd (D.-W.Va.), quoted in David J. Vogler, *The Politics of Congress* (Allyn and Bacon, 1983), p. 77.

27. See the case studies in Richard F. Fenno, Jr., *Senators on the Campaign Trail: The Politics of Representation* (University of Oklahoma Press, 1996), p. 331. See also Benjamin Bishin, "Constituency Influence in Congress: Does Subconstituency Matter?" *Legislative Studies Quarterly* (August 2000), pp. 389–415.

28. www.senate.gov, www.house.gov. See also thomas.loc.gov.

29. See a fascinating comparison of two Rhodes Scholars, one a liberal from Maryland and the other a conservative from Indiana, and what has shaped their votes over several terms in the U.S. Senate: Karl A. Lamb, *Reasonable Disagreement: Two U.S. Senators and the Choices They Make* (Garland, 1998).

30. See Richard Morrin, "Tuned Out, Turned Off: Millions of Americans Know Little About How Their Government Works," *The Washington Post National Weekly Edition*, February 5–11, 1996, pp. 6–7.

31. A 1999 CBS survey reported in "Poll Readings," *National Journal*, October 9, 1999, p. 2917.

32. Bradley, *Time Present, Time Past*, chap. 4.

33. Mary Lynn F. Jones, "For Top Hill Aides, Raising Money Is Part of the Job," *The Hill*, May 24, 2000, pp. 1, 30.

34. Jackie Clames, "House Divided: Why Congress Hews to the Party Line on Impeachment," *The Wall Street Journal*, December 16, 1998, p. 1.

35. *Congressional Quarterly Weekly*, January 6, 2001.

36. For reflections from a leading member of the Black Caucus, see Ronald V. Dellums, *Lying Down with the Lions* (Beacon, 2000).

37. Ornstein et al., *Vital Statistics on Congress, 1999–2000*, pp. 103–106.

38. Lieberman, *In Praise of Public Life*, p. 109.

39. Constance Ewing Cook, *Lobbying for Higher Education* (Vanderbilt University Press, 1998). See, too, Ken Kolman, *Outside Lobbying* (Princeton University Press, 1998).

40. Lieberman, *In Praise of Public Life*, p. 118.

41. Carroll J. Doherty, "Clinton's Big Comeback Shown in Vote Score," *Congressional Quarterly Weekly Report*, December 21, 1996, pp. 3427–30.

42. See Jeffrey S. Peake, "Presidential Agenda Setting in Foreign Policy," paper presented at the American Political Science Association Annual Meeting, Boston, September 3–6, 1998.

43. "Resumé of Congressional Activity," 105th Congress, *Congressional Record, Daily Digest*, January 19, 1999, p. D29.

44. Editorial, *Kansas City Star*, June 25, 2000, p. B10.

45. Sinclair, *Unorthodox Lawmaking*, p. 58. For a defense of riders as a means to cut wasteful spending, see Slade Gorton and Larry E. Craig, "Congressional Riders Rein in Excesses," *Walla Walla Union-Bulletin*, July 31, 1998, p. 4.

46. See David W. Brady and Craig Volden, *Revolving Gridlock: Politics and Policy from Carter to Clinton* (Westview Press, 1998). For two case studies on the way bills get treated in Congress, see Janet M. Martin, *Lessons from the Hill: The Legislative Journey of an Education Program* (St. Martin's Press, 1993); Steven Waldman, *The Bill—How Legislation Really Becomes Law: A Case Study of the National Service Bill* (Penguin, 1996).

47. Woodrow Wilson, *Congressional Government* (Houghton, Mifflin, 1885; reprint, Johns Hopkins University Press, 1981), p. 69.

48. Christopher J. Deering and Steven S. Smith, *Committees in Congress*, 3d ed. (Congressional Quarterly Press, 1997).

49. Karen Foerstel, "Chairman's Term Limits Already Shaking Up House," *Congressional Quarterly Weekly*, March 24, 2000, p. 628.

50. Joel D. Aberbach, *Keeping a Watchful Eye: The Politics of Congressional Oversight* (Brookings Institution, 1990).

51. "Resumé of Congressional Activity, 105th Congress," *Congressional Record*, Daily Digest, January 19, 1999, p. D29.

52. For an example of intense bargaining on a major defense appropriation bill, see Pat Towell, "Camouflage-Green Defense Bill Poised for President's Signature," *Congressional Quarterly Weekly*, July 22, 2000, pp. 1819–22.

53. William S. Cohen, "Why I Am Leaving," *The Washington Post National Weekly Edition*, January 28–February 4, 1996, p. 29. Four years later, as secretary of defense, Cohen allowed that he enjoyed generally positive relations with members of Congress except when it came to their resistance to closing more military bases. Quoted in "The Hill Interview," *The Hill*, May 17, 2000, p. 41.

54. James Madison, *The Federalist*, No. 57, in *The Federalist*, ed. Jacob E. Cooke (Meridian Books, 1961), p. 385.

55. See Kenny J. Whitby, *The Color of Representation: Congressional Behavior and Black Interests* (University of Michigan Press, 1998); Barbara Mikulski, Kay Bailey Hutchison et al., *Nine and Counting: The Women of the Senate* (Morrow, 2000).

56. See Clymer, *Edward M. Kennedy*.

57. See Charles Lewis and the Center for Public Integrity, *The Buying of the Congress: How Special Interests Have Stolen Your Right to Life, Liberty and the Pursuit of Happiness* (Avon, 1998).

58. For an excellent treatment of ethical problems faced by members of Congress and what has been and might be done about them, see Dennis F. Thompson, *Ethics in Congress* (Brookings Institution, 1995).

59. Brady and Volden, *Revolving Gridlock*, p. 178.

CHAPTER 12

1. Charles O. Jones, *The Presidency in a Separated System* (Brookings Institution, 1994), p. 295. See also Jean Reith Schroedl, *Congress, the President, and Policymaking* (M.E. Sharpe, 1994).

2. William E. Leuchtenburg, "The Twentieth Century Presidency," *Miller Center Report* 16, no. 1 (Spring 2000), pp. 15–23.

3. Glenn A. Phelps, *George Washington and American Constitutionalism* (University Press of Kansas, 1993).

4. It is difficult for the average citizen to assess systematically the health and character of presidential candidates, but voters still try to do so. For various efforts, see Fred Greenstein, *The Presidential Difference* (Free Press, 2000); David Gergen, *Eyewitness to Power: The Essence of Leadership—Nixon to Clinton* (Simon & Schuster, 2000); and Stanley A. Renshon, *The Psychological Assessment of Presidential Candidates* (New York University Press, 1996).

5. For a penetrating and realistic analysis of Abraham Lincoln, see David H. Donald, *Lincoln* (Simon and Schuster, 1995). See also, on the paradoxes and the heightened expectations we place on presidents, Thomas E. Cronin and Michael A. Genovese, *The Paradoxes of the American Presidency* (Oxford University Press, 1998).

6. See, in general, Joseph G. Dawson III, ed., *Commanders in Chief: Presidential Leadership in Modern Wars* (University Press of Kansas, 1993).

7. See Thomas J. Weko, *The Politicizing Presidency: The White House Personnel Office, 1948–1994* (University Press of Kansas, 1995).

8. See G. Calvin MacKenzie and Robert Shogan, eds., *Obstacle Course: The Report of the Twentieth Century Fund Task Force on the Presidential Appointment Process* (Twentieth Century Fund Press, 1996).

9. See James P. Pfiffner, *The Strategic Presidency: Hitting the Ground Running*, 2d ed. (University Press of Kansas, 1996).

10. *United States v Curtiss-Wright Export Corp.*, 299 US 304 (1936).

11. For those who believe the *Curtiss-Wright* ruling was too sweeping, see Harold H. Koh, *The National Security Constitution* (Yale University Press, 1990); Louis Fisher, *Presidential War Power* (University Press of Kansas, 1995); David Gray Adler and Larry N. George, eds., *The Constitution and the Conduct of American Foreign Policy: Essays on Law and History* (University Press of Kansas, 1996).

12. On the president's major involvement in the budget process, see Allen Schick, *The Federal Budget: Politics, Policy, Process* (Brookings Institution, 1995).

13. Albert R. Hunt, "Clinton Ends His Tenure on High Note," *The Wall Street Journal*, December 14, 2000, p. A9.

14. See Kenneth T. Walsh, *Feeding the Beast: The White House Versus the Press* (Random House, 1996). See also Richard Morris, *Behind the Oval Office* (Random House, 1997).

15. See Howard Kurtz, *Spin Cycle: Inside the Clinton Propaganda Machine* (Free Press, 1998).

16. See also the vigorous criticism of the Washington media and their biases by former U.S. Senator Alan K. Simpson, *Right in the Old Kazoo* (Morrow, 1997).

17. See Sidney M. Milkis, *The President and the Parties: The Transformation of the American Party System Since the New Deal* (Oxford University Press, 1993); James W. Davis, *The President as Party Leader* (Praeger, 1992).

18. See Bradley H. Patterson, Jr., *The White House Staff: Inside the West Wing and Beyond* (Brookings Institution, 2000).

19. For the views on presidents and the White House staff of a highly placed White House aide in several administrations, see Gergen, *Eyewitness to Power*.

20. See Shelley Lynne Tomkins, *Inside OMB: Politics and Process in the President's Budget Office* (M. E. Sharpe, 1998).

21. See Cronin and Genovese, *Paradoxes of the American Presidency*, chap. 9.

22. Information provided to Thomas E. Cronin in a letter, February 1997, from Kathryn Hughes, secretary of the cabinet in the Clinton White House. See also Robert B. Reich, *Locked in the Cabinet* (Knopf, 1997).

23. There has been a certain amount of controversy about the Twenty-fifth Amendment. See Herbert L. Abrams, *The President Has Been Shot: Confusion, Disability and the Twenty-fifth Amendment* (Stanford University Press, 1994); Laura Myers, "Transfer-of-Power-Rules Urged for Impaired Presidents," *Seattle-Post Intelligencer*, December 4, 1996, p. A3.

24. Former Vice-President Dan Quayle's views are of interest: *Standing Firm* (Harper Paperbacks, 1995). Three useful general treatments on the vice-presidency are Jules Witcover, *Crapshoot: Rolling the Dice on the Vice Presidency* (Crown, 1992); Paul Light, *Vice Presidential Power* (Johns Hopkins University Press, 1984); Joel Goldstein, *The Modern Vice Presidency* (Princeton University Press, 1982).

25. Mark Hertsgaard, *On Bended Knee: The Press and the Reagan Presidency* (Farrar, Straus, Giroux, 1988). See also John A. Maltese, *Spin Control: The White House Office of Communications and the Management of Presidential News* (University of North Carolina Press, 1992).

26. Political scientists are unsure of these relationships. See Jeffrey E. Cohen et al., "State-Level Presidential Approval and Senatorial Support," *Legislative Studies Quarterly* (November 2000), pp. 577–90; Lyn Ragsdale, "Studying the Presidency," in Michael Nelson, ed., *The Presidency and the Political System*, 6th ed. (Congressional Quarterly Press, 2000), pp. 29–63; Paul Gronke and Brian Newman, "FDR to Clinton . . . : A 'State of the Discipline' Review of Presidential Approval," paper prepared at the American Political Science Association Annual Meeting, Washington, D.C., August 31–September 3, 2000.

27. These points are more fully developed in Cronin and Genovese, *Paradoxes of the American Presidency*, chap. 3.

28. Clinton Rossiter, *The American Presidency* (Harcourt, Brace and World, 1956), p. 257.

29. Harold J. Laski, *The American Presidency: An Interpretation* (Harper and Brothers, 1940), p. 38.

CHAPTER 13

1. David S. Broder, "A Weak Hand," *The Washington Post National Weekly Edition*, December 25, 2000–January 1, 2001, p. 4.

2. George C. Edwards, "Building Coalitions," *Presidential Studies Quarterly* (March 2000), pp. 60–61.

3. See the arguments in David Gray Adler and Michael A. Genovese, eds., *The Presidency and the Law: The Clinton Legacy* (University Press of Kansas, 2002); Louis Fisher, *Congressional Abdication on War and Spending* (Texas A & M Press, 2000).

4. James A. Thurber, "An Introduction to Presidential-Congressional Rivalry," in James A. Thurber, ed., *Rivals for Power: Presidential-Congressional Relations* (Congressional Quarterly Press, 1996), p. 6.

5. Sarah A. Blinder, "Going Nowhere: A Gridlocked Congress?" *Brookings Review* (Winter 2000), p. 18.

6. See, for example, former Republican Senator Warren G. Rudman's memoir, *Combat* (Random House, 1996), chaps. 2, 3. See also former Democratic Congressman Timothy Penny and Major Garrett, *Common Cents* (Little, Brown, 1995).

7. John R. Hibbing and Elizabeth Theiss-Morse, *Congress as Public Enemy: Public Attitudes Toward American Political Institutions* (Cambridge University Press, 1995).

8. David W. Brady and Craig Volden, *Revolving Gridlock* (Westview Press, 1998), p. 176.

9. Abraham Lincoln to his Illinois law partner W.H. Herndon, February 15, 1848, in *Abraham Lincoln, Speeches and Writings, 1832–1858* (Library of America, 1989), p. 175.

10. Leonard C. Meeker, "The Legality of U.S. Participation in the Defense of Vietnam," *Department of State Bulletin*, March 28, 1966, pp. 448–55.

11. Madeleine Albright, in *Congressional Record*, July 30, 1998.

12. David Gray Adler, "The Clinton Theory of the War Power," *Presidential Studies Quarterly* (March 2000), p. 167.

13. Fisher, *Congressional Abdication*, p. 184.

14. Ibid., p. 170. See also Louis Fisher and David Gray Adler, "The War Powers: Time to Say Goodbye," *Political Science Quarterly* (Spring 1998), pp. 1–20.

15. Lee Hamilton, "The Role of the Congress in U.S. Foreign Policy," speech delivered to the Center for Strategic and International Studies, Washington, D.C., November 19, 1998, p. 1.

16. See Henry J. Abraham, *Justices, Presidents, and Senators: A History of U.S. Supreme Court Appointments from Washington to Clinton*, 4th ed. (Rowman and Littlefield, 1999); Sheldon Goldman, *Picking Federal Judges* (Yale University Press, 1997).

17. Orrin G. Hatch, "Senate Isn't Guilty of Racism in Confirming Judges," *The Wall Street Journal*, September 5, 2000, p. A34.

18. William Bradford Reynolds, "Etiquette for the Senate," *The New York Times*, January 12, 2001, p. A23.

19. Raoul Berger, *Executive Privilege: A Constitutional Myth* (Harvard University Press, 1974).

20. Mark J. Rozell, "The Law: Executive Privilege—Definition and Standards of Application," *Presidential Studies Quarterly* (December 1999), p. 924.

21. *U.S. v Nixon*, 418 U S 683 (1974).

22. See Mark J. Rozell, "Something To Hide: Clinton's Misuse of Executive Privilege," *PS: Political Science and Politics* (September 1999), p. 551. See also Mark J. Rozell, *Executive Privilege: The Dilemma of Secrecy and Democratic Accountability*, 2d ed. (University Press of Kansas, 2000).

23. See Richard A. Posner, *An Affair of State: The Investigation, Impeachment and Trial of President Clinton* (Harvard University Press, 1999); Mark J. Rozell, "Executive Privilege and the Modern Presidents: In Nixon's Shadow," *Minnesota Law Review* (May 1999), pp. 1069–1126. See also Mark J. Rozell, "An Old (or New) Understanding of Executive Privilege," in Adler and Genovese, eds., *The Presidency and the Law*.

24. www.nara.gov/fedreg/eo.

25. See Nancy Kassop, "A New (or Old?) Understanding of the Separation of Powers: The Expansion and Contraction of Presidential Power under Clinton," paper presented at the American Political Science Association Annual Meeting, Washington, D.C., August 31–September 3, 2000. See also Christopher J. Deering and Forrest Maltzman, "The Politics of Executive Orders: Legislative Restraints on Presidential Power," *Political Research Quarterly* (December 1999), pp. 767–83.

26. Terry Moe and William Howell, "Unilateral Action and Presidential Power: A Theory," *Presidential Studies Quarterly* (December 1999), p. 856.

27. Ibid., p. 856.

28. For a useful history of the veto power, see Robert Spitzer, *The Presidential Veto: Touchstone of the American Presidency* (State University of New York Press, 1988).

29. *Clinton v City of New York*, 521 US 811 (1998).

30. Fisher, *Congressional Abdication*, p. 124.

31. Donald F. Kettl, "Presidential Management of the Economy," in James Pfiffner and Roger H. Davidson, eds., *Understanding the Presidency*, 3d ed. (Addison, Wesley, Longman, 2000), p. 363.

32. Adapted from Edwards, "Building Coalitions."

33. Ibid., pp. 49–58.

34. Ibid., p. 63.

35. See Charles Walcott and Karen Hult, *Governing the White House: From Hoover through LBJ* (University Press of Kansas, 1995); Bradley H. Patterson, Jr., *The White House Staff: Inside the West Wing* (Brookings Institution, 2000).

36. James MacGregor Burns, *Roosevelt: The Lion and the Fox* (Harcourt Brace, 1956), p. 186.

CHAPTER 14

1. Alexis de Tocqueville, *Democracy in America*, ed. Phillips Bradley (Knopf, 1944), 1:278–80.

2. Harold J. Laski, *The American Democracy* (Viking, 1948), p. 110.

3. Jerome Frank, *Courts on Trial: Myth and Reality in American Justice* (Princeton University Press, 1949), pp. 80–103.

4. *Chicago Grand Trunk Railway Co. v Wellman*, 143 US 339 (1892).

5. Philip J. Cooper, *Hard Judicial Choices: Federal District Court Judges and State and Local Officials* (Oxford University Press, 1988), p. 15.

6. *Luther v Borden*, 7 Howard 1 (1849).

7. Quoted in Paul E. Freund, *Understanding the Supreme Court* (Little, Brown, 1949), p. 3.

8. For one of the great classics, see Benjamin N. Cardozo, *The Nature of the Judicial Process* (Yale University Press, 1921).

9. Quoted in H.L.A. Hart, *The Concept of Law* (Oxford University Press, 1961), pp. 121–22.

10. David M. O'Brien, *Storm Center: The Supreme Court in American Politics*, 5th ed. (W.W. Norton, 2000), p. 30, and as updated by the author through the 1999–2000 term.

11. C. K. Rowland, "The Federal District Courts," in *The American Courts: A Critical Assessment*, ed. John B. Gates and Charles A. Johnson (Congressional Quarterly Press, 1991), pp. 61–80.

12. Quoted in Christopher E. Smith, *United States Magistrates in the Federal Courts: Subordinate Judges* (Praeger, 1990), p. 183.

13. *Peretz v United States*, 501 US 923 (1991).

14. See Donald R. Songer, "The Circuit Courts of Appeals," in Gates and Johnson, eds., *American Courts*, pp. 35–37; Deborah J. Barrow and Thomas G. Walker, *A Court Divided: The Fifth Circuit Court of Appeals and the Politics of Judicial Reform* (Yale University Press, 1988); Arthur D. Hellman, ed., *Reconstructing Justice: The Innovations of the Ninth Circuit and the Future of the Federal Courts* (Cornell University Press, 1991).

15. John Gruhl, "The Impact of Term Limits for Supreme Court Justices," *Judicature*, September/October 1997, pp. 67–68.

16. *Bordenkircher v Hayes*, 434 US 357 (1978). See also James Eisenstein, *Counsel for the United States: U.S. Attorneys in the Political and Legal Systems* (Johns Hopkins Press, 1978).

17. Joan Biskupic, "For Court Advocate, a Nominee Who Seeks 'Different Solutions,'" *The Washington Post*, April 19, 1993, p. A21.

18. For a critical analysis, see Lincoln Caplan, *The Tenth Justice: The Solicitor General and the Rule of Law* (Knopf, 1987). For a defense, see former Solicitor General Charles Fried, *Order and Law: Arguing the Reagan Revolution—A Firsthand Account* (Simon & Schuster, 1991). For a more neutral account, see Rebecca Mae Salokar, *The Solicitor General: The Politics of Law* (Temple University Press, 1992).

19. *Legal Services Corporation v Velazquez*, 120 S. Ct.(2001).

20. Neil D. McFeeley, *Appointment of Judges: The Johnson Presidency* (University of Texas Press, 1987), p. 1.

21. Harold W. Chase, *Federal Judges: The Appointing Process* (University of Minnesota Press, 1972), pp. 3–47; and Sheldon Goldman, *Picking Federal Judges: Lower Court Selection from Roosevelt Through Reagan* (Yale University Press, 1998).

22. Lettie McSpadden Wenner and Lee F. Dutter, "Contextual Influences on Court Outcomes," *Western Political Quarterly* 41 (March 1988), pp. 115–34; Ronald Stidham and Robert A. Carp, "Exploring Regionalism in the Federal District Courts," *Los Angeles Daily Journal* 18 (Fall 1988), pp. 113–25.

23. See Amy Goldstein, "Bush Curtails ABA Role in Selecting U. S. Judges," *The Washington Post*, March 23, 2001, p. A1.

24. Lisa M. Holmes and Roger E. Hartley, "Increasing Senate Scrutiny of Lower Federal Court Nominees," *Judicature*, May/June 1997, p. 275.

25. George Watson and John Stookey, "Supreme Court Confirmation Hearings: A View from the Senate," *Judicature*, December 1987/January 1988, p. 193. See also John Massaro, *Supremely Political: The Role of Ideology and Presidential Management in Unsuccessful Supreme Court Nominations* (State University of New York Press, 1990).

26. Barbara A. Perry and Henry J. Abraham, "A 'Representative' Supreme Court? The Thomas, Ginsburg, and Breyer Appointments," *Judicature*, January/February 1998, pp. 158–65.

27. Goldman, *Picking Federal Judges*, pp. 161, 327–36.

28. Sheldon Goldman, "Bush's Judicial Legacy: The Final Imprint," *Judicature*, April/May 1993, p. 291.

29. Robert A. Carp and C. K. Rowland, *Politics and Judgment in Federal District Courts* (University Press of Kansas, 1996).

30. Sheldon Goldman, "Reagan's Judicial Legacy: Completing the Puzzle and Summing Up," *Judicature*, April/May 1989, pp. 318–30.

31. Leo V. Hennessy, "Redrawing the Political Map? An Impact Analysis of the Reagan Appointments on the U.S. Courts of Appeals," paper presented at the Southern Political Science Association, Tampa, Florida, November 7–9, 1991.

32. Robert A. Carp, Donald Songer, C. K. Rowland, Ronald Stidham, and Lisa Richey-Tracey, "The Voting Behavior of Judges Appointed by President Bush," *Judicature*, April/May 1993, pp. 298–302.

33. Naftali Bendavid, "Diversity Marks Clinton Judiciary," *The Recorder*, December 30, 1993, p. 11.

34. Dan Carney, "Battle Looms Between Clinton, GOP over Court Nominees," *Congressional Quarterly Weekly Report*, February 8, 1997, p. 369.

35. David M. O'Brien, "Judicial Legacies: The Clinton Presidency and the Courts," in Colin Campbell and Bert A. Rockman, eds., *The Clinton Legacy* (Chatham House, 2000), pp. 96–117; and http://afj.org/jsp/home.html.

36. William Howard Taft to Horace Taft, November 14, 1929; quoted in Henry Pringle, *The Life and Times of William Howard Taft* (Farrar, 1939), 2:967.

37. Sue Davis, "Federalism and Property Rights: An Examination of Justice Rehnquist's Legal Positivism," *Western Reserve Political Quarterly* 39 (June 1986), pp. 250–64.

38. David M. O'Brien, *Judicial Roulette: Report of the Twentieth Century Fund Task Force on Judicial Selection* (Priority Press Publications, 1988), pp. 10–11.

39. White Burkett Miller Center of Public Affairs, *Improving the Process of Appointing Federal Judges* (Miller Center, University of Virginia, 1996).

40. Donald Santarelli, quoted in Jerry Landauer, "Shaping the Bench," *The Wall Street Journal*, December 10, 1970, p. 1. See also J. W. Peltason, *Federal Courts in the Political Process* (Doubleday, 1955), p. 32.

41. Michael A. Kahn, "The Appointment of a Supreme Court Justice: A Political Process from Beginning to End," *Presidential Studies Quarterly* 25 (Winter 1995), pp. 26, 39.

42. Ex parte *McCardle*, 74 U S 506 (1869).

43. Barry Friedman, "Attacks on Judges: Why They Fail," *Judicature*, January/February 1998, p. 152.

44. Tony Mauro, "Yipes! Stripes!" *The Recorder*, February 8, 1995, p. 8.

45. Tony Mauro, "Supreme Court Calendar Begs for More Arguments," *The Recorder*, February 13, 1996, p. 1.

46. David M. O'Brien, "The Rehnquist Court's Shrinking Plenary Docket," *Judicature*, September/October 1997, p. 58.

47. O'Brien, *Storm Center*, p. 63. See also Tony Mauro, "Jumping into the Pool," *The Recorder*, September 14, 1993, p. 6.

48. Sidney Ulmer, "The Supreme Court's Certiorari Decisions: Conflict as a Predictive Variable," *American Political Science Review* 78 (December 1984), pp. 901–11.

49. Quoted in John R. Vile, "The Selection and Tenure of Chief Justices," *Judicature*, September/October 1994, p. 98.

50. Robert J. Steamer, *Chief Justice: Leadership and the Supreme Court* (University of South Carolina Press, 1986).

51. Sue Davis, "The Supreme Court: Rehnquist's or Reagan's," *Western Political Quarterly* 44 (March 1991), p. 98.

52. David G. Savage, "The Rehnquist Court," *Los Angeles Times Magazine*, September 29, 1991, p. 13; David W. Rohde and Harold J. Spaeth, "Ideology, Strategy and Supreme Court Decisions: William Rehnquist as Chief Justice," *Judicature*, December 1988/January 1989, pp. 247–50. See also Joseph F. Kobylka, "Leadership on the Supreme Court of the United States: Chief Justice Burger and the Establishment Clause," *Western Political Quarterly* 42 (December 1989), pp. 545–68.

53. David Danelski, "The Influence of the Chief Justice in the Decisional Process of the Supreme Court," in Thomas P. Jahnige and Sheldon Goldman, eds., *The Federal Judicial System: Readings in Process and Behavior* (Holt, Rinehart and Winston, 1968), p. 148.

54. Edward Lazarus, *Closed Chambers: The First Eyewitness Account of the Epic Struggles Inside the Supreme Court* (Times Books, Random House, 1998), p. 423.

55. Gregory A. Caldeira and John R. Wright, "Organized Interest and Agenda Setting in the U.S. Supreme Court," *American Political Science Review* 82 (December 1988), p. 1110; Donald R. Songer and Reginald S. Sheehan, "Interest Groups' Success in the Courts: Amicus Participation in the Supreme Court," *Political Research Quarterly* 46 (June 1993), pp. 339–54.

56. *Webster v Reproductive Health Services*, 492 US 490 (1989); *Roe v Wade*, 410 US 113 (1973). See also Susan Behuniak-Long, "Friendly Fire: Amici Curiae and *Webster v Reproductive Health Services*," *Judicature*, February/March 1991, pp. 261–70.

57. *United States v Lopez*, 514 US 549 (1951).

58. Karen O'Connor, "The *Amicus Curiae* Role of the U.S. Solicitor General in Supreme Court Litigation," *Judicature*, December 1982/January 1983, pp. 256–64; Jeffrey A. Segal, "*Amicus Curiae* Briefs by the Solicitor General During the Warren and Burger Courts," *Western Political Quarterly* 41 (March 1988), pp. 134–44.

59. Tony Mauro, "The Supreme Court as Quiz Show," *The Recorder*, December 8, 1993, p. 10.

60. Joyce O'Connor, "Selections from Notes Kept on an Internship at the U.S. Supreme Court, Fall 1988," *Law, Courts, and Judicial Process* (Department of Political Science, Purdue University) 6 (Spring 1989), p. 44.

61. Tony Mauro, "No Comfort for Counsel After Court Review," *The Recorder*, November 10, 1997, p. 8.

62. Mauro, "Yipes! Stripes!" p. 8.

63. Joan Biskupie, "Supreme Court Film Offers Glimpse Behind Justices' Closed Doors," *The Washington Post*, June 17, 1997, p. A15.

64. William H. Rehnquist, *The Supreme Court: How It Was, How It Is* (William Morrow, 1987), pp. 289–90.

65. Daniel M. Berman, *It Is So Ordered: The Supreme Court Rules on School Segregation* (Norton, 1986), p. 114; Walter F. Murphy, *Elements of Judicial Strategy* (University of Chicago Press, 1964), p. 66; O'Brien, *Storm Center*, pp. 262–72.

66. Charles Evans Hughes, quoted in Donald E. Lively, *Foreshadows of the Law: Supreme Court Dissents and Constitutional Development* (Praeger, 1992), p. xx.

67. *Brown v Board of Education*, 347 U S 483 (1954).

68. *United States v Nixon*, 418 US 683 (1974).

69. Gerald N. Rosenberg, *Hollow Hope: Can Courts Bring About Sound Change?* (University of Chicago Press, 1991).

70. J. W. Peltason, *Fifty-eight Lonely Men: Southern Federal Judges and School Desegregation* (University of Illinois Press, 1971), p. 19.

71. Cooper, *Hard Judicial Choices*, pp. 347–50.

72. Arthur S. Miller, "In Defense of Judicial Activism," in Stephen C. Halpern and Charles M. Lamb, eds., *Supreme Court Activism and Restraint* (Heath, 1982), p. 177. See also, by the chief justice of the West Virginia Supreme Court, Richard Neely, *How Courts Govern America* (Yale University Press, 1981).

73. *United States v Carolene Products*, 304 US 144 (1938). Variations on this basic position have been restated in dozens of books. Halpern and Lamb, eds., *Supreme Court Activism and Restraint*, and Mark Tushnet, *Red, White, and Blue: A Critical Analysis of Constitutional Law* (Harvard University Press, 1988), provide analysis from all perspectives. For another analysis of this great debate, see Lief H. Carter, *Contemporary Constitutional Lawmaking* (Pergamon Press, 1985). See also Terri Jennings Peretti, *In Defense of a Political Court* (Princeton University Press, 1999); Stephen Macedo, *The New Right v the Constitution* (Cato, 1986). Leslie F. Goldstein, "Judicial Review and Democratic Theory: Guardian Democracy vs. Representative Democracy," *Western Political Quarterly* 40 (September 1987), pp. 391–412, also contains a bibliography.

74. J. W. Peltason, "The Supreme Court: Transactional or Transformational Leadership," in Michael R. Beschloss and Thomas E. Cronin, eds., *Essays in Honor of James MacGregor Burns* (Prentice Hall, 1988), pp. 165–80; Mark Silverstein and Benjamin Ginsburg, "The Supreme Court and the New Politics of Judicial Power," *Political Science Quarterly* 102 (Fall 1987), pp. 371–88.

75. *Planned Parenthood v Casey*, 505 US 833 (1992).

76. Thomas R. Marshall, *Public Opinion and the Supreme Court* (Unwin Hyman, 1989), p. 193. See also Thomas R. Marshall, "The Supreme Court and the Grass Roots: Whom Does the Court Represent Best?" *Judicature*, June/July 1992, pp. 22–28; Michael Comiskey, "The Rehnquist Court and American Values," *Judicature*, March/April 1994, pp. 261–67; William Mishler and Reginald S. Sheehan, "The Supreme Court as a Counter-Majoritarian Institution? The Impact of Public Opinion on Supreme Court Decisions," *American Political Science Review* 87 (1993), pp. 87–101; along with Mishler and Sheehan response, Helmut Norpoth and Jeffrey A. Segal, "Popular Influence on Supreme Court Decisions," *American Political Science Review* 88 (September 1994), pp. 711–24.

77. Rosenberg, *Hollow Hope*, p. 343.

78. Rehnquist, *Supreme Court*, p. 98.

79. Chief Justice Edward White, "The Supreme Court of the United States," *American Bar Association Journal* 7 (1921), p. 341.

CHAPTER 15

1. Data on U.S. budget projections and employment can be located at www.whitehouse.gov/omg and www.gpo.gov/usbudget and in *Statistical Abstract of the United States*, 2000.

2. Barry Bozeman, *Bureaucracy and Red Tape* (Prentice Hall, 2000), p. xi.

3. See data provided in Andrew Kohut, ed., *Deconstructing Distrust: How Americans View Government* (Pew Research Center for the People and the Press, 1998), p. 124.

4. An exception is a useful book of essays in praise of innovations by federal agencies, John D. Donahue, ed., *Making Washington Work: Tales of Innovation in the Federal Government* (Brookings Institution, 1999).

5. Shelley L. Davis, *Unbridled Power: Inside the Secret Culture of the IRS* (Harper Business, 1997).

6. Philip K. Howard, *The Death of Common Sense: How Law Is Suffocating America* (Random House, 1994), p. 9.

7. Many of these ideas are reported in Al Gore, *The Best Kept Secrets in Government: How the Clinton Administration Is Reinventing the Way Washington Works* (Random House, 1996). See, too, Donald F. Kettl, *Reinventing Government: A Fifth Year Report Card* (Brookings Institution, 1998).

8. Bush's campaign promises were discussed and quoted in Gerald F. Seib, "A Big Bush Idea Rises Amid Fluff, But It Is Private," *The Wall Street Journal*, August 2, 2000, p. A24.

9. Adapted from Dennis Palumbo and Steven Maynard-Moody, *Contemporary Public Administration* (Longman, 1991), p. 26.

10. For an analysis of the use and abuse of the civil service system in the early twentieth century, see Stephen Skowronek, *Building a New American State* (Cambridge University Press, 1982).

11. A history of the old Hatch Act is provided in James Eccles, *The Hatch Act and the American Bureaucracy* (Vantage Press, 1981).

12. For the 1994 revisions of this act, see Jeanne Ponessa, "The Hatch Act Rewrite," *Congressional Quarterly Weekly Report*, November 13, 1993, pp. 3146–47.

13. Paul C. Light, *The New Public Service* (Brookings Institution, 1999), p. 25.

14. Ibid., p. 2.

15. Donahue, ed., *Making Washington Work*, chaps. 12, 14.

16. Gore, *Best Kept Secrets in Government*, p. 24.

17. See the discussion in Alvin Felzenberg, ed., *The Keys to a Successful Presidency* (The Heritage Foundation, 2000), chaps. 3, 4.

18. See David E. Lewis, "The Presidential Advantage in the Design of Bureaucratic Agencies," paper presented at the American Political Science Association Annual Meeting, Boston, September 3–6, 1998.

19. Morris P. Fiorina, "Flagellating the Federal Bureaucracy," *Society* (March/April 1983), p. 73.

20. Francis E. Rourke, "Whose Bureaucracy Is This, Anyway?" *PS: Political Science and Politics* (December 1993), p. 691.

21. Surveys discussed in Bozeman, *Bureaucracy and Red Tape*, p. 39.

22. For the general philosophy of the congressional Republican leadership in the 1990s, see Newt Gingrich, *To Renew America* (HarperCollins, 1995); Dick Armey, *The Freedom Revolution* (Regnery, 1995).

23. Jonathan Weisman, "Republicans Showing Less Zeal to Cut Cabinet Departments," *Congressional Quarterly Weekly Report*, January 18, 1997, p. 171.

24. Ibid., p. 172.

25. The strategies used in these places and elsewhere are detailed in David Osborne and Ted Gaebler, *Reinventing Government: How the Entrepreneurial Spirit Is Transforming the Public Sector* (Addison-Wesley, 1992); and in David Osborne and Peter Plastrik, *Banishing Bureaucracy: The Five Strategies for Reinventing Government* (Addison-Wesley, 1997).

CHAPTER 16

1. *Felker v Turpin*, 518 US 651 (1996); *Winthrow v Williams*, 507 US 680 (1993); *McCleskey v Zant*, 499 US 467 (1991); and *Stone v Powell*, 428 US 465 (1976).

2. Neil H. Cogan, ed., *The Complete Bill of Rights: The Drafts, Debates, Sources, and Origins* (Oxford University Press, 1997); Robert A. Rutland, *The Birth of the Bill of Rights, 1776–1791* (University of North Carolina Press, 1955).

3. *Barron v Baltimore*, 7 Peters 243 (1833).

4. *Gitlow v New York*, 268 US 652 (1925).

5. Richard C. Cortner, *The Supreme Court and the Second Bill of Rights: The Fourteenth Amendment and the Nationalization of Civil Liberties* (University of Wisconsin Press, 1981).

6. Dorothy Toth Beasley, "Federalism and the Protection of Individual Rights: The American State Constitutional Perspective," in *Federalism and Rights*, ed. Ellis Katz and G. Alan Tarr (Rowman & Littlefield, 1996).

7. *Witters v Washington Department of Services for the Blind*, 474 US 481 (1986); *Zobrest v Catalina Foothills School District*, 509 US 1 (1993).

8. *Everson v Board of Education*, 333 US 203 (1947).

9. *Lemon v Kurtzman*, 403 US 602 (1971).

10. *Capital Square Review Board v Pinette*, 515 US 753 (1995).

11. *Lynch v Donnelly*, 465 US 669 (1984).

12. *Allegheny County v Greater Pittsburgh ACLU*, 492 US 573 (1989).

13. *Bowen v Kendrick*, 487 US 589 (1988); *Lee v Weisman*, 505 US 577 (1992); *Board of Education of Kiryas Joel Village School District v Grumet*, 512 US 687 (1994).

14. *Agostini v Felton*, 521 US 74 (1997).

15. *Lee v Weisman*, 505 US 577 (1992); *Santa Fe Independent School District v Doe*, 120 S.Ct. 2266 (2000).

16. *Engel v Vitale*, 370 US 421 (1962).

17. *Edwards v Aguillard*, 482 US 578 (1987).

18. *Marsh v Chambers*, 463 US 783 (1983).

19. *Employment Division of Human Resources of Oregon v Smith*, 494 US 872 (1990).

20. *City of Boerne v Flores*, 117 S.Ct. 2157 (1997).

21. *Rosenberger v University of Virginia*, 515 US 819 (1995).

22. *Board of Regents of the University of Wisconsin System v Southworth*, 120 S.Ct. 1346 (2000).

23. Oliver Wendell Holmes, in *Abrams v United States*, 250 US 616 (1919).

24. John Stuart Mill, *Essay on Liberty (1859)*, in Arthur Burtt, ed., *The English Philosophers from Bacon to Mill* (Random House, 1939), p. 961.

25. Robert Jackson, in *West Virginia State Board of Education v Barnette*, 319 US 624 (1943).

26. *Brown v Hartlage*, 456 US 45 (1982), reversing a decision of the Kentucky Court of Appeals based on the bad tendency test.

27. Oliver Wendell Holmes, in *Schenck v United States*, 249 US 47 (1919).

28. *Dennis v United States*, 341 US 494 (1951).

29. *The New York Times v Sullivan*, 376 US 254 (1964).

30. *Yates v United States*, 354 US 298 (1957).

31. *Brandenburg v Ohio*, 395 US 444 (1969).

32. *The New York Times v Sullivan*, 376 US 254 (1964).

33. *Hustler Magazine v Falwell*, 485 US 46 (1988).

34. *Masson v New York Magazine, Inc.*, 501 US 496 (1991).

35. *Gertz v Robert Welch, Inc.*, 418 US 323 (1974).

36. Potter Stewart, concurring in *Jacobellis v Ohio*, 378 US 184 (1964).

37. John Marshall Harlan, in *Cohen v California*, 403 US 15 (1971).

38. *Miller v California*, 413 US 15 (1973).

39. *Young v American Mini Theatres*, 427 US 51 (1976); *Renton v Playtime Theatres, Inc.*, 475 US 41 (1986).

40. *Barnes v Glen Theatre, Inc.*, 501 US 560 (1991); *City of Erie v Pap's A.M.*, 120 S.Ct. 1382 (2000).

41. *New York v Ferber*, 458 US 747 (1982).

42. *General Media Communications v Cohen*, 118 S.Ct. 2367 (1998).

43. See Catharine A. MacKinnon, *Only Words* (Harvard University Press, 1993), and compare another feminist, Nadine Strossen, *Defending Pornography: Free Speech, Sex, and the Fight for Women's Rights* (Scribner's, 1995).

44. *Butler v Her Majesty the Queen*, 1 S.C.R. 452 (1992).

45. *Chaplinsky v New Hampshire*, 315 US 568 (1942).

46. *Cohen v California*, 403 US 115 (1971).

47. *R.A.V. v St. Paul*, 505 US 377 (1992). See also *Wisconsin v Mitchell*, 508 US 476 (1993); *Apprendi v New Jersey*, 120 S.Ct. 2348 (2000).

48. *44 Liquormart, Inc. v Rhode Island*, 517 US 484 (1996).

49. *New York Times Company v United States*, 403 US 670 (1970); *Near v Minnesota*, 283 US 697 (1930).

50. *Hazelwood School District v Kuhlmeier*, 484 US 260 (1988).

51. *R.A.V. v St. Paul*, 505 US 377 (1992). See also *Wisconsin v Mitchell*, 508 US 476 (1993).

52. *Branzburg v Hayes*, 408 US 665 (1972).

53. *Richmond Newspapers, Inc. v Virginia*, 448 US 555 (1980). See also David M. O'Brien, *The Public's Right to Know: The Supreme Court and the First Amendment* (Praeger, 1981).

54. Oliver Wendell Holmes, dissenting in *Milwaukee Pub. Co. v Burleson*, 255 US 407 (1921).

55. *Lamont v Postmaster General*, 381 US 301 (1965).

56. *Rowan v Post Office Department*, 397 US 728 (1970).

57. *McIntyre v Ohio Election Commission*, 514 US 334 (1995).

58. *Southeastern Promotions, Ltd. v Conrad*, 420 US 546 (1975).

59. *Federal Communications Commission v Pacifica Foundation*, 438 US 726 (1978).

60. *Turner Broadcasting System v Federal Communications Commission*, 518 US 180 (1997).

61. *United States v Playboy Entertainment Group*, 120 S.Ct. 1878 (2000); *Denver Area Educational Television v Federal Communications Commission*, 518 US 727 (1996).

62. See and compare *Federal Communications Commission v Pacifica Foundation*, 438 US 726 (1978), and *Sable Communications v Federal Communications Commission*, 492 US 115 (1989).

63. *Reno v American Civil Liberties Union*, 117 S.Ct. 2329 (1997).

64. Freedom Forum Online: www.freedomforum.org/assembly/1998/9/2/march.asp.

65. Lee C. Bollinger, *Images of a Free Press* (University of Chicago Press, 1991).

66. *Walker v Birmingham*, 388 US 307 (1967).

67. *Madsen v Women's Health Center*, 512 US 753 (1994); *Schenck v Pro-Choice Network*, 519 US 357 (1997); *Hill v Colorado*, 120 S.Ct. 2480 (2000).

68. *West Virginia State Board of Education v Barnette*, 319 US 624 (1943).

CHAPTER 17

1. *Vance v Terrazas*, 444 US 252 (1980).

2. G. Pascal Zachary, "Dual Citizenship Is Double-Edged Sword," *The Wall Street Journal*, March 25, 1998, pp. B1, B15, quoting T. Alexander Aleinikoff of the Carnegie Endowment for International Peace. See also Mark Fritz, "Dual Citizenships Create Dueling Family Allegiances," *Los Angeles Times*, April 6, 1998, p. A1; William Branigin, "Pledging Allegiance to Two Flags," *The Washington Post National Weekly Edition*, June 8, 1998, p. 14.

3. *Plyler v Doe*, 457 US 202 (1982).

4. *Sale v Haitian Centers Council, Inc.*, 509 US 155 (1993).

5. *Chicago Home Building & Loan Assn. v Blaisdell*, 290 US 398 (1934).

6. *Chicago, Burlington & Quincy Railway Co. v Chicago*, 166 US 226 (1897).

7. *First English Evangelical v Los Angeles County*, 482 US 304 (1987). See Richard A. Epstein, *Taking: Private Property and the Power of Eminent Domain* (Harvard University Press, 1985).

8. *United States v 564.54 Acres of Land*, 441 US 506 (1979).

9. *Mathews v Eldridge*, 424 US 319 (1976), restated in *Connecticut v Doeher*, 501 US 1 (1991).

10. *Meyer v Nebraska*, 262 US 390 (1923).

11. *Griswold v Connecticut*, 381 US 479 (1965).

12. Philip B. Kurland, *Some Reflections on Privacy and the Constitution* (University of Chicago Center for Policy Study, 1976), p. 9. A classic and influential article about privacy is S. D. Warren and L. D. Brandeis, "The Right to Privacy," *Harvard Law Review*, December 15, 1890, pp. 193–220.

13. *Roe v Wade*, 410 US 113 (1973).

14. *Planned Parenthood of Southeastern Pennsylvania v Casey*, 505 US 833 (1992).

15. *Stenberg v Carhart*, 120 S.Ct. 2597 (2000).

16. *Bowers v Hardwick*, 478 US 186 (1986).

17. *Baker v Vermont*, 744 A.2d 864 (1999); *Powell v Georgia*, 510 S.E. 2d 18 (1998); *Kentucky v Wasson*, 842 S.W. 2d 487 (1992).

18. *Boy Scouts of America v Dale*, 120 S.Ct. 2446 (2000).

19. Antonin Scalia, dissenting in *Romer v Evans*, 517 US 620 (1996).

20. *Tennessee v Garner*, 41 US 1 (1985).

21. *Katz v United States*, 389 US 347 (1967).

22. *County of Riverside v McLaughlin*, 500 US 44 (1991).

23. *California v Hodari D.*, 499 US 621 (1991).

24. *Terry v Ohio*, 392 US 1 (1968).

25. *Minnesota v Dickerson*, 508 US 366 (1993).

26. *Almeida-Sanchez v United States*, 413 US 266 (1973); *United States v Ortiz*, 422 US 891 (1975).

27. *United States v Ramsey*, 431 US 606 (1977).

28. *Coolidge v New Hampshire*, 403 US 443 (1971); *Arizona v Hicks*, 480 US 321 (1987).

29. *United States v Ross*, 456 US 798 (1982).

30. *Pennsylvania v Mimms*, 434 US 110 (1977), reaffirmed in *Ohio v Robinette*, 519 US 33 (1997).

31. *Michigan v Tyler*, 436 US 499 (1978); *Mincey v Arizona*, 437 US 385 (1978).

32. *Chandler v Miller*, 520 US 305 (1997).

33. *Treasury Employees v Von Raab*, 489 US 656 (1989); *Skinner v Railway Labor Executives' Assn.*, 489 US 602 (1989); *Vernonia School Dist. 47J v Action*, 515 US 646 (1995); *Chandler v Miller*, 520 US 305 (1997).

34. *Mapp v Ohio*, 367 US 643 (1961).

35. Senate Committee on the Judiciary, *The Jury and the Search for Truth: The Case Against Excluding Relevant Evidence at Trial: Hearing before the Committee*, 104th Cong., 1st sess., 1997.

36. *United States v Leon*, 468 US 897 (1984); *Arizona v Evans*, 514 US 1 (1995).

37. *Miranda v Arizona*, 384 US 436 (1966).

38. *Dickerson v United States*, 120 S.Ct. 2326 (2000).

39. Justice Felix Frankfurter, dissenting in *United States v Rabinowitz*, 339 US 56 (1950).

40. *United States v Enterprises, Inc.*, 498 US 292 (1991).

41. *Williams v Florida*, 399 US 78 (1970); *Burch v Louisiana*, 441 US 130 (1979).

42. *J.E.B. v Alabama ex rel T. B.*, 511 US 127 (1994); *Batson v Kentucky*, 476 US 79 (1986); *Powers v Ohio*, 499 US 400 (1991); *Hernandez v New York*, 500 US 352 (1991); *Georgia v McCollum*, 505 US 42 (1990).

43. *Benton v Maryland*, 395 US 784 (1969). See also *Kansas v Hendricks*, 117 S. Ct. 2072 (1997).

44. *Graham v Collins*, 506 US 461 (1993).

45. Jerome Frank, *Courts on Trial* (Princeton University Press, 1949), p. 122. See also Steven Brill, *Trial by Jury* (American Lawyer Books/Touchstone, 1989).

46. Harry Kalven, Jr., and Hans Zeisel, *The American Jury* (University of Chicago Press, 1971), p. 57. See also Jeffrey Abramson, *We, The Jury: The Jury System and the Ideal of Democracy* (Basic Books, 1994).

47. George Edwards, *The Police on the Urban Frontier* (Institute of Human Relations Press and the American Jewish Committee, 1968), p. 28. See also Jerome G. Miller, *Search and Destroy: African-American Males in the Criminal Justice System* (Cambridge University Press, 1996).

48. Sandra Bass, "Blacks, Browns, and the Blues: Police and Minorities in California," *Public Affairs Report* (IGS, University of California, Berkeley) 38 (November 1997), p. 10.

49. See David Cole, *No Equal Justice: Race and Class in the American Criminal Justice System* (New Press, 1999); and Randall Kennedy, *Race, Crime, and the Law* (Pantheon, 1997).

50. See "Understanding Community Policing" (Bureau of Justice Administration), at www.community_policy.org.

51. Robert H. Jackson, *The Supreme Court in the American System of Government* (Harvard University Press, 1955), pp. 81–82.

CHAPTER 18

1. Michael R. Belknap, *Federal Law and Southern Order: Racial Violence and Constitutional Conflict in the Post-Brown South* (University of Georgia, 1987), pp. 128–204.

2. Taylor Branch, *Parting the Waters: America in the King Years, 1954–1963* (Simon & Schuster, 1988). See also Harris Wofford, *Of Kennedys and Kings: Making Sense of the Sixties* (Farrar, Strauss and Giroux, 1980).

3. See Robert D. Loevy, *To End All Segregation: The Politics and Passage of the Civil Rights Act of 1964* (University Press of America, 1990).

4. Aldon D. Morris, *The Origins of the Civil Rights Movement: Black Communities Organizing for Change* (Free Press/Macmillan, 1985); James Farmer, *Lay Bare the Heart: An Autobiography of the Civil Rights Movement* (Arbor House, 1985).

5. National Advisory Commission on Civil Disorders, *The Kerner Report* (Washington, D.C.: Government Printing Office, 1968), p. 1.

6. Ellen Carol DuBois, *Feminism and Suffrage: The Emergence of an Independent Women's Movement in America, 1848–1869* (Cornell University Press, 1978); Joan Hoff-Wilson, "Women and the Constitution," *News for Teachers of Political Science* (American Political Science Association), Summer 1985, pp. 10–15.

7. Susan M. Hartmann, *From Margin to Mainstream: American Women and Politics since 1960* (Temple University Press, 1989); Susan Gluck Mezey, *In Pursuit of Equality: Women, Public Policy, and the Federal Courts* (St. Martin's Press, 1992).

8. Celia W. Dugger, "U.S. Study Says Asian-Americans Face Widespread Discrimination," *The New York Times*, February 29, 1992, p. 1, reporting on U.S. Civil Rights Commission, *Civil Rights Issues Facing Asian Americans in the 1990s.*

9. Won Moo Hurh, *Korean Immigrants in America* (Fairleigh Dickinson University Press, 1984).

10. Antonio J. A. Pido, *The Filipinos in America: Macro/Micro Dimensions of Immigration and Integration* (Center for Migration Studies of New York, 1986).

11. Harold L. Hodgkinson, *The Demographics of American Indians: One Percent of the People, Fifty Percent of the Diversity* (Institute for Educational Leadership/Center for Demographic Policy, 1990), pp. 1–5. See also *New York Times Almanac–2000* (Penguin, 1999), p. 289.

12. Charles F. Wilkinson, *American Indians, Times, and the Law* (Yale University Press, 1987), p. 62; Vine Deloria, Jr., and Clifford M. Lytle, *The Nations Within: The Past and Future of American Indian Sovereignty* (Pantheon Books, 1984).

13. *County of Yakima v Yakima Indian Nation*, 502 US 251 (1992).

14. Theodora Lurie, "Shattering the Myth of the Vanishing American," *The Ford Foundation Letter* 22 (Winter 1991), p. 5.

15. Spencer Rich, "Native Americans, They Can Still Get Free Health Care If They're Indian Enough," *The Washington Post National Weekly Edition*, July 14, 1986, p. 34, quoting the Office of Technology Assessment.

16. *Idaho Employment v Smith*, 434 US 1 (1974).

17. *San Antonio School District v Rodriguez*, 411 US 1 (1973).

18. *Frontiero v Richardson*, 411 US 677 (1973).

19. *Califano v Webster*, 430 US 313 (1977).

20. *Mississippi University for Women v Hogan*, 458 US 718 (1982); *United States v Virginia*, 518 US 515 (1996).

21. *San Antonio School District v Rodriguez*, 411 US 1 (1973).

22. Sandra Day O'Connor, in *Kimel v Florida Board of Regents*, 120 S.Ct. 631 (2000).

23. Ibid.

24. *Washington v Davis*, 426 US 229 (1976). See also *Hunter v Underwood*, 471 US 522 (1985).

25. Justice Sandra Day O'Connor, concurring in *Hernandez v New York*, 500 US 352 (1991).

26. *Personnel Administrator of Massachusetts v Feeney*, 442 US 256 (1979).

27. *Smith v Allwright*, 321 US 649 (1944).

28. *Gomillion v Lightfoot*, 364 US 339 (1960).

29. *Harper v Virginia Board of Elections*, 383 US 663 (1966).

30. Harold W. Stanley, *Voter Mobilization and the Politics of Race: The South and Universal Suffrage, 1952–1984* (Praeger, 1987).

31. Abigail M. Thernstrom, *Whose Votes Count? Affirmative Action and Minority Voting Rights* (Harvard University Press, 1987), p. 15.

32. *Report of the United States Commission on Civil Rights* (Government Printing Office, 1959), pp. 103–104.

33. Thernstrom, *Whose Votes Count?* For a contrary view, see Bernard Grofman, Lisa Handley, and Richard G. Niemi, *Minority Representation and the Quest for Voting Equality* (Cambridge University Press, 1992).

34. *Morse v Republican Party of Virginia*, 517 US 116 (1996).

35. *Shaw v Reno*, 509 US 630 (1993). See also *Shaw v Reno*, 509 US 874; *Johnson v De Grandy*, 512 US 997 (1994).

36. *Abrams v Johnson*, 518 US 74 (1997); *Miller v. Johnson*, 515 US 900 (1995).

37. Orlando Patterson, *The Ordeal of Integration: Progress and Resentment in America's "Racial" Crisis* (Civitas/Counterpoint, 1997), p. 67.

38. *Plessy v Ferguson*, 163 US 537 (1896).

39. *Brown v Board of Education of Topeka*, 347 US 483 (1954). See also J. W. Peltason, *Fifty-eight Lonely Men: Southern Federal Judges and School Desegregation* (University of Illinois Press, 1971), p. 248.

40. *Brown v Board of Education*, 349 US 294 (1955).

41. William Celis III, "Study Finds Rising Concentration of Black and Hispanic Students," *The New York Times*, December 14, 1993, p. A1.

42. *Missouri v Jenkins*, 495 US 33 (1990).

43. See Gary Orfield, Susan E. Eaton, and the Harvard Project on School Desegregation, *Dismantling Desegregation: The Quiet Reversal of Brown v Board of Education* (New Press, 1996). See also Peter Appelbome, "Schools See Reemergence of 'Separate But Equal,'" *The New York Times*, April 8, 1997, p. A8.

44. Raymond Hernandez, "NAACP Suspends Yonkers Leader After Criticism of Usefulness of School Busing," *The New York Times*, November 1, 1995, p. A13.

45. Quoted by Peter Appelbome, "Opponents' Moves Refueling Debate on School Busing," *The New York Times*, September 26, 1995, p. A1.

46. Justice William O. Douglas, dissenting in *Moose Lodge No. 107 v Irvis*, 407 US 163 (1972).

47. *New York State Club Association v New York City*, 487 US 1 (1988).

48. *Boy Scouts of America v Dale*, 120 S.Ct. 2446 (2000).

49. *Civil Rights Cases*, 109 US 3 (1883).

50. *Heart of Atlanta Motel v United States*, 379 US 421 (1964).

51. Darryl Van Duch, "Plagued by Politics, EEOC Backlog Grows," *The Recorder*, August 18, 1998, p. 1; David Rovella, "EEOC Chairman Casellas, 'We Are Being Selective,'" *The National Law Journal*, November 20, 1995, p. 1.

52. Charles M. Lamb, "Housing Discrimination and Segregation," *Catholic University Law Review* (Spring 1981), p. 370.

53. *Shelley v Kraemer*, 334 US 1 (1948).

54. Timothy Noah, "Housing Report Says Racial Bias Remains Prevalent," *The Wall Street Journal*, August 30, 1991, reporting on findings of report prepared by the Urban Institute commissioned by the Department of Housing and Urban Development.

55. Daniel Mitchell, quoted in CQ Researcher, *Housing Discrimination* 5 (February 24, 1995), p. 174.

56. Justice John Marshall Harlan, dissenting in *Plessy v Ferguson*, 163 US 537 (1896).

57. *University of California Regents v Bakke*, 438 US 265 (1978).

58. Sandra Day O'Connor, in *Richmond v Croson*, 488 US 469 (1989).

59. See *Adarand Constructors, Inc. v Pena*, 515 US 2000 (1995).

60. *Shaw v Reno*, 509 US 630 (1993); *Miller v Johnson*, 515 US 900 (1995).

61. *Hopwood v Texas*, 518 US 1016 (1996).

62. "Affirmative Action in California Passed," *The Economist*, April 8, 2000, p. 29.

63. Romel Hernandez, "Universities Will End Offers of Scholarships Based on Race," *The Oregonian*, March 21, 1998, at www.oregonlive.com/todaynews.

64. Carol M. Swain et al., "When Whites and Blacks Agree: Fairness in Educational Opportunities," Institute of Governmental Studies, University of California at Berkeley, Working Paper 98-11, 1998, p. 6. See also Lee Sigelman and Susan Welch, *Black Americans' Views of Racial Inequality: The Dream Deferred* (Cambridge University Press, 1994); Peter Skerry, "The Affirmative Action Paradox," *Society* 35, no. 6 (September/October 1998), p. 11.

65. James Farmer, quoted in Rochelle L. Stanfield, "Black Complaints Haven't Translated into Political Organization and Power," *National Journal*, June 14, 1980, p. 465.

66. National Academy of Science, *A Common Destiny: Blacks and American Society* (National Academy Press, 1989).

67. Gary Orfield, "Separate Societies: Have the Kerner Warnings Come True?" in Fred R. Harris and Roger W. Wilkins, eds., *Quiet Riots: Race and Poverty*

in the United States—The Kerner Report Twenty Years Later (Pantheon, 1988), p. 103. See also Madeline Landau, "Race, Poverty and the Cities: Hyperinnovation in Complex Policy Systems," *Public Affairs Report* (Bulletin of the Institute of Governmental Studies, University of California, Berkeley) 30 (January 1989), p. 1; Margaret C. Simms, ed., *Black Economic Progress: An Agenda for the 1990's* (Joint Center for Political Studies, 1988); Nicholas Lehmann, *The Promised Land* (Knopf, 1991).

68. Patterson, *Ordeal of Integration*, p. 54.
69. Gary Orfield and Carole Ashkinaze, *The Closing Door: Conservative Policy and Black Opportunity* (University of Chicago Press, 1991), p. 26.
70. William J. Wilson, *The Truly Disadvantaged: The Inner City, the Underclass, and Public Policy* (University of Chicago Press, 1987), esp. chap. 5.
71. Orfield and Ashkinaze, *Closing Door*, pp. 221–34.

CHAPTER 19

1. Edith Hamilton, *The Echo of Greece* (W.W. Norton, 1957), p. 47.
2. John F. Kennedy, *Profiles in Courage* (Pocket Books, 1956), p. 108.
3. See Warren Bennis and Patricia Ward Biederman, *Organizing Genius: The Secrets of Creative Collaboration* (Addison-Wesley, 1997).
4. See Lawrence R. Jacobs and Robert Y. Shapiro, *Politicians Don't Ponder* (University of Chicago Press, 2000); Christopher Beem, *The Necessity of Politics* (University of Chicago Press, 1999); and John E. McDonough, *Experiencing Politics* (University of California Press, 2000).
5. See Kareem Abdul-Jabar and Alan Steinberg, *Black Profiles in Courage* (Morrow, 1996).
6. Reinhold Niebuhr, *The Children of Light and the Children of Darkness* (Charles Scribner's Sons, 1944), p. xi.

7. See Bernard Crick, *In Defense of Politics*, rev. ed. (Pelican Books, 1983); Stimson Bullitt, *To Be a Politician*, rev. ed. (Yale University Press, 1977).
8. See the essays in Benjamin R. Barber, *A Passion for Democracy* (Princeton University Press, 1998).
9. See Nat Hentoff, *Free Speech for Me—But Not For Thee: How the American Left and Right Relentlessly Censor Each Other* (Harper Perennial, 1993).
10. William J. Brennan, commencement address, Brandeis University, Waltham, Mass., May 18, 1986.
11. Arthur M. Schlesinger, Jr., *The Disuniting of America* (W.W. Norton, 1993), p. 134.
12. John W. Gardner, *Self-Renewal*, rev. ed. (Norton, 1981), p. xiv.

PHOTO CREDITS

Chapter 1: 1 Library of Congress **2** S.E. McKee/AP/Wide World Photos **3** Corbis Digital Stock; White House Collection, courtesy White House Historical Association **6** Bob Daemmrich/Corbis/Sygma **7** Jeffrey Markowitz/Corbis/Sygma **15** *(left)* The Granger Collection; *(right)* Corbis **16** Liaison Agency, Inc. **21** Courtesy Louise Turner Arnold

Chapter 2: 25 The Granger Collection **31** The Granger Collection **32** Theo Westerbenger/Liaison Agency, Inc. **34** *(top)* The Granger Collection; *(middle)* Fabian Bachrach/FPG/International LLC; *(bottom)* Ron Edmonds/AP/Wide World Photos **39** AP/Wide World Photos

Chapter 3: 51 Mike Williams, Preamble, 1987; painted metal on vinyl and wood; National Museum of American Art, Smithsonian Institution; Gift of Nissan Motor Corporation; Art Resource, N.Y. **52** *(top)* Greg Baker/AP/WideWorld Photos; *(bottom)* Donald McLeod/AP/Wide World Photos **60** Jim Wilson/New York Times Pictures **66** AP/Wide World Photos

Chapter 4: 73 Spencer Grant/Photo Reseaachers, Inc. **76** *(top)* Richard Shock/Liaison Agency, Inc; *(left)* Stephen McBrady/Photo Edit: *(right)* Michal Heron/Pearson Education/PH College **78** Jean Catuffe/SIPA Press **80** UPI/Corbis **84** Richard Ellis/Liaison Agency, Inc. **85** Librado Romero/New York Times Pictures **86** Greg Gibson/AP/Wide World Photos **87** Courtesy of Libertarian National Committee, Inc. **88** SIPA Press **89** Mitchell Cohen

Chapter 5: 95 Jake Schoellkopf/AP/Wide World Photos **97** Library of Congress **98** LouKrasky/AP/WideWorld Photos **105** Liaison Agency, Inc. **107** *(left)* Liaison Agency Inc., courtesy of National Archives/Newsmakers; *(center)* Les Stone/Corbis/Sygma; *(right)* Laura Rauch/AP/WideWorld Photos

Chapter 6: 117 John Chiasson/Liaison Agency, Inc. **123** Liaison Agency, Inc. **124** Celano Lee/Liaison Agency, Inc. **125** Susan Hunt/SIPA Press **126** Bob Daemmriach/Stock Boston **127** Cynthia Howe/Corbis/Sygma **132** *(left)* Corbis; *(right)* Roswell Angier/Stock Boston **134** © Sam Mircovich/Reuters New Media Inc./Corbis **135** Crandall/The Image Works

Chapter 7: 143 Daniel MacDonald/Stock Boston **146** Bob Daemmmrich/The Image Works **149** John Harrington/Black Star **150** Ed Betz/AP/WideWorld Photos **153** Paul Conklin/PhotoEdit **154** Dennis Paquin/AP/WideWorld Photos **155** *(top)* Ron Edmonds/AP/Wide World Photos; *(bottom)* Mark HumphreyAP/WideWorld Photos **164** Dennis Cook/AP/Wide World Photos **165** AP/Wide World Photos

Chapter 8: 171 Joe Raedle/Liaison Agency, Inc. **172** Bob Daemmrich/Stock Boston **176** UPI/Corbis **178** Bob Daemmrich/Stock Boston **179** Alexis DCLOS/Liaison Agency, Inc. **183** Julia Malakie/AP/Wide World Photos **184** Liaison Agency, Inc. **186** Walter Michot/AP/Wide World Photos

Chapter 9: 193 © Brian Snyder/Reuters New Media Inc./Corbis **196** Liaison Agency, Inc. **199** Richard Drew/AFP/Corbis **205** Mike Fiala/SIPA Press

206 *(left)* © Don Emmert/AFP/Corbis; *(right)* © Jeff Mitchell/Reuters New Media Inc./Corbis **212** *(top)* AP/Wide World Photos; *(bottom)* Charles Rex Abrogast/AP/Wide World Photos **216** Lawrence University **217** AP/Wide World Photos

Chapter 10: 223 Lisa Quinones/Black Star **225** © AFP/Corbis **227** Geostock/PhotoDisk, Inc. **229** UPI/Corbis **230** © Mitchell Gerber/Corbis

Chapter 11: 243 L. Mark/UPI/Corbis **244** © Mike Theiler/Reuters New Media Inc./Corbis **246** *(top)* Corbis; *(bottom)* Corbis **249** Robert Trippett/ SIPA Press **251** *(top)* J. Scott Applewhite/AP/Wide World Photos; *(bottom)* Robert Trippett/ SIPA Press **253** Robert Trippett/SIPA Press **257** AP/Wide World Photos

Chapter 12: 273 Reuters/Jeff Mitchell Archive Photos **280** Dennis Brack/Black Star **282** Liaison Agency, Inc. **284** Bruce Chambers/SABA Press Photos, Inc. **285** Beaudenon/SIPA Press **289** © Reuters New Media Inc./Corbis

Chapter 13: 297 AP/Wide World Photos **298** The Nashua Telegraph/SIPA Press **303** AP/Wide World Photos **305** Alex Wong/AP/Wide World Photos **306** AP/Wide World Photos **311** Joe Marquette/AP/Wide World Photos

Chapter 14: 317 Brad Markel/Liaison Agency, Inc. **324** *(left)* Clary/UPI/Corbis; *(center)* Carol T. Powers/AP/Wide World Photos; *(right)* Reuters/Corbis **325** *(left)* Reuters/Gary Hershorn/Corbis; *(right)* Reuters/Steve Jaffe/Corbis **328** Susan Walsh/AP/Wide World Photos **329** Supreme Court Historical Society **333** Reuters/Gary Hershorn/Corbis

Chapter 15: 343 © Roger Ressmeyer/Corbis **344** Sue Klemens/Stock Boston **357** Robert Trippett/SIPA Press **359** © Gail Mooney/Thomas A. Kelly/Corbis

Chapter 16: 363 Rob Crandall/The Image Works **367** Joe Raedle/Liaison Agency Inc. **369** LM Otero/AP/Wide World Photos **371** Charles Tasnadi/AP/Wide World Photos **372** Tom Uhlman/AP/Wide World Photos **377** Jean Catuffe/SIPA Press **379** *(left and right)* Adam Nadel

Chapter 17: 383 Andrew Lichtenstein/Stock Boston **384** David McNew/Liaison Agency, Inc. **386** Corbis **390** Joe Marquette/AP/Wide World Photos **392** *(top)* Chris Hondros/Liaison Agency, Inc.; *(bottom)* Blair Seitz/Photo Researchers, Inc. **393** Bob Daemmrich/Stock Boston **394** James Wilson **398** Seth Perlman/AP/World Wide Photos **399** Damian Dovarganes/AP/Wide World Photos

Chapter 18: 403 Raynor/SIPA Press **406** AP/Wide World Photos **407** *(top)* AP/Wide World Photos; *(bottom)* L.P. Winfrey/Woodfin Camp & Associates **408** Corbis **409** AP/Wide World Photos **410** Eric Haase/Contact Press Images Inc. **415** UPI/Corbis **416** AP/Wide World Photos **419** AP/Wide World Photos **420** McKinney & McDowell Associates **421** Curiale Dellaverson Hirschfield/ Kelly & Kraemer

Chapter 19: 427 Reza Estakhrian/Stone **428** Bob Daemmrich Photography Inc.

INDEX

A

ABC/Capital Cities, 230
Abortion
  privacy rights and, 390
  public opinion and, 173
Accommodations. *See* Public
  accommodations
Adams, Abigail, 14
Adams, John, 31
Adams, John Quincy, 151, 196
Adler, David Gray, 303
Administrative law, 318
Administrator, president as, 286–88
Admiralty law, 318
Adversary system, 317, 319
Affirmative action, 404, 419–23
  attack on, 421
  Bakke decision, 419–20
  continuing conflict over, 422–23
  defense of, 420
African Americans
  in cities, 101
  civil rights and, 405–7
  education and, 112
  judicial selection and, 326, 327
  judicial system and, 398–400
  political diversity and, 101–2
  in South, 99
  voting rights, 180–81
  wealth distribution and, 101–2
Age
  classification and, 412
  political diversity and, 110–10
  political ideology and, 82
Age Discrimination in Employment
  Act (1967), 414
Agenda setting
  by media, 234
  by president, 282–83
Aid to Families with Dependent
  Children (AFDC), 67
Albright, Madeleine, 303
Aliens
  rights of, 386–87
  undocumented, 386, 387
Alliance for Justice, 324
Amendments to U.S. Constitution.
  See also specific amendments
  list of, 36
  methods of proposing, 36–38
  ratifying, 38–39
American Association of Retired
  Persons, 119
American Association of University
  Professors, 122
American Automobile Association
  (AAA), 119
American Bar Association (ABA),
  122
  death penalty and, 398
  Standing Committee on the Fed-
    eral Judiciary, 324
American Cancer Society, 123
American Civil Liberties Union
  (ACLU), 92, 122
  Women's Rights Project, 130
American Committee on Africa, 124
American Conservative Union, 131
American Dream, 78–79
American Farm Bureau Federation,
  120
American Federation of Govern-
  ment Employees, 352

American Federation of Labor
  (AFL), 120
American Federation of Labor-
  Congress of Industrial Organi-
  zations (AFL-CIO), 117, 121
American Federation of State,
  County, and Municipal
  Employees (AFSCME), 167
American Federation of Teachers,
  122
American Heart Association, 123
American Independent Party, 149
American-Israel Political Action
  Committee (AIPAC), 124
American Medical Association
  (AMA), 122
American Political Science Associa-
  tion, 122
American Realtors Association, 122
American Revolution, 13
Americans for Democratic Action
  (ADA), 131, 154
Americans with Disabilities Act
  (1990), 67, 414
America OnLine, 230
Amicus curiae briefs, 130, 334
Amnesty International, 92
Anderson, John, 205
Annapolis Convention, 13–14
Anthony, Susan B., 104
Antifederalists, 19–20
Anti-Saloon League, 123
Antiterrorism and Effective Death
  Penalty Act (1996), 364
Anti-trade/globalization movement,
  125
Antitrust legislation, 79
Appellate jurisdiction, 319
Appointive powers, presidential,
  281–82
Armey, Dick, 152
Articles of Confederation, 12, 13
  weaknesses of, 14
Ashcroft, John, 287, 385
Asian Americans, 101, 103
Assembly, freedom of, 9, 378–80
Associated Press, 230
Association, right of, 416–17
Association of South East Asian
  Nations (ASEAN), 51
Athens, ancient, 427
AT&T, 167
Attentive public, 178, 255
Australian ballot, 181
Automobile exception, searches/
  seizures and, 393

B

Bad tendency test, 370, 371
Baker v. Carr, 245
Bakke, Allan, 419
Balanced government, 16
Bankruptcy judges, 322
Baptists, 107, 108
Bauer, Gary, 84
Beard, Charles, 20
Beauty contests, presidential pri-
  maries as, 202
Bernstein, Carl, 229
Bicameralism, 17
  consequences of, 246–47
  in Germany, 246

Billboards, constitutional protection
  of, 377
Bill of Rights, 9
  Second, 80
  state bills of rights, 13, 364, 366
  states and, 364–66
Bills of attainder, 363, 364, 365
Blanket primaries, 147
Block grants, 66
Bork, Robert, 131, 324, 326
Bowers v Hardwick, 390
Boy Scouts of America v Dale, 391,
  417
Brandeis, Louis, 55
Brennan, William J., Jr., 326, 328,
  330, 412
Breyer, Stephen, 7, 65, 325, 367
Broadcasting
  constitutional protection of,
    377–78
  impact of, 228–29
Broder, David, 233
Broker rule, 430
Browne, Harry, 87
*Brown v Board of Education of
  Topeka*, 405
Buchanan, Patrick, 149, 205–6
Buckley v Valeo, 209
Budde, Bernadette, 130
Bull Moose Party, 149
Bundling, 135
Bureaucracy, federal, 343–60
  accountability
    to Congress, 357–58
    to president, 356–57
  bureaucrats in, 346–47
  case study, 353–56
  Clinton-Gore reform efforts, 344
  congressional oversight of, 248
  defined, 344, 345
  evolution of, 345–46
  operating procedures, 350–53
    bureaucratic realities, 352–53
    hiring practices, 351, 352
    management principles, 351
    reform efforts, 352
    regulation of employees, 351–52
  organization
    formal, 347–49, 350
    informal, 349–50
  policy implementation by, 347
  as political issue, 344–45
  privatization and, 356, 357
  public opinion of, 358–60
Bureaucrats, 346–47
  defined, 344
  drug testing issue, 352, 353
Bureau of Indian Affairs, 410
Bureaus, 348
Burger, Warren, 330, 334
Burr, Aaron, 196
Bush, George, 64
  judicial appointments, 324–25,
    326, 327, 331
Bush, George W., 1, 6–7, 137, 153,
  187–88, 206, 208
  faith-based social service initia-
    tive, 107
  on federal bureaucracy, 344–45
  immigration issues, 95
  judicial selection, 325
  traditional conservatism and, 84
Bush, Laura, 293
Bush v Gore, 1, 6–7

Business, as interest group, 119
Business and Industrial Political
  Action Committee (BIPAC),
  130
Business Higher-Education Forum,
  119
Business-Industry Political Action
  Committee, 134

C

Cable communications, constitutional protection of, 377–78
Cable television, 229
Calhoun, John C., 64
California
  economic/political importance
    of, 100
  Proposition 187, 408
  Proposition 209, 422–23
Campaign finance, 207–13
  in Canada, 219
  candidates' personal wealth, 211
  current, consequences of, 211–13
  in Great Britain, 219
  independent expenditures, 211
  issue advertising, 210–11
  reform efforts, 208–9
  scandals involving, 207–8
Campaigns
  for House of Representatives,
    199–200
  presidential, 206–7
  for Senate, 201
Campbell, Ben Nighthorse, 411
Canada
  campaign financing, 219
  constitution, 31
  federalism, 61
  multiparty system, 149
Candidate activists, 159
Candidate-centered party system,
  145
Candidates
  appeal, voting on basis of, 187–88
  media's role in choice of, 235
  personal wealth of, 211
  reasons for and against becom-
    ing, 432, 433
Cantwell, Mary, 193
Capitalism, defined, 78
Carter, Jimmy, 187, 206
  judicial appointments, 326
Categorical-formula grants, 66
Caucus/convention system, 144,
  146, 203
Cavazos, Laura F., 103
Census, controversy over, 96, 97
Centralists, decentralists *vs.*, 63–64
Certiorari, writ of, 333
Chamber of Commerce of U.S.,
  119, 131
Checks and balances, 9, 27–30
  modifications of, 28–29
Cheney, Dick, 205
Chicago Tribune, The, 229
Chief Justice of Supreme Court,
  333–34
Child Care and Development Block
  Grant (CCDBG), 67
Child Online Protection Act (1998),
  373
Child pornography, 373
Chinese Americans, 409

Christian Coalition, 84–85, 92, 107, 117, 123
Cisneros, Henry G., 103
Cities, African Americans in, 101
Citizenship rights, 383–87
Civic organizations, political culture and, 76
Civil disobedience, 379
Civil law, 318, 364
Civil liberties, 364, 403
  Supreme Court and, 400
Civil rights, 364, 403, 404–23
  affirmative action and, 404, 419–23
  African Americans and, 405–7
  Asian Americans and, 408–9
  Chinese Americans and, 409
  contemporary issues, 423–24
  education and, 415–16
  equality and, 404
  Hispanics and, 408
  Japanese Americans and, 409
  Native Americans and, 410–11
  racial justice and, 405–7
  voting and, 413–15
  women and, 407–8
Civil rights acts
  1957, 414
  1964, 58, 63, 406, 414
    Title II, 417–18
    Title VI, 416
    Title VII, 418
  1991, 414
  list of, 414
Civil Service Commission, 346
Civil Service Reform Act (1978), 346, 349
Civil War, rise of Republicans and, 151
Class action suits, 318, 319, 418
Classifications, Constitutional
  quasi-suspect classifications, 412
  suspect classifications, 411–12
  tests for, 411–12
Clay, Henry, 196
Clear and present danger test, 370, 371
Cleveland, Grover, 196
Clinton, Bill, 28–29, 206, 232, 234, 376
  federal mandates, 67
  impeachment of, 34
  judicial appointments, 325, 326, 327, 330
  welfare reform, 67
Clinton, Hillary, 293
Closed primaries, 147
Closed shop, 121
Cloture rule, 251
CNN, 13, 30
Coalition builder, president as, 283–84
Coalition for a Democratic Majority, 154
Coalition government, 148
Coattail effect, 197
Cohen, Mitchell, 89
Cohen, William, 265–66
Commerce clause, 58, 416, 417
Commercial speech, 374
Commission on Presidential Debates, 206
Committee of the whole, 248
Committee on Political Education (COPE), 120–21, 134
Common law, 318, 364
Communications Decency Act (1996), 373, 378
Communist party, 149
Community policing, 400
Competitive federalism, 53
Concurrent powers, 59
Concurring opinion, Supreme Court, 336
Confederate flag, controversy over, 98

Confederation, 54
  federalism compared to, 54, 55
Conference Board, 119
Conference committees, 264
Confirmation politics, 304–5
Confirmation power of Senate, 28, 248, 251–52, 254, 326
Congress, 243–69
  accountability of bureaucracy to, 357
  Connecticut Compromise and, 18
  Constitutional powers of, 247–48
  criticisms of, 266–68
  defense of, 268–69
  elections for, 197–201, 244–46
  50/50 split in, 263
  functions of, 248
  impeachment and removal power, 34–35
  judicial system and, 319
  legislators
    attentiveness to constituents, 255
    colleagues' influence on, 255–56
    interest groups' influence on, 257–58
    as lawmakers, 255–58
    party influence on, 256–57
    policy/philosophical convictions of, 255
    president's influence on, 258
    as representatives, 254–55
  New Jersey Plan for, 17, 18
  107th, profile of, 267
  party unity score in, 166
  political parties in, 158
  as presidential constraint, 290
  reform of, 264, 265
  staffs of, 256
  structure/powers of, 246–54
  Supreme Court and, 64–65
  Virginia Plan for, 17, 18
Congressional Budget Office (CBO), 67
Congressional campaign committee, 155
Congressional elections, 197–201, 244–45
  for House of Representatives, 199–200
  presidential popularity and, 197–98
  safe seats in, 197, 244
  for Senate, 201
Congress of Industrial Organizations (CIO), 120
Connecticut Compromise, 18
Consensus, in public opinion, 173
Consensus building, congressional function of, 248
Conservatism, 84, 88
  criticisms of, 85–86
  social, 84–85
  traditional, 84
Constitution, U.S., 43–49. See also First Amendment rights; specific amendments
  amending, 36–39
  checks and balances in, 9, 27–28
  commerce clause, 58
  congressional elaborations of, 34
  contract clause, 388
  custom and usage, 35
  due process clause, 364–65
  equal protection clause, 411
  establishment clause, 366–69
  extradition clause, 61–62
  federalism and, 9
  framers of, 14–15
  free exercise clause, 369
  full faith and credit clause, 60–61
  impeachment and removal power, 34–35
  importance of reading, 42
  interstate compacts, 62

interstate privileges and immunities, 61
interstate relations, 60–62
judicial interpretation of, 35–36
national supremacy article, 57
as natural law, 25
necessary and proper clause, 56–57
presidential practices and, 35
ratification of, 19–21
roots of, 12–21
separation of powers in, 9, 26–27
taxation/spending, 58
war power, 58
Constitutional Convention (1787), 14–19
  Connecticut Compromise, 18
  consensus achieved at, 15–16
  delegates to, 14–15
  New Jersey Plan, 17
  three-fifths compromise, 18
  Virginia Plan, 17
Constitutional courts, 319, 322
Constitutional democracy
  American, 12–21
    Articles of Confederation, 13
    colonial beginnings, 12–13
    Constitutional Convention (1787), 14–19
    overview, 2–4
    participation/representation in, 428–30
    politician's role, 430–31
    ratification debates, 19–21
  British, 33
  conditions conducive to
    educational, 10
    ideological, 11
    social, 10, 11
  defined, 4
  judicial power in, 337–39
  leadership for, 431
Constitutionalism, defined, 4
Constitutional law, 318
Content-neutral laws, 375
Contract clause, 388
Conventions, national party, 144, 146, 154, 203–6
Converting realignment, 151
Cooperative federalism, 53
Cooperative lobbying, by interest groups, 131
Council on Foreign Relations, 124
Counsel, right to, 394
County committees, 156–57
Court of appeals, 320
Crawford, William, 196
Crime Control and Safe Streets Act (1968), 391
Crimes, rights of persons accused of, 364, 391–96
Criminal law, 318
Crisis manager, president as, 279–81
Cross-cutting cleavages, 96
Cross-cutting requirements, 68
Cross-over sanctions, 68
Crossover voting, 147
Cruel and unusual punishment, 396
C-SPAN, 13, 30
Cuban Americans, 102–2
Cuomo, Mario, 226
Custom and usage, Constitution and, 35

D

Dahl, Robert A., 79
Daley, Richard, 166
Dealignment, partisan, 162
Death penalty, 396, 398
Decentralists, centralists vs., 63–64
Declaration of Independence, 5, 13
De facto segregation, 416
Defendants, 322
Defense lawyers, federal, 322

Defense of Marriage Act (1996), 60
De jure segregation, 416
DeLay, Tom, 152
Delegates, 255
  legislators as, 254
Democracy. See also Constitutional democracy
  defined, 4
  derivation of word, 4
  difficulty of sustaining, 11
  direct, 4
  reconciling leadership and, 431–32
  representative, 4
  as system of
    interacting values, 5, 8
    interdependent political structures, 5, 9–10, 12
    interrelated political processes, 5, 8–9
Democratic consensus, 12, 75
Democratic faith, 432–33
Democratic Leadership Council, 154
Democratic values
  conflicting, 8
  equality of opportunity, 5
  personal liberty, 5
  popular consent, 8
Democrats/Democratic party, 31, 99, 150, 151
  ideological diversity, 154
  midterm elections, 198
    1998, 189
  platform, 156–57
  reform among, 166
  2000 presidential election, 189
Demographics, 96
Descriptive representation, 254
Devolution revolution, 51, 52, 69
Direct democracy, defined, 4
Direct orders, 68
Direct popular election of president, 218
Direct popular participation, 428–29
Direct primary, 29, 146–47
Discharge petitions, 262
Discrimination
  affirmative action and, 419–23
  age, 412
  education, 415–16
  employment, 418
  ethnic, 408–11
  housing, 418–19
  poverty and, 412
  proving, 413
  public accommodations, 417–18
  racial, 405–7
  reverse, 419
  sex, 407–8
  voting, 413–15
Disney corporation, 230
Disparate impact, 413
Dissenters, protection of, 429
Dissenting opinion, Supreme Court, 336
Distribution, in public opinion sampling, 172
District courts, 319–20
Divided government, 28
  political parties and, 152–53
Dole, Bob, 206
"Don't ask, Don't tell" policy, 105
Double jeopardy, 396
Douglas, William O., 416–17
Dual citizenship, 385
Dual federalism, 53
Due process
  clause, 364–65
  defined, 388
  rights, 388–89
DuPont, Pete, 88

E

Eagleton, Tom, 187

Harrison, William Henry, 151
Hastert, Dennis, 249
Hatch, Carl, 351
Hatch, Orrin, 325, 327
Hatch Act (1939), 351
  revised, 351
Hate speech on campus, 374, 375
Havel, Vaclav, 428
Hayes, Rutherford B., 196
Heightened scrutiny test, 412
Henry, Patrick, 21
Heritage Foundation, 324, 327
Hersh, Seymour, 229
Hibbing, John, 243
Hill, Anita, 325, 408
Hines, Richard Towell, 117
Hispanics
  civil rights for, 408
  education and, 112
  federal judgeship appointments,
    327
  judicial selection and, 326
  judicial system and, 398–400
  political diversity and, 101, 102–3
  wealth distribution and, 102
Holds, 250
Holmes, Oliver Wendell, Jr., 376–77
Honeymoon period, 145–46
Hoover, Herbert, 152
Hopwood v Texas, 422
House of Commons, 33
House of Representatives, 28
  elections for, 199–200, 244–46
  fixed terms of office for, 194
  impeachment power, 34
  organization/procedures, 248–50
  redistricting by states for, 245–46
  Senate compared to, 247
Housing and Urban Development,
  Department of, 419
Housing discrimination, 418–19
Hughes, Charles Evans, 333–34, 336
Hustler magazine, 372

I
Idealism, as American value, 77
Ideological interest groups, 122–23
Ideology, 81–92
  conservatism, 84–86
  defined, 12, 81
  environmentalism, 86–87
  judicial selection and, 326–30
  labeling by, 87, 90
  liberalism, 81–84
  libertarianism, 87
  political parties and, 149, 154
  role of, in U.S., 90–91
  socialism, 86
  tolerance and, 91–92
Immigrants
  Asian, 103
  Cuban, 102, 103
  ethnic bonding by, 103
  growth in population of, 103–4
  Mexican, 103
  Puerto Rican, 102–3
Immigration Act (1965), 387
Immigration and Naturalization
  Service (INS), 384
Immigration policy, controversy
  over, 95
Immunity, grant of, 393–94
Impeachment power, congressional,
  28, 34–35, 247–48
Implied powers, 56
Impoundment, 35
Income, political diversity and,
  108–9
Incumbency advantage, 245
Independent agencies
  executive, 29
  regulatory, 29, 348
Independent expenditures, 211

Indictment, 394–95
Individualism, as American value,
  74–75
Individual preference, in public
  opinion sampling, 173
Industrial transformation, political
  culture and, 79–80
Information Committee on Federal
  Food Regulations, 131
Inherent powers, 57
Initiative petitions, 29
Initiative 200, 423
INS v Chadha, 28
Intensity of public opinion, 174
Interested money, 207
Interest group pluralism, 119
Interest groups, 117–41. *See also*
  Lobbying; Lobbyists; PACS
  characteristics/power of, 126–32
    cohesiveness, 127–28
    leadership, 128
    size/resources, 126–27
    techniques, 128–31
  criticisms of, 136
  overview, 117–18
  regulation/reform of, 136–40
  social movements and, 116–17
  types of
    economic, 119–22
    foreign policy, 124
    government, 124–25
    ideological, 122–23
    public interest, 123–24
  U.S. as nation of, 118
Internet
  constitutional protection of, 378
  as news source, 225
  politics and, 227
  voting and, 188, 189
Interstate Commerce Commission
  (ICC), 29
Interstate compacts, 62
Interstate privileges and immunities
  clause, 61
Investigating power, congressional,
  248, 264
Investigatory journalism, 229
Iron triangles, 133, 353
  defined, 352
Isikoff, Michael, 229
Israel, multiparty system in, 148
Issue activists, 159–60
Issue advocacy, 117
Issue advocacy advertising, 210–11,
  225–26
Issue framing, by media, 234–35
Issues
  media framing of, 234–35
  voting on basis of, 188

J
Jackson, Andrew, 151, 345
Jackson, Robert H., 3, 370, 380, 400
Japan
  bureaucracy, 354
  Constitution of 1947, 29
  media, 228
  soft money, 208
Japanese Americans, 409
Jay, John, 20
Jefferson, Thomas, 3, 5, 14, 26, 31,
  64, 111, 149, 196, 293
  executive privilege and, 306
  greatness of, 293
Jeffersonian Republicans, 31
Jeffords, Jim, 257
Jews, 108
Jim Crow laws, 415
Johnson, Andrew, 34, 331
Johnson, Lyndon, 80, 187, 198, 203,
  406
Joint committees, 261
Jones, Brian W., 421

Jones, Charles O., 28, 274–75
Jones, Paula, 408
Journalism
  investigatory, 229
  objective, 228
Journalists, politics of, 234
Judicial activism, 330
Judicial circuits, 320
Judicial restraint, 330
Judicial review, 28, 30–32, 34, 317,
  319
Judicial Selection Monitoring Pro-
  ject, 324
Judicial system. *See also* Federal
  judges; State courts; Supreme
  Court
  adversarial nature of, 317
  criticisms of, 396–400
  federal court system, 62–65,
    319–21
  judicial power, 317–18
    in constitutional democracy,
      337–39
  political parties in, 158–59
  prosecution/defense in, 322–23
Judiciary Act of 1789, 32, 34
Justice, as American value, 75
Justice Department, 322
Justiciable disputes, 317

K
Keating, Charles, 208
Keep It Flying, 117, 129, 135
Kennedy, Anthony, 353
Kennedy, John F., 80, 107, 108, 231,
  406
Kentucky and Virginia Resolutions,
  31
Kerner, Otto, 406–7
Kerner Commission, 406–7
Key, V.O., 150
Keyes, Alan, 226
Keynesian economics, 152
King, Larry, 224
King, Martin Luther, Jr., 107, 378,
  379, 406
Knights of Labor, 120
Korean Americans, 409

L
Labor
  as interest group, 120–21
  unions
    election activities, 130–31
    membership, U.S. *vs.* other
      countries, 120
    membership decline, 121–22
Ladd, Everett C., 13
Laissez-faire policy, 152
Larry King Live, 29
Laski, Harold, 317
Latency, in public opinion, 174
Latinos. *See* Hispanics
Law clerks, Supreme Court, 333, 334
Law making, congressional function
  of, 248
Laws, types of, 318
Leadership
  for constitutional democracy, 431
  reconciling democracy and, 431–32
Leadership, interest group, 128
Leadership Conference on Civil
  Rights, 131
Lee, Frances, 246
Legal privileges, 364
Legal Services Corporation (LSC), 323
Legislative courts, 319, 322
Lemon v Kurtzman, 366–67
Less drastic means doctrine, 374
Lewinsky, Monica, 35, 232
Lewis, John L., 134
Leykins, Tom, 226

Libel, 372–73
Liberalism, 81–84, 89
  contemporary, 82–83
  criticisms of, 83–84
Libertarianism, 87
Libertarian party, 149, 151
Liberty, as American value, 74
Liddy, G. Gordon, 226
Lieberman, Joseph, 106, 107, 108,
  154, 194
Life-cycle effects, politics and, 111
Light, Paul, 352
Limbaugh, Rush, 226, 233
Limited public forums, freedom of
  assembly in, 379
Lincoln, Abraham, 64, 151, 293
Lincoln, Blanche, 253
Literacy tests, 414
Litigation by interest groups, 130
Litt, Edgar, 176
Lobbying, 132
  cooperative, 131
  regulation, 136–36
Lobbying Disclosure Act (1995), 137
Lobbyists
  activities, 133
  identity, 132–33
  influence, 131–32
Local government, political parties
  in, 159
Locke, Gary, 103, 409
Locke, John, 26
Log rolling, 256
Los Angeles Times, 229, 233
Lott, Trent, 152, 250
Lujan, Manuel, 103

M
Madison, James, 4, 15, 20, 26, 31,
  54, 106, 109, 118, 246, 292, 303,
  306, 380
Magistrate judges, 320
Mails, constitutional protection of,
  376–77
Majority leader
  House of Representatives, 249
  Senate, 250
Majority-minority districts, 415
Majority rule, 9, 148
  as American value, 75
  in British system, 33
Mandamus, writ of, 32, 34
Mandatory partial preemption, 68
Mandela, Nelson, 428
Manifest destiny, 98
Mapp v Ohio, 393
Marble cake federalism, 53
Marbury, William, 32
Marbury v Madison, 31–32, 34, 158
Maritime law, 318
Marshall, John, 30, 31–32, 62–63,
  64, 65, 317, 388
Marshall, Thurgood, 32, 330
Martin, Luther, 62
Martinez, Mel, 103
Marx, Karl
Mason, Mary, 226
Mass mailing, by interest groups,
  128, 129
Mass media
  appeals, by interest groups, 128
  defined, 224
  political culture and, 76
  public opinion and, 176
Mayhew, David, 133
Mayhew, David R., 28
McCain, John, 128, 155, 164, 203,
  208, 227
McCain-Feingold campaign finance
  reform bill, 155, 212
McCarthy, Eugene, 203
McConnell, Mitch, 165
McCulloch, James William, 62

Senatorial courtesy, 252, 323
Seneca Falls Women's Rights Convention, 407
Senior Executive Service, 349
Seniority rule, 263
Sentencing, 395–96
Separation of powers, 9, 26–27, 247–48
Seventeenth Amendment, 29, 151, 246
Sexual harassment, 408
Sexual orientation
  political diversity and, 105
  rights, 390–91
Shaw, Theodore M., 420
Shaw v Reno, 415
Shays, Daniel, 14
Shays Rebellion, 14
Shield laws, 375
Sierra Club, 117
Silent, right to remain, 393–94
Simpson, O.J., murder trial, press and, 376
Single-issue interest groups, 122–23
Single-member districts, 195
Sixth Amendment, 395
Skocpol, Theda, 13
Slaughterhouse Cases, 385
Smith, Alfred E., 108
Smith, Jeremiah, 318
Smith Act (1940), 372
Smith v Allwright, 413
Snowe, Olympia, 253
Social capital, defined, 10, 73
Social class, political diversity and, 110
Socialism, 86
Social movements, interest groups and, 118–19
Socioeconomic status (SES), 110
Soft money, 135, 145, 155, 164–65, 209–10
  in Japan, 208
  stronger parties and, 166–67
Solicitor general (SG), 322
Sound trucks, constitutional protection of, 377
Souter, David, 65, 324, 327, 333, 335, 367
Speaker of House of Representatives, 248–49
Special elections, 182
Speech
  freedom of, 370–75
  nonprotected, 371–74
  protected, 374–75
Spoils system, 344–45
Staggered terms of office, 194
Standing committees, 258
Standing to sue, 245, 318
Stare Decisis, 318–19
State chair, 155
State committees, 155
State constitutions, bills of rights in, 364, 366
State courts, federal courts and, 321
States
  Bill of Rights and, 364–66
  constitutional limits/obligations, 59–60
  constitutional powers, 58–59
  political parties, 159
States' rights, 102
States' Rights party, 149
Statism, 5
Statutory law, 318
Stenberg v Carhart, 390
Stevens, John Paul, 7, 64–65, 367
Stewart, Potter, 373, 399
Stone, Harlan F., 334, 338
Straight ticket voting, 144
Strict scrutiny test, 411–12
  fundamental rights and, 412–13
Substantive due process, 389
Substantive representation, 254
Sun belt, 99
Sunshine laws, 375
Supremacy clause, 17
Supreme Court, 18–19
  centralist/decentralist positions of, 64
  civil liberties and, 400
  confirmation politics, 324–27, 330–31
  Congress and, 64–65
  jurisdiction of, 319
  operation of, 332–37
    amicus curiae briefs, 334

choosing cases, 333
conference, 335
law clerks' role, 334
opinions, 336–37
oral arguments, 334–35
powers of Chief Justice, 333–34
original jurisdiction of, 319
people and, 338–39
selective incorporation by, 365–66
Supreme Court decisions
  abortion, 334, 338, 366, 390
  affirmative action, 419, 422
  association rights, 417
  campaign financing, 209
  citizenship rights, 385
  civil rights, 58
  commercial speech, 374
  constitutional democracy, 3
  contract clause, 388
  death penalty, 396
  disparate impact, 413
  electoral recounts, 1
  equal protection clause, 411–12
  establishment clause, 366–67
  exclusionary rule, 393
  federalism, 62–63
  freedom of assembly, 379–80
  freedom of speech, 365, 371, 372
  free exercise clause, 369
  gun control, 334
  implementation of, 337
  judicial review, 31–32, 34
  mails, 376–77
  Miranda warning, 394
  obscenity, 373
  parochial school aid, 368
  pornography, 373
  press freedom, 365, 376–78
  privacy rights, 390–91
  protected speech, 374–75
  redistricting, 245
  school prayer, 367
  searches and seizures, 392
  sexual orientation, 390–91
  term limits, 195
  unannounced drug testing, 353
  voting rights, 413, 415
Surface Transportation Board, 29
Suspect classifications, 411–12
Switzerland, federalism in, 61
Symbolic representation, 254

T

Taft, William Howard, 330
Taney, Roger B., 330
Tauzin, Billy, 223
Taxation, Congress's power of, 58
Tax-exempt public charities, 123
Teapot Dome scandal, 207
Technology, media, 236
Telecommunications, constitutional protection of, 378
Television
  impact of, 229
  pervasiveness of, 225–26
  ratings systems, 232, 233
Tenth Amendment, 64, 65
Term limits, 194
Terry v Ohio, 392
Texas v Johnson, 371
Theiss-Morse, Elizabeth, 243
Theocracy, defined, 12
Third parties, 148
Thirteenth Amendment, 405
Thomas, Clarence, 64, 65, 229, 324–25, 327, 333, 335, 367, 408
Thompson, Tommy, 90
Three-fifths compromise, 18
"Three strikes and you're out" laws, 396
Tilden, Samuel, 196
Times/Mirror, 229
Time Warner, 230
Title IX, Education Amendment (1972), 414

Tocqueville, Alexis de, 5, 97, 98
Tolerance, ideology and, 91–92
Total preemption, 68
Totenberg, Nina, 229
Trade associations, as interest groups, 119
Travel rights, 386
Trials by jury, 395
Truman, Harry S., 293, 405
Trustees, 255
Turner Broadcasting System, 230
Turnout, voter, 182–83
Twelfth Amendment, 195
Twenty-fourth Amendment, 180
Twenty-seventh Amendment, 38
Twenty-sixth Amendment, 184, 413
Twenty-third Amendment, 180
2000 elections, 193
  in Florida, 1, 6–7, 186
  issue voting in, 189–90
  media coverage of, 223–24
  political parties and, 153, 161–62

U

Unanimous consent motion, 248
Underclass, 423
Undocumented aliens, 386
Undue burden test, 390
Unfunded Mandates Reform Act (1995), 67
Unions. *See* Labor
Unitary systems of government, 54
United Press International, 230
United States Court of Veteran Appeals, 322
United States-Israel Free Trade Agreement, 124
United States Supreme Court Reports, 336
United States v Eichman, 371
United States v Lopez, 334
United States v Playboy Entertainment Group, 378
Unit rule, 166
Universe, in public opinion sampling, 173
University of California Regents v Bakke, 419–20
Unreasonable searches and seizures, 391–94
  automobile exception, 393
  drug testing issue, 393
  exclusionary rule, 393
  exigent circumstances, 392
  foreign agent exception, 393
  plain-view exception, 392
  search warrants and, 391
  stop and frisk exception, 392
Upton, Jonas H., 104
U.S. Court of Appeals for the Armed Forces, 322
U.S. Court of Claims, 322
U.S. Court of International Trade, 322
USA Today, 30, 226

V

Vagueness doctrine, 374
Van Buren, Martin, 151
V-chip, 232, 233
Ventura, Jesse, 147, 227
Veterans interest groups, 126
Veto
  pocket, 260
  politics of, 307–8
  presidential, 28
  override of, 260
Vice-presidential nominee, 205–6
Vietnamese Americans, 409
Violence Against Women Act, 65
Virginia Plan, 17, 18
Voting, 180–85
  choices, elements of, 185–89
    candidate appeal, 187–88
    issues, 188–89
    party identification, 187
  eligibility standards, expansion of, 180
  by mail and internet, debate over, 188, 189
  nonvoting, seriousness of, 184
  patterns, in former Confederate states, 99
  turnout, 182–83
    demographic factors, 183, 185